Where the Whaups Are Crying

A DUMFRIES AND GALLOWAY ANTHOLOGY

Edited by

INNES MACLEOD

Birlinn

For Scarlett

First published in 2001 by
Birlinn Limited
West Newington House
10 Newington Road
EH9 1QS

www.birlinn.co.uk

ISBN 1 84158 149 6

British Library Cataloguing-in-Publication Data
A catalogue record for this book is available from the British Library

Typeset by Textype, Cambridge
Printed and bound by
Creative Print and Design, Ebbw Vale

Contents

✝

12. HEROES AND HEROINES

ABREVIATIONS

DGC	*Dumfries and Galloway Courier*
DGS	*Dumfries and Galloway Standard*
DMM	*Dumfries Monthly Magazine*
DT	*Dumfries Times*
DWJ	*Dumfries Weekly Journal*
DWM	*Dumfries Weekly Magazine*
GA	*Galloway Advertiser and Wigtownshire Free Press*
GG	*Galloway Gazette*
KA	*Kirkcudbrightshire Advertiser and Galloway News*
NSAS	*The New Statistical Account of Scotland*
OSAS	*The (Old) Statistical Account of Scotland*
SM	*The Scots Magazine*
TDGNHAS	*Transactions of the Dumfries and Galloway Natural History and Antiquarian Society*

Acknowledgements

✝

The editor and publisher acknowledge their gratitude to those copyright-holders and agents who have given permission for extracts to be reproduced in this anthology. Whilst every effort has been made to identify copyright-holders, in some cases we have been unable to do so. We will be pleased to hear from copyright-holders in such cases.

A.P. Watt on behalf of The Lord Tweedsmuir and Jean, Lady Tweedsmuir for excerpts from *The Thirty-nine Steps*, *Sir Quixote and the Moors* and *Andrew Jameson Lord Ardwall* by John Buchan

I. Niall for 'Adders' and 'The Cry of the Whaup'

Mainstream Publishing for extract from *Scottish Journey*, by Edwin Muir

Canongate Books for 'Hauntings' from *Whereabouts*, by Alastair Reid and extract from *Torwatletie*, by Robert McLellan

Dumfries and Galloway Libraries, Information and Archives for extracts from School Log Books and the Rainy Trust volume

The Estate of T.G. Gracie for *The Grey Glen*

I.G. Henderson for extract from *Lockerbie* by T. Henderson

The Estate of F.W. Crofts for *Sir John MacGill's Last Journey*

The Estate of Dorothy L. Sayers for extract from *Five Red Herrings*

Carcanet Press Limited for 'Country Life' and 'The Dog Pool' from *Collected Poems*, by Hugh MacDiarmid

Samuel French Ltd on behalf of the Estate of J.M. Barrie for *Gretna Green Revisited*, by J.M. Barrie

A.E. Truckell for extracts from *Unpublished Witchcraft Trials*

The late Mrs Murray Usher for the Broughton and Cally Muniments, now deposited in the National Archives of Scotland GD10 1091

The Stair Society for extracts from *Select Justiciary Cases 1624–1650*

The National Library of Scotland for extracts from MS. 874

Mrs W. Edwards for the Virginia City Letters

The Mitchell Library, Glasgow; The Central Library, Edinburgh; The National Library of Scotland; The Ewart Library, Dumfries and the Stranraer and Newton Stewart Branch Libraries

1

A SENSE OF PLACE: JOHN BUCHAN AND *THE THIRTY-NINE STEPS*

†

John Buchan's Great European War story The Thirty-Nine Steps *(1915) – as Richard Hannay put it, 'I had done my best service, I think, before I put on khaki' – and Alfred Hitchcock's 1935 film with Robert Donat, Madeleine Carroll, Peggy Ashcroft and John Laurie have been enjoyed by millions of people.*

Buchan (1875–1940) was a prolific writer. In his biography of Andrew Jameson Lord Ardwall, published in 1913, he reveals his already intimate knowledge of the Galloway landscape and his deep affection for a place [Ardwall] and a way of life to which he seemed to belong. Buchan met Andrew Jameson (1845–1911), the Sheriff, at Oxford in 1898. Jameson's wife inherited Ardwall estate when her father, Walter McCulloch, died in 1892. Jameson was 'one of those who are born with a mission to improve the face of the globe . . . and his efforts were directed to sober practical reforms, like draining, fencing, and setting farm steadings in order'. The house at Ardwall was about a mile from Samuel Rutherford's Anwoth kirk. 'To the east are the wooded slopes of Cally park, and to the south Wigtown Bay, with a flotilla of little islands guarding the river mouth. To the west and north rise the heathery outposts of the great Galloway hills. It is one of the most exquisite sites for a dwelling even in Galloway, that home of fortunate sites.'

Late in life Jameson became a successful stock-farmer, specialising in black-faced sheep and Galloway cattle, especially his prized dun and belted Galloways. Once he had left the Courts behind he found that 'Providence had built him for the part of a South-country laird. Clad in knickerbockers he bestrode the world like a Colossus.' Buchan loved the shooting parties at Ardwall, in spite of the perils of being driven by the Sheriff up and down hill-road precipices in a four-wheeled dog-cart. 'Fishing, however, was Andrew Jameson's great pursuit, and, so long as business allowed, he was an indefatigable angler. . . We would return in the small hours from expeditions to the Dungeon of Buchan, and go to bed in broad sunlight; or we would indulge in the precarious game of swimming horses across the Fleet at high tide, or the still more precarious sport – a Jameson patent – of pursuing hares on horseback with a greyhound over the briar-clad dykes and bogs of a Galloway moor... On Sabbath there was a different scene. His lordship, splendid in kirk-going clothes, mounted the box-seat of the waggonette and drove a contingent to the Free Church in Gatehouse... Usually of a Sabbath afternoon he... would conduct his guests to view his Galloways, much as the Psalmist walked round the bulwarks of Jerusalem.' Fishing, hunting, adventure, a friend of the laird, was Buchan, 'the Presbyterian Cavalier', ever happier?

It was a remarkable coincidence that it was through a McCulloch of Ardwall that Buchan came to know Galloway, just as it was David McCulloch of Ardwall who introduced the young Walter Scott to the ecclesiastical politics of the Presbytery of Kirkcudbright and the General Assembly of the Church of Scotland in the scandalous case in 1792–93 of the Rev. John McNaught of Girthon.

In The Thirty-Nine Steps *we discover Galloway in (Chapter II) 'The Milkman Sets Out On His Travels' and in (Chapter III) 'The Adventure Of The Literary Innkeeper'.*

✝

Then I got out an atlas and looked at a big map of the British Isles. My notion was to get off to some wild district, where my veldcraft would be of some use to me, for I would be like a trapped rat in a city. I considered that Scotland would be best, for my people were Scotch and I could pass anywhere as an ordinary Scotsman... I fixed on Galloway as the best place to go. It was the nearest wild part of Scotland, so far as I could figure it out, and from the look of the map was not over thick with population.

A search in Bradshaw informed me that a train left St Pancras at 7.10, which would land me at any Galloway station in the late afternoon... As soon as I got to Euston Road I took to my heels and ran. The clock at Euston Station showed five minutes past the hour. At St Pancras I had no time to take a ticket, let alone that I had not settled upon my destination. A porter told me the platform, and as I entered it I saw the train already in motion. Two station officials blocked the way, but I dodged them and clambered into the last carriage.

Three minutes later, as we were roaring through the northern tunnels, an irate guard interviewed me. He wrote out for me a ticket to Newton-Stewart, a name which had suddenly come back to my memory, and he conducted me from the first-class compartment where I had ensconced myself to a third-class smoker, occupied by a sailor and a stout woman with a child. He went off grumbling, and as I mopped my brow I observed to my companions in my broadest Scots that it was a sore job catching trains. I had already entered upon my part. . . I reminded myself that a week ago I had been finding the world dull. . . .

I fell asleep and woke at Dumfries just in time to bundle out and get into the slow Galloway train. There was a man on the platform whose looks I didn't like, but he never glanced at me, and when I caught sight of myself in the mirror of an automatic machine I didn't wonder. With my brown face, my old tweeds, and my slouch, I was the very model of one of the hill farmers who were crowding into the third-class carriages.

I travelled with half a dozen in an atmosphere of shag and clay pipes. They had come from the weekly market, and their mouths were full of prices. I heard accounts of how the lambing had gone up the Cairn and the Deuch and a dozen other mysterious waters. Above half the men had lunched heavily and were highly flavoured with whisky, but they took no notice of me. We rumbled slowly into a land of little wooded glens and then to a great wide moorland place, gleaming with lochs, with high hills showing northwards.

About five o'clock the carriage had emptied, and I was left alone as I had hoped. I got out at the next station, a little place whose name I scarcely noted, set right in the heart of a bog. It reminded me of one of those forgotten little stations in the Karroo. An old station-master was digging in his garden, and with his spade over his shoulder sauntered to the train, took charge of a parcel, and went back to his potatoes. A child of ten received my ticket, and I emerged on a white road that straggled over the brown moor.

It was a gorgeous spring evening, with every hill showing as clear as a cut amethyst. The air had the queer, rooty smell of bogs, but it was as fresh as mid-ocean, and it had the strangest effect on my spirits. I actually felt light-hearted. I might have been a boy out for a spring holiday tramp, instead of a man of thirty-seven very much wanted by the police. I felt just as I used to feel when I was starting for a big trek on a frosty morning on the high veld. If you believe me, I swung along that road whistling. There was no plan of campaign in my head, only just to go on and on in this blessed, honest-smelling hill country, for every mile put me in better humour with myself.

In a roadside planting I cut a walking-stick of hazel, and presently struck off the highway up a bypath which followed the glen of a brawling stream. I reckoned that I was still far ahead of any pursuit, and for that night might please myself. It was some hours since I had tasted food, and

I was getting very hungry when I came to a herd's cottage set in a nook beside a water-fall. A brown-faced woman was standing by the door, and greeted me with the kindly shyness of moorland places. When I asked for a night's lodging she said I was welcome to the 'bed in the loft', and very soon she set before me a hearty meal of ham and eggs, scones, and thick sweet milk.

At the darkening her man came in from the hills, a lean giant, who in one step covered as much ground as three paces of ordinary mortals. They asked no questions, for they had the perfect breeding of all dwellers in the wilds, but I could see they set me down as a kind of dealer, and I took some trouble to confirm their view. I spoke a lot about cattle, of which my host knew little, and I picked up from him a good deal about the local Galloway markets, which I tucked away in my memory for future use. At ten I was nodding in my chair, and the 'bed in the loft' received a weary man who never opened his eyes till five o'clock set the little homestead a-going once more.

They refused any payment, and by six I had breakfasted and was striding southwards again. My notion was to return to the railway line a station or two further on than the place where I had alighted yesterday and to double back. . . .

It was the same jolly, clear spring weather, and I simply could not contrive to feel careworn. Indeed I was in better spirits than I had been for months. Over a long ridge of moorland I took my road, skirting the side of a high hill which the herd had called Cairnsmore of Fleet. Nesting curlews and plovers were crying everywhere, and the links of green pasture by the streams were dotted with young lambs. All the slackness of the past months was slipping from my bones, and I stepped out like a four-year-old. By-and-by I came to a swell of moorland which dipped to the vale of a little river, and a mile away in the heather I saw the smoke of a train.

The station, when I reached it, proved to be ideal for my purpose. The moor surged up around it and left room for the single line, the slender siding, a waiting-room, an office, the station-master's cottage, and a tiny yard of gooseberries and sweet-william. There seemed no road to it from anywhere, and to increase the desolation the waves of a tarn lapped on their grey granite beach half a mile away. I waited in the deep heather till I saw the smoke of an east-going train on the horizon. Then I approached the tiny booking-office and took a ticket for Dumfries.

The only occupants of the carriage were an old shepherd and his dog – a wall-eyed brute that I mistrusted. The man was asleep, and on the cushions beside him was that morning's *Scotsman*. . . . As we moved away from that station my companion woke up. He fixed me with a wandering glance, kicked his dog viciously, and inquired where he was. Clearly he was very drunk.

'That's what comes o' bein' a teetotaller,' he observed in bitter regret.

I expressed my surprise that in him I should have met a blue-ribbon stalwart.

'Ay, but I'm a strong teetotaller,' he said pugnaciously. 'I took the pledge last Martinmas, and I havena touched a drop o' whisky sinsyne. No even at Hogmanay, though I was sair tempit.'

He swung his heels up on the seat, and burrowed a frowsy head into the cushions.

'And that's a' I get,' he moaned. 'A heid hetter than hell fire, and twae een lookin' different ways for the Sabbath.'

'What did it?' I asked.

'A drink they ca' brandy. Bein' a teetotaller I keepit off the whisky, but I was nip-nippin' a' day at this brandy, and I doubt I'll no be weel for a fortnicht.' His voice died away into a stutter, and sleep once more laid its heavy hand on him. . . .

2

NATURAL HISTORY AND 'SCIENCE'

†

The everchanging landscapes and seascapes of Dumfries and Galloway include an amazing variety of habitats, from the strange and silent places in and behind the Gallowa' Hills to the green rolling sheep pastures in Annandale and Nithsdale, the tidal bore on the Nith and the forgotten ways on foot across the Solway, the cliffs and tidal races at the Mull of Galloway and the Scares out from Luce Bay, the moorland of the old Grey Galloway where 'the sun and the rain are flying' and 'the whaups are crying', the Grey Mare's Tail and the path to Loch Skene, the Dalveen and Mennock and Enterkin passes, and the forests and woodland with a place for red and roe deer and for peregrines and hen harriers. Some of the stories and accounts in this chapter may be more reliable than others!

†

THE INUNDATION
6th November, 1627

Much about this time an alarming accident happened on the south-west coast of Scotland. A south wind, blowing directly from the isle of Man, threw the sea upon Blackshaw, within the parish of Carlaverock, and upon Old-cock-pool, and several other parts within the parish of Ruthwal, in such a fearful manner as none then living had ever seen the like. It went at least half a mile beyond the ordinary course, and threw down a number of houses and bulwarks in its way, and many cattle and other bestial were swept away with its rapidity; and, what was still more melancholy, of the poor people, who lived by making salt on Ruthwal lands, seventeen perished; thirteen of them were found next day, and were all buried together in the church-yard of Ruthwal, which, no doubt, was an affecting sight to their relations, widows, and children, etc. and even to all that beheld it. . . .

The house of Old-cock-pool being environed on all hands, the people fled to the top of it for safety; and so sudden was the inundation upon

them, that, in their confusion, they left a young child in a cradle exposed
to the flood, which very speedily carried away the cradle; nor could the
tender-hearted beholders save the child's life without the manifest danger
of their own: But, by the good providence of God, as the cradle, now
afloat, was going forth of the outer door, a corner of it struck against the
door-post, by which the other end was turned about; and, going across
the door, it stuck there till the waters were assuaged. . . .

– Andrew Stevenson, *The History of the Church and State of Scotland
from the Accession of Charles I to the Restoration of Charles II*, vol. 1,
1853, pp. 28–29

ANDREW SYMSON
A Large Description of Galloway (1684)

*Andrew Symson (c.1638–1712) was educated at the High School of
Edinburgh and Edinburgh University. He was licensed to preach by the
Bishop of Edinburgh in January 1663 and was rector of Kirkinner parish
in Wigtownshire from 1663 to 1686. As archivist and clerk to the Synold of
Galloway he was the obvious person for Sir Robert Sibbald, the
Geographer Royal for Scotland, to approach for a detailed report on the
area for his projected* New Atlas and Description of Scotland.

Symson's Large Description of Galloway, *completed in 1684 and revised in
1692, is especially useful as a record of farming methods and technological
levels from the tilling of oats to obtaining oil for lamps from stranded whales,
dyes from cork-lit and lichens, and sacks and ropes from hemp-rigs. In his
response to Sibbald's* Querie concerning plants *he smoothly integrates information on cures for men and beasts and the industrial uses of 'excrescences'.*

*He was of course writing for an audience for whom biblical stories and
metaphors were rich in meaning: close attention was paid by everyone to
reports of eclipses, apparitions in the sky, thunder, lightning and
earthquakes in Jamaica, as portents of judgements to come.*

*The story of herrings raining from the sky is probably a factual report of
what happened when a waterspout came in from the sea over the moors of
Minnigaff parish. There are recorded falls of herring from the sky over
Melford House in Argyll in 1821 and near Loch Leven in Fife in 1825.
Shoals of herring were common in the Solway at much later dates, for
example off Wigtownshire in the 1820s and off Dumfries-shire and the
Cumberland coast between 1848 and 1852.*

✝

Monnygaffe . . . in the moors of the parish . . . not many years since at a place called La Spraig, not far from the water of Munnach, but sixteen miles distant from the sea, there fell a shower of herring, which were seen by creditable persons who related the story to me; some of the herring were, as I am informed, taken to the Earl of Galloway's house and shown to him. . . .

As to the second Querie concerning plants . . . I have observ'd these following to grow more plentifully here than I remember to have seen in other places, viz. at the seaside, glasswort, eringo, sea-wormwood, scruvy-grass, sea kale; and on the rocks, paspier, scurvy grass, hind-tongue; in the moors, spleenwort, heath or heather with the flower; in boggs, mosses and soft ground, ross solis (the countrey people call it muirill-grass and give it to their cattel to drink against the disease call'd the muir-ill), pinguicula or butterniat or Yorkshire sanicle (which being made into an ointment is very good to anoint the udders of their kine, when they are rocked or chapped), hasta regia or Lancashire ashphodele; as also the true osmunda regalis or filix florida, many horse loads whereof are growing in the Caumfoord near the Loch of Longcastle in this parish of Kirkinner: this plant the countrey people call the lane onion or, as they pronounce it, the lene onion, the word lene in their dialect importing a soft, grassie meadow ground; they call this plant also by the name of stifling grass and they make much use of it for the consolidating of broken bones or straines, ether in man or beast, by steeping the root thereof in water till it become like to glue water or size, wherewith they wash the place affected with very good success.

Danewort also grows very plentifully on the southeast of Wigton; in the churchyard of Anwoth; and in a place in this parish of Kirkinner call'd the Cruives of Dereagill; this vegetable, whether herb or shrub I shall not dispute, is found by experience to be very useful against paines in the joynts or the contraction of the nerves and sinews, by bathing the place affected in a decoction of the leaves and stalks of the said plant in sea water . . . .

In the parish of Monnygaffe there is ane excrescence, which is gotten off the Craigs there, which the countrey people make up into balls; but the way of making them I know not; this they call cork lit and make use thereof for litting or dying a kind of purple colour. There is also in the said parish another excrescence, which they get from the roots of trees and call it woodraw; it is a kind of fog or moss with a broad leaf; this they make use of to lit or dy a kind of orange or philamort colour.

JOHN MACTAGGART
'Elfrings'

The 'Elfrings' passage is a good example of pseudo-science. The obvious nineteenth-century parallels are ley lines, mesmerism and phrenology and, for the late twentieth century, crop circles. Mactaggart (see Chapter 3) could be very mischievous, so it is difficult to know to what extent he is playing games with his readers. The circles he describes are more like the rutting rings which are worn in the grass by deer.

✝

ELFRINGS. On old pasture land, that slopes about at right angles to the rays of the Midsummer sun, circles, of all diameters, from three to thirty feet, are to be seen; and these circles are beautifully defined by a kind of white mushroom growing thickly all round the circumference, except about a foot or two in some; these spaces, unstudded with fungi, are called the 'elfdoors', the openings by which elves go into their circle or ring to hold the lightsome dance . . . . No sage nor naturalist hath yet shewn the cause why these rings are formed . . . . That they are formed by the solar rays, I doubt not a moment; no animal on earth has any thing to do with their formation, because, on places where the ground is not of the same declivous nature, these 'rings' deviate from the true circle, and the unevener the slope, the greater the variety of circles, or ellipses of various eccentricities; and where the rays strike at about a right angle to the plane, there they are of equal radii.

But here comes the difficulty; if the figures and situations of the 'elfrings' prove them to be the work of the sun's rays, how do the sun's rays produce them? Before the mushrooms grow, the grass of the ring seems as if it had been withered by a scorching heat; now, this must either proceed from lightning, or from the sun . . . About the summer solstice, the rings are first observed 'singed', and in August they get covered with mushrooms: this is a natural consequence, because wherever grass is 'singed' or blasted, there start up clusters of the mushroom tribe . . . As for the elves having anything to do with them, is at least rustic nonsense; let the superstitious hold it out so or not.

– Mactaggart, *The Scottish Gallovidian Encyclopedia*, 1824, pp. 196–97

THE SILVER FLOW, THE SOLWAY
MOSS AND DORNOCK FLOW

The floating bogs in the Galloway hills, the welcoming quicksands and shifting channels and fast tidal races of the Upper Solway, the Dumfriesshire mudflats and saltmarshes, even the modest tidal bore on the river Nith and the old pedestrian way over the Cree estuary from Ferrytown to Wigtown, all have their own scintillating and occasionally terrible beauty. The most dramatic sounding location is perhaps the Murder Hole in a bay at the north-west end of Loch Neldricken; but it is really only an anomaly, a shallow circular lagoon of more or less clear water surrounded by a ring of vegetable matter and submerged mud which fills the rest of the inlet. The 'murder hole' title was added for dramatic effect by S.R. Crockett as a relocation of the story of the murder of a tramp who was buried in a deep water-hole, long filled in, in the valley of the Minnoch.

The Silver Flow, or Flowe, underneath Craignaw and Dungeon Hill, is one of the most famous and studied floating bogs in Britain. The Flow is a sort of enclosed plateau of 472 acres with peaty pools up to 20 feet deep, ditches, hummocks and ridges, the whole full to brim with water, and a growing thing as decaying vegetation marginally heightens the whole each year. Kilhern Moss, south-east of New Luce, is another peat-bog site, but unusual as a crater type on top of a hill and possibly a lake 10,000 years ago; and Kirkconnel Flow, between New Abbey and Dumfries, is a raised bog greatly altered by peat cutting and nineteenth-century ditches. The Solway Moss or Flow is on the English side of the Border, north-west of Longtown and to the west of the river Eden. It burst its peat banks on 16th and 17th November, 1771, moving forward as a mass 'like a cataract of thick ink' for about a mile. It covered between 600 and 900 acres of land to a depth of up to 15 feet and ruined eleven or twelve 'towns' or multiple-tenancy farm holdings. The Rev. Dr John Walker reported that thirty-five families lost their homes, and most of their cattle.

Loss of life is these incidents is fortunately rare, but the Dornock Flow tragedy in 1862 is an example of the extreme danger of bogs and mosses.

✝

The Silver Flow

I guess it to be about a third of a square mile in area, and it lies on a low plateau somewhat elevated above its contiguous surroundings. It is as flat as a loch on the same site would be, for its surface is determined by its watery content. It is irregularly circular in shape, and it is held up all round by natural embankments with the top of which it is nearly flush . . . . It is a true floating bog, and one who sought to cross it would do so at his peril.

For the Silver Flow is an expanse of mud, though not an unbroken expanse, but rather a network of ditches with watery surface and substratum of mud of unknown depth, running in all directions, and communicating at all angles, with narrow banks between, on which a man might find precarious footing. These channels are comparable to nothing but stagnant open sewers filled with slush that smells with the smell of the dead and decaying debris of vegetable and insect life . . . Many of these arteries can be stepped across, some of them jumped across, but others are yards wide, and even expand into small lochans. I have never plumbed the depth of their semi-liquid contents, but I have often pushed a walking-stick down into the narrowest of some of them as far as I could push it without ever finding bottom. Immersion in the smaller of these channels would be a disagreeable experience, but to get into one of the wider ones would be dangerous, much more dangerous than to fall into the same depth of water, for the mud gets dense as it descends and becomes tenacious.

There is little to tempt the ordinary holiday tramp into this marsh, but on the other hand there is nothing to keep him out of it . . . . There is the authentic record of an old female tramp having many years ago lost her life in the Silver Flow, not by drowning, but from exposure. She was making her way up the valley in the dark, stumbled into one of the sloughs and could not get out till she was dragged out the following morning. She died a few hours after being released.

– J. McBain, *The Merrick and the Neighbouring Hills*, 1929, pp. 244–47

Solway Moss

The original moss, which contains about 1400 acres, was raised above all the circumjacent grounds, in some places three feet, and in others as many yards. The surface of it in summer was generally so firm and dry, that people could safely walk over the whole of it, and in some places it could even bear horses; but in winter even foot-passengers durst venture only upon the skirts of it . . . . for many years it has been gradually increasing in height. . . . On Saturday, Nov. 16 . . . a large body of the moss was forced, partly by the great fall in rain, and partly by some springs below it, into a small beck or burn. . . . It was carried down a narrow glen between two banks about thirty feet high into that wide and spacious plain opposite to Langtown; over part of which it immediately spread with great rapidity. The moss continued for some time to send off considerable quantities. . . .

The 17th of November presented a most melancholy prospect to the miserable inhabitants of that country. They beheld . . . rich arable land covered with moss from three to twelve and fifteen feet deep. Many of them saw their houses, out of which they had narrowly escaped the preceding night, rendered inaccessible, or tumbled into ruins, and their corn, built up in stacks for their winter's provisions, and the payment of their rents, floating on the surface of this new moss. . . . There cannot be less than 800 acres of rich arable ground over-run . . . on which there were eleven different steads, containing twenty-seven families, and one hundred and ten inhabitants.

– *SM*, vol. 33, December 1771

Dornock Flow: Drowning in a Moss-Hole

On Monday week Alex. Nicholson, a lad about 14 years of age, son of Maxwell Nicholson, tailor, Creca, was accidentally drowned in a moss-hole at Dornock Flow. He was living at service with Mr Glendinning, Niven Hill; and on Monday was assisting at peat-casting in the moss with others of Mr Glendinning's work-people. He had retired a little distance from the past breast, and as he was longer in returning than he ought to have been, another boy was sent in search of him. The boy found Nicholson's cap floating on the water in a moss hole, and putting his hand into the water, he got hold of the hair of his companion's head, and thereby lifting the body in the water, and then succeeded in getting it out of the hole, in a lifeless state . . . . The hole was 8 or 9 feet long, by 5 feet wide at one end, and about 18 inches at the other, and there was about 6½ feet depth of water in it, and the brow was about 2 feet high above the water.

– *KA*, 30th May, 1862

LOCHAR MOSS

In the eighteenth century the Lochar Moss peat bog covered an area some ten to twelve miles long and up to three miles wide. It ran south and south-east from Tinwald parish through Torthorwald, Dumfries, Caerlaverock, Mouswald and Ruthwell. The traditional view expressed in 1790 in Laurie's description of Tinwald parish, that the sea once covered this whole tract, seems to be correct. The sea level, about 5000 BC, at 25 to 30 feet above the present level, was clearly enough to have made most of Lochar Moss a part of the Solway. Over the next few thousand years sea levels were at different times below or variously above the present level, for example the 23 feet (8m) and 4 or 5 feet (1.2 and 1.5m) raised beaches along Caerlaverock parish marking some of these changes.

The small medieval and post-Reformation burgh of Dumfries had its own bogs and swamps outside and inside the town wall: the Goosedubs Bog and Reid's Dub south of St Michael's Church, the Braidmyre, including Creynlar Moss to the north, the Watslacks Bog to the east, and Laripotts Bog, Craneberry Moss and the Gallows Myre.

Extensive nineteenth- and twentieth-century drainage and improvements transformed the old Lochar Moss. There are now some five distinct areas of the old moss left: 'the Lochar Moss', north-east of Dumfries, Craigs Moss, Racks Moss, Ironhirst Moss, and the Longbridge Moor raised bog north-west of Ruthwell.

James Laurie (c.1752–1799), the minister of Tinwald parish from 1784 to 1799, and James Macmillan (1736–1808), the minister of Torthorwald from 1762 to 1808, provided readable and useful descriptions of Lochar Moss. The canoes mentioned are probably Iron Age period. The very large 45 feet (13.7m) Loch Lotus (or Loch Arthur, near Beeswing) canoe found in 1874 has been radiocarbon dated to c. 150 BC–AD 200. Other, usually much smaller, canoes have been found at Catharinefield farm near Locharbriggs, Carlingwark Loch at Castle-Douglas, and in the Moss of Cree and the River Cree in Wigtownshire.

✝

The Rev. James Laurie, The Parish of Tinwald

An extensive moss, called Lochar Moss, 11 or 12 miles in length, and in some places 3 in breadth ... supplies the inhabitants of Dumfries, and the surrounding neighbourhood with fuel .... There are ... several good farms in different places on the higher parts of the moss, on both sides of the Lochar, which divides it nearly into two equal parts. There is a tradition, universally credited, that the tide flowed up this whole tract above the highest bridge in the neighbourhood. In the bottom of the moss sea-mud is found; and the banks are evidently composed of sea-sand. A few years ago, a canoe of considerable size and in perfect preservation, was found by a farmer, when digging peats, 4 or 5 feet below the surface, about 4 miles above the present flood-mark; but it was destroyed before any Antiquarian had heard of it. ... Antiquities of various kinds are found in every part of this moss where peats are dug, even near its head, such as anchors, oars, etc.; so that there is no doubt of its having been navigable near a mile above the highest bridge, and fully 12 miles above the present flood mark ....

– OSAS, vol. I, 1790

The Rev. James MacMillan, The Parish of Torthorwald

RIVER AND MOSS. The river Lochar . . . is about 25 feet broad at a medium . . . and so much on a level in its course through Lochar Moss that it has a descent of only 11 feet in that space, which measures 12 miles in a direct line. It contains pike, perch, trout, and eel. . . . Several otters frequent this river, and make great havoc among the pike. Wild duck and teal abound here all year round, and many wild geese visit this place in stormy winters. A few swans also come hither, and several bitterns and herons. In the adjacent moss and meadows, curlews, plovers, and moor-fowl breed. Lochar Moss . . . is a tract of 12 miles in length, and betwixt 2 and 3 in breadth, extending down to the Solway firth. That this moss was once an arm of the sea appears from several circumstances: Sea-sand and sleech are found at the bottom; and sometimes boats, almost entire, with anchors, cables, and oars. . . .

– OSAS, vol. II, 1790

THE FAMOUS FOSSIL OAK FURNITURE

When Robert Young retired from his cabinet making business in Newton Stewart in May 1850, his unique fossil oak furniture was famous throughout Britain. He had had the imagination to take out of the bed of the river Cree scores, perhaps hundreds, of great prehistoric oaks: to sell them to furniture makers in Edinburgh and London and Liverpool: and to make in his own workshop cabinets, bookcases, sideboards, sofas and chairs in what turned out to be a wonderful rich dark sable oak. His marketing strategy attracted aristocratic customers. The Earl of Galloway purchased a fossil oak cabinet for Galloway House and the Duke of Marlborough ordered another of the same design for Blenheim Palace. Lady Heron Maxwell of Kirroughtree furnished her Swiss style 'Hermitage' (in the south-east corner of a ¼-acre artificial grotto in an old quarry managed by 'Old John Gordon') with Young's brown and black fossil oak.

Young recruited good staff, notably in 1844 Mr Duncan, a clever and original designer from Liverpool. Duncan also taught drawing and perspective in Newton Stewart, and built up a business as an itinerant photographer, working out of Stranraer and Newton Stewart. His Daguerrotype portraits included family groups at Galloway House and a photograph of W.G. Cumming, the rector of Douglas Academy, with his assistants and boarders (18 in total) in May 1849.

Robert Young died at Threave farm in Penninghame parish on 10th May, 1851. He was 36 years of age.

Two questions remain. Firstly, how did Young get the great oaks out of the bed of the Cree? A possible explanation appears in the New Statistical Account of Scotland *entry for Minnigaff parish compiled by Mr Thomas Hogg of Minnigaff Mill in 1842. He refers to Joseph Train's description of Mr Newall in Machermore farm who devised a method of doing just this in 1819: 'Mr Newall ... collected all the empty casks he could find in the neighbourhood, bunged them up, and fastened them by ropes to the wood in the bed of the river, and as they rose, the casks raised the timber to which they were affixed.'*

Secondly, what elemental forces could have snapped these trees and piled them up in the river? The same phenomenon of a huge number of oaks (in the Moss of Drumcrieff near Moffat) is described by Sir John Clerk [letter to Roger Gale, September, 1729, The Surtees Society, *80, 1887, 394–5]. The local newspaper in Stranraer has the following account:*

✝

... Mr Young's Fossil Oak Furniture ... manufactured from oak trees raised from the River Cree ... from a little below Newton-Stewart to near the bay of Wigtown. ... There seems to have been deposited above the trees a series of beds of clay and gravel alternately, with layers of decayed leaves and hazel nut shells. Some of the layers are about 3 inches deep, through an extent varying from 12 to 15 feet. Many of the trees are of prodigious dimensions, some of them measuring from 12 to 24 feet in circumference, and from 30 to 50 feet in length.

The period when, or the cause that first placed them in their present position, and the locality of their growth, are subjects of speculation to many, but still remain a mystery to all. We do not, however, consider them as having grown in the vicinity where they lie, but rather to have been swept there by some mighty current, as in some places they are found lying in all directions, crossing each other two or three in height. They must also have been subjected to some extraordinary force, as many of the largest in circumference have been found snapped across as if they had been but twigs. Mr Young succeeded in raising one lately broken in this manner, a few feet below where the branches spring off, that measured 16 feet in circumference. The timber was as hard and fresh as on the day it had fallen.

... this now valuable timber was looked upon as nothing more than a venerable memorial of a remote period in our earth's history, until the sagacity of Mr Young suggested the probability of its value in his own profession, and having obtained liberty from the Earl of Galloway, on whose property it is, he commenced the operation of raising, and after having spent a great deal of time, and expended a large sum of money, he has succeeded in raising six or seven cargoes, which have met with a ready sale in Edinburgh, London, and the chief towns in Britain, besides retaining an immense quantity for his own use.

The wood . . . shews forth a beauty and variety of shade and figure, which is not to be found in any oak or walnut of the present age. Such is the growing demand by the higher classes for furniture made out of this material that one extensive house in Liverpool has been obliged to devote itself to its manufacture exclusively, and so great is the run put on Mr Young for articles made of it, that he finds it impossible to get hands to accomplish his orders. Mr Young lately completed a Cabinet for the . . . Earl of Galloway, made of the fossil oak . . . which has brought . . . an order for one exactly similar from the first ducal mansion in England . . . .

– *GA*, 15th January, 1846

S.R. CROCKETT
The Raiders (1894)

In his own time S.R. Crockett (1859–1914) was a prolific and popular author. The great strengths of his treatment of landscape in his novels lie in his remarkably poetic and visionary sense of time and place and in his almost pedantic attention to topographical detail:

> *Along the long cliff line, scarred and broken with the thunderbolt, the clouds lay piled, making the Merrick, the Star, the Dungeon, and the other hills of that centre boss of the hill country look twice their proper height. The darkness drew swiftly down like a curtain. The valley was filled with a steely blue smother. From the white clouds along the top of the Dungeon of Buchan fleecy streamers were blown upwards, and swift gusts spirted down. (Chapter 25).*

The Raiders is the story of Patrick Heron of Rathan and Silver Sand who is also Johnny Faa, the Cameronian gypsy (educated in Paris!) and a leader of the broken clans and wild gypsies whose last refuge was in the mountains around Loch Enoch. When Patrick first knew him, Silver Sand went to all the farmhouses and cothouses with keel in winter and scythe sand in summer. John Mactaggart (1824) notes that the sand was sold in shops in the mowing season 'at about twopence the Scotch pound'. One of the last of the itinerant sand vendors, Johnnie Morgan, died in Thornhill in 1901. The sand was still being collected from Loch Enoch in the 1930s for sharpening scythes and knives.

One of the best descriptions of Loch Enoch, 'The Mecca or Samarkand' of sand vendors, is in the essay by Bernard Fergusson (of Barr in Carrick) on Galloway in G.S. Moncrieff's Scottish Country (1935). On a dry day

the hard and white as ivory sand seemed 'to whisper as you walk on it'.
Fergusson also describes swimming in the icy cold Loch-in-Loch, a lochan
in an island on Loch Enoch.

✝

Silver Sand's White Magic

Silver Sand . . . had set up his tent again, and . . . he went back to his trade
of selling the scythe sand, all made out of the hardest white grit of the
granite where it is ground down and sifted by the rain and the wearing of
the rocks on the edges of the lochs in the granite districts.

Three kinds of sand he brought me to see, but not being a scytheman I
could not tell the difference. Then, very willingly, Silver Sand instructed me.

'This,' he said, running his hand through the fine, white, sandlike meal
that he had in his bag, 'is the sand which I gather from the edge of the little
Loch of Skerrow near to Mossdale that Sammle Tamson kens so weel.
This is the commonest kind, yet good for coarse work, such as mowing
ordinary grass, or the weeds and girse about a field's edge. This sort is also
the cheapest; but this,' he said, showing me another very fine sand, 'is the
sand from Loch Valley, which, when last we passed, I had not time to
show you . . . . It is fine, and sticks smoothly on the strake, and is used for
corn on the braes, and for short hay that is easy won.

'But this,' he said, taking up a smaller bag as if it had been the finest
gold, 'is the silver sand from Loch Enoch itself. It is the best, the keenest,
and lies closest to the blade of the scythe. It is used for the mowing of
meadow hay, which is hard to win, because it has to be cut about the
Lammas time, when the floods come. Then it is sore work to mow for a
long summer's day, and a great swing of the scythe is needed. At that time
of the year you can hear the *strake, strake* of the mower in the shade as he
puts an edge of his tool, and nothing else is used for this purpose through
all Galloway, Carrick, and the Upper Ward of Lanarkshire than the Loch
Enoch sand – that is, when they can get it.'

– *The Raiders*, Chapter 35

FRANK BUCKLAND AND CAPTAIN COLVIN STEWART OF CAIRNSMORE
The Wild Goats of the Stewartry

The black, brown and cream coated goats in the 'Wild Goat Park' off the
A712 and on Cairnsmore of Fleet National Nature Reserve, including the

Clints of Dromore, are probably the descendants of goats held as stock on eighteenth-century farms. Samuel Brown and Robert Ramsay, for example, who were the tenants of Drumruck, Murraytoun and Orquhers on the Broughton and Cally estate between 1751 and 1776, had 800 goats on their three farms.

Frank Buckland (1826–80) was both a popular author and journalist and a scientist with a special interest in improving British fisheries and the condition of fisherfolk in general. Buckland was on the staff of The Field *from 1856 to 1865 and then started his own weekly journal,* Land and Water, *in 1866. On occasion splendidly eccentric (as a student at Christ Church, Oxford, he kept tame monkeys and a bear), he had a very wide range of interests. His four-volume* Curiosities of Natural History *(1857–72) included Japanese mermaids, Chang the Chinese giant from Fychow, performing fleas, and 'wild men of the woods' on show in London halls in the 1860s and 1870s. He was also, however, a thoroughly competent and reliable scientist and co-author of a number of official reports to HM Government, including* Scotch Salmon Fisheries *(1871), based on surveys between May and September 1870, and* Scotch Herring Fisheries *(1878). He was inspector of salmon fisheries from 1867 to 1880. His study on* Fish Hatching *(1863) and his collection of models of fish-passes and hatching apparatus were important.*

In the summer of 1870 Buckland was in Galloway inspecting salmon rivers, including the Cree and the Minnoch, with Captain Stewart of Cairnsmore. Stewart presented him with a fine horned head of a goat fresh from the taxidermist and gave him a very useful account of the goats in the Galloway hills.

Buckland enjoyed his Scottish visits and was impressed with the enthusiasm of the children he saw crowding the streets at 9 o'clock in the morning eager to get to school 'as if learning was worth having':

> *At Dumfries I especially noted the door of an infant school. There was a regular swarm of little urchins playing about until the clock struck, and they went like bees into a hive. Few, if any, of these little things had shoes and stockings. They were all exceedingly cleanly dressed, and their hair nicely brushed and oiled . . . Few of the children in the summer towns and villages wear shoes and stockings. An excellent custom: it saves expense, and makes them healthy. The more you walk upon shoe leather the thinner it gets, the more you walk upon human leather the thicker it gets. I examined the soles of some fisher girls . . . the skin was thick and as hard as the foot of an elephant . . .* ['Buckland's "Impressions of Scotland", notes written on the railway train between Berwick and London in September, 1870', in G.C. Bompas, *Life of Frank Buckland*, 1885, p. 241].

Captain Colvin Stewart

These animals are semi-wild, and live high up among the grand mountains to the east of Wigtown Bay. They are all owned by somebody; the farmers catch them as kids, and put their own mark on the ear; and then let them go again. When harvest time comes round the farmers begin to 'drive the goats', and they feed the harvest labourers upon the goats' meat. They surround the flock of goats as well as they can, and drive them towards the steepest precipice in the neighbourhood; they then send in dogs which pin the goats, which are at once slaughtered. If I understand right, the dogs are let loose at the goats just before they get to the precipice, and so the goats are cut off by the men behind and the dogs in front; the dogs are done if the goats get to the precipice, as they are terribly active among the rocks. One gentleman kills as many as 20 goats every year, and in the hills about Newton-Stewart, at least 50 goats are killed every year; a good goat will give about 60 lbs of meat. When a goat is caught and killed in the common hunt, his ear is examined and he is at once sent to the farmer who has fixed his mark upon the beast. This is done with the greatest fidelity; each farmer has his own mark. If a goat is unmarked he becomes the property of whoever catches him. The billy goats are in best order in August and September. The farmers never shoot the goats, they only catch them at the proper time of 'goat gathering'. If they can't catch the goats this year they hope to catch them next. The goats are very artful and wary, and require careful 'gathering'; many escape every year.

– Stewart, *The Wild Goats of the Stewartry*, 1870

ADDERS
'A Good Place to Steer Clear Of'

John McNeillie (b.1916), who is also Ian Niall, came as a boy to live with his grandfather and great-grandfather at North Clutag near Wigtown. He became a reporter on the local newspaper and had three early novels published, The Wigtown Ploughman *(1939),* Morryharn Farm *(1940), and* Glasgow Keelie *(1940). They could fairly be described as harsh and coarse tales dealing with the brutal realities of rural and urban life.* The Wigtown Ploughman *undoubtedly created a furore of scandalised and pursed lips – worse, much worse, it was serialised in the* Scottish Sunday Mail.

The Ian Niall, with some forty-five books to his name and many beautifully composed commentaries on rural life in Galloway and in England and Wales in the Country Life *column, 'A Countryman's Notes', provided a different, gentler, kinder perspective on the countryside. A*

Galloway Childhood *(1967)*, Country Matters *(1984), and* The Galloway Shepherd *(1970) will be in everyone's Dumfries and Galloway library. The illustrations by C.E. Tunnicliffe are also charming and evocative.*

'A good place to steer clear of' is taken from a 1979 Country Life *column in which Niall writes about adders. It is a perfect example of how good Niall was at being at once stimulating, informative and elegant. Adders are, of course, a favourite of mine. There are few things better than watching young or baby adders bravely basking in the sun on a rocky access path to a popular beach: or coming across a 'plague' of adders travelling more or less at the same time from their winter hibernation quarters in earth burrows or under scree boulders to their summer feeding grounds.*

✝

We are not now in the kind of crackling heat with the drone of bees and the song of the grasshopper to which the adder takes its siesta, but far from it, with a more than generous dusting of snow on the foothills and a glazing on the higher peaks. I was, however, warmed out of my winter depression by reading a letter in the correspondence column of *Country Life* which referred to a clipping from *The Galloway Gazette*, a country newspaper that was compulsory reading in my childhood, mainly because the national newspapers tended to have an historical flavour by the time they filtered through to us.

The clipping was a letter from a gentleman named Scott who was something of an adder killer in his part of Wigtownshire before the First World War. He claimed to have killed adders right, left and centre, 20 here and I don't know how many there on another day, but what brought me up was his reference to big adders, snakes of 26 or 27 inches in length, because these were legendary in Galloway in my childhood and, with the passing of time, seemed to be creatures of the imagination.

People talk of big adders being 20 inches. The average length seems to be around 14 or 15 inches. I have hesitated all my life to speak of one that was as long as a man's walking stick, being afraid that someone would say it was a grass snake and I didn't know one from the other. . . . with the passing of time I have wondered about the indistinct markings on my monster – whether it was a very dull female grass snake, and a very big one at that, or the monster adder I was convinced it was at the time. It was as long as a walking stick because as it slithered to the stoneheap I tossed the walking stick and it fell alongside the snake. The snake's body matched the length of the stick but its girth was almost double.

I went home to tell of my experience which took place on a rough knoll on a farm belonging to a neighbour. There had always been big adders there, I was informed, and it was *a good place to steer clear of*. There were tracks of big adders in the moss and ferns, tracks as broad as the handle of a stable brush. But mine wasn't the biggest adder of them all.

At Monreith, back in the days of my grandfather's early manhood, there had been an adder that matched the length of a man. The man who killed it had been rewarded with as much corn as would bury it, presumably when it was held up by the tail. I have often thought to go back to the knoll of the big adders and see if they are there yet. . . . All the banks beside drystone walls were havens for adders in the old days and there was no spraying to keep down herbage and destroy the kind of food on which the adder thrives.

– I. Niall, 'A Countryman's Note', *Country Life, 25th January, 1979*

GALLOWAYS
Roadsters, Racers and Pack Ponies

The common ancestors of the Galloway, Highland, Cumberland Fell, Dales, Exmoor, Dartmoor and Welsh ponies were the wild horses that roamed across Europe thousands of years ago, surviving three Ice Ages. Their varying characteristics from the shaggy coated Exmoors to the thickset Highland garrons no doubt evolved depending on local climate and topography. The Welsh Pony and Cob Society recognises four types, and had the Galloway ponies survived as a distinct breed they too might have been divided into four categories of up to 12, 13, 14 and over 14 hands. An examination of the details of Galloways listed as stolen or strayed in early Scottish newspapers between 1699 and 1730 provides some evidence of size variations. Examples from the Edinburgh Evening Courant *include 'a small Galloway, well made, about 12 hands high' stolen from Leith Links on 27th October, 1720, 'a light Gray Galloway about 13 hands high' taken from one of the* Horse Closses *in Edinburgh on 19th June, 1727, and 'a Dark Bay Galloway, of a Hunting kind, near 14 hands high' lost near Duddingston Mill on 3rd May, 1730. Descriptions mentioning colour include light, sandy, dark and 'blew gray', 'milk white', 'blackish bay', 'black man'd' and 'black tail'd'.*

During the first half of the eighteenth century Galloways were valuable and therefore vulnerable, as were spaniels and greyhounds, to the schemes of organised criminal and gypsy gangs. They were prized in Edinburgh and in towns and on estates in central and southern Scotland and in the

*north of England as roadsters and racers. Their almost legendary
reputation for stamina and reliability – 60 miles a day without complaint,
12 to 15 miles without breaking trot, 100 miles a day for three days with
no difficulties at Newmarket trials in 1754 – made them ideal for country
gentlemen travelling from, for example, Stranraer to Ayr or from
Kirkcudbright to Dumfries or Annan, and for excise officers, including
Burns, on their itineraries. The 1716 advertisement shows just how
determined Colonel Agnew was to exact retribution for the theft of his
Galloway.*

*Because of the demand for Galloways in England, the term 'Galloway'
seems to have become synonymous there with any strong 13 to 14 hands'
saddle horse. Considerable confusion also arose later from the use of
'Galloway' for 11 hands' pit ponies, more probably Fell or Dales ponies or
'Fell Galloways,' in coal mines in Northumberland and Yorkshire.*

*In the later eighteenth century, Galloway roadsters were replaced by
horses imported from England and their progeny. Very large sums were
invested in 'improvements' in livestock breeding and even on gambling
on the merits of roadsters. A wager of £200 in January 1769 between Mr
Maxwell of Dalswinton and Mr Blair of Dunrod near Kirkcudbright
ended up in court when the loser, Mr Blair, died before his bill became
due.*

The Dumfries Weekly Journal *carried advertisements between 1788
and 1793 for 15½, 16 and even 17½ hands' stallions –* Alfred, Merry
Batchelor, Diamond, Aske *and* Suffolk *– based at Kirkbean, Kelton and
Glasserton and available to travel to cover mares in the Stewartry and
Wigtownshire. A new breed of horses for the road, for carriages and for
draught work was acquired by landowners and prosperous tenant
farmers. Galloways were still wanted for a time on hill and moorland
farms. Joseph Train, in a letter to Walter Scott dated 9th May, 1817,
described the kirking of a newly married couple in Newton Stewart:
parties of forty to fifty people came in from the moors of Penninghame,
Kirkcowan and Minnigaff, each man with a woman behind him on his
Galloway. [*National Library of Scotland, M.S. 874*] The long-term
process of decline was, however, inevitable as there was by then almost no
interest in maintaining Galloway blood lines.*

*The lightly built racers or 'racing Galloways' competed at York and
Thirsk and the Sands of Leith racecourses in the early eighteenth century.
In 1717 and 1720 Galloways ran at Leith for substantial prizes of 30
guineas and 20 guineas, but already by then faster racehorses with Arab
blood lines imported from England were competing for the larger purses
of 100 guineas. Increasingly Galloways, and 'country Galloways' at*

provincial racecourses, were pushed into second-class plates for modest purses. Systems of handicapping were sometimes applied, for example at Linton in the county of Peebles on 21st June, 1717, with 'the least siz'd Galloways being allowed a proportionable desalcation of weight for their want of size'. Although on 5th March, 1763 a bay Galloway belonging to the Earl of Erroll started a race at Leith for a 20-guinea purse, this is probably exceptional by that date. By the end of the eighteenth century Galloways are only occasionally mentioned at racecourses, even at Dumfries and at local country fairs and races at Gatehouse-of-Fleet, Castle-Douglas, Kirkpatrick-Durham, Rhonehouse, Creetown and on the Sands of Luce in the 1790s and 1800s. The attempt at Dumfries in 1801 to provide opportunities for the recovery of the Galloway breed was a failure.

Most Galloways in the south-west of Scotland in the eighteenth century were employed as pack ponies, moving goods, including smugglers' cargoes, along the roads and over hill tracks to Ayrshire, Lanarkshire and the Lothians. Some Galloways may have been used on farms along with imported English and Irish work horses in mixed plough teams. Oxen, of course, were used on heavy ground. In the early and middle nineteenth century Clydesdales were introduced in large numbers to replace smaller horses and ponies as farm work horses. To confuse matters further Fell ponies from Cumberland were crossed with Galloways, Highland ponies were sold in Stranraer in 1845, and Welsh and Icelandic ponies were present in Castle-Douglas and Kirkpatrick-Durham in 1861–62. By the middle of the nineteenth century the general consensus among contemporary commentators was that only a small number of Galloways as a distinct breed were left in the south-west. The last Galloway stallion, bred in Wigtownshire, died in Kirkmabreck parish in the 1930s. Unlike the Eriskay ponies, down to one stallion in 1968, there was to be no reprieve for the Galloways.

†

Whereas, One John McFarland, who was Colonel Agnew's Footman, run away on Thursday's Night, being the Nineteenth Instant, from Lochryan in the Shire of Galloway, and stole from his Master a dark bay Coloured Galloway, very well Paced, about 13 Hands high, of 8 Years old, cut half Mane back, the Hair shorn on his far Thigh, and a little mealie Mouthed; he took likewise a light Pad-Sadle, a Pair of Pistols and a Firelock; the Sadle is mounted with blew Cloath and Gold Lace, and over it a plain mourning Cover: the Pistols are mounted with Iron, some cutting on their Taps, and Royal Scotch Dragoons on their Barrels, but the Letters are almost worn out; the Firelock is plain, mounted with iron, L.C. burnt, and I.W. cut on the stock.

He is a young Man, about 5 Foot high, a little Ruddie Fac'd, thick Bodied, with dark Colour thick hair. He took with him a Suit of black Cloaths, and a light gray coloured Coat lined with red, and red Button Holes, with Brass Buttons, and a Silver-trac'd Hat; he served some time in Flanders in Brigadier Preston's Regiment, he speaks a little with the Highland Accent.

'Tis said that his Relations live about Camstroden, near Loch-Lomond, in the Shire of Dumbarton; he passed by Maybole on the Friday following.

Whoever apprehends and secures the said John McFarland, so as the Horse and the other stolen Goods may be recovered, and give Notice thereof to Mr Wallace of Carnhil Merchant in Glasgow, at his Dwelling-House at the Head of the Bridgate, or to the Printer hereof, at the Printing-House in the College, shall receive 5 Guineas Reward.

– The West-Country Intelligence, 26th–28th April, 1716

Edinburgh, November 19, 1722. This Day is to be run for at Leith the Silver Plate of 20 Guineas, by three Horses; the Owners are, Mr James Steuart, a sorrel Stone Galloway, called *Wanton Willy*, Rider's Name, Kenneth Wright, Livery, striped Cotton Satin.

Captain William Areskine, a Gray Stone Galloway, called *Small-hopes*, Rider's Name, John Slaeman, Livery, White Fustain.

William Morgan, a Bay Stone Galloway, called *Murecock*, Rider's Name, James Ronald, Livery, Red Satin.

– The Edinburgh Evening Courant, 15th–19th November, 1722

Dumfries Races by Galloways: In the month of September, or in the beginning of October next, as will be hereafter more particularly advertised, a *Plate of Fifty Pounds* will be given by the Dumfries and Galloway Hunt, to be run for over the Course of Tinwald Downs, by Horses Bred in Scotland not exceeding 14 hands high, and carrying not less than 12 stone. The object of the Hunt in giving this Plate, being to recover the breed of Galloways now almost lost, it is in their contemplation annually to give a Plate on similar terms at the Dumfries Races.

– The Edinburgh Evening Courant, 15th–19th November, 1722
– DWJ, 21st April, 1801

THE MINES
At Jamestown, Wanlockhead and Blackcraig

The long history of coal, iron, lead, copper, silver, antimony and barytes mining in Dumfries and Galloway is one part of our history of which many visitors are largely unaware. The Sanquhar and Kirkconnel coalfields, the lead mines at Wanlockhead, the Blackcraig mines near Newton Stewart, and the Closeburn limestone quarries were all at one time a major source of employment and profitable investment. As recently as the late 1950s the Sanquhar mines were producing some 400,000 tons of coal annually and employing 1,500 men.

The account by William Little (c. 1746–1820), the minister of Westerkirk parish from 1779 to 1820, is a clear and concise picture of the short-lived mining community in the new village of Jamestown up the Megget Water from the B709 near Langholm. The antimony mine on Glendinning farm was only open from 1793 to 1798. Some 100 tons of regulus antimony was produced before it closed. The Westerkirk Library (known locally as 'the Bentie') benefited from the gift of books and a legacy from Thomas Telford, who was born nearby at Bentpath.

✝

The Rev. William Little: The Parish of Westerkirk

Minerals. . . . Sir James Johnstone had, for more than 30 years back, been in search of lead in the grounds of Glendinning. In the year 1788, metal was discovered; but, on trial, it was found to be antimony. . . . Of the mines in the grounds of Glendinning, Sir James Johnstone retains two fourth shares. He has let one fourth share to Captain Cochrane, and another to Mr Tait. The company has built a smelting house in the neighbourhood of the mines, in which the ore is manufactured. . . . Regulus antimony is a common ingredient in speculums, in bell metal, in types for printing, etc. . . .

Miners, Village, etc. . . . There are 40 people, exclusive of an overseer, employed at present in the mines, and in preparing the antimony. A miner's wages are from £23 to £26 a year, and, as such, he enjoys many other advantages. The company has built a village, which is pleasantly situated on the banks of the Megget, and named *James' Town*, in which every miner is provided with a comfortable lodging for himself and his family, at a moderate rent: he has grass for a cow, during the summer, for which he pays no more than 20s., and 10s. for coarse hay for her provision in the winter; and may have as much land as he has occasion for, at the rate of 10s. per acre, for cultivating cabbages and potatoes. A storehouse is built by the company, in which they mean to lay up grain when the prices are low, and sell it out to the workmen, at all times, even in a season of dearth and scarcity, at the rate at which it was purchased. The miners are at work only 6 hours a-day; and, to encourage them to read, a present was, some months ago, made them in books, by the company, to the value of £15; and these, with others, which the workmen have since been able to purchase, amount at present to 120 volumes. To render the situation of the miners as comfortable as possible, the company has built a school-house, for the purpose of having their children educated; has granted considerable advantages to the teacher, and purposes to give £10 per annum, to which each of the workmen is to add 1s. a quarter, as a fund for the relief of such individuals among them, as may be disqualified for following their employment by sickness and old age.... The mining company ... has done an essential service to the public, by making an excellent road, along the E. side of the Megget, between James' Town and Waulk-Mill; and, in the line of the road, which is three miles and a half, has built 4 stone bridges, of one arch each.

– OSAS, vol. XI, 1793, pp. 560–561

THE TRUCK SYSTEM
At Wanlockhead in 1871

The 1871 Commission appointed to investigate the operation of the truck system of paying wages in industrial areas, in mines, and in the Shetland Isles, wholly or partly in goods rather than in cash earnings, found that the practice was particularly prevalent in Ayrshire and Lanarkshire and in 'remote' areas where procurator-fiscals were unable to enforce the already existing prohibitions against truck under the 1831 Act. The attraction for employers of a system of 'long pays' was that it tied skilled workers who, unless they were very prudent, found themselves almost perpetually in debt to company stores.

The 250 men in the Duke of Buccleuch's mines at Wanlockhead were paid every January twelve months in arrears. The only cash paid out during the year was 6s. in April to buy seeds for their plots of ground, £2 in July to buy coal, and £4 mart (Martinmas) money in October to buy a beast killed and salted for the winter.

The evidence of the mine manager and the store cashier (who was also the pay clerk!) showed that twelve months' credit was allowed to the miners and their wives to buy meal and flour from the cashier's store: coal, groceries, potatoes and, of course, candles and gunpowder for their work in the mines, from the underground manager's store: dairy produce and mutton from the manager's farm: and clothes from the drapery shop kept by the cashier's wife. The stores, shops, the farm and the miners' houses all belonged to the Duke. The cashier/pay clerk/storekeeper was paid a generous £80 a year salary, which perhaps helped to ensure the appointment of an honest man to a position in which the opportunities for fraud (the greatest weakness of the system) were obvious.

Report of the Commissioners appointed to inquire into the Truck System, 1871

John Nicoll examined.

16,735.	What are you? – I am a lead miner at Wanlockhead.
16,736.	To whom do the works here belong? – To the Duke of Buccleuch.
16,737.	How long have you been a lead miner in the duke's works? – I have been there nearly 40 years, but not all the time in the duke's works.
16,738.	How long have you been in the duke's works? – I could not say, but I think it will be somewhere about 27 years.
16,739.	How many men are there in the duke's works? – I don't exactly know that.
16,740.	How often are you paid at Wanlockhead? – Once in the 12 months.
16,741.	Are you paid then for the previous year, or for the year before that? – When the month of January 1871 comes round, we will be paid for the year 1869.
16,742.	Do you mean to say that in January 1871, you will be paid what you earned in the year 1869? – Yes.
16,743.	Then you have a lie year? – Yes, a lie year.
16,744.	Or rather a lie two years? – Yes.
16,745.	From twelvemonth to twelvemonth, what money do you get? – Any regular money that we get is 6s. in April, £2 in July, and £4 in October.
16,746.	What is the 6s. in April for? – It is for buying seed for planting our plots of ground with corn or potatoes, or anything we like to plant in them.
16,747.	Do you get plots of ground from the duke? – Yes, for cultivating them by our own industry.
16,748.	But they are the duke's ground? – Yes.
16,749.	And you cultivate them by your own industry? – Yes.

16,750.   In July you say you get £2; what is that for? – Formerly it was termed *peat money*; it was to buy fuel.

16,751.   What is it called now? – It is called coal money.

16,752.   Is it to buy coals with? – Yes.

16,753.   Where do you get your coals? – A good many of them come from Hurlford and Sanquhar, and so on.

16,755.   But where are the collieries that you get the coal from? – I think it is generally from Bankhead.

16,744.   Whose colliery is that? – I think it is Mr Wigham's.

16,756.   You say that in October you get £4, what is that called? – It is termed *mart money*. . . .

CANDLE IN HELMET
Down a Blackcraig lead mine in 1873

Lead mining began at Blackcraig about 1764 with peak periods of production in the 1770s and 1780s until closure in 1795. Speculative ventures with a number of new companies from 1825 to 1839, from c. 1848 to 1861, and from 1865 to 1884 had varying degrees of success. There was a final revival for a few years from 1917. Perhaps the last Blackcraig miner died in 1992.

In the 1870s the East Blackcraig Mining Company extended operations down to 900 feet below ground level with new cuttings and galleries. It employed between 170 and 200 miners, lead washers, carters, engine drivers, office cleaners and others.

The following account of a visit to Blackcraig mine in 1873 is a vivid and indeed terrifying portrayal of the claustrophic and dangerous working conditions. The author may have been Dr Alexander Trotter (1835–1901), whose medical practice was in the coal-mining area of Blyth in Northumberland. He contributed many articles on a wide range of subjects to Galloway newspapers. He describes coming down the New Galloway road to Newton Stewart on a raw, haze-ridden Monday November morning accompanied by Mr Ashe, one of the managing directors of the mining company. He could well have been staying for a few days with his father, Dr Robert Trotter, who had retired in 1864 to Dalry, where he died in 1875.

✝

. . . outwardly as one who earns his crust with pick, crowbar, and gunpowder . . . and under the guidance of Captain Crogar, we soon make a dash from the office fire through the chill air to the pit's mouth, the appearance of which causes us to open ours in amazement as the truth is made manifest that the 132 fathoms between bank and bottom have to be gone through on almost perpendicular ladders. We had seen coal pits and noted how snugly the miner ensconces himself in a cage to be reeled therein to the bottom . . . hence the dismay when the narrow hole, with a ladder poking out of it, presented itself as the one means of communication for everything human with the depths below . . . .

Dimmer and dimmer grows the light as step after step is taken on the perpendicular and ever-darkening ladder: and as twilight is succeeded by gloom, and gloom by a darkness which may be felt, the fact that a false footstep, a rotten rung, or a weakened wrist may precede a hurl in the gulf below is far from reassuring. . . . 'Were a man to fall from the ladder, what then?' . . . 'Well, he wouldn't be worth picking up, that's all' . . . and clink-clank, clank-clink go our heavy hob-nailed boots on the iron bars of the ladder. . . .

When Captain Cogar arrives at the bottom of this, the first of a series of ladders, the end of a shaft which runs out upon the distant valley . . . he strikes a light and soon a couple of candles make the surrounding darkness visible. By means of clay, reserves of which the miners seem to keep at frequent intervals, we each stick the dip in front of our helmet-like caps (some two or three pounds weight these seem by the way). . . . The surroundings seen thus are dismal in the extreme: jagged rocks adown which trickle and drop the ever-present water, slime, and round on every hand props to keep the less solid sides from falling in. On the left is the shaft proper, a yawning gulf, up and down which comes and goes at intervals a huge jug-like kibble, in which the ore is taken to the top.

The left arm meanwhile runs uneasily against a moving iron rod as we descend, the means of communication between top and bottom, and every now and again the body has to be squeezed through a man-hole, our candle being more than once extinguished in the operation. . . . At certain stages we come upon cranes, planking, and other working materials, the lumber legacies of former owners, now only in the way when the mine has been sunk deeper and deeper and newer workings opened out. . . .

We stop at the various levels, the 30 fathom, the 60 fathom, the 80 fathom, and so on, and candle in hand now pick our way warily over masses of ore and under rugged archways like unto tunnels. Bump! every now and again goes the head against some rocky promontory . . . and it is then that we bless the thickness of the helmet-like hat. . . . There is no wintry weather down a mine: summer and winter, seed-time and harvest, it is all the same here, and the perspiration has by this time come out on the forehead like great beads. Were such a thing procurable, a pint of bitter would be worth its weight in silver. Above and around us meanwhile gleams the welcome lead, now appearing in clumps and patches and again in streaks running away and losing themselves in the dim distance. . . . Every now and then the lead will disappear entirely and we come upon giant blocks of whinstone and masses of coal-like rock. . . . Most of the new cuttings are into what is called *kindly* or *fitty* ground, and when the new engine is at work above and more hands blasting and digging below, the valuable ore . . . will be taken more rapidly and in larger quantities to the top to the joy and profit of the ever-expectant shareholders.

But down we must go and, with candle once more firmly fixed in helmet, we prepare to again hand-and-foot it on the now familiar ladder. Every now and then we come upon a goblin-like miner, candle-illumined and grimy, prosecuting his work as cheerily as though his workshop were door'd and window'd and opened out upon a street. Down, down we go, clink-clank, clink-clank, the rumbling of the trucks and the echoing of the blast below sounding weirdly in this ghostly hole, while the smell of the villanous saltpetre suggests thoughts too horrible for utterance.

Here we are at last at the very bottom, 900 feet from daylight, every inch of which has been gone over . . . hand over hand, foot over foot. We sit down here to rest, hot and tired, the sinews of wrist and arm standing out like whip-cords, a strange weakness about the ankles and knees, and a feeling of all-overishness as though this deep depth was the hottest chamber of a Turkish bath. Chatting here, we learn from our guide, who has inhabited a mine, as it were, ever since he was so high, many hitherto unknown facts. . . . It takes . . . the workmen twenty minutes steady tramping to come from top to bottom . . . while the upward journey occupies fully half-an-hour. They work in shifts, eight hours at a time, and are paid either by the piece or hour according to the nature of the work. They generally work in twos and each couple receives weekly three pounds of candles and a supply of gunpowder for blasting purposes. . . .

We begin to explore the bottom-most workings and soon find that lead is here in great abundance. In . . . the bottom of the shaft . . . a man is busy filling up the kibble from a mass of ore before him, brought here by little wagons from all the galleries by means of ingeniously contrived trapdoors. Round and round we go, east and west, north and south, to the extremity of each working, lead and blend glistening in the candle-light on roof, wall and floor almost everywhere. . . .

'Do you think you could come up here?' queries our guide, pointing to a swinging chain-ladder about five feet from where we stand ... the climbing of chain-ladders, each step of which is a joint, is not our strongest point. ... Up goes Captain Cogar, as easily as though he were not a grandfather and Mr Darwin was in the right of it, and after him we wriggle, tossed about by every moving link, struggling to keep the perpendicular and straining every nerve to make the difficult task seem easy. ... Along several chambers and galleries we prowl, dodging a rocky headland here and splashing and wading and jumping there: pass the sump near a tramway, an ugly-looking mass of water: crawl through various holes and climb innumerable masses of ore on all fours, finally sliding down an inclined plane of wood and dropping upon our level several feet below.

'Yes, I think we will really begin to go up now...' and a weary, fatiguing task it is, each successive ladder seeming less standindicular and wider apart in the steps than that which has gone before. ... About midway up we meet the descending shift, and sitting down on a convenient plank behind the water-pipe we listen to the clink-clanking of the coming men, to whom the journey comes as easy as to walk along a pavement. As each emerges from the darkness with a candle in his hand and a bunch at his button-hole and disappears in the depths below, to be succeeded by another in like manner, and another, and another, the effect is as weird-like as it is novel. ... It was nearly 11 o'clock when we went down: it was nearly 3 when we came up. ...

– *GG*, 22nd November, 1873

H.G. MacCREATH
The Farmers of the South-West

The Scotia Review was a quarterly journal, begun in 1880, devoted specifically to 'the cause of the independence of Scotland'. MacCreath came from farming stock in Carrick on both his father's and his mother's side. His article is a mixture of old-fashioned nineteenth-century physical anthropology, early social anthropology or sociology, and sound agricultural economics. Dr Beddoe's work was a classic example of not very useful 'science'. The anthropology and sociology now make amusing reading. Believe it if you must!

This study of farming and farming incomes before and during the Great War of 1914–18 deals in some detail with the problems of small and hill farmers as compared to the relative affluence of the 'farming aristocracy' of the Rhins of Wigtownshire, and the role of 'crofters', tinkers, and casual labourers.

✝

The average farmer in the south-west of Scotland is, physically, a very fine man. Strangers visiting the markets of Ayr, Newton Stewart, and Castle-Douglas are often surprised to see the large proportion of men of six feet in height, while the average stature must be over five feet ten inches. With their spare and sinewy frames, many of the farmers are models of athletic grace and symmetry. About thirty years ago Dr Beddoe, the well-known anthropologist, stated that the natives of these parts were the tallest men in Scotland. The men of the parish of Balmaclellan, in the Stewartry, were found to be the tallest and heaviest men in Europe. The average height was almost six feet, and the average weight was about fourteen stone. At these gathering places of farmers I have mentioned, one observes few mean or unintelligent faces. Taking the Galloway man at his best, he is high of brow, aquiline of nose, with short upper lip, firm wide mouth, and strong jaw. His hair is dark brown, seldom black, and his eyes dark blue and clear. His mental characteristics are equally pronounced. He is not slow of speech, but has great fluency of utterance. His intelligence is not unmixed with cunning, and he has a profound delight in getting on the right side of a bargain. He will seldom tell a deliberate lie, but has a distaste for telling the whole truth, if something less than that will better serve his turn. He has a great fund of humour, and is usually a good story-teller. One of his strongest features is his admiration for intelligence. The man who rises in the world commands his respect more than any other, perhaps too much, because this passion is wont to be indulged, irrespectively of the means by which success is achieved. . . .

The farmers of the south-west are as urbane and well-spoken a set of men as any of their class in Scotland. Indeed, in old Ayrshire, the Galloway men were always accused of being too sweet to be wholesome. Whenever you meet a brusque pushing sort of person in Galloway, you may be tolerably sure that he is an incomer. Those who have the old blood of the province are invariably men of much geniality and natural politeness. Their hospitality is unbounded. There are many farmers who may be said to keep open house all the year round so continuous is the stream of callers, who are all treated to the best the house can provide. . . . At the present day, few farmers are anything but moderate drinkers, and, among the younger men, many are total abstainers. Accordingly, the bottle is not so often produced, and when it is, it is more sparingly partaken of. . . .

A Stewartry parish minister said not long ago that lying was a well-developed Galloway trait. Doubtless that was a hard thing to say, but candour obliges me to admit that it has a foundation of truth. As I have already observed, our Galloway people will seldom tell a deliberate lie; that is far too clumsy and inartistic a weapon of speech for them to use. On the other hand, there is an excessive tendency among them to wish to keep fair with the person they are talking to, to agree with his opinions for the sake of good fellowship, while all the time their private sentiments are running in an entirely different direction . . . strangers who visit this part of Scotland without knowing anything about the local tendency for flattery, are very apt to be misled, and, when undeceived, to think harshly of the natives, since nothing is so galling to individual human pride as the consciousness of having been deceived. So, in Galloway, a stranger may go far and converse with many without meeting one who will contradict him outright. The natives will willingly engage in conversation with him – the true Galloway man being always ready to talk, and even to lay aside his work for the sake of a crack. They will politely defer to his opinions, and amiably admit there is a deal in what the stranger says that is worthy of consideration, but all the time the old opinions remain unbroken, and the laugh . . . will presently be exploded at the stranger's expense. . . . In fine, though possessing sterling qualities, the Galloway character tends rather to disingenuousness than to outspoken simplicity . . . .

As far back as I can remember there was, until a few years ago, much pessimism among farming families as to the prospects of the calling. . . . the advice was invariably the same – 'Get the lads away to the towns; put them to anything, as long as you don't let them stay at home.' The cry was, that there was no money in farming, nothing but hard work all your days, and little to show when the best in a man was spent. So the fiat went forth that lads should be given *an education*, and put to the local bank, or placed in a city office, if they had a kinsman of sufficient influence to give them a start, or, failing this, they should be sent to the *pack*, i.e. the credit drapery trade in England. The last-mentioned employment was, however, long past its palmy days when I was a youth. Before the decline set in, many a packman returned to his native district in early middle life with a capital of £5,000 or £10,000, and set up as a gentleman farmer. . . . Moreover, not a few families have been enriched by legacies bequeathed by packmen who had made fortunes in England. . . .

As a rule, however, the advice which was lavished on such of us as belonged to the younger generation fell on deaf ears. When one is come of a stock that has been rooted in the soil time out of mind, and is at an age when the handling of a pair of Clydesdales seems the grandest thing on earth, it is not easy to persuade a lad, whose instincts are all for the country, the clean sweet air of the fields, and the homely merriments of the rustic ball that the better and the finer life is to add up figures in a city office. . . . I alone broke with the land and went to town. . . .

This evening, as I write, visions of the farmhouses among which I spent my boyhood rise up before me. Kinder, better people never lived than lived in those homesteads. . . . No one was very rich, but all had the means to live comfortably. Scandal among the farming families was practically unknown, and the social atmosphere was remarkably pure. On entering the sitting-room of one of these plain moderately-sized farm-houses, one saw at a glance that here there lived or had existed, men of thought and reading. Behind their glass doors the old bookcases showed many a volume of theology, history, and biography. . . . Here, you would be pretty sure to find *Jane Eyre, Lorna Doone, The Scottish Chiefs*, and, of course, the works of Burns. The girls of the household pored over the stories of Mrs Braddon, Augusta Evans Wilson, and the Rev. E.P. Roe. The periodicals most favoured were the *Quiver, British Weekly,* and *Chambers's Journal*.

It was not without reason that the old farmers were pessimistic touching the future of their calling. Twenty years of hard times had set their mark on the district. 'Yin to saw, yin to gnaw, and yin to pey the laird witha'' was all that the average small farmer could wring from a year's heroic toil. . . . Their mild diversion consisted in a day at the 'ice-playing' or a quiet glass with a neighbour, when they forgathered in the town. For years on end, the business accounts of some of them showed a balance on the wrong side, but they struggled on, and managed to bring up their families creditably, and to preserve a cheerful countenance through it all. . . .

About the year 1910 came the first decided change for the better, and ever since the farming industry has shown an upward tendency. In my native parish the farmers are now making money fast, but they are not spending a penny more than they used to do in pre-war times. . . .

. . . the small Galloway farmer class . . . The house consists of a kitchen, a 'room', a wee bedroom, and a pantry, on the ground floor, and two attic bedrooms. . . . The outhouses are in keeping, small, old-fashioned, and inconvenient. In front of the dwelling-house is a garden, large, but almost useless for cultivation and overgrown with willow-bushes and nettles. The extent of the holding is 300 acres, of which the greater part is moorland. The rent is about £65. The farmer started his tenancy of this holding with a capital of about £150. This was a quarter of a century ago and he is now worth probably £1000. . . .The family of this particular farmer cost him but little as regards their upbringing and placing in life. . . . His wage-bill was never large. At times he had in his service a servant-lad at, perhaps, £8 for the half year, but for years past now he has found it possible to work his holding single-handed, only employing casual labour. It is to such farms as these that tinkers are accustomed to resort, and at times of peat-cutting, hay and corn harvest, turnip shawing and potato lifting, a hardy old ex-soldier is generally to be found at work on this farm.... His wife, assisted by her daughter, manages the small dairy of half-a-dozen cows. The daughter also sometimes gives a hand in the fields. Eight or ten years ago, even if, out of his hundred ewes or so, the farmer succeeded in realising as many as ninety lambs to take to market, the sale would probably only realise £80. His annual sale of ten or eleven queys would give him another £80 or £90. His wool-clip would bring in £10 or £11.... In the present year ... I should estimate my friend's incomings for the year at £300....

As a rule the crofter makes of his own few acres but headquarters, from which to go forth to earn the greater part of his living by working for other men. Labour being always scarce, he finds his services in much request. At the peat-cutting he can have 5s., or at war rate 7s. a day, with all found. Taking a contract for hay-mowing, he can, by swinging the scythe for fourteen hours a day, make £3 a week clear. At harvest, six shillings a day is his wage.... Some crofters, and also a good many farmers' sons, are accustomed to supplement their earnings by taking up, temporarily, other employment. Rabbit-catching is one such occasional employment. To carry heavy loads of rabbits for miles, as the men often have to do, requires exceptional strength, but £5 a week can often be made in this way, board and lodgings being thrown in. Again, a couple of men, strong enough to work many hours a day ankle deep in water, subsist on bread and tea, and sometimes sleep in old disused cothouses and barns, can make £50 between them by taking a two months' draining contract in the hills....

The farming aristocracy of the south-west is principally located in the Rhinns of Wigtownshire, and around the county town of Kirkcudbright.... order and cleanliness reign supreme, and the effects of the presence of a large and well-organised staff are everywhere agreeably manifest. Range after range of outbuildings present themselves to the eye, all being obviously constructed with a view to convenience and efficiency. Yonder are the cotmen's well-built houses. Almost do they form a hamlet of themselves. The dwelling-house ... generally contains two or three public rooms, four or five bedrooms, and a bathroom. Almost every farmer in the favoured Rhinns district is at least well off, and many of them are even rich, as 'riches' are ranked among farmers....

They whose fortunes rest upon a solid foundation have here, as elsewhere, added farm to farm, with the result that many of the successful men are now tenants of from three to seven or eight holdings each.

Indeed, one sheep-farmer in Kirkcudbrightshire is credited with the tenancy of twenty farms. In Wigtownshire alone, a certain farming firm pays some £3000 of rent.... At Castle-Douglas mart every Monday farmers attend whose ordinary dealings run into hundreds of pounds. These men, too, have many sources of income. From their dairies of from 50 to 100 cows they rail daily a large quantity of milk to Glasgow, for which they are paid at the rate of 1/3 or 1/4 per gallon, the pre-war prices being 10d and 11d.. Others who devote themselves to cheese-making, and who in former years obtained 60s. per cwt. of cheese, have also greatly benefited by the war. Two years ago the price of cheese, as sold by the farmer, was up to 80s., but latterly sales have taken place by which the farmer realised at the rate of 105s. per cwt.... At all the great national and provincial shows the big men are much in evidence, debonair and prosperous-looking....

The Scotia Review, 40, Spring 1917, 99–117

IAN NIALL
'The Cry of the Whaup'

My earliest positive recollection is of being measured against a wall to see how far I still had to grow to reach the bracket holding a small oil-lamp. The oil lamp was exactly three feet from the form on which I stood, I discovered when I was older. I was three-feet tall at three years of age it was recorded. Well, I knew the cry of the whaup long before that. It was part of my life. I was born where they flew and brought up where they nested. Like the sound of the peewit, the liquid call of the lone curlew was a milestone in spring when it was heard above the moss. We didn't call them curlews however. I was in my teens before I accepted that name for the *long-nebbed birds*, known as whaups until that time. Only when I found that the local and doric names like shilfie, skart, mavis, yellowyoite and whaup got in the way of communication did I adopt the standard names. But a curlew is still a whaup to me. There is no name that fits it so well. I hear its call when it flies to the pasture beyond my house, and the sound still fills me with nostalgic memory.

I also remember my grandfather whipping up emotion in me at the fate of *our folk* when the cry of that bird betrayed my ancestors to the soldiers of Bloody Cumberland. Being a born alarmist the curlew can't help its hysterical outbursts when someone rises on the skyline. It was known as the *cursed curlew*, but it was a whaup when someone went poaching across the boundary or a pair of dogs were worrying sheep. Immediately it became the *auld whaup*.

Not far away from us was the place of whaups – Whauphill, where the moss with its bog cotton and myrtle on one side and green pastures on the other encouraged a congregation of whaups that gave the place its name. I often went to Whauphill on foot or on a rattling old bicycle to bring back some small item of grocery from the village shop. Memory suggests that these excursions took place on days of mist and rain, although I have no doubt that half of them were bright and sunny with the air drenched in the sweet scent of hawthorn blossom. Whaups cried endlessly as they stood on the slope of the hill beyond the straggling clachan or made wheeling flights in the rain.

I used to look for whaup eggs. They were as good to eat as the peewit's, and larger. There was no law against gathering them, although I can't recall seeing them parcelled and posted to London as the eggs of the peewit were.

There was a limit to the number of whaup eggs one could manage for breakfast, and a limit to the number of days on which the feast could be faced. The plough boys gathered the peewit eggs to make money, and when the market was supplied they left the peewit to nest in peace, and the whaup too, but I never got tired of looking for the nest. The whaup always seemed much more wily than the peewit, especially in its take-off from the nesting area, and it was much more wary in going back to settle on the clutch. The way to locate the nest was to take note of the little rise in the ground where the curlew was spotted, place a twig in the ground there and walk in a circle round it, going farther and farther out on each circuit so that every yard of ground was inspected.

The eggs are so wonderfully camouflaged and so perfectly shaped and marked that among the grass and dead moss and scorched rushes they are almost invisible. Most children are taken by the beauty of eggs. I certainly was. I could find a nest and stand and stare at it in wonder for minutes on end. It wasn't long before I wanted to preserve the whole thing. I would leave the nest undistrubed and come back again to look at it on another day. I felt a deep sense of loss when at last the eggs were gone....

– *Country Life*, 4th July, 1974

3

HISTORY AND TRADITIONS

✝

Many of the excerpts in this chapter are very different from the 'hard facts' and detailed evidence on which professional historians depend. They rather provide an opportunity to explore other sources and to enjoy reading about the past through the use of annals, of chronicles and traditional tales, and of reminiscences and oral history sources.

✝

NEW ARCHAEOLOGY AND
GEORGE CHALMERS'S CALEDONIA (1824)

The recent discovery of the site of three wooden concentric circles, initially as a result of aerial photography in 1993 and then through excavation in 1999, has opened up a whole new perspective on the organisational and engineering capabilities of the people living in Dumfries and Galloway c. 2500 BC. The sheer scale of this prehistoric gathering place and centre for 'religious' ceremonies is staggering. Oddly, it lies partly north, but mainly south, of the railway line at Dunragit, near Stranraer. A long avenue of wooden 'oak' posts led to the concentric circles, the largest 300+ metres in diameter and the two smaller circles inside 150 and 130 metres in diameter. The post holes suggest that the 'totem poles' were between 15 and 30 feet high. The adjacent mound, Drochduil 'mote', usually regarded as a medieval timber and earthwork motte castle, may have to be redefined as an integral part of the complex, a sort of observation platform with a terrace which might also have been useful during the planning, layout and building stages.

The local stone circles, Torhouse, Glenquicken, Cauldside, are utterly dwarfed by the Dunragit complex. A source of information for other [stone] circles is the generally regarded as unreliable Chalmers's Caledonia, *an historical and topographical account of North Britain, already 'out-of-date' when published in three volumes in 1807, 1820 and 1824. George Chalmers (1742–1825) collected information as late as June*

1820 from local correspondents, in particular from Joseph Train. Train in turn accumulated data from replies to his letters and queries sent out to friends and colleagues throughout Ayrshire and Dumfries and Galloway. Chalmers's account of the antiquities of Kirkcudbright included 'lost' sites with a number of 'temple/circle' locations listed in Kirkbean, Lochrutton and Southwick in the eastern Stewartry. Perhaps there are more 'Dunragits' waiting to be discovered.

✝

George Chalmers: Antiquities of Kirkcudbright

In this stewartry, there are Druid remains, which are the superstitious relics of the early times of the first settlers. . . . In Kirkbean parish, on the farm of Airdrie, there is a Druid temple, consisting of a circle of upright stones, which continue entire. In the same parish there was a similar temple, which was destroyed about the year 1790, when the stones were cleared away, for the purpose of building a farmstead, on the hallowed ground. At Southwick, there are the remains of a Druid temple. . . . And there is a similar remain in the neighbouring parish of Kirkgunzeon. On a hill, in Lochrutton parish, there is a Druid temple, which consists of nine large upright stones, in a circular form, which surrounds a rising ground and is 170 feet in diameter: it is called the *Seven* grey stones, though there are, in fact, nine. From this rising ground, there is an extensive prospect over the circumjacent country, particularly, by an opening, to the *east*. In Parton parish, on a gentle eminence, there are the remains of a Druid temple, consisting of the usual circle of standing stones: distant from it, two hundred yards, there is a very large artificial mound, about two hundred yards in circumference, at its circular base, which is surrounded by two ditches of considerable depth. From this mound, half a mile, south, near the church of Parton, there is a similar mound, whose circumference is only one hundred and twenty yards, at its base, which is also surrounded by a ditch, that is from six to nine feet deep. . . . In Kelton parish, there is another Druid temple, though without an accompanying barrow; yet, with a copious spring. . . . two neighbouring farms are named Tors. . . . There are the remains of two Druid temples in Rerwick parish. On Glenquicken-moor, in Kirkmabreck parish, there are the vestiges of a Druid temple, consisting of a circle of standing stones. In the neighbouring parish of Minnigaff, near the banks of the Cree, there is another Druid temple, which also consists of a circle of upright stones. . . .

At a little distance from the Druid temple at Airdrie, in the parish of Kirkbean, there was discovered in the earth a *kistvaen*, or stone coffin, which inclosed an urn, containing ashes: the sides and ends of this kistvaen were built up with small stones, and it was covered with thin flag stones. Another kistvaen was discovered at a little distance, southward from the former.

– G. Chalmers, *Caledonia*, vol. III, 1824

THE 'WICKED ARMY'
In the Twelfth Century

The problems in trying to make sense of Northern English propaganda versions of twelfth-century 'Galloway' life and of 'Galwegians' at war are not essentially different from those which arise in assessing early twenty-first century reports from Sierra Leone or Lebanon. To ecclesiastical chroniclers in the north of England the vassals and tribes [from various parts and with very different languages and customs] following the kings of the Scots were dangerous and savage enemies. The 'wicked army', as Richard of Hexham put it, of Normans, Germans, English, of Northumbrians and Cumbrians, of men of Teviotdale and Lothian, of 'Picts' [who are commonly called Galwegians] and Scots, were a highly diverse horde. Galwegians in the twelfth century meant not just men from Galloway in the modern sense of the term, but from a much larger and more loosely defined geographical area, running east into Nithsdale and beyond and north towards Strathclyde. They were accused in the English annals of slave trading with barbarian foreigners, of extraordinary cruelties against clergy, women and little children, of regarding 'as nothing adultery and incest', and of practising a kind of pagan sorcery in blood-letting wed-brotherhoods.

One of the more significant writers was the great Cistercian administrator and abbot, Ailred of Rievaulx (c. 1109–66). His biographer, Walter Daniel, described Ailred's 1164–65 visit to Galloway – 'a wild country where the inhabitants are like beasts, and is altogether barbarous. . . . There chastity founders as often as lust wills, and the pure is only so far removed from a harlot that the more chaste will change their husbands every month and a man will sell his wife for a heifer' (ed. F.M. Powicke, The Life of Ailred by Walter Daniel, *1950, p. 45). How much in these annals is fact; how much propaganda-enhanced stereotyping?*

Ailred of Rievaulx, 'Saints of Hexham', in J. Raine (ed.), *The Priory of Hexham*, Surtees Society, 1864–65 (c. 1079):

Ailred of Rievaulx, 'Saints of Hexham', in J. Raine (ed.), *The Priory of Hexham, Surtees Society*, (c. 1079):

At a time when Malcolm, king of the Scots, ravaged Northumbria with cruel slaughter, he ever preserved peace with the church of Hexham, through honour for the saints who rest in it. But on one occasion his messengers fell among robbers near the lands of that church, and returned robbed and wounded to the king, they laid the charge of this cruelty against the innocent people. And the king was enraged and furious . . . and summoned his Galwegian vassals, more cruel than the rest; and said in the hearing of the messengers, 'So soon as the day dawns, cross the river and fall upon them: let not your eye spare or pity rank, or sex, or age. Whatever the sword cannot, let fire destroy; and leave of them no remains.'

Ralph de Diceto, in W. Stubbs, (ed.) *Imagines Historiarum 1148–1202, Rolls Series* no. 68 (1173):

William king of Scots . . . collected an army, with an endless host of Galwegians – men agile, unclothed, remarkable for much baldness; arming their left side with knives formidable to any armed men, having a hand most skilful at throwing spears, and at directing them at a distance; raising their long lance as a standard when they advance to battle.

Having a safe journey through the lands of Hugh, bishop of Durham, the king of Scotland began to harry England, to burn down villages, to collect incalculable spoil, to lead away young women captive, to take out the half living infants from the wombs of the pregnant.

Ailred of Rievaulx, *Relation de Standardo*, in R. Howlett (ed.), *Chronicles of the reign of Stephen, Henry II and Richard I, Rolls Series*, no. 82 (1138):

The Galwegians . . . saying that it was their right to fill the front line, to make the first attack upon the enemy, to arouse by their courage the rest of the army . . . persisted, demanding that their right be granted to them. . . . Then the king . . . yielded to the will of the Galwegians. The second the king's son arranged with great wisdom; with himself the knights and archers, adding to their number the Cumbrians and Teviotdalesmen. . . . The men of Lothian formed the third rank, with the islanders and the men of Lorn. The king kept in his own line the Scots and Moravians. . . .

And the column of the Galwegians after their custom gave vent thrice to a yell of horrible sound, and attacked the southerns in such an onslaught that they compelled the first spearmen to forsake their post; but they were driven off again by the strength of the knights. . . . And when the frailty of the Scottish lances was mocked by the denseness of iron and wood they drew their swords and attempted to contend at close quarters. But the southern flies swarmed forth from the caves of their quivers, and flew like closest rain; and irksomely attacking the opponents' breasts, faces and eyes, very greatly impeded their attack. Like a hedgehog with its quills, so would you see a Galwegian bristling all round with arrows, and none the less brandishing his sword and in blind madness rushing forward now smite a foe, now lash the air with useless strokes.

Richard Prior of Hexham, *De Gesti Stephani*, in *Chronicles of . . . Stephen* (1138):
So that execrable army, savager than any race of heathen, yielding honour to neither God nor man, harried the whole province and slaughtered everywhere folk of either sex, of every age and condition, destroying, pillaging and burning the vills, churches and houses. For they slaughtered by the edge of the sword or transfixed with their spears the sick on their pallets, women pregnant and in labour; the babes in their cradles, and other innocents at the breast or in the bosoms of their mothers, with the mothers themselves; and worn-out old men and feeble old women, and the others who were for any reason disabled, wherever they found them. And the more pitiable a form of death they could destroy them by, the more did they rejoice. . . . It is even reported that in one place they slew many little children gathered together, and draining their blood collected it in a stream which they had previously dammed up, and thus drank that bloody water, nay, now for the most part blood. . . .
    – in A.O. Anderson, *Scottish Annals from English Chroniclers, 1908*
pp. 101, 247, 198, 202–03, 180

JOHN BARBOUR
The Bruce

John Barbour (?1320–95) completed The Bruce *about 1375. Remarkably it is both a national epic on the theme of 'fredome' written in the vernacular 'Inglis' and, at the same time, a carefully prepared, scholarly, and generally reliable history of the violent events and desperate battles as Robert Bruce fought to 'mak him king'. W. M. Mackenzie's* John Barbour: The Bruce *(1909) is based on the earliest [1487] manuscript copy.*

Nothing is known of Barbour's early life. By 1357 or earlier he was archdeacon of Aberdeen. Safe conducts for travel in England indicate that he visited the universities at Oxford in 1357 and 1364 and Paris in 1365. In 1372 he was employed as a clerk in Robert II's household and in 1373 he was auditor of the exchequer. Various bounties and pensions were paid to him between 1377 and 1388.

Barbour would have been well placed to discuss the events he describes with men who themselves, or whose fathers or uncles or brothers, fought in the wars before and after Bannockburn. The amount of gory detail of the battles between hard fighting men, of the topography whether of a pass or a ford, and even of weather conditions, is impressive. More important, Bruce (1274–1329) is not presented as a blameless hero bound by romantic codes. The murders at Dumfries where Bruce, no doubt 'getting his retaliation in first', sinned greatly 'in giving no heed to the sanctuary of the altar', and his early recklessness are not ignored. It makes the character development of Bruce from a merely immensely brave warrior into an imaginative, shrewd, cautious and careful guerilla tactician and campaign strategist and king all the more convincing.

The extracts dealing with Dumfries and Lochmaben in 1306, the guerilla war in Carrick and the engagement at Glentrool in 1307, and Edward Bruce's 'fire and sword' campaign in Galloway in 1308 bring out the importance of the south-west of Scotland in the long struggle for 'fredome'. Galloway in particular, with the Balliols at Buittle Castle, was hostile territory for the Bruces of Carrick and Annandale. John Comyn was Balliol's nephew and his wife was a sister of Aymer de Valence.

John Comyn comes down from Dalswinton and is murdered near the high altar in the church of the Friars Minor [Franciscans] in Dumfries on 10th February, 1306.

✝

Sa fell it in the samyn tid,
That at Dumfres, rycht thar besid,
Schir Jhone the Cumyn sojornyng maid;
The Brus lap on and thiddir raid;
And thocht, for-owtyn mar letting,
For to quyt hym his discoveryng.
Thidder he raid, but langir let,
And with Schyr Jhone the Cumyn met,
In the Freris, at the hye awter,
And schawyt him, with lauchand cher,
The endentur; syne with a knyff,
Rycht in that sted, hym reft the lyff.

Schyr Edmund Cumyn als wes slayn,
And othir mony off mekill mayn. . . . [Book II, lines 25–38]

He mysdyd thar gretly, but wer,
That gave na gyrth to the awter.
Thar for sa hard myscheiff him fell,
That Ik herd nevir in romanys tell. . . .[lines 43–6]

Till Louchmabane he went agayne;
And gert men, with his lettres, ryd
To freyndis apon ilke sid,
That come to hym with that mengyhe;
And his men als assemblit he:
And thocht that he wad mak him king.
Over all the land the word gan spryng,
That the Bruce the Cumyn had slayn. [lines 72–9]

Bruce in Carrick in 1307 and the hostility of the Galloway men; Bruce's battle courage, taking and giving many wounds ['rowtis ryde' or 'woundis wyde'].

Sik speking maid he of the King,
That ay, forouten sudjornyng,
Travalit in Carrik heir and thair.
His men fra him sua scalit war,
Till purches thame necessite
And als the cuntre for to se,
That thai left nocht with him sexty.
And quhen the Gallowais wist suthly
That he wes with a few menyhe,
Thai maid a preve assemble
Of weill twa hundreth men and ma;
Ane sluth-hund with thaim can thai ta,
For thai thoucht him for to suppris;
And gif he fled on ony wis,
To follow him with the hunde swa,
That he suld nocht escape thaim fra. . . . [Book VI, lines 25–40]

In this maner that I haf tald,
The King, that stout wes, stark and bald,
Wes fechand on the furdis syde,
Gyffand and takand rowtis ryde;

Till he sic martirdome thair maid
That he the furde all stoppit had,
That nane of thame mycht till him ryde. [lines 285–91]

The engagement at Glentrool in 1307: Bruce's personal bravery and organisation of his 300 men against 1500.

In Glentruell a quhile he lay,
And went weill oft to hunt and play,
For to purchase thame venysoun,
For than the deir war in sesoun.
In all that tyme Schir Amery,
With nobill men in cumpany,
In Carleill lay, his poynt to se;
And quhen he herd the certante
That in Glentruell wes the King,
And went to hunt and to playing,
He thoucht than with his chevelry,
To cum apon hym suddanly;
Fra Carleill all on nychtis ryde,
And in covert on dayis byde.
And swagat, with sic tranonting,
He thoucht he suld suppris the Kyng,
Than he assemblit a gret menyhe
Of folk of full gret renowne,
Bath of Scottish and Inglis men. . . . [Book VII, lines 494–512]

Quhen at the King herd that tithing,
He armyt hym but mair duelling;
Sa did thai all that evir thar war,
Syne in a sop assemblit ar:
I trow they war thre hundreth ner.
And quhen thai all assemblit wer,
The King his baner-gert display,
And set his men in gude aray. . . . [lines 564–71]

The noyis begouth soyne and the cry;
For the gud King, that formast was,
Stoutly towart his fayis gais,
And hint out of a manis hand,
That neir besyde him wes gangand,
A bow and a braid arrow als,

And hyt the formast in the hals,
Till throppill and wassand yheid in twa,
And he doune to the erd can ga. . . . [lines 577–85]

For thai falyheit of thair entent,
Thai war that tym sa fowly schent,
That fiften hundreth men and ma
Wyth fewar war rebutit swa,
That thai with-drew thaim schamfully. [lines 614–18]

*The King's brother, Edward Bruce, in Galloway; the battle beside the
Cree (Fordoun has the Dee); thirteen castles are taken in 1308.*

The Kingis brothir, quhen the towne
Wes takyn thus and doungyn doune,
Schir Edward, that wes so worthy,
Tuk with him a gret cumpany,
And tuk his gat toward Galloway.
For with his men he walde assay
Gif he recover mycht that land,
And wyn fra Inglis mennys hande. . . . [Book IX, lines 472–79]

This gud knycht, that I spek of heir,
With all the folk that with hym weir,
Weill soyn to Galloway cummyn is,
All that he fand he maid it his;
And ryotit gretly the lande. . . . [lines 496–500]

Bot he with fewar folk thaim met
Besyde Cre, and so hard thame set,
With hard battale in stalwarde ficht,
That he thame all put to the flicht.
And slew twa hundredth wele and ma,
And the chiftanis in hy can ta
Thair way to Buttill, for till be
Resavit in-to gude savite.
And Schir Edward thame chasit fast. . . . [lines 516–24]

Ande he duelt furth in-to the land,
Thame that rebelland war warrand,
And in a yheir so warrait he,
That he wan quytly that cuntre

Till his brothiris pes, the king;
Bot that wes nocht but hard fichting.
For in that time thair him befell
Mony fair poynt, as I herd tell,
The quhilk that ar nocht writin heir.
Bot weill I wat that, in that yheir,
Thretten castellis with strynth he wan,
And ourcom mony a mody man. [lines 648–659]

HENRY THE MINSTREL, COMMONLY KNOWN AS BLIND HARRY
The Actis and Deidis of . . . Schir William Wallace

Blind Harry's epic poem on Wallace, written in the Inglis of the Lothians, was put together in the 1470s and 1480s. The events he described took place between 1297, when Wallace emerged as a national figure, and his death in London on 23rd August, 1305. Blind Harry may well have been able to use some lost sources and lives, including a work by the Benedictine, John Blair, but essentially his work depended on bringing together the popular legends and myths in circulation in fifteenth-century Scotland. In other words, Blind Harry is, to put it mildly, un unreliable source. To English commentators in Cumberland, Northumberland and Durham, Wallace and his raiders were savages, murderers and thieves. In Blind Harry's history Wallace is an heroic warrior, protecting the poor with the impudence of a 'master of thieves', storming and breaking down castles, and even burning English ships and joining forces with a French pirate, Thomas Longueville, after the defeat at Falkirk in 1298: all this accomplished with the wild outlaw bravado of a Robin Hood.

His Actis and Deidis include the taking of Lochmaben and Crawford Castles and, in the Sext Buik, a castle 'on the wattir off Cre'. Blind Harry's story about the 'strenth' on the Cree recalls the passage in the Norman French Roman de Fergus, written by William the Clerk for Alan of Galloway in the first quarter of the thirteenth century, in which he describes the castle [Cruggleton?] of Somerled and his son Fergus of Galloway, who died in 1161.

> *Upon a great dark-coloured rock*
> *He had his house right nobly set. . . .*
> *The Farmer was full glad to own*
> *So fair a home above the sea. . . .*
> *For thirty leagues he had a view*

Around him if he cast his gaze.
Who is within need have no fear
Of escalade and engineer.'

 Any attempt, however, to identify precisely the 'strenth' on the Cree is ultimately futile as Blind Harry was more than capable of describing battles and sieges that happened only in his imagination. Either Cruggleton Castle or Kirkclaugh motte and bailey on opposite sides of Wigtown Bay fit well enough. The motte and bailey in Minnigaff is also a possibility.

✝

Schir William Wallace . . . The Sext Buik (ed. James Moir, 1889)

 A strenth thar was on the wattir off Cre
 With in a roch, rycht stalwart wrocht off tre;
 A gait befor mycht no man to it wyn;
 But the consent off thaim that duelt within.
 On the bak sid a roch and wattir was;
 A strait entre forsuth it was to pass.
 To wesy it Wallace him selff sone went;
 Fra he it saw, he kest in his entent
 To wyn that hauld; he has chosyne a gait,
 That thai with in suld mak litill debait.
 His power haill he gert bid out off sycht,
 Bot iij with him qwhill tyme that it was nycht.
 Than tuk he twa, quhen that the nycht was dym,
 Stewyn off Irland, and Kerle, that couth clyme
 The wattir wnder; and clame the roch so strang:
 Thus entrit thai the Sothrone men amang.
 The wach befor tuk na tent to that syd:
 Thir iij in feyr sone to the port thai glid.
 Gud Wallace than straik the portar him sell;
 Dede our the roch in to the dik he fell;
 Leit doun the brig, and blew his horne on hycht.
 The buschement brak, and come in all that mycht;
 At thair awne will some entrit in that place;
 Till Inglishmen thai did full litill grace.
 Sexty thai slew; in that hauld was no ma,
 Bot ane auld preist, and sympill wemen twa.
 Gret purweance was in that roch to spend;
 Wallace baid still quhill it was at ane end:

Brak doune the strenth, bath bryg and bulwark all;
Out our the roch thai gert the temyr fall;
Wndid the gait, and wald no langar bid.

[lines 803–33]

HECTOR BOECE
History of Scotland (1527)

Hector Boece or Boethius (?1465–1536) came from an Angus family of Boyis or Boyce. While studying at Paris between c. 1492 and 1498 he met Bishop Elphinstone, who engaged him to assist in planning over the next ten years the foundation of a new 'studium generale' or university at Aberdeen. He must have been a capable administrator or the very able Elphinstone would not have employed him. However his History of Scotland *(up to the accession of James III), published in Latin in 1527 [a translation into Scots followed in 1536] is now generally regarded as of interest only as a curiosity. It is surprising just how credulous he seems to be when repeating wildly inaccurate and unlikely or fabulous tales. His account of Annandale is obviously over-the-top.*

†

On the tothir side, fornence the Ireland seis, lyis Annandail, fra the watter of Annand. It marchis sum times with the out boundis of Nidisdail, quhair all thir thre rivers forsaid, Eus, Annand, and Sulway, discendis togidder, under ane streme, in the Ireland seis. In Annandail is ane loch namit Lochmaben, five milis of lenth, and four of breid, full of uncouth fische. Beside this loch is ane castell, under the same name, maid to dant the incursion of thevis. For nocht allanerlie in Annandail, bot in all the dalis afore rehersit, ar mony strang and wekit thevis, invading the cuntre with perpetuall thift, reif, and slauchter, quhen thay se ony trublus time. Thir thevis, becaus thay have Inglismen thair perpetuall ennimes, liand dry marche apon thair nixt bordour, invadis Ingland with continewal weris, or ellis with quiet thift; and leiffis ay ane pure and miserabill life. In the time of peace, thay ar so accustomit with thift that thay can nocht desist, bot invadis the cuntre (howbeit thay ar ay miserabilie put doun), with ithand heirschippis [rapid forays]. Mony riche and plentuus boundis of Scotland lyis waist, for feir of thair invasion. Nocht far fra Sulway ar mony sinkand sandis, sa perilus, that na peple may transport thaim self throw the samin, but gret difficulte and danger of thair livis. This vale of

Annand wes sum time namit Ordovitia, and the pepill namit Ordovices; quhais cruelteis wes sa gret, that thay abhorrit nocht to eit the flesche of yoldin prisoneris. The wivis usit to slay thair husbandis, quhen thay wer found cowartis, or discomfist be thair ennimes; to gif occasioun to otheris to be more bald and hardy quhen danger occurrit: Quhill at last thay wer finalie distroyit by the weris of Romanis.

HEADLESS HORSEMEN AND HOLY WELLS

Folk memories based on the beliefs and associated with the sacred places of the Celtic tribal confederations in Dumfries and Galloway two thousand years ago were still strong in the seventeenth and early eighteenth centuries. The persistence of these traditions suggests just how much fear and longing remained over the centuries from the European Celtic cults of hunting and collecting the heads of enemies to bring them back to trophy rooms and sanctuaries, and of going to wells and waterways for healing and sympathetic magic. Stories of headless men and women and horses, sometimes with their heads sailing through the air in front of them [severed heads were capable of movement and speech] are variously associated with Tynron Doon near Penpont, where heads were rolled down the hill into [St Bride's] Well at the edge of Clonrae meadow; with Piltanton [Lodnagappal] Plantation on Genoch Moor in Stoneykirk parish; with the grounds at Park near Glenluce; with Corsock Hill; with Buckland Glen near Kirkcudbright; and, as late as the 1930s and 1960s, with Kirkdale Bridge and Glen.

Celtic stone heads, some two-faced and so looking backwards and forwards into the underworld, have been found in Dumfries-shire at Middlebie in Annandale, in Lochar Moss near Collin, and at the chapel site at Rockhallhead, in Dunscore or Auldgirth, and, in 1986, in Locharbriggs where a head from Tinwald Down had been in use as a doorstop. Animals, in particular the boar, the stag and the horse, were given a special place as deities: the discovery of a horse's head under the altar in the pre-Reformation church at Rerrick near Kirkcudbright was a remarkable example of the persistence of the old ways long after the apparent triumph of Christianity.

Celtic sacred pools and wells and streams and lochs were the homes of gentler gods and godesses. Treasures for the gods were sometimes left as offerings, for example, and both near Castle-Douglas, the Carlingwark hoard and the Torrs pony cap and drinking horn terminals sent by Joseph Train to Sir Walter Scott. The early Christian church wisely took over many pagan sites, erecting chapels at what became holy wells. In the seventeenth century contemporary offerings of clothes and money were left by local folk at wells and lochs which were believed to have healing properties. The Dowloch in Penpont parish, for example, was believed by 'the vulgar' to offer 'medicinal for both man and beast': 'Clothes' and 'Shackle or Teather' belonging to their cows or horses were left in or around the loch. The Dowloch also gave predictions of recovery: if the items left floated it was a good omen of recovery and if they sank then recovery was hopeless.

A brief Description of the bounds of the Presbytery of Penpont (c. 1720?) in Walter Macfarlane, Geographical Collections relating to Scotland, *vol. III, 1908, p. 203*

The Rev. George Smith (1793–1866), writing the Penpont parish entry in the Dumfries-shire volume of the New Statistical Account of Scotland *in 1836, included a detailed account of the legend of the Dowloch. He adds that*

> it is not long since the virtue of Dowloch was put to the test, as individuals are now alive of undoubted veracity and intelligence, who have seen the votive offerings floating on the lake, or scattered around its banks. And to such a degree had the habit prevailed in earlier times, that Mr Murray, the minister who lived till 1736, was regularly in the habit of debarring from the sacrament those who had engaged in the heathenish practice. (pp. 504–5)

Kirk sessions and presbyteries endeavoured to suppress these activities without seemingly much success. Minnigaff Kirk Session, for example, 'rebooked and exhorted' a number of young people, Patrick Stewart, James Reid, Jo. Roxburgh, Robert Roxburgh, Margaret Martine and Jean Reid, on 29th May, 1720 for visiting the Gout Well on the first day of May [H. Paton (ed.), Minnigaff Parish Records. The Session Book of Minnigaff 1694–1750, *1939, p. 358]. The Dumfries Kirk Session, which approved a number of similar entries, punished Dorothy Herais and Marione Hair on 19th June, 1645 for going to 'the idolatrous' well at Cairgen [Cargen] called St Jargon's [St Queran's] Well on the first Sunday in May. However, when the well was cleaned out in 1891, hundreds of coins were taken out, including William and Mary bodles and George II and George III pennies and halfpennies and farthings.*

Doctour George Archbald, Account of the Curiosities at Drumfreis and Further Account anent Galloway **(?1700)**
As for Wells, the three shires abound with many, unto which people resort, more famous from fables than fates.... Here are many superstitiously used, but Physical I know none, save Moffet Wells in

Annandale. A Well in Closeburn Parish in a Moss belonging to the Laird of Closeburn. Another at Tothorwald belonging to the D. of Queensberry. A third at Kirkbeen in Galloway within a mile of the black Lake in a meadow. These are used after the same manner, have the same colour, tast and smell but the ill luck of a lesser fame. Many run superstitiously to other Wells and obtain, as they imagine, health or advantage. But I know of no Physical influence. Only ... they are deceived and there they offer bread and cheese or Money, by throwing them in into the Well.

– Walter Macfarlane, *op. cit.*, pp. 188, 192–193

Andrew Symson, A Large Description of Galloway *(1684)*

Bootle ... about a mile from the kirk towards the north is a well, called the rumbling well, frequented by a multitude of sick people for all sorts of diseases the first Sunday of May, lying there the Saturday night and then drinking of it early in the morning. There is also another well about a quarter of a mile distant from the former, towards the east; this well is made use of by the countrey people when their cattel are troubled with a disease called by them the Connoch; this water they carry in vessels, to many parts, and wash their beasts with it, and give it to them to drink. It is too remember'd that at both the wells they leave behind them some thing by way of thankoffering. At the first they leave ether money or cloathes; at the second they leave the bands and shacles wherewith beasts are usually bound. ...

Mochrum ... Myreton pronounced Merton ... On the north side of this house and hard by it is the White Loch of Myrton, but why call'd white I know not except, as Sir William Maxwell informes me, it be so called because the water, as he saith, hath this property that it will wash linnen as well without soap as many others will do with it; and therefore in my opinion it is an excellent place for whitening or bleeching of linnen, holland and muzlin webbs. ... I dent not but the water thereof may be medicinal, having receaved severall credible informations that severall persons, both old and young, have been cured of continued diseases by washing therein; yet still I cannot approve of their washing three times therein, which, as they say, they must do, nether the frequenting thereof the first Sunday of the quarter, viz. the first Sunday of February, May, August and November, although many foolish people affirm that not only the water of this loch, but also many other springs and wells, have more vertue on those days than any other. ...

Kirkmaiden ... about a mile and an halfe from the parish kirk is a well call'd Muntluckwell; it is in the midst of a little bogg, to which well severall persons have recourse to fetch water for such as are sick asserting, whether it be truth or falsehood I shall not determine, that if the sick person shall recover the water will so buller and mount up, when the messinger dips in his vessel, that he will hardly get out dry shod by reason of the overflowing of the well, but if the sick person be not to recover then there will not be any such overflowing in the least. It is also reported, but I am not bound to beleeve all reports, that . . . there is a rock at the seaside opposite to the coast of Ireland, which is continually dropping both winter and summer, which drop hath this quality, as my informer saith, that if any person be troubled with chine-cough, he may be infallibly cured by holding up his mouth and letting this drop fall therein. . . .

THE DEFENCES OF DUMFRIES IN 1715

The Rev. Peter Rae (1671–1748), clockmaker, precentor, clerk, printer, and parish minister of Kirkbride (1703–32) and Kirkconnell (1732–48), brought out an excellent History of the Late Rebellion *in 1718. It was printed and published in Dumfries by his son Robert Rae (1698–1759) and reprinted in London in 1748. Although Rae did see the Rebellion in too simplistic terms as a struggle to prevent the reimposition of 'Popery and Tyranny', it was nevertheless a well-researched, wide-ranging and detailed 388-page account of the course of events in 1715.*

The Jacobite rebels in the south of Scotland, led by the Earl of Nithsdale, the Earl of Carnwath and Viscount Kenmure, were a small and relatively insignificant force in Scottish and British terms: they eventually joined the northern English rebels led by the Earl of Derwentwater to defeat at Preston. However, overall the 1715 rebellion in Scotland should have been, on paper, a Jacobite triumph. The men led by the predominantly Episcopalian, and Jacobite by conviction, landowners from Angus, Perthshire, Aberdeenshire and the north-east, plus the Highlanders out in 1715, greatly outnumbered the army put together by the Duke of Argyll.

In the south of Scotland Ayrshire, Renfrewshire, Lanarkshire including Glasgow, and Dumfries and Galloway, were overwhelmingly Presbyterian and loyal to George I. Landowners, the Marquis of Annandale, Col. Maxwell of Cardoness (1663–1752), who was sent to Glasgow in October to organise its defences, Alex. Ferguson of Craigdarroch, Thomas Gordon of Earlston, Sir Thomas Kirkpatrick of Closeburn and Sir William Johnston of Westerhall, joined with

Presbyterian parish ministers, notably in Tynron, Glencairn, Moniaive, Keir and Penpont, and the town of Dumfries to organise watches and trained bands. The Cameronian John Hepburn of Urr brought 300 men in eight companies to Corberry Hill outside Dumfries; and country folk from Tinwald, Torthorwald and Sanquhar came in to join in the defence of Dumfries.

Rae shows the town of Dumfries responding to the emergency and the Jacobite threat with an amazing display of energy and enthusiasm. Militias were organised, billets and provisions arranged, and weapons collected, improvised and distributed. These included 100 'war scythes' for those inhabitants 'with least skill of fire-arms'. Trenches were dug and filled with water, the medieval ports fortified, barricades raised on avenues and highways, perimeter walls strengthened, and on one Sabbath morning work continued in ditches and on a half-moon bastion. St Christopher's Chapel was almost demolished for building material.

✝

The Reverend Mr Peter Rae, The History of the Rebellion, Rais'd against His Majesty King George *(1718): the Second Edition 1746*
The Magistrates of Drumfries, being, on the 23d of July (1715), appriz'd, by Letters from London, of the Pretender's Design to land in Scotland . . . their Train'd Bands were drawn out, and strong Guards were constantly kept for the Safety of the Town. And for their more orderly Procedure, they choos'd of the Inhabitants seven Companies, of Sixty effective Men in each Company . . . and assign'd unto each of 'em their proper Officers. . . .

    I John Crosby of Holm, late Provost, Captain. John Kennan, late Bailey, James Gordon, Writer, Robert Gordon, Ensign, Lieutenants.

   II John Irving, Convener, Captain. Walter Newal, late Convener, George Michel, late Convener, Lieutenants.

 III William Craik of Duchrae, Collector of his Majesty's Excise, Captain. Thomas Edgar, Merchant, John Reid, Merchant, Lieutenants.

 IV James Young of Goolihill, Comptroller of his Majesty's Customs, Captain. Mr. Alexander Ker, Schoolmaster, Hugh Fraser, Younger of Laggan, Lieutenants.

  V John Neilson of Chappel, Captain. John Johnston, Merchant, Edward Maxwel, Merchant, Lieutenants.

 VI William Lawrie of Barnsoul, Captain. Robert Edgar, Writer, Joseph Currie, Writer, Lieutenants.

VII John Paterson, late Baillie, Captain. William Martin of Kirkland, Andrew Crosby, Son to Provost Crosby, Lieutenants.

These Companies were under the Command of the Provost, and carefully trained up in Military Exercises: And, for the more effectual training of the younger sort, a Company of Batchelors was formed out of the rest, who assumed the Title of, The Company of loyal Batchelors. . . . The well-affected Gentlemen, Ministers of the Gospel, and People in Nithsdale and Galloway . . . took care to make ready their Arms, and rendezvoused frequently; sometimes each Paroch apart by themselves, and sometimes in conjunction with others. (pp. 182–84)

The Half-Pay Officers, whom his Grace the Duke of Argyle, at the Desire of the Marquis of Annandale, had sent from Glasgow to train the Militia . . . being come to Dumfries by the 24th of October, many Hands were set on Work to entrench and fortify the Town: All the Gates and Avenues were built up with Stone, except the Bridge and Lochmabengate. A Line was drawn from the River to the Church-Yard (which was strongly fortified on the East and North Quarters), and from thence through the Meadow and Grounds to the Highway, without Lochmabengate: And on the other Side of the same, it run East, turning round towards the North West, and then to the South-East Corner of the Christal Chappel, making a Covered Way, in Form of a Half-Moon and Bastion. From the South-West Corner of the same Chappel, another Line was drawn somewhat parallel to the former, for the Safety and Convenience of the Men, in Case the Enemy should form on the Fields betwixt that and the Loreburn, which was also entrench'd and made fit for Service. The Inclosure, or Meadow, betwixt that and the Highway leading to the Townhead (which was built up with stone, as above), was sufficiently fortify'd by a strong Trench on the Inside of the Hedge: And on the other Side of the same Highway (at the Moat) betwixt it and the River, another Trench was cast up, in form of a Bastion. . . .

Upon Sunday, October 30th, the Rebels march'd from Hawick to Langholme. . . . That same Forenoon, about Nine a Clock, the Provost of Dumfries, and Deputy Lieutenants . . . ordered a Bank to be beat, and Intimation to be made to the Workmen (who had scrupled to work on the Lord's Day) to repair in the Trenches immediately with suitable Instruments for carrying on that Work; which they did accordingly. The Wrights cut down several Trees in the Church-Yard in Time of Sermon, and clave them for Stakes to secure a Dam thro' the Milburn, to cause the Water flow up to fill that Part of the Trenches, and to stop the Passage of the Enemies Horses through the Meadows: The Masons threw down the East Gravel of the old Chapel, which was then a fine Arch, and levell'd the same, and the Back-Wall, to a convenient Height as placing of Firelocks thereon; the Stones being drawn down to the Highway, a Redoubt was built to cover the Enemy. (pp. 274–75)

THE GRAITNEY AND PORTPATRICK MARRIAGE MARKET

Although Portpatrick was, in a sense, the Gretna Green for Ireland, the situation at Portpatrick was quite different that at Graitney [Gretna]. Marriages of Irish runaway couples were performed by the parish minister who 'accepted' a fee of £5 [latterly £10], until the practice was banned by the church courts in 1826. It was a neat racket, 'a nice little earner' for the benefit of the parish minister between 1773 and 1836, the Rev. John Mackenzie (his stipend in 1790 was a handsome £80), and the session clerks. Urquhart was parish minsiter between 1832 and 1843 as assistant and then successor to Mackenzie. He joined the Free Church in 1843.

Gretna, however, was always scandalous and a fit subject for ridicule and satire in newspapers and journals. The 'irregular' marriages were performed by a series of rogues, charlatans and showmen. In the eighteenth century it seems to have been mainly fools and fortune-hunters from the ranks of the English nobility and gentry who exposed themselves to the miscreant marriage brokers of Gretna. By 1834 it seems to have been rather the silly and vulgar from the 'the lowest ranks of the population' who resorted to Gretna or to rival 'priests' in Annan or Coldstream. Morgan was the parish minister between 1790 and 1828 and his successor, Roddick, remained at Gretna from 1828 until his death in 1869.

✝

The Rev. John Morgan, The Parish of Graitney *(1793)*
Clandestine Marriages. – This parish has been long famous in the annals of matrimonial adventure, for the marriages of fugitive lovers from England, which have been celebrated here. People living at a distance erroneously suppose that the regular and established clergyman of this parish is the celebrator of those marriages: Whereas the persons who follow this illicit practice, are mere imposters, priests of their own erection, who have no right whatever, either to marry, or to exercise any part of the clerical function. There are, at present, more than one of this description in this place. But the greatest part of the trade is monopolised by a man who was originally a tobacconist, and not a blacksmith, as is

generally believed. He is a fellow without literature, without principles, without morals, and without manners. His life is a continued scene of drunkenness. His irregular conduct has rendered him an object of detestation to all the sober and virtuous part of the neighbourhood. Such is the man (and the description is not exaggerated) who has had the honour to join, in the sacred bonds of wedlock, many people of great rank and fortune from all parts of England. It is 40 years and upwards since marriages of this kind began to be celebrated here. At the lowest computation about 60 are supposed to be solemnized annually in this place. Taken at an average throughout the year, they may be estimated at 15 guineas each; consequently this traffic brings in about £945 a-year. The form of ceremony, when any ceremony is used, is that of the Church of England. On some occasions, particularly when the parson is intoxicated, which is often the case, a certificate only is given. The certificate is signed by the parson himself, and two witnesses under fictitious signatures. The following is a Copy of one of these Certificates, in the original Spelling: 'This is to ȝartȝay all perȝons that my be conȝernid, that A.B. from the pariȝh of C. and in county of D. and E.F. from the pariȝh of G. and in the county of H. and both comes before me and declayred themȝeleȝs both to be ȝingle perȝons, and now mayried by the forme of the Kirk of Scotland, and agreible to the Church of England, and givine ondre my hand, this 18th day of March, 1793.'

Is it not a disgrace to the police of a civilized country, to permit such irregularities to be practised with impunity? And is it not a reflection on the good sense and discernment of the Nobility and Gentry of England (for some of the English Nobility have been married here), to suffer themselves to be imposed upon, and their pockets to be picked by such miscreants?

– *OSAS*, IX, 1793, p. 531–32

An elopement from Carlisle

On the 25t ult. was married at Gratney-Green, Mr Edward Ward, of Castle Sowerby dry-salter, to Miss Bell, of Kingmoor, near Carlisle; the envied hope of many wooers. On the night appointed by the lovers for the elopement, the bridegroom went from Carlisle to Kingmoor, in a chaise, attended by a British tar, who more than once had seen the united navies of France and Spain fly before him. . . . On their arrival, they were greatly mortified to find the father had obtained intelligence of Miss's intention, and had locked every door to prevent her escape. What cannot love devise? they found means to converse through a key hole, and she informed her lover, that if he could get a rope, and ascend the top of the house his attempt would be crowned with success; for he might easily *draw her up the chimney*. A rope was accordingly procured, and the lover, assisted either by the wings of love, or a peat-stack which stood adjacent to the house, ascended, and instantly enlarged the lady: who, though besmeared with soot, retained her pristine charms, and vows, and the indissoluble knot was tied without further interruption. This (we presume) is quite *a new stratagem*, which may with great propriety enter into the composition of the next *soporific* administered in the shape of a *novel*.

– *DWJ*, 29th October, 1793

The Rev. Andrew Urquhart, The Parish of Portpatrick *(1838)*
Portpatrick was long celebrtated as the Gretna Green for Ireland. Parties who could not obtain ecclesiastical sanction of their marriage on the other side of the channel, with all the expedition or secrecy which the opposition of relatives or other circumstances rendered desirable, found their way to this place, and on satisfying the minister that there was no legal objection to their union, were admitted to the benefit of proclamation in the parish church immediately on their arrival, and were married without delay. These marriages are registered in the records of the kirk-session, and attested by the minister and the witnesses. The fees exacted on these occasions varied according to the rank and ability of the parties. The lowest sum that was accepted at one time was £5, but it was latterly raised to £10, payable to the minister, and £1 to the session-clerk. This practice was abandoned in 1826, in consequence of the interference of the church courts; but during the preceding period of about fifty years, the records of these marriages exhibits the names of 198 gentlemen, 15 officers of the army or navy, and 13 noblemen.

– *NSAS*, vol. IV, 1845, *Wigtonshire*, p. 140

The Rev. James Roddick, The Parish of Graitney *(revised March 1834)*
The far-famed marriages of Gretna Green are celebrated, it is said, to the number of three or four hundred annually. The parties are chiefly from the sister kingdom, and from the lowest ranks of the population. . . . Parties have been known to betake themselves hither, from the north of Scotland itself, to celebrate a marriage which, a few lines written by a magistrate, a lawyer, a shoemaker, or a sexton, and signed by two witnesses at home, might have effected equally well, according to the present law of Scotland. . . . Great numbers resort to these altars of Baal, whose priests are numerous in this district and others, more particularly about Annan and Coldstream. Their number, indeed,

has sadly injured the trade, for the fees are now only half-a-crown a-pair. One of these functionaries, who breaks stones daily on the verge of England, has the best chance of succeeding, for he accosts every party as they pass, and tries to strike the best bargain. Tippling-houses have each their rival priest, some of whom satisfy the parties by merely giving lines signed by witnesses, and others by jabbering over a portion of the service of the church of England. Wherever such irregularities are practised, they are calculated to bring *all* law and *all* religion into contempt and ridicule. . . .

– *NSAS*, vol. IV, 1845, *Dumfries-shire, p. 273*

JOSEPH TRAIN AND THE 'REVERED SIR WALTER'

Joseph Train (1779–1852) is best known as the post-1814 supplier of stories and ideas and of objects of antiquarian interest to Sir Walter Scott. The 'objects' included everything from battle-axes and the Torrs chamfrein to thumbkins and a cow's tail charm, to protect cattle against witchcraft, from Scroblemore in Minnigaff parish.

Brought up in Sorn parish and, from 1787, in Ayr itself, Train found employment as a weaver before serving in the Ayrshire Militia from 1799 to 1802 as a substitute for James Stevenson, Erroch, Carsphairn. His first book, The Poetical Reveries of Joseph Train, *published by subscription in Ayr in 1806, has a sharpness and a savage innocence in, for example,* The Cabal o' Witches *and the epitaphs, which is good fun.* Strains of the Mountain Muse *(1814), although the rich historical footnotes attracted Scott's attention, is a much more prosiac and indeed rather dull collection.*

Train's long career in the Excise service, in Ayr from 1806, and in Balnaguard near Aberfeldy, Largs, Newton Stewart (1813–20), Cupar, Queensferry, Falkirk, Wigtown, Dumfries, and Castle-Douglas (1826–31) gave him a wide range of contacts and informants. On retirement in 1831 he lived at Lochvale, Castle-Douglas.

In Newton Stewart Train and the local antiquarian, Captain James Denniston, sent out a printed circular to schoolmasters and parish clerks in the south of Scotland asking for information on forts, Roman camps, moats, and local manners and customs. The history of Galloway project and any ideas Train might have had of publishing a collection of local traditions and tales lapsed, perhaps because he became completely overawed by Scott's friendship and his own role as a collector and supplier to Scott. The letters to Train now in Hornel's Broughton House archive (MS. 2/26A) from Denniston and from William Dobie of Beith, Hugh

Hamilton of Belleisle, David Wallace of Newton (Ayr), James Wright of Greenock, Hugh Jeffrey of Dumfries, William Todd of Kirkmaiden, Robert Malcolmson of Kirkcudbright, William Smith of Moniaive and Alexander Murray (on the Craigenrae murder hole) cover a vast range of subjects. Denniston and Mr Broadfoot, the schoolmaster at Clachan of Penninghame, who supplied a story to Train for Scott's Doom of Devorgoil, gave him an excellent description of the Barholm (later a Dirk Hatterick) Cave entered then, as now, by a narrow vent and involving sliding down a 20-feet rockface into an area furnished with recesses and pigeon-house type rectangular storage compartments; and McKerlie sent in a report on the tenant farmer at Cruggleton, after 1838, filling up the castle ditch and using stones from the castle to build a new farm house and offices.

Scott himself recognised in the prefaces and introductions to his novels how much he owed to Train. In Guy Mannering, Old Mortality and Redgauntlet in particular Scott had depended on Train's knowledge of Dumfries and Galloway locations and characters. Eddie Ochiltree (Andrew Gemmell) in The Antiquary and Madge Wildfire in Heart of Midlothian (the Galloway Feckless Fanny or the Wife wi' the Sheep) are other examples. One difficulty is that people in ninteteenth-century Dumfries and Galloway did want too much to identify fictional with real people and precisely located places and sometimes pushed possible parallels to excess.

Train's letters to Scott (MS 874, National Library of Scotland) included information on Robert Paterson, 'Old Mortality'; on the Levellers; the Fife Gypsies; William Marshall, 'The King of the Randies', and his wife Flora Marshall, sometimes identified with Meg Merrilees; Captain Yawkins and the smugglers (information to Train from James Copeland); the Torthorwald Fire Raid; the Waponschaws at Dumfries and Kirkcudbright; the Dunscore kirkyard funeral of Excise officer Farkine; traditions of Stoneykirk and Kirkmaiden (from William Todd); Andrew Gemmell's grandson, the surgeon on Pellew's flagship in 1812; Galloway customs and stories (from Alexander McCreadie of Kirkinner, who was in his 106th year in 1829); Manx history and traditions (from James McCrone, the factor to the Duke of Atholl); the Amorous Abbot of Dundrennan (from John Anderson, Kirkcudbright); and, in a letter of 8th October, 1830, the story of the blind fiddler and harpist William ap Prichard of Llandegai, 'the chief gutscraper' at Bridals and Merry Making from Gretna Green to the Braes of Glenapp (including information from John Rain and the Rev. John Williamson of Twynholm).

The stories of Cooper Climent, used in Old Mortality, and the 'Civil

War' at Lockerbie suggest that Train would have been a more than merely
competent author and editor of a Dumfries and Galloway anthology. His
Buchanities from First to Last *(1846) is a useful book. Train's work was*
also used by Chalmers in his Caledonia, *including the story of* The Deil's
Dyke *(from Samuel Wilson of Burnbrae, Crossmichael); by William*
Mackenzie in his History of Galloway; *and by the ministers of Buittle,*
Crossmichael and Minnigaff in the New Statistical Account of Scotland.

✝

The Civil War in Lockerbie: Letter from Joseph Train to Sir Walter Scott, 4th September, 1829

Revered Sir Walter . . . The anecdote in Guy Mannering page 271 of the
old woman at Lockerby asked for a person of the name of Christian and
received in answer that there were no Christians there brought to my
recollection an affray that happened there at Old New Years Day 1827 of
which I happened to be an eye witness.

It had previously been the practice of the inhabitants of that village
who considered themselves of the first class to observe the first day of
January as a Festival, but there were others who thought Old New Years
Day a more proper time to rejoice and make merry as being the true
commencement of the year as handed down to them by their fathers – but
the uproar made on the street that morning was so very offensive to the
modern party that they resolved to prevent the celebration of Old New
Years day at all and a Mandate was issued to that effect.

On Hogmanay the Guisards go round the village of Lockerby as
in other places in the South of Scotland and instantly on the clock striking
twelve the Town Drummer beats up a kind of tattoo at the Market place
and from thence proceeds through each vennel of the village rolling
and rattling . . . for the purpose of calling up the inhabitants to usher in
the New Year. Young women are in attendance by every stream and
around every well anxious to obtain a draught of the limpid eliment ere
the first moment of the year is past in the belief that each one will thereby
obtain more certainly the object of her affections. This custom which
is now falling into disuse is perhaps of even higher origin than drinking
out of Wells dedicated to Saints on certain days of the year for similar
purposes.

At the first tap of the midnight Drum the most convivial part of the
community sallies forth from their dwellings each with a flagon of mulled
Ale but the highest over proof Mountain Dew is now the most favourite
beverage there as it is in other parts of Scotland.

In Clydesdale and even in Galloway it was once a prevailing belief that the good and bad fortune that was to follow a family during the year was influenced by the person who first crossed the threshold on the first morning of the year being soncy or otherwise therefore a person whose concerns in life had been prosperous was generally solicited to be First Fet. . . .

The superstitious notions that gave rise to these observances . . . in Annandale . . . have wholly passed away. To drink and be merry seems now to be the sole object of the people of Lockerby mustering at midnight to the roll of the drum. As they meet in the street with their bottles and their buns they greet each other with hearty cheers rank together and visit in a body their friends and neighbours. . . . they are frequently under the influence of evil spirits even after the crowing of the Cock.

The mandate of the New Style gentry as they were denominated by the other party had a different effect from what they intended. It appeared to the Old Style people to be a direct infringement on their liberties. It operated as a War Cry to call each other to stand forward in defence of his legitimate rights. On Old New Years day morning the bottles and the bun circulated more freely than they had done for many years before. By the dawn of day all the Carts and Casks that could be found in the Town were piled up together in the centre of the streets thereby forming a barrier between the New and the Old Style villagers.

There having been a heavy fall of snow during the night the Old Style people collected such a quantity that they completely imbedded out of sight in it all the Carts and Casks gathered to that place. This formed a hill resembling the arch of a Bridge upon which they placed Centinels to prevent people either searching for their property concealed below or passing over the ridge from one part of the town to another.

The village then presented a scene of tumult. The Old Style people to the amount of at least two hundred were assembled at the outside of the Snow barrier round a large fire over which hung a pot of capacious dimensions full of water to make Toddy in a tub placed hardby which brought to my remembrance the recruiting sergeants Punch Bowl at the Hallow Fair 'that like the Sea would swim a large Dragon'. Wooden ladles were used to fill the glasses that circled merrily round till in the slang language of topers all were glorious. In this state man woman and child passed over the Snow bridge rank and file upon the Town as if to take it by storm vociferating most ludicrously as they went along.

The New Style people were provoked by their conduct and were angry at being deprived of their Carts Casks and wheel barrows buried in the snow heap assembled at the Market place for another purpose than to strype straes. As the Old Style people advanced they began to pelt them with snow balls. a general engagement immediatley insued. shreds of caps and ribbons and of sacksuns were soon seen twirling in the air. The finger nails of the females sank deep into the faces of their opponents whilst the clenched fists of the men seemed to deal mute-mete at every blow.

Since the last time the Cumberland Reavers pillaged the Town of Repentance such Blood and Battery had not been seen in Annandale. There were not any prisoners taken but the number of the wounded carried off the field of battle was nearly equal on each side. Both parties claimed the victory and were equally proud . . . but the result is that any person may now celebrate the New Year on any day they want or in any way he chuse without being molested for doing so. . . .

– J. Train, Castle Douglas, 4th September, 1829
The National Library of Scotland, MS874, f. 163–169

Cooper Climent of Borgue: Letter from Train to Scott, 12th May, 1829

Honoured and Revered Sir Walter . . . When I wrote last I omitted to mention the following anecdote of Old Mortality. . . . He was working at his usual employment in the Kirkyard of Girthon when the sexton turning up large fragements of old coffins out of a grave which he was making attracted the notice of some schoolboys passing through the churchyard on their way homewards, one of whom asked the Grave digger what use he made of the old coffins which he seemed to collect with so much ease and of which he had such a store. The sexton not giving an immediate answer Old Mortality in his usual facetious manner said what makes you ask that question when you know well enough that he sells all he can gather to your Grandfather to make luggies of.

Cooper Climent the person referred to carried on his business to considerable extent at Borgue Kirk not many miles from Girthon and served all the neighbouring farmers not only with luggies pails naps and milk dishes but with coops of every kind required in that part of the country. But it was frequently remarked that his vessels tinged whatever was first put into them with a reddish colour. A stripling who had often hesitated himself at taking his pottage out of some of cooper Climents coges ran instantly homewards to the farm house where he was servant. It being the harvest time the shearers were accidentally placed round one of those large dishes taking their kale out of it and as soon as the boy made the disclosure every spoon was thrown to the ground in disgust at the idea of supping out of the remains of an old coffin.

The report soon spread over the country. Some farmers destroyed the vessels which they had purchased from Cooper Climent even many years before; others returned them to him demanding repayment of the same, without taking time to examining into the report which spread so fast to the prejudice of the poor cooper but none was more unfortunate than the Laidi Wife of Borgue at thinking she had been so long plagued with scouring and scalding old coffins.

The coopers business having left him suddenly and even his life endangered by the hatred of the public he summoned Old Mortality to a Court at Kirkcudbright where he obtained damages against him for defamation of character, and although he proved to the satisfaction of every unprejudiced person that the vessels complained of were made out of the staves of Old Wine Pipes purchased from smugglers with whom the country abounded at that time, and although Old Mortality frankly made oath that he had no grounds whatever for the assertion he made, yet the coopers business continued to decline and he died a few years ago in abject proverty solely it is said in consequence of the report raised against him by Old Mortality. . . . J. Train Castle Douglas 12 May, 1829

The National Library of Scotland, MS874, f. 126–127

MARIA TROTTER
Galloway Gossip

Maria Nithsdale Maxwell (1803–79) married Dr Robert Trotter (1798–1875) at Creetown c. 1831. Four sons, Robert, Alexander, James and John all practised medicine in Northumberland, where the eldest, Robert (de Bruce) Trotter (1833–1907), edited and published Galloway Gossip Sixty Years Ago *(Choppington, 1877, 2nd edition 1878). The 392-page-long collection of her memories of the manners, customs, peculiarities and language of the people of* Wigtonshire *was 'to a great extent in the old lady's own words'. S.R. Crockett thought it was by far the best and most accurate Galloway [Wigtownshire] book ever written.*

†

Birth . . . I was born at Baraar in Penninghame, on the 3d of October, 1803 . . . my mother, whose name was Agnes Stewart, died two days after I was born, so of course I know little aboot her. I had an only full brother called Thomas, who died when about 14 years of age. The same doctor attended him that had attended my mother, and I mind of quarrelling my father for paying him for curing my brother when he had just let him die, and had let my mother die into the bargain. . . . (p. 2).

Farmers of Old. Farmers in my young days hadn't so much pride as they have now, and did not treat their servants as if they were a kind of nowt, or some kind of brute beasts for chirting work out of, and fit for naething else, as seems to be the fashion at present; but then the farmers were all natives and the servants natives too, and very often near friens forbye, but it's a' altered now-a-days – mair's the pity. The farmer and his family, and the men, and the lasses, all sat at the wan table, and sat round the same fireside, and conversed with one another as if they were all human beings alike, and I don't think they were anything the waur o't; and in the lang winter forenichts we teazed oo, and carded lint, and span, and workit stockin's, and dippit candles, while the men sang, and told us funny stories, and tales about ghaists, and fairies, and wutches, and the farmer was maistly the heartiest and drollest o' them a'; and when a' our work was done, the farmer gied out a psalm, and read a chapter of the Bible to us, and then put up a prayer, and after that we went to our beds. I mostly sleepit with one of the servant lasses, and I don't think it ever did me any ill. . . . (p. 6)

A Farm-House Dinner. It was the custom when I was young for the farmers and their families and all their servants to take their meals together in the kitchen, which was also the usual sitting room; and all the moderate-sized lairds followed the same fashion. It was usual for the gude wife, sometimes assited by the farmer, to rive up the (boiled) meat into convenient pieces before setting it down to the people; for knives were very scarce then, and there was seldom more than one in an ordinary farm-house. The first thing that was brought forward was the broth, or broos, as they used to call them, and they were set down either in a hooped wooden dish, or a big bowl, or a hand-basin, and each person had a horn spoon, and they all suppit out of the wan dish, farmer or laird and all. Then a hooped dish like a butter-nap, full of potatoes coarsely bruised with a three-toed thing like a graip, the ca't a rauhhel, which was stirred up and down in the pot to break them, was brought forward and set down to them. Then the meat was set down on an ashet, and the farmer lifted a junk with his hand, and reached it out to the one next him, and said 'hae!' then to the next and the next, till they were all served. Sometimes the potatoes were set down whole in a small basket or a nap, and then they took a potato in one hand and the meat in the other, and took rive about at them with their teeth; but when the potatoes were bruised they ate them with the same spoon they suppit the broth with, and took a rive at the meat and a mouthful of the potatoes time about. When the potatoes and meat were done, there was a big bowl of milk set down at each end of the table, and a basket of cake-bread in the middle, and they ate the bread, and suppit the milk to it, with the spoons they had for the broth and potatoes. Neither knives, forks, nor plates were used, except the plate to set the meat on. Before they begood to eat, the gudeman always askit a blessing, and returned thanks as soon as they were done. . . . (pp. 8–9)

Babby Vance. When I was young there was an old buddy they ca't Barbara Vance lived down in Glasserton, at a pit they ca't Craigdow, and she was very religious, and she had lost her man. . . . when the minister was visiting Barbara, the cat was sitting at the fireside during the interview, bisily hunting for fleas. Barbara remarked –

'What an odious torment sir, a flae is tae a cat, let alane a Christian; deed sir! it's a beast I canna thole ava.'

'You know, Barbara,' says the minister, showing off his knowledge, 'a flea, strictly speaking, is not a beast at all.'

'Bless me! sir,' says Babby, 'is't no! what is't then?'

'An insect, Barbara, an insect,' was the reply.

'In a sack sir, or oot o' a sack sir,' says Barbara, 'it's a' yin tae me; but yae thing I ken, sir, it can take a gude stanning jump.' . . . (p. 215)

Clogs. Despite the decrees of fashion and folly, clogs are now common enough in Galloway, and in the Stewartry and the eastern part of The Shire nearly all the young folk waer them in the winter. In the Rhinns they're ower proud to wear them; they wad raither gang barefit. I mind when there wasna sic a thing. The first time ever I saw clogs, I was a little lass about eleven. It was at Penninghame kirk, and they created a great sensation. Mrs Boyd of Mertonhall had been a' the way at London, and had brought this pair of clogs with her, and had worn them at the kirk and on several other occasions before I saw them. This Sunday when the kirk came out, I saw a lot of farmers' daughters and young women crowding round the Mertonhall carriage, and I pushed forward to see what was the ferlie, and was told that they wanted to see the 'shoon wi' wudden soles' that Mrs Boyd had brought from London. I managed to get a look at them as she entered the carriage, and thought them very curious, but I was nearly trampit down by the young ladies and the shoemakers in their struggles to get near enough to catch the fashion – the better day the better deed, they say. They soon became quite the rage, and for long after, every woman with any pretentions to gentility, used to wear clogs on all grand occasions, and to go to the kirk in; but after a while they got quite common, and not only the gentry, but just ordinary people, had them for Sunday before long. There's naething but puir people wears them noo. (pp. 3–4)

JAMES SHAW
Tynron in the 1860s

James Shaw (1826–96) was born and brought up in Barrhead in Renfrewshire. From the age of 13 he trained and worked as a calico pattern designer and printer at Gateside and Crosshill. Changing careers, he trained as a teacher at the Established Church Training College in Glasgow in 1855–56. After a year teaching in Melrose and three or four years in West Kilbride, in October 1862 he became the Tynron parish dominie at the school on the Shinnel Water two miles up from Tynronkirk. He remained there for the last thirty-four years of his life.

His many articles, papers and letters were brought together posthumously by Professor Robert Wallace of Edinburgh University and published under the title A Country Schoolmaster *(1899). Lecturer, author, poet, Church of Scotland elder, his very diverse interests included botany, biology and astronomy, curling, antiquarian research, and collecting local folklore, childrens' rhymes and riddles, and words in the Dumfries-shire dialects. He could be persuaded to give recitations from his collections.*

✝

When I arrived in Tynron, and for years afterwards, water was obtained almost universally from open wells; chimneys were swept by setting fire to them; messages were conveyed across straths by shrilly whistling on fingers; towns were reached by bridle paths. The mountain tracks then used for driving sheep to the great stock markets, such as Sanquhar, not being much employed for this purpose now, are falling into decay. The people around me to a greater extent than at present knitted their stockings, plaited their own creels, carved their own crooks, made their own curling brooms or 'cows', bored their own 'bod-and-lamb' boards, squared their own draught-boards. A very few women smoked tobacco like men, and many men had chins like women. Broom was boiled, the juice mixed with hellebore and tobacco, and used as a sheep-dip. The sheep, in fact, were not dipped at all, but their wool was shed into ridges, and the composition carefully poured on the skin from an old teapot.

There were no wooden frames for bees, only the cosy-looking straw 'skeps'. The Shinnel drove several mill-wheels, now it drives only one ... there was a method of announcing the arrival of letters, by depositing them in a water-tight chamber of a cairn on an eminence a mile perhaps from the shepherd's house, and then erecting a huge pole or semaphore, which soon attracted a messenger. The limbs and backs of boys were stronger, and carried for you heavy carpet bags at 1d per mile. Watches were worn in trousers' pockets. The school children were fitted out with stronger leather bags like soldiers' haversacks, containing their dinner as well as their books. . . .

When I found myself in the interior of shepherds' and dairymen's houses, the old eight-day clock, with wooden door and painted dial, was common. It kept company with the meal-ark, a huge chest divided into two compartments, one for oatmeal, one for wheaten flour. Bacon, hams, and flitches, then as now, wrapped in newspapers, hung from kitchen rafters. Puddings were wreathed round suspended poles. . . . An inner ladder was stationed in the porch or between the but-and-ben, up which the children or serving men mounted to their obscure attic shake-downs. On great nails, here and there in the walls, hung, and still hang, crooks, shears for clipping sheep, lanterns for moonless nights, mice traps with holes, rat traps with strong iron teeth and springs. There were no carpets in the rooms, but the floor was mottled with home-tanned sheep-skins in their wool, and the mat before the room fire was home-made, with all sorts of dark rags stitched together, having a fluffy, cosy look. . . .

On Sundays, waggon loads of children, carefully packed in straw, presided over by the maternal or paternal owner, or both, would pass my house on the road to church; wives and maidens who could not command such a conveyance walked past, their shoes and stockings in a napkin, ready to be put on at the rivulet's side nearest the church. At that time the greater portion of the families in my district were Cameronian or Reformed Presbyterian. . . .

It is well known that Kirkconnel in Tynron was a haunted house. Weird faces, with grinning teeth and fiery eyes, were wont to peep in at the windows on winter evenings. Eldritch sounds and low moanings proceeded in the darkness from the copse around. Indeed, had there not been a considerable use made of cast horse shoes, of rowan branches cut when no eye saw the cutter, of 'fow' (house-leek) growing on the thatch, and a careful observance paid to certain new moon and other duties, life would hardly have been worth living in that lonely shieling. Satan himself was once seen sitting on the ledge of the bridge which crosses the dark defile near it, but, scared, he fled beneath the starlight noiselessly down into a deep recess. . . .

Words from Dumfriesshire Dialect...

Faildykes, a wall built of sods .... *Fawns*, rough wet places on the hills, white spots on moorish or mossy ground .... *Flake*, a bar (sheep hurdle); *Flapper-bags*, burdocks; *Flapperbags*, butter-burs ... *Fleem*, phlegm, spume (the lancet used for bleeding cattle) .... *Flichen*, anything small or light, as 'flichens of soot'; *Flosh*, a swamp, a bog .... *Flype*, to turn inside out; *Foisonach* or *Fushloch*, waste straw, dried grass, chips of wood, or refuse of that sort; *Footy*, in good condition, applied to cattle; *Fow*, a pitch-fork; *Fow* or *Fooze*, the house-leek ... *Frem* or *Fremmit*, strange, foreign ... *Friggle*, to work vainly, to work at trifles....

Children's Rhymes ... sung in a low monotonous tone:

> No a beast in a' the glen/Laid an egg like Picken's hen;
> Some witch wife we dinna ken/Sent a whittret frae its den,
> Sooked the blood o' Picken's hen/Picken's hen's cauld and dead,
> Lying on the midden head. ...

The children's Hogmanay rhyme in Dumfries-shire is more polite than its Renfrewshire version:

> Hogmanay, troll lol lay,
> Gie's a piece o'pancake/And let us win away;
> We neither came to your door/To beg nor to borrow,
> But we came to your door/To sing away sorrow.
> Get up guidwife and shake your feathers,
> Dinna think that we are beggars,
> But boys and girls come out to play,/And to seek our Hogmanay.

– *A Country Schoolmaster* (1899), pp. 18–20, 35–36, 347–48, 377–78

JOHN MACTAGGART
The Scottish Gallovidian Encyclopedia (1824)

John Mactaggart was born on 26th June, 1797 at Plunton in Borgue Parish. His father, James, the tenant farmer, and his mother, Mary Sproat, had ten other children. After attending Borgue School, Mr Caig's school at Torrs near Kirkcudbright, and Kirkcudbright Academy from c. 1803 to 1810, his only other formal education was two winter sessions at the University of Edinburgh in 1817. After a few years on the farm he tried his hand in London, but his attempt at a weekly newspaper, the London Scotsman, *failed. However, he had his* Encyclopedia *published in London in 1824; 'printed for the author' and sold by, amongst others, A. Constable and Co., Edinburgh, J. Sinclair, Dumfries, J. Nicholson, Kirkcudbright, and J. Dick, Ayr. He had gathered his material for his long 504-page book over the years post-1817. Unfortunately it included an all too detailed and libellous account of the many scandalous liaisons across social/class boundaries of 'The Star O'Dungyle', Miss Heron of Ingleston, and under the threat of legal action the greater part of the print run was suppressed.* The Encyclopedia *was reprinted in a run of 250 copies in 1876 and again in 1981. Copies of the first edition were selling at prices of £100 and upwards in the 1970s.*

The skills in mathematics and engineering he had somehow acquired enabled him to obtain an appointment as Clerk of Works (1826–28) to the 160-mile-long Rideau Canal in Upper Canada. He proved to be a thoroughly competent surveyor and engineer. His Three Years in Canada *(1829) is a detailed account of his experiences. Returning home in June 1829 with swamp fever, he died at Torrs on 8th June, 1830.*

The Encyclopedia *was an extraordinary achievement by a reckless, mischievous and sceptical young man endowed with enormous energy and ability. It was at once a dictionary of 'singular Words, Terms and Phrases', including the rude and the crude, and a collection of poems, incantations, spells, gossip, anecdotes, tales and epitaphs. It had a very mixed reception.* The Scots Magazine and Edinburgh Literary Magazine *for October 1824 ran an overwhelmingly hostile nine-page review article on what it called 'the most extraordinary, not to say, monstrous production of the present age', written by a blockhead who indulged 'in the most loathsome obscenities' and filled page after page with his own and other poetry from 'senseless Sawnies'.*

Nevertheless, the Encyclopedia *is a great book. The arrangement of everything in alphabetical order makes it difficult to identify, without close study, some of the subjects in which Mactaggart was particularly well-informed, for example, curling or channle-stanes, bee-keeping, food (few could forget, having once read them, his definitions of 'braxy ham' and 'jumpers'), and 'bairnsplay' or children's games.*

The poetry poses some problems. To what extent, for example, were his 'cantrips' or witch spells really 'yet afloat on the atmosphere of traditions' and to what extent merely Mactaggart's own invention? His description of the 'gill-gatherers' is wonderful:

> *People who gather leeches in the marshes. These are commonly old women: they wade about with their coats kilted high; the vampires lay hold of them by the legs, when the gill-gatherers take them off, and bottle them up. These persons have commonly a long stick, called a gill-rung, with them. When they come to a deep hole, they plunge in it with this, and start the leeches, singing a strange song at the same time to the rouses of the pole.*

But was the song collected or edited or rewritten or invented by Mactaggart? The 'Bairnsplay' collection is probably much more straightforward from this point of view as a presentation of the games of Borgue and Kirkcudbright parishes in particular and Galloway in general.

✝

Bairnsplay
Allicomgreenzie: A little amusing game played by young girls at country schools. They form themselves into a circle; one goes round on the outside with a cap, saying, while so doing –

> I got a letter from my love,
> And by the way I drop'd it – I drop'd it.

Then she lets the cap fall behind some one, the which seeing, takes it up and runs after the other in order to catch her; but she eludes her as well as possible, by crossing the circle frequently, and the follower must exactly follow her steps; if she fails doing this, she must stop, and stand in the circle, face out all the game afterwards; if she succeed in catching the one, the one caught must so stand, and the other take up the cap and go round as before.

Rules o'Contrary: A female school game, much like *Allicomgreenzie.*

Dools: A school game; and school games are by no means things unworthy of observation, as many of them bespeak matters of the olden time, the one of dools then, amongst others, hints at something of this nature; the dools are places marked with stones, where the players always remain in safety – where they dare neither be caught by the hand nor struck with balls; it is only when they leave these places of refuge that those out of the doons have any chance to gain the game, and get in, and leave the doons they frequently must; this is the nature of the game. Now this game seems to have been often played in reality by our ancestors about their doon-hills.

Bucks and Kids: A school-game. See *Dools.*

Spy-ann: A game of hide and seek, with this difference, that when those are found who are hid, the finder cries *spyann*; and if the one discovered can catch the discoverer, he has a ride upon his back to the dools.

Chucks: A game with marbles played by girls.

Cuddy and the Powks: An ass with bags hanging about it; also a school game – two boys join hands and feet over the back of a third, the which creeps away with them on hands and knees to a certain distance, and if able to do this, he, the cuddy, must have a ride as one of the powks, on some other's back.

Hammer, Block, and Study: A school game. A fellow lies on all fours, this is the block; one steadies him before, this is the study; a third is made a hammer of, and swung by boys, against the block; it is a rude game.

Hinnie-pigs: A school game; also pots to hold honey. The boys who try this sport sit down in rows, hands locked beneath their hams. Round comes one of them, the honey-merchant, who feels those who are sweet or sour, by lifting them by the arm-pits, and giving them three shakes; if they stand these without the hands unlocking below, they are then sweet and saleable, fit for being office-bearers of other ploys. . . .

King and Queen o' Cantelon: A chief school game. Two of the swiftest of the boys are placed between two doons, or places of safety; these, perhaps, two hundred yards distant. All the other boys stand in one of these places or doons, when the two fleet youths come forward, and address them with this rhyme –

> King and Queen o'Cantelon,
> How mony mile to Babylon;
> Six or seven, or a lang eight,
> Try to win there wi' candle-light.

When out, they run in hopes to get to Babylon, or the other doon, but many of them get not near that place before they are caught by the runners, who taen them, that is, lay their hands upon their heads, when they are not allowed to run any more in that game, that is, until they all be taend or taken. This sport has something, methinks, of antiquity in it; it seemeth to be a pantomime of some scenes played off in the time of the Crusades. . . . Babylon in the rhyme, the way they had to wander, and hazard the being caught by the Infidels, all speak as to the foundation of the game.

Shuggie Show: The amusement of boys on the slackrope, riding and shoving one another in the curve of the rope; they recite this to the swings:

> Shuggie Show, Druggie Draw,
> Haud the grup, ye canna fa',
> Haud the grup, or down ye come,
> And danceth on your braid bum.

Whurlie-Birlie: Any thing which whirleth round; children have little toys they spin, so termed. . . . There is another poem in my wallet respecting the peasantry, termed *Auld Wullie Birlie* . . . I feel inclined to give it; and be it understood, when I name not the author of any piece, I want my readers to guess that, or let it alone, just as they feel. . . .

Rickety: Dickety. A toy made of wood, for children.
Dingle Dousie: A piece of wood burned red at one end as a toy for children. The mother will whirl round the ignited stick very fast, when the eye, by following it, seems to see a beautiful red circle. She accompanies this pleasant show to her bairns with the following rhyme –

> Dingle dingle dousie,
> The cat's a' lousy;
> Dingle dingle dousie,
> The dog's a' fleas. . . .

HOGMANAY
Belzies and Busked Boys

Anthropologists looking today for a New Year flambeaux procession, a swinging fireball display, a massive bonfire, or the old Burning the Clavie [clevies = torches] tradition would go to Comrie, Stonehaven, Biggar and Burghead: and to Foula or Berneray [North Uist] to bring in the Old New Year on January 11th/12th. But they would have been able to see all of these and much more exotica in nineteenth-century Dumfries and Galloway, in spite of the disapproval and opposition of the unco good. Reporting is selective, but some newspapers carry reports of bonfires of animal bones and wood [fire as a cleansing agent]; of marchers with flaming torches and blazing tar barrels; of parades of Belzies with black faces and Guisers; of mummers plays [sympathetic magic]; of a tradition of spreading mischief and disorder, removing fences, gates, shutters, carts and barrels; of dressing up as Busked Boys, not so much Ethiopian Minstrels as figures of darkness, 'whose name are legion', and malevolent spirits, or more innocently as cowboys, the 'Daring Dead Shots' of Whithorn in 1893, and 'Indians'; of gangs of 'beggars' going round the doors with rhymes that carried an unpleasant threat of violence –

> *Gin ye dinna gies our Hogmanay*
> *We dunner a' yer doors the day;*

of keeping the Old New Year in Lockerbie, Millburn Kirkcudbright, and Wigtown (The Oracle, Wigtown, February 1832) as late as the 1820s and 1830s; to all kinds of games from foot races and climbing the greasy pole to fottball in fancy dress, for example the Kirkcudbright Grand Character Football Match between two St Cuthbert Wanderers teams, an Ordinary XI with Buffalo Bill, Annie Roonie, Aly Sloper and Mrs O'Shea, and the Ethiopian Darktown XI; the cutty hunt in Kirkcudbright and Newton

Stewart; and the firing of guns and pistols by all and sundry and the 'discharge of squibs, crackers, and such like miniature artillery missiles' in all the villages along the road from Dumfries [GA, 1843]

✝

Kirkcudbright in the 1810s and 1820s

On New Year's Eve ... the apprentice lads and juveniles took to the streets, the harbour, and suburbs, collecting carts, boats, barrels, gates, the plants of masons and joiners, and hauled them to the market cross, where they deposited them to loud hurrahs. ... In the morning the owners knew where to find their missing property. ... There was wantonness, devilry it may be, but no malice in the absurd proceedings. Many of the boys, some even in the middle rank, itinerated the town and country as 'Busked Boys', two of them dressed in white, generally a shirt worn in blouse fashion, and one of them with blackened face and dark clothing. ... They used to return in the evening with a good purse, and a large stock of oaten cakes, supple scones and whangs of indigestible skimmed-milk cheese. ... Every man, lad, and boy, who could command a fowling piece or pistol took to the fields to try their luck at hares or birds. ... Boys during their fortnight of holidays went in greatly for catching birds by grins on a hoop, or by riddles supported on one side by a stick, having a string attached within reach of the setter. Then in very severe weather we used to follow the cruel practice of hunting cutties (wrens), dykeies (hedge sparrows), and other birds in hedges. The birds were weak from short commons. Two boys took to each side of the hedge, with stones provided, and kept firing away at the bird, which became stupid and confused owing to the fusilade, and generally succumbed at last. The sport was called 'the cutty hunt'.

... The Millburn folks ignored the modern New Year, but held Old New Year's Day. The only person in town who concurred with them in doing so was Mr Johnston, merchant, opposite the Meikle Yett. Their feasting took place on 12th January, and the boys and lads had noble sport at the shinty. ... The Millburn 'Busked Boys' made their rounds on Old New Year's Day. ...'

– Senex, 'New Year's-Day in the Olden Time', *KA*, 28th January, 1881

Creetown in 1874

The New Year was observed here in the usual manner. ... At an early hour of the morning, a number of boys denuded gardens and other places of their liggets, and evinced their bump of destructiveness to some extent.

The oft recuscitated flute band paraded the streets at six o'clock in the morning, preceded by tar-torches . . . that left miniature bonfires in their train, and burned two or three boys who were following them. Sports came off during the day . . . A leg of mutton was temptingly exposed for several hours on the top of the greased pole, at the Cross, and was eventually knocked off by Mr Alexander Stitt, after many fruitless attempts had been made by others. . . .

– *GG*, 3rd January, 1874

Hogmanay 1873

In Newton-Stewart . . . about 11.30 on Tuesday night a large crowd of boys and girls, men and women, many of them dressed as guys, guisers, belzies, or whatever the name is – faces black, fantastically dressed, and armed with huge sticks – assembled between the Angle and the Crown; pistols being fired and squibs and crackers set off meanwhile as of yore. At midnight a blazing tar-barrel was produed from somewhere, mounted somehow on two long poles; and these poles were perched on the shoulders of a dozen of the biggest of the belzies. . . . then a fife and drum band struck up, the crowd gave a yell, the belzies frantically flourished their sticks after the manner of wild Indians, and off the procession moved . . . surging crowds tramped from the Angle to the Brewery and back, and then over to Minnigaff. . . .

Kirkcowan. New Year's day passed off very quietly here . . . partly owing to the fact that the working-classes have little to sport, as the hours of labour have been so broken by the constant wet weather. Mr William McDowall, jun., originated a series of out-door sports, and collected in a short time upwards of two pounds, which was given in prizes from 5s downwards. The races took place in the street, and brought out a great number of onlookers. John Muir, shoemaker, showed that he was possessed of pedestrian powers of no mean order, and won the men's race in great style. John Tonner won the youth's race, and was most active when tied up in a sack. John Moore, although the smallest, came first in the boy's race. Alick McGarva cleared most ground in the hop, step, and leap. Wm Thomson showed most power and agility in putting the stone.

– *GG*, 4th January 1873

WALTER GREGOR
Folklore in Galloway

Walter Gregor (1825–97) was born at Forgieside farm near Keith. Educated at King's College, Aberdeen, he was first a schoolmaster at Gamrie, and then parish minister at Macduff (1859–63) and then at Pitsligo (1863–95). A formidable linguist and one of the leading British folklorists and ethnographers of his day, he combined his ministry with a vast output of scholarly books and articles on the language, dialect, traditions and customs of the farming and fishing communities of Aberdeenshire and Banffshire. He also edited Rolland's 1575 Ane Treatise Callit The Court of Venus *for the Scottish Text Society (1884) and provided the notes and a glossary for an edition of* The Poems of William Dunbar *(1893), including* Ane Ballat of the Fenzeit Freir of Tungland. *He was not popular in his own parish – perhaps the professional detachment with which he dealt with the 'coarse' and 'rude' material he collected and published was misunderstood by the embarrassed and puzzled good folk at Pitsligo.*

In 1895 he was commissioned by the Ethnographical Survey of the UK to undertake a survey of the traditions and popular superstitions of Galloway, which he visited in October and November 1895 and in Spring 1896. As a guest of Sir Herbert Maxwell at Monreith, and of parish clergy at Soulseat, Kirkmaiden, Minnigaff, Mochrum and Kells, he completed a detailed survey based on data collected from his 'informants' (many in their 80s), gamekeepers, blacksmiths, farmers, shoemakers, lead miners, carpenters, gravediggers and policemen. Kirkmaiden parish proved to be an especially rich area. His work was published in two parts as a Preliminary Report on Folklore in Galloway, Scotland *(1896) and a* Further Report on Folklore in Galloway *(1897).*

The following excerpts, out of at least 730 entries, give some idea of the range of his report. Mumming plays from Balmaghie and Laurieston are included in Chapter 9.

✝

The New Year. 449. Kirkmaiden. On the morning of New Year's Day the boys used to go in company to catch wrens. When one was caught its legs and neck were decked with ribbons. It was then set at liberty. This ceremony was called *the deckan o' the wren*. My informant has assisted at the ceremony.

Halloween. 641. Dalry. On Halloween the fairies rode on cats at the

Holme Glen, Dalry. On that night considerate housekeepers shut up their cats, to prevent them from being laid hold of by the fairies.

The Adder. 520. Kirkmaiden. A farmer of the name of Milnmine occupied the farm of Myroch. One day he went to an uncultivated hillock that was covered with whins to cut some. Near it was a hollow, and looking down into it from the hillock he saw a great number of adders, as many as would fill the box of a cart, all squirming through each other, with a white one in the middle of them. He threw among them the axe with which he was to cut the whins, and turned and fled. Next day he returned to search for his axe. In his search he found an adder-stone, a white stone with a hole through the centre of it. He preserved it carefully by putting it into his kist. He was never without money afterwards.

Human Hair. 601. Mochrum. Human hair was never burned. Burning the hair made one cross. It was twisted up, and put commonly on the wa' head, but at times into crevices of the walls of the dwelling-houses. My informant has seen tufts of human hair in holes of the walls of old uninhabited houses.

Death by Drowning. 335. Balmaghie. A blue light appears over the spot where the body of one that has been drowned lies on the ninth day after death, when the gall-bladder breaks.

338. Newton Stewart. My informant, an ex-policeman, in his investigation into a case of drowning in the river Cree, heard old people say, 'She has not got her complement yet.'

Marriage: Telling the Future. 206. Inch. Young women sometimes pin a piece of bread and cheese under the baby's dress when attired for baptism. After baptism the bread and cheese are divided and put below the pillow to call forth dreams as to the young women's future husbands. It is called dreaming cheese.

225. Minnigaff. To find out who was to be her husband, the young woman took an apple in one hand and a lighted candle in the other on Halloween, and placed herself in front of a mirror, and ate the apple in the name of *Uncle Geordie*, i.e. the devil. The face of the future husband appeared in the mirror when the last mouthful was eaten. My informant once went through this incantation, but when she came to the last bit she turned and fled in fright lest Uncle Geordie should make his appearance.

Cures and Spells. For the Sting of an Adder. 352. Kirkmaiden. Tear a fowl sindrie, i.e. asunder, and put it hot and bleeding over the wound. This was done, according to my informant, about thirty years ago, in the case of a man named James Garva.

For Deafness. 371. Kirkmaiden. Hare's urine was used as a cure. The bladder is taken from the animal, and the urine is squeezed out of it, and allowed to drop into the ear. Mr MacDouall of Logan has given a hare for this purpose.

For Mumps. 368. Corsock. The mumps is called branks. The mode of cure is to put a horse's branks over the patient's head and lead him or her to water as one does a horse.

For Cholera. 396. Mochrum. When cholera visited the country in 1832, pieces of raw beef were fixed to long poles, and the poles were erected on Mill Hill near Port William to catch the disease.

Some Old White Magic. 672. Corsock. The farmer of Crogo Mill had in the byres some of the stakes to which the cattle are fastened, made of rowan tree, as a safeguard from witches. He died about ten years ago.

684. Penninghame. In the cattle watering trough on the farm of Garchew in the parish of Penninghame, a holt stone was kept for the protection and luck of the cattle. It was called Old Nanny's mother's trough stone. Old Nanny Wilson died about 1891 at the age of ninety years.

698. Kirkmaiden. A byre girl sprinkles her urine over a cow's back when she is going to calve. This is done to keep off witches and ill-luck. Not long ago a farmer's widow ordered her byre girl to do this.

708. Rerrick. The skeleton of a horse's head was found below the pulpit when the old parish church was pulled down.

LANGUAGE AND PROVINCIAL DIALECTS

The story of the growth and decline of languages in Dumfries and Galloway is one for specialists with a knowledge of Welsh, Gaelic, Northumbrian English, Danish and Norse. At the Langholm and Canonbie end the vocabulary, phraseology and accents we hear to-day are reminiscent of the dialect and sounds of Cumberland and Carlisle; at the Stranraer and Portpatrick end we are very aware of the proximity of Ireland. Very few clergy use the Statistical Accounts as an opportunity to discuss language or dialect. The Rev. John Russell, the minister of 'Canoby' from 1784 until his death in 1814, provided a neat cameo of the situation in his parish in the 1790s:

> *Language. A mixture of the provincial dialects of Cumberland, Annandale and Eskdale seems to form the language commonly used here, which is very incorrect in point of grammatical propriety; and with respect to accent, harsh and unpleasant. The plainest rules of syntax are much violated: for example,* I is, thou is: I'se gaan, *for I am going;* thou'se get, *thou shalt get;* how'se' t'ou, *how art thou.* I wite is't, *a common expression meaning, I wot*

it is: in plain English, it is so. The word canny *is much in use here, as well as on the other side the border, and denotes praise. A canny person, or thing; a good sort of person, etc.. In you, the dipthong is sounded as in trout; and the vowel in me, as the dipthong in feign.'*

– OSAS, vol. XIV, 1794, p. 429

Many of the great figures of the Scottish 'Enlightenment' were also the leaders of the movement in Edinburgh, Glasgow and Aberdeen in the second half of the eighteenth century for the eradication of Scotticisms, i.e. for systematically and deliberately replacing the use of Scotch words and 'improprieties' of phraseology in speech and in writing with 'correct' English pronunciation and prose. David Hume, Adam Smith, James Beattie, Sir John Sinclair, and the historian and Principal of Edinburgh University, William Robertson, embarrassed and/or ashamed of the handicap of their spoken Scots, took very good care to write essays and books in the standard English 'of a united Britain', acquired by 'study and observation' [Henry Mackenzie] and careful preparation. A six-page list of Scotticisms was attached to the 1752 edition of David Hume's Political Discourses. *Hume, it was sometimes said, when he died confessed not his sins but his Scotticisms. Courses of lectures on elocution, for example by Mr Thomas Sheridan from Drury Lane in 1761 (repeated in 1762 and 1764), were attended by lawyers and politicians and aspiring literati, including the members of the Edinburgh Select Society for promoting the Reading and Speaking of the English Language (1761). Major books, Sir John Sinclair's* Observations on the Scottish Dialect *(1782) and, in particular, James Beattie's* Scotticisms arranged in alphabetical order, *published by Creech in Edinburgh in 1787, became standard readers.*

The course of lectures given by Hugh Mitchell in Dumfries in 1779 is a good example of the long reach of Edinburgh culture in south-west Scotland.

Elocution

Dumfries, June 22, 1779

Hugh Mitchell, M.A. proposes, on Thursday the 23d current, to begin, in the Town-house, Dumfries, A Course of Five Lectures on Elocution and English Pronunciation. Specimens from the most celebrated English Poets will be delivered at the conclusion of each Lecture. . . .

Lecture 1st.   An Address to the Company. . . .

Lecture 2d.   Of Articulation.

Lecture 3d.   Of Pronunciation and Accent.

Lecture 4th.   Of Emphasis and Cadence.

Lecture 5th.   Of Reading and Speaking Tones, and the Management of the Voice. . . .

A Ticket for the Course, 7s. 6d. For a Single Lecture, 2s. To begin at Seven o'Clock in the Evening. Tickets may be had of Mr Jackson, Printer; of Messrs Wilson and Boyd, Booksellers; from Mr McConchie, Preacher; and from Mr Mitchell, at Mrs Perry's, Middle of the Old Flesh-Market-Street.

– DWJ, 22nd June, 1779

Authors whose work contains discussion of language and dialect include Mactaggart on Borgue, Shaw on Tynron, William Todd on Kirkmaiden, J.F. Cannon on Whithorn, Gordon Fraser (1836–90) on Wigtown and Whithorn, Maria Trotter on Wigtownshire in general, and J.G. Horne on 'Some Dumfriesshire Dialects' (TDGNHAS, 18, 1931–33). It is interesting to compare their approach with more recent academic studies by John MacQueen, 'Welsh and Gaelic in Galloway' (TDGNHAS, 32, 1953–54) and 'The Gaelic Speakers of Galloway and Carrick' (SS, 17, 1973), and W.A.D. Riach's 'Dialect Study of Comparative Areas in Galloway' (SLJ, 9, 1979 and 12, 1980). Riach's work, based on interviews with older Gallovidians in 1971–72 and a follow-up survey in 38 local primary schools in 1980, demonstrated the changes as one moves across Galloway from west to east, so that a slatternly woman is a scutt, a huggery, a tudderie, a slitter and a clart.

✝

Maria Trotter, *Galloway Gossip* (1878)

Local Languages. It is a popular belief in Galloway that the language changes every four miles, and there is a good deal of truth in it, for there is a great deal of difference in the speech of the different parts of The Shire, one dialect prevailing in the Machars, one in the Muirs, one in the Rhinns, and another among the Fingauls of Kirkmaiden, and the one takes off the other and makes fun of them.

The side next the Stewartry, I think, speaks better Scotch than the Western side, which gives a stronger Irish twang to it, till a stranger is apt to get confused west of Stranraer, and wonder which side of the Channel he is on.

Lately however, the whole talk of Galloway is rapidly getting spoiled by a mixture of the lowest Lanarkshire Irish, Ayrshire Irish, and Liverpool English, elegantly embellished by the addition of the Glasgow snivel, which makes everything they say sound as if they wanted the roofs of their mouths, and had somebody holding them tightly by the nose all the time they were speaking. ... And then they have brought their horrid Glasgow-Irish-English grammar into Galloway too, to make things worse, and in defiance of all rules of Scotch, English, or any grammar but that of the Keelies of the High Street, they say *I seen* for I saw . . . *he has went* for He Has Gone . . . and a lot of others in the same strain. . . .

We used to have a rhyme or saying, when we lived in Penninghame, that we cried at the Machars folk when they came to Newton-Stewart to the fair or the market; it was supposed to hit off the peculiarities of their language.

> Luk in the n'yuk,
> An' g'yim me the cruk,
> Or A'll hit ye on the faice wi a raid blaizin pait, so A wull.

That is about as near the way they pronounced it as I can make it. . . . (pp. 151–2)

Gaelic. Although in old times Gaelic used to be the common language of Galloway, very few folk now-a-days have any idea that it was ever spoken here, and still fewer would ever guess that any remnants of it now exist.

I have heard my man say that when he was a boy there were still a few old women in the Glenkens that could speak a few words of it; and that in his father's time there were plenty of old folk among the hills that used it for talking among themselves. . . . The only traces of it now left, as far as I can find out, are to found among . . . the Fingauls or Heehhenders of Kirkmaiden; though when I was young there were some Gaelic words used in the Machars too, but I didn't know they were Gaelic then. . . . (p. 263)

Gordon Fraser, Lowland Lore, or the Wigtownshire of Long ago *(1880)*
. . . the major part of the provincial speech is still in the pithy native tongue, and for long any attempt on the part of a native to substitute English equivalents for certain peculiarly Scotch terms; or, still more, any inclination to 'speak English' (even without imitation of the disliked English accent), was sure to exite ridicule or contempt, and the delinquent would, with much scorn, be stigmatized as a creature of pride and vanity . . . when there arose a necessity for 'speaking proper' (as it was phrased), the unwonted effort was often attended with difficulty, not unfrequently with confusion of thought as well as speech, and occasionally with amusing blunders. . . .

High-sounding words, often mistaken as an indication of wisdom or learning, no doubt had a charm and influence over some of the burgh's indwellers. There is a story told of a young woman who, on her return to Whithorn from a visit to Liverpool, remarked to a neighbour: 'Oh, George, I learned sic nice expressions when I was in England! . . . *Infuse*

the tea (Isna' that beautifu'?) and *Mysterious Visions* (oh! that's gran!) . . .'
(pp. 146–48)

A Chapter of Gallovidian Proverbs, Phrases, Similes, and Characteristic
Sayings. . . .
A person with a sour countenance is said to 'hae a face like the far 'en o' a
French fiddle. . . .'
'What's that yin yawpin' at: he haes surely got a crack in the lug wi' a
Carlisle biscuit.' This allusion is to a Scot indulging in high-flown
English. . . .
'He (or she) is nae scone o' yesterday's bakin' . . . .'
A miserly individual is sometimes alleged to be one 'that would skin a
louse for its hide. . . .' (pp. 155–61)

4

A MATTER OF LIFE AND DEATH

✝

It is almost impossible to 'see' the people of Dumfries and Galloway behind the crosses and holy wells of the Early Church or beyond the shining piety of the ruined medieval abbeys and chapels – how they thought? How important to them was protective magic? What did the central concept of the life passage of the soul mean to them? How real for them were the stories of famines and the savagery and ethnic cleansing of the Old Testament? For example, David's treatment of his defeated enemies from the city of Rabbah where 'he brought forth the people that were therein, and put them under saws, and under harrows of iron, and under axes of iron, and made them pass through the brick-kiln: thus did he unto all the cities of the children of Ammon' (II Samuel, XII, 31). There are saints' lives and biographies replete with miracle stories to authenticate the saintliness of Ninian and Ailred of Rievaulx: and no doubt many of the Cistercian abbots and priors at Dundrennan and Glenluce and Sweetheart were able and good men, who brought with them from France a new order and discipline and skills in land reclamation and sheep ranching.

Indeed some of the most interesting evidence for the twelfth and thirteenth centuries is in the register and records of Holm Cultram abbey in Cumberland. The Cistercians at Holm Cultram held properties in Kirkgunzeon, Kirkconnel, Lochrutton and Southwick, vills, granges, saltworks, fisheries, pastures for sheep and oxen and pigs, and land reclaimed from the sea with access rights to landing places: properties whose boundaries, marked by burns and streams and cairns and crosses and oaks which had crosses on them, were perambulated over hills and through woods and across mosses, for example in Kirkconnel between Polleychos and Grenesiche and from Polleroth to the Nid: properties they defended with their own armed retainers, servants with bows and arrows.

The extracts in this chapter, however, provide an opportunity to look at some of the better documented 'heroic' figures of the seventeenth, eighteenth and nineteenth centuries, from Samuel Rutherford, ever ready to turn love of God into hatred of anyone who disagreed with his version of Presbyterianism, to eccentrics (Mother Buchan) and good and decent men (Young, Gibson, McFarlane). It also explores some of the work of

*'good' and 'bad' and 'indifferent' Christians and of how 'piety' and
'goodness' (or madness) could turn religion all too easily into a matter of
life or death.*

✝

GAVIN YOUNG OF RUTHWELL
A Tranquil and Useful Life

*Gavin Young (c. 1586–1671) took his MA from the University of St
Andrews in 1612. As the minister of Ruthwell parish (1617–71) he lived
through a period of extraordinary turmoil in Scottish church history. A
good and brave man, he managed to find the best and middle way
between the wild excesses and mutual intolerance of Episcopalian and
Presbyterian forms of government. He endured and accepted them all.*

The description by Robert Chambers sums up his life and significance:

Ruthwell church-yard contains . . . a monument to the Rev. Mr Gavin
Young, once minister of Ruthwell, and a sort of Scottish Vicar of Bray.
This reverend person was ordained minister in 1617, when the church
was presbyterian. Soon after, the king established an episcopalian form of
church government, which was followed up, in 1637, by the introduction
of a liturgy. Mr Young treated these matters very differently from his
brethren, being apparently more concerned about the spirit of religion
than its forms.

By and bye came the Covenant; and presbytery flourished again in its
plenitude of acrimony, corrugation, and baldness. It was all one to Mr
Young.

Next came Cromwell's time, when sectaries of all sorts, like a variety of
carrion flies, arose from the prostrate carcase of the church – all equally
hating, persecuting, and being persecuted in their turns. But Mr Young
had a fair word to every one, and in secret made the church and living of
Ruthwell the chief object of his care.

At the Restoration, Episcopacy got once more upon his legs, and,
putrid and gouty as they were, contrived to stagger through the six and
twenty years which ended in the Revolution. Good old Gavin still held
fast by his integrity and the kirk of Ruthwell. What is more, he
maintained his character; was respected by all parties for his moderation
and learning; lived a tranquil and useful life; and died in peace, after
enjoying his cure for fifty-four years.

There is surely no impropriety in supposing that it would have been much better for Scotland had all the ministers, instead of canyelling for two generations about visionary points of doctrine, administered the practice of the church with the gentleness, faithfulness, and effect of the minister of Ruthwell. . . .

Ruthwell church-yard contains . . . the fragments of a Runick monument, which is said to have been brought from heaven, and planted here, before a church existed upon the spot. The church was built over it some time after, in consequence of the worship which the people paid to it . . . to prevent the venerated object from taking another flight. It was broken down from its place in the church, by order of the General Assembly of 1644, who were scandalized at the respect still paid to it by the far descended prejudice of the people.

– Robert Chambers, *The Picture of Scotland* (1827), 3rd edition, 1834, I, pp. 204–05

As Chambers also pointed out, the tombstone epitaph to Gavin Young, his wife Jean Stewart, and their children and grandchildren is 'worthy of commemoration':

> Far from our own,
> Amid our own we lie;
> Of our dear bairns,
> Thirty and one us by.
>
> Gavinus Junius
> Unius agni usui
> Jean Stewart
> A true saint.
>
> A true saint I live, so I die it;
> Though men saw not, my God did see it.

Note also the inscription for their daughter, Christian Young or Wilson, who died in 1653:

> Heir lyis the earthly pairt
> Of Christian Young, 'spous
> To John Wilson, who depairted I of
> March, 1653, of hir age 27.
>
> My Dear Mother, Heir I ly,
> Ten before me, the 11th am I.
> Dear Spous while you behold
>
> This Shryne, Think on your
> Bony babs and myne.

SAMUEL RUTHERFORD
'ALL CHRIST'S GOOD BAIRNS GO TO HEAVEN'

Samuel Rutherford (c. 1600–61) was held in high regard in eighteenth- and nineteenth-century Scotland as 'the Saint of the Covenant', as a man of 'true Godliness'. Some part of this reputation stemmed from the lyrical qualities of his Letters, *which greatly appealed to Victorian readers in particular.*

Rutherford was born at Nisbet in Roxburghshire and educated in Jedburgh and at the University of Edinburgh (1617–21). Appointed by competition as Professor of Humanity [Latin] in 1623, he had to demit his charge after antenuptial fornication with Euphame Hamilton, who was shortly to become his first wife [Edinburgh Town Council Minutes, 3rd February, 1626]. She died in June 1630, and in March 1640 he married Jean McMath, who died in May 1675. He was appointed minister of Anwoth parish in 1627 through the influence of John Gordon of Lochinvar and Rusco, who became Viscount Kenmure in 1633.

Rutherford's strongly held Presbyterian and anti-Episcopalian views brought him into conflict with Thomas Sydserf, the Bishop of Galloway, and in 1636 he was exiled to Aberdeen in the strongly Episcopalian north-east. He remained there from 20th September, 1636 to June or July, 1638, when he was able to return to Anwoth. He took part in the General Assembly in Glasgow and in the Presbyterian triumph, the religious and political revolution against Charles I and Episcopacy, led by nobles, lairds and clergy. In 1639 he was appointed Professor of Divinity at the University of St Andrews and in 1647 Principal of St Mary's College. He was in London from 1643 to 1647 as a commissioner to the Westminster Assembly. In 1651 he was in the minority opposed to the support given by the Scottish Parliament to Charles II. After the Restoration of the monarchy and a diluted form of Episcopacy in 1660 he was stripped of his offices and cited to appear before the Scottish Parliament on a charge of high treason, but died on 29th March, 1661 without having had an opportunity to plead his case.

One reason for the charge of treason was his Lex Rex, *or the Law and the Prince (1644), which, although it may seem now a tedious and pedantic textbook was in the seventeenth century seen as a revolutionary statement of something like popular sovereignty as against the Divine Right of Kings and of the duty of men to resist tyrannical rule: government is from God – the best form of government is a mixed monarchy – but the power of creating a man king is from the people alone.*

However Rutherford believed in absolute certainties and in the idea of a totalitarian Presbyterian Godly State able, with the full apparatus of the General Assembly, Synods, Presbyteries and kirk sessions, to wage war against heresies, nonconformity, blasphemy, adultery, disorder and petty mischief. Rutherford and his colleagues believed that the Devil or AntiChrist and his agents were at large in the world and were identified as bogus churches, the Pope and the Catholic Church, bishops and the Episcopalian establishment, and, by 1648, the English sectaries or Independents who had been allies in 1639. As Rutherford himself declared, 'I am made of extremes' [letter to the Rev. David Dickson, who in 1642 was made Professor of Divinity in the University of Glasgow, 1st May, 1637]; and his Letters *and books with their Old Testament imagery confirm this assessment.*

†

The ceremonies now entered in the kirk . . . are superstitious, idolatrous, and antichristian, and come from hell. . . . Its plain Popery that is coming among you . . . and wo be to a dead, time-serving, and profane ministry; they are but a company of dead dogs.
  – Rutherford, *The Last and Heavenly Speeches, and Glorious Departure, of John, Viscount Kenmure,* 1649. [Kenmure died on 12th September, 1634.]

Our clergy is upon a reconciliation with the Lutherans . . . Let us not fear or faint. He will have His Gospel once again rouped in Scotland, and have the matter going to voices, to see who will say, 'Let Christ be crowned King in Scotland'. It is true that Antichrist stirreth his tail; but I love a rumbling and raging devil in the kirk . . . rather than a subtle or sleeping devil. (Letter to the Rev. John Livingstone, 7th February, 1637)

For the rest, I write it under my hand, there are days coming in Scotland when barren wombs, and dry breasts, and childless parents shall be pronounced blessed. (Letter to John Gordon of Cardoness, Younger, c. 1637)

I desire to see no more glorious sight, till I see the Lamb on His throne . . . and the crown put upon Christ's head in Scotland again. And I believe it shall be so, and that Christ will mow down his enemies, and fill the pits with their dead bodies. (Letter to Bailie William Glendinning, Kirkcudbright, 21st September, 1637)

I would fain both believe and pray for a new bride of Jews and Gentiles to our Lord Jesus, after the land of graven images shall be laid waste; and that our Lord Jesus is on horseback, hunting and pursuing the Beast; and that England and Ireland shall be well-sweeped chambers for Christ and his righteousness to dwell in. (Letter to Dr Alexander Leighton, 22nd November, 1639)

But who can blame Christ to take me on behind Him (if I may say so) on His white horse, or in His chariot, paved with love, through a water? (Letter to the Rev. David Dickson, 7th March, 1637)

Rutherford's letters were gathered together and published by the Rev. Robert McCuard [or McVaird or MacWard], a lad from Glenluce and a former student of his at St Andrews, when in exile in Rotterdam in 1664. The definitive collection of the Letters was edited by the Rev. Andrew Bonar, a moderator of the Free Church of Scotland, in 1891. The letters contain some remarkable and extravagantly lyrical and opulent passages, combining erudite scholarship and erotic imagery with some very direct, not to say rude, counselling and instruction. One feature of the collection of 365 letters is that 220 were composed during his period of exile in Aberdeen. Fifteen and ten letters are dated respectively to the 13th and 14th of March, 1637 – perhaps Rutherford added the dates when an opportunity arose to send a packet south with a reliable messenger.

Forty-four letters were addressed to Marion McNaught, the wife of William Fullerton, the provost of Kirkcudbright, and the niece of John Gordon, Viscount Kenmure, and forty-two to Lady Kenmure [Lady Jane Campbell, the daughter of the 7th Earl of Argyle]. Rutherford's brother George, a schoolmaster in Kirkcudbright between 1630 and 1636, when he was removed from his post, is mentioned in some letters, but his own [first] wife only features in two letters and his children in one. Some of the most interesting letters are those sent to the lairds of Cally, Rusco, Cardoness and Earlston; to his parishioners at Anwoth en masse *and individually, for example to John Clark and to John Henderson, the tenant of Rusco farm; and to Jean Brown, the mother of the Rev. John Brown of Wamphray parish (1655–62), who died in exile at Rotterdam in 1679.*

Woe, woe to the inhabitants of this land! for they are gone back with a perpetual backsliding. These things take me so up, that a borrowed bed, another man's fireside, the wind upon my face (I being driven from my lovers and dear acquaintance, and my poor flock) find no room in my sorrow. I have no spare or odd sorrow for these; only I think the sparrows and swallows that build their nests in the kirk of Anwoth, blessed birds. (Letter to Lady Boyd, from Aberdeen, 1st May, 1637)

Let your children be as so many flowers borrowed from God: if the flower die or wither, thank God for a summer loan of them. . . . (Letter to Lady Earlston, 7th March, 1637)

There be two herbs that grow quickly in our souls in summer weather: security and pride. Humility is a strong flower that grows best in winter weather, and under storms and afflictions. (*Sermon preached in the parish of Anwoth*, published by John Nicholson, Kirkcudbright 1842)

Rutherford to Viscount Kenmore: What will you think, My Lord, when Christ shall dry your watery eyes, and wipe all tears from your face, and lay your head upon his breast, and embrace you in his arms, and kiss you with the kisses of his mouth? (*The Last and Heavenly Speeches . . . of John, Viscount Kenmure*, 1649)

I beseech you, in the Lord Jesus, to mind your country above; and now, when old age (the twilight going before the darkness of the grave, and the falling low of your sun before your night) is come upon you, advise with Christ, ere ye put your foot into the ship, and turn your back on this life. (Letter to John Bell, elder, Anwoth, from Aberdeen, 1637)

Remember, when the race is ended, and the play either won or lost, and ye are in the inmost circle and border of time, and shall put your foot within the march of eternity, and all your good things of this short night-dream shall seem to you like the ashes of a bleeze of thorns or straw, and your poor soul shall be crying, 'Lodging, lodging, for God's sake!' then shall your soul be more glad at one of your Lord's lovely and homely smiles, than if ye had the charters of three worlds for all eternity. (Letter to John Gordon, elder, Cardoness, 1637)

The advice Rutherford gave could be extremely specific, even to his patron John Gordon:
My worthy and dear brother, Misspend not your short sand-glass, which runneth very fast. . . . I beseech and obtest you in the Lord, to make conscience of rash and passionate oaths, of raging and sudden avenging anger, of night drinking, of needless companionry, of Sabbath-breaking,

of hurting any under you by word or deed, of hating your enemies. (Letter to John Gordon, at Rusco, 14th March, 1637)

Lady Cardoness was given her instructions:
Stir up your husband to mind his own country at home. Counsel him to deal mercifully with the poor people of God under him. They are Christ's, and not his; therefore, desire him to show them merciful dealing and kindness. (Letter to Lady Cardoness, 6th March, 1637)

In his letters to John Gordon, younger, of Cardoness and William Gordon of Earlston, Rutherford shares something of his own experiences as a young man: Forsake the follies of deceiving and vain youth: lay hold upon eternal life. Whoring, night-drinking, and the misspending of the Sabbath, and neglecting of prayer in your house, and refusing of an offered salvation, will burn up your soul with the terrors of the Almighty, when your awakened conscience shall flee in your face. Be kind and loving to your wife: make conscience of cherishing her, and not being rigidly austere. . . . Ye know that this world is but a shadow, a short-living creature, under the law of time. Within less than fifty years, when ye look back to it, ye shall laugh at the evanishing vanities thereof, as feathers flying in the air, and as the houses of sand within the sea-mark, which the children of men are building. (Letter to Cardoness, younger, 1637)

I must first tell you, that there is not such a glassy, icy, and slippery piece of way betwixt you and heaven, as Youth; and I have experience to say with me here, and to seal what I assert. The old ashes of the sins of my youth are new fire of sorrow to me. . . . The devil in his flowers (I mean the hot, fiery lusts and passions of youth) is much to be feared: better yoke with an old grey-haired, withered, dry devil. For in youth he findeth dry sticks, and dry coals, and a hot hearth-stone. . . . Yet I must tell you, that the whole saints now triumphant in heaven, and standing before the throne, are nothing but Christ's forlorn and beggarly dyvours. What are they but a pack of redeemed sinners? . . . All Christ's good bairns go to heaven with a broken brow, and with a crooked leg. (Letter to Gordon of Earlston, younger, 16th June, 1637)

Much honoured sir . . . I long to hear how your soul prospereth. . . . I beseech you, in the Lord, to give more pains and diligence to fetch heaven than the country-sort of lazy professors, who think their own faith and their own godliness, because it is their own, best; and content themselves with a coldrife custom and course. . . . It is impossible that a man can take his lusts to heaven with him; such wares as these will not be welcome there. . . . What was the cause of Solomon's falling into idolatry and multiplying of strange wives? What, but *himself*, whome he would rather pleasure than God? What was the hook that took David and snared him first in adultery, but his *self-lust*? and then in murder, but his *self-credit* and *self-honour*?. (Letter to John Lennox of Cally, 1637)

To his parishioners: I instructed you of the superstition and idolatry in kneeling in the instant of receiving the Lord's Supper, and of crossing in baptism, and of the observing of men's days, without any warrant of Christ our perfect Lawgiver. Countenance not the surplice, the attire of the mass-priest, the garment of Baal's priests. The abominable bowing to altars of tree [wood] is coming upon you. Hate, and keep yourselves from idols. Forbear in any case to hear the reading of the new fatherless Service-Book, full of gross heresies, popish and superstitious errors, without any warrant of Christ, tending to the overthrow of preaching. You owe no obedience to the bastard canons; they are unlawful, blasphemous, and superstitious. All the ceremonies that lie in Antichrist's foul womb, the wares of that great mother of fornication, the kirk of Rome, are to be refused. . . . I have heard, and my soul is grieved for it, that since my departure from you, many among you are turned back from the good old way to the dog's vomit again. . . . I arrest their souls and bodies to the day of our compearance. Their eternal damnation standeth subscribed and sealed in heaven by the hand-writing of the great Judge of quick and dead. . . .

Ye were witnesses how the Lord's day was spent while I was among you. . . . What will the curser, swearer, and blasphemer do, when his tongue shall be roasted in that broad and burning lake of fire and brimstone? And what will the drunkard do, when tongue, lungs, and liver, bones, and all, shall boil and shall fry in a torturing fire? . . . and there is not a cold well of water for him in hell. . . .

I know there are some believers among you, and I write to you, O poor broken-hearted believers: all the comforts of Christ in the Old and New Testament are yours. . . . Your lawful and loving pastor. (Letter of 13th July, 1637)

To his parishioners: Remember that I forewarned you to forbear the dishonouring of the Lord's blessed name, in swearing, blaspheming, cursing, and the profaning of the Lord's Sabbath; willing you to give that day, from morning to night, to praying, praising, hearing of the word, conferring, and speaking not your own words but God's, thinking and meditating on God's nature, word, and work. . . . And that crossing in baptism was unlawful and against Christ's ordinance. And that no day besides the Sabbath . . . should be kept holy. . . . Also, that Idolatry, worshipping of God before hallowed creatures, and adoring of Christ by kneeling before bread and wine, was unlawful. And that ye should be humble, sober, modest, forbearing pride, envy, malice, wrath, hatred, contention, debate, lying, slandering, stealing, and defrauding your neighbours in grass, corn, or cattle, in buying or selling, borrowing or lending, taking or giving, in bargains or covenants; that ye should work with your own hands, and be content with that which God hath given you. . . .

But if there be any among you that take liberty to sin because I am removed from amongst you, and forget that word of truth which ye heard, and turn the grace of God into wantonness, I here, under my hand, in the name of Christ my Lord, write to such persons all the plagues of God, and the curses that ever I preached in the pulpit of Anwoth, against the children of disobedience! . . . Your loving and lawful pastor. (Letter of 23rd September, 1637)

THE MAIDEN AND THE GOOD WIFE OF BALMACLELLAN

Margaret Thomson was a daughter of the manse. Her father, Robert Thomson, was minister of Muiravonside (1613–15) and Torryburn (1615–28), and her brother Patrick was a minister in Ireland. She was baptized on the 4th of February, 1606. She married James Keir, who became minister of Glenluce or Old Luce parish in Wigtownshire in 1630: he was only about 27 years of his age when he died in 1632. Her second husband was Robert Murray, the minister of Balmaclellan parish in the Stewartry of Kirkcudbright from 1625 until his death in 1644: they had two children, James and Elizabeth.

Murray was deposed by a Commission of Kirkcudbright appointed by the General Assembly in Glasgow in 1638 on charges of oppression, drunkenness, railing, selling the sacraments, sacrilege, bribery, etc. He was allowed to return to return to his charge in 1643. At the same time in 1638 Patrick Adamson in Buittle parish was deposed for his disobedience and 'insufficiencie for the Ministrie' and 'frequent drunkenness on the Sabbath, and dancing in his drunkenness'; Robert McClellan in Kelton for his disobedience and 'insufficiencie' and intemperate drinking; and James Scott in Tongland for his disobedience and absence from his flock for eight

Sabbaths. However, 'oppression', 'disobedience' and 'insufficiencie' may only be code words applied to ministers whose record lacked the 'correct' strongly Presbyterian and anti-Episcopalian sentiments necessary in 1638–39. Murray's reputation may have left a shadow of doubt over the quality of life in his manse at Balmaclellan and is unlikely to have helped his widow during her trial before the Court of Justiciary in 1645.

Margaret Thomson was beheaded by the Maiden on the Castlehill of Edinburgh on 28th May, 1646, for adultery in June, 1644, while her husband was still alive, with John Edmonston of Gravaland, the minister of Mid Yell in Zetland, who was also 'ane mareit man'. The case against her also included the fraud and false testimony she used to have her 'adulterous chyld', a 'maidin bairne, baptised. She was tried before a jury of fifteen Edinburgh merchants and craftsmen, including a goldsmith, a stabler, an armourer, two fleshers and a tailor. She does not seem to have had any legal representative to present a defence and at the trial confessed her guilt to the charges. She was accused in court of

the filthie cryme of adulterie committit be hir (hir husband being leveand) with Mr Johne Edmestoun, minister at Yell in Zeitland, committit in the moneth of Junii 1644 yeiris, in the Cannogait, neir to the burght of Edinburgh, to the quhilk Mr John Edmestoun scho bure ane maidin bairne . . . in the moneth of Merche thaireftir 1645 yeiris . . . eftir the birth of the said adulterous chyld, and to get the samyn baptizet, the said Margaret presentit ane counterfute testimoniall (subscryvit be George Walker and Johne Inglis, bailyeis of Edinburgh for the tyme) to Mr Patrik Hendersone, keiper of the kirk register, nameing hirself falslie Margaret Murray, the spous of Johne Brown, ane souldiour in Ingland under Sir Thomas Fairfax . . . the said adulterous chyld borne be hir was baptizet, commitin thairby manifest fraud and falsett. . . . the said Margaret Thomesone . . . to be tane to the castell hill of Edinburgh upone Monondy nixt the first of Junii nixt, and thair betwix twa houris and fyve in the eftirnoone to be execute to the daith . . . be streking hir heir fra hir body and hir moveabill guidis to be escheit to his Majestis use. . . .

(ed. J. Irvine Smith, Select Justiciary Cases 1624–50, The Stair Society, III, 1974, pp. 689–692). Another manuscript version (MS 1945), more in English than in Scots, i.e. maidin bairne *becomes* female child, *is in the National Library of Scotland.*

The Maiden was the ten-feet-high guillotine made in Edinburgh in 1564–65 and in use until 1710. It was presented to the Society of Antiquaries of Scotland in 1797 and can now be seen in the Museum of Scotland, where it seems to attract much more attention than the fine 1598 carved oak pulpit from Parton and the bookcase made of panels c. 1600 from Threave Castle. It was in a sense a distinction reserved for the élite to be taken by the 'Heiding Axe' or the 'Madan'. Even John Gordon, the 'sone naturall' of John Gordon of Knockschean (west of Dalry), found guilty in 1645 of bigamy in marrying 'twa wyffis' and of adultery with Janet Thomson in Kelso and of stealing sheep from Kellystown in Dumfries-shire and cattle from Barskeoch, was only hung on the Castlehill. The Maiden was for the likes of John Johnstone of Lochwood (1603), Lord Maxwell of Caerlaverock (1613) or Sir Godfrey McCulloch (1697), and for those guilty of what were seen as especially heinous offences, for example Alex. Blair, a tailor in Currie, for incest with his first wife's half-brother's daughter (1629), for Janet Embrie for incest with two brothers (1643), and for Grissel Hamilton for adultery and returning after being banished (1649).

Margaret Thomson was caught up in the post 1638-39 venomous evangelical enthusiasm and ambitious zeal of the Presbyterian extablishment to enforce Biblical prohibitions and penalties against adultery, bigamy, incest, homosexuality and bestiality. These were laid down for all to see in the King James Bible in Leviticus, Chapters XVIII and XX, in verses which encapsulated all too much of the savagery and madness found in parts of the Old Testament. The consequences were tragic and ludicrous. In Dumfries, for example, John Forsythe in 1639 and John Wright in 1665 were burnt to death for bestiality offences. Jean Knox, tried before the same assize as Margaret Thomson, was convicted of incest for becoming pregnant to William Murray in 1644 and then marrying his brother John, and was sentenced to be hanged. But 'justice' could be very uneven. It is surprising in the Margaret Thomson case that there is no mention of a punishment for John Edmonston and he was a son of the manse.

In general in seventeenth-century Scotland the state did not sanction execution for adultery, but persistent or 'notour' adultery, involving cohabitation which was not ended after warnings and excommunication and when a child was born, did make it a capital offence. Very few people were executed for adultery: scourging through the streets of a town, branding, banishment and fines were much more likely consequences. John Maxwell of Castlemilk, for example, was excommunicated before the Tundergarth kirk session in June, 1627, for adultery with Janet Chalmers, the wife of John Park, and fornication with Jean Irwing. At the local parish level a complex scale of penalties was imposed upon guilty parties, requiring them to appear in sackcloth before their congregations to purge their guilt in public: three appearances for one instance for fornication, six for a 'relapse' or second offence, twenty-six for a third offence and for adultery, three-quarters of a year or thirty-nine appearances for a fourth offence and a 'relapse' into adultery, and a whole year for incest.

WITCHES, CHARMERS AND LIBBERS

It is perhaps difficult today to begin to understand the terrible, absurd, and intoxicating enthusiasm with which Presbyterian and Episcopalian Christians in seventeenth-century Scotland, in particular in Berwickshire, the Lothians and Fife, set about strangling and setting on fire numbers of their fellow citizens as witches. At least 1,000 for certain, and more probably between 2,500 and 3,000 people, were executed as 'enemies of God', the worst of all heretics, men and women who were supposed to have made a pact with the Christian Devil. The standard textbook on witchcraft, used by Catholics, Lutherans, Episcopalians and Presbyterians alike, was the Malleus Maleficarum *(1494) by the Dominicans Heinrich Kramer and Jokob Sprenger, who were commissioned by Innocent VIII to bring together all the evidence from Biblical and classical sources. In Scotland James VI's* Daemonologie *(1597) had a special place and prestige as a local textbook. The new Bible in English had some very specific texts in* Deuteronomy, XVIII, v. 10–12, *in* Exodus, XXII, v. 18; *'Thou shalt not suffer a witch to live', and in* Leviticus, XX, v. 27; *'A man also or woman that hath a familiar spirit, or that is a wizard, shall surely be put to death; they shall stone with stones. . . .'*

Witchcraft prosecutions under the parliamentary legislation of 1563 and the General Assembly Acts of 1640, 1643, 1644, 1645 and 1649 were typically initiated at a local neighbourhood level with accusations, often going back several years, and evidence being taken before kirk sessions and presbyteries. Cases were then referred upwards to Edinburgh and trials followed before commissions appointed by the Privy Council or before the Court of Justiciary or before circuit courts, for example in Dumfries or Ayr. In Scotland in general there were peaks, with large numbers of trials in the 1590s and in 1620–30, 1640–49, 1650–59 and 1660–69. Cases in south-west Scotland do not fit neatly into this pattern, but the 1630s and 1650s seem to show the witch hunts at their worst. Changes from Episcopalian to Presbyterian dominance and vice versa seem to suggest that the new regimes tried to establish a reputation for sound orthodoxy and evangelical zeal by engaging in purifying witch hunts soon after coming to power.

Courts looked for evidence, to coincide with the fantasies of the clergy, that a witch had made a pact with the Devil consummated by a 'nipp', Satan's mark, on her or his body. It was believed that the witch was insensible to pain at that place. Confessions were important and these were obtained using torture, sleep deprivation, hair shirts (the Dumfries Burgh Council ordered their shirts from Langholm) dipped in vinegar to lift the skin off, pinniewinks or *thumbsrews,* boots *to crush the legs, turcas for tearing out nails, thrawing with ropes. . . . Itinerant consultants, specialist witchfinders or prodders or prickers, were employed by the burgh councils. In Dumfries, for example, Thomas Crawford the Prodder was paid £8.6s. for his services in November 1650. Elsbeth Maxwell was*

> tryit be the man who professit to discover witches by Satans mark, before she put off her shoes and stockings said God help us we have meslet skins we sit neir the fyer, and being blindfolded notwithstanding that shoe was sensible in the chyne and shrinked, yet being questioned thairefter whare shoe fand pain, shoe could not point the pairt nor did any blood appeir at all, the pin being thrust in a place fill of vains and sinews in her leg. . . . (Justiciary Court Processes, *1650*)

It was also necessary to establish that the witch had done actual damage to people or their property. The proportion of men to women varied from one to eight to one to ten: women were known to male theologians as more prone to malice and more susceptible to the snares of the Devil. 'Witches' in Dumfries and Galloway were often women who had a reputation for being difficult, aggressive, quarrelsome, 'libbers', revengeful, 'by habit and repute a witch', prone to cursing and ill-wishing, lewd, having a vicious tongue and a filthy temper; 'charmers', pretending to have special skills in cures and spells; and the poor and dispossessed, vulnerable, mentally unbalanced, the despair of their neighbours and blamed by them for the disasters which befell them, their cows and horses and livestock in general, their crops and their property. Elspeth McEwen, for example, was accused in 1698 of causing her neighours' hens to stop laying and of having a wooden pin at her command which could draw off milk from their cows, and of causing the minister's horse to tremble with fear and sweat blood when she was on its back. Janet Hairstanes was accused at her trial in May 1709 by Mr Andrew Reid, the minister of Kirkbean from 1699 to 1713, of moving his cow by magic and leaving it upside down in a hedge, of causing his house to fall down and of almost drowning him in a stream, and of vanishing from him when he was admonishing her only to reappear some distance away.

It is difficult to avoid concluding that Mr Reid and the eight ministers appointed by the Presbytery to assist their brethren at the day of the execution of nine witches in Dumfries in 1659 would have benefited from a week in hair shirts (with vinegar)! The eight ministers included John Welsh of Kirkpatrick-Irongray and John Brown of Wamphray.

The old legislation was repealed in 1735 and under the new Witchcraft Act it was only possible to charge someone with pretending to be a witch. It is interesting to speculate whether Scotland would have followed England in this respect in 1735 if the Union of 1707 had failed. Opposition to the repeal was strongest in the University of Glasgow. As it was, tolerance and good sense were imposed by the government upon a somewhat reluctant population.

✝

Privy Council Cases

4th February, 1630: A Commission to Sir John Charters of Amisfield and others to search for, apprehend, imprison and try Katherine McCheyne in Lochmaben, Marion Hannay and Janet Robsoun in Dumfries, Agnes Kirkpatrick in Hills of Lochretoun, Jonet Clerk in Hollowyairds of Hills, Marion Martine Alias Malie Martine, sometime in Barfill, Marioun Johnestoun alias Hauche and Margaret Affleck, long suspect of witchcraft.

9th February, 1630. Mansie Aslowane was executed to death as a witch in Dumfries.

1st June, 1630. A Commission to Sir Robert Grier of Lag and others to hold court and try Janet Herreis in Stelingtrees, Janet Ferguson in Torskechane, Isobel Moffat in Dumfries, Agnes Weir in Larbreck, all long suspected of witchcraft.

6th November, 1644. A Commission to James McDougall of Garthland and others to hold court and try Marion Shewan in Drochdoole, Afrik Elam in Knockbuie, Marion Russell in Glenluce and Isobell Bigham in the parish of Stranrawer, all delate guily of witchcraft.

Tried before Judges Mosley and Laurence, Commissioners in Criminal Cases to the people in Scotland. 2nd to 5th April, 1659. Drumfreis, the 5th of Apryle, 1659. The Commissioners adjudges Agnes Comenes, Janet McGowane, Jean Tomson, Margt. Clerk, Janet McKendrig, Agnes Clerk, Janet Corsane, Helen Moorheid and Jennat Callen, as found guilty of the several charges of witchcraft . . . to be tane upon Wednesday come eight days to the ordinary place of execution for the burgh of Dumfries, and ther, betuing two and four hours of the afternoon, to be strangled at staikes till they be dead, and thereafter their bodies to be burnt to ashes.

Helen Tait, at the same assize, was found 'not cleirly proven' and was banished from the parish and required to find £50 Sterling, a massive sum, for future good behaviour. A Bessie Stevenson was also executed in Dumfries in March and Biggie Cairnes and Jennat McKnight in April, 1659.

The evidence taken by the Presbytery and given before the Justiciary Court in Dumfries in 1671 in the case of Janet Mackmuldroch, spouse to James Hendrie in Airds, is a good local case study. Airds was near the end of a road from Cally Mains to Sandgreen Hill and Airds Bay in Girthon parish. Cuffington, Laik and Clene (Clyn or Cloan) are all in the same area between the Fleet and the old parish church. Boghall Wood is on the road by Blackloch to Anwoth Church and Barley is north of Gatehouse. Miniboui or Monybuie is in Balmaclellan parish and was held in 1662 by a William Gordon. John Cannones, John Cairns and James Hendrie were tenants in the multiple tenancy farm toun of Airds. Jean Sprot was married to Rott. Cairns, the brother of John Cairns. Robert More or Muir was the parish minister of Girthon between 1668 and 1686.

Depositions against Janet Mackmuldroch

Johne Moor of Barley . . . depones yt about four zears since he having poyndit the sd. Janet she promised him ane evill turne and yr efter one of his oxin died therupon he challenged her and she told him he should gett ane worse turne and yr efter his chyld died of ane exterordinarie sickness sueting to death. . . .

Johne Murray of Laik . . . depones that about ane zear since he being at the Clyn wt the ad Janet wher by ane accidentall tuitch of the deponers feet she gott ane fall and went away cursing and within the space of fyve or six weiks yr efter he had two calffs ran wood and ramished to death. . . .

Jeant Sprut . . . depones that a bout 7 zears since or yr by that Janet Mackmuldroch came to borrou some meall from her which because she refused the sd Janet told her she should rue it more then the worth of the meall and yt same night she milked her cou the Milk was mixed with blood and flesh. . . .

Wm Gordoune of Miniboui . . . depones yt about 3 zears since finding the sd Janets guids upon his gras he turned ym off whereupon she folloued him scolding and told him that she hoped that he should not have soe many geir as he had then to eat the nixt grasse. . . . the nixt May ther was tuelve of his oxin and ky zoung and old and sevin or eight of his horse died befor Beltoun next and that she hes bein under ane evill report this long tyme bypast.

Rott Broun in Cuffitoun . . . that Janet . . . hir goods being upon his grass he turning the same she declaired that he should not have no many Nolt to eat the nixt grasse and that before John Cannones in airds and Jean Sprot and Cristian gordon which was found to be too trew for before hir sett tyme all his goods to his great lose dyed.

John Cairnes in airds deponed . . . that his broyr lying on his deathbed desyred James Hendrie to bring in the sd Jannet to pray god send him his helth and she refuised it and the sd Rott left his death upon hir and ordained him to persue hir to the death. . . .

Jean Sprot deponed . . . yt qun she Came first to the toune she went thryse withershines round about all the zeards bare-footed. . . .

John Naires in Clean deponed that when he poynded hir horse for eiting his grasse and corn she . . . went away Murmoring but he kneue not qt she Spake and he neuer gat rest nor sleipe afteruard till his Chyld drouned in ane peit pot. . . . Mr Rott more minister examined the sd Janet she declared that Jean Sprot ought not to be receaved a witnes in regaird she was a witch alse weill as she hirself. . . .'
[*For full text see A.E. Truckell, 'Unpublished Witchcraft Trials'*]
TDGNHAS, vol. 52, 1976–77, pp. 96–100.

Elspeth McEwen from Bogha near Cubbox was examined before Dalry kirk session in 1696, imprisoned in Kirkcudbright Tolbooth, and tried before a Privy Council Commission in March 1698. She was found guilty, strangled and burnt to ashes. The Kirkcudbright Burgh accounts on 24th August, 1698 include

> *For peits to burn Elspet wt . . . for twa pecks of colls . . . for towes, small and great . . . for ane tarr barle to Andrew Aitken . . . to Hugh Anderson for carrying of the peits and colls . . . to William Kirk qu she was burning, ane pint of aill . . . to James Carson his wife threeteen shillings drunken by Elspet's executioner . . . spent by the Proveist Wt Howell and Ba Dunbar, the day of Elspet's execution, ane gill brandie. . . .*

PETTY MISCHIEF

'thair be secreit spyes appoynted'

The tragedy of seventeenth-century Scotland lay not so much in the waste and loss in the Civil Wars and the Scottish/English/Irish wars, the plaque in 1647–48, and the famines of the 1690s, but rather in the clash between the Episcopalian and Presbyterian varieties of Protestantism. The totalitarian authoritarianisms of the Episcopalians (1660–89) and of the Presbyterians (1638–60 and post-1690) were not essentially different, although in the south-west of Scotland the Presbyterian establishment was more popular and therefore more successful in imposing its own tyranny. One sad commentary on their 'Christianity' was the refusal of Episcopalians and Presbyterians alike to recognise the validity of what they defined as 'irregular' marriages celebrated by 'clergy' other than their own. Any substantial degree of personal freedom and religious liberty only emerged in the eighteenth century when it was imposed by the British government and the Scottish aristocracy.

The burgh councils in Dumfries, Kirkcudbright and Wigtown and the kirk sessions (the merchants and craftsmen on one were often the elders in the other) worked together to control an unruly people. The burgh courts punished deviants, thieves and harlots, who might be branded, scourged, fined, flogged or whipt through the streets and banished; the kirk sessions, rural and urban, imposed their own cycle of public humiliation and retribution, and fines, banishment and excommunication. Kirkcudbright Town Council used one memorable phrase in introducing new rules on Sabbath observance in January 1639 'for trying quherof are secreit spyes appoynted'.

However well-intentioned, some of the new policies look like a crusade, and one which left little room for loving kindness or sweetness, to control and suppress even simple pleasures, games and football on a Sabbath, music and dancing at 'pennie-bridals', described in a 1645 Act of the General Assembly of the Church as 'fruitful Seminaries of all lasciviousnesse and debaushrtrie', and the observance of 'Yule-Day'. In Dumfries the piper, John Laurie, was refused permission to use and exercise his calling and told 'to tak himself to some honester way of living'. The Dumfries kirk session in 1643 stopped the old way of 'bringing in or birks at May games', accompanied, they suspected, by 'a number of suspicious and heathenish ceremonies'. George Richardson in Minnyhive [Moniaive] was cited before Glencairn kirk session in May 1715 'for keeping up people all night in his house playing and dancing to minstrels'.

The church in each parish, as the education authority and social welfare agency, controlled the appointment of schoolmasters and the allocation of bursaries for poor children and the distribution of money, of clothes and of blankets on loan and of meal to the poor and destitute, including travelling poor, provided they carried testimonials from their parish of origin. Money was allocated from fines, weekly collections, and legacies, and occasional appeals for charitable causes from the dependants of the captives of Algerian pirates (Penninghame, 1701) to destitute Protestants in France and Ireland.

The duties of the elders, for example in Dumfries and Holyrood parishes, included ensuring that no scandalous person without a testimonial (almost like an internal passport) was allowed to settle in their burgh or parish, checking in particular the position of any new servants. These controls on population movement and settlement could be quite brutal: Jonet Cairnes, for example, a servant to James McCairntney, was expelled from Kirkcudbright because she wanted 'ane testimoniall of her guid life' in Tongland where she lived, and Janet Boddane was warned (February, 1639) that if she or any of her 'bairnis' were found in Kirkcudbright she would be burnt in the cheek with 'ane het irne and skurgit' through the town. The worst offenders were permanently banished or excommunicated, that is cut off from all, even everyday business contacts with other people in their parish.

Strenuous efforts were made to enforce Sabbath observance and make attendance at morning and afternoon services compulsory. Elders in, for example, Dumfries, Glencairn, Minnigaff and Wigtown, were to go among the houses, looking in the windows searching for anyone keeping company and reporting their absence from public worship, and also visiting ale-houses to chase up stragglers for afternoon services. In Minnigaff (1702) a 'Drunken Bell' was rung one hour after the end of the sermon to remind drinkers to come back from the ale-house to the church. Attempts were even made, usually without much success, to require fractious lairds, Colvenan, Lady Elshieshields, Lady Craigs, to attend services.

Profaning the Sabbath, and there was an infinite variety of ways to do so, resulted in fines or worse. In Dumfries in 1685 the 'perverest knaves in all the burgh for Sabbath-breaking' were punished by being whipped before the kirk session. The ministers at Portpatrick and Kirkmabreck complained to the Episcopal Synod of Galloway in 1666 that boatmen going for Ireland and ferrymen at the Water of Craise [Cree] crossing to Wigtown were profaning the Sabbath. The Synod, also in 1666, ordered that Monday markets should be closed because they entailed Sunday *travel. You could be fined for playing cards, for cutting kale in the yard, for threshing corn, for looking for stolen or strayed livestock, for feeding fodder to horses or cleaning their stalls, for unnecessary travel, and even, by order of the Dumfries Burgh Counil in 1664, for walking idly from house to house or gossiping in the street on the Sabbath day. Wives, of course, were expected to walk in an 'orderly' way, that is, behind their husbands.*

All this left far too much scope for the purveyors of tittle-tattle, the malicious scandal-mongers, to do their worst. They had more opportunities for mischief making in keeping a watch on young girls and newly married women for evidence of [antenuptial] fornication and in carrying reports of 'uncleanness' to the kirk sessions. It is quite clear from the evidence of the Session Books of Minnigaff 1694–1750, of Penninghame 1696–1724, and of Wigtown 1701–45, that elders spent an enormous amount of their time there, as elsewhere, in examining in nauseating detail cases of fornication, adultery and incest among their neighbours. The processes and retribution dragged out over months and not infrequently years. Women were brought to the sessions and interrogated at length about the place and time and circumstances and frequency of their 'uncleanness' and, in cases of childbirth, of evidence of paternity. Offenders were publicly humiliated further by appearing in sackcloth at Sabbath services and, in a burgh, they might be placed in the jougs. Women who kept 'departing from virtue' were likely to be carted from the town [Dumfries]. In Wigtown in 1706 'several singing young women' living in the town and responsible for 'much sin and lewdness' were banished by the Town Council at the request of the kirk session.

A good detail of attention was paid to the activities of charmers and necromancers, 'cany' women and wizards: Thomas Stark in Drungone in Wigtownshire using his 'charmes, inchantementis, sorcerie and otheris divelishe and detestable practizes' (Register of the Privy Council, *15th May, 1622); the witch-wife in Dundrennan giving a salve to John McQuhan from Urr parish for his sick wife in 1656; the charmer Alexr Heron in Barskeoch in Penninghame parish in April 1670* (Register of the Synod of Galloway); *the smith to whom William Anderson in Hall of Forest in Irongray parish took his child in 1691 to be charmed with 'ane forge hammer'; and Alexander Douat, the gardener at Maxwelton, brought before Glencairn kirk session in November 1707 for finding and bringing back by charm and enchantment and some pretended occult quality [in herbs] the sheets and aprons and a silver tumbler stolen from Maxwelton. Douat was 'sought unto by persons from diverse corners of the country'. He told Sir Walter Laurie of Maxwelton: 'Lock me ever so close in a room and I will cause all the cloaths that were taken away hang down upon the spouts of the tower upon the morrow morning.' He also admitted going backwards from the fire to the door, round the close backwards, up the stair backward, and into bed backward!*

The charmers were at once marriage guidance counsellors advising on choosing husbands and wives and supplying love potions and aphrodisiacs, fortune tellers, and problem solvers finding lost objects and finding out thieves. Simple magic, turning the riddle, metting the belt, winnowing straw, turning the key in the Bible, was often attempted without recourse to the experts. Some of the nobility, including the 2nd Earl of Galloway, consulted the London astrologer, William Lilly (1602–81), for his advice on more weighty matters such as how to determine propitious dates before undertaking a voyage.

The charmers practised white magic, giving protection [spells, incantations] against the machinations of witches and brownies and spirits, and offering simple practical advice, for example, to place stones with circular holes on the lintels of their cow houses to protect their milk yield. This may have been important because the Reformers had taken away all the old Catholic defences of holy water, saints' relics, blessings on ships and crops and cattle, and inscriptions on crosses and bells and amulets. They were also healers sought out for their expertise in the use of herbs and pyscho-drama, for example in using South running water, to protect and cure people and their livestock.

Every little help mattered, as the near panic caused by the evil spirits and apparitions in three famous cases suggests. The Devil of Glenluce invaded the house of a weaver, Gilbert Campbell, between 1654 and 1658: the blame here was eventually laid on to a beggar, Alexander Agnew, who had threatened hurt to Campbell's family when he was not given the alms he asked for [he was later executed in Dumfries for blasphemy]. An evil spirit in the form of a bee or a black man possessed Jonet Fraser or Frissel in Closeburn c. 1684–87: she confessed to the Presbytery in 1691 that she had pretended to be a prophetess and to see visions. And a stone-throwing, minister-attacking spirit invaded the house of Andrew Mackie in Ringcroft of Stocking near Auchencairn between February and May of 1695: in this case the blame was put on the previous occupant, one Macknaught, who had sent his son to a witch-wife at Routing-bridge in Irongray parish. The Glenluce and Ringcroft visitations were published in George Sinclair's Satan's Invisible World *(1685) and in Alexander's Telfair's* A New Confutation of Sadducism *(1996) and generated enormous interest.*

✝

Banished to Borgue (or Tongland)
14th October 1601. The quhilk day it is statut that Bessie Lichtoun, Helene Lichtoun, Jonet Lichtoun, Bessie McKerrollie, Jonet Murray, Grissell Maxvell, Meg Herroun, Jonet Henrysoun, Barscob, Jonet Vakir, Lillie Schennan, Agnes McBirnie be expellit out of the toun for confessit and tryit fornicatiounes and adulterres commitit be thame and ordainis thame to be poindit for thair penulteis conforme to the actis of the kirk.
     – *Kirkcudbright Town Council Records 1576–1604*, 1939, p. 399

The following extracts are from the Minnigraff, Penninghame and Gretna kirk session records:

Penningham, 1703. The minister represents to the Session that there are several scandalous persons come in to be inhabitants of this paroch without sufficient testimonials. . . . and the Session appoints Thomas McKeand and John Martin to go to [the laird of] Castlestewart to discourse with him to remove the aforesaid persons out of his lands and to get his answer and report.

Penningham, 1701. Alexander McKeand cited, called and compearing and interrogat concerning breach of the Sabbath acknouledgeth that in complyance with his goodmothers desire de drave her cow to a bull on the Sabbath, esteeming it a work of necessity. He is informed and admonished that he be not found in the lyke again. . . .

Penninghame, 1709. The Session is informed that the people in the Newtown carry in water from the river to their houses and cutt their pot herbs on the Lords day and meet in companies for idle discourse. . . . They are to be discharged of this from the pulpit through all the parish under pain of censure for Sabbath breaking. . . .

Minnigaff, 1719. William McBurnley . . . confessed he had travelled upon the Sabbath day from Carick Miln through the parish of Bar and went past the church of Bar in time of sermon. . . .

Minnigaff, 1703. Andrew McMillan . . . confessed that he had driven sheep on the Lords day. . . . the session . . . appointed him to be rebuked before the congregation. . . .

Minnigaff, 1702. . . . ye members of ye session that live in ye toun of Minigoff are hereby appointed, each Sabbath evening after ye touling of ye bell, two and two persons, to go throu ye toun of Minigoff and search ye several alehouses yrof, and if they find any persons drinking beyond ye said tyme, to delate ym and the head of yr families. . . .

Minnigaff, 1705. . . . a flagrant report yt Margaret Heron, lawfull daughter to the Laird Heron, who hath been for some tyme out of the country without desiring testimoniall from us, was with child before she left the place. . . . The Session . . . appoints the minister to write to the said Margaret Heron . . . to attend the Session Wadensday next. . . .

Minigaff, 1726. John McClave . . . confessed that he had for 20 years begone had a custom to ly in that bed in the kitching of Machimore with whatever kitchen maid was there for the time . . . added that it had been a custome for the men and women of Machirmore to do so for a hundred years. . . .

Minnigaff, 1721. It being noised commonly that William Stewart daily haunts the hous of Agnes Young, spous to William McDouel, wright, notwithstanding they were both discharged of haunting one anothers company, the Session appoints one of their number to acquaint them that if they do not dishaunt their being togither their names shall be read out in the congregation as obstinate, and if persisting cited to the Presbyterie. . . .

Minigaff, 1720. Their being likewise a report of charming the falling sicknesse . . . by putting straw ropes about the persons middle and afterwards cutting it in three pieces and burning it in the fire, practised in this place, the Session appoints the minister to commun with the woman whose sone is the person affected.

Minigaff, 1729. Janet Barrie . . . having left her fathers hous and gone the lenth of Dumfrice in company with a soldier. . . . the Session thought fit to enquire into her end in so doing . . . she said she believed he had given her something in a pice of bread that he gave her which had inchanted her to follow him. . . .

Penninghame, 1706. Jean Brown, calld, compears and interrogat if she converses ordinarily with spirits answers affirmatively. . . . being interrogat if these spirits ly carnally with her as men and women do when they beget children. . . . she answered they do . . . they are invisible spirits and do not appear visibly to her but she feels them and they speak to her when they please but not allways when she would. . . .

Graitney, Februart 1733 and April 1741. It was represented by some of the members that the Charms and Spells used at Watshill for Francis Armstrong, Labouring under distemper of mind, gave great offence and 'twas worth while to enquire into the affair and publickly admonish the people of the evil of such a course that a timely stop may be put to such a practice. . . .

Several of the members gave account that in Barbara Armestrang's they burned Rowantree and Salt, they took three Locks of Francis's hair, three pieces of his shirt, three roots of wormwood, three of mugwort, three pieces of Rowantree, and boiled alltogether, anointed his Legs with the water and essayed to put three sups in his mouth, and meantime kept the door close, being told by Isabel Pott, at Cross, in Rockcliff, commonly called the *Wise* Woman, that the person who had wronged him would come to the door. . . . Mary Tate, Servant to John Neilson in Sarkbridge, is to be cited as having gone to the Wise Woman. . . .

Mary Tate . . . confessed that She had gone to Isabel Pot in the Parish of Rockliff, and declared that the sd Isabell ordered South running water to be lifted in the name of Father, Son, and Holy Ghost and to be boiled at night in the house where Francis Armstrong was. . . .

ROBERT WODROW
'ears erect at every tale of wonder'

Robert Wodrow (1679–1734) was a member of a famous Presbyterian dynasty of ministers. His father, James Wodrow (1637–1707), was a minister in Glasgow and, from 1692, Professor of Divinity in the University. Robert Wodrow graduated MA at Glasgow in 1697 and, after working as the University librarian, became the minister of Eastwood parish (1703–34). In 1708 he married Margaret, the daughter of Patrick Warner of Irvine parish, and widow of Ebenezer Veitch, the minister of Ayr from 1703 to 1706. They had sixteen childen, including Robert, Patrick and James, respectively ministers of Eastwood, Tarbolton and Stevenston.

Perhaps best known for his History of the Sufferings of the Church of Scotland *between 1660 and 1688 (2 vols., 1721–22), Wodrow was referred to by clergy and laity for opinions and advice. His voluminous correspondence, published in the* Private Letters . . . 1694–1732 *(1829),* Letters from Lord Pollok . . . 1703–1710 *(1835) and* The Correspondence of the Rev. Robert Wodrow *(3 vols., 1842–43), and his* Analecta *(4 vols., 1842–43) contain a vast range of subjects from Samuel Rutherford's last words, the McMillanites, the Levellers, witchcraft and devilry, precognitions and apparitions, and rumours of scandals, to the geography and anthropology of Mull, Guiney, Virginia and Caledonia Nova and Neu Edinburgh.*

Forever exchanging gossip and compiling data, he was nevertheless essentially a credulous gossip, 'ears erect at every tale of wonder' [H.G.

Graham], a real blethsrakate and a bit of a 'misery'. In 1728, for example,
he is lamenting the appearance of Allan Ramsay's lending library with its
'villanous profane and obscene books and plays' from London spreading
'abominations, and profaness, and leudness' in Edinburgh, and in 1731 the
presence of Strollers and Commedians, 'a most scandalouse way of
disposing of our money' and 'a dreadfull corruption of our youth'.
– Analecta, III, pp. 515–16, and IV, p. 214

✝

I am weel assured that the Countess of Dumfreice, Stair's daughter, was
under a very odd kind of distemper, and did frequently fly from the one
end of the room to the other, and from the one side of the garden to the
other; whither by the effects of witchcraft upon her, or some other way, is
a secret. The matter of fact is certain. January 1712.
– Analecta, II, p. 3

Mr A. Simson tells me, that about thirty years agoe, he had this accompt
from the Minister of Penpont and his wife, who wer witnesses, and from
many others. The thing was noture and knouen. In the parish of Penpont
ther was a child found buryed in a yeard. The child was discovered when
it was fresh, and the Minister told of it, who ordered the child to be raised
and brought to the Church, and caused conveen all the inhabitants about
to see if they kneu any thing about the child. After many had come, a man
came near to the child, and the child lift up its hand and pointed at him!
Which soe struck his conscience, that immediately he confessed to the
Minister and all that wer present, that he was the father of the child; that it
was begotten in incest on his wife's sister, and (I think) that he was privy
to its murder. He was secured and delivered to the Shirrife, and I think the
sentence of death was passed on him; but having means, he bribed the
Shirrife and gote off. November 1706.
– Analecta, I, pp. 86–87

This month I have the lamentable accompt of Mr Thomas Laury,*
Minister at Closeburn, his adultery with Barbara Gaudy, clothed with
very agravating circumstances; for which he is deposed, and the Synod
are upon passing the higher sentence of excommunication upon him.
This is the only instance I heard of, since the Revolution, of a Minister's
falling into this sin; and is like to breed a terrible stumbling in that
part of the Church. I remember only of Mr J.M. his antenuptial
fornication, for which he left the nation; and Mr J.A. in Steutarton,

was was jealoused of ill-carriage, and left that place and went to Ireland. February 1710.

– Analecta, I, 236

*Thomas Lawrie was the parish minister at Closeburn from 1693 to *c.* 1709, when he was deposed for adultery.

My wife tells me she has this accompt from good hands: That the Laird of Baldoun, father, I think, to Lord Basile's Lady, was marryed to another woman, before her mother. His first lady, it seems, was under a promise and oath to another gentleman. Houever, shee had given him over. That day shee was contracted, her first choice came to the house, and was denyed access; he desired one word of the lady, and told he would not goe away till he gote it, and if it could noe otherwise be had, he would speak it before company. She came to the dore to him. . . . Shee would not hearken to him. Then he desired that she might remember he had warned her that Baldoun and shee would not long enjoy each other; and ther would be a sad accompt of her! Shee went on, and they wer marryed. That night they wer marryed, or in the morning after, they wer in bed, ther was a great noise heard, and when people came up she was gote at the dore sitting youldering like a dog, and he lying speechless in another part of the room! She continued youling and houling for some dayes till she dyed, and she continued very ill, but after her death recovered. October 1711.

– Analecta, I, p. 355

September 1712. The beginning of this month I went in to Galloway by Balmaclellan to Dumfreice. In that country I observed severall things not soe ordinary with us. I find they have noe great quantity of strau, and necessity has learned them to make thrift of what we very much neglect, fearn or brackens, which grou there very throng. They thatch their houses with them; it makes excellent thack when pulled up by the roots and stript of the leaves, and they say it lasts long, six or eight years, in their great stormes. . . . I notticed beside many of their Churches, that of Balmaclelland, that of Partan, that of Kirkmichaell, and they tell me it is beside many Churches, litle green mounts, artificiall certainly, with a ditch about them. What they have been is very hard to say. Some of the gentlmen I talked with reacon them Pagan places of worship; buriall-places I scarce take them to be. Perhapps they wer old places for keeping of Barron Courts, which we call Laues. It were a pitty some of them wer not digged throu, to see what is in them. . . . The largest and compeatest mount that I saw was at Demellingtoun, which belongs to the Earle of Stair. . . . I nottice throu all the Steuarty which I went throu, the houses very litle and lou, and but a foot or two of them of stone, and the rest earth and thatch.

– *Analecta*, II, pp. 81–83

I have this account of the state of the Separaters, or Mountain-folk, in this country. In the Steuartry they make very little noise, and have made nou converts these many years; they are presently at a stand. Mr Boyd of Dalry said to me, they wer the baggage-horse of the Papists in that country, and just made use of as tools by them! September 1712.

– *Analecta*, II, p. 88

I hear the McMillanites are very much broken and crumbled among themselves of late, and most part of the Separatists. Mr Hepburn's followers, since his death, have all joyned in ordinances. Mr Taylor's party is very much sinking, and Mr McMillan is lately marryed, wher they say he has met with a disappointment of much money he was expecting. His Kirk, for he still keeps the Church of Balmagie, was very throng for some Sabbaths after his marriage, but is since turning much thinner. Upon this occasion, some rumours being given out that he had made some complyance in his marriage, his people sent some to him to enquire by whom he was married; he declined to give accounts. However, a story was spread that he was by Mr Fork, but that was found groundless; another, that some Minister in Angus had married him, which he seemed not to deny; but when that was enquired into, it was found false, and his people were told that no Presbyterian Minister in the Church would marry an excommunicat person, as he was. This, with his own declining to give account of how he was married, has raised a great *summ* among his followers. November 1725.

[*summ* = displeasure, umbrage, dissatisfaction]

– *Analecta*, III, pp. 243–44

SCANDALS?

The single issue which led to the most serious dissension and purges and schisms in the Scottish Church in the eighteenth century, including the secession of the Associate Presbytery in 1733 and the Relief Church in 1761, and the culmination finally in the Disruption in 1843, was the question of patronage, that is, who appointed the ministers. The

Episcopalian church in 1662, still with its kirk sessions and presbyteries, had reverted to the presentation of parish ministers by the feudal landowners as patrons. The triumph of Presbyterianism in 1690/91 meant the abolition of patronage: ministers were to be chosen by the parish heritors (of whom there might be one or ten or fifteen or more) and the elders, subject to the consent of the congregation. In March 1712 the British Parliament, in imposing the Act of Toleration, which permitted Episcopalian clergy to conduct public worship provided they took an oath of allegiance and renounced Jacobitism, incensed many Presbyterian clergy, who were also indignant because they themselves were required to take the oath. In April 1712 the British government restored patronage, raising the ultimately central issue of power, of whose was the ultimate authority, the Church or the Crown in Parliament. For the next 162 years the Crown and the aristocracy, Dukes and Earls and lesser men, not necessarily titled, could exercise their right to present parish clergy.

Many landowners seem to have reasserted their right to present ministers during the 1730s and 1740s. The 'Moderates', the clergy and laity who controlled most annual General Assemblies, used their authority to affirm the rights of patrons in disputes referred up to them from kirk sessions and presbyteries. Evangelical zealots and extremists were kept under control and, as far as possible, out of office: they might have found a congenial home in the Reformed Presbyterian Church established in 1743 by some of the heirs of the conventiclers or Covenanters, Cameronians, Hebronites, Macmillanites, who had remained outside the established Church of Scotland. The Moderates were, mostly, decent Christians – sensible, 'progressive', tolerant, even sceptical, practical men who supported agricultural improvement and were part of the ordered hierarchy of North British society and of the Scottish Enlightenment.

Nevertheless there was something 'scandalous' in patronage. There were too many anomalies. Some patrons were themselves Episcopalians rather than Presbyterians. The stream of disputes which reached the General Assembly had many causes: vice, that is joint, patrons could not always agree on the arrangements for alternatively nominating a minister; groups of heritors and elders objected to the minister nominated by the patron; heritors attempted to appoint an alternate candidate; appeals and delays occurred when more than one party claimed to own the patronage of a parish; reports and libels were issued against the character and suitability of a nominee. Some Presbyterians thought that each congregation should have the right to 'call' or elect their minister. It could be even worse; for example, in 1788 the General Assembly received overtures from the Synods of Galloway and of Glasgow and Ayr asking it 'to consider the evils which may arise from the sale of patronages during vacancies'. And in 1792 the patronage of Dalry parish, along with half of Carsphairn parish, where there were two vice-patrons, the Crown and Mr Newall of Barskeoch, was advertised for sale:

To be Sold by public auction, within the George Inn in Dumfries, on Thursday the 26th day of April next ... The Lands of Drummanister, lying in the parish of Balmaclellan ... presently in the proprietor's natural possession, but ... formerly set at 44L. 4s. sterling of yearly rent. For the encouragement of purchasers, they will be exposed at the low price of 900L. sterling. Also, the Sole Patronage of the parish Church of Dalry, with elegant gallery, and fire-room off it, and fourteen pews in the said Church; and the Vice Patronage of the parish Church of Carsephairn ... to be exposed at the low price of 400L. sterling; and, if purchasers rather incline, the Patronage of Dalry, with gallery and pews, shall be exposed in one lot, at 250L. sterling; and the Vice Patronage of Carsephairn in another lot at 150L. ... The title-deeds, and conditions of roup, to be seen in the hands of John Hunter, writer to the signet; to whom, and David Newall, writer in Dumfries, or to the proprietor John Newall, Esq. at Rammerscales, near Lochmaben, persons inclining to make a private bargain may apply.

– *DWJ*, 10th April 1792

Dumfries and Galloway was unusual in the 1790s in that one man, the Duke of Queensberry, owned the patronage of Kirkbean, Lochrutton and Terregles in the Stewartry, and Caerlaverlock, Dornoch, Durisdeer, Glencairn, Keir, Kirkconnel, Kirkmahoe, Morton, Mouswald, Penpont, Sanquhar, Torthorwald and Tynron in Dumfries-shire; he was also vice-patron of Tinwald, Hoddam and Kirkmichael. The Crown held Glasserton, Inch, Leswalt, Mochrum, Old Luce, New Luce, Sorbie, Stranraer and Whithorn and the vice-patronage of Kirkinner and Stoneykirk in Wigtownshire; Balmaclellan, Borgue, Buittle, Colvend, Girthon, Kells, Kelton, Kirkcudbright, Kirkpatrick-Durham, Minnigaff, New Abbey, Rerrick, Tongland, Troqueer and Urr and the vice-patronage of Carsphairn and Kirkmabreck in the Stewartry; and Cummertrees, Dryfesdale, Dumfries St Michaels and Dumfries New, and Dunscore and the vice-patronage of Langholm, Kirkmichael and Tinwald in Dumfries-shire. In comparison, the Duke of Buccleugh only owned Canonbie and the vice of Langholm and Westerkirk; the Earl of Selkirk – Twynholm; the Earl of Stair – Kirkmaiden; the Earl of Galloway – Kirkcolm, Penninghame and Wigtown; David Maxwell of Cardoness – Anwoth; Sir

John Hunter Blair – Portpatrick; Mr Ferguson of Craigdarroch and Mr Oswald of Auchencruive jointly – Kirkpatrick-Irongray. . . .

The Carsphairn case (1780–83), which began after the death of the Rev. John Cambell on 28th May, 1780, is a good example of the way disputes escalated. Here it was Mr Newall's turn to present, and he nominated Mr Robert Affleck on 5th July, 1780. The Crown, however, also nominated a candidate (a Mr Blain). Most of the heritors in Carsphairn were against Mr Affleck: when he first appeared to preach on 16th July he found the church locked and the beadle missing! Then seven heritors, six elders and eighty heads of families signed a representation against him and requested permission to call Mr Smith. The Presbytery refused in May 1781 to sustain Mr Affleck's nomination. The General Assembly on appeal reversed the decision of the Presbytery by 74 votes to 72. In 1782 the General Assembly heard a Libel from Mr McMillan of Holm and others charging Mr Affleck with fornication with Elisabeth Collier while he was at the College in Edinburgh, with antenuptial fornication with his wife, and with simoniacal practices. The Libel had been passed from the Presbytery of Kirkcudbright to the Synod of Galloway before reaching the Assembly. The General Assembly sustained the Libel and recalled Mr Affleck's licence as a probationer and preacher. Affleck appealed unsuccessfully in 1783. The Rev. Samuel Smith was finally ordained at Carsphairn on 28th August, 1783 (The Scots Magazine, vol. 43, 1781, pp. 274–77; vol. 44, 1782, p. 329; and vol. 45, 1783, pp. 332–33.)

One of the longest delays was in Kirkmabreck parish. The Rev. John Inglis was deposed in April 1804 for drunkenness and adultery with Janet Tait. A dispute then arose between John McCulloch of Barholm, who proposed a probationer, James Mitchell, and the Crown, which nominated the Rev. William Gillespie of Kells. Gillespie subsequently withdrew, but the Rev. John Sibbald, nominated by George III in November 1806, did not take up his post until 20th April, 1809.

A minister, of course, was only another and all-too-fallible human being having to cope with the additional pressures of the attentive interest elders and parishioners paid to life in the manse. As far back as June 1646 the General Assembly expressed its concern about the 'Enormities and Corruptions observed to be in the ministry' and specifically, 'In Our Callings', the problem of men 'entering into the ministry as a way of living in the world'. The Church in 1789 was again addressing itself as to how best to recruit persons 'of good report, of sufficient learning, of sound principles, of a pious, sober, grave and prudent behaviour, and of a peaceable disposition'.

Scandals involving fornication and adultery were no doubt inevitable, *but a new embarrassment in the 1770s, 1780s and 1790s was the hothouse atmosphere in which newspapers reported the details not only of the defrocking of ministers in the Presbyteries and the Synods and in the General Assembly as the final court of appeal, but also the growing number of divorce cases coming before the Scottish Commissary Court in Edinburgh; for example the divorce of the notorious Mrs Barberie de la Motte, who lived up to her name, from Sir William Jardine of Applegarth in 1786–87 (DWJ, 14th November, 1793).*

Even cases in Orkney were reported in The Scots Magazine. *These included the Rev. William Nisbet of Firth and Stenness, who was tried before Inverness Assize Court in 1765 for adultery with Margaret Agnew, the wife of John Agnew, the supervisor of Excise at Arbroath, and the daughter of Sir James Agnew of Lochnaw. Nisbet was sentenced to two months on bread and water in Inverness Tolbooth and transportation thereafter to the American Plantations.*

In addition to press reporting, the Libels, with the evidence of witnesses in the processes against clergy, for example Inglis of Kirkmabreck, McNaught of Girthon and Bryden of Dalton, were published separately. And the Dumfries Weekly Journal *for 23rd October, 1792 even carried an advertisement for* Remarkable Cases of Adultery, *newly published at 1s. 6d., with 'interesting scenes' from the examples of Viscountess Belmore with the Earl of Ancram and Fanny Wilmot, the wife of John Wilmot, MP, with Edward Washborn, her Footman.*

Ministers in cases of scandal included the Rev. James McEwen of Moffat, deposed in December 1741 for adultery; the Rev. Robert Grier or Grierson of Durisdeer, deposed for immorality in May 1757; the Rev. Robert Carson of Anwoth, charged in 1764 and 1765 with fornication with Grizel Macmaster and with smuggling and encouraging that practice, and found guilty at the General Assembly in 1767 of forging evidence in his defence; the probationer, Mr William Macmaster of Portpatrick, presented by Captain John Blair of Dunskey in August 1770, and deprived of his licence to preach in May 1772 for criminal intercourse with a young woman; the Rev. David Donaldson of Wamphray, who had to resign and retire to Moffat in December 1793 because of his dissipated habits; the Rev. Thomas Henderson of Dryfresdale, deposed for drunkenness in April 1799; the Rev. John Inglis of Kirkmabreck; and the Rev. John McNaught of Girthron, charged in 1786 with an aggravation of wickedness, in particular ratifying irregular marriages and baptisms. McNaught was finally deposed after taking the case to the General Assembly in May 1793. He was certainly not a man of 'a peaceable disposition', but the record of his work with poor sinners suggests that he had more in common with Jesus Christ than any of the one hundred plus Christians bearing witness against him. The very young Walter Scott, in his first case, defended McNaught before the General Assembly; but that is another story.

The case of the Rev. Dr William Bryden of Dalton, who was charged in 1782 with 'abandoned profligacy' and escaped with 'a sharp rebuke' from the Moderator at the General Assembly in 1788, was an altogether more squalid affair. Was he guilty as charged or was there a plot by the heritors to get rid of him? There was at least one incident, at the meeting of the Presbytery of Lochmaben in August 1784, when Mr Murray of Murraywaithe gave Bryden a lesson in manners he richly deserved! The declaration of the principal witness, Anne Dalziel, in the Proof in the Cause, the Parish of Dalton; against the Reverend Doctor William Bryden *was taken at Lochmaben on 19th August, 1783. She was followed by Janet Anderson in Luss in Hoddam parish, Mary Dalziel in Kirkwood, Robert Brown in Cumrue, John Kennedy, jun. in Hitae, Janet Richardson, Charles Dalziel in Hitae, Mary Edgar, and Margaret Carruthers late in Townhead of Hitae. Janet Adamson and Margaret Carruthers were servants in Bryden's manse.*

✝

Anne Dalziel . . . declares . . . that she resided at the manse of Dalton in the years 1779 and 1780 . . . and that her husband, Robert Rae, left this country to go to India in the month of December 1778 . . . And being interrogate, What was the cause of her leaving this country in the month of October 1780, to go to Ireland? declares, That it was because she was with child to Doctor Bryden . . . and she went to Ireland to bear the child with great privacy, at the desire of Doctor Bryden: That she was begot with child by Doctor Bryden in the manse of Dalton, in the month of April 1780, and she was delivered thereof in the house of Mrs Margaret Clark, No. 27, Great Ship-Street, Dublin, upon the 23d day of January 1781 . . . And being interrogated, If she could condescend upon the number of times she had had carnal connection with Doctor Bryden prior to April 1780? declares, It was no matter how often, or how seldom. . . . she generally sleeped in the room above the parlour; but sometimes sleeped in the parlour; and that she at different times sleeped with Doctor Bryden, both above and below stairs, in said rooms . . . they were so employed upon different Saturday's nights, and Sunday's nights. . . . one of these nights . . . she so sleeped in the parlour . . . because the bed she usually occupied was then occupied by

Mr Nicol, one of the teachers of the High School of Edinburgh.

Doctor Bryden and Mr Nicol had been a jaunt to Ireland together ... after the Doctor's return from Ireland with Mr Nicol ... Doctor Bryden told the declarant, That Mr Nicol informed him, that there were things might be given to a woman that would make her miscarry ... but the declarant refused to hear of it. ... That at different times, Doctor Bryden desired her to father her said child upon his nephew, Ensign James Douglas, who went to Holland. ... That when the declarant had agreed to go to Ireland to be delivered, she received from Doctor Bryden, to defray her expenses, eight guineas in gold two guinea notes, and four half guineas; but after she had received the money, the Doctor told her, He would have occasion to go to the synod, and was scarce of money, and therefore desired to have one of the half guineas back, which she gave him. ...

And being further interrogated, whether she received any money ... after her return from Ireland? declared, That upon her return to the house of Charles Dalziel in Hitae, the Doctor, who had formerly employed him as a weaver ... the Doctor ... threw a letter down upon the table at which the declarant was sitting sewing, directed for her, in which was inclosed two guinea notes, and one guineas in gold, And when she was at Carlisle, she received two letters from Doctor Bryden, each of which had one guinea note inclosed. ... at Carlisle in June 1782 ... an attempt was made by two gentlemen, ministers of this Church, to make her retract the declaration she had emitted ... the reverend Mr Thomas Henderson, minister of Dryfsdale ... the reverend Mr Thomas Smith, minister of Cumbertrees. ... That Mr Smith farther told the declarant, That Mr Laurie, preacher at Kirkwood, had spoken a deal of ill of her, and that he was a snifling brat; and he supposed the said Mr Laurie wanted the kirk of Dalton. ...

Proof in the Cause, *The Parish of Dalton* ... 1783, pp. 1–5, 7–8, 10–12

Case of Doctor William Bryden ... against Robert Henderson of Cleughheads, a non-residing Heritor, and others. ... John Carruthers, late patron of the parish, and proprietor of the estate of Holmains, which is since sold, had, of this date (May 26, 1777), accepted a bill of 72L. 12s. Sterling ... for behoof of the poor. Not long after this ... Mr Carruthers had fallen into a bankrupt state. ... The session, after four years indulgence ... resolved in Summer 1781 ... to use legal measures for recovering payment of said bill. ... Mr Carruthers ... so effectually practised with the elders in private, that he prevailed with them to urge Doctor Bryden to rescind said deed of session: and because he declined this ... a torrent of obloquy was poured out upon him by Mr Carruthers and his friends. . . . two of his elders left the church; a general flame was raised in the parish; and the other heritors . . . were prevailed upon to take a warm part in the affair. . . .

Doctor Bryden . . . had, a little after this, obtained a decreet of Presbytery, for some necessary repairs, and enlargement of his manse and offices. Mr Carruthers prevailed with the other heritors to suspend that decreet. After warm opposition, the heritors lost their cause; and the Court of Session . . . found more repairs necessary, than appointed by the Presbytery. . . . The heritors, who . . . had their passions considerably inflamed, suffered their resentment to transport them beyond all bounds of honour and decency. . . . Bent upon revenge, they entered into a concert against Doctor Bryden, which would have disgraced the darkest ages. . . . Those heritors, and their agents, who were most active against Doctor Bryden, endeavoured to impress the husband with the belief of his wife's guilt, and of Doctor Bryden having seduced her, because she sometimes visited in his family. . . . The heritors exulted. They convened the whole parish in the church. They harangued their tenants, and others, and urged them to join in a zealous prosecution. . . .

Lastly, Doctor Bryden . . . hopes the Venerable Assembly will think it dangerous, to make the character and office of one of the ministers of her Establishment, depend upon the testimony of persons of another Establishment, without the kingdom, and in the lower ranks of life. Doctor Bryden would in charity believe well of all men; but he is informed, that the common people in the small sea-port towns in Cumberland are very ignorant, and very corrupt in their morals; and that persons may be got from among them, who, for a very little money, will swear any thing. . . . (pp. 1–4, 20)

On Monday March 9, came before the High Court of Justiciary, at Edinburgh, the trial of John Murray of Murraywaithe for an assault upon and beating and bruising of the Rev. Dr. William Bryden, Minister of the Parish of Dalton. The facts that give rise to this singular trial are as follows: the Rev. Dr. Bryden being libelled by several of his parishioners before the presbytery of Lochmaben for several alledged scandals, at a meeting of the Presbytery on the 5th of August last Mr Murray, on being present as a heritor, uttered these words – 'Some persons, perhaps, find it in their interest to protract this cause.' Upon which Dr Bryden asked him, do you mean me, Sir? – Mr Murray having replied, I do mean you, Sir; the Doctor, in return, said he was an impertinent puppy; upon which Mr Murray seized him by hair or toupee with one hand, and the other, in which he held his cane, he applied to the brow and forehead of Dr

Bryden. The cause being remitted to a jury, consisting mostly of landed gentlemen, who made choice of William Tytler, Esq., of Woodhouslie for their Chancellor, and of Thomas Tod, Esq., of Hayfield, for their Clerk, they returned an unanimous verdict to the Court finding Mr Murray not guilty. Whereupon Mr Murray was dismissed from the bar; and the Court, upon application of the counsel for Mr Murray, found Dr Bryden the prosecutor, liable in expenses.

– *SM*, vol. 46, 1784, pp. 220–21

'A GREAT WONDER IN HEAVEN'
The Friend Mother in the Lord and the Buchanites

Elspeth Simpson, Mother Buchan (1738–91) and her contemporary millenarian prophetesses, Ann Lee or Mother Lee (1736–84), the leader of the Shaking Quakers in New England, and Joanna Southcott (1750–1814) in England, offered an intoxicating mix of imminent salvation and deliverance. They each had their own special belief that God had chosen them to announce the Second Coming of Jesus Christ and identified themselves with the great woman in heaven in Revelation, *XII. Mrs Buchan believed she was the Friend Mother in the Lord and that her disciple, the Rev. Hugh White, was her spiritual man-child.*

Driven out of Irvine, the Buchanites moved en masse through Ayrshire into Dumfries-shire and settled for three years (1784–87) at New Cample farm between Closeburn and Thornhill. The tenant farmer, Thomas Davidson, allowed them to build their own house, Buchan Ha'. The stresses during the forty-day Great Fast and the abject failure of the attempted Ascension from Templand Hill greatly weakened the movement. Charges of blasphemy and profligacy before the Presbytery of Penpont and Closeburn kirk session failed, but the Justice of Peace Court required them to leave the county by 10th March, 1787.

The smaller group settled at Auchengibbert near Crocketford. There the Buchanites followed a quieter lifestyle, in effect a closed community, albeit with their own brand image of light green dyed clothes. The sad and bitter story of the death of Mother Buchan in 1791 and her itinerating corpse accompanying the dwindling flock of believers to Larghill and lastly to Newhouse is all too well known. Fifty years after her death her last devoted follower, Andrew Innes, was still waiting for her resurrection.

Many questions remain. Did the Buchanites live together like brother and sister or in a ferment of free love? Do the views expressed by Burns reflect his own disappointment at his failure to captivate the 'darling Jean' of his Epistle to Davie, *the Buchanite Jean Gardner? Did Mother Buchan develop her views from reading the Bible or from some of the many English eighteenth-century millenarian pamphlets in circulation?*

> *And there appeared a great wonder in heaven; a woman clothed with the sun, and the moon under her feet, and upon her head a crown of twelve stars. . . . And she brought forth a man-child, who was to rule all nations with a rod of iron: and her child was caught up unto God, and to his throne.*
> – The Revelation of St John the Divine, Chapter XII, v. 1 and 5

✝

Glasguensis Mercator, Account of the Buchanites

The Buchanites pay great attention to the Bible, being always reading it, or having it in their pocket, or under their arm, proclaiming it the best book in the world. They read, sing hymns, preach, and converse much about religion, declaring the last day to be at hand, and that no one of all their company shall ever die, or be buried in the earth, but soon shall hear the voice of the last trumpet, when all the wicked shall be struck dead, and remain so for 1000 years. At the same moment they, the Buchanites, shall undergo an agreeable change, shall be caught up to meet the Lord in the air. . . .

Since the Buchanites adopted their principles, they neither marry nor are given in marriage, nor consider themselves as bound to any conjugal duties, or mind or indulge themselves in any carnal enjoyments; but having one common purse for their cash, they are all sisters and brothers, living a holy life as the angels of God. . . . Rude people, who visit them, impose much on the public, by propagating falsehoods concerning them. . . . I found the Buchanites a very temperate, civil, discreet, and sensible people, very free in declaring their principles, when they were attended to; but most of their visitants behaved in a rude, wicked, and abandoned way.

– The Scots Magazine, vol. 46, 1784, pp. 589–90

Letter from Robert Burns to his cousin, James Burness, 3d August, 1784

. . . We have been surprized with one of the most extraordinary Phenomena in the moral world, which, I dare say, has happened in the course of this last Century. We have had a party of the Presbytery Relief as they call themselves, for some time in this country. A pretty thriving society of them has been in the Burgh of Irvine for some years past . . . a Mrs Buchan from Glasgow came among them, and began to spread some fanatical notions of religion among them, and in a short time made many converts among them, and among others their preacher, one Mr Whyte . . . . in spring last the populace rose and mobbed the old leader Buchan, and put her out of the town . . . and after several stages, they are fixed at present in the neighbourhood of Dumfries. Their tenets are a strange jumble of enthusiastic jargon, among other she pretends to give them the Holy Ghost by breathing on them, which she does with postures and practices that are scandalously indecent; they have likewise disposed of all their effects and hold a community of goods, and live nearly an idle life, carrying on a great farce of pretended devotion in barns, and woods, where they lodge and lye all together, and hold likewise a community of women, as it is another of their tenets that they can commit no moral sin. I am personally acquainted with most of them, and I can assure you the above mentioned are facts.

– Joseph Train, *The Buchanites from First to Last*, 1846, pp. 56–58

Andrew Innes on the Buchanites at New Cample near Closeburn (1784–87)

Here, like the disciples of Christ after Pentecost, our apostolic life commenced. 'All that believed were together, and had all things in common.' Our money was put into a common stock, and placed at the disposal of John Gibson, as treasurer, to purchase all that might be requisite for the use of the society. All unoccupied clothes were placed under the care of Janet Grant, formerly Mrs Muir, who had kept a cloth-shop in Irvine. She had the charge of seeing them kept clean and whole, and of giving them out when a change was wanted by any person. The other women assisted in washing, in knitting, and in mending the stockings. We had tailors who mended our clothes, and coblers who repaired our shoes. . . . All sat at the same table, and partook of the same food, with the exception of our Friend Mother, who either served those at table herself, or was employed in directing others to do so. . . .

Having neither hay nor straw for bedding, and Mr Davidson having none to give us, we were obliged to go to the moor and gather heather for that purpose. This we bound in bundles of about six feet long, and four feet broad, thereby forming a bed for two persons. These bundles were placed in a double row on the barn-floor, leaving room scarcely for a single person to pass between them. These beds were not hard . . . but we had at first no more bed-clothes than a single blanket to each bed, and all made pillows of their body-clothes. When we had nearly completed our up-putting, Mr Hunter and several other persons arrived from Irvine, and contentedly lay down on heather beds – there being now no distinction of persons among us – those who had wives, being as if they had none. But if our Friend Mother and Mrs Gibson be excepted, the women were greatly behind the men in their compliance, for there was scarcely one, either old or young, who did not retain a partial hankering after either husband or sweetheart; but, as there was no law to be put in force, and no punishment to be apprehended, it was all matter of choice with us.

– Joseph Train, *op. cit.*, pp. 68–71

After a Great Fast for forty days in 1786 the Buchanites assembled at sunrise on Templand Hill for the glorious day when they expected to be taken up to heaven:

Platforms were erected for them to wait on, until the wonderful hour arrived, and Mrs Buchan's platform was exalted above all the others. The hair of *ilka* head was cut short, all but a tuft on the top for the angels to catch them by when drawing them up. The momentous hour came. Every station for ascension was instantly occupied. Thus they stood, expecting to be wafted every moment into the land of bliss, when a gust of wind came ... capsized Mrs Buchan, platform and all! and the fall made her all *hech* again on the *cauld* yard. . . .

– Mactaggart, *The Scottish Galloviuian Encyclopedia*, 1824, pp. 98–99

THE MAN IN THE MOONLIGHT
David Gibson of Auchencairn

David Gibson was born in Irvine in 1778. After early experience in missionary work in Ayrshire for the Baptist Evangelical Society (later The Home Missionary Society for Scotland), he was sent to Galloway in 1814 to preach the Gospel. The rest of his long life was spent in a routine of long-distance preaching tours throughout south-west Scotland. 'His excursions are made in winter by moon-light' [Report of the Baptist Home Missionary Society for Scotland, 1829]. After 1817 he was based in Auchencairn where he established a chapel and a thriving Sabbath School. His journal or diary gives some idea of not only his work, but also of many aspects of life in early nineteenth-century Galloway. He died in 1853 and was buried in the choir of Dundrennan Abbey.

The diary covers parts of 1814, 1816, 1819, 1826–27 and 1831–35, with notes on the Auchencairn Sabbath School 1820–21 and the Rerrick Bible Society.

†

1831. July 5. Preached out of doors at Gatehouse to a considerable audience. George Hannay, son of Captain Hannay of Rusco, is a subject of much conversation in Gatehouse, having been lately baptised in Edinburgh.

July 6. Walked to Creetown. Found that the quarrying stones for Liverpool Harbour, which was lately carried on near Dalbeattie, is now to be in this neighbourhood. About 100 men, they say, are employed at the work, which is, as yet, preparatory. A pier is making for shipping the stones. A child between two and three years of age was nearly drowned at Carsluith to-day in a dam made by the hoopers for steeping their wood. Preached at Creetown at 8 o'clock in the evening. Lodged in Young's Inn.

July 7. Crossed from Creetown to Wigtown and preached to a small audience in the Court House, and heard sermon in the Seceder meeting-house in the evening.

July 8. Left Wigtown for Kirkcowan. Found Mr Love, the innkeeper, died about a year ago. Mr Hunter, the schoolmaster, whom I formerly met here, having been put off, a Mr Livingstone from Edinburgh is parish schoolmaster now. There had been disagreements for a number of years between the parishioners and Mr Hunter, the late schoolmaster. Dr Stewart is said to have sided with Mr Hunter. The affair came before the Presbytery, who decided against Mr Hunter; hence it was carried to the Synod, who confirmed the sentence; hence to the General Assembly, who also confirmed. Mr Hunter has taken a farm in the parish.

Preached in Kirkcowan schoolhouse to a considerable audience. Mr Livingstone precented. . . . July 12. Preached this evening at Glenluce at 8 o'clock at the end of the King's Arms to a large audience. Lodged at the King's Arms. . . .

July 14. Went to-day and saw the fish-pond at Portnessock, which belongs to Col. McDowall of Logan. It is certainly a great curiosity. Whenever the door is opened the fish are all in motion towards the place where food is given them. Some of them are large fish. There are different kinds of fish, cods, blocks and salmon, and a great number of them. The large codfish allow you to stroke their heads and take meat out of your hand. I saw some of the little fish, which did not put their heads above water as others did, take food out of the hand when the hand was just under water. The fish are completely tame, and it is not long, I understand, until they are thus tamed. . . .

Preached this evening at Sandhead. Audience large, although John McCulloch had taken ill, and influenza was raging. I lodged in Peter Dalrymple's inn. . . .

July 19. Left Stranraer and walked to Portpatrick, which I reached in the evening, and preached in Mr Gordon's coachhouse just opposite his own door, where the mail coach at present is kept. A very large audience, so large that some could not get admission. I intimated sermon for to-morrow evening. A young man of the name of Wright from Dalry in the Glenkens promised to precent. He said when I preached in the open air at Dalry it was always before his father's door.

The mail coach leaves Portpatrick for Dumfries at 7 o'clock in the evening, and the mail coach comes in from Dumfries at 11 o'clock at night. About 100 men are at present working at the harbour of Portpatrick. I understand that 700 wrought at it at one time. There are two diving bells employed at present. There are 3 men in each bell. Two men is the number that these bells ought only to have in them. They are down four hours at a time, and so are eight hours down each man each day, for each goes down twice; four and a half hours is the time for each party, but I observe half an hour is employed each time in coming up and going down. They begin at 3 o'clock in the morning and leave off at 9 o'clock that night. These men in the bells I mean. Portpatrick is 84 miles from Dumfries. There is but one packet since one was lost last winter, but they expect another.

JOSEPH TRAIN
The burial of an old Cameronian – James Maclune

Train's letter to Sir Walter Scott, with a decription of a funeral in Rerrick parish, was sent so that he could compare it with the details of the burial of Robert Paterson, 'Old Mortality,' which Train had already given to him. The routine of having seven, nine and even twelve rounds of spirits and wines seems to have been common at funerals in the eighteenth and early nineteenth centuries. The practice, or at least the worst excesses, had largely disappeared by the 1830s and 1840s.

✝

A vain display of pomp and family pride at Funerals then extended down to the peasantry in such a degree that the person who had arrived at the age of thirty years without having set apart from his earnings however scanty his income might be a sum sufficient to defray the expenses of a Funeral in a style becoming his rank in society was accounted very improvident indeed. . . . The last burial in this quarter conducted in the true Cameronian style was that of James Maclune Farmer of Castlegower . . . who died in May 1823 and having a little money saved by great frugality it was his wish and request that his funeral should be conducted with the same liberality as had always for many generations past been observed at the funerals of his forefathers.

The persons invited to the funeral of the old farmer of Castlegower to the number of about one hundred assembled in the Cameronian Meeting House at Castle Douglas. Upon entering the place of mourning each individual was presented with a glass of plain spirits and a biscuit. When the company was fully assembled the blessing was asked by the Reverend pastor of the congregation of which the deceased was a worthy member.

Each time the drinks is handed round the company is at funerals in the West and South of Scotland called a *service*. Upon the occasion here allowed to the finest service that was handed round after the blessing was asked consisted of Whisky and shortbread of which all were invited to partake with freedom. The second of Brown Stout and Edinburgh Ale . . . with Buns and cheese. The third of Port and plumb cakes. The fourth of White Wine and sugar biscuits. The fifth consisted of Sherry and Port with sugar biscuits and plum cakes, that everyone might take which he pleased. The sixth consisted of Rum and Whisky and the seventh of Brandy and shortbread of which and of all the various kinds of liquor here mentioned many of the people partook plentifully. The whole concluded with the Rev. Mr. Osborn returning thanks for the mercies offered and gratefully received.

The family burial place of the Maclunes of Castlegower being in the Churchyard of the Old Abbey of Dundrennan the funeral procession moved from Castle Douglas toward the place of interment preceded by two gentlemen on horseback acting like . . . Blue Mantle Pursuivant Kings at Arms did of old. Upon arriving at the consecrated ground in which the deceased was to be laid the riders alighted and according to ancient custom the Boys of the Parish School were in attendance each to take a horse under his charge whilst the people were employed in laying the corpse in the grave and in taking a refreshment in the village for which an allowance in Scotch money was usually claimed that is now paid in sterling.

On the present occasion whilst the horses were eating the hay and corn in the churchyard that was provided for them in abundance after the funeral was over the people retired to the Schoolhouse immediately adjoining where after a blessing being asked by the Reverend Mr Thomson, the Minister of Rerwick, the company was again entertained in like manner as they were in the Cameronian Meeting House in Castle Douglas first with Plain Spirits and biscuits, next with Beer and Buns, then with Port and Plum cakes, next with Sherry and Sugar biscuits, and after ale with Brandy and Shortbread for which thanks were returned by Mr Osborn the Cameronian minister in an able manner.

On this occasion as in former times all the poor people in the neighbourhood who chused to attend were presented with a glass of spirits and a penny, nor was any person allowed to pass without being required to partake of the funeral service.

The spirits and wine consumed at this funeral appears from the books of Mr William Young spirit dealer Castle Douglas who furnished the same to have amounted to nearly £20 and the bread to upwards of £7.

Mr Young has obligingly furnished me with all the particulars here stated – he was present at the funeral – and I have conversed with several persons who were so likewise and they all assure me that notwithstanding the great quantity of liquor that was consumed the whole was conducted in the most orderly manner. . . .

– Letter from Joseph Train to Sir Walter Scott, from Castle Douglas,
7th June, 1829 (National Library of Scotland, MS. 874, f. 146–49)

CHURCH ATTENDANCE IN 1838
Opportunity and the Want of Decent Clothes

The Report of the Royal Commission for Inquiry into the Opportunities of Public Religious Worship, and Means of Instruction, and Pastoral Superintendence . . . Scotland 1835–38 (and the 1851 Census of Religious Worship and Education) contain an enormous amount of information on the health of the churches in Scotland, the accommodation in them, and the number of people attending services. The Seventh Report from the Royal Commission includes the Presbytery of Wigton. The detailed return for Penninghame Parish Church, visited on 9th September, 1836, suggests something of the overall scale of the report. The Penninghame section contains information on the Church of Scotland Parish Church, the Relief Church, and the Roman Catholic Congregation: the minister of the Reformed Presbyterian Church, no doubt on principle, did not take part in the exercise.

✝

Parish Church. Rev. Samuel Richardson, A.M., Minister. . . .
Extent and Circumstances . . . about 80 square miles . . . partly landward, partly the village of Newton-Stewart, which contains 2241 inhabitants.

Population. . . . The minister stated the present population at 3556 . . . Belonging to the Established Church 2723 To other denominations 833. . . . A great proportion of each class are of the poor and working classes. The population in the landward part of the parish is chiefly composed of farmers and agricultural labourers, and in the village of Newton-Stewart of merchants, tradesmen, a considerable number of cotton weavers and labourers. . . .

Average attendance in July, August, and September about 550. November, December, and January about 400 . . . from the want of accommodation, the attendance of a considerable number is so deficient, that it cannot, with propriety, be termed a habit. . . . Communicants rather more than 700. . . . Increased about 130 within the last five years which the minister attributes to the last enlargement of the accommodation.

The church was built in 1777–78. Enlarged about 18 years ago, by erecting additional galleries, capable of holding upwards of 100 sittings. A change was made in the arrangement of the body of the church about four years ago, by which about 60 additional sittings were gained. Another gallery could not be put up. . . .

Rather above 200 families are distant more than two miles from the parish church; rather above 100 families more than four miles; about 55 more than six miles. The greatest distance is 12 miles or more. . . .

The minister states that the church is not in a good state. Apprehensions have been entertained in regard to its safety, and a builder, who was employed to examine it, stated . . . that it would not be safe for more than two or three years, and he suggested that by putting cross joints on the principal couples above the ceiling (which has been done) it might be rendered safe for that time. The two principal heritors have stated . . . that they were disposed to enter into arrangements for a new church. . . .

Accommodation. . . . Total number of sittings, at 15 and 16 inches 700. On account of the narrowness of the pews, the church cannot hold 700 with comfort. Allocated to heritors and their tenants, minister and elders, 406. Free 25. Set apart for letting 269. All the allocated sittings are occupied by those entitled to them, with the exception of a few attached to farms held by Dissenters, some of which are retained for the use of servants on the farms, and others are occupied by the friends of the parties having right, by a private engagement. The free sittings are generally well filled by the poor. The minister states that 575 sittings are necessary to complete the number required by law. . . . The poor and working classes are principally in want of seats. The families in this situation are chiefly in . . . Newton-Stewart. . . . there are only about 370 sittings for a population of 946 examinable persons. . . . A considerable number of the allocated sittings belong to families at a distance, who do not fill them every Sabbath. The minister had intimated that the parishioners generally might occupy vacant sittings at a reasonable time after the commencement of public worship, but they do not avail themselves of this to any extent, as it is considered an intrusion. . . . Sittings let at each rate in 1835 – not more than 1s. 30. More than 1s and not more than 2s. 87. More than 2s. and not more than 3s. 152. . . . All let.

Seat Rents Nearly L.43 13s yearly, prior to 1835.

Ordinary Collections 1835 L.68-10-2 Extraordinary Collections 1835 L.7-0-0 The seat rents are received by the heritors, to whom the seats belong, except the rents of about 30 sittings belonging to the session, formerly let at 2s., now 1s., which are paid into the poor-funds. The ordinary collections are all applied to the poor, after paying dues to church-officer, clerks, etc. The extraordinary collections were paid thus: To board of health, during cholera L.23-14-3; To society for the church in Canada L9-3-6; For Bibles to the poor of Penninghame L.7-0-0.

The minister's stipend is 16 chalders, half meal, half barley, with L.10 for communion elements, derived from the teinds. The minister is allowed L.30 yearly in lieu of a manse. He has a glebe, the yearly rent of which is L.22-17-2d. He has the privilege of cutting peats.

A considerable number, of the poorer classes especially, are prevented attending public worship regularly, by want of church accommodation and distance. Some state they are prevented attending by the want of decent clothes. . . .

A Sabbath school was established in Newton-Stewart in 1821 by the united efforts of the members of the Establishment and of the Relief body . . . average attendance 140 children of all denominations.

– *Seventh Report by the Commissioners of Religious Instruction,*
Scotland 1838, pp. 358–61

THE PRECENTOR OF WAMPHRAY
'Now Israel may sing, and that truly'

During the week he might be a tailor, or a souter, or a dominie, but on Sundays he was the patriarchial precentor, a difficult man to deal with, the eminent autocrat who, decked out in his 'best blacks', occupied a miniature pulpit below the minister, 'read the line' and 'repeated the tune' and sounded the tuning fork, leading the kirk in singing the Psalms of

David in the days before any such innovation as a choir or a 'kist o' whistles'. He might also be the bellman and 'the minister's man'. Even in a country parish he might have other duties, for example, Crossmichael in 1864 was offering a salary of £10 a year for a new precentor who would also conduct a Psalmody class during part of the season [KA, 21st October, 1864].

Under the Rev. Charles Dickson, the minister of Wamphray parish from 1825 to 1853, the precentor was Mr John Gibson, so well described by John Paterson in his Wamphray *(1906).*

✝

In former days the precentor was a great and indispensable institution in the kirk. Seventy and more years ago, John Gibson, a slater by trade, led the psalmody in Wamphray kirk. He had a really good tenor voice, and he knew it, prided himself on it, and was not slow to say that he had heard few or none to equal it. He had also a fairly good knowledge of music. There was no keeping upsides with him, not to say beating him, except when old Nannie Macmoran, hearing him begin a tune that she thought not adapted to the sentiment of the psalm, 'skirled' up the 'Bangor' or some other more suitable tune in her opinion, and so divided the musical honours with him. . . .

John was once asked by an elder of the church to attend a singing class that was being conducted in the school one winter by a rather famous musician. John excused himself by saying, 'Me gang! I have forgotten more tunes than ever that man kenned,' and John did not go. . . .

John Gibson was very short of stature, and his weight corresponded therewith. The latter stood him in good stead at the time he fell from the roof of the manse. The minister, sitting in his study, saw something like a great bird falling past the window. In mortal terror he threw up the window and cried aloud, 'John, are you killed?' 'Na, a'm no killed,' was the tart reply. Strange to say he was not a bit the worse for his aerial journey, but mounted the roof again and finished his job, and thenceforward watched his feet better. John's pastime was angling and fly-hook dressing.

The beadle was an entirely different person in every way from the precentor. . . . His figure . . . was large, and his clothes, to meet a probable expansion, were always made 'lucky'. The old minister never bothered him to dress for Sunday duty, or stand at attention and then follow upstairs to shut the pulpit door. He just carried up the Bible below his 'oxter' under the plaid, laid it on the pulpit bookboard, and retired to his seat. The old minister's successor stuck a black coat and white tie on him, and made him mount the pulpit stairs and shut the door. William did not like these innovations. . . . Another innovation followed, the church was artificially heated. William blamed the railways for bringing in these new ideas. . . . The church had never in its history been heated before. It was, inside, as white as whitewash could make it, and when matched by snow on the ground and snow falling, there was too much purity to be seen, in and out, even for a kirk. The heating process can not be said to have improved church attendance, but it was more comfortable for those who did attend. The protection from cold feet on a cold winter day formerly was to wash them in cold water, put on clean stockings, and put dry wisps in the clogs, just before setting out for church.

– J. Paterson, *Wamphray*, 1906, pp. 112–15

RUTHWELL
'Away from the hum of the city'

There were many good men who spent their lives in relative anonymity ministering in country parishes. James McFarlan, the minister of Ruthwell parish from 1871 to 1889, was a fundamentally decent, sensible and conscientious man, a caring pastor, and innovative, for he not only introduced his parishioners to the new Scottish Hymnal and the idea of the possibility of marriages taking place within rather than outside the church, but he also had the Ruthwell Cross itself brought inside the church in October 1887. All this might have been forgotten but for his wife.

James McFarlan's father was the minister of Muiravonside from 1834 to 1871. James was born on 6th January, 1845. He was educated at Edinburgh Academy and the University of Edinburgh. Presented to Ruthwell in April, 1871 by the Earl of Mansfield, he married Helen Menzies, the niece of Dr Robert Menzies, the minister at Hoddom, on 24th October, 1871. The description of their reception in Ruthwell is a good example of the status enjoyed at that time by parish clergy.

They had six children between 1873 and 1881, James, the twins Allan and William, Helen Elizabeth [Elsie], Patrick, and Robert. Life at the manse was hectic, as the minister's wife, brought up in Edinburgh, had to look after pigs, hens, a cow, and lambs kept over the winter to sell in the spring. James McFarlan died while on holiday in the Lake District on 4th October, 1889 and his widow on 29th January, 1914.

Helen's biography of her husband, James McFarlan, including examples

of his poems and sermons, was privately published in 1892, and her
Selections from Letters and Journals of Ruthwell Manse 1871–1889 *was*
published in Ediburgh in 1914. She had a happy knack of recording
Ruthwell folk reminiscencing about the old customs and traditions of the
parish, as well as aspects of their happy and occasionally hilarious family
life at the manse and on holiday in the Lake District and in Harris.

The first extracts are from James McFarlan *(1892).*

✝

Ruthwell . . . in 1871 . . . was even more rural than it is now; for then,
although there was a railway station of a humble kind, there was no
telegraph or money-order office in the parish, the postman walked to and
from Annan with the letters of Ruthwell. . . . The newly-married pair
were received with a warm and brilliant welcome on their arrival in the
parish. A bonfire on the Aiket heights, an arch of evergreen, and
illumination of every house and cottage on their way, awaited them. At
the glebe the horses were taken from the carriage and a crowd of young
men drew it with much cheering up the avenue to the manse door. (pp.
49–51)

Over the length and breadth of this flat little bit of land . . . the new
minister went to and fro, over arable and pasture, moor and merse land,
in fair weather and foul, making acquaintance with his flock, learning
much from them of the cares and anxieties of agricultural life, and seeing
the comfort and happiness of it too. . . .The people . . . spoke the same
pure old Scotch that the village had known for centuries. They kept
their cottages beautifully clean, they lived hardworking, frugal, and
thrifty lives, and each house had its peat-stack and pig. . . . Old women
loved to tell of the busy life of their youth, when women, they said, really
had plenty to do, when there was lint to spin, and straw to plait, and
all the bread of the house to bake, mostly 'haver-breid' [oat-cakes].
(pp. 54–55)

. . . he gave his congregation an address on Church Service, and asked
them to adopt the Scottish Hymnal, to stand while singing, to kneel at
prayer, and to remain still and silent for a few moments after the blessing
had been pronounced. At the same time, small bags for the collections
were substituted for the noisy and clumsy wooden ladles hitherto is
use. . . . The parishioners were by no means unanimous about these
innovations in church, and protested in various ways. A few left the
church altogether, many continued to sit while singing, some stood to

sing the Psalms of David, but sat with well-closed lips during the singing of the hymn. (pp. 62–63)

Extract from Sermon. A very unnatural and quite unwarranted view of Christianity, or rather of religion generally, is that melancholy becomes it. It is thought by holders of this view that it is unbecoming in a truly religious person to appear too happy in this world. A redeemed person should not jest, nor make merry with his friends; the mirth even of children should be restrained; there should be little laughter in a Christian home! . . . Surely if they had any true perception of the solemn meaning of self-dedication unto God in Christ . . . they could afford to dispense with the sham of being grave for the sake of being grave, and, facing the real facts of life and death, condescend to meet the world as brightly as even Jesus did. . . . (pp. 200–01)

The following extracts are from the Selections *(1914):*

On February 10th, 1881, your father was presented with Carlyle's works in volumes by the ladies of Cummertrees. . . . The very day on which this welcome gift was presented, Thomas Carlyle was buried at Ecclefechan. . . . One old dame who had been at school with him said, 'Ay, he was a gey forrit chiel.' . . . Calling one day on Mrs Austen (Mary Carlyle), his sister, at the Gill' we found her with many illustrated papers on the table. . . . In October . . . J. paid her another visit and asked her in the course of their talk if she had ever seen Edward Irving.

'Yes, often,' she said. 'He used to come aboot my faither's. I can see him now, as well as I see you sittin' there. It was a wild e'en – sic anither as this. He and my brither Tom cam' riding through the close. They baith o' them had big cloaks on, and they were a' filled up wi' the wind. Irving's face had the wind in't tae, and his lang black hair was a' blawn back ower his heid. . . . Irving hadna beguid wi' the squeakin' tongues then.'

. . . At Lady Hall Farm Mrs Johnston told us, 'Yes, I've seen Tom Carlyle many a time. He used to come riding down the road and through the close here on to the merse, and then away out to the very edge of the ride, and there he would sit on his white horse for half an hour or more just glowerin' out over the water.' (pp. 70–71)

November 6th, 1881. The twins are off to school. Baby sleeping and Elsie and Patrick playing at being gypsies. They have hung the old plaid round the side table, books keeping it in place, and inside they are very happy with books and work, a lighted candle, and two scones. . . .

On one Saturday afternoon in June of this year the twins had been more mischievous than usual. Wandering in to the back kitchen they found a basket full of flounders, fresh from the Solway, and proceeded to pass them one after another through the mangle. (pp. 74–75)

1885 . . . talk about getting up a soup-kitchen, to give the school children warm soup at dinner time. Seven ladies came, and we settled to have it at Clarencefield. . . . Mrs Fisher of Horseclose was the only one who did not approve. She wrote me a letter to say that when she was four she had to be at school every morning with a peat under her arm and a bit of oatcake for her dinner but she often had finished it by the time she reached Summerfield, and she does not think children should get any more now. . . .

October 31st. I was in Dumfries yesterday and brought out 2s. 6d. worth of bones and a pot to hold fourteen gallons of soup. To-day Maclean is taking the cart with some potatoes over to the cottage, and on Tuesday the soup is to be ready. Some people oppose the scheme, but most of the farmers are kind and willing to help, and I am collecting half and whole crowns from friends to pay for the pot, bowls, spoons, etc. . . .

November. Patrick and Robert have been making tickets for the soup-kitchen. Yesterday there were over seventy children. Mrs Broatch was at the door, and as they crowded in she said, 'Keep bawk, keep bawk.' Then they all began to say it too and crowded in still, and there was a great row. The hounds meet at Comlongon to-morrow, and we are going to see them.

November 7th. To Janet Henderson. . . . I have made my velveteen bonnet; it is very neat, with lace and pheasants' feathers. Now I must away. If I can get twelve farmers to promise 2 cwt. of potatoes each for the soup-kitchen, that will do. I should like an illuminated 'Grace before meat' to hang up for the children. (pp. 106–08)

February 6th, 1886. To-day I visited Betty Grierson at the Glebe Cottage. Hard frost, and she a delicate old body in her bed, but her door was wide open as usual. She was very interesting. In her young days, she said, women had far more work to do than they have now. There was all the knitting, and the lint to sort and to spin. At that time there was a bleaching-green which belonged to the village. It lay up the burn from Thwaite Pond, and there the wives bleached their webs and the young folk met to play games. The men had a quoiting-ground there too. There was also a common pasture-ground, which extended from the kirk yett up the hill. Many of the cottagers then had their own cows and they all fed together. When that pasture-land was thrown into Aiket Farm they all had to sell their cows.

Betty believes that long ago the old Cross stood in the village of Ruthwell, through which the Glasgow road passed. The Cross, she says, stood near the four cross roads in the middle of the village, at the top of what is still called 'the Auld Manse brae'. The old manse is supposed to have stood on the right hand there, as you look towards Criffel, and the kirk further from the road, behind the manse. Betty's father and mother lived in a thatched house which stood where the sawmill is now. (p. 115)

5

TRAVELLERS

†

Travellers, as authors, are traditionally allowed to choose where they go and when, to exaggerate the difficulties and dangers they faced, and to write about the more exotic and unusual pleasures and personalities they 'discovered'. They do also sometimes plagiarise, one from the other: it is curious, for example, how many writers mention encountering barelegged young women outside Dumfries!

From the late eighteenth century onwards there was a ready market for travel books whether merely 'in search of the picturesque', or, as RLS put it a hundred years later, to carry one 'body and mind, into some different parish of the infinite'.

†

C. LOWTHER, MR R. FALLOW, AND PETER MANSON

Lowther, perhaps Sir Christopher Lowther who died in 1644, and his companions travelled from Carlisle to Edinburgh via Langholm [Langham] and Selkirk in November 1629. Their journal included notes on 'The Bleaching of Linen', Scottish weights and measures and coinage, 'The Scottish Dialect', and the law courts in Edinburgh. 'Maxfeild' was, in fact, Lord Maxwell, the Earl of Nithsdale.

Langham . . . My Lord Maxfeild hath gotten it to be a market within this 5 years, and hath given them of Langham and Erkenholme land to them with condition to build good guest houses within a year. We lodged at John a Foorde's at my Lord Maxfeild's gate where the fire is in the midst of the house; we had there good victuals, as mutton, midden fowle, oat bread cakes on the kirdle baked the 5th part of an inch thick; wheat bread, ale, aquavitae. . . .

At Langham, Arche my Lord Maxfeild's steward, bestowed ale and aquavitae; we laid in a poor thatched house the wall of it being one course of stones, another of sods of earth, it had a door of wicker rods, and the spider webs hung over our heads as thick as might be in our bed. Mr

Curwen, parson of Arthuret sent his man over to Langham to get Arche to get us a lodging in Lord Maxfeild's house, because of the outlaws in the town at that time, but the keys were at Arche's house 4 miles off so that we could not otherwise. . . . Mr Robert Pringle . . . writ commendatory letters for us to Sir James Pringle sheriff of Ethrick, and to Edinburgh. . . . All the churches we see were poor thatched and in some of them the doors sodded up with no windows in almost till we came at Selkirk. . . .

– C. Lowther, R. Fallow & P. Manson: *Our Journall into Scotland* (1629)

WILLIAM LITHGOW

William Lithgow (1582–c.1645) was a native of Lanark. His comments upon Scotland in 1628 come at the end of his book, which is a mixture of fact and fiction, in journeys to places as far away as Poland and Moldavia and Syria and Palestine. His remarks on 'Gallowedian Nagges' have been widely quoted. He came over to Galloway after visiting Arran.

✝

I coasted Galloway even to the Mould that butteth into the Sea, with a large Promontore, being the South-most part of the Kingdome. And thence footing all that large Countrey to Dumfries, and so to Carlile: I found heere in Galloway in diverse Rode-way Innes, as good Cheere, Hospitality, and Serviceable attendance, as though I had beene ingrafted in Lombardy or Naples.

The Wooll of which Countrey, is nothing inferior to that in Biscai of Spain: providing they had skill, to fine, Spin, Weave, and labour it as they should. Nay, the Calabrian silke, had never a better luster, and softer gripe, then I have seene and touched this growing wooll there on Sheepes backes: the Mutton whereof excelleth in sweetnesse. So this Country aboundeth in Bestiall, especially in little Horses, which for mettall and Riding, may rather be tearmed bastard Barbs, then Gallowedian Nagges.

Likewise their Nobility and Gentry are as courteous, and every way generously disposed, as eyther discretion would wish, and honour Command: that (Cunningham being excepted, which may bee called the Accademy of Religion, for a sanctified Clergy, and a godly people) certainly Galloway is become more civill of late, then any Maritime Country, bordering with the Westerne Sea. . . .

– W. Lithgow: *The Totall Discourse of the Rare Adventures and painfull Periginations of long Nineteene Yeares Travayles* (1632)

SIR WILLIAM BRERETON

Sir William Brereton (1604–61) was a Member of the English Parliament for Cheshire in 1627–28 and in the Short and Long Parliaments of 1640. He was a successful commander in Parliamentary Army campaigns between 1642 and 1646 in Cheshire and the neighbouring counties to the south and south-west. On his Scottish tour in June and July of 1635 he travelled from Berwick to Edinburgh, and hence via Falkirk to Glasgow, Irvine, Ayr and Carrick before arriving at The Chapell [of St John] or Stranraer on July 3 en route to Portpatrick and Ireland. He returned to England from Waterford on July 25/26. He was the first visitor to Dumfries and Galloway to recommend lodgings for travellers in Carlingwark and Dumfries.

✝

Julii 3. . . . This day we were exceedingly punished for want of drink and meat for ourselves and our horses, and could not meet with any good accommodation in riding forty long miles; the entertainment we accepted, in a poorer house than any upon Handworth Green, was Tharck-cakes, two eggs, and some dried fish buttered; this day, as many days before, I drunk nothing but water; and divers of our horses, and Will. Baylye almost fainted for lack of relief. This day we passed up and down many high and steep hills, which you cannot ride, and very much hard and stony beaten way, exceeding much moorish barren land.

We came into Galloway about six miles from the chapel, and therein observed one of the widest, broadest, plainest moors that I have seen . . . About eight hour we came to this long desired chapel, the town is thence denominated and so called. This is situate upon a long loch, four miles long, wherein the sea ebbs and flows. Here we found good accommodation (only wanted wheat bread) in Hughe Boyde's house; ordinary 6d., good victuals, well-ordered, good wine and beer, lodging, and horse meat. This house is seated four miles from the Port Patrick, whence it is to Carlingworke 32 miles; best lodging there is Tho. Hutton; thence to Don-Frise 28 miles; best lodging is John Harstein; thence to Carleil 24.

Julii 4. We went from hence to Port Patrick, which is foul winter way over the mossy moors, and there we found only one boat, though yesternight there were fifteen boats here. We hired a boat of about ten ton for five horses of ours, and for five Yorkshiremen and horses; for this we paid £1 and conditioned that no more horses should come aboard, save only two or three of an Irish Laird's, who then stayed for a passage, and carried his wife and three horses. . . . Here we shipped our horses before we went aboard. It is a most craggy, filthy passage, and very dangerous for horses to go in and out; a horse may easily be lamed, spoiled, and thrust into the sea; and when any horses land here, they are thrown into the sea, and swim out. Here was demanded from us by our host, Thos. March-banke, a custom of 2s. an horse, which I stumbled at, and answered that if he had authority to demand and receive it, I was bound to pay it, otherwise not; and therefore I demanded to see his authority, otherwise I was free to pay or refuse; herewith he was satisfied, and declined his further demand. Here is a pretty chapel lately built by Sir Hugh Montgomeries, laird of Dunskie on this side, where he hath a castle, and of Newton de Clanboyes on the Irish side, where he hath a market-town. . . .

– W. Brereton, *Travels in Holland, the United Provinces, England, Scotland, and Ireland*. Chetham Society, 1844

THOMAS TUCKER

Tucker was sent to Scotland in 1655 by Cromwell's British government, which had already incorporated Scotland 'into one free State and Commonwealth with England'. He was to report to the Commissioners for the Excise in England and 'to give his assistance in settling the excise and customs' in Scotland. His report is a useful account of Scotland towards the end of a period of international war, civil unrest and economic decay.

✝

The next and last head port of Scotland is Ayre. . . . The lymitts or district of this port are of a very large extent and circuit, being all the shoare that bounds and terminates the shires of Kyle, Carrick, and Galloway, places fuller of moores and mosses then good townes or people, the same being in many places not planted, and all of it voyde of tradeing, except the towne of Ayre, Kircowbright, and Dunfreeze; nor in any liklihood of obtayneing any when there is not a shippe or barke belonging to any port in these parts except to Ayre. . . .

Stranrawer, otherwise called the Chappell, being a small mercate towne the side of the lough, which would prove a pretty harbour for shelter of vessells, in time of storme to putt in there, which is certainely very seldom and rare, in respect there is not now nor ever was any trade to bee heard of here.

Next to Stranrawer is Girvellen, a creeke, whether boates come and goe to and from Ireland, and next to these two is Port-patrick, a place much frequented by those who have any trade or affaires towards Ireland, because of its nearnesse to that countrey, and conveniency of transporting horse, cattell, and other materialls for planting thither, which is the sole trade of these parts; as there is noe harbour soe noe vessell of any burden can possibly come in.

The next to these are Whithorne and Wigton, to the latter of which there comes sometimes a small boate from England, with salt or coales.

Betwixt these and Kircowbright there is noe creeke nor port, but one creeke at the foot of the water of Fleete, not worth the nameing. As for Kircowbright, it is a pretty and one of the best ports on this side of Scotland, where there are a few, and these very poore merchants, or pedlars rather, tradeing for Ireland. Beyond this, there are the small creekes of Balcarie, the Water of Ore, and Satternis, whither some small boates come from England with salt and coales. And last of all Dunfreeze, a pretty mercat towne, but of little trade, that they have being for most part by land, either for Leith or Newcastle. The badness of comeing into the river upon which it lyes, hindering theyre comerce by sea, soe as whatever they have come that way is comonly and usually landed at Kirkcowbright. This towne of Dumfreeze was formerly the head port of these parts . . . but there being nothing to doe, the comissioners thought fitt to remove the collector to Ayre . . . where there is a checque and three officers; one of which officers attends constantly at that town, one other of them resides at Port-patrick . . . and the last of them at Kircowbright. . . .

– T. Tucker, *Report upon the Settlement of the Revenues of Excise and Customs in Scotland* (1655)

CAPTAIN RICHARD FRANCK

Captain Richard Franck (c. 1624–1708) was a cavalry officer with Cromwell's army in Scotland. His journey c. 1657 took him through Dumfries and Galloway and on to Glasgow and as far north as Sutherland and Caithness. His Northern Memoirs, *written in 1658 and published in 1694, were reprinted for Sir Walter Scott in 1821. The awkward format, an interminable dialogue between Arnoldus [Franck] and Theophilus,*

*makes it difficult to recognise that it is essentially an account of a fishing
tour by master and pupil, a sort of guide to salmon and trout fishing in
Scotland, a land 'immerged with rivers and gliding rivulets where every
fountain overflows a valley and every ford superabounds with fish'. His
pictures of Dumfries and Sanquhar [Zanker] are critical, but not
malicious.*

†

Arnoldus. . . . the river Eden floats near the skirts and the fortifications of
Carlisle. . . . another river commonly known by the name of Annan, of a
more rapid motion and more resolute streams . . . issues from the famous
top of Ericstane, not far from as famous a mountain called
streams . . . issues from the famous top of Ericstane, not far from as
famous a mountain called Tintan. . . . another river the natives call
Esk . . . tumbles into the sea . . . as near as I can guess at Quaking
Sands. . . .

I'll gratify you with a breviate of Dumfreez . . . It was anciently a
town girt about with a strong stone wall; but the late irruptions, or
perhaps some State disagreement, has in a manner defaced that regular
ornament, otherwise the cankrous teeth of time have gnawn out the
impressions, as evidently appears by those ruinous heaps. . . . In the
midst of the town is their market place, and in the centre of that stands
their tolbooth, round which the rabble sit, that nauseate the very air with
their tainted breath, so perfumed with onions that to an Englishman
it is almost infectious. But the kirk is comely . . . the outside than the
inside is more eminently embellished, if sepulchres and tombstones
can be said to be ornaments; and where death and time stand to guard the
steeples. . . . Here also you may observe a large and spacious bridge that
leads into the county of Galloway, where thrice in a week you shall rarely
fail to see their maidmankins dance corantos in tubs. So on every Sunday
some as seldom miss to make their appearance on the stool of
repentance. . . .

Theophilus. . . . Zanker, farewell! I am glad to see thee behind me, and
no need of a chirurgeon. Zanker stands situate on a flat or level,
surrounded with excellent corn fields; but more remote it's beseiged with
mountains that are rich in lead mines, and though the people hereabouts
are destitute of ingenuity, and their fields for the most part impoverished
for want of cultivation, yet their rivers and rivulets replenished with
trout, because undisturb'd with the noosy net. . . . Zanker is a town and a
corporation too, though not bulky in buildings. . . . There is also a

market-place, such as it is, and a kind of a thing they call a tolbooth. . . . There is also a kirk, or something like it, but I might as reverently call it a barn, because there is so little to distinguish between them, and the whole town reads daily lectures of decay, so do her ports, her evenues, and entrances. It's true I was not murdered, nor was I killed outright, yet I narrowly escaped as eminent a danger when almost worried to death with lice. . . .

– R. Franck, *Northern Memoirs, calculate for the Meridian of Scotland to which is added the contemplative and practical angler* (1694)

JOHN RAY

John Ray (1627–1705) of Trinity College, Cambridge, was the most distinguished naturalist of his day. His accounts of his itineraries, 'simpling voyages' or botanical study tours in Western Europe, including the British Isles, were published in various collections. In 1661 he travelled through Northumberland and Cumberland and in the south of Scotland from Berwick to Edinburgh and Glasgow and back through Lanarkshire to Dumfries and Carlisle. Like many others traversing the Southern Uplands he was widely out in his estimates of the height of the hills. Thirstane Hill and Steygail above the Enterkin [Anderkin-Hill] Burn south of Wanlockhead reach only 1912 feet and 1876 feet [583m and 572m].

✝

August the 24th. We rode to Dumfries . . . 28 miles, and in the way saw lead mines, at a place called the Lead-Hills, which will in time, it is likely, increase to a good considerable town. We also passed over much hilly ground; the highest place was called Anderkin-Hill, upon the top whereof the air was sharp and piercing . . . neither yet were we on the highest apex of it, by the ascent of near half a mile, as we guessed. This hill we judged to be higher than any we had been upon in England or Wales, Snowdon itself not excepted. This is a dangerous passage in winter time, the way being narrow and slippery, and a great precipice on the one hand, besides the descent steep, so that we led our horses down about a mile.

At Dumfries they have two ministers, one a young man named Campbell . . . the other, an elder man, by name Henderson, who has married his daughter to the younger. Campbell prayed for the preservation of their church government and discipline, and spake openly against prelacy and its adjuncts and consequences. Here, as also at Dunbar, and other places, we observed the manner of their burials, which is this: when any one dies, the sexton or bell-man goeth about the streets, with a small bell in his hand, which he tinkleth all along as he goeth, and now and then he makes a stand, and proclaims who is dead, and invites the people to come to the funeral at such an hour. The people and minister many times accompany the corpse to the grave at the time appointed, with the bell before them, where there is nothing said, but only the corpse laid in. . . . Before sermon, commonly, the officers of the town stand at the church-yard gate, with a join'd stool and a dish, to gather the alms of all that come to church. The people here frequent their churches much better than in England, and have their ministers in more esteem and veneration. They seem to perform their devotions with much alacrity. There are few or no sectaries or opinionists among them; they are much addicted to their church government, excepting the gentry, who love liberty, and care not to be so strictly tied down. The country abounds with poor people and beggars.

Their money they reckon after the French manner. A bodel (which is the sixth part of our penny) they call tway-pennies, that is with them two-pence; so that, upon this ground, 12 pennies, or a shilling Scotch (that is, six bodels), is a penny sterling. The Scotch piece mark'd with xx, which we are wont to call a Scotch two-pence, is twenty-pence Scotch, that is, two-pence sterling, wanting two bodels, or four pennies Scotch; the piece with xl is four-pence sterling – 4 bodels; and so one shilling sterling is 12 shillings Scotch. Thirteen pence half-penny English, a mark Scotch. One pound Scotch, 20d. sterling. One bodel they call tway-pennies (as above), 2 bodles a plack, 3 bodels a baubee, 4 bodels 8 pennies, 6 bodels 1 shilling Scotch.

– J. Ray, Itineraries (1661)

JAMES BROME

James Brome became rector of Cheriton in Kent in 1676. He died in 1719. On his Scottish journey in 1669 he arrived at Dumfries after an exhausting two-day journey from Hamilton 'over meers and dangerous mountains . . . where the weather was ill, the ways worse, and the long miles with their way-bits at the end of them worst of all.' The complaint about the 'wee bits' stemmed from the fact that the Scotch, as opposed to the English, mile was a 'mile and a bittock'!

✝

But coming at length to Dumfries in the County of Nidisdail it made us some amends for being situate between two hills upon the mouth of the river Nid, over which is laid a bridge of large fine stones, it appears to be one of the most flourishing towns in this tract, notable no less for its ancient castle and manufacture of cloath, than for the murther of John Cummins ... whom Robert Bruce, for fear he should fore-stal his way to the crown, run quite through with his sword in the Fryars Church, and soon obtain'd his pardon from the Pope, though he had committed so great a murder in so sacred a place.

   After this we came to Anandale at the mouth of the river Anan in the County of Anandale, bordering upon our own nation, which lost all its glory and beauty upon the war, which was raised in Edward the Sixth's days; in these two last-named counties have been bred a sort of warlike men, who have been infamous for robbery and depredations, for they dwell upon Solway-Frith, a fordable arm of the sea at low water, through which frequently they have made many inroads into England to fetch home great booty's, and in which they were wont after a delightful manner on horseback, with spears to hunt salmons. . . .

– J. Brome, *Three Years' Travels over England,*
Scotland and Wales (1700)

ANONYMOUS

The identity of the author is not recorded. Extracts were published in vol. II of Blackwood's Edinburgh Magazine *for February, 1818. The route the author took from Dunbar to Edinburgh, Glasgow and Hamilton was straightforward, but he found the journey from Douglas and Elvanfoot to Moffat a terrifying experience. He ended up lost and stranded overnight in a bog. From Moffat he continued by Poldean and Annanbank to Lockerbie and Ecclefechan [Arkle Forken].*

†

16th April, 1704 . . . I was got past Elwin ffet, and the road, or rather sheep tracts . . . were so obscure, I could hardly find a way, and the rocks were so thick and close, that I had often much ado to get myself and horse between them. Now I were on a vast precipice of a high rock, with the river running under me, and anon I was in a bogg, and by and by my horse began to tyre and jade. . . . and considering that I was in the South Highlands, and did not know how I might be besett, I moved further up the hill side-ways of it . . . I hung my pistolls on my wrist . . . my knees and harnessing sunk into the bogg . . . I often groped my watch, and wish't for morning . . . As the day began to dawn . . . I went a mile one way, and then back, and a mile the other . . . at length I resolved to go eastward . . . and so this 17th of April, 1704, I got to Moffat. This is a small straggling town among high hills, and is the town of their wells. In sumer time people comme here to drink waters, but what sort of people they are, or where they get lodgings, I can't tell, for I did not like their lodgings well enough to go to bedd, but got such as I could to refresh me, and so came away.

From hence I came through Pudeen, and to Annan or Annand House, and at the last place I dined at a good Scotch house, and so came to Lockerby, a small town, where I lay. It had rained all this day from before noon till night; and to comfort me more, the room wherein I was to lay was overflown with water, so that the people layd heaps of turf for me to gett from the door to the fireplace, and from thence to the bed; and the floor was so worn in holes, that had I tread aside a turf, I might have sunk up to my knees in mudd and water, and no better room was to be had in this town; nay, what was worse, my room had but halfe a door, and that to the street; and the wall was broke down between the gable, so that the room lay open to the stable. . . . but I was forced to bear it so, layd 2 case of pistolls that I had with me by my bedd's head, and slep dogg's sleep till morning, and had the advantage of overhearing if any one attempted to steal my horse; and yet the people here had French wine, though it was always spoiled for want of being well cellar'd.

I went out early in the morning the next day, and came through Arkle Forken, a small village, and so to Allison Bank, another small village, and the last I was at in Scotland. . . .

– Anon., *An Old Tour in Scotland* (1704)

JOHN MACKY

Nobody seems to know where Macky came from, though it is just possible that he had some connection with Alexander Mackye of Palgowan whose seat at Loch Trool he admired so much. John Macky was a spy or secret agent working for the governments of William III and Queen Anne. Between c. 1688 and 1695 he was in Paris and, specifically, at the Court of St Germain to gather intelligence for his masters in London. His View of the Court of St Germain *(1696) is a propaganda exercise designed to discredit James II by showing that his Court was infiltrated by a swarm*

*of spies and pensioners to England. In 1691 he was in Scotland working
for Secretary of State Melville, posing as an emissary from St Germain,
and reporting back on the Jacobite sympathies of the Episcopalian bishops
of Glasgow and St Andrews and the plots of the Earl of Arran and
Archibald Paterson of Glasgow. His network provided advance warning
of the Jacobite invasion in 1708. In 1697 he married a daughter of Sir
William Spring, a Suffolk landlowner. He died in exile in Rotterdam in
1726.*

His Journey through Scotland *(1723) was the third volume to complete*
Great Britain, beside his earlier Journey through England *(1714,*
*reprinted with a second volume in 1722). It took the form of a series of
fourteen letters, from Letter I in Kirkcudbright and Letter II in Dumfries
and the Borders through most of mainland Scotland, and returning via
Maybole to Galloway in Letter XIV. The three volumes served as a model
for the much better known* Tour Thro' the Whole Island of Great Britain
in which Defoe made very free use of some of Macky's ideas.

✝

Letter I ... In five hours from the Isle of Man I arrived at
Kircudbright ... an ancient town, with the prettiest navigable river I have
seen in Britain ... this little town ... consists of a tolerable street, the
houses all built with stone, but not at all after the manner of England;
even the manners, dress and countenance of the people differ very much
from the English. The common people wear all bonnets instead of hats;
and though some of the townsmen have hats, they wear them only on
Sundays and extraordinary occasions. There is nothing of the gaiety of
the English, but a sedate gravity in every face, without the stiffness of the
Spaniards; and I take this to be owing to their praying and frequent long
graces, which gives their looks a religious cast. Taciturnity and dulness
gains the character of a discreet man, and a gentleman of wit is call'd a
sharp man.

I arriv'd here on Saturday night, at a good inn; but the room where I
lay, I believe, had not been washed in a hundred years. Next day I
expected, as in England, a piece of good beef or a pudding to dinner; but
my landlord told me that they never dress dinner on a Sunday, so that I
must either take up with bread and butter, a free egg, or last till after the
evening sermon, when they never fail of a hot supper. Certainly no nation
on earth observes the Sabbath with that strictness of devotion and
resignation to the will of God; they all pray in their families before they
go to church, and between sermons they fast. After sermon every body

retires to his own home and reads some book of devotion till supper, which is generally very good on Sundays, after which they sing psalms till they go to bed.

This, with the adjacent Shire of Galloway, is reckon'd one of the coarsest parts of Scotland ... The Macdweles, Mackys, Macqhys, Maclurgs, Maclellans and Maxwells are the common names here; but gentlemen are never called by their names here, but, as in France, by their estate ... for example I know six gentlemen each called John Maxwell in this Stewartry: when you ask for any, you never name him, but his lairdship, as they call it. ... If you meet a man in the streets, and ask for Maxwell of Gribton, you ask for the laird of Gribton. ... There are lairds here of 500 Pounds a year, and of 15 only; a Galloway laird of 20 or 30 Pounds a year is a frequent thing, and all gentlemen, as in Wales. ...

There is a fine salmon-fishing in this river, and no place can be finer situate for a white fish-fishing on the Bank of Solway and the north coast of Ireland; but the inhabitants neglect both, there being never a ship and scarcely any boat belonging to the whole town. But the Union having encouraged both English and Scots to improve the fishing on the coasts and in the rivers of Scotland, it's to be hoped that this well situated town for that trade may in time come to flourish. ...

Letter XIV ... I came to the town of Stranrawer, a royal borough on Lockrian, but hardly a house two stories high in the whole town and a most miserable place ... I got to Port-Patrick, a miserable place, where the packet-boats pass between Scotland and Ireland, and makes for a short passage, having a full view of the coast of Ireland all the way; but the boats are not so good as those that pass the Frith of Forth from Lieth to Fife. ...

Near Wigton is the seat of Stuart, Earl of Galloway ... Here are the breed of little strong pads, called from the country Galloways, which are very strong and hardy. ...

There are several other mountains and lakes, well stor'd with fish, within the barony of Esbuchan, and the Forest belonging to Alexander Mackye of Palgoun, who hath a very commodious and romantick seat on the lake Lochtrool, in a valley invironed with mountains on the north and east a mile high: he keeps at least ten thousand sheep on these mountains, besides an incredible number of black cattle and wild horses call'd Galloways, and is one of the greatest grasiers in Britain, and has vast parks and inclosures.

Not far from this is the famous mountain of Carnsmure, full of dear and wild cattle . . . and to the south-west a handsome seat call'd the Caily, belonging to Alexander Murray of Brouchton, with a large park, which feeds one thousand bullocks, that he sends every year to the markets of England. . . .

– J. Macky, *A Journey through Scotland* (1723)

DANIEL DEFOE

Daniel Defoe (1660–1731) was sent to Edinburgh by government ministers, Harley in 1706–07 and Goldolphin from 1708 intermittently through to 1711, to report back on the situation in Scotland and to take a creative role in influencing opinion in favour of the Union (of 1707). His last visit was in 1712. As an English Dissenting Presbyterian, Defoe was particularly suited for his work in infiltrating Church of Scotland synods and presbyteries to calm away the fears and alarms of the Scottish Presbyterian establishment. As a journalist he played an active part in the pamphlet war in 1707 and for a short time, from December 1709, took over two newspaper sheets, the Scots Postman *and the* Edinburgh Courant. *At that point in his life the great novels,* Robinson Crusoe *(1719) and* Moll Flanders *(1722) and the* Journal of the Plague Year *(1722) were still to be written.*

Neither John Macky nor Daniel Defoe really wrote travel journals. Their books were compilations based on memories of places they had visited, accounts based on information miscellaneously collected, and plain straightforward plagiarism. Defoe's excellent account of John Hepburn's conventicle, for example, is directly taken from a letter dated 26 December, 1706 from another agent 'John Pierce' (perhaps John Kerr of Kersland) who had spent three days with 'the Cameronian Bishop'! The Cameronians were opposed to the Union, but Pierce claimed that he had received assurances from Hepburn that there would be no danger from him. And Defoe's lively description of Kirkcudbright is quite probably little more than a brilliant rewriting of John Macky. The third volume of Defoe's Tour, *taking in the north of England and Scotland, was published in 1727.*

Defoe is always consistent in his enthusiasm for a Protestant and a United Britain and for the increase of trade and manufacture and shipping and commerce. He was also adept at making friends of people who mattered. The good Sir John Clerk of Penicuik (1676–1755), scholar, antiquary, MSP for Whithorn from 1703 to 1707, who had married, in 1701, Lady Margaret, the daughter of the 3rd Earl of Galloway, was one

of his best contacts. Clerk in his private journal of 'A Journie to Gallouay'
in 1721 (SRO GD 18 2101) described the Galloway trade in black cattle in
some detail and estimated, probably overoptimistically, the value of cattle
sold to the English markets at £100,000 sterling a year. Clerk also
mentioned that Galloway horses were bred in the moors of Minnigaff and
about the hills of Craignelder and Poultrybuie.

†

Letter XII . . . Dumfries was always a good town and full of
merchants . . . in the sense that word is taken and understood in England,
not mercers and drapers, shop-keepers, etc., but merchant-adventurers
who trade to foreign parts and employ a considerable number of ships.
But if this was so before, it is much more so now: and as they (with
success) embark'd in trade to England as to the English plantations, they
apparently encrease both in shipping and people. . . .

While I was at Drumlanrig . . . I, in particular, view'd some of the
hills to the north of the castle . . . Here we were surpriz'd with a sight,
which is not now so frequent in Scotland as it has been formerly, I mean
one of their field meetings, where one Mr John Hepburn, an old
Cameronian, preach'd to an auditory of near 7,000 people, all sitting in
rows on the steep side of a green hill, and the preacher in a little pulpit
made under a tent at the foot of the hill; he held his auditory, with not
above an intermission of half an hour, almost seven hours; and many of
the poor people had come fifteen or sixteen miles to hear him, and had all
the way to go home again on foot. . . . if there was an equal zeal to this in
our part of the world, and for that worship which we acknowledge to
be true, and of a sacred institution, our churches would be more throng'd
and our ale-houses and fields less throng'd on the sabbath-day than they
are now. . . .

Galloway . . . the first town on the coast of any note is Kirkubright, or,
as vulgarly call'd, Kirkubry. . . . Here is a pleasant situation, and yet
nothing pleasant to be seen. Here is a harbour without ships, a port
without trade, a fishery without nets, a people without business; and, that
which is worse than all, they do not seem to desire business, much less do
they understand it. I believe they are very good Christians at Kirkubry,
for they are in the very letter of it, they obey the text, and are contented
with such things as they have. . . . In a word, they have no notion of being
rich and populous, and thriving by commerce. They have a fine river,
navigable for the greatest ships to the town-key . . . But, alas! there is not
a vessel, that deserves the name of a ship, belongs to it; and, though here

is an extraordinary salmon fishing, the salmon come and offer themselves, and go again, and cannot obtain the privilege of being made useful to mankind; for they take very few of them. They have also white fish, but cure none; and herrings, but pickle none. . . . I doubt not, were two or three brisk merchants to settle at Kirkubry, who had stocks to furnish out ships and boats . . . they would soon find the people as industrious and as laborious as in other places . . . 'tis the poverty of the people makes them indolent.

. . . the common people all over this country, not only are poor, but look poor; they appear dejected and discourag'd, as if they had given over all hopes of ever being otherwise than what they are. They are, indeed, a sober, grave, religious people . . . conversation is generally sober and grave; I assure you, they have no assemblies here, no balls; and far from what it is in England, you hear no oaths or prophane words in the streets; and, if a mean boy, such as we call shoe-blackers, or black-guard boys, should be heard to swear, the next gentleman in the street, if any happen'd to be near him, would cane him and correct him. . . .

It is the honour of Scotland that they are the strictest observers of the Lord's-Day of any nation in the world; and, if any part of Scotland are more strict observers of it than the rest, it is their part, and all the country from Dumfries, and the parts adjacent to Glasgow and the Clyde, inclusive of both the towns of Dumfries and Glasgow; and tho' this country of Galloway may be the poorest and empty of commerce, it is, perhaps, the most religious part of all Scotland. . . .

The people of Galloway do not starve . . . they have other business, that is to say they are meer cultivators of the earth and in particular breeders of cattle, such as sheep, the number of which I may say is infinite, that is to say innumerable; and black cattle, of which they send to England, if fame lies not, 50 or 60,000 every year . . . they have the best strong breed of strong low horses in Britain, if not in Europe, which we call pads, and from whence we call all small truss-strong riding horses Galloways: these horses are remarkable for being good pacers, strong, easy goers, hardy, gentle, well broke, and above all that they never tire, and they are very much bought up in England on that account . . . the gentlemen here are the greatest sheep-masters in Scotland . . . and the greatest breeders of black cattle and horses.

– D. Defoe, *A Tour Thro' the Whole Island of Great Britain* (1724–27)

RICHARD POCOCKE

Richard Pococke (1704–65), 'Pococke the Traveller', was born in Southampton. His career as a clergyman in the Church of Ireland from Precentor of Lismore [Waterford] in 1725 to Archdeacon of Dublin, Bishop of Ossory and finally Bishop of Meath, allowed him time to travel extensively in Europe, Italy, Greece, Austria, Prussia (1733–36) and in the Eastern Mediterranean and Egypt, Syria and Mesopotamia (1737–42). His six month long Scottish journey in 1760 took him as far north as Cape Wrath, Stroma and Kirkwall. It was published by the Scottish History Society in 1887.

The first three weeks after crossing to Portpatrick on 29/30 April were spent between Whithorn, Newton Stewart ('in a narrow valley, much like the face of Switzerland'), Auchencairn, Rascarrel, Munches, Dumfries and Moffat. He was, like Sir John Clerk, especially interested in antiquities, but also in natural hisory and folklore. Were the 'wild cats' in the eastern Stewartry an exotic import, or were they Scottish wild cats?

✝

Whithern . . . A quarter of a mile to the southeast of the town, towards the sea, is what they call the Castle of Bishopstown, which, it is said, was the Bishop's house. It seems to have been an oblong square. They speak of the garden extending towards the sea, and it is indeed a most delightfull situation. This town consists mostly of farmers and a few tradesmen and manufacturers in woollen and linnen for home consumption. There is a square tower in the middle of the street, which they always keep well whitened. . . .

Going to the isle, I saw they had been digging for coal, and had raised a fine sandy clay, but were obstructed by the water. I could learn no other reason for their sinking for coals, but that it was in the right line from Whitehaven, I suppose north-west. I came to the isle, which is a little harbour formed by a pier, within which they have 18 feet water at high tydes, and a ship of 300 tuns can come in. They export barley, and import plank and iron from Gottenburgh in Sweden, and send it by boats to Wigtown, as the entrance and harbour there are not good. There is a bridge over to the island, under which the sea passes at high water. The principal houses are on the west side of it, and on the Isle near the bridge is a row of poor houses. . . .

To Aghakern . . . a village so called from a carn near. They found some iron ore about this place, bit it did not answer in the smelting. They have also searched for coal at Roscorriel, at a small distance, and propose to carry it on by subscription. This place is near the river Our or Orr, in which they have a bed of oysters, and they catch in the sea cod and Mackrel. . . . They have many mounts in this country, which they call motes. . . .

About twelve years agoe they found . . . on the estate of Mr Maxwel of Minches, a bed of cockle-shells about a foot under ground, and four feet deep, extending over three acres of ground, which are most excellent manure. They use also sea-shells in this country for the same purpose, at the expensive carriage or seven or eight pounds for an acre. They have grouse and the black game on the mountains, and abundance of foxes. They have also a wild cat three times as big as the common cat, as the pollcat is the less. They are of a yellow red colour, their breasts and sides white. They take fowls and lambs, and brede two at a time. . . .

Moffet is a small town. . . . It is the estate of the Marquis of Anandale, who is lunatic, and Lord Hopton is the curator, who is setting on foot a manufacture of shalloons and serges here. . . . The old Spaw was found above a hundred years agoe by Bishop Whiteford's daughter. It comes out of a rock over a rivulet that runs down the rocks in a deep glyn adorned with wood in a very romantick manner. . . . There are two springs. One comes out of the top of the rock, and is the strongest of sulphur, which settles on the rock. This is carried to Moffet to bathe in, and may be drank. But they commonly drink the other which comes out lower on the other side of the cave, and is softer. It is esteemed particularly good in all scorbutick disorders, both to bathe and drink, and is particularly good for sores . . . a long room and conveniences here for the people to come and drink the waters on the spot. . . .

> – R. Pococke, *A Journey round Scotland to the Orkneys* (1760)

JAMES BOSWELL

Journal of My Jaunt. Harvest, 1762
The 'great' Boswell (1740–95), scribbler, journalist, gossip, Scotsman on the make, was the son of the advocate Alexander Boswell, Lord Auchinleck (1706–82). Until the discovery of the vast collection of his journals and private papers in Malahide Castle near Dublin in the 1920s and also at Fettercairn House in 1930–31, Boswell's reputation had rested on his Life of Samuel Johnson *(1791) and his* Journal of a Tour to the Hebrides with Samuel Johnson *(1786). The transfer of his papers to Yale in*

1949 and the publication of a series of these journals, James Boswell. The Earlier Years 1740–1762 *(1966),* Boswell on the Grand Tour 1762, Boswell in Search of a Wife 1766–69, Boswell for the Defence 1769–1776 *. . . established Boswell's reputation as a recorder of eighteenth century life.*

The Journal of My Jaunt. *Harvest 1762 [Harvest in this context means 'hairst' or Autumn] was prepared for the press by Geoffrey Scott and privately printed in the USA in 1928 as part of the first of twenty volumes of the* Private Papers of James Boswell *from Malahide Castle. Boswell, accompanying Lord and Lady Kames, left Auchenleck in Ayrshire on 14th September, 1762. They itinerated throught the Stewartry of Kirkcudbright, Wigtownshire, Dumfries-shire and Cumberland, and hence via Northumberland and Berwickshire to reach Edinburgh on 14th November. Boswell already knew parts of Dumfries-shire, in particular the Moffat area, having been sent there first as a child in 1752 and then as a young man in 1757 to take the sulphur springs and warm baths as a cure for his 'scorbutic' and 'scrofulous' condition and his melancholy (depression). He was back in Moffat again in 1766 with the same problems.*

As a guest at Lagwine, Kenmure Castle and Kirroughtree in the Stewartry, at Galloway House in Wigtownshire, and at Kelhead and Springkell in Dumfries-shire, and as a visitor to other estates, including Baldoon, Merton and Bonshaw, Boswell met a wide cross-section of greater and lesser country house society. Boswell already saw himself as someone with 'no sort of turn for farming', so there is virtually no information about changes and improvements in land use and agriculture. However his gossipy notes (he was at 22 a thorough snob, a spoiled brat, and something of an expert in character assassination) do give a lively picture of life 'at the top'.

At Lagwine Boswell played on his German flute and took the part of Macheath in The Beggar's Opera *to Miss Macadam's Polly. He already had a clear view of his own importance: at Lagwine as a cousin he 'had their affections', 'as being very clever their Admiration', and as Mr Boswell of Auchinleck 'their Respect'. But to Boswell their 'landlady', who entertained them to dinner at Berbeth near Dalmellington, before they continued in the afternoon to Lagwine, was 'of little service to us'. After all, although a good-looking young woman and a niece of the laird of Craigengillan, her employment had 'always been with the Cows, and her Companions the Inhabitants of the Kitchen'. These sharp distinctions of rank and worth were not, of course, peculiar to Boswell. Mr Macartney, the tutor at Kirroughtree, who had been in the same class as Boswell at the*

University of Edinburgh, was treated by the Heron family 'as a sort of cringing animal little better than a livery servant'. Meanwhile, at Kirroughtree, Mr Boswell was reading letters by Swift (with the worst of intentions) 'to a young lady newly married'.

Boswell provides neat and damning snapshots of character. At Lagwine he met Mr Shaw, a writer from Edinburgh who had retired to Dalmellington, 'precise, starched and proud' 'with a lank iron countenance and 'a weather-beaten Scotch wig,' who sat 'erect up on his chair' while singing 'Tarry Woo' with an English accent.

At Kirroughtree he met James Murray of Broughton, 'a most amiable man' with 'very good sense, great knowledge of the world and easy politeness of manners', and his wife, Lady Katie, the daughter of the 6th Earl of Galloway, 'very beautiful', 'very agreeable', and 'posest of the most engaging Affability'. [The portraits by Allan Ramsay and Angelica Kauffman fully confirm this assessment.] 'They present a pleasing picture of matrimonial felicity. They seem like a Couple who have been married but a year and are indeed Evergreen in love.'

At Galloway House he found Lady Galloway formidable, a 'Jacobite in Politicks', a 'highchurchwoman in religion', whereas Lord Galloway was a good father, husband and Master. Lord Garlies was a little man with a great flow of animal spirits, but he had been 'indulged and idolized' by his father, the Earl, and this explained his 'petulant forwardness'. Lady Garlies was very little and very young, sweet and composed, a turn for all the little amusement, 'such as painting flowers and cutting paper'. But at Galloway House 'their table, tho' plentifull, was yet narrow, and you seemed to be fed by measure.'

At Sir William Maxwell's at Springkell, Boswell met his sister, Miss Maxwell, who played on the guitar and sang Italian airs, English ballads and Scotch songs 'with a thorough bass voice'. And Sir William Maxwell of Monreith, formerly 'a genteel, pretty looking man', now looked 'like an overgrown Drover'.

JOHN WESLEY

Over the Sands to Skinburness
John Wesley (1703–91) was not only a good and a great man, a noble spirit, a major force in eighteenth-century British religious life; he was also a traveller who routinely tackled journeys of fearsome length and difficulty. In a long life he covered vast distances on horseback, including twenty-three visits to Scotland between 1751 and 1790, the great majority

preaching tours, although in 1767, unable to arrange a passage by sea to Ireland, he left Bristol (March 16th) to travel to Belfast via Portpatrick. He rode 430 miles in six days and, with a Friday to Monday stopover in Liverpool, reached Portpatrick on March 28th. In the next four months (up to July 29) he itinerated via Belfast, Armagh, Ennis, Cork, Kilkenny and Athlone to Dublin, before returning by Donaghadee to Stranraer en route to Newcastle (August 6th).

On his last Scottish tour, at the age of 87, in the relative 'comfort' of various chaises, he left Queensferry on May 17th, 1790, and itinerated via Dundee and Aberdeen to Banff, returning by Brechin and Auchterarder to Moffat and Dumfries (May 31st) and Carlisle (June 2nd). On May 31st he left Glasgow at 1.30 in the morning, hence by Hamilton 4.30, Douglas Mills 8.15, Elvanfoot 12 noon for dinner, and Moffat 3 afternoon, to reach Dumfries at 6.30 for tea, followed by preaching a sermon. The Dumfries preaching-house came under the Carlisle circuit. It should perhaps be added that, in comparison to England and Wales, Wesley's success in Scotland was relatively limited, and there were only some 1,000 Methodists in Scotland at the time of his death in 1791.

Some of the most interesting sections in the 1909 edition of Wesley's Journal [edited by Curnock] are the descriptions of the crossings of the Solway on horseback and of the short 'ferry' from Portpatrick to Donaghadee. He was fortunate on more than one occasion to escape with his life. He may not have fully appreciated the dangers which he and his companions faced, or perhaps just felt that ultimately he was in God's hands 'as God should please'.

✝

April 27th, 1761 [from Wigton in Cumberland] Before noon we came to Solway Firth. The guide told us it was not passable, but I resolved to try, and got over well. Having lost ourselves but twice or thrice, in one of the most difficult roads I ever saw, we came to Moffat in the evening.

April 30th, 1765 [from Girvan] We rode over high and steep mountains between Ballantrae and Stranraer, where we met with as good entertainment of every kind as if we had been in the heart of England. We reached Port Patrick about 3 o'clock, and were immediately surrounded with men, offering to carry us over the water. But the wind was full in our teeth. I determined to wait till morning, and then go backwards and forwards, as God should please.

May 1st, Wednesday The wind was quite fair; so, as soon as the tide served, I went on board. It seemed strange to cross the sea in an open boat, especially when the waves ran high. I was a little sick, till I fell asleep. In five hours and a half we reached Donaghadee; but my mare could not land till five hours after, so that I did not reach Newtownards till past 8. . . .

June 24th, 1766 [from Thornhill] Before eight we reached Dumfries, and after a short wait pushed on in hopes of reaching Solway Firth before the sea came in. Designing to call at an inn by the Firth side, we inquired the way, and were directed to leave the main road and go straight to the house which we saw before us. In ten minutes Duncan Wright was embogged. However, the horse plunged on, and got through. I was inclined to turn back; but Duncan telling me I needed only go a little to the left, I did so, and sunk at once to my horse's shoulders. He sprang up twice, and twice sank again, each time deeper than before. At the third plunge he threw me on one side, and we both made shift to scramble out. I was covered with fine, soft mud from my feet to the crown of my head; yet, blessed be the Lord, not hurt at all. But we could not cross till between 7 and 8 o'clock. An honest man crossed with us, who went 2 miles out of his way to guide us over the sands to Skinburness, where we found a clean little house, and passed a comfortable night.

March 26th, 1767 [from Cockermouth] We rode through miserable roads to Solway Firth; but the guides were so deeply engaged in a cock-fight that none could be procured to show us over. We procured one, however, between 3 and 4. But there was more sea than we expected, so that, not withstanding all I could do, my legs and the skirts of my coat were in the water. The motion of the waves made me a little giddy; but it had a stranger effect on Mr Atlay – he lost his sight, and was just dropping off his horse when one of our travellers caught hold of him. We rode on 9 or 10 miles, and lodged at a village called Ruthwell.

THOMAS PENNANT

Thomas Pennant (1726–98) was born at Holywell in Flintshire and went to school in Wrexham. He became a prolific author of books and articles on British zoology and mineralogy and antiquities. His accounts of his Scottish journeys in 1769 and 1772, planned and executed with a view to authorship, were published as A Tour in Scotland *(1771) and* A Tour in Scotland and Voyage to the Hebrides *(1774–75). They were received with great popular acclaim. Sales were immediate and profitable. On his second tour, in particular, he had travelled 'to the remotest part of North Britain, a country almost as little known to its southern brethren as Kamschatska'. The subjects he covered included prehistoric and Roman antiquities, for example, the canoes from Lochar Moss and the Roman statues and coins from Netherby near Longtown, the brochs in Glenelg, and ruined, and therefore 'romantic', castles and abbeys. He had the happy knack of noting what was easily missed, for example the motte at Lincluden, where 'there are the vestiges of a flower-garden, with the parterres and scrolls very visible; and near that a great artificial mount, with a spiral walk to the top, which is hollowed, and has a turf seat around to command the beautiful views.'*

Pennant also included sections on mineralogy and zoology, botanical notes by the Rev. J. Lightfoot, the staggering and completely new account of Staffa by the great Sir Joseph Banks (1743–1820), some aspects of the way of life of people on Jura and Canna and Skye, and plates from drawings by his own draughtsman, Moses Griffiths, and others, including Paul Sandby. The Staffa plates were eminently collectable, a source of never-ending wonder and amazement.

His success and celebrity status not only inspired Johnson and Boswell's visit to the Hebrides, but also led to a veritable flood of Scotch travel books in the 1790s and 1800s.

On the 1769 tour Pennant returned to England on the west coast route via Moffat, Lockerbie and Longtown. In 1772 he travelled north by Canonbie, Annan, Ruthwell, Kirkconnel, Hoddam, Lochar Moss, Dumfries, Lincluden, Keir, Drumlanrig and Durisdeer, before working his way up to Jura, Islay, Kintyre, Oronsay, Iona, Canna, Skye, Assynt and Mull. The following extracts are from his 1772 tour.

✝

Ruthwell. As soon as the warm and dry weather of June comes on, the sun brings up and incrusts the surface of the sand with salt: at that time they gather the sand to the depth of an inch, carry it out of the reach of the tide, and lay it in round compact heaps, to prevent the salt being washed away by the rains: they then make a pit eight feet long and three broad, and the same depth, and plaister the inside with clay, that it may hold water; at the bottom they place a layer of peat and turf, and fill the pit with the collected sand; after that they pour water on it: this filters through the sand, and carries the salt with it into a lesser pit, made at the end of the great one: this they boil in small lead pans, and procure a coarse brown salt, very fit for the purpose of salting meat and fish.

Dumfries. a very neat and well-built town . . . containing about 5000 souls. It was once possessed of a large share of the tobacco trade, but at present has scarce any commerce. The great weekly markets for black cattle are of much advantage to the place; and vast droves from Galloway and the shire of Air pass through in the way to the fairs in Norfolk and Suffolk. . . . This place like most other considerable towns in Scotland has its seceders chapel: these are the rigid presbyterians who possess the religion in all its original sourness: think the church is in danger because their ministers degenerate into moderation, and wear a gown; or vindicate patronage. To avoid these horrid innovations, they separate themselves from their imaginary false brethren; renew a solemn league and covenant, and preserve to the best of their power all the rags and rent bequeathed to them by John Knox, which the more sensible preachers of this day are striving to darn and patch. . . .

Mr Hill, surgeon, favoured me with the sight of the head of an old lady, excellently painted, about forty years ago, by Mr John Patoun, son to a minister in this town. After painting three years in Scotland, about the year 1730 he went to London, where he read lectures on the theory of his art: at length was tempted to make a voyage to Jamaica, where he died in a few weeks, leaving behind him the character of a good man, and able artist.

Drumlanrig. In my walks about the park . . . the white breed of wild cattle . . . still retain the primaeval savageness and ferocity of their ancestors: were more shy than any deer; ran away on the appearance of any of the human species, and even set off at full gallop on the least noise . . . during summer they keep apart from all the other cattle, but in severe weather hunger will compel them to visit the out-houses in search of food. The keepers are obliged to shoot them, if any are wanted: if the beast is not killed on the spot it runs at the person who gave it the wound, and who is forced . . . to fly for safety to the intervention of some tree. These cattle are of a middle size, have very long legs, and the cows are fine horned: the orbits of the eyes and the tops of the noses are black: but the bulls have lost the manes attributed to them by Boethius.

– T. Pennant, *A Tour in Scotland and Voyage to the Hebrides* (1774–75)

WILLIAM GILPIN

William Gilpin (1724–1804) was born at Scaleby Castle near Carlisle. His books, published in the 1780s and 1790s on the theory of the picturesque, established very precise British canons of good taste and refinement on what constituted for landscape painters and landscape architects, for country gentlemen and travellers alike, 'the correctly Picturesque'. Mountains with rounded swelling forms or with regular mathematical terraced lines were vulgar and unpleasing; lakes should have rushing torrents and sharp and steep rocky mountains; ruined abbeys and towers were romantic and essential for 'Picturesque Travel'; foregrounds should be broken up with moving objects, wagons, cattle, ships; cattle were more picturesque than horses; an improved and properly developed landscape was acceptable, even if not strictly picturesque.

Gilpin's *Observations . . . on* Cumberland and Westmoreland (1786) *was followed by his* Observations on several parts of Great Britain, particularly the High-Lands of Scotland, relative chiefly to Picturesque Beauty, made in the year 1776 *(1787), which included some discussion of the presence or abscence of aesthetic pleasures around the Solway Firth and at Gretna Green, Dumfries, Lincluden and Kirkcudbright.*

In the countryside outside Dumfries 'various surfaces appear ambiguous, and are melted together by light mists into one mass. They are beautiful in that ambiguity . . . to make pictures of them . . . the foregrounds must be adorned with objects – masts of ships, figures, cattle, or other proper appendages, to break the lines of distance.'

At Kirkcudbright 'on the West side of Saint Mary's isle, a creek runs up, which forms the harbour . . . This town, tho of no extensive trade, employs coasting vessels enough to people the bay with shipping; which is a great advantage to it in a picturesque light.'

At Drumlanrig the Duke of Queensberry has 'built comfortable houses for his tenants through his whole estate. Many of them are ranged within sight of his castle, at proper distances along the sides of the hills.'

– W. Gilpin, Observations . . . relative chiefly to Picturesque Beauty *(1787)*

THOMAS NEWTE

Thomas Newte was no English gentleman. His name was, in fact, William Thomson, and he was born in Forteviot in Perthshire in 1746. He died in London in 1817. After studying at the University of St Andrews he was appointed assistant and intended successor at Monzievaird parish in the Presbytery of Auchterarder on 20th March, 1776. He was removed from office on 1st October, 1778. He mentions in his Tour *that in that Presbytery 'the frailty that excites the severest indignation and vengeance is fornication . . . such of the clergy as are the least strict in their own private lives are often the severest in the censure of backsliders in public.'*

He was perhaps too liberal in his theology and too tender in the administration of discipline. He was given an LL.D. by the University of Glasgow in 1783.

Thomson spent thirty-five years in London making a living as a professional author of travel books and histories. As well as being 'Thomas Newte' he was also 'the Rev. James Hall' of Travels in Scotland (1807). Newte's Tour in 1785 was published in 1788. It contains much original material, not least his suggestion that the problem of the two small and competing universities, King's and Marischal, in Aberdeen should be solved by fixing on one as 'the' university in Aberdeen, with the other moving to Inverness with a new Professor of Gaelic or Erse.

†

19th June, 1785. Dine at Carlisle, and in the afternoon, crossing the sands at the upper end of Solway Firth, enter Scotland. . . . The land between the Solway Sands and Annan is poor, being chiefly a black gravel, and bog, producing nothing but heath. The country here is for many miles low and flat, but the road exceedingly good. Immediately on crossing the Solway Firth, we found the children, and even many of the men and women, without either shoes or stockings. The cottages are miserable huts, made of mud, intermixed sometimes with round stones, such as are found in the beds of rivers . . . and covered with turf. Sleep at Annan, where there are two very good inns, particularly the Queensberry Arms. . . .

On Monday, the 20th June, ride in the afternoon, eighteen miles to Dumfries. On the road from Annan . . . the cottages are built of mud, covered with turf or thatch, the poorest habitations that can be imagined, and extremely dirty. The inhabitants are turned yellow with the smoke of the turf, which is their only fuel. The connection between climate, soil, food, vegetable effluvia, and other physical causes, and the complexions or colours of man . . . is for the most part as mysterious as it is various; but here it is abundantly manifest. Till you come within two miles of Dumfries, the land is so exceedingly bad, that it must baffle every effort towards cultivation. It seems to produce nothing but peat, which is cut here, in large quantities, and supplies all the country round. . . .

Tuesday, 21st June. Leave Dumfries in the morning; pass Lord Hopetoun's house, around which we find some tolerable woods; but the adjacent country is very barren. The farm houses are in general miserable huts, the people very poor, and the lower class of females exceedingly dirty. The old women, frightful enough of themselves, are rendered still more so by their dress, the outer garment being a long dirty cloak, reaching down to the ground, and the hood drawn over their heads, and most of them without shoes and stockings. Others among them wear what they call *huggers*, and in the Northern parts of Scotland *huggermuggans*, that is, stockings with the feet either worn away by long and hard service, or cut from them on purpose: so that the leg is covered by these uncouth teguments, while the foot, that bears the burden, and is exposed to brakes and stones, is left absolutely bare.

– T. Newte, *A Tour in England and Scotland by an English Gentleman*
(1788)

DAVID LOCH

David Loch of Over Carnbee in Fife was a merchant and shipowner in Leith. In 1776 the Board of Trustees for Fisheries, Manufactures and Improvements in Scotland appointed him insepctor-general of the woollen manufactures of Scotland. He died in Edinburgh on 14th February, 1780. His Tour *(1788) was really a survey in a slim 70 pages of some 132 towns and villages from Cromarty and Fortrose to Lochmaben and Yetholm. The data had been collected for his earlier* Letters Concerning the Trade and Manufactures of Scotland, *particularly the Woollen and Linen Manufactures (1774) and* Essays on the Trade, Commerce, Manufactures and Fisheries of Scotland *(1775). He clearly had a close personal acquaintance with many of the places he describes. Certainly no one could have described Peterhead as 'the Scarborough of North Britain' unless they had been there. The accounts of Sanquhar, Moffat and Langholm are richly detailed.*

✝

Sanquhar . . . The manufacture, called stuffs, made here, is from the wool of the country. These stuffs are twenty-seven inches broad, and the price six-pence per yard. There are about 30 looms all employed in the woolen way. Here are five frames in the stocking way, and a great deal of stockings knit and sold here, from one shilling to five shillings per pair, and a great demand for them. There are four markets in the year. Provost Wiggam has much public spirit, and is bringing a better breed of sheep, and tars little. He likewise carried on a shalloon manufactory, in company with others. A tilt mill is erected here for making spades, and all such implements for country use, in the iron way, equal to any in Britain. It cost 800 L. Sterling. His Grace the Duke of Queensberry . . . has made twenty miles of road at his own expence. . . . His Grace likewise contributes 40 L. annually, and the Honourable Board the like sum, which are given as premiums to the people in this neighbourhood, in order to promote industry; and, by this means, spinning of wool and knitting of stockings, which they do better here than any where in my tour (Aberdeen excepted), has of late greatly increased, and is daily increasing. The fabric of these goods is of an excellent quality, and find ready sale. Mr Commissioner Clerk has been of great service here, and all over these parts.

Thom-Hill (Thornhill) . . . Here are four markets or fairs in the year, and much coarse linens and woolen goods are sold at these fairs, as people from England come to them. A good deal of woolen yarn is likewise spun here, which goes to Kilmarnock for the carpet manufactory. A number of looms is employed in these parts, and the proprietors send all their goods to Thom-Hill markets. . . .

Dumfries . . . There are twenty-one looms now employed in the linen branch, two making carpets, and thirty frames in manufacturing stockings. . . . There are two breweries, and two roperies here. The town is neat and clean, good buildings, and about 600 inhabitants.

Lochmaben . . . There are eight looms employed in the jobbin way. About three tons of Riga flax is spun annually, and all the yarn goes to England to be manufactured. . . .

Moffat . . . Here are strong, well built, warm houses, well situated for carrying on coarse woolen manufactures, and at present much is done in that way. Hugh Beattie manufacturer deals in the woolen goods considerably. Their market is to Edinburgh, Glasgow, Paisley, and England. Spinning is much wanted, and the practice of tarring the sheep greatly complained of. Here are excellent woolen weavers, and the reputation of the goods well established. Thomas, John, and Adam Reids, manufacturers at Moffat, give an account of a particular kind of goods called stuffs, made at this place, which are sold on the English side, and the demand is so great that it cannot be answered. This fabrick is carried on intirely with coarse. . . . They also manufacture plaids or mauds, and blankets to a great extent, of which article they made upwards of 3000 yards last year. There is another article they manufacture, called checked serge, of the above kind. It is made into hunting coats, a light garb for summer wear, and answers very well for children's cloaths. They also make lastings, mancoes, flannels, and serges, which are mostly exported to Holland. The ordinary quantity of wool manufactured in and about Moffat annually is about 1250 stones. . . . Mr Bell of Scotbridge, a tenant of Mr Clark, has the best wool in that country . . . at fifteen shillings per stone. . . . At Moffat there is a waulk mill built and fitted up by Lord Hopeton. Adam Dickson dyer and cloathier does a good deal of business on his own account, and is well employed by all the country round. He works two woad fats, and finds much benefit by using them; he gets his wool from Yorkshire. Here are about fifty looms all in the woolen branches, and all for sale. Serges, shalloons, duffles, blankets, coarse cloths of all denominations, and great demand for them at present. . . Mr Ewart has a fine breed of sheep, of Bakewell and Cowley's kind.

Langholm . . . A good deal is spun here for sale on the English side, and about seventeen looms are employed mostly on woolen goods. William Turnbull and others, farmers, and considerable dealers in wool, in this neighbourhood and about Hawick, purchase wool annually for the English market. . . . Most of this wool, after being combed in England, comes down to this country to be spun into yarn of different grists, as ordered; and, after so spun, carried up to the manufacturing towns to be wove and dressed; and great part of it, after being so manufactured, comes to Scotland for sale.

– D. Loch, *A Tour through most of the Trading Towns and Villages of Scotland* (1788)

CAPTAIN FRANCIS GROSE

Captain Francis Grose (c. 1731–91), 'The British Antiquarian', was born at Greenford in Middlesex. His father, a jeweller in Richmond, came from Bern in Switzerland. Grose specialised in military and ecclesiastical architecture, but also wrote about 'buckish slang' and vulgar dialect. A fine draughtsman, he reduced and finished the drawings for the engravers, preparing plates for his Antiquities, *of England and Wales, of Scotland, and of Ireland. He was a Captain in the Surrey militia.*

Burns, who genuinely liked and admired him, described him as 'a cheerful-looking grig of an old, fat fellow, the precise figure of Dr Slop' [see also the portrait by John Kay of Edinburgh]; and, more to the point, noted in a letter to Mrs Dunlop of Dunlop that he had 'never seen a man of more original observation, anecdote and remark'.

The Antiquities of Scotland included castles in Fife, Angus, Moray, Perthshire, etc., but the Dumfries and Galloway and Ayrshire sections were particularly well researched and planned. Grose spent two months in 1789 enjoying the hospitality of Robert Riddell at Friars Carse and studying his papers. Riddell introduced him to Alexander Gordon of Greenlaw and the amateur antiquarian, Adam de Cardonnel. They all helped to direct or accompany him to the best sites. Grose and Burns were responsible for a quite unique distinction in the second volume, published in April 1791. As Grose explained 'my ingenious friend, Mr Robert Burns . . . not only was at the pains of marking out what was most worthy of notice in Ayrshire . . . but he also wrote, expressly for this work, the pretty tale' of Tam O' Shanter *to go with the plate of Alloway Church, a church 'famous for being the place wherein the witches and warlocks used to hold their . . . sabbaths . . . here too they used to amuse themselves with dancing to the pipes of the muckle-horned Deel.'*

✝

Sweetheart Abbey . . . the principal parts remaining, are the church and part of the chapter-house, said to have been an elegant piece of architect demolished . . . for the sake of the stone. It was feared the whole building would have undergone the same fate; whereupon a number of the neighbouring gentry raised a sum of money by subscription, and the minister was employed to enter into an agreement with the tenant to prevent it, for which forty pounds was paid him. It is but justice to Mr Copeland, the proprietor, who had purchased this abbey of Mr Spotswood, to take notice that he had in his lease prohibited and guarded against all such dilapidations; but hurt that his neighbours should suppose him capable of such a piece of barbarism as to permit so great an ornament to the country to be demolished for the paltry sum of six or seven pounds, the price he was said to have gotten for the stones, he, as a fine or amende, honourable to his character and taste, permitted his tenant to take the sum above-mentioned. The ministers and subscribers are, however, justly entitled to the thanks of the country for their public-spirited behaviour on this occasion.

– F. Grose, *The Antiquities of Scotland*, 2 vols (1789, 1791)

JOSEPH FARINGTON

Joseph Farington (1747–1821) was born in Leigh in Lancashire. A pupil of Richard Wilson in London, he achieved some considerable success as a watercolourist of landscapes, notably of the English Lakes. The National Gallery of Scotland has two Farington Edinburgh townscapes. On his Scottish tours in 1788, 1792 and 1801 he continued to add to his notebooks or diaries. Extracts from the 1788 and 1792 notebooks were published in The Scotsman *in 1935 and* The Glasgow Herald *in 1930. The complete set of* Farington Diaries 1793–1814, *edited by J. Greig, was published in 1922.*

Farington spent a fortnight in Dumfries and Moffat in 1792. He had excellent contacts everywhere, in Edinburgh Raeburn and Nasmyth, in Dumfries Robert Riddell, who introduced him to Burns, with whom he 'passed part of a day in His company'. He mentions in 1801 that 'a small print' of Burns offered with one edition of his works 'resembles his countenance'. His own description in 1792 is very useful.

In 1801 he made his headquarters for a time at Gretna Hall Inn. The rogues and charlatans who officiated at 'marriage' ceremonies were much despised at the Gretna Hall Inn, who would not receive couples travelling for that purpose. The 'drunken and improvident' seventy-year-old tobacconist, Joseph Paisley, who had been 'the chief person' for forty years, was performing in 1801 at Springfield village. David Lang, a labouring man whose son was a chaise driver, and Andrew Lekel were at Gretna Green. The whole disreputable farce was 'managed' by the drivers of chaises or carriages, who brought couples to Paisley and negotiated terms of from 5 to 50 guineas, depending on their appearance, mode of travelling and potential gullibility. Half the money went to the drivers.

✝

July 10, 1792: At 5 this morning left Long Town and at 4 miles distance entered Scotland . . . Gretna Green a straggling village at the South end of which some small Houses are erecting on a regular Plan, one of which is a publick House at present the House of resort for such couples as apply for marriage at this celebrated spot. Present *Parson* a weaver, the Blacksmith being dead. . . .

Reached Dumfries, 16 miles from Annan. People going to market there. Women generally wearing long Blue Cloaks, without Hats – white Caps with long lappets and loose, and bare-legged, as the men universally wear stockings and shoes. We put up at the King's Arms, Dumfries –

Master and Mistress careless of showing respect to travellers. Inn dirty, waiters uncivil. Name of Master, Clint. The other Inn, the George and Dragon. . . . By the Town a broad river runs under a Bridge 8 – arches. A new Bridge is begun. Land we are told lets in this neighbourhood well in some parts for 3 or 4£ an acre. A Scotch acre 1-5th more than a statue acre. . . . Price of labour is low. Labourers' wages 10d a day in summer, 8d a day in winter. Wednesday is market day at Dumfries and fully attended. After dinner we went to Mr Riddel's, at Friars Carse, 6 miles from Dumfries. . . .

July 20th: This morning I was employed in taking notes from Mr Riddell relative to the River Clyde. . . . Mr Burns, the Scottish Poet, at present an Exciseman in Dumfries, on 170£ a year. He is married and has a family. He is a middle-sized man, black complexioned, and his general appearance that of a tradesman or mechanick. He has a strong expressive manner of delivering himself in conversation. He is not acquainted with the Latin language. His Father was a gardener in Ayrshire. . . .

Saturday, July 22d: This morning Mr Riddel accompanied us to Moffat. . . . We passed Mr Miller's of Dalswinton on the right, and as we proceeded had a beautiful view of Dumfries with Criffel for a background. . . . we stopped at a place where there were a few cottages. A young woman came to the door of one of them, with her throat very much wrapped up. On Mr Riddel putting some questions to her we found she was under the operation of mercury, on procuring which He would not suffer us to enter the House, apprehending the girl might be infected with a very Dreadful disease called the Sivvens, or Yaws. . . . Dr Gilchrist, Physician in Dumfries, who about 20 years ago wrote a pamphlet on this subject, was informed it was introduced into this country by Cromwell's soldiers. . . .

Moffat . . . assumes the apperance of an Italian Town . . . is covered by a Hill with plantations on it. Arrived at Rae's Inn, Moffat, the Town small, consisting of no more than an open kind of market place irregularly built. The waters drank here are a mild Harrogate. Some years ago this place was much frequented, but of late few come here as we are told in consequence of the extravagant demands for Lodgings, etc.. Mr Riddel, Mr Hughes, and Mr Clarke, an ingenious man, school master of Moffat, joined me in undertaking to trace the source of the Clyde. . . .

– J. Farington, *In Scotland* (1792)

ROBERT HERON

Robert Heron (1764–1807) was born in New Galloway, where his father, John Heron, was a weaver. He went up to the University of Edinburgh in 1780 and paid his way by working years out as tutor to the children of farmers in Borgue and by teaching at a school in Kelton parish. Finally licensed to preach in 1789, he spent six months as assistant to Dr Hugh Blair, but decided to make a living in Edinburgh as an author of geographies and histories and travel books, as the translator from the French of travel books and scientific textbooks, as editor of James Thomson's Seasons *(1789), as an occasional preacher and lecturer, as contributor of articles and translated texts to the* Encyclopaedia Britannica, *and as sub-editor of Sir John Sinclair's* Statistical Account of Scotland. *He rushed out the first biography of Burns,* A Memoir of the Life of the late Robert Burns *(1797), a perceptive and embarrassingly revealing study of a poet, whom he ranked with the Miltons, the Popes and the Grays, and of a human being whose habitual failings and wit he knew all too well. Heron's play, a comic drama with the unlikely title* St Kilda in Edinburgh *(1798), was a disastrous failure. Heron emigrated to London in 1799 and died there in 1807.*

His two-volume 'Journey' (1793), undertaken in 1792, was a very long and ambitious examination of 'scenery, antiquities, customs, manners, population, agriculture, manufactures, commerce, political condition, and literature'. The greater part of the second volume covers Galloway. Some of his descriptions, of genteel Dumfries, of the devils, brownies, fairies and witches who were 'becoming every year less numerous and less frequent in their appearance in Kirkcudbright-shire', and of the gypsy tinkers, 'those savage animals which increasing population and order expel or exterminate', are not easily forgotten.

✝

The Schools of *Dumfries* have long been eminent. Many very able scholars received their initiatory classical education here. . . . Hither, too, are many of the little Misses of Galloway and Dumfries-shire sent to receive their education in boarding-schools for young ladies.

Dumfries is perhaps a place of higher gaiety and elegance than any other town in Scotland of the same size. The proportion of the inhabitants who are descended of respectable families and have received a liberal education is greater here than in any other town in this part of the island. These give by consequence a more elevated and polished tone to the manners and general character of this city. The mode of living which prevails here is rather shewy than luxurious. To be esteemed genteel, not to sit down to a board overloaded with victuals, is the first wish of every one.... The citizens of Dumfries are frugal of their money, but hold idleness a proof of gentility: and they value only such enjoyments as they can be seen to share and can be esteemed the greater for sharing. They delight in fine and fashionable clothes. They are fond of assemblies and plays. A playhouse has been lately erected here and the players have fared better than in many more populous and opulent towns....

Both the Dumfries and Galloway and the Caledonian Hunts were assembled here at this time. Every inn and ale-house was crowded with guests. Many, even of the more respectable citizens, had been persuaded by the tempting offers of very high rent to let their best rooms for a few days. In the mornings the streets presented one busy scene of hair-dressers, milliner's apprentices, grooms and valets, carriages driving and bustling backwards and forwards....

The bottle, the song, the dance and the card-table endeared the evening and gave social converse power to detain and to charm till the return of morn. Dumfries, of itself, could not afford ministers of pleasure enough for so great an occasion. Here were waiters, pimps, chairmen, hairdressers, and *ladies*, the priests and priestesses of these festivities, from all those more favourite haunts where pleasure ordinarily holds her court....

New-Galloway ... Its present population may be between four and five hundred souls. The inhabitants are mechanics, labourers in husbandry, a few alehouse-keepers, two or three shop-keepers. It consists of two small streets crossing each other at right angles. It rises at the foot of an irregular ridge of ground. The houses are low, ill-built, thatched with straw, and very imperfectly repaired within. A sashed window was lately a curiosity not to be seen here.... But a few slate houses, rising to the height of two stories, or a story and a half, are interspersed among the lower and thatched houses.... Most of the inhabitants of this little burgh possess, beside their houses and gardens, small crofts, on which a cow or two are fed and a few bolls of potatoes and corn raised, and a small spot of meadow upon the river which affords winter fodder for their cattle....

This little burgh ... has a weekly market to which meal is brought from the low country and to which the farmers, but more especially the cottagers from the remoter muirs, repair to supply themselves. It has a post-office.... It has a mill to which the little crops of the neighbourhood are brought to be made into meal. . . . Here is a school, too, which, like the other parish schools in Scotland, contributes happily to the preservation and the diffusion of useful knowledge among the poor. . . .

A tannery . . . has been repeatedly tried here. . . . abundance of hides are to be obtained in Galloway. What more may be wanted are easily imported from Ireland. Bark is to be procured by the purchase of young oak wood. . . . A manufacture of coarse woollens has been lately proposed here. . . . It is to be hoped that the manufacturers will attempt none but those coarse woollen stuffs which have been most neglected in other places . . . or, if they make cloth, would sell it raw and undressed to the . . . manufacturers of York-shire. . . . The Irish, too, who come over into Galloway and eagerly truck their linen for old woollen clothes, would still more readily accept in exchange coarse new cloth. . . . A small manufacture of coarse hats might be profitably enough tried at New-Galloway. . . . Here are also in considerable quantity skins of hares, fulmarts, otters. . . . The manufacture of linens might succeed here. . . . But the cotton manufacture is the favourite object at present with all the inhabitants of these parts. . . .

– R. Heron, *Observations made in a journey through the Western Counties of Scotland* (1793)

DOROTHY WORDSWORTH

Dorothy Wordsworth (1771–1855), her brother William Wordsworth (1770–1850), and his friend, Samuel Taylor Coleridge (1772–1834) were experienced travellers. They had toured in Germany together in 1798–99. By 1803 the Wordsworths and Coleridge were settled in the Lake District. They set out from Keswick on the 15th of August on a tour which was to take them through Dumfries-shire and on to Glasgow, the Trossachs and Glencoe, returning via the Borders in October. Coleridge, beset by illness and his addiction to opium, got as far as Inversnaid before retiring from the enterprise.

The Recollections *were first published in 1874. Dorothy Wordsworth had a happy knack of incorporating the thoughts and words of her companions, without in any way leaving the reader in doubt that this was very much her own journal.*

†

Wednesday, August 17th . . . The town of Annan made me think of France and Germany; many of the houses large and gloomy, the size of them outrunning the comforts. One thing which was like Germany pleased me: the shopkeepers express their calling by some device or painting; bread-makers have biscuits, loaves, cakes painted on their window-shutters; blacksmiths horses' shoes, iron tools, etc., etc.; and so on through all trades. . . .

Friday, August 19th . . . Passed through the village of Thornhill, built by the Duke of Queensberry. . . . we were reminded at every turning of the road of something beyond by the coal-carts which were travelling towards us. Though these carts broke in upon the tranquillity of the glen, they added much to the picturesque effect of the different views. . . .

After some time our road took us upward towards the end of the valley. . . . Just as we began to climb the hill, we saw three boys . . . one carried a fishing-rod, and the hats of all were braided with honeysuckles; they ran after one another as wanton as the wind. I cannot express what a character of beauty those few honeysuckles in the hats of the three boys gave to the place. . . . They told us that they lived at Wanlockhead, the village above, pointing to the top of the hill; they went to school and learned Latin, Virgil, and some of them Greek, Homer. . . . round the village, which consisted of a great number of huts, all alike, and all thatched, with a few larger slated houses among them, and a single modern-built one of a considerable size, were a hundred patches of cultivated ground, potatoes, oats, hay, and grass. We were struck with the sight of haycocks fastened down with aprons, sheets, pieces of sacking. . . . Every cottage seemed to have its little plot of ground, fenced by a ridge of earth; this plot contained two or three different divisions, kail, potatoes, oats, hay; the houses all standing in lines, or never far apart . . . it was indeed a wild and singular spot – to use a woman's illustration, like a collection of patchwork, made of pieces as they might have chanced to be cut by the mantua-maker, only just smoothed to fit each other. . . . The village, as we guessed, is inhabited by miners; the mines belong to the Duke of Queensberry. . . .

Our road turned to the right, and we saw . . . a tall upright building of grey stone, with several men standing upon the roof, as if they were looking out over battlements . . . a kind of enchanter's castle. . . . When we drew nearer we saw, coming out of the side of the building, a large machine or lever, in appearance like a great forge-hammer, as we supposed for raising water out of the mines. It heaved upward once in half a minute with a slow motion, and seemed to rest to take breath at the bottom, its motion being accompanied with a sound between a groan and a 'jike'. . . . it was impossible not to invest the machine with some faculty of intellect; it seemed to have made the first step from brute matter to life and purpose. . . . William made a remark to this effect, and Coleridge observed that it was like a giant with one idea. . . .

– D. Wordsworth, *Recollections of a Tour made in Scotland* (1874)

WILLIAM DANIELL AND RICHARD AYTON

The great project William Daniell (1769–1837) began in 1813 was to travel along the whole coast of England, Wales and Scotland, beginning at Land's End in Cornwall, using open boats and sailing vessels. The original plan was soon abandoned in the face of rapid tides and foul winds and instead the 'voyage' was completed riding or walking along cliffs and estuaries and inlets and over mosses and swamps. Daniell was already a highly successful artist and businessman. He had travelled through North and South India with his uncle, Thomas Daniell, between 1785 and 1794 and worked on their great Oriental Scenery *(1795–1808).*

On the 1813 and 1814 tours from Cornwall to Holyhead and from Holyhead to Newton Stewart or Wigtown, Daniell was accompanied by Richard Ayton (1786–1823), who provided the text for the first two of the eight volumes (1814–25). Daniell, using a miniature camera obscura, worked on the drawings and plates and the final exquisite acquatint prints. The complete text and plates for Cumberland and Westmoreland and Dumfries and Galloway, edited by Innes Macleod, was published as Sailing on Horseback *in 1988.*

Ayton, a solicitor and freelance author and playwright, was a good man who understood something of the tragedy of poor suffering humanity. He used the Voyage *as an opportunity to write about the lot of the poor and the deprived, including the condition of the women, children and men in the Whitehaven coal mines. He was capable of the occasional lyrical passage, for example on the Solway at Carsethorn:*

> *The Firth lay extended in an immense desert of sand, warmed by a golden hue from the broad and level beams of the sun, which had not yet mounted far above the horizon. The figures of some shrimpers appeared far remote on this wide plain, looming up as if they trod on air; here and there was a flock of gulls, enlarged to a monstrous size, and occasionally a solitary heron sprung with a piercing scream from its marshy borders.*

Ayton also had an excellent sense of humour, not least in his much copied description of the Scottish economy practised by the lasses, the 'nudipedes', coming into Dumfries from the country for Sunday kirk carrying their shoes and stockings 'wrapped up in their handkerchiefs' until the last moment.

✝

When engaged in their ordinary occupations, and dressed in coarse and suitable garments, their bare legs and feet do very well, and a lover of the picturesque might probably prefer them, rough, dirty, and weather-beaten as they are, to shoes and stockings. . . . Here you may see a lady with a white gown, a silk shawl or spencer, and a straw bonnet with artificial flowers in it, nay, with gloves on too, and all this finery terminated by a huge pair of bare, begrimed legs and feet, which look as if they could hardly belong to her. The legs and feet, from exposure to wet, and cold, and the sun, become red and puffy, resembling in surface and colour a great over-grown radish, most unfortunately set off certainly when seen peeping from beneath a white muslin gown.

Annan . . . contains about eighteen hundred inhabitants, and consists principally of one broad unpaved street . . . flanked on each side by respectable houses and shops, of various elevations, and jutting out in various degrees of projection, with here and there a hut amongst . . . singular from their being permitted to take their places in a great street. They are built with unhewn stones thrown together as if by accident, and covered with a thatched roof black with rottenness, but giving nourishment to a harvest of rank grass and weeds, and topped by most uncouth chimneys, each formed by four stakes placed about a foot asunder, and wrapped round with bands of straw, or filled up with sods of earth. . . . There are two or three alleys in Annan filled with such huts. . . .

That whisky is the favourite drink of the people is very evident, not only from the prevalence of red noses, but from a direct notice that it is to be bought at every other house in the place. The vending of it is combined with every other trade. . . . Opposite to me, as I sat in the inn, I perceived a 'draper and dealer in spirits'; a little lower down is a 'grocer and dealer in spirits'; and in the town is a still more extraordinary union, a 'banker and dealer in spirits'. . . .

At a short distance west of Comlongan, I came to the village of Powhellin. . . . It contained twelve mud hats, with walls full of grooves and hollows, the effects of the rains, thatched roofs, ready for the scythe, and the same kind of grotesque and preposterous chimneys that I had seen at Annan. . . . These mud-huts, however . . . are far superior in positive comfort to many stonebuilt cottages . . . cottages with a better name, and of a less wig-wamish appearance, but not half so warm and substantial, admitting wind and water through numberless chinks and crevices. . . . Mud-huts have the cardinal merit of being perfectly water-proof. Those of Powhellin have a foundation of stone three feet high, on

which is raised a wall two feet thick, composed of clay mixed with straw. A hut so constructed will last thirty or forty years, wasting away only on the side that is exposed to the stormy rains from the south. The insides of them baffle all description. As each usually contains only one room, in which the family with all their worldly property must somehow be packed, it would be harsh and unreasonable to complain of a want of neatness and tidiness of arrangement; but the dirt that shews itself amidst the jumbled litter of children, dogs, chickens, beds, chairs, old coats, and breeches, and stockings, scythes, shrimp-nets, pitchforks, and spinning wheels, and an incredible number of other materials that are and are not wanted, is quite abominable. . . . Yet in these miserable hovels I found the people exceedingly decent in their manners, with their minds improved and refined by education . . . highly civilized, intelligent, and moral. There was not a man or woman in the village that could not read and write, nor a single hut without a book.
– W. Daniell & R. Ayton, *A Voyage Round Great Britain*, vol. II (1815)

JOHN KEATS AND CHARLES BROWN

John Keats (1795–1821) was surprisingly one of the great distance walkers along with Wordsworth, Coleridge, William Hazlitt, Thomas De Quincey, George Borrow and Robert Louis Stevenson. Keats and his companion, Charles Brown (1786–1842), a wealthy Scottish stockbroker, began their long 1818 summer walk at Kendal on June 26th and trekked through Dumfries and Galloway, Ayrshire, Argyll, Mull, Staffa, Fort William and the top of Ben Nevis, to reach Inverness on August 8th. There Keats collapsed from an exhaustion that may have been the first onslaught of the tuberculosis that was to kill him less than three years later.

The letters Keats sent to Fanny and Tom Keats included the 'knapsack' song of the road, written while walking to Kirkcudbright:

He took	*In his knapsack*	*A book*	*Full of vowels*
And a shirt	*With some towels*	*A slight cap*	*For night cap*
A hair brush	*Comb ditto*	*New stockings*	*For old ones . . .*

The portable canvas tents and waterproof sleeping bags used by Borrow and Stevenson had not been thought of in 1818; Keats and Brown stayed in lodgings and inns. They were warned off the inn at Ballantrae because the landlord was 'a little in trouble', i.e., he had been 'taken' for robbing the Paisley bank. At Dumfries they were taken for 'travelling jewellers, razor sellers and spectacle vendors'. The landlady at Creetown, where

Keats thought the children seemed to 'jabber away as if in a foreign language', confirmed how unusual it was to see 'Southrens' in Galloway. In Newton Stewart they dined 'on dirty bacon, dirtier eggs, and dirtiest potatoes, with a slice of salmon', but in Glenluce they breakfasted in 'a nice carpeted room, with sofa, hair-bottomed chairs, and green-baized mahogany'.

Charles Brown kept his own journal, Walks in the North, *first published in the* Plymouth and Devenport Weekly Journal *in October, 1840. He introduced Keats to Scott's* Guy Mannering *and inserted Keats's impromptu ballad on Meg Merrilies in his journal:*

> Old Meg she was a gipsey
> And liv'd upon the moors . . .
> Alone with her great family
> She liv'd as she did please . . .

Both Keats and Brown mention the women at Dumfries who avoided wearing shoes and stockings, with Keats expatiating on the 'beautiful effect of colour when a young lassie's foot was on the green grass'. Brown in general is perceptive and sensible, although the parties they encountered on the seaside road were perhaps only returning from a market day in Creetown rather than, as they claimed, taking part in a seabathing expedition.

✝

Walks in the North: . . . Dumfries stands in a delightful situation. Neither of us expected to remark much difference between English and Scotch towns, generally speaking; but it appeared as if we had stepped into a foreign country. It might be difficult to define in what the distinction lies; perhaps it consists in numerous small particulars, each unimportant in itself. . . . To our minds the people we had seen and conversed with, both in and out of the town, were more serious and solidly inanimated than necessary. They had a quiet expression and manner. . . . They are, also, in their speech, tedious, slow, and drawling. Except two or three girls, who returned our 'speerings' – alias, usual salutations – on the road, with a sort of grin, we did not perceive an approach to a laugh.

. . . We had been recommended to seek entertainment at the village of Dalbeattie from a Mr Murray. Besides keeping a 'Public', he kept a shop below, supplying every one in the district with almost every article, from tea down to candles and brick dust, ironmongery of all sorts, whiskey, broad cloth, sheeting, printed cottons, pens, ink and paper.

It was a day appointed by the Kirk for a fast in that parish; and, therefore, the shop was shut, and Mrs Murray only at home. From some unexplained cause, she was at first unwilling to let us enter – she 'didna ken what to say'!

. . . Taking the sea-side road to Cree Town, four miles longer than the usual road, we became acquainted with a custom which I wish were more general in all countries. We soon met, returning to Gate House, men, women and children, of all ages and descriptions. It looked like an emigration, and we inquired the reason; when 'The salt water' was reply; and truly the greater proporton of the population had taken the opportunity of high tide to wash and be clean, where a jutting rock on the coast separated the sexes; and, moreover, they told us it was their daily custom. There was nothing else remarkable in this stage except a deep glen, full of large trees, with a mountain stream running below, a spot that Meg Merrilees must have often frequented. . . .

– J. Keats, *Songs of the Road*

LORD COCKBURN

Henry Thomas Cockburn (1779–1854) was born on Cockpen estate near Edinburgh. His father was Sheriff of Midlothian. He took the title Lord Cockburn in 1834 as a judge of the Court of Session. His Memorials *(1856) and* Journals *(1874) are a useful record of Whig politics and the Scottish legal world centred in Edinburgh.* Circuit Journeys *(1884) is an account of his extra-mural experiences on the North, West and South (Ayr, Dumfries and Jedburgh) Circuits. His notes for 1839, 1841 and 1844 are devastatingly frank, when not plainly rude. Turnerelli's statue of Burns is 'horrid' (1839); the Commercial Hotel in Dumfries is the perennially 'wretched' establishment where, in 1844, he endured a public dinner 'of unexplained abomination', Gelston (1839) is 'ugliness itself', Minnyhive (1839) is 'a wretched, half-dead village':*

> Durisdeer (1841) is as shabby inside as most Scotch villages, but outside, and seen from a distance . . . I . . . have never lost the impression made upon me early in the morning by the loneliness of that still, smokeless and silent village . . . like a town one would expect to meet in the wilds of Arabia.

Creetown and Newton Stewart (1844) are

> beautifully situated, and seen at a distance amidst the sheltering trees, look like capitals in Areadia; but . . . when they are entered . . . Styes for human swine

and Gatehouse (1844) is 'too visibly a village at the Great Man's Gate'.
Cockburn invariably stayed as a guest at Cumpston and his notes on
Kirkcudbright and area are particularly detailed.

†

Dumfries, 21st September, 1839 I never enter mad-houses, but the new
Lunatic Asylum is very striking outside, and stands on a fine site. While
asking a little boy on the road some questions about it, he used a word,
which it is to be hoped does not truly indicate the character of the internal
treatment. He pointed out a man who was walking in a gallery, as 'the
Breaker'! 'What do you call the Breaker?' 'The man that *breaks* the daft
folk.' A lad beside us also used the term as one familiar.

13th April, 1841. I was told a singularly pleasing fact about the Lunatic
Asylum. A box is occasionally taken in the theatre for the patients, who
go respectably in coaches, and sit happily and enjoy the play. A very
curious and delightful fact.

Cumpston, 27th September, 1839. To-day we went and saw the Abbey of
Dundrennan. Though greatly abridged, it is still a beautiful and
interesting mass. But every other feeling is superseded by one's horror
and indignation at the state in which it is kept. . . . Five pounds worth of
draining, £20 worth of cleaning and levelling, and £200 of masonry would
preserve it, in decency, for centuries. But . . . it is left a victim to every
element, man included. . . . My excellent and esteemed host, in whose
house I now am, and on whose ground this abbey stands, is the chief
delinquent. . . . the mischief proceeds . . . from that absence of right
feeling which, on such subjects, seems to be nearly universal among
Scotch proprietors. . . . It is a humiliating, national scandal.

Cumpston, 23d September, 1844. I have revisited Dundrennan Abbey, and
claim the principal merit of its being in the state it now is. The objurgation
which I have recorded in 1839 was freely administered verbally. This
roused Thomas Maitland, now of Dundrennan, and he roused Lord
Selkirk and others; and the result is that the Commissioners of Woods
and Forests have cleaned out the rubbish, and drained the ground, and
made some judicious repairs, and cleared away the abominable offices
of the manse, and enclosed the whole. . . . Mr Maxwell of Terregles, the
owner of Lincluden, a most liberal gentleman . . . complained to me
that he could not get that building preserved from the mischief of tourists
and Dumfries picnickers. And what had this man of fortune, residing

only two miles off, done to preserve it? . . . he leaves it unenclosed, and may see the tenants' cattle in it any time he may choose, and lets spoliation proceed unchecked, and leaves every new ton of rubbish to lie, for the nettles, where it may fall. . . . Does he do no more for his pheasants?

Cumpston, 29th September, 1839. The prospect from Tongueland Hill is beautiful and peculiar. Kirkcudbright stands like a little Venice, in the midst of its surrounding waters.

Cumpston, 27th September, 1844. To-day I went to Tongueland Hill to have another view of Kirkcudbright. I doubt if there be a more picturesque country town in Scotland. Small, clean, silent, and respectable; it seems . . . the type of a place to which decent characters and moderate purses would retire for quiet comfort. . . . the dismal swamps of deep, sleechy mud, by which it is nearly surrounded at low tide . . . is a dreadful composition. And what fields, and streaks, and gullies of it! . . . I believe that painters don't dislike this substance, which they don't require to touch. It is not unpicturesque. Of a leaden grey colour, very shiny, in the sun even silvery in appearance; utterly solitary, except to flocks of long-billed and long red-legged sea birds . . . a town surrounded by a lake of bird-lime! It is only at full tide, or nearly so, that Kirkcudbright is to be viewed . . . And then, how beautifully does it stand! . . . surrounded by wooden hills and apparently glittering sea. . . . From several aspects it is the Venice of Scotland.

Cumpston, 26th September, 1844. Yesterday was given to an expedition to the lighthouse on the island of Little Ross. . . . Some rode and some drove, and George Maitland walked, till we came to the alehouse on the peninsula of Great Ross, where we took boat. . . . Eleven people lunched at the alehouse on our return upon the oatcakes, cheese, butter, and ale of the house. In a frenzy of generosity I resolved to pay the bill, and was rewarded by finding it amounted to only *one sixpence*. There's a hotel for you. I shall tell this to William Clerk, and he'll take up house there.

– Lord Cockburn, *Circuit Journeys in 1839, 1841 and 1844*

GEORGE BORROW

George Borrow (1803–81) was born in Norfolk, but spent some of his school years in Edinburgh. Perhaps the most famous exponent of pedestrianism, during a long life he walked vast distances, for example 112 miles from Norwich to London in 27 hours in November 1832. Quite without any false modesty or silly gentility, he proclaimed himself as 'a lad who twenty tongues can talk', 'can turn a song a make a verse', 'can read Dante... charm snakes... and horses too' [a horse whisperer, he could tame the most vicious of the breed]. He delighted in feats of strength, for example diving into a 16-foot-deep pool in the Dee near Threave Castle on July 23rd, 1866, getting to the bottom, and bringing up a flagstone which he flung onto the shore.

By the time of his tour from Stranraer to Berwick (July to August 1866) he was already famous as the author of The Zincali *(1841),* The Bible in Spain *(1843),* Lavengro *(1851),* The Romany Rye *(1857) and* Wild Wales *(1862). His tours in the Isle of Man in 1855, the Scottish Highlands and the Northern Isles in 1858, Ireland in 1860, and Galloway, Dumfries-shire and the Borders in 1866 were recruiting grounds for material for more books and articles. The notes for his Galloway tour were part of the manuscripts and notebooks collected by Professor W.L. Knapp for his standard* Life, Writings and Correspondence of George Borrow *(1899). They were published with his permission by Andrew McCormick in* The Gallovidian *in 1905. The notes from Stranraer on July 17th to Gretna on July 28th take the form of prompts to recall happenings and conversations; for example, to the Scotch Pedlar on July 18th. They show up some of his likes and dislikes, his preference for the company of pedlars and gypsies and fiddlers and his anti-Popery sentiments. Andrew McCormick, of course, shared his lifelong interest in European and British gypsies.*

✝

July 18. Noble breakfast – tea, rolls, fish, whiting, turkey's eggs.... Glenluce two miles... The man on wall on the left side of the road.... cattle in the water – stay and look at them. Overtaken by a man who had a pack on his back – Scotch pedlar – been every-where.... Discourse with the pedlar bound for Glenluce.... regular old-fashioned Scottish town; very beautiful scenery hollow and upland dells lined with woods; MacLellan's Hotel – ale; stroll about the town, old and thoroughly Scottish; up the hill by the end; man in kirkyard – discourse.... Capital dinner – salmon, mutton and sweets; first-rate water. Stroll behind the inn. The glen, the little bridge, the rivulet and trees; child playing in the water; strong smell of turf smoke throughout the village; cool, delightful evening; stroll up and down. People in the street sitting or standing enjoying the cool. Pedlar again – discourse; the kirk, the minister, and school; prices of food....

July 19. Breakfast – egg, ham, honeycomb . . . go to the sea to bathe . . . two miles distant . . . some people bathing; none could swim; seemed surprised that I could. . . . Return from Abbey. The miller and his friends seated on the stone wall drinking cool water out of a basin; discourse about the war and the Pope of Rome. Many Papists in the neighbourhood, but all Irish, the natives all Protestants.

July 21. . . . village of Black Craig. Discourse with a man at a cottage door. . . . There was a mine a little way up the hills; the miners were people from all parts – Highlanders amongst them. . . . The horners, people who make hornspoons; proceed, the village of Palnure on a river of that name; public-house. . . . Creeton . . . crowds of workmen along the road coming into town. 'What is the name of that house?' said I to a man, pointing to a building far up the hill on the left. 'That? the quarry house.' 'And why are there so many people?' 'We always drap at 3 o'clock every Saturday afternoon.' 'And where do the stones go?' 'All to Liverpool; there are always three ships loading in the river.' Extensive stone works on the right. . . . came to an inn on the left hand called Raven's Hall, went in and had some ale . . . Gatehouse Hotel, full of noisy farmers and riflemen; vagabond and girl, regular tramps, singing before the door. Joe Dunbar. . . .

July 22. . . . Caylay, Minto Cottage . . . Lions Inn . . . Wander slowly and heavily up a steep hill; day frightfully hot; pass under a railway arch; descend; sit down under some trees on a road leading to Kirkcudbright, 6 miles; proceed; come in sight of a river on the right; go on gasping with heat. Inn – no admittance – 'We dinna sell onything on a Sunday.'

– George Borrow, *Notes of his Tour through Galloway in 1866*

ROBERT LOUIS STEVENSON

Stevenson (1850–94) was plagued with ill-heath from childhood. Vacations away from Edinburgh in Italy and on the Riviera and the early walking tours in Buckinghamshire and Galloway were essentially remedial and recuperative. In 1876 the great books still lay ahead – Travels with a Donkey in the Cevennes *(1879),* Treasure Island *(1883),* Kidnapped *(1886),* The Master of Ballantrae *(1889).*

The walking tour from Ayr by Maybole, Girvan, Ballantrae, Stranraer and Glenluce to Wigtown was completed between January 8th and 17th, 1876. This is confirmed in a letter from Stevenson written in February 1876 in which he mentions that he is as fit as a fiddle after the walk and that he intends to make an article of it under the title A Winter's Walk in Carrick and Galloway. *The essay which was published in the* Illustrated London News *in the Summer of 1896 is unfortunately only a fragment, taking the account as far as the road from Turnberry to Girvan. Did Stevenson complete the article? Was the rest lost after his death in 1894? The essay that has survived is an excellent, flowing, scholarly piece, with references to ballads and songs and good use being made of James Paterson's* History of the County of Ayr *(1847).*

†

Next morning there was sun and a flapping wind. From the street corners of Maybole I could catch breezy glimpses of green fields. The road unferfoot was wet and heavy – part ice, part snow, part water; and any one I met greeted me, by way of salutation, with 'A fine thowe'. My way lay among rather bleak hills, and past bleak ponds and dilapidated castles and monasteries. . . . As I came down above Turnberry, the sea view was indeed strangely different from the day before. The cold fogs were all blown away; and there was Ailsa Craig, like a refraction, magnified and deformed, of the Bass Rock; and there were the chiselled mountain-tops of Arran, veined and tipped with snow; and behind, and fainter, the low, blue land of Cantyre. Cottony clouds stood, in a great castle, over the top of Arran, and blew out in long streamers to the south. The sea was bitten all over with white; little ships, ticking up and down the Firth, lay over at different angles in the wind. On Shanter they were ploughing lea; a cart foal, all in a field by himself, capered and winnied as if the spring were in him.

– R.L. Stevenson, *A Winter's Walk in Carrick and Galloway* (1896)

EDWIN MUIR

Edwin Muir (1887–1959) was born in Deerness in Orkney. From 1889 to 1895 he lived at The Bu on the island of Wyre. In his An Autobiography *(1954) his Orkney childhood seems like 'an image of Eden' compared to the deprivation and disillusionment of life in Glasgow. He moved to Glasgow when he was 14. Muir had a distinguished career as a poet and literary critic. His* Scottish Journey *was an opportunity to put forward in what appeared to be a travel book his own bitter and wildly pessimistic view of Scotland in the 1930s, of unemployment, of industry 'vanishing like a dream', of Scotland being 'emptied' of its spirit, its art, its intellect and its innate character. The Dumfries and Galloway journey is not typical of the book as a whole, as it has almost a warm lyrical glow and is certainly remote from the realities of rural life. Perhaps because he was travelling by car from Moffat to Dumfries, Kirkcudbright, Newton Stewart, Barrhill and Girvan, it was only in Kirkcudbright overnight that he encountered real people in any depth as opposed to landscapes.*

✝

When one takes the road from St Mary's Loch westward to Moffat one soon finds oneself in a completely different country. The very names have a different ring. One . . . is among comfortable, substantial, beefy names like Beattock, Moffat, Lockerbie, Lochmaben, Dumfries, Annan. . . . the hills become large, plain, green, heavy, grand, prosaic; hills for sheep, shepherds, Bible-readers and a sober peasantry devoted to plain living and high thinking . . . they look like mud-castles on a gigantic scale, over which a good thick padding of fat turf has been drawn, so that though they are apparently solid and immovable they give a feeling of insecurity; for they are smooth as well as steep, and quite treeless; smooth as a crowd of vast and stupid shaven conical heads. . . .

When one is past Moffat . . . one begins to penetrate the rich agricultural county of Dumfriesshire. The soil seems to get deeper and deeper; everywhere signs of fruitfulness press in upon one; and one's mind is insensibly filled with thoughts of live stock, cattle-shows, prize bulls, and Scots love in the Burns style. These fields, one tells oneself, must be well manured. Fertility here is a solid, organized industry. Even the woods have a rank look, as if primitive rites have gone in them for centuries. . . .

Dumfriesshire looks to the passer's eye like the classical incarnation of the trinity which Matthew Arnold disliked so much: Scotch drink, Scotch love and Scotch religion. It is solid, fertile and handsome. There may be found in certain districts of it, I have been told, a great number of people who look very like Burns. . . .

Dumfries itself is a blowsy, overgrown country town. . . . I did not stop in Dumfries, but from a number of men, young and old, standing at the street corners, I could see that it was suffering from unemployment. . . .

I reached Kirkcudbright, hot and covered with dust. I stopped at the first hotel I saw and asked if I could have a room for the night. The hotel proprietor first gave me a look, then went to the door, gave a look at the car, seemed to hesitate for a moment, but then said yes, I could have a room. . . . After dinner I went for a walk through the town. It has a great number of handsome houses, which I believe have been looked after and preserved by the colony of painters who are settled in the town. Most of the houses round the harbour square and in the streets leading off it are painted in various colours, black, dark blue, Payne's grey, yellow – a pleasant surprise in a Scottish street. . . . Presently I found myself at a gate leading into a field adjoining the river, and asked two men, who were also dark and gipsy-like . . . and by their appearance seemed to be fishermen, if the path would take me down to the sea. They stopped their conversation and looked at me for a minute, then one of them said in a reluctant voice: 'Ay, ye *could* get to the sea that way.' . . . I struck out across the field, keeping to a little footpath. It was after eight; the sky was cloudless and blue; the sun was bright on the lush, wet-looking grass, and lit up brilliantly a line of green hills in the distance; the squat solid trees dotting the field cast long broad shadows. The path wound this way and that, taking me into another field with black cattle and along a ditch filled with meadow-sweet which breathed out a palpable bank of scent into the stagnant air. The place was quite still and deserted, except for the children's cries coming from the harbour square.

– E. Muir, *Scottish Journey* (1935)

6
AGRICULTURAL REVOLUTIONS
✝

The Agricultural Revolution *is a blanket phrase often used by historians
to describe the changes in farming, in land use, and in estate management
in the eighteenth and early nineteenth centuries. These included the
amalgamation of small holdings to create larger farms; the elimination of
mutiple-tenancy ferm-touns in favour of units held by a single tenant; the
end of the old runrig system of cultivation; enclosures and the creation of
fields separated by dykes and hedges; the introduction of new grasses,
lucerne, clover, fiorin, and of new root crops, including turnips and carrots;
experiments to improve the weight, size and calibre of cattle, sheep and
pigs; the development of woodland plantations; the building of new
farmhouses, stables and barns; the introduction of leases of 19 or 21 years
carrying inbuilt requirements upon tenant and landowner in relation to
draining, liming, manuring, crop rotation and dyking, etc.; increases in
rents by three or ten or twenty times the old amount, which still allowed
tenant farmers to prosper from improvements in productivity and
profitability; competition between tenants to secure leases; improvements
in road transport and shipping; the investment of surplus profits in the
development of ancillary industries, tanneries, breweries, grain mills, and
in planning and building new villages and towns. It was not a technology-
based revolution, although new ploughs, harrows and carts were useful, as
were the premiums awarded by the Highland and Agricultural Society in,
for example, 1802 and 1803 for the best ploughteams competing at
Blackpark near Castle Douglas and Longbarns near Kirkcudbright, and
to Samuel Bland, the ploughwright at Tongland Bridge, for the best
modern plough made in the Stewartry in 1803.*

*The 'fever for improvement' was most apparent in the south-west
between c. 1770 and 1820, but some of the new ideas and practices can be
traced back to the legislation passed by the Scottish Parliament before
1707; for example, the Enclosure Acts of 1661, 1685 and 1695 and the
Division of Commonties Acts of 1695. This legislation is evidence of the
intention to encourage growth, rather than of action taken; nevertheless
there were some large-scale cattle ranching enterprises requiring a
substantial investment of capital; for example Sir David Dunbar's*

Baldoon estate. Symson described Baldoon in 1684 as capable of keeping 'winter and summer, about a thousand bestiall', cattle bought in from the country, and from Dunbar's own breed of '200 milch kine', to go to the English markets.

The Agricultural Revolution was not a smooth, seamless, gradually evolving transition from scarcity and famine to enhanced profitability and productivity. It was characterised rather by a number of stops and starts, of growth and recession, of successes and failures. Overoptimism and rash investment could easily end in bankruptcy. William Craik of Arbigland (1703–98) was successful in the long term, but he was a careful and prudent improver. Robert Maxwell of Arkland (1695–1765), the secretary of the Society of Improvers and the author of the essays and papers published in 1757 as The Practical Husbandman, *had to sell his estate to his creditors in 1750.*

Ultimately what determined the condition of an estate was the calibre and personality of the proprietor. Some landowners were too idle to initiate improvements; others, even if they might have wished to be seen by their peers as far-sighted and benevolent gentlemen, just did not have the capital to invest for long-term returns. Some of the most extensive improvements were carried out by Edinburgh and Glasgow merchants and bankers who became country gentlemen by acquiring estates in Ayrshire and Dumfries and Galloway, for example, Patrick Miller of Dalswinton (1731–1815).

Some of the best descriptions of the Agricultural Revolution are in the reports of the parish ministers for The Statistical Account of Scotland *(1791–99). The clergy depended on the landowners for their stipends and for the maintenance of their churches and manses. They do, therefore, tend to uncritically approve the work of improving landowners. Opposition is dismissed as ignorant and backward-looking. In any case many ministers were themselves enthusiastic improvers, interested in farming as a science and supporters of the new Farming Clubs and Agricultural Societies, such as the Society for the Encouragement of Agriculture in Galloway and Dumfries-shire (1776). Moreover the glebe provided the manse with food and a supplementary income.*

The 1793 account of Tongland parish by the Rev. Alex. Robb (for his brother William, the parish minister from 1769 to 1797 – whom he succeeded in 1797) is exceptionally good. The two sets (1793–95 and 1809–15) of reports with the titles, a General View of the Agriculture of the various Scottish counties, *included two Galloway and two Dumfries-shire volumes. Three are by parish ministers, the Rev. Dr Bryce Johnston (1747–1805) of Holywood from 1771, was the author of the 1794 Dumfries-shire* View, *the Rev. Dr William Singer (1765–1840), of*

Wamphray from 1794 to 1799 and Kirkpatrick-Juxta from 1799, was the author of the very long (696 pages) and excellent 1812 Dumfries-shire View, *and the Rev. Samuel Smith (1757–1816), whose father was the tenant farmer in Craigmuie in Balmaclellan, was the minister of Carsphairn from 1788 to 1792 and of Borgue from 1792, and author of the Galloway 1810* View. *In comparison the Galloway 1794* View *by James Webster, the farmer at Fowlis Easter in Perthshire, is much less satisfactory.*

Another important source is The Present State of Husbandry *(6 volumes, 1778 and 1784) by Andrew Wight, the farmer at Ormiston in East Lothian. He was appointed by the Commissioners of the Annexed Estates to survey their properties in 1773, a remit later extended to Scotland as a whole. Extracts from the estate papers of James Murray of Broughton (1727–99) and from the* Reminiscences of Samuel Robinson *(1786–1875) are also included in this chapter.*

✝

'AGAINST THE POOR THEY STILL PREVAIL'

When the Union had opened an unrestrained market for lean cattle in England, the gentlemen of the country seem to have perceived the possibility of deriving a better income from their lands . . . and cattle were the chief source from which gentlemen might expect a revenue. . . . to encrease the quantity of the grass . . . they knew of no other means, than to give the land a longer respite from tillage, either by throwing farms wholly into grass, or at least by cropping them to a much less extent. About the year 1715, or 1720, it appears to have been the intention of most landlords to reduce the tillage from one-half to one-third, and in some cases to one-fourth of the arable land. This violent innovation created a dreadful alarm among the tenantry, and all the lower orders. . . . Improvements, thus carried on by turning many people out of their farms, excited a general odium; which was greatly increased by the ill-judged precipitation of the gentlemen in ejecting too many at one time, and without affording them any resources of occupation, or means of subsistence. . . . in 1720, an insurrection actually took place; and the peasantry in the lower parts of Galloway assembled in parties of several hundreds, throwing down the stone dykes which had been built for inclosures. . . . From this circumstance they got the name of *levellers.* . . .

– The Rev. Samuel Smith, *General View of the Agriculture of Galloway,*
1810, pp. 43–45

Letter from John Maxwell of Munches to W.M. Herries of Spottes,
8th February, 1811

... I was born at Buittle, in this parish ... on the 7th day of February, old style, 1720 ... in 1722 ... many of the proprietors enclosed their grounds to stock them with black cattle, and, by that means, turned out a vast number of tenants at the term of Whitsunday 1723, whereby numbers of them became destitute, and, in consequence, rose in a mob; when, with pitchforks, gavellocks, and spades, they levelled the park-dykes of Barncailzie and Munshes, at Dalbeattie, which I saw with my own eyes. The mob passed by Dalbeattie and Buittle, and did the same on the estates of Netherlaw, Dunrod, etc., and the Laird of Murdoch, then proprietor of Kilwhaneday, who turned out sixteen families at that term. ... some were banished to the plantations, whilst others were imprisoned. ... This misfortune, with what happened to the Mississippe Company in the year 1720, did most generally distress this quarter of the kingdom. ... In 1725, potatoes were first introduced into this stewartry by William Hyland, from Ireland, who carried them on horses' backs to Edinburgh, where he sold them. ... At that period, there was only one baker in Dumfries, and he made bawbee baps of coarse flour, chiefly bran, which he occasionally carried in creels to the fairs of Urr and Kirkpatrick. ...

At this period, few of the proprietors gave themselves any concern anent the articles of husbandry, their chief one being about black-cattle. William Craik Esq. of Arbigland's father died in 1735, and his son was a man of uncommon accomplishment, who, in his younger days, employed his time in grazing of cattle, and studying the shapes of the best kinds, his father having given him the farm of Maxwelltown to live upon. The estate of Arbigland was then in its natural state, very much covered with whins and broom. ... That young gentleman was among the first that undertook to improve the soil; and the practice of husbandry, which he pursued, together with the care and trouble which he took in ameliorating his farm, was very great. ...

[John Maxwell died in 1814. His letter was published in *The New Statistical Account of Scotland,* vol. IV, Kirkcudbrightshire, pp. 206–08].

May, 1724. In the beginning of this moneth we hear accounts from Galloway, and Nidsdail, and Dumfreice, of a great gathering of people, to the number of 500 or 600, for demolishing of inclosures and gentlemen's parks. They began about Dumfreice, and are come the lenth of Kircudbright, and have the name of *Levellers* and *Dyk-breakers*. They have a manifesto, and sent one to the Justice-Clerk. ... It's certain, great depopulations have been made in the South, and multitudes of familys turned out of their tacks and sent a wandering. The Lairds of Murdoch, Herron, and others, have turned much of their estates into grass. Some parishes, particularly that of Girtoun, are almost whole inclosed, and scarce six or seven familys left; and these gentlemen take leases of other gentlemen's lands, and inclose them. . . .

June, 1724. Mr David Warner, who has been in Galloway for some weeks, gives me a quite other representation of the affair of the Levellers than I formerly heard. . . . He tells me that the common people there are very lazy, and they generally run out the ground prodigiously . . . and that, generally speaking, the tenants are all very poor, and many of them behind in their rents, three, four, five, or six years. This brought the gentlmen to make inclosures, and they wer forced to it by the constant failour of their tenants, throu lazines and idlnes. That this last spring ther was a generall grumbling among many broken tenants upon ther masters' putting to them for bygone rents, and threatening to eject them; but, generally speaking, it's among none but such as wer very poor, and could not pay their rent. . . . These inclosures are no great matter, only stone dicks, where the great charges is in leading the stones. They began with the Lady Kenmuir's, and wer about sixty or a hundred pence; and then went to the barrony of Airds, taken by Herron at Earlstoun's desire. . . . They prepared gavelocks, and other instruments, and did their work most dexterously; and had herds and young boyes that first turned over the head and loose stones; then the weemen, with the hand and shoulders, turned doun the dyke; then the men came last, and turned up the foundation. From thence they went to Mr Andreu Euart's inclosure next week; and then to Mr Basil Hamiltoun's; and thence, about thirty men, to Kircubright, and published their manifesto. . . . That there is none among them of any note, save Mr Cluny, the deposed Curate, who draues their papers: That many of them are Hebronites [Hepburnites]. . . .

I hear that toward the end of the last moneth [October], the Levellers are falling to work in the shire of Galloway; before, they wer only in the Steuartry, and they are pulling doun inclosures in the night time. They put out a manifesto, and fixed it on Sorbie Church dores . . . and when Mr Anderson ordered the beddel to take it doun, next night his yeard-dyke was pulled doun. . . .

May 1725 . . . the Levellers have been very quiet since summer last, and the forces there keep them in au; that except a little brustle they made in Sorby, and of late in throuing doun some of Mr Basil Hamiltoun's dykes. . . .

    – The Rev. Robert Woodrow: *Analecta*, vol. III, 1843, pp. 152, 154, 157–58, 160, 170, 210

An Account of the Reasons of Some People in Galloway, their Meetings anent Public Grievances through Inclosures (1724)

... To complete our ruin they have now proceeded beyond all the bounds of former years. ... They this year have warned a very great number of families to remove at Whitsunday, the 15th of May, 1724, viz.: upwards of sixty in some parishes and more than thirty in others, and scarce any other places can be found for their relief, so that we expected nothing but the open fields for ourselves, wives and little ones ... and thus almost distracted by hearing the doleful cries and lamentations of our wives and children we did arise in a considerable body, without any arms or ammunition, until we were necessitate for our self-preservation ... but our far greater number have nothing but staves or clubs to drive the Irish cattle, of which we have seized upon and slaughtered fifty-three ... some country tenants, or rather drovers, have taken all the grounds they can get and stockt the same with black cattle and sheep by which many an honest man is straitened as well as by the gentlemen's parks themselves. ... And lately the said Mr Basil Hamilton hath cast out thirteen families upon the 22d day of May instant who are lying by the dykesides. Neither will he suffer them to erect any shelter or covering at the dykesides to preserve their little ones from the injury of the cold ... they would make Galloway a hunting field. ...

James Charters, Kirkland of Dalry – *The Levellers' Lines*:

> A generation like to this
> Did never man behold,
> I mean our great and mighty men
> Who covetous are of gold.
> Solomon could not well approve
> The practice of their lives,
> To oppress and to keep down the poor,
> Their actions cut like knives. ...
>
> They from the hungry take the sheaf
> And of them corn do crave,
> They turn them out to ly in fields
> Nor house nor shelter have. ...
>
> The lords and lairds they drive us out
> From maillings where we dwell,
> The poor man says 'Where shall we go?'

The rich says 'Go to hell.'
These words they spoke in jest and mocks,
But by their works we know,
That if they have their herds and flocks,
They care not where we go.

Against the poor they still prevail
With all their wicked works,
And will enclose both moor and dale
And turn corn fields to parks.

'AGRICULTURAL REVOLUTIONS'

If Farmers will read my Papers with as much Attention as I have wrote them, will be convinced of Errors, will depart from them, and will practise the Husbandry which I have directed, we must soon become rich, and may be happy: But as few of them will yield to Reason, and relinquish Ways of their Forefathers which are destructive to the ground, and so to themselves; I have shown, how they may be covenanted with in such a Manner, that their Possessions must be highly improved, and their Profits must be at the same Time become far greater than they before could be. . . .

– Robert Maxwell of Arkland, *The Practical Husbandman*, 1757,
p. VII

Dumfries-shire Farmers. Among so great a body of men, supposed to consist, in this county, of above 1300, it is natural to think that a great variety of character must appear. The division that has been made of them into farmers of the old school, and improvers, is not unsuitable. . . . Of the farmers of the old school, there is not much to be said; and fortunately their number diminishes every year. Indeed, under most new leases, improvements are necessary, in order to afford a chance for paying the stipulated rents. With this view, open fields, and slovenly or scourging modes of cultivation, are out of the question. . . . Improving farmers are now appearing in every district of the county. But, considering that some of these have been regularly going on with their operations for thirty or forty years, it seems unaccountable that others have been so slow in beginning . . . those gentlemen who were able to improve, and interested in doing it, have often felt inclined to ascribe the delay among tenants to ignorance and obstinacy, when they were slow in imitating superior examples. The truth is, that under a lease drawing towards a close, prudential motives affect the tenant. New leases either do or ought to bring new motives to improve; and until private interest shall be visibly promoted by them, no person ought to expect expensive improvements from any farmer whatever. . . .

– The Rev. Dr William Singer, *General View of the Agriculture, State of Property, and Improvements in the Country of Dumfries*, 1812, pp. 105–106

Galloway: Husbandry. The condition of the peasantry of Galloway, at a period not very remote, appears to have been depressed, and the state of husbandry rude and barbarous in the extreme. . . . Estates appear to have been broken down into very small farms; or when farms were large, they were held in *common* by two, three, or even four different tenants, who divided the labour and produce in a proportion corresponding to their rent. These, when in tillage, were sometimes *run-rigg*, where each had his portion allotted; sometimes the whole was ploughed, sowed, and reaped in common, and the produce divided in the field, barn, or barn-yard. . . . Their houses were commonly wretched dirty hovels built with stones and mud, thatched with fern and turf; without chimnies; filled with smoke; black with soot: having low doors, and small holes for windows, with window shutters; or, in place of these, often stopped with turf, straw, or fragments of old clothes. . . .

The farms were always overcropped and overstocked. Ten, twelve, or fourteen horses would not have been reckoned sufficient for operations of husbandry which are now performed by two or three. . . . The plough-team sometimes consisted of six or eight. . . .

The Reporter . . . has been struck, in the course of his survey, with the very different state of improvement upon estates possessing similar advantages; and which must be ascribed to the proprietors themselves, or to those entrusted with the management of their property. On some estates, the same poor accommodation of buildings, the same awkward subdivision of farms, or total want of fences and inclosures; in a word, the same wretched plans of husbandry which prevailed forty or fifty years ago, are still continued. . . . In the managment of other estates, and perhaps the greater number, attention and judgement are displayed on the part of the proprietors, with sufficient liberality in giving encouragement to the possessors. . . . They are judicious in sizing and subdividing their farms; careful in the selection of their tenants; liberal in advancing money for buildings, fences, drains, manures, roads, etc. and some of them, also, not remiss in forming plantations, which Galloway so much wants. . . . But there are many landlords, and among these some of the most considerable in the district, who lay out no money on their farms, and whose management consists wholly in receiving their termly rents . . . and the mischief is sometimes aggravated when the management of estates is committed to gentlemen of the law as factors. . . .

While the example of Mr Craik and his disciples had . . . excited a spirit of improvement in the neighbourhood of Dumfries, various attempts were made to carry the new system farther into Galloway. The late Dunbar Earl of Selkirk, whose friendship and confidence Mr Craik had long enjoyed, and who was an early convert to his mode of management, was desirous of introducing it upon his own estate. With this view, his lordship induced a gentleman (Captain Ewart) of Mr Craik's school to take a large farm in the neighbourhood of Kircudbright; but this, and every other effort which was made to extend and perpetuate the liberal and enlightened practices of Mr Craik ultimately failed. . . . although the Ayr Bank gave, at first, an impulse to the spirit of improvement . . . the facility with which credits were obtained induced speculative individuals to engage rashly in extensive agricultural operations: these were often conducted with too great disregard of expences, and when the Bank stopped payment, were followed in some instances by such ruinous consequences as could not fail to bring a certain degree of discredit upon agricultural improvements in general. . . .

– Smith, *op. cit.*, pp. 38–39, 33–35, 49–52

Memorial anent the Moss-Husbandry, 8th March, 1754

It is preferable to any Grounds in the Country in this, that a Man of a very small Stock is capable to labour a Farm of the Moss: He does not want a Number of Horse, Kine and Sheep, which cost a great deal of Money, and by the loss of which a Farmer is too often broke: the Moss Farmer needs only a few Lads to work; and if any of these die, or break a Leg, it is a Misfortune surely, but it is no great Loss to the Farmer. If he wants Seed, the Laird can safely advance it, till the Crop comes from the Ground. . . . What a happy Thing this is for a Day-labourer, to get himelf so easily stocked into a good profitable Farm, and have People working under him, bring up his Family creditably, and set out a new Stock of Farmers, instead of a Breed of idle Beggars; and every Day-labourer, who is honest and industrious, may in this Manner get himself set up in a small Farm at First, and a Few Years may make him able to take more, to take a large Farm. . . .

– Maxwell, *op. cit.*, pp. 75–79

Memorial . . . to the Duke of Queensberry and Dover, relating to the
Improvement of his Grace's Mosses upon Locher Water. . . . (c. 1754)
. . . having viewed the great Moss of Locher, at the Desire of the
Honourable Patrick Boyle, one of your Grace's Commissioners . . . it is
more than probable, that, upon proper Trials, and even by the Draining,
great Quantities of Shell-marl may be discovered. . . . That Moss
is . . . become a Morass so impassable, that Cattle have only Access to
feed upon it in very dry Seasons. . . . It is certain, that the greatest Part of
this very Moss of Locher, if once sufficiently drained, might, on a very
reasonable Expence, be made as profitable Ground as perhaps any in
either of the Counties of Nithsdale and Annandale . . . and it is far from
being impossible to drain all your Grace's Property of it, if the Lord
Maxwell's Mill was removed; for the Dam of this Mill, together with the
Narrowness of several of the Passages of the water above the Dam, swells
it back . . . and that by collecting the Water that falls down from
Mousewall Side into the Moss, at a very convenient Place above
Horseholm House, and carrying it by a Canal to a Runner of Water that
passes under a Bridge into Locher, a little below the Stankhouse, where
there is a very proper Station for a new Mill . . . and by thus diverting the
Water . . . the swelling of Locher would be so far prevented. Besides, if
the Course of Locher Water was widened and deepened, it would contain
a far greater Quantity of Water than at present . . . and the Ditches from
Locher up through the Mosses . . . will also contribute to prevent the
Overflow. . . . it is possible . . . that your Grace may, on very moderate
Charges . . . make two considerable Estates, the one out of Moss of
Mousewall, and the other out of the Moss of Craigs. . . .
– Maxwell, *op. cit.*, pp. 50–60

Craik of Arbigland
. . . fortunately for the country, a gentleman of great worth and abilities,
Mr Craik of Arbigland, turned his attention to country matters and made
farming his study. The want of experience, example, or instruction, and
the backwardness of people to new methods, threw many difficulties in
the way of his first essays; and it was but in the latter end of a course of
many years farming, that he adopted the valuable system he now
follows. . . . his own property . . . in the space of 35 years, he raised to five
times the value at which he received it. His example was soon followed by
other proprietors, and a new system of agriculture began to be
understood. . . .
– James Webster, General View of the Agriculture of Galloway,
1794, p. 13

Letter from John Maxwell of Broomholm to Lord Kames, 2nd March, 1777

... the Duke of Buccleugh's proceedings with his estate in the parish of Cannobie ... which contains 21,549 acres ... altogether the property of his Grace. ... With a few exceptions, the farm-houses, or rather the small villages, were situated on the banks of these rivers (Esk and Liddell); and besides the pieces of dry holm land, occupied by the villagers in the way of runrig, each farm, or village, had a share of the back grounds, extending in a long narrow strip, often to the distance of two miles; and these outfields ... common to the village ... were used for summer pasturage to young cattle. ... and it is now about three years since these back grounds were begun to be divided into new farms, containing from 60 to 150 acres each. Upon each of these there is already built, or to be built, at his Grace's expence, a commodious dwelling-house and offices; to which the tenants are removed from the old villages, upon tacks for twenty-one years; and the rent charged upon them is very moderate. ... The tenants are obliged to inclose the farms, and to divide them properly; and the thorns for the hedges are furnished from the Duke's nurseries, or purchased at his expence; and, at his expence also, people are employed to keep the hedges clean, and in order. The tenants ... are bound by their tacks to follow a regular course of husbandry. The Duke has ordered £100 per annum to be expended in making or repairing ... roads. ... the good effects of what is already done begin to shew themselves to great advantage, and to the disgrace of evilspeakers; for it has not been unattended with opposition from malice and ignorance: and the tenants themselves, of the remaining undivided farms, in spite of old prejudices, are become so sensible of the advantages their neighbours are likely to reap, that they are keenly petitioning for an extension of it to themselves.

– Andrew Wight, *The Present State of Husbandry*, vol. II, 1778, pp. 420–25

Canonbie: State of Agriculture

The late Dr. Grahame of Netherby, a gentleman of extensive views, and uncommon enterprise ... improved his estate from £2500 a-year, the rental when he came to the succession in 1753, which, at the same time, was seldom paid up, to £8000, the rental at his death in 1781, which was well paid: while the tenants lived more comfortably and respectably than formerly, when they paid little more than a quit-rent. ...

When the present Duke of Buccleugh came of age ... it did not escape his Grace's observation, that this part of his estate was also capable of improvement.... A gentleman of distinguished talents and activity was at length found to direct and superintend improvements upon the estate in this country, Mr Keir ... whose chief attention came naturally to be turned to Canoby.... The consequence now is, that luxuriant crops of corn are reaped, where heath, and bent, and moss, had predominated, perhaps, since the deluge; population increased; the spirit of industry roused; the face of the parish beautified; and the inhabitants, in point of civilization, proportionably improved.

– The Rev. John Russell, 'Parish of Canoby', *OSAS*, vol. XIV, 1794, pp. 36–37

The estate of Torthorald, belonging to the Duke of Queensberry, has been greatly improved since the year 1769.... The estate is now divided into farms, upon a plan extremely judicious. The whole tenants had been collected into two villages, and their houses consequently at a most convenient distance from the grounds they occupied. The bulk of them are removed to the center of their new farms. The rest, who remain in the villages, have lands adjacent to their houses. There are thirty farms in the whole, from 60 to 200 acres, as best suit the soil and other conveniences. Inclosing was the next step, done with ditch and hedge, or with stone walls.... No less than £4000 Sterling has been bestowed on these operations; and well bestowed, for it produced an additional rent suitable to the sum laid out.

– Wight, *op. cit.*, vol. II, 1778, pp. 441–42

Mr Jaffray, Minister of Ruthwell, who was several years in East Lothian, acquired considerable skill in farming, and directs his parishioners in their temporal concerns as well as spiritual. His glebe consists of forty acres, poor, wild, and wet, when he got possession. He fallows, limes, and lays down with grass-seed, after a crop of potatoes. He limed a second time, partly on grass, partly on fallow. The first answered by far the best.

– Wight, *op. cit.*, vol. II, 1778, pp. 434–35

The Hon. D. Gideon Murray of Kirkhouse ... living at his benefice in England ... does his part as a landlord, by advancing money for building houses, for inclosing land, and for lime, for which he never demands more than 5 per cent.... Mr Alexander, minister at Kirkbean, is another of Mr Craik's disciples. His little farm is high and exposed, and access to it with manure difficult.... Mr Alexander has ... undertaken a reform on his flock of sheep. He is among the very few that have ventured to introduce a mixture with English breed. He is justly of opinion, that the present

debased race is unworthy to be seen in the pasture of an improver.
                          – Wight, *op. cit.*, vol. III, 1784, pp. 67–68

Mr Scot, minister of Twineholm, gives his parishioners a good example in husbandry, as well as in morals. . . . Lime is the manure he uses, though shell-marl is at hand. His present crop of oats, pease, barley, wheat, are all good. His potatoes in drills make a fine appearance; hay and pasture-grass excellent. . . . an example to his brethren of the clergy who have country parishes. There can scarcely be imagined a harder situation, for a man of industry and talents, than to be tied to a country parish, with a numerous family and a small stipend, and seldom a person of reading or conversation within his reach. Husbandry . . . is an occupation that will enable him with comfort to rear a numerous family and . . . will enable him to instruct the tenants in his parish, and introduce among them a habit of industry, and consequently of honesty.
                          – Wight, *op. cit.*, vol. III, pp. 86–87

Progress at Ingleston-lodge [Terregles]
Excited by the great fame of Mr James Rome, I hastened to Ingleston-lodge, where he possesses a large farm belonging to Mr Heron of Heron. The bargain between them was uncommon; they joined in the lease; the landlord advanced the money, and the profits were divided. . . . I saw, with rapture, inclosures with ditches and hedge in perfection, luxuriant crops of corn, and grass fields, both hay and pasture, filled with choice grass plants . . . what surprised me most is a round hill of 180 acres, so steep that I was scarcely able to crawl up to the top on horseback, and yet all laid over with shell-marl in one season.

An account by Mr Rome of his progress
I employed eight men and an overseer . . . in raising marl the first half year. . . . When the tenant's crops were off, I began to plough a field of 67 acres, at first across the old crooked ridges, and a second time, about Candlemas, with three horses in a plough. . . . In April 1764, I, without harrowing, ploughed across these winter ridges. . . .

I was determined with all my force to undertake the marling improvement of Ingleston-hill. . . . I employed 24 men by days wages to throw marl. . . . We sometimes had upwards of 90 horses employed in this work; many of these were hired from the neighbouring tenants at two shillings for a man and two horses per day. These were divided into companies of eight horses each, who had two men and a woman allotted to fill and lay on bags to each company. . . . A boy in the morning, at setting off with the first gang, winded his horn. . . . we allowed an acre . . . 335 bags of about four Winchester bushels each . . . which we did effectually on 32 working days and four hours. In that time we carried up 48,346 bags to the parts of the hill that were inaccessible to carts. . . . We opened it into ridges, with six large oxen and three men to the plough; the ridges were ploughed up with four horses. . . . Thus we marled and broke up in less than a year, 144 acres of perhaps the worst lying land that was ever ploughed up. . . . loose stones . . . I gathered for division dykes, and what was not wanted for them, I built into thick walls on different places, for shelter, like this figure +.

Summer 1767, we raised marl, and marled 200 acres, called Clouden-park. . . . In April 1771, I had 87 fat bullocks sold in Smithfield, the charges on driving, etc. were from 18s. to 24s. . . . At the rate of 15 miles a day, they go from Dumfries to London in 29 or 30 days. . . . I sowed, about the first of June 1768, about 50 acres of turnips. . . . My greatest difficulty was to get them hoed properly, as not one of my men had ever had a turnip hoe in their hand, except John Linton, the overseer, who was bred a gardener. . . . next year, when I had 130 acres turnips, I had about 30 hoers, that would have passed in any field in Norfolk. . . .

– Wight: *op. cit.*, vol. III, 1784, pp. 53–66

A very speculative gentleman

Mr Miller, of Dalswinton, in the course of twenty-five years, has realised a plan which, to many landholders, even to those of great understanding and spirit, has been merely utopian. He has gone over a large estate, said to contain above 5000 acres, and has improved the whole of it, with the exception of a portion which is now under process. . . . His plan is, not to farm his lands himself, but to prepare them by improvement for being let to farmers. . . . Mr Miller found this property, when he entered to his purchase, in the most miserable state of exhaustion and barrenness. It is now, perhaps, one of the most improved and beautiful estates in this county. . . . This gentleman's intelligence and accuracy in business are well and long known; and he is of opinion . . . that very poor lands, fully improved, are capable of yielding twenty times their original produce. This is undoubtedly the case on the high and naturally barren lands now improving by Mr Miller, where the crops of grass, and of potatoe oats, are as fine as any in the county, and the flock of new Leicester sheep are thriving.

The farm of Pennyland . . . which was lately rented at £50, and for which only £78 could be obtained, is likely, in Mr Miller's hands, to return £1000 a year: nor is this wonderful, for though high situated, it contains 985 acres. . . .

Different pieces of ground have been laid down into fiorin meadows.... In laying down 14 acres at present, Mr Miller has caused the whole surface, consisting of rough coarse black moss, to be taken off and consumed by paring and burning, and the soil to be well dug and levelled. He then lays down the fiorin, and covers it with ashes, and also with compost of earth and lime. Two men were mowing the grown fiorin in order to furnish the plants to lay down; four girls were beating into fine mould, and mixing up the compost; one woman was drawing up some of the fiorin, in small parcels ... and another was chopping these parcels into cuttings ... to be scattered on the land; six men followed each other, with wheelbarrows, laying down compost earth and ashes, in regular order; and two persons were occupied laying the cuttings, and spreading the mould and ashes over them. In respect of wages, the men were allowed two shillings and three-pence, and the girls nine-pence per day each, without victuals.... It is Mr Miller's intention soon to lay down more and more, to the amount in all of above 200 acres.

Letters from P. Miller, Esq., of Dalswinton

24th September, 1810 ... I have now gone over all of this estate, which is let, except two or three trifling farms, containing about 120 acres of arable ground; and this I have done without the aid of a tenant.... I need not inform you that the first steps in improvement are, draining when necessary, inclosing sufficiently, removing stones, roots, and rubbish of every kind and liming. These operations cost me, I reckon, £11 per acre upon an average.... I reckon there are about 180 acres upon this estate of plantations of forty years of age and downwards, besides a very great number of fine old trees about the mansion-house.... I have, besides, planted myself about 150 acres ... generally Scotch fir and larch mixed.... I keep 20 work-horses. I employ about 70 men as ploughmen, labourers, ditchers, dikers, girls and boys....

13th February, 1812. ... I intend, and hope to be able, to lay down, before the middle of November next, 220 acres of ground in fiorin grass. This ground I advertised to be let a few years ago, and the highest offer made to me was a shilling per acre, which would have been for the 220 acres, £11. I reckon it will cost me, to lay it down all with plough and harrows, £6 per acre.... when the work is finished, I would not give a lease ... under £15 a-year for each acre....

For sheep I am building two folds, one of which is 60 yards, on two sides, by 30 yards: in short, a parallelogram of 60 yards by 30, and the other 50 by 30. These I cover, and I intend to feed my sheep, when sheltered there from bad weather, or vermin in hot weather, with short-cut fiorin grass, or fiorin hay, given in mangers. In their pasture grounds, fiorin ricks will be placed open for their use. . . .

– Singer, *op. cit.*, pp. 63–64, 249–51, 549–54

Wigtown and Baldoon

Wigton is inhabited by a drowsy people, who make no figure in trade or manufactures, nor are they more eminent in husbandry, though the soil near the town is good. . . . William McConnel has turnip and potatoes in drills, and a field under summer fallow, absolute novelties about the town of Wigton. . . . Peter Warwick has turnips and potatoes in drills, very well dressed. These are disciples of Mr Jaffray, factor to the Earl of Selkirk at Baldoon. . . .

Account by Mr Jaffray, Baldoon, 27th July, 1778

The greater part of the soil of Baldoon is a low marsh. . . . The ridges were broad, high, crooked, and unequal, some of them terminating in narrow points in mid land: Betwixt these ridges lie baulks, covered with rushes and small dwarf willows. Such was the situation of the soil when our operation was begun in . . . 1760. The lands were first ploughed up as the ridges lay, baulks and all, and sowed with oats. This crop was repeated the second year, and the ploughings directed to lower the ridges as much as possible . . . reckoning the men at 10d per day . . . and . . . a ploughman and a pair of horses at 3s 6d a day, the whole operation was performed, on an average, at the rate of 25s sterling per acre. . . .

The field, after the operation of levelling, lay in broad round reversed ridges. . . . I covered it with sea-shells . . . at the rate of 25 tons or 550 Winchester bushels to an acre. . . . the levelling was completed, and the new ridges laid out in the sixth year after the land was broke up. . . . near 300 acres have been managed in this manner. . . . I am now sowing out this farm in grass for pasture. . . . You saw in summer 1777 twenty Galloway cows feeding up twenty acres of this grass. I bought them at the first of May for £2-8-6 each, and sold these twenty cows, on the 15th of November following, to the butcher, at one hundred guineas neat, ready money. . . .

I have two rows of carrots upon a five feet ridge. . . . I have used them in feeding horses, cattle, sheep, and hogs . . . even geese eat them with greediness. . . . I was in use . . . to give the whole farm-horses here one feed of oats, and a feed of carrots in the day. . . .

I have used cabbages as a common green crop for a long time . . . in single rows on . . . ridges four and one-half broad. . . . Cabbages, where

they succeed, are a better food for cattle . . . than turnips.
– Wight, op. cit., vol. III, 1784, pp. 92–104, 116–17

Baldoon in the 1790s

. . . during the last eighty years . . . In no other part of the country has a greater change taken place than in the holm portion of the Baldoon Estate. I shall begin with the low land bordering the Wigton Bay . . . four miles north and south . . . its breadth at the north end say two miles, narrowing to a few hundred yards at Orchardton on the south. When I first saw it, it was an immense unbroken field of pasture land, the then proprietor Basil, Lord Daer, being just commencing operations by dividing it into fields of different sizes by double ditches, with strips of plantations, which still exist. He also intersected the land with two excellent roads and built a few excellent cottages, out of one of which our family was driven by the sea. . . . No doubt centuries had passed since that great field had been thrown up into ridges, varying from fifteen to fifty feet broad, with corresponding spaces. . . . In rainy weather the spaces between the ridges were so flooded that a canoe would have been useful when crossing. They ran from the hard land in an unbroken curved line into the sea at high-water, the tide ebbing out nearly three miles. . . .

One monster ridge claims particular attention. It occupied a space nearly in the middle of the strath and was a full mile in length, much broader and higher than the others, and was called *par excellence*, Rosie's Rigg. . . . It is not possible to say whether Rosie was a fairy, a brownie, or a fire or water kelpie, perhaps a cross between some of the parties; but she must have been of some note in the district, as a lovely green bank facing the sea on the farm of Orchardton at the end of the strath is called Rosie's Brae and a delightful spring at its foot also bears her name.

These ridges lay undisturbed till early in the present century, when drains were put in the spaces and a gradual levelling process by the plough reduced the whole strath into a flat plain of as rich wheat-bearing land as any in the kingdom.

With a few feeble, though praiseworthy, attempts at improvement, agriculture was in a very low state in Wigtonshire at the end of the eighteenth century. Great quantities of surface water lay undisturbed from generation to generation, every little hollow having its loch of water, swarming with leeches and water fowl, and every little burn alive with fine spotted trout. Numerous marshes of all sizes, covered with rushes, other portions with dwarf alder, slae-thorn, and all manner of obnoxious things that delight in moisture abounded through the whole country, importing to it a dreary and desolate aspect.

... when the lands of Baldoon fell by purchase into the possession of the house of Galloway ... a new era was introduced. This was brought about by the letting of the Baldoon lands for a term of nineteen years by public competition in the court-house of Wigton, when rents were offered that never had been dreamed of by a Galloway farmer. Farm rents had in the course of ages crept up from a few pounds a year to a few hundreds, but on that occasion farms of moderate extent were let at above two thousand a year. ...

– Samuel Robinson, *Reminiscences of Wigtonshire about the close of last century*, 1872, pp. 54–58

Memorandum from James Murray of Broughton and Cally to John Bushby, 23rd January, 1775, Respecting the Lands of Broughton

The Large Marle bog is already open and the drain completely finished but there are other bogs in which it is supposed there are considerable quantitys of Marle contained, and if Drains can be made at a moderate expence it might be proper to open them, but on Account of the uncertainty of the expence of making Drains in that part of the Country, Mr Murray would not undertake them at his own risque, but on the bogs being bored and the appearance being promising he would give a sum of money to assist the Tenant who should take the risque of making the Drains. The first is the little Moss on the march of Broughton Skeoch ... and he would allow the one half of the expence of the Drain provided it did not exceed in whole Thirty pounds Sterling – The Second the Moss in Oultoun it is expected contains a large and valuable quantity of Marle, there is a Drain already made, but it will require cleaning and deepening and as it passes thro one of Lord Galloway's Farms, it is probable some obstruction may be given by the tenants. ...

Method Mr Murray had in view to sett this Estate: Broughton Mains – Andrew Broadfoot in Belsier had been with Mr Murray frequently about this Farm and from what has passed Mr Murray thinks will give twelve shillings Sterling per acre for it upon a Nineteen years Lease and during the first five years, for which his Tack of Belsier subsists, require only a sufficient Barn which must be made. This is a Tenant much to Mr Murray's mind and not to be parted with for trifles. William Drew in Newton Stewart, Alexander Stewart in Cults and one Hannay a grain Merchant have also been applying about this Farm.

John Dunie in Broadwig has offered Mr Murray twelve shillings Sterling per Acre for Archibald McCaul's last possession and for the little Park below the road next to Sir Stair Agnews march for a Nineteen year lease – This Tenant having houses on his present Farm requires no houses but a Barn – Mr Murray thinks him an Industrious, careful Man he is desirous to prefer this Tenant.

Alexander Dickson Tenant to Mr Keith Stewart has offered Mr Murray eleven shillings Sterling per acre for the whole of Broughton Skeoch, but Mr Murray is desirous to have Dunie for the part mentioned above and therefore wishes to deal with Dickson for the midle part of Broughton Skeoch. And as Mr Murray considers the midle part to be inferior in soil, tho' more convenient for Marle, he thinks it will be convenient and proper to sett it before the other parts are Lett.

The possession of the Miln and Eighteen acres of Land thereby. George Scamble is so generally liked by the Country that Mr Murray wishes him to have a Nineteen year Lease of his possession on the best terms he will agree to, being subjected to the whole expence of having the Miln in repair – But as this is a kind of personal favour to the Miler, so powers must be reserved to Mr Murray to resume the Tack in the event of Scambles death during the Currency thereof, unless the Tenants concur in approving of the Millers successor as a proper peaceable and sufficient man. . . .

The Oultons are possessed by John Hawthorn and John Coning and the Lease thereof expires at Whitsunday (1777). There is therefore more time for Letting this Farm, at the same time Mr Murray has no objection to its being sett immediately. The present Tenants are not so attentive in every respect to the improvement of these Lands as Mr Murray could wish, but he inclines however to prefer them on the same terms to any other – This Farm is lett so low as Fifty pound Sterling at present and is in a very bad state, but it is so conveniently situated for Marle that Mr Murray thinks it may be sett for half a Guinea an Acre or perhaps more – It will be necessary to restrict the Tenants to three successive crops and to reserve the previlidge of taking Marle from one Farm to another where it can be spared and roads the most convenient for both parties to lead it away with, on payment of damages.

Stewartry Farms – Laigh Lag presently possessed by William and William Nishes – The Farm contains Sixty five acres and is now sett at Eleven pounds Sterling and the Lease expires at Whitsunday (1775) – William Nish the Younger has offered Eighteen pounds, and Mr Murray expects £25 Sterling of yearly rent at least and he has had it valued at £29 Sterg. per year – Mr Murray wishes to prefer Young William as an Encouragement and he would furnish him over board, with three hundred Carlisle Bushels of Shell Lime the Tenant paying along with the

Rent Six per Cent yearly for the expence thereof.

Laigh Creoch and Tanny Fad possessed by John McClure and Anthony Cowan, at the rent of £28 or thereby, but Mr Murray never intends to treat with the old Tenants as being indolent and in every respect bad managers – They contain 231 Acres and Mr Murray has offered it at £69, tho' Dunbar has valued it at £77 of yearly Rent. . . .

Fleularg – This Farm Mr Murray has offered the upper part thereof to Alexr McClure at £25 Sterling per year – A dyke to be drawn along the Ford road from Gatehouse, to the corner of Alexr McClures house, and if McClure wont give that Rent, Robert More's son in Barley will take it and who Mr Murray thinks a better Tenant tho' he will let McClure have it if he desires – What remains of Fleularg Mr Murray meant to have thrown into small parks and have sett for the accommodation of the Inhabitants of Gatehouse. . . .

Plunton – This Farm is presently sett for £90 Sterg. per year – Mr Murray offered it to the Tenants for £200 a year, and they offered £160 Sterg. a year – It contains 460 Acres and is a valuable Farm, but has been under very bad management and therefore on Mr Murrays setting his Shire Lands, he intended to have it taken into his own hands and to have keept it as a Stock Farm for a few years, until got into some heart. . . .

Mr Murray . . . hopes the hints will be of some use to Messrs Agnew McDowell Syme Gordon Stewart and Bushby whome he has requested to take charge of his affairs in his absence, but Drumruck Murraytoun and Orquhers three farms now in the possession of Robert Ramsay will also be sett before Whits. 1776 when the Current Tack Expires – The present Rent is about £140 Yearly, but Mr Murray expects a very great rise upon these farms . . . he imagines they will bring more than Double the present Rent, he has been informed the tenant keep 3000 Sheep between 30 and 40 Milk Cows and sells yearly about a hundred Stotts which he keeps over Summer and perhaps part of them over Winter and he has also 800 Goats – He has also sufficient Corn Land for two families. . . .

– *Broughton and Cally Muniments*, Scottish Record Office GD 10 1091

Glasserton: The late Admiral Keith Stewart of Glasserton had, for many years, applied himself, with great earnestness, to beautify and improve his estate in that parish. He built on it a stately mansion-house, formed an excellent garden, and scattered plantations over his grounds . . . to afford the most useful shelter, and the most to gratify the eye of taste. In his own natural possession, he reserved nearly two thousand acres of land. . . . For managing the husbandry of this tract of ground, he hired his upper farm servants from those counties of England, of which the agriculture is deemed to be the most skilful. He formed ... a square of farm office-houses, possessing every requisite accommodation for every sort of animal-stock ... he provided all the best instruments of improved agriculture, and breeds of the best races of the different sorts of animals to be fed upon his lands. ... four hundred black cattle, forty score of sheep, and a proportionate number of horses, formed his animal stock. A number of day-labourers, varying from 50 to 70, were constantly employed in the farm-work ... The use of oxen, for drawing the cart and plough, were zealously adopted. ... the stoutest and largest boned oxen were usually selected out of those droves of Irish cattle, which were continually imported ... towards England. At the age of 4 years, these were yoked in the draught: They were wrought, in this labour, for the next four years: On the 9th year, they were freed from the yoke, and fattened for the butcher. ...

All the agricultural improvements ... were prosecuted on a large scale, and at a great expence. So many of them were, of necessity, merely experimental, that they cannot be supposed to have every one already repaid the expence at which they were made, with a reasonable surplus of profit. ...

The church stands near to Glasserton-House, and is romantically embosomed in wood, which sheds around it a venerable gloom, as if it were a druidical temple. ... it was built in the year 1752. The wood was at a much later period planted around the church yard, by the late Admiral Stewart, to hide the church, that it might not deform the aspect of his ornamental grounds.

– The Rev. Dr Davidson, 'Parish of Glasserton' *OSAS*, vol. XVII,
1794–95, pp. 590–94

Sir William Maxwell of Monreith has commenced farmer, and with great success, so far as he has proceeded. He is very capable of making it a business. ... Inclosing with stone dikes near the coast goes on briskly. ... Wool in the parish of Mochrum bears a great name. ... The sheep here are original; no remembrance of any change of breed, nor of any attempt to improve either the body or fleece.

– Wight, *op. cit.*, vol. III, 1784, pp. 133–36

Letter from Major Ross in Balkail, 1st November, 1777
It only contains about 400 acres in all, part my own property, part feued on a lease of 100 years, upwards of 80 to expire, and part on a lease of 42 years, about 37 to expire. From the length of the lease, I have been induced to improve mountainous ground, that otherwise I would not

have engaged with, from the severity of the labour. . . . My breed of black cattle is esteemed the true Galloway, and the best in Scotland. My father was at least 30 years before he brought them to what they are now.

– Wight, *op. cit.*, vol. III, 1784, pp. 137–38

The Earl of Stair: His Lordship thinks the most substantial improvement for a gentleman is to procure industrious and improving tenants. He treats them kindly, and is ever ready to give them good instructions. But words will not do; example is necessary; and in that view he takes farm after farm into his own hand, and, upon dressing high, lets them out to the most enterprising. . . . The great fund for improvement in that country is lime, brought raw from Ireland; it is burnt in a draw-kiln, and can be laid on the land for about £3-10-0 per acre. The Earl holds 400 acres in his natural possession, as a farm for the family conveniences. . . . Above all, I admired a large inclosure, on account of the rich pasture in it, and the substantial wall that surrounds it, six feet high, copped in the manner of Galloway snap-dikes. . . . This fine park serves for sheep walk, deer park, horses and black cattle, all feed promiscuously on it . . . every kind keep by themselves. . . .

– Wight: *op. cit.*, vol. III, 1784, pp. 140–43

Dumfries-shire: Besides the dung produced by the cattle on the farms, by that collected in all the towns, and by . . . compost dunghills of rich earth, corrupted vegetables, and lime, a very large quantity of lime is used as a manure in this county. . . . The lime-stone hath been manufactured, for many years, in the east-side of the county on the estates of Springkell, Braes, and Kellhead; for several years near the middle of it, on the estates of Comlongon and Closeburn; and for some years near the west side of it, on that of Barjarg. . . .

– Bryce Johnston, *General View of the Agriculture of the County of Dumfries*, 1794, p. 37

Letter from Sir James Kirkpatrick to Sir John Sinclair, respecting the lime husbandry of Dumfries-shire, etc.
The lime quarry of Barjarg . . . the property of the Rev. Dr. Hunter, was discovered in the year 1785, and the first lime was sold from it in summer 1786, when the sale amounted to 12,640 Dumfries measures . . . 1787 . . . 27,263 measures . . . 1791 . . . 27,722 measures . . . 1792 . . . 22,260 measures.

The Dumfries measure contains two heaped Dumfries pecks, or 43½ Scots pints, and is sold at nine-pence. . . . The demand is chiefy from the parishes of Dunscore, Glencairn, Tynron, Penpont and Keir; in small quantities also Closeburn, Morton, Durisdeer, Kirkmahoe and Irongray; and within these two or three last seasons, a good deal has been carried into the parishes of Kells, Dalry and Balmaclellan. . . .

– Johnston, *op. cit.*, Appendix III, pp. XV–XVI

Carlingwark: Marl from the Carlingwark Loch is sometimes driven 3 miles, and 40 or 50 cart loads of 22 cubical feet each, are applied to the acre, which cost is 1s per load. Shells . . . the most valuable bank . . . is on the estate of Cassencary, the property of Alexander Muir Mackenzie, Esq., of Delvine. Vessels ly to, to load, within a few paces of the shell bank, which runs from 5 to 8 feet deep. They cost 8d per ton, and from 1s to 2s 6d, according to the distance of water carriage. 25 or 30 tons are allowed to an acre.

– Webster, *op. cit.*, p. 8

Galloway cattle: . . . all the prime cattle are appropriated for the English markets, whither by far the greatest number are sent at three, or three and a half years old. Many of them are driven at once to Smithfield, but the principal sales are at St Faith's, and other markets in Norfolk. . . . The whole number of cattle sold annually from Galloway . . . may be stated at 20,000. . . . Next to St Faith's, Bungby and Hampton are the most considerable. The average prices of the cattle sent to these markets, for two or three years preceding 1809, may be stated at £13. Many of the inferior cattle are sold in Dumfries, or sent to the north of England, probably to the amount of 3000, at the average price of £8 or £8 10s. . . . a vast number of transfers are made among the farmers. . . . the following weekly or monthly trysts are held: Kelton, Gatehouse, Wigton, Glenluce, Stranraer, and Whithorn. Prime cattle, however, are seldom brought to any of these markets.

– Smith, *op. cit.*, pp. 249–50

Cattle: Mr Murray of Broughton has given great attention to perfect the breed of the true Galloway kind of cattle . . . he sold in one drove 100 bullocks, for which he was paid by the drover £925. . . . They were not of a great size, but their figure and fat captivated the purchaser, who was as complete a judge of cattle as any in England. Mr Murray's method of rearing cattle is to give them coarse grass when young, but in great plenty. . . . the young stock are never housed, but all winter over are left to the foggage in a sheltered field. At the age of three they are led to rich pasture, to fit them for the market. Those that are kept till they are 4 or 5 years old are fit for the butcher any time during winter or spring, with the aid only of a few turnip thrown to them once a day. No stall-fed beef is comparable. . . .

Forty cows I saw all in one shed tied up to be milked; not a dirty spot to be seen. Nor can I omit the cleanness of the milkers, and of the vessels. The maid that had the distinction was from England: She sat so upright as to preserve her fashionable high head from being ruffled. Her head-dress, however, did not altogether equal the fashionable heads in Edinburgh.

– Wight, *op. cit.*, vol. III, 1784, pp. 89–90

Sheep: The mountain flocks at present consist either of the Cheviot breed of sheep, or of the short heath sheep, with black faces and coarse wool. . . . At the present time it is believed that all Eskdale is under Cheviot stocks; and also by far the most part of Annandale . . . including the vales of Evan and Moffat. . . . other breeds are found in the lower farms, in the hands of intelligent farmers. Mr John Church, at Hitchill, has a flock of thirty score of Leicester sheep; and the same breed is kept by Mr Thomson, Charlesfield . . . Mr Miller of Dalswinton, Mr Menteath, General Dirom, and some other gentlemen. Mr Stewart of Hillhead has for many years had a small flock of Spanish original, and Major Harte of Castlemilk has a flock of South Downs. The last-introduced and fine-woolled Negrette and Paular breeds from Spain, have not yet been naturalized in this county. . . . The oldest native sheep of Scotland, small in size, and having dun faces and knees, although still in Galloway, are no where to be seen in this county.

– Singer, *op. cit.*, pp. 358–59

Mochrum: This parish has long been famous for excellent wool, on account of its still retaining some of the ancient breed of the Galloway sheep. Of these sheep, the most distinguishing marks are, orange coloured face and legs, short thick wool, and very small size. When at full growth, and tolerably fat, the wedder would not exceed 30, nor the ewe 27 lib.; and it would require 18 or 20 of their fleeces to make a stone of 26½ lib..

– The Rev. John Steven, 'Parish of Mochrum', *OSAS*, vol. XVII, 1794–95, p. 568

The Earl of Selkirk at St Mary Isle: His Lordship, willing to improve the breed of sheep, entered keenly into the fashionable mode of bringing rams from England. Mr Bakewell's, Mr Culley's tups were got, and ewes from Mr Thomson of Northumberland.

– Wight, *op. cit.*, vol. III, 1784, p. 84

A cunnigary in the sandy district near Glenluce: A rabbit warren . . . is rented at £100 a year. The skins go to the English market, and the carcases are sold in the country at 4d the pair.
  – The Rev. William Learmont, *OSAS*, 'Parish of Old Luce', vol. XIV, 1790–91, p. 494

Dumfries. Many noblemen and gentlemen have formed themselves into a society for the encouragement of agriculture. Their constant president is Mr Craik of Arbigland. . . . The society hold regular meetings every month at Dumfries, and publish from time to time printed instructions for advancing the tenants in the art. . . . The society does not stop at giving precept and example. They generously contribute their money; and in a most patriotic spirit confine these premiuns to tenants, without having any share themselves. These premiums are given to promote summer-fallow, to raise crops of turnip, and to improve the breed of horses, horned cattle, and sheep.
  – Wight, *op. cit.*, vol. II, 1778, p. 443

Planned villages (Holywood and Gretna parishes)
Since the middle of last March, a village was begun by Dr Bryce Johnston; six houses are finished, and inhabited a considerable time ago; three more will be finished before Martinmas. . . . The village is built at a small distance from the scite of the Druidical temple. . . . It is called *Druidville*; and he intends, this Winter, to plant a grove of oaks around it, in memory of the holy grove of the Druids. . . .
  – Bryce Johnston, 'Parish of Holywood', *OSAS*, vol. XXI, pp. 4–5

In the year 1791, a new village was begun on the farm of Springfield, belonging to Sir William Maxwell, where upwards of 40 houses have been already built, or are now building. The plan of the village is perfectly regular. The streets are 50 feet wide, and the houses are all built of freestone or bricks, and covered with blue slate. A great part of the land adjacent to the village, and belonging to the proprietor, has been inclosed, and the fences planted with quicks and hedge-rows of trees. Each settler is accommodated with an inclosure of 6 or 4 acres at a moderate rent, and upon a lease for 19 years.
  – The Rev. John Morgan, 'Parish of Graitney', *OSAS*, vol. IX, 1793, p. 529

FARMHOUSES AND COTTAGES

Dornock: Mud-houses. The farm-houses in general, and all the cottages, are built of mud or clay; yet these houses, when plaistered and properly finished within, as many of them are, are exceeding warm and comfortable. The manner of erecting them is singular. In the first place, they dig out the foundation of the house, and lay a row or two of stones, then they procure, from a pit contigous, as much clay or brick-earth as is sufficient to form the walls: and having provided a quantity of straw, or other litter to mix with the clay, upon a day appointed, the whole neighbourhood, male and female, to the number of 20 or 30, assemble, each with a dung-fork, a spade, or some such instrument. Some fall to the working of the clay or mud, by mixing it with straw; others carry the materials; and 4 or 6 of the most experienced hands build and take care of the walls. In this manner, the walls of the house are finished in a few hours; after which, they retire to a good dinner and plenty of drink which is provided for them, where they have music and a dance, with which, and other marks of festivity, they conclude the evening. This is called a daubing. . . .
 – The Rev. James Smaill, 'Parish of Dornock', *OSAS*, vol. II, 1790, p. 22

Galloway (1794): With the exception of a few particular estates, these are in general bad, having but one floor, a thatch covering, and very poorly fitted up within. The offices are of a piece with the house, and seldom put down in proper order. The dwellings of the mechanics and labourers are wretched hovels, built of turf and moss, with a covering of the same materials.
 – Webster, *op. cit.*, p. 15

Dumfries-shire (1794): For the last twenty years farm-houses and offices are much improved in point of situation and quality; but in many parts of the county they still stand in much need of improvement in both. . . . Some time ago the best farm-houses were built in the form of the three sides of a square: the dwelling-house formed the front, the stable and byre the second, and the barn, cart-house, and grainery, the third side. In some instances the back part, or fourth side, was filled up with shades for young cattle, and houses for hogs and poultry. This is a convenient and beautiful form . . . in this country, where the wind is frequently very high, the square form . . . occasion such swirle-blasts, as very frequently unroof them. If large and heavy slates are used in order to resist the blast, the walls and timber must be proportionally stronger, and the expences of building greater.

To remedy ... these evils, several farm-houses and offices are now built in a long range, the dwelling-house being at the east end of it. On this plan several gabled walls are saved ... and houses are very seldom unroofed. ...

– Johnston, *op. cit.*, pp. 74–75

Kirkcudbright: ... Basil William Lord Daer ... began his operations on his father's estate in the year 1786. ... The farms on this estate, though considerably different in extent, are generally however of a proper size; and almost every tenant is accommodated with a good dwelling-house, and a complete set of offices. The dwelling-house commonly consists of two stories, and always of four, five, or six apartments. Barns, stables, cow-houses and sheds are provided ... built with stone and lime, and covered with good slates. Almost every farm has also a good threshing machine driven by water, or wrought with horses. Mr Corrie of Dunrod, Sir William Douglas, and many others soon followed the example. Mr Oswald of Auchencruive has lately built, and Mr Gordon of Balmaghie is now building farm-houses on a scale which, by many, is deemed extravagant.

– Smith, *op. cit.*, pp. 57–58

Dumfries-shire: The Duke of Buccleuch allows wood, slates, and lime; and the tenants carry these, and all other materials, and pay also for building and fitting up. But the situation, plan, and extent of the buildings must first be approved of by his Grace's man of business. ... Many of these farming sets of buildings have been estimated, some years ago, as high as £1500 on each farm; and yet the Duke has not laid out very deeply; the tenants have done the greater part themselves. ... A common ... cottage is put up ... stone and lime walls, seven feet high, thirty-six feet long, and fourteen to sixteen feet wide within; the roof of Scots fir, which is preserved from the worm by smoke, and covered with thatch; a chimney at one end, and an open passage for smoke in the other ... it would let at £3 a year or more. ...

– Singer, *op. cit.*, pp. 86, 98

THE CIRUMSTANCES AND CHARACTER OF THE PEOPLE

Canonbie: Population. The account transmitted to Dr. Webster in 1755, fixed the population of this parish to the number of 1733 souls. At present, in the beginning of 1794, it reaches to 2725 souls. ... There are

20 widowers and 54 widows; batchelors, or such as live single in their own houses, do not exceed 6. The taste for matrimony universally prevails here. . . . Of the inhabitants, 201 are enrolled upon his Grace's rental-book as tenants, possessing land. The farms are generally small, at an average about £15 a-year. The rent of some is so low as £2 or less; and of others as high as £80, £120, and even near to £300.

The rest of the inhabitants that are come to maturity, consist of artificers, labourers, and work servants. The state of the first class is as follows, viz. weavers, 40; one stocking weaver; masons, 14; wrights, 16; blacksmiths, 8; tailors, 10; shoemakers, 4; coopers, 6; clogmakers, 3; wheelwright, 1; bakers, 4; ale and spirit venders, 9; shopkeepers, 4; and surgeons, 2. Of labourers, including coal miners, 98; male servants, 54; female, 62. Of the description of gentry, there are only 4 or 5 families. Many have fixed their residence here, who are not natives; several of whom are from England.

> – The Rev. John Russell, *Parish of Canonby*, OSAS, vol. XIV, 1794,
> pp. 423–25

Balmaghie: Population. Souls in 1793 – 862; Males . . . 433; Females . . . 429; No. of families – 152 . . . Male farming servants – 63; Female servants – 51; Labourers engaged by the year, called benefit-men, living in separate houses – 18 . . . *Religious Persuasion.* Roman Catholicks – 11; Children of ditto – 3; Antiburghers – 2; Cameronians – 8; Established Church – 838. *Occupations.* The Minister – 1; Schoolmasters – 2; Small heritor resident – 1; Farmers whose rents are from £240 to £30 – 30; Do. renting below £30 – 34; Servants and labourers on farms as above – 132; Blacksmiths – 2; Millers – 3; Shoemakers – 8; Weavers – 12; Masons – 7; Carpenters – 8; Tailors – 8; Boatmen – 2; Dram sellers – 8; Families of the above – 604. *Place of Birth.* Ireland – 30; England – 2; Galloway, etc. – 831.

> – The Rev. James Thomson, *Parish of Balmaghie*, OSAS, vol. XIII, 1793,
> p. 644

Whithorn: Population. The population of this parish, about 55 years ago, was placed at 1300; now it is 1890. . . . The town contains . . . 756. The Isle of Whithorn, the only village, contains . . . 396. The country part of the parish contains . . . 738. . . .
Professions. There is 1 clergyman, 1 writer, 1 attorney, 1 plasterer, 1 saddler, 18 masons and 1 apprentice, 16 joiners and 11 apprentices, 2 slaters, 25 weavers and 2 apprentices, 22 shoemakers and 2 apprentices, 16 tailors and 2 apprentices, 8 blacksmiths and 1 apprentice, 1 landwaiter,

and 1 tideman, 12 shopkeepers, 2 coopers and 1 apprentice.
        – Isaac Davidson, D.D., *'Parish of Whithorn'*, OSAS, vol. XVI, 1794,
                                                    pp. 289–90

Dumfries-shire (1794): The wages of labouring men are, for the long day
one shilling and twopence, for the short day of elevenpence; for casting
peats one shilling and threepence, and for mowing one shilling and
sixpence; and those of women are, for working at peats, ninepence; at
turnip-weeding, hay-making, and other farming work in summer,
sevenpence, and for shearing (reaping), those of both men and women are
one shilling and twopence. The day wages of a joiner, mason, bricklayer,
and slater are two shillings. All these labourers and tradesmen provide
their own bed and board at these wages. A taylor receives one shilling and
twopence without, and eightpence with, his meat, per day.
                                        – Johnston, *op. cit.*, p. 58

Dornock: Labouring Poor. The expences of a common labourer, with a
wife and four children, may be nearly as follow.

	£	s	d
House-rent, with a small garden or kail-yard	£1	0	0
Peats or fuel	0	6	0
A working jacket and breeches, about	0	5	0
Two shirts, 6s. a pair of clogs, 3s. 2 pair of stockings, 2s.	0	11	0
A hat, 1s. a handkerchief, 1s. 6d	0	2	6
A petticoat,. bedgown, shift, and caps for the wife	0	9	0
A pair of stockings, 1s. clogs, 2s. 6d. apron, 1s. 6d. napkin, 1s. 6d. for ditto	0	6	6
A shirt, 2s. clogs, 2s. stockings, 1s. for each of the four children	1	0	0
Other clothes for the children, about 4s. each	0	16	0
School wages, etc. for the four children	0	10	0
Two stone of oat meal, per week, at 20d. per stone	8	13	4
Milk, 9d. per week, butter, 3d. per ditto	2	12	0
Salt, candle, thread, soap, sugar, and tea	0	13	0
The tear and wear of the man and wife's sunday cloths	0	10	0
Total outlays	£17	14	4

At the rate of 6s. per week, for 48 weeks, in the year, the man may earn
about £14-8; the expence of maintaining the family, will therefore exceed
the man's annual earnings, about £3-6-4 per annum; but the deficiency is
generally made up by the wife's industry, by her working in hay-time and
harvest, when she can earn about £1-10s. and by her spinning through

winter and spring, when she may gain from 1s. to 1s. 6d. per week, besides taking care of her family. The labourers usually get some potatoes set by the farmers who employ them, with any manure they can gather, which is a great help to their family, particularly in the article of oat meal. With that saving they are enabled to buy better clothes, and a little butcher meat for the winter. Indeed, such as are industrious, sober, and economical, live pretty comfortably, and are in general wonderfully well contented with their situation.

  – Rev. James Smaill, 'Parish of Dornock', *OSAS*, vol. II, 1790, pp. 20–21

Galloway (1794): As soon as the whole field of reapers are collected together in the morning, they receive what is called their *handsel*, which consists of as much as bread and milk as they can destroy. This once finished, they proceed to work; at which they continue till 9 o'clock in the morning, when a plentiful breakfast of pottage and milk is brought them. That being over, and a sufficient rest afterwards administered, they proceed again to work, from which they are stopped about 12 by another refreshment. A dinner of broth, beef, and ale arrives at 2; and they are allowed a sufficiency of time before dark to take their supper, which is the same with their breakfast. The reader will probably wish to be informed, how it is possible that these people, crammed with victuals to the mouth at all times, can perform any work; or why at this season, and in a climate too so precarious for a corn crop, so much valuable time should be thus wasted? These are questions which it remains with the farmers of Galloway to answer.

  – Webster, *op. cit,*. p. 16

Dalry (1791–93): The inhabitants of this parish are in general a peaceable, social, hospitable, obliging, humane and well disposed people. Many of the principal farmers, not to speak of heritors, besides all the qualities mentioned, possess a measure of information and politeness, which render them agreeable companions to men of superior rank and education. It is remarkable, that even the most idle, dissipated, and worthless part of the inhabitants, are not destitute of all those good qualities which distinguish the rest. Scarcely any of them, for a long period, have been convicted of capital crimes, though there are a few, especially in the village, who are said to be addicted to fraud, pilfering, lying, evil speaking, and several other immoralities.

  – Rev. Alexander McGowan, 'Parish of Dalry', *OSAS*, vol. XIII, 1791–93, p. 65

Kirkcudbright (1792): The people of Kirkcudbright are, in general, of a pleasant, social and agreeable disposition, and their morals are fully as good as those of their neighbours. Few or none are ever incarcerated for crimes or misdemeanors. . . . In point of taste, they are much superior to most people of the parishes around them. Their reading is extensive; and being furnished with an excellent subscription library of the best modern books, they have access to all the improvements in literature and politics. They are all loyal to government; and no less attached to the principles of the British Constitution, than averse to divisions in the Church. No minister in the church of Scotland can boast of such unanimity amongst his people: For among the whole 2,295 that compose the parish, there is not one dissenter, or seceder, of any denomination whatever.

– Rev. Robert Muter, 'Parish of Kirkcudbright', *OSAS*, vol. XI, 1792, p. 23

Kirkinner (1791): Are there any means by which the condition of the people could be ameliorated? is the most amiable of the Statistical Queries. . . . perhaps, the greatest barrier against household industry and manufacture among us, is the scarcity of fuel in many parts of the country. A human being pinches with cold, when confined within doors, is always an inactive being. The day-light, during the winter, is spent by many of the women and children in gathering *elding*, as they call it, that is, sticks, furze, or broom, for fuel, and the evening in warming their shivering limbs before the scanty fire which this produces.

– Rev. John Graham, 'Parish of Kirkinner', *OSAS*, vol. IV, 1791, pp. 146–47

Tongland (1792): Character and Manners of the Inhabitants. They are, in general, a decent and respectable people in their different ranks of life; sensible and rational in their religious principles. No sectaries. They are all warm friends to the principles of the Revolution Government, and the succession of the Family of Hanover. There is not an old woman in the parish, but would debaub *Tom Paine* with dirt, if he presumed to set his foot within the verge of it. They hear that the King and the Royal Family go constantly to church on the Sabbath day, and hate Tom Paine for abusing so good a Prince. Numbers of them are terrifed that the French Revolution Government should be introduced among them, for every one chooses to keep what he has lawfully got, and not make an equal division of it among his neighbours.

– Rev. Alex. Robb, 'Parish of Tongland', *OSAS*, vol. IX, 1792, pp. 323–24

Kirkmichael: State of the Poor. The poor receiving alms are only 5; who are supported, partly, by weekly collections, which, with small fines exacted from delinquents, and dues paid for marriages and baptisms out of the church, amount, annually, to £14 or £15, and partly by alms, in meal and other victuals, given them from house to house, or sent to them when unable to go about the parish. . . . In extraordinary cases of distress, we have a custom which deserves to be taken notice of in a paper of this kind; and that is, when any of the lower people happen to be reduced by sickness, losses, or misfortunes of any kind, a friend is sent to as many of their neighbours as they think needful, to invite them to what they call a *drinking*. This drinking consists in a little small beer, with a bit of bread and cheese, and sometimes a small glass of brandy or whisky, previously provided by the needy persons, or their friends. The guests convene at the time appointed, and, after collecting a shilling a-piece, and sometimes more, they divert themselves for about a couple of hours, with music and dancing, and then go home. Such as cannot attend themselves, usually send their charitable contributions by any neighbour that chooses to go. These meetings sometimes produce 5, 6 or 7 pounds to the needy person or family.
– Rev. Dr John Burgess, 'Parish of Kirkmichael', *OSAS*, vol. I, 1790, p. 59

Langholm: Of Distilleries. . . . when whisky, of all other liquors the most subversive of the health, the industry, and the morals of the people, became so cheap and so common as to supersede the drinking of beer, the good old wholesome beverage of our fathers. Religion, morality, health, and industry, are the dreadful sacrifices. . . . Tradesmen, some of whom at times have been able to earn a guinea a-week by the loom, etc instead of living comfortably with their families, and saving a little for a reverse of circumstances, have not often on Saturday night wherewithal to subsist during the ensuing Sabbath. . . . But every paltry hamlet, from Graham's Dyke to John o'Groats, is feeling, and while it is permitted, will continue to feel, its woeful effects. It has engendered that depravity, that dissipation and profligacy of manners, which, like the destroying angel, is stalking forth, and with rapid strides, dealing destruction every where around it. . . . Licentiousness, under the sacred, though prostituted, name of Liberty, fraud, robbery, murder, insanity, and suicide, every where mark its fatal progress! . . . Let the distilleries then, those contaminating fountains, from whence such poisonous streams issue, be, if not wholly, at least in a great measure, prohibited; annihilate unlicensed tippling-houses and dram-shops, those haunts of vice, those seminaries of wickedness, where the young of both sexes are early seduced from the paths of innocence and virtue, and from whence they may too often date their dreadful doom. . . . Beer is the natural and the wholesome beverage of the country. . . .

– Rev. Thomas Martin, 'Parish of Langholm', *OSAS*, vol. XIII,
pp. 603–05

A NEWSPAPER MISCELLANY

Cleaning the Streets of Dumfries
The Magistrates and Council of Dumfries have this day resolved to let the Cleaning of the Streets, and Dung arising therefrom, for One year after Candlemas next. The town at present pays six pounds yearly to the persons employed, besides furnishing besoms, and allowing them the whole profit of the Dung, which must be considerable; but as there has been much reason to complain that the streets have not been properly cleaned, they wish to enter into a new bargain with any one, two, or more persons, who will undertake the same, and engage to keep them properly clean. Any person or persons who are willing to undertake this business, may give in their proposals to the Town Chamberlain immediately.

– *DWJ*, 26th January, 1779

William Hope, Peruke-maker and Hair-dresser, at the End of the Coffee-house, Dumfries . . . proposes to sell . . . Violet Powder, Lavender Water, Hungary Ditto, Oil of Lavender, Do. of Bergamotte, Do. of Lemons, Wash Balls, Swan Puffs, Powder Boxes, Silk Puffs, Roll Pomatum, Soft Pomatum, Hair Pins, and Dressing Combs of all kinds. . . .

– *DWJ*, 28th September, 1779

A Farm to let in Annandale
To let, upon a lease for 10 or 15 years, and to be entered to at Whitsunday or Martinmas next, as shall be agreed on, the Lands of Robbiewhat, lying in the parish of Mousewald and county of Dumfries. The farm consists of near 100 acres of arable land, including eight acres of meadow, and is compleately surrounded and bounded by new march dykes and ditches, and also subdivided by new dykes, ditches, and drains, into about 16 inclosures, and the whole dykes planted with thorn hedges and trees, and gate or yett posts, for spars, placed at the entry to a number of the inclosures; all which has lately been done at considerable expence to the proprietor.

The houses on the farm are in exceeding good repair, and consist of a

Dwelling house, containing a parlour, mid-room, kitchen and garret, dairy, barn, barn-yard, byre, stable, washing-house, cart-house, hog-yard, and workman's-house (which last is to be excepted from the lease, and the possessor employed in taking care of the plantations and hedges, at the proprietor's expence).

The lands of Robbiewhat are situated very near the new turnpike road, leading betwixt Dumfries and Annan, at the distance of 8 miles from the former, and 7 from the latter; and there is a new road lately made by the proprietor, from the turnpike road into the farm. The limestone quarry at Kelhead is only 4 miles distant; and the Earl of Mansfield's limestone quarry at Clarencefield is within a mile and a half of the lands; so that great improvement may be made upon the farm, at an easy rate.

As the farm has been in the natural possession of the proprietor for two years, and considerable meliorations and improvements made by liming, etc. the tenant will have the benefit of them. Persons wishing to take a lease of the premises, are desired *instantly* to transmit their *proposals* to John Dickson, writer to the Signet, Edinburgh. N.B. The tenant may be accommodated with the Stock and Crop, and Husbandry Utensils, on the farm, at a valuation, upon his entry, otherwise they will be sold by public roup.

– *DWJ*, 10th February, 1795

Farm in the Stewartry of Kirkcudbright

To be Let for seventeen years from Whitsunday 1798, and entered to at that term, or *immediately* as to the arable Lands, as may be agreed on, the Farm of Drumcoltran, in the parish of Kirkgunzeon, situated eight miles from the town of Dumfries, and five from the port of Dalbeaty. It contains about 213 acres, and (excepting 10 acres of meadow) is nearly all arable. Fifty acres were limed *last year and this*, of which 14 (the holm) have this year been also completely dunged and fallowed. Part of the Hill is broken up, and has been lying in fallow since the summer of 1796. Twenty acres have been sown out with grass seeds, and the Holm falls to be sown out with the ensuing crop.

The proprietor is bound to rebuild and repair the march-dykes free of interest, and has so far finished them. The division dykes are in great forwardness, for executing which he is bound to allow 100L. on the tenants paying at the rate of 7½ per cent.. The tower or dwelling-house was this year repaired at a considerable expence, and will accommodate a large family. The whole of the Offices are newly built, and form a square behind the House, on a plan remarkably convenient. The soil is in general excellent – part of it, indeed, is scarcely to be equalled in this part of the country, and the whole is now in good condition. In short, a farm in such a situation, and with such advantages, at a tenant's entry, is very rarely to be met with.

The farm will be let upon a grassum, the present rent being 120L. 10s. which includes the interest for building and repairing the Houses. Apply to G. Duncan, merchant, Dumfries. The servants at Drumcoltran will shew the lands. 18th December, 1797.

– *DWJ*, 19th December, 1797

A Wind-mill to be sold

To be Sold by public roup, within the Court-house of Whithorn, upon Tuesday the twenty-ninth day of August current, the Windmill at Whithorn, with the Kiln, and spot of Ground around the same, belonging to John Davis, Miller there. The Kiln is almost new, being only built about three years ago, and has an iron head; and the Mill is in an excellent state of repair for grinding any kind of Grain, and making Shilled Barley. The subjects hold feu of the town of Whithorn, and may be seen at any time before the sale, and entered immediately. For particulars apply to the proprietor.

– *DWJ*, 15th August, 1797

Tannery, etc. to be sold

There is to be Sold by public roup, within the Coffee-house of Dumfries, on Friday the 29th day of August instant, between the hours of 3 and 4 afternoon, All and Whole the Heritable Subjects, which belonged to the deceased Wm. Wilson, late Deacon of the Skinners and Glovers in Dumfries, in two lots, as follows:

Lot I – Will consist of a Dwelling-house, consisting of two storeys, covered with slate, with an excellent cellar, garrets, back shades, a garden containing some fruit trees, and berry bushes; having a capital pump well, which yields or throws excellent water for all purposes; and Seven Tanning Pits, in very good order. And,

Lot II – Will consist of a Tan Yard and Shades, of every proper description, lately prepared and fitted up by the said William Wilson, lying on the South side of the Milnburn of Dumfries, on the opposite side of the street to Lot 1st, and contains twelve large tanning pits, six handler pits, two lime pits, three scouring pits, and a bating pit; proper back presses, and every other-thing necessary for carrying on an extensive tanner's work, properly walled about, and adorned with cherry trees of the best kind. . . .

– *DWJ*, 19th August, 1794

To Sell, or Let, for a Term of Years – Entry Immediate. That *Old Tan-Yard in Stranraer*, lately occupied by Anthony McMaster, consisting of Water Pit, Two Lime-Pits, Eleven Handlers, Twenty-two Lapping Pits, with Four Spenders, Bark Loft, Bark Mill, Drying Shed, and Two Leather Cellars, etc., etc.. And also, Conveniences for carrying on the Currying Trade, which may be let separately or together with the other premises. For a person with a moderate capital these premises prevent a temptation which does not occur often . . . apply to John Kerr, Banker; or to Anthony McMaster, here.

– GA, 25th January, 1844

Kelp Shores

To be let immediately, for cutting and working into kelp, the Sea Weed on the Shores of the estate Monrieth, extending about ten miles in the parishes of Glasserton and Mochrum. For full information apply to Mr Walker, the factor of said estate, at Airlour.

– DWJ, 2nd December, 1794

Wanted Immediately. A person who will undertake to Cut The Kelp in the Bay of Kirkcudbright. Kelp Cutters may apply to Caleb Grayson and Co., Kirkcudbright.

– DWJ, 1st August, 1797

Brewery and Water-fall. To be set, or sold, and entered to immediately, all and whole that newly-erected Distillery, or Brewery, at Stakeford, in the parish of Troqueer . . . with the Utensils, Cellars, Cattle Shades, Malt Work and Granaries thereto belonging – the whole erected within these three years, upon an extensive plan, and at present in complete repair. Also, a Mill calculated for grinding malt, barley, or oats, having a fall of 32 feet of water, well supplied. The premises are situated within a quarter of a mile of the town of Dumfries, in a country abundantly supplied with grain, fuel, etc. and where labourers can be had in plenty, at very moderate wages. It is worthy of notice, that there are no manufactories within thirty miles of the premises; and that the supply of water to the above Mill, is not only sufficient for the purposes of a Brewery, but for a Cotton, or other work. . . . apply to William Hyslop, baker in Dumfries, who will shew the works, and inform as to particulars.

– DWJ, 10th October, 1797

Flax-Dressing, Kirkcudbright. Alexander Gordon begs leave to intimate that he has commenced the manufacture of Flax in Kirkcudbright; and has on hand a quantity of excellent Dutch and White Lint, which he is now selling wholesale and retail. A. Gordon begs leave to add, that he continues to carry on the Stationary Business as Bookseller and Binder. . . . Schoolmasters and Country Shopkeepers supplied on his usual moderate terms.

– DWJ, 10th October, 1797

Shirmers Flax Mill to let . . . at Whitsunday next. The Flax Mill of Shirmers, in the parish of Balmaclellan . . . with a Dwelling-house, and Ten Acres of Land adjoining, and well inclosed. The Mill is intirely new, has a fine command of water, and will have a large share of business – none being nearer than fifteen miles. . . . Apply to Mr John Hutton in Shirmers.

– DWJ, 12th March, 1805

To be let . . . the *Flax Miln at Maryfield*, in the vicinity of the village of New Abbey . . . also the Miln Croft with the houses therein. The above miln was built within these few years, its machinery of the most approved construction, and in good repair; and being situated in a populous neighbourhood, where a considerable quantity of flax is usually produced, an attentive and industrious tacksman cannot fail to meet with suitable encouragement. . . . to Thomas Golding, Commissary, or Robert Threshie, writer, Dumfries.

- DWJ, 9th February, 1802

Wanton depradations. The Stranraer Agricultural Society, supported by the Noblemen and Gentlemen of the Landed Interest of the Upper District of the County of Wigton, taking under their serious consideration the great discouragement given to the improvements of the District, by the wanton depradations of the public, committed on Turnips, Pease, and Beans and other improving articles of husbandry, and by the breaking down of Hedges and Fences on the Roads and Highways leading thereto, have entered into an Association to prosecute, to the *utmost rigour of law*, all and every person who may be found leaping over Hedges or Fences, or pulling up Turnips, Pease, Beans, or other improving articles of husbandry, without consent of the Owner, in any Field, Garden, or Croft, within this District. . . . the Society above alluded to hereby offer a Reward of Two Guineas, to any person giving such information to their Secretary, as may lead to a discovery of those guilty of these mean and abominable practices. . . . And they accordingly order this Advertisement to be published in the *Edinburgh Advertiser* and *Dumfries Journal*; and printed Copies hereof to be affixed to the market Cross of Stranraer, and to the several Parish Church Doors within this District.

– *DWJ*, 22nd October, 1799

7

LONG GONE AND FAR AWAY

JAMAICA, NOVA SCOTIA, OLD CALIFORNIA, VIRGINIA CITY, AUSTRALIA AND THE NEW HEBRIDES

✝

The great majority of those who left southern Scotland, including Dumfries and Galloway, to live in the West Indies, North America and Australia, went there by choice. This includes even many of the felons charged with theft, assault, forgery, child murder, who petitioned the Circuit Court in Dumfries for banishment to the plantations and colonies as indentured servants. Some were sentenced to serve for a fixed period, frequently seven years; some were banished from Scotland for life. A random list might include James Hownam, the son of Andrew Hownam, a weaver in Langholm, banished for life in 1750 for riot and assault; William Nicholson in Dyke in Dalton parish transported for seven years in 1754 for stealing a horse; Agnes Walker from Crossmichael parish sentenced in Kirkcudbright in 1762 for child murder and transported to the plantations (a certificate issued in Fort George in the City of New York in 1765 confirmed her arrival there); Janet Hepburn, spouse to Alexander Walker, chaise-driver in Dumfries, banished on petition for life for fire-raising in 1767; George Willis given seven years in 1786 for picking the pocket of John Armstrong, a farmer in Hoddom-toun, at the Ecclefechan fair; and John Wilson, lithographic printer, and John Stewart, twister, given seven years' transportation to Australia in 1843 for breaking into Cuil farm (Mrs McKie) in Kirkmabreck parish and Mrs Nicholson's shop in Newton Stewart. Some paupers were given assisted places on ships going out to the colonies, for example the Parochial Board of Anwoth agreed in 1858 to allocate £6 for an outfit for William Milligan, a boy in Kirkcudbright Poor House, in response to an offer from Robert Gordon in Kirkcudbright to procure a situation for him on board the Alive *bound for Australia.*

The letters, journals and notes from the Caribbean, North America, Australia and the Pacific tend to reaffirm traditional images and stereotypes of the achievements of Scots overseas – the clannishness and retention of ethnic identity in Caledonian Societies and the 'Wild Scots of

Galloway', and the sheer cussedness of retaining the rigid barriers between varieties of Presbyterianism; the respect for success defined by property and savings in the bank; the energy and durability of men and women made to last, as J.K. Galbraith put it, whether in crossing the Great Plains or at the diggings or mines in two continents; the contrast between the good intentions of missionaries and the decimation or extermination of 'aboriginal' peoples; and the memories retained of birthplace, of 'native glens' and mountains, or, as Alistair Reid has it, 'my personal Eden'.

CARIBBEAN CONNECTIONS

In the eighteenth and early nineteenth centuries the West Indies were a magnet for young men from Dumfries and Galloway looking for adventure and for opportunities to make their fortunes. There were many vacancies for craftsmen, carpenters, coopers, wheelwrights and surgeons, and for men, farmers' sons, lairds' sons, willing to start as clerks and overseers. Liverpool, of course, as a major port in the British slave trade, was a way out to the West Indies from south-west Scotland, whether on merchant ships or slave traders. There were many useful family and business links between Dumfries and Galloway and Liverpool, where Messrs Twemlow and McDowal were among the largest owners and investors in shipping. Between 1786 and 1806 Samuel McDowal invested in 79 vessels (14,550 tons) and Thomas Twemlow in 71 vessels (13,311 tons). Samuel Robinson (1786–1875) from Kirkinner, sailed, aged 13, in 1800 from Liverpool on the Lady Nelson *(licensed to carry 294 slaves) for the West African slave emporiums and hence to Demerara. His mother's cousin was a member of Twemlow and McDowal, and her brother, Captain Cowan, was the master of a Liverpool merchant ship engaged in the slave trade. The* Lady Nelson's *crew included Thomas Hannah from Wigtown and John Clark from Castle Douglas.*

A number of Dumfries and Galloway men became plantation owners, for example, Samuel Douglas in Jamaica and Thomas Rainy in Dominica (see Chapter 8), William Dunns from Arbrack near Whithorn in Grenada, the McDowalls of Garthland in St Kitts, Niven McKenzie from Cairnryan in St Vincent, and Robert and James McKie in Antigua. Some retired to Scotland and brought a slave page boy or servant back with them. The Visit of the Patron and Patroness to the Village School *(Dundee Art Gallery), a wonderfully organised genre painting by Thomas Faed (1825–1900) from Gatehouse-of-Fleet, has a black page boy gazing at the some fifteen small children 'controlled' by the artist, but clearly not by the middle-aged schoolmaster; and a portrait of one of the eighteenth-century Maxwells of Monreith also has a 12–14-year-old black page boy (Untold: Britain's Slave Trade, Channel 4 Television, 24th October, 1999).*

The account by James Murray McCulloch of Ardwall (1769–1857) is a useful record of some of the hazards of the Caribbean experience. He was fortunate to encounter Dr James Nasmyth from Kirkcudbright, a friend of Smollett, and a man whose experiences in the Mediterranean, India, China and Canada, and as a doctor and planter in Jamaica, is almost a mini-history of the British Empire in the middle of the eighteenth century.

✝

Wanted to go to Jamaica, A Young Man bred a House Carpenter, and who understands the business of a Wheelwright . . . to engage for a short term of years . . . applying to Mr Stothart of Cargen, or Thomas Stothart, writer in Dumfries. . . .

– DWJ, 22nd December, 1789

To Farmers Sons etc. Wanted for a Cattle Farm, in the Island of Jamaica, A Young Man of a good character, who understands perfectly the breeding and fattening of Black Cattle, spaying of Heifers, etc. An adequate salary will be given to one who can be well recommended, particularly from Galloway. Apply to Mr Thomas Williamson, writer in Dumfries and Mr Gilbert Laing, merchant in Edinburgh.

– DWJ, 7th November, 1797

Wanted immediately, Two Young Men to go out to the island of Granada, to be employed as Overseers and Clerks upon a very healthy Estate there. . . If they understand farming, they will be more acceptable. . . . Apply to Mrs Johnstone, near the Kings-Arms Dumfries.

– DWJ, 14th November 1797

Died . . . 3rd September of fever, in St Kitts, Mr John Mundell, surgeon, in his 24th year. . .

– DWJ, 19th December, 1797

A Bond of Freedom: Wigtown, 13th February, 1772

. . . In presence of Thomas Dundas, Esq. Advocate Sheriff Depute of Wigtown Compeared David Anderson Writer in Wigtown as pror. for the Black man named Jacky formerly belonging to Charles Warner Dunbar Esq. of Machermore and gave in the Bond of Freedom. . . .

Machermore 14th June 1771. Know all men by these presents that I Charles Warner Dunbar of Machermore in the Stewartry of Kirkcudbright in the County of Galloway North Britain have hereby voluntarily discharged the Black man, Jacky, from the Bonds of Slavery, in consideration of his services during Twenty years, and I do hereby renounce all Claim, right, Title and property in and to the said Man named Jacky.... the forementioned person Jacky has full power and authority in himself to enter into the Service of any Gentleman in Great Britain or elsewhere, as his Inclination or Interest may direct him....

– The Gallovidian Annual, 1939, p.105

Whereas a black servant called Thomas (the real property of Robert Riddick of Corbitoun) has of late behaved in so licentious and turbulent a manner, that other servants were afraid to live in the house with him; on which account his master was obliged, on Friday night last, to shut him out to the company of his worthless companions; since which time, he has not made any offers of returning to his duty. The other Gentlemans' servants in his situation may not have encouragement to behave as he has done; it is hoped and requested that no person in this county will give him employment, or harbour him about their house.

– DWM, 4th April, 1775, back cover.

Leswalt, Wigtownshire, Population c. 1790

... The present population of the parish, from an accurate survey lately made, amounts to 1194 souls. Of this number there may be about 150 Irish, three English, and one Mulatto. These are in general either hired servants or labourers....

– Rev. John Rose, 'Parish of Leswalt', OSAS, vol. III, p. 321.

James McCulloch of Ardwall: A Voyage to the West Indies in 1786

Not considering myself as perfectly qualified to discharge my duty as fourth mate of an East Indiaman, I resolved to employ my time in making a voyage to the West Indies and that too, in doing my duty before the mast. My friend Thomas Gordon, Esq. of Balmaghie, a very eminent Madeira merchant, recommended me to Captain Cleveland, who commanded the *Caroline*, bound on a voyage to Madeira, Port Antonio, Annotta Bay, and Port Maria in the island of Jamaica. I went on board of the ship in November 1785; we sailed in the beginning of 1786 ... we were ... above a month on our passage to Madeira.

We laid for three weeks in Funchal Roads and sailed again early in March; made the Canary Islands, and took a fresh departure from the

Peak of Teneriffe; crossed the Atlantic with a fresh N.E. trade wind and made the island of Antigua; we ran through the passage betwixt Antigua and Montserat, seeing as we sailed along the smaller islands of Nevis and Deseada; we made the coast of Hispaniola; then the east end of Jamaica, and anchored in Port Antonio about the beginning of April, 1786, having been about three months from England.

We took in some part of our cargo, consisting of rum and sugar, at Port Antonio, some part of Annotta Bay, and the remainder at Port Maria; we sailed again from Jamaica on the 25th of July, came round the west end of the island of Cuba, through the Gulf of Florida, recrossed the Atlantic, and arrived in the Thames about the end of September 1786.

I then left the ship, returned to Mr Laidlaw's family, and attended Mr Dunn and Hamilton Moore in order to improve myself in navigation and practical astronomy.

When I went on board the *Caroline* . . . I had letters from my friend Mr Gordon to his partners, Mr Johnston and Mr Murdoch, in Madeira; while the ship remained there I lived on shore in their hospitable house, and in this charming island I spent three of the happiest weeks of my early life. When I left Mr Johnston, he gave me a letter to Dr Js. Nasmyth in Jamaica. My friend Mr Gordon had already done so. On Board after leaving such kind friends I found a sea-stock of wine, fresh provisions and fruit, sent on board by these gentlemen for my use. . . .

Mr Johnston sent, under my care, some slips of the Madeira wine to his friend Dr Nasmyth, and I was allowed to go and deliver them by a Bristol ship going to Annotta Bay. Dr Nasmyth's estate of Watervalley being in that neighbourhood, I delivered the vines . . . and my two letters and was very kindly received. . . .

It was then usual for the Jamaica ships to collect their cargoes from the different plantations. This was done by a sloop-rigged long boat, large enough to carry eight or nine hogsheads of sugar. . . . on one occasion I was sent to a place called Buchaness Bay to the westward and leeward of Port Maria. As no cargo was ready for us, we had to wait there some days. I then had been exposed to a burning sun during the day, and to sleep under a heavy dew during the night. . . . My pulse rose and I became very sick. . . . in a high fever and drenched with rain, I desired my two comrades to bare away for Port Maria to endeavour to get sick quarters . . . they were at last told that the wife of an American pilot lodged sick sailors. . . . on her being assured that I had a great many clothes, nine or ten guineas in money, besides a hogshead of Madeira wine as an adventure, and that I would be well looked after, being somewhat better than a common sailor, they were told that I might be brought on shore.

... Having been seated in an arm chair in the sitting apartment of the pilot's house, in a very weakly state, with a slight degree of delirium, I saw the corpse carried out of the apartment of which I was destined to be the succeeding tenant. . . .

Next day a medical gentleman of the name of McEwen called and saw me. He said I was very ill and prescribed some medicine. When he was about to leave me, he asked my name? I said, Sir, my name is James McCulloch. He then asked if I was from Scotland. I said, I was so. He then said yours is a common name in Galloway where I am from, and asked if I came from Galloway. I told him I did so. He asked me who my father was? I said, Sir, I am the son of the present Mr McCulloch of Ardwall. He seemed surprised and asked how I came to be in such a place and in so low a condition. I then told him my history, which seemed to satisfy him. . . . He recommended me strongly to the great care of my landlady and confirmed what my two shipmates had previously told her. . . . Dr Nasmyth, having heard of my illness, sent a servant . . . requesting Dr McEwen to attend me and to inform him whenever I might be in a state to remove to Watervalley.

With that good constitution with which Providence had blessed me, together with the care bestowed on me by my landlady, my medical attendant, and others, I was ready to go to Watervalley in three weeks, at which time a servant and horses were sent for me; but my fever became an intermittent, and I remained under the care of Dr Nasmyth until the *Caroline* sailed. . . .

Some account of the life of Doctor James Nasmyth . . . a friend and benefactor . . . James Nasmyth was born in Kirkcudbright about the year 1700. His father was of the profession of the law and of high respectability. James, after receiving a good education, was bred to the medical profession. He left his relations and the place of his nativity in very early life, like so many of his young countrymen, to push his fortune in foreign parts.

I believe his career began by entering the service of the Old Turkey Company. In this he made several voyages and in the course of that time had many opportunities of visiting the countries and lands in the Mediterranean and Levant. . . . When war broke out with Spain in the year 1739, he entered the naval service of his country and was present in the year 1741 at the memorable but unfortunate siege of Carthagena. He also served in Lord Anson's fleet on the 3d of May 1747, when he defeated the French in the Bay of Biscay.

After the peace of Aix-la-Chappelle, he entered the service of the East India Company and made several voyages to India and China. He returned to the navy on the breaking out of the war in 1756. In the year 1759 he served under Admiral Saunders at the siege of Quebec, when the renowed General Wolfe so gallantly fell on the heights of Abraham. He was on the most intimate terms with the celebrated Doctor Smollett, and was well known to have been the person alluded to in drawing the character of Thomson in his popular work of *Roderick Random*. Some say Beau Jackson, but this is a mistake.

After so many adventures he became desirous of settling in London as a medical practitioner, but in this he did not succeed. He then took out his medical degree, went to Kingston, in Jamaica, and there his success as a practitioner was great, almost beyond any example. At Kingston he married a lady of great fortune and purchased the fine estate of Watervalley in the parish of St Mary's. He lost his wife without her having born children. . . . he settled there, built an elegant house on his fine estate of Watervalley, lived many days . . . and died greatly lamented at the advanced age of nearly ninety years.

Dr Nasmyth, at the outset in life, had the advantage of a liberal education. He possessed an inquisitive turn of mind, with great powers of observation; he had read a great deal, and hardly had ever any man seen so much of the world. He was unobstrusive with the narrative of his own adventures, but, when induced to enter on it, he was eloquent and attractive without affectation and accurate without prolixity. Hence he was an instructive and very entertaining companion. In his manners he was perfectly the gentleman of the old school. In his stature he was tall and in his youth he had been handsome, which left a dignified and venerable mien in his advanced years. His temper mild and steady, his disposition was benevolence itself. He was a generous protector of his own kindred, a zealous and sincere friend, a kind acquaintance, and an indulgent and humane master. . . . .

– *The Castle-Douglas Weekly Visitor*, vol. II, 10th June, 1831

LETTERS FROM MUSQUODOBOIT, NOVA SCOTIA

The earliest, and surprising, link between the south-west of Scotland and Nova Scotia was the plan (never implemented) put forward between 1621 and 1625 by Sir Robert Gordon of Lochinvar to establish a Scottish colony on Cape Breton. His proposals, published in Edinburgh in 1625, as 'Encouragements, For such as shall have intention to bee Under-takers in the new plantation of Cape Briton, now New Galloway, in America', were directed at the bonnet lairds and the younger sons of country gentlemen. Lochinivar was offering to them new opportunities for the 'private and particular gaine' which, he suggested, would be theirs lawfully and easily for the taking in this 'New Galloway'. He did not fail either to point out that it was their duty as Christians to propagate the Gospel and as patriots to gain 'a Kingdom' where they could plant and build 'a foundation for... posteritie'. This New Galloway would also provide employment for the excess numbers of soldiers, mechanics and beggars who traditionally adventured across the North Sea to the Netherlands, Germany and Poland. As a plan it was much more possible and practical than the later absurd Darien Scheme or, indeed, Lochinvar's other idea of a colony placed on an island off the coast of Brazil.

A steady and profitable trade in timber from New Brunswick, Nova Scotia and Prince Edward Island and in trade goods (oatmeal, salt hams, textiles) and people (carpenters, shipbuilders, seamen, entrepreneurs) from Scotland had developed during the later eighteenth century. After the end of the Napoleonic Wars there was an unprecedented exodus from Dumfries Port, Annan, the Water of Urr, and Kirkcudbright to New Brunswick and Nova Scotia, with a peak between 1816 and 1818. The Dumfries and Galloway Courier *(10 June, 1817) noted that 547 emigrants had left 'this season' from Dumfries Port alone and another 100 had gone from Annan. Thomson's Dumfries Port based fleet included the* Jessie, *the* Nile *(180 tons), the* Queen Charlotte *(150 tons), and* Thomson's Packet. *Some shipping advertisements included attractive-sounding offers of land for sale. A letter in the* Courier *(10 June, 1817) attacked a dissenting clergyman in Lockerbie for encouraging emigration to America where he had been offered a meeting-house; a blacksmith from Dumfries-shire, who had gone to the Bay of Fundy in Nova Scotia c. 1805–07 and had sent back misleading reports of his instant prosperity as a 1,000-acre Nova Scotian laird, although he had been unable to send any remittances home to his aged mother; and a Mr Campbell, who went out to Pictou in 1815 and sent back such 'flaming accounts' of his success that two vessels sailed from Maryport filled with people from his neighbourhood. The* Courier *shipping reports for 9th June, 1817 listed, as having cleared Dumfries Port, the* Nancy *with 149 passengers for St John's, New Brunswick, the* Success *with 37 for Miramichi, and the* Queen Charlotte *with 27 for St John's.* Thomson's Packet *sailed in late May, 1818 with 186 passengers for St John's.*

The Rev. John Sprott (1780–1869), the author of the letters from the Manse of Musquodoboit, was part of the 1818 exodus, sailing on the Nile *from Kirkcudbright for New Brunswick and hence over to Nova Scotia (the sea was always better than the land route). He was born on 3rd*

February, 1780 at Caldons Park in Stoneykirk parish, which is south of Stranraer. His letters, many written forty, fifty, sixty and seventy years later, describe the farmhouse in which his father, James Sprott, and his mother, Margaret Hannay, brought up their family, and his schooldays in Stoneykirk and in Stranraer. Although brought up in the Church Of Scotland, he was also immersed in the Coventanting traditions of Galloway and was well aware of the continuing work of the Reformed Presbyterian congregations in Newton Stewart under the Rev. James Reid (between 1783 and 1828) and in Stranraer. Their congregations in Stoneykirk and Stranraer were merged in 1796, but the new Stranraer congregation split between 1800 and 1804 into Smeatonites and McMillanites. After four years at the University of Edinburgh he attended the Reformed Presbyterian Divinity Hall, also for four years, and was licensed in the RP Church in 1809. Although twice called to the Water of Urr near Castle Douglas, on each occasion the proposal fell through after internal disputes in the congregation (a not infrequent problem in the RP Church). He joined the Relief Church in 1815, and in 1818 was accepted by the Presbyterian Church of Nova Scotia as a missionary. After years as an itinerant missionary and as pastor for Windsor, Newport and Rawdon, he moved to Musquodoboit, some forty miles east of Halifax, in 1825 and remained there – for twenty-eight years as their minister, and then, while still active, throughout Nova Scotia as a visiting preacher until 1867. He died on 16th September, 1869 in the 90th year of his age.

His contemporaries included Charles James Stewart (1775–1837), the son of the 7th Earl of Galloway and the brother of General Sir William Stewart. Much respected by Sprott, Stewart graduated BA, MA, BD, and DD from Oxford and worked for a number of years as the rector of Orton in Huntingdonshire. In 1807 he went out to Canada as a missionary for the Society for the Propagation of the Gospel, based at Saint Armand and Misisquoi Bay, and then at Hatley with a responsibility for visiting mission stations in remote parts of Quebec. He took up the post of Bishop of Quebec in January 1826 in charge of work in Upper and Lower Canada. He died in London in 1837 on a visit home to Britain.

John Sprott's brother James, who was also in Nova Scotia, took a farm at Windsor in March 1822 and married Lamira Smith from Newport. He died in 1837 leaving his widow and seven children. John had more than his own share of grief to bear. He married Sarah Clarke from Windsor in October 1821. A Donegal girl with 'an Irish heart, a Scottish head, and English hands', she died in childbirth in April 1823. He married his second wife, Charlotte Leslie from Shelburne, 'a sprig of Caledonia' from a

Perthshire family, in June 1824. She died in July 1825.

In 1826 John came back home on Thomson's Packet, *leaving Halifax on 9th June and reaching Wigtown on 9th July. He returned to Musquodoboit on the 29th of August on the* Margaret Pollock *(900 tons), reaching New Brunswick on 13th October and then taking the* Relief of Truro *over to Nova Scotia. He had with him his third wife, Jane Neilson, a young widow whose sister Agnes was married to his friend John McCaig of Kilhilt. She died in April 1873. They had two daughters, Jane and Elizabeth, and three sons, Charles, who inherited his father's land at Musquodoboit, John, who studied medicine in Edinburgh, and the eldest, George (1829–1909), who was sent over to study for the ministry at the Univeristy of Glasgow. Graduating in 1849 he became the Rev. George W. Sprott and went on to a distinguished career in Kandy in Ceylon and as a parish minister in the Chapel of Garioch and at North Berwick.*

John Sprott, as he often said, crossed the Atlantic seven times, in 1818, in 1826, in 1834, and in 1844. The second last was the best crossing, leaving Halifax on the Hibernian *on the 3rd, catching the* Harrington *from Liverpool to Kirkcudbright on the 15th, and reaching Stoneykirk on the 18th of January.*

A man of two worlds, Sprott had in abundance that enormous energy and physical stamina that was needed to cope with years of travel through the harsh terrain and during the hard winters of his adopted land. His journeys became legendary. 'His horse had been in almost every station in the province.' 'He trod the wilderness with a firm step and a light heart.' And in the 1820s and 1830s journeys to Windsor, the Bay of Fundy, Digby: to Lunenburg, Liverpool, Shelburne, Barrington: to Truro, Pictou, Tatamagouche: and to Sheet Harbour and Sherbrook: and indeed through his own enormous 'parish', involved, as his letters show, real hardship and exposure to danger. As a Nova Scotia pastor he built his house at Musquodoboit, drained swampland and cleared forty acres of hill land. He enjoyed travel, visiting the United States, Maine, Massachusetts, Boston, New York, and Chicago, where his nephew Archie Sprott from Windsor, was living, in 1850; and Newfoundland in 1854. He had been well prepared for 'the battle of life'. Year after year he had walked from Stoneykirk to Edinburgh, and back, when attending the Univeristy and Divinity Hall.

His letters were addressed to a vast range of correspondents, to the Rev. John Inglis in the New Hebrides; his brother William in Stoneykirk; his father-in-law, Charles Neilson; John McCaig, Kilhilt and his son, also John McCaig, Barnultoch; Archdeacon Willis of St Paul's in Halifax; Mr McKinnon, a student in Edinburgh; Mrs McClymont in Corkfeckloch,

*Minnigaff parish (both she and her husband were cousins of Jane Neilson);
more letters were forwarded to newspapers in Nova Scotia and Scotland,* The
Halifax Citizen, The Colonial Standard, The Scottish Presbyterian, The
Galloway Register, The Kirkcudbrightshire Advertiser, The Galloway
Advertiser and Wigtownshire Free Press. *The 'Stranraer Free Press' in return
reached Musquodoboit, the banks of the Mohawk, and Kandy. The Rev.
G.W. Sprott brought together some extracts from his letters, journals, diaries,
sermons and addresses in his* Memorials of the Rev. John Sprott *(1906).*

  *His letters bring us to a man who was pious and devout, impatient,
plain-speaking, tough, a temperance total abstinence enthusiast,
interested in everything – schools, churches, sawmills, farming, commerce,
customs and traditions, the 'MicMac' Indians, changes and improvements
in Nova Scotia and in Galloway. Welcoming controversy, he was an
experienced writer, giving to using telling phrases in different contexts, for
example his 'flies dancing in windows' in Newfoundland and in
Galloway. He had a fine sense of humour and a smooth, graceful, 'almost
musical' style. 'His sentences would almost sing themselves off the reader's
tongue' (obituary notice in* The Presbyterian Witness). *'Some of his best
friends were Episcopalians.' And there are unexpected delights, not least
discovering him playing* shinty *in Stoneykirk in the 1780s!*

✝

Letter to the family of John McCaig, Kilhilt, 12th June, 1849

I have travelled a great deal, and, owing to the watchful care of Providence,
I have not met with a scratch of a finger. I have slept securely surrounded
by a camp of Indians with their long knives and guns. I have frequently
met the bear in the green woods. I was lately followed by a pack of hungry
wolves so anxious to get my dog that they chased him below the horse's
feet, yet they offered no violence to me. I have crossed many seas, and the
Atlantic seven times. I have seen the ocean heaved from its bed, and the
ship staggering and plunging so that nothing but the most dexterous
management of the helm could preserve her buoyancy. . . .

– *GA,* 13th July, 1849

January 1851. I have crossed the Atlantic seven times . . . travelled by
land and water 80,000 miles since I left my father's house. I have preached
the Gospel in the crowded schoolhouse in the backwoods and the
splendid church, or the quarter-deck on the high seas, and in the open air,
under a cloudless sky, in the green glens of Galloway.

– *Memorials of John Sprott,* p. 123

25 July, 1851. When I first visited Tatamagouchhe, thirty years ago, I crossed the French river, where the noble bridge now stands, on a cake of floating ice for want of a canoe.... James McNab will remember Pugwash when it had only three huts. It is now a rising village with splendid buildings and more than 1000 people.

– Memorials, pp. 126–27

Address at the Jubilee of the Rev. Mr. Brown (1795–1845)

When ... the country was a wilderness ... it took ... several days for a man and horse to go to Halifax, with a tomahawk attached to the saddle to free the horse's feet from the roots of the trees ... gigs and waggons ... then unknown, and the best farmers rode to church on horseback with their wives behind them and their children in their arms....

– Memorials, pp. 72–73

18 April, 1845. From the moment I set my foot on the new world, I entered on the rugged road of privation, self-denial, and labour. The ministry here is not a sinecure, or an affair of gentility; it is a post of high responsibility, severe duty, and slender reward. We preach often, have long rides, deep roads, and sometimes bitter cold nights.... Our meetings were like green spots in the wilderness, and, though surrounded by dreary wastes, shall be remembered when the sunshine of other landscapes has faded from the mind. When your ministers go from home, they have railroads, steamboats, and all the appliances of modern art. When the snow becomes too deep for us, we must dismount from our horses, and carry our portmanteaus on our shoulders, and are sometimes glad to reach the 'glittering haunts' of men, thought the stars stream through the crevices of the log-hut, and the snow drifts over our head....

– GA, 18th September, 1845

1845. Some of the old people remember when the moose were as plentiful on the river as black cattle, and Francis Cape, the Indian hunter, has been seen go down the river with a hundred moose skins in his canoe.... I have rode to church on an ox shed .... The first goose bonnet in the church belonged to an English woman. It was a leghorn bonnet, which stood high like a Scottish church and attracted all eyes. ... We had three poor school-houses like hog pens. ... now there are fifteen schoolhouses on the river, shingle palaces finely painted....

– Memorials, pp. 210–11

Progress in Nova Scotia 25 December, 1860. Forty years back...
schoolhouses were log hovels...schoolmasters often old soldiers or
broken-down sailors who ... boarded with their employers, petted their
children, took snuff with the old women, and did little jobs for them
which their careless husbands neglected...going the round of the
neighbourhood with all his chattels in a cotton handkerchief, his
garments fluttering and begging in the wind...now teachers are well
qualified and paid...there is a network of schoolhouses with books,
map and globes....

– Memorials, pp. 168–69

Jubliee at Londonderry, 30 July, 1845. Long rows of carriages moved on,
crowded with people, like the deck of a steamboat. I counted twenty-five
carriages in one of these rows...in all they must have amounted to
hundreds.

– Memorials, pp. 67

Account of a Mission to Shelburne, August 1846. To assist a young brother
officer at the communion....more than 200 miles through a rough
country....The land along the southern shore...has many rising
villages, and many happy homes....You might travel a whole day
without meeting a single traveller.... The landscape is tranquil, nothing
to be heard but the woodpecker, with a bill like a carpenter's mallet,
hammering a decayed tree, the saw mills, or the sound of a huntsman's
horn....I saw several well frequented taverns completely in
ruins.... The dark forests between Windsor and Chester are beginning
to be opened, and some settlers have made a clearing; but when I travelled
that road 27 years ago there was 20 miles without a house.... Lunenburg
is rich in cultivation – a people laborious, frugal and cheerful. The
Germans were blowing up the rocks and planting cabbage.... They have
a little money and know how to take care of it; none can surpass their
women for managing a boat or dressing a field of potatoes....

New Dublin is a beautiful township. The splendour and neatness of the
buildings at Mill Village must surprise every traveller.... I learned that it
was chiefly owned by working people.... It has 20 sawmills and carries
on a prosperous trade with the West Indies. The handsome town of
Liverpool is built on both sides of the river Mersey on rocks; and the
clearing of one garden has been known to cost £500. It has 47 sawmills,
and 27,000 logs has been known to be in the stream at one time.... It has
3 ships, 20 brigs, and 40 schooners; a prosperous trade to the West Indies;
and seven places of worship handsomely finished.

It is twenty years since I was at Shelburne and the place is greatly improved. ... every morning at 5 o'clock I could hear the sound of the copper and carpenter's hammer. Twenty years ago whole streets were deserted ... but now ... they have five or six vessels which trade regularly to the West Indies, and many coasters. Three vessels are on the stocks.... Ragged Island is 20 miles to the east of Shelburne.... It is thickly studded with fine houses and stores ... has 5 vessels which trade regularly to the West Indies; has 30 fishing vessels, and has been known in one year to ship 24,000 quintal of fish for the West Indies. ...

– *GA*, 20th August, 1846

Pictou County and New Glasgow. August 1847

Ship building and the coal trade bring an immense treasure to Pictou ... New Glasgow, with its rich meadows, fine buildings, railroad trains, and the forest of shipping in the harbour ... when I first visited Glasgow forty years ago there were only five small shallops at the Broomielaw, but here I could count sixty vessels.... I spent the Sabbath at the West River and preached at Milford Bridge for the Rev. James Ross.... The church is seated for 800 and it was filled.... I met a few old acquaintances, who had not seen me since they heard me preach in times long gone by among the green hills of Galloway; for Scottish men are as numerous abroad as they are at home, and you meet with them in all parts of the world, and they are so clannish that Divine truth has double its sweetness when they hear it from one of their own countrymen. At the church door I met with a numerous staff of grey-haired elders keeping guard over the treasury, and from their deep and reflecting foreheads I concluded they could be nothing but Calvinists of the first water.... There are 14 or 15 congregations on this side of Mount Tom, who all sing the same psalms, offer up the same prayers, and preach the same doctrine, and to all appearances are the same people; yet the unnatural distinctions of Kirkmen, Seceders, and Free Church form an enchanted line which they cannot pass, and keeps them pure. It is doing them no injustice that those unholy contentions have wasted their tabernacles, lessened them in the esteem of their friends, and exposed them to the censure of their enemies. ...

– *GA*, 23rd September, 1847

Visit to Newfoundland, 1854

On the first of November the stocks of oats were standing in the fields, the Irish girls were digging the potatoes, the sheep nibbling in the meadows, and the flies dancing in the windows. ...

– *Memorials*, p. 142

The Indians

2nd October, 1846. Formerly the Indians abounded on the river Musquodoboit, but there is a sad uncertainty in the human lot – 70 years ago they were the sole occupants of the soil where our buildings and orchards now stand – now they are strangers in the land of their fathers. . . . reduced to a few beggarly chiefs, who hang on the skirts of our settlements and derive a precarious living by hunting, fishing and basket-making. . . . The American Government is now driving the Indians beyond the Rocky Mountains; and they are making the same complaints which the natives in New Zealand and the Caffres in Africa made against the enroachments of the British Government. The Aborigines have been peeled and robbed in the east and west. We all know what has been the influence of the intercourse of the Europeans with the Indians. Where he found them poor, he left them poorer, where he found an evil passion, he planted many. . . . and when it raged against him, he commenced the work of extermination. The settlement of the whites in America is with few exceptions a foul blot on Christendom. . . .

– *GA*, 29th October, 1846

20 March, 1849. Towns and villages rise on their camp ground, and the graves of their forefathers are torn up with the ploughshare. Small-pox and measles have entered their dwellings and are scattering the cold damps of death over their families; and the once powerful tribes of the Micmacs in Nova Scotia are reduced to about 1500. . .

– *GA*, 4 May, 1849

30th December, 1845. They cannot live when the wild animals are frightened away and their hunting grounds are destroyed. . . . Now we seldom see a moose or an Indian. They . . . are still too independent to beg, unless they are hungry. In general appearance and habits they would remind you of the Scottish gipsies, but their principles are better and dispositions are milder. An Indian would not curse and swear like a gipsy. He has not a word in his language which corresponds to profane swearing. Neither would he steal your poultry or your hams. I have known a hundred of them encamp for a whole week very near to our house, without doing us the smallest harm.

Isidore, the chief of Musquodoboit, died lately, and his ten sons had all crossed the dark lake and gone to the pleasant mountains before him. This venerable old hemlock, through whose branches the storms of ninety years had whistled, often visited me, kissed my hand, and called me his father. . . . he still claimed the sovereignty of the soil, for the land of Musquodoboit, he said, belonged to him and we were all intruders. I visited his camp a few minutes after his son died. They were all on their knees, engaged in prayer and praise. . . . They are all Roman Catholics and so highly devotional in their way that their little boys will not touch a meal of victuals without first making the sign of the cross. They would not hunt on the Sabbath, unless they were hungry. . . . I have often in my long journeys met with strolling parties of redskins, with their long knives and fire-arms in their hands, but never felt the least apprehensive of danger. If I missed my way I would seek no better guide than an Indian. I could sleep in their camps as soundly as I could do in your house. . . .

– Memorials, pp. 80–82

Letter to Mr McKinnon, a student in Edinburgh, on a preaching excursion in 1856 to the Bay of Fundy – a visit to an Indian camp. The squaw was at the door of the wigwam to give me a hearty welcome, the papooses were waiting for a biscuit from my wallet, the dogs were wagging their tails for a crust of bread, and the rooster, like a Mormon gentleman with his wives, was ready to collect his tithe from the horse's feed of oats. . . .

– Memorials, p. 148

From Dumfries and Galloway to America

January 1847. Thirty years ago emigration to America was all in fashion in Galloway. It resembled the slave trade. The Thomsons of Dumfries owned a little fleet of timber vessels, which were all employed in carrying passengers to America. A splendour was thrown around the undertaking which concealed the difficulties of the case. Flaming accounts were published of the beauty and fertility of the new world, and of the happy lot of the new settlers. The ships were decorated with flags and adorned with music, while people rushed on board as thoughtlessly as they would go to a county fair. I recollect that Captain MacDowall of Kirkmaiden, Peter Hanna of Caldons, Archibald Stevenston of Freugh, and myself often spent whole evenings in talking over our hopes and prospects in America. We believed that as soon as we landed we would cast off the evils of the old world and acquire wealth and independence. It was all a dream! These men met with broken hearts and an early grave, and their friends who have survived them have not made fortunes. It is a good country for a poor man, but no country for a gentleman. It is the land of universal labour . . . If a farmer wishes to live by farming he must rise by 5 o'clock in the morning and his spouse must rise at the same early hour to milk the cows. The cooper and the carpenter must be at work at the same hour. The Squire must feed his pigs and drive his own team. The Colonel of the

Militia must shoe his own horse and build his own waggon and his lady must take the fleece and convert it into a garment. The pastor must plough potatoes and rake hay; and a member of our colonial Parliament has been known to hawk beef in the streets of Halifax. . . . It would be but humble praise for a captain's lady to write to her relations in Scotland that, after 12 years of hard labour, her family . . . had cleared thirty acres of land, had two steers, three cows, three pigs, ten hens and three ducks. . . .

– *GA*, 25th February, 1847

His Reminiscences of Galloway
4th September, 1843. I have grown old in the service and must soon give in my account; but were I young again, I would go home and join the ranks of the Welshes, Buchanans, and Candlishes, and preach the gospel with them in the moorlands and mountain-solitudes, already consecrated by the labours of Cargill, Renwick, and Peden. . . . I am glad to hear that the old Cameronian garrison at Newton Stewart is repaired and its banners unfurled. I well recollect that, near half a century ago, it was regarded by the old dissenters as one of the strongholds of truth in Galloway. . . . The Rev. James Reid was then in the flower of his flame and his charge extended from Portpatrick to Dumfries. . . . About the second Sabbath of June . . . the well-known tent was erected in John Gordon's garden, or some retired spot near the town. . . . Many came thirty miles – from Stranraer, from Castle Douglas, Colmonell, and Whithorn. . . . We had neither leisure nor inclination to look at the landscape, but it abounded in natural beauties. The rich valleys around the town, the green woods, the sloping hills, the majestic river, and the wild mountains of Minnigaff in the back ground, hiding their heads in the clouds and often mantled with snow. . . .

– *The Scottish Presbyterian*, vol. 4, January, 1844, pp. 324–26

January 1846. Mr Reid's elders did not make such a high profession as some of our new light ranters who have been several times converted and who are waiting for another cast, but they were men of intelligence, integrity and piety. . . . Robert Milroy of Kirkcowan was a remarkable man on his knees. Peter McMaster of Stranraer was an angel of peace to the sick room. Henry Duggan had a strong memory stored with scripture truth and the traditions of the martyrs, well acquainted with business and often chosen to settle knotty points which baffled the wit and wisdom of the sheriff of Wigtown. Thomas Thorburn of Stoneykirk had great gifts for devotional exercise, but his affectation for speaking fine English marred his edification. But for deep-rooted piety and a ready hand with the pen,

Alexander McCarley, miller, Soleburn, surpassed all the elders. . . .

– *GA*, 22nd January, 1846

August 1846. His mission to Shelburne. Twenty years had passed since his last visit. Pastor Dripps, with all his good elders and most of his communicants, had dropt their clay mantle and gone home. . . . David White, from Wigtownshire, had been spared . . . and is a kind of golden link between the distant and the near. He is in his 96th year and is still able to illustrate the manners of Galloway in the last century. I thought myself very near to heaven while in company with this venerable cedar from the Bridge of Bladnoch.

– *GA*, 20th August, 1846

10th March, 1855. Few sects can boast of such venerable men as the Erskines and their early companions. . . . A century has passed away since they spread their tents on the Rhins of Galloway. . . . In early life my mother was occasionally a hearer of the older Mr Ogilvie of Wigtown, and her relations were staunchly Anti-burghers. Peter McNair, a cottar, lived at one time on my father's farm at Caldonpark and a willow tree still marks his garden lot. This venerable patriach was a full-blooded Seceder of the highest caste. He had a memory like a camel and never forgot that which he had seen and heard. . . . Dissent . . . at that time was regarded as a stunted plant and the religion of the barns; its adherents were few in number and exposed to much opposition. . . .

– *GA*, 19th April, 1855

Notes on his last journey back to Stoneykirk

1844. 3rd Jan. At twelve o'clock embarked on board the steamship *Hibernian* for Liverpool.

13th. Reached Liverpool early in the day.

15th. Went on board the *Harrington* for Kirkcudbright.

18th. Reached Stoneykirk. A happy meeting with my brother and family. Met Sergeant McWhirter. We had been together in Captain Maitland's Volunteer Company in the year 1799. Met with John McMaster of Auchencloy. . . . nearly sixty years ago we paddled about the burn and fished for trout with a crooked pin.

1st Feb. Had a delightful drive up the Loch of Cree . . . visited Glencaird and spent the evening in company with Mr Murray and his wife. . . . I resided for one year on the farm of Stroan, thirty-eight years ago.

– *Memorials*, pp. 55–56

Galloway fifty years ago

June 1848. With some exceptions, the country had a desolate and neglected appearance. It was open and few fields were enclosed. There was not a fence on the road between Balgreggan House and Stranraer, except at the Garthland, where there were some plantations. The roads were nearly all unbridged and scarcely passable. The farmers subsisted on the productions of the soil, and had some comforts suited to their tastes, but their houses were generally miserable bothies with earthern floors and roofs of straw. Their churches were a disgrace to religious feeling – places where you might catch a cold or a rheumatism, but not suitable temples for divine worship. Gigs and wagons were highly taxed and were totally unknown among the common people. . . . About the end of last century carts were introduced as travelling carriages. This was reckoned a great improvement and you might have seen a long row of horse-carts streaming away to the house of God full of worshippers. Though at first opposed as a breach of the fourth commandment, the practice gained ground and became general. The mail coach came to Dumfries and Ayr, and the letter bag was carried on horseback in Galloway. I have known the mail for Ireland detained at Portpatrick by a head wind.

Stranraer . . . . in the year 1793 . . . consisted chiefly of one long street, many of the houses of which were roofed with straw. It had about thirty little sloops, but no foreign trade. . . .

I see you now have a coach which runs to the village of Drummore and another to Wigton. At that time John Chalmers rode post to Kirkmaiden every Saturday. His horse was about the size of an Ayrshire ram, and besides carrying the mail he did many little errands for the farmers' wives which their careless husbands neglected. He was a worthy wight with an easy and well-oiled disposition, and very obliging. Peace be to his ashes. He had an astonishing memory, kept every person's money and parcel wrapped up separately, and generally did his business with much punctuality, but in declining years he was rather a thirsty soul, and in the cold winter nights on the Stoney Kirk road he sometimes took one glass, and then another, till his parcels at times got into confusion, and in that case the Kirkmaiden women had a hard scramble to recover their rights. . . .

We had a regular set of drunkards at Stoney Kirk who often met at the tavern to discuss the politics of the parish, and they seldom ventured on any weighty undertaking till they had cleared their heads with a cooling draught of whiskey and water. (A set of the same kind of people clustered about the villages of Kirkcowan, New Luce and Clachan Easy.) I have known several persons killed by hard drinking. Gauger Wilson of Port o'

Spittal would have spent the whole week in a tavern at Portpatrick, and when the Saturday evening arrived, he refused to go home till he would attend divine service and take with him the blessings of the church.

We had few newspapers and no periodical literature, but we had a plentiful supply of ghosts, brownies, and fairies to amuse us in the winter evenings. The ghost of the Galdenoch was such a regular visitant in the family, that it often attended at family prayers; and when the goodman gave out the psalm it pitched a high key above all the singers. The ghost at Ballochabrig near Balgreggan House was often seen late in the evening by persons returning home from Robert Munn's whiskey shop; but when the shop broke up it never appeared again, and it is probable it would join the fairies. The fairies were a beautiful little people who usually frequented green knowes and thorn bushes. A woman in Nithsdale returned after she had been several years in Fairyland, and suckled several of their children, and gave much information regarding their habits and manners. . . .

– *Memorials*, pp. 96–99

Letter to the Rev. T. Neilson, Rothesay, 1844

The town of Stranraer is much improved and several of the fields in its vicinity are laid out as handsome streets. Its harbour is improved and adorned with steamboats. Of its former fleet of coasting vessels I could see no memorial except the little sloop *Industry*, owned by John Kerr. She has the same appearance which she had forty years ago. I met with Mr Charles Paterson and asked him for his brother officers in Colonel McDowall's Regiment of Dragoons. He said the regiment was raised in the year 1795, and nearly all the men and officers had gone to the unseen abode, where the noise of war is unknown. . . . There are new merchants in the shops, new lawyers at the bar, new judges on the bench, and new priests at the altar. . . . I crossed the long sea to repair the stock of friendship and renew the intercourse of early years, but this was impossible. . . .

– *Memorials*, p. 59

Reminiscences of the 1790s. March 1850

Regiment after regiment was raised and hurried away to the harvest of death. I have seen at that time twenty-eight recruiting parties at a Stranraer fair, besides a party of sailors recruiting for the navy with a full-rigged frigate in miniature with colours streaming, which carried the crowd. In 1794 Colonel McDowall raised a regiment of horse and many of the nobility and the flower of the country went away with the army and never returned. My brother Robert joined the Wigtonshire Cavalry, and I entered the volunteer company of Captain John Maitland. I was then at school and read the Latin poets in the forenoon and attended drill in the afternoon (I mounted guard with a Virgil in one hand and a musket in the other). The war spirit had fallen upon the school and fifes and drums were the usual amusement. . . .

– Memorials, p. 114

23rd April, 1850. I am sorry to see from your paper that little groups of thirsty neighbours, on the market night at Stranraer, still cluster and linger about the taverns and take first one glass and then another before they turn their horse's head to their home. On reaching their own fireside, their thrifty wives will give them their 'kale through the reek'.

– GA, 16th May, 1850

17th March, 1851. When I was at school few took the newspapers but the laird and the parish minister. . . . I scarcely remember what Stranraer was sixty years ago. I can see it only through the dim shadows of the past; many of its dark and dingy dwellings were thatched with straw; its bridges were ragged; its streets ill-paved; and the Clayhole was scarcely passable at the time of a high tide. The school-boys were ill-conditioned and carried on an incessant warfare with little chaps from the countryside. When I reached the keystone of the old bridge, on my way home, I durst not look behind me till I reached the Spoutswells, for fear of being assailed with showers of stones by mischievous boys. The Stranraer fleet consisted of about 30 sloops, chiefly employed by the herring fishing. . . .

– GA, 24th April, 1851

18th April, 1845. Letter to Mr John McCaig, Kinhilt
When at home last winter I actually made a pilgrimage to the village of the Inch, with your son, to see the old schoolhouse where I had planted some Greek and Latin roots under the direction of that excellent linguist, the late Mr Wallace. The schoolhouse had disappeared and another was built. . . . The dwelling-house of the old teacher was the same as formerly, but has now two doors, and this alteration greatly puzzled me. . . .

– GA, 18th September, 1845

15th May, 1850. Almost every *Free Press* newspaper announces that some early schoolfellow has gone to the home of the departed. . . . The sun of many of our early companions went down at noon. Some of them lie in the coral beds where the sunbeams never play. Some of them have slept their long sleep in Africa or India, and not a few of them ahve breathed their last on the soldiers's battlefied.... The rocks, streams and heath-covered mountains of Galloway often rise on my view, and I would always wish to see them once in seven years; and almost every Scotchman would rather be buried in his native glen than in Westminster Abbey....

In the year 1793 all Europe was a barracks and a vast battle-ground.... We were threatened with a French invasion and an Irish rebellion. On the hill side attending divine service we heard the firing of the great guns across the Irish channel at the battle of Balinahench and soon after saw the Wigtownshire horsemen sweeping the country in quest of fugitives....

– *GA*, 13th June, 1850

30th September, 1851. I do not regret that I sent my son to Glasgow University to seek knowledge.... There is a degree of energy and intelligence among John Knox's children seldom found in other lands.... It is the purity of the standard of our National Zion and the fidelity with which ministers and schoolmasters discharge the duties of their office which has given North Britain such a high rank....

Near the close of last century I attended the school of Mr Carnochan of Stranraer. The council of black coats held their meetings in the schoolroom. The oldest member of the Presbytery was Mr Mochery of Colmonell.... The chief conveyance to Glasgow was by the *John's Packet*, Captain Gibson, once a month....

– *GA* 6th December, 1851

5th February, 1854. It is almost seventy years since I first went to Stoneykirk school, with a Catechism in one hand and a piece of fuel for the fire in the other. The Catechism and the Scriptures were the class books in use. We were taught reading, writing, and figures. Grammar, geography and science ... were not at that time introduced into the schools in the Rhins.... We knew nothing of the Newtonian system; and we believed the earth to be a great extended plain, reaching as far as Jerusalem or Babylon, or other countries mentioned in the Bible.... we knew little of the holy places except what the Scriptures told us. If a young man returned from the West Indies or the whale fishing, we gathered round to learn the wonders of other lands.... the common people got most of their domestic news from pedlars and travelling beggars, who greatly abounded at that time in Galloway....

I well recollect the earthern floor and roof of straw in the Caldons Park, where we spent so many cheerful evenings.... We never felt want;

but our table did not abound with luxuries, for when our venerable parents treated themselves with a cup of tea on Sabbath mornings, they shut the door and drew down the curtains on the windows, not because drinking tea was sinful, but because it might be reckoned extravagant. The farm was small, but like a kitchen garden, rich and well cultivated. A dried apple or a crust of bread from the Caldon Park would be as pleasing to me as the wine of Lebanon. With the exception of the minister's glebe, the fields around Stoneykirk village were nearly all open, and they formed a battle ground for many at terrible struggles at the shinty and the ball. . . .

– *GA*, 5th December, 1854

NEWS FROM CALIFORNIA

A letter from Charles Annan to his brother in Kirkmaiden parish:

Pleasant Valley, Upper California   10th February, 1850
Dear Brother, I take this opportunity of informing you that after a long and toilsome journey we all arrived in this far distant country alive, after a tedious six months travelling in waggons. We left Milwaukie, in Wisconsin, on the 15th day of March, 1849, for St Louis, on the Mississippi, distant from Milwaukie 500 miles. From St Louis up the Missouri river to Fort Independence, another 500 miles. This was the starting place.

Alexander was there two weeks before us buying cattle for the remainder of our journey. We left Fort Independence on the 5th of May to cross the continent; the distance to California being 2200 miles, through the wilderness inhabited by the Red Man. We thought little about this journey at starting, but we were heart sick of it, believe me, before we got through. In fact, if we had known aught of the difficulties we had to encounter, before starting, we never would have undertaken it; but now that we are in a country abounding in gold, we have a good prospect of being well paid for all that we suffered in reaching it. . . .

After leaving Fort Independence, we crossed the boundary of the United States, and in three days entered the Indian territory, or Great Plains as they are called. After travelling 350 miles we reached the great Plat river, which heads in the Rocky Mountains: which mountains we had to cross. We travelled up the river some hundreds of miles; there the wild buffalo range in tens of thousands. After leaving this river we entered upon the Black Hills, or Snake country, as it is called, a wild barren mountainous country far from the dwellings of civilized men. The next place of note we came to was 'The Poisoned Waters', or Alkali Lakes, of which, if cattle drink, they are sure to die in a few hours thereafter. Farther on we came to another river called 'The Sweet Water'. We wended our way along the banks of this river, and on the 5th day of July we were at the south pass of the Rocky Mountains.

This is the great dividing ridge betwixt the Atlantic and Pacific Oceans. Before we came to it the water ran in an easterly direction, but after passing it, the water ran west. After travelling 300 miles farther through a wild romantic country, we reached the 'Great Salt Lake', the settlement of the Mormons. After staying there five days, during which we got fresh cattle, we started again to travel the remaining 850 miles of our journey over the wilds. The next place of note we came to was 'The Humboldt River', named after Humboldt the great traveller. We travelled along the banks of this river 300 miles, till, as many rivers here do, it sinks in the sand; we then entered the desert, fifty miles wide, where we could neither get grass nor water for our cattle. In all directions here the wrecks of waggons, and carcases of cattle, appear. We suffered much, but got through safely, thank God. The next place we came to was the great Sierra Niveda, or 'Snowy Mountains' of California. In crossing these we were far above the limits of eternal snow. After passing over these mountains 150 miles, we reached 'Pleasant Valley' gold mines, where we now are.

Our brother Hugh, with his wife and son, are here with us. They came to this country a little after us. We are thinking of returning to the United States in the fall of the year. You need not write till you hear from us again. If God spares us health this summer, we have a good prospect of making our fortunes. Alexander has just returned from a five weeks' ramble among the mountains. He and his party fought a battle with the Inidans, and killed a number of them. He has discovered rich gold mines, and we will be working there this summer. This is the great country to make money in. Martha has earned, herself, 25 dollars per week (or over £5) all this winter, cooking for miners. Alexander and I work in the mines, taking out from £5 to £10 a day. . . .

– *GA*, 9th May, 1850

LETTERS FROM VIRGINIA CITY 1877–84

James McDade died on the 23rd of May, 1886 after a fall down a mine shaft while working near the pumps. The mine belonged to the Gould and Curry Mining Company of Virginia City, Nevada. Still at 33 a bachelor, he was rooming with a Mrs Kaiser and her family. Numerous letters of condolence from his many friends, including the Rev. Isaac White of the

*1st Presbyterian Church, were addressed to his mother, Mrs Captain McDade in Gatehouse-of-Fleet. They suggest that he was a popular and highly respected figure in Virginia City. A fine singer (*Far Away *and* Robin Gray *were among his favourites), he was described as 'the life and soul of the entertainment' at the annual Burns Birthday Celebrations of the Virginia City Caledonian Club. His occasional letters back home to Gatehouse-of-Fleet, to his mother and father, his sister Jessie and his brother Willie, are full of humorous asides. As little snapshops of life in Virginia City and Gatehouse they raise a number of issues of more general interest than merely family history.*

✝

Virginia City Nov. 6th 1877. Dear Mother, You will be looking for a letter. . . . There is one thing I would like the folks at home to DO, that is viz. to put enough postage on the letters . . . it looks as if they all come from the bogs that is the simple remark here when such a thing happens – the only ones that has put the postage on right are my father and Willie. Hugh is the worst of the whole lot. I have to pay 15 cents for every one he sends. Wee Pete and Hannah and Jessie are very near as bad.

My uncle and I are getting along first rate. he is working in one of the big bonanza mines. . . . Vernon was telling me in his letter that Kattie Tait and (Whaty) Carson have got married and off to London. . . . How is Dick getting on, I hope he will get into the Bank, any kind of a situation is better than hard work. . . . How long will Jessie be in mourning for old Charlie. I think her last chance is gone except she can put Miss Smith's eye out and get Douglas McMillen. . . . From your aff. Son Jas. McDade.

June 9th 1878. Dear Bro. Willie, I should earlier have acknowledged the receipt of yours of three or four months ago, but I am such a 'putter-off' of things unless it is business importance. I am very 'slow in stay's' . . . I think you over dosed your last with the science of elocution. At least I call it a science. Why don't you confine yourself to categorical statements and facts, unincumbered by metaphorical allegory. . . .

You say Jessie has left school, I think it would not hurt her one bit to be sent to some 'high-tone' school for six months or a year if Father and Mother would approve the proposition. . . . Dick must be a fine big fellow, 'as big as a skinned horse', from all accounts. . . . Hugh must cut a terrible dash with his 'stovepipe' hat every day. . . . The lady uncle and I stay with . . . thinks Hugh is too much like a Turkish pasha . . . .

James McDade   Taylor St   Virginia City.

July 15th 1878. Dear Father, When I received your last I was along with
Tom Gracey you had mentioned his name sending your respects which I
passed over to him. . . . Gracey and uncle have advised me to buy more
mining stocks. . . . I have thirty shares of Crown Point at $7 per share, 20
of Kentuck at $3 and 50 of Imperial at 90 cents. . . . besides I have 200 in
the bank. . . . How are all the Ferry folks. It is about five or six years since
I had a letter from any of them.

April 5th. Dear Father . . . tell me how you are getting along with the
Keith. I am sure she must bother you a great deal with her making so
much water. if I had it in my powr I would send you a few pounds but I
can not at present. it took about £35 to fetch me out here and keep me
here until I got work, but I have paid it all up now to my uncle and I have
invested about 135 dollars in mining stocks . . . my uncle says he thinks I
will make about 1000 dollars . . . I hope that I am not building castles in
the air as we are all very apt to do. . . . McKenzie treats me very well but
he gave me one of the hardest jobs around the mine and when I tell him
aboute it he only says grow fat and get married. There were two weddings
at McKenzie's house on the 17th of March. one of the girls was Mrs Mc's
cousin and the other was the one she brought out from Liverpool with
her. they were both married to Scotchmen. my uncle and I were both
there and we enjoyed ourselves A.1 at Loyd's as Mr Helme used to say.
   Dick was saying in his letter that Sanders had failed and Helme had
bought up all his wood and engine so he will have command of
everything now. . . .
   There is a great excitement here just now about gold diggings
discovered at the Black Hills about 1100 miles from here. . . .

Virginia City Nevada. Christmas. My Dear Mother . . . You mention in
yours about me having to work in the hot mine, but I have got a place to
work on the surface at the same mine as my uncle but it is very hard
work. . . . and Sunday is just the same as any other day. one is kept at it all
the time. I am up at 5 o'clock every morning and it is half past six when I
get home at night. . . .
   I was very poorly all the time when I came here at first but I am all right
again. . . . I was very ill and confined to my room for 17 days. The doctor
told me it was tiphod fever that I had but I did not believe him. doctor's
charges are very dear they are only five dollars a visit, there were five and
six deaths every day when I came at first but there are not so many
now. . . . it is not safe to be out after dark there are so many shot or
stabbed. There is never a week but there are 2 or 3 killed. within the last

eight days there were no less than five shot dead and one stabbed. . . .

I have a very comfortable house to live in. they are German's that we stop with and they are very nice people. . . . my uncle would tell you all about the great fire we had here. it was an awful sight while it lasted. there was about three or four times the size of Gatehouse burned down in less than six hours. McKenzies house was burned in about fifteen minutes to the ground. . . .

When you write to me spell my name Daid as there is another party of the same name as me here. . . . P.S. Tell Jenny and Jeannie that I have not forgot them not forgetting old grany Gilmour. . . .

June 30th 1879. Dear Bro. Willie . . . The fourth of July is close at hand. The one hundred and third anniversary of *our* independence. The citizens have chosen McKenzie Grand Marshal of the day and the best of the joke is Mc does not know the first thing about riding a horse . . . everybody is making great fun of an old *whale* on a horse. . . .

Without doubt Mr Dick thinks himself something away beyond the average youth, so far as comelyness, that is judging from the quiver of his upper lip in his photr. . . .

Sept 30th 1880. Dear Mother . . . I would a hundred times rather live among the Americans, with their free and easy state of manners, nevertheless polite to the point, than I would among the bigoted and prejudiced beef eating Johnney Bull of Old *England*. They think they know every thing, but they have just got to live in this country about five years to find out they know nothing. . . .

Mrs Kaiser's brother was killed about a month ago, by a block of wood thrown from a circular saw . . . he was only 24 years old and only a few months married. . . .

I think times are going to be better here this winter than they have been on account of two of the most prominent men of the Coast going to run for the U.S. Senate, viz. Colonel Jim Fair and Senator Billy Sharon, they are both millionaires and equally anxious to get elected, and I expect they will give us a stock boom or something of that sort, to brighten our blighted hopes of the last two years. . . .

April 21st 1881. Dear Sister Jessie . . . Times are very dull at present. . . . There has been quite a controversy in the papers about the reduction of wages but so far the miners have avoided any parley in the conference whatever, and will not interfere until they are put to the test in the reduction, then I am afraid there will be some trouble. Uncle has been working for the past few months at Crown Point, but he told me the other day he did not know how long it would last. I dont think he has any intention of going to Arizona now, unless the aspect becomes more gloomy. . . .

April 23, 1885. My Dear Mother . . . I am glad that Father is doing well with the schooner, tell him to remember me to Jim Vernon or Cook as we used to call him. Jessie was asking me in one of her letters whether Jim McMichael or I was the elder. she can give him my regards, and tell old smoothy that he is about five years my senior. . . .

My old friend Tully has got back to the Comstock. And one went away last night. he says if he goes home to Annan he will take a trip up to Gatehouse to see you. he was foreman of the mine McKenzie was Supt. of. I think he has a good sack to. he knows Dr Cox well. they went to school together.

[no date] 'Dear Jessie . . . I see by your letter that Heleme's mill was burned down. I was very sorry when I read it, and that he had been so unfortunate, not to have it insured. I hope you seen it so that you can have an idea what the fire here was like. there were hundreds of houses and plenty of them as big as the mill and some of them biger were burned in a very short time. . . .

They are trying to reduce the miners wages here but I do not think they will succeed. and if they do, there will be a wild time here. it is pretty rough at any time. there is always some shooting going on. just last night there were two men shot one of them a young man about twenty one whom I was intimately acquainted with so that is the way they go on here.

You can tell Hugh when you write to him that I do not enjoy life very well in the *antipodes* yet, that is one of his many long nebbers that he had in his last letter, I think he was swallowed another dictionary. . . .

God Bless you is the prayer of your Affectionate Brother James McDade   Taylor Street   Virginia City.

AUSTRALIA AND 'THE WILD SCOTS OF GALLOWAY'

The most important single person to reach Australia from Dumfries and Galloway was the coach and chaise painter and 'Convict Artist', Thomas Watling. Found guilty in 1789 of forging Bank of Scotland notes, he was sent off to New South Wales in June 1791. After escaping from the Good

Ship Pitt *at the Cape of Good Hope, he enjoyed seven months in prison there and only reached Port Jackson in October 1792. In his five years in Australia he produced a marvellous series of paintings of animals and birds and the aboriginal peoples and a book,* Letters from an exile in Botany Bay to his aunt in Dumfries *(1794). For further details see* Hugh Gladstone, Thomas Watling. Limner in Dumfries *(1938).*

However, only some 8,000 of the 160,000 men, women and children transported to the Australian colonies between 1777/1778 and 1868 were Scots. And certainly the vast majority of Scots in New South Wales and Victoria in the middle of the nineteenth century were farmers, shepherds, miners, bankers, engineers, shopkeepers, entrepreneurs who chose to go there. The letters they sent back home and notices of goods exported from Newton Stewart and Kirkcudbright provide an interesting picture of colonial life.

✝

The Wild Scots of Galloway. As is common with Gallovidians wherever they assemble . . . . a society was formed under the denomination of 'The Wild Scots of Galloway'; which has for its objects the promotion of good fellowship and kindly feeling among Gallovidians resident in, and visitants to, the Colony; the relief of Gallovidians in distress; and the assistance of Gallovidian immigrants on their arrival on our shores. Of this society the following gentleman are the office-bearers, viz. William Kerr, Larbrax, President; R. Macmicking, Miltonies, Secretary; A. McMaster, Stranraer, Treasurer. Committee: Captain John McLean, Portnessock, William Martin, Belvidere, Caleb Emerson, Stranraer, John Rankin, Cairnbrock, and Alexander McGeoch, Crouse.

'The Wild Scots of Galloway' already include in their ranks a very considerable number of Gallovidian residents, and at the date of the formation of the society there were either six or seven vessels in port commanded by Gallovidian captains. . . . William Kerr, Melbourne, 19th June, 1852.

– The Melbourne Argus, June 1852

Kirkcudbright. Amongst the exports per the *Countess of Galloway*, which left this port at eight p.m., on the 21st curt., there were six carts with suitable sets of harness, etc., and a gig, all for Australia; shipped by a gentleman in the neighbouring parish of Borgue, per order for a relative now successfully pursuing his fortune in that distant land. The carts, which were in every way substantially finished, were made by Mr

William Brown, Townhead, of Tinwald, near Dumfries. The gig, also a very substantial and well finished vehicle, was made by his brother Mr James Brown, coach-builder, in Castle-Douglas. The carts and gig were more than ordinarily high in the diameter of the wheels, being 4 feet 9 inches, for this reason – as assigned by the gentleman who sent home the order – 'because our roads here are more indebted to nature than to art for their construction, and, by making the wheels higher in diameter, we shall have less friction in the draught of the load.

– DGC, 25th January, 1853

Goods for Australia. During the last few weeks a large quantity of miscellaneous articles manufactured in Newton-Stewart have been transmitted to Liverpool for shipment to Australia, consisting of chests of drawers, presses, wearing apparel, home-knit stockings, from 1,200 to 1,500 pairs of boots and shoes, a large assortment of tin utensils, spades, picks and shovels for the diggings, horse shoes and nails, from 200 to 250 glazed double window sashes and frames, and a quantity of fowling pieces, rifles, and revolvers, the manufacture of our respected townsman, Mr Erskine, who has already attained considerable celebrity in the sporting world by the invention of some very ingenious improvements in fire arms, and though last not least, a portable dwelling house capable of comfortably accommodating a number of individuals and in every respect adapted to the migratory habits of a large portion of our antipodal brethren. . . . Last week about 200 of the most necessitous of the population of Newton-Stewart received quantities of coals, varying from two to four bushels each, according to their circumstances – the proceeds of Captain Williams' lecture on Australia, together with donations from a number of benevolent individuals. . . .

– GA, 17th March, 1853

The Australian Gold Regions [a letter from John Hutchinson to his brother in Newton Stewart]:
Bathhurst, 23d September, 1851. . . . In my last letter to you I spoke of the discovery of gold in this district; no doubt you have heard all the particulars of it ere this time, therefore I need give you none. Many people are realising rapid fortunes; some cannot earn anything at it. A gentleman named Dr Kerr picked up a piece which weighed 106 lbs., which was sold for upwards of £4,000. A party of six of the name of West, by regular work, obtained from £3,000 to £4,000 worth during the last two months. . . . I turned gold digger myself, and I think I have been as fortunate as the best of my neighbours. There are three of us together, and

we have obtained as much as £100 per day! I have been at it for the last five weeks. . . . I am saving money now very fast. . . .

The district of Bathurst is very mountainous. The fells we were brought up in are nothing in comparison to the hills and mountains here. . . . When a party starts they buy 20 or 30 yds. of calico, 1 cwt. flour, 30 lbs. sugar, 6 lbs. tea, 2 lbs. coffee, salt, tin pints, a tin teapot, and an iron pot. Sheep can be got any part of the country at 10s. a piece. We bake our own bread as we require it, and have bread and mutton, with tea, three times a day: this is our way of living. For our nights' comforts we have a bed stuffed with straw, between this and the ground we put a sheet or two of bark, and have two pairs of blankets and two or three rugs to throw over us, and we are pretty comfortable. . . .

The things we require for work are two picks, a cradle, two spades, a tin dipper or ladle, two tin dishes, two buckets, a crowbar, and sometimes a pump. . . . Parties of five men keep two cradles going, parties of seven keep three. . . . I should say there are at least 20,000 people here digging for gold. We have a licence imposed upon us of 30s. per month for each digger, which goes to government. . . .

– GA, 19th February, 1852

From the Diggins [A letter from Patrick Douglas to his father in Stranraer]:
Daisy Hill Diggin's, 18th August 1855. Dear Father, I duly received your welcome letters per *Marco Polo*, *Blue Jacket*, and *Mermaid*. . . . I will just write as thoughts strike me, sitting here, as I am to-night, while we all are a sleep around me, in what I call my parlour and bed-room, with a capacious slab chimney piece at one end with a fire that would roast a bullock. I am writing on the little desk I brought with me, a lamp on my right, and two candles stuck into two bottles as a substitute for candlesticks, my day book laid aside, the kettle steaming on the fire, with a cup of good chocolate to keep up the old tabernacle. . . .

The dress I am rigged in to-night is top boots, duck trousers, white shirt, black silk tie, Panama hat, with red shirt over, so I daresay you would think me a very flash cove in a small way, if you chanced to meet me in George Street. . . . I am just returned from Melbourne, where I have been for the last eight days. I was busy all the time buying goods and getting deeds completed for land bought lately. I saw five loaded drays despatched at £19 per ton carriage. Business is very dull in town, but all kinds of goods are on the rise, especially provisions. I have been eight days coming up, owing to the late heavy rains, a number of the bridges being swept away. I bought a horse in town this time and rode him up, which saved me £8 10s., and only cost £13. I was offered £18 for him on the road, but I expect to turn £25 out of him before two months. My partner has just bought an iron store, which will cost us £300 when up on Daisy Hill, and which makes our third. Business continues brisk, having taken £680 over the counter in course of the last 18 days.

The plot of ground I purchased from Government lately is only half a mile from this, and is beautifully situated and is fit for garden or agricultural purposes. . . . I bought it for 21s per acre, and was offered £100 next day for my bargain. I intend to bring it into cultivation . . . it is . . . situated within a few miles of three of the best markets, viz. Maryborough, Avoca and Black Creek, where produce generally commands double that of Melbourne. Diggers, if steady and persevering, make good wages. . . . I have seen me having to give a poor hardworking unfortunate digger his breakfast upon credit, and being worth £100 by dinner time. . . . William Owens happened on a good claim the other day when looking for the horses on Jeffray's Flat . . . when he found a bag containing 47 oz., which had in all probability been left there by some Bushranger. . . . He would have waited long about Cairnryan before he would have picked that up. . . .

I lately returned from an excursion up the country: I was some 60 miles up at a Mr Russell's for fruit. We stopped at Loch Moria one day, and shot 33 wild ducks, a black swan, and a number of wild cats, etc.. The fruit sold very well and the ducks brought 10s. a pair. . . .

Numerous gangs of bushrangers continue prowling about, and hardly a night passes without some tent being robbed; we are, however, generally prepared for them, as we always lye with loaded pistols under our heads, besides having the assistance of four good dogs. It was only the other day that a party of diggers secured a gang of bushrangers known by appellation of the 'Black Douglas' gang . . . and who would undoubtedly have lynch-lawed them, the rope being thrown over a tree for the purpose, when the authorities interposed to prevent it.

20th. This is Sunday morning. . . . being generally put in with playing cricket, shooting, and such like amusements, we have much need of some of your spare ministers here. . . .

– *GA*, 13th December, 1855

THE REV. JOHN INGLIS

Report of a Missionary Tour to the New Hebrides (1851)

John Inglis (1807–91) was born in Moniaive. After years working as a mason, he went up to the University of Glasgow and the Reformed Presbyterian Hall in Paisley. During the vacations he earned money tutoring and teaching in a school in Rothesay. He was licensed as a minister by the R.P. Presbytery of Paisley in June 1842, but instead of working in Scotland he was adopted by the Mission Committee and ordained as a missionary to go to New Zealand in September 1843. John Inglis and his wife, Jessie McClymont (see Chapter 12), sailed for Wellington in July 1844.

With the support of the Governor-in-Chief of New Zealand, Sir George Grey, he was sent on HMS Havannah on a three-month tour of the New Hebrides, Queen Charlotte's Islands, the Solomon Islands and New Caledonia between August and November, 1850. His Report, forwarded to Grey and published in the New Zealand Government Gazette, is a remarkably thorough, careful and detailed analysis of the populations, the languages, the resources and customs of the islands and of the difficulties of establishing permanent mission stations in the New Hebrides. Perhaps unaware of the dangers, he visited the volcano on Tanna – two of the seven or eight craters were in a state of great activity with showers of molten matter being discharged every five minutes.

In 1852 Inglis was settled on Aneityum,* where his mission seems to have been very successful (see Chapter 12). He retired to Kirkcowan in 1876 and died there on 18th July, 1891. Working with another missionary, Dr Geddie of Nova Scotia, he translated the Old and New Testaments into Aneityumese, and subsequently the Shorter Catechism and the Pilgrim's Progress. His publications included a Dictionary of Aneityumese (1882) and In the New Hebrides (1887). In 1883 he was honoured with a DD by the University of Glasgow.

✝

The Havannah left Auckland on the 8th of August, 1850. . . . The inhabitants of all these four groups . . . are quite a distinct race from the inhabitants of Eastern Polynesia. . . . Their clothing throughout all the groups is essentially the same. . . . The men everywhere, except Pate, wear only a narrow cincture and a wrapper of leaves or native cloth. . . . The women wear around their middle a mat manufactured from the rind of a tree. In the New Hebrides this dress is much fuller than in New Caledonia. . . . in New Caledonia they have a large mat to cover them

*Anatom, Tanna and Erromango are the southernmost islands of the modern state of Vanuato.

completely, and protect them, when necessary, from rain or cold. . . . In Aneiteum, Tana, and to a small extent in Erumanga, the men dress their hair in a peculiar manner. The hair is separated into small locks, and tied round from the roots to the top with a narrow rind; when fully dressed in this way it has the appearance of a bunch of small whip cord, spread over the head and fastened behind. In New Caledonia the chiefs and influential men wear their hair long, and tie it up in a semi-conical form on the top of their head. . . .

Their food consists chiefly of indigenous fruits and vegetables; as the cocoa-nut, breadfruit, tare, yams, kumeras, bananas, sugar cane, etc.. They also use fish, fowls, and pigs. In New Caledonia they boil and eat locusts in great quantities. To these they are now adding maize, pumpkins, melons, the paypaya apple, and other exotic productions. . . .

Their principal occupation is clearing, fencing, and cultivating their plantations, which they keep with great care. They practice irrigation to a great extent. In Aneiteum we saw canals cut along the sides of hills more than a mile in length. . . . In the New Hebrides they excel on the making of mats, baskets, armlets, and in the constructing of fences. . . . The largest canoes and the best houses are found in New Caledonia. The houses are constructed of a wattled frame, and thatched with grass; the walls are round, and the roofs conical; in appearance they are like corn-ricks; in the other islands, they are simply oblong roofs, some small, others very large. At Port Sandwich, in the island of Malicola, we found in every village, so far as we were allowed to examine them, images as large as life, dressed as men, and apparently looked upon as sacred, but their precise object we could not discover. The images seemed to be made of some kind of native cloth, stuffed with some firm but malleable substance . . . the face was painted like an Egyptian mummy. We found three or four in the sacred house of each village. . . .

War appears to be universal. The Missionaries in the New Hebrides have ascertained that the natives are occupied fighting for ten months in the year. . . .

Throughout all these groups *dancing* appears to be the principal amusement. In the New Hebrides, for two months at one season of the year, the natives meet daily about mid-afternoon and continue dancing till daylight next morning. In returning from the volcano in Tana, we came upon a dancing party, from four to five hundred in number. They were assembled in an open circular space, shaded by spreading banian trees to celebrate the ripening of the bread fruit and the removal of the tapu from the trees. . . . The figure of the dance was circular, the men were in the centre, and the women, two deep, formed a ring outside. . . . The dancing was a continuous earnest leaping or jumping, rather than a series of elegant artificial or acquired movements. . . . The women had their faces besmeared with a black pigment; their heads were decorated with figures; they were dressed with flowing petticoats of the dracaena plant, surmounted behind with monster bustles of fern leaves, and each one carried a club or a spear. The men were besmeared with a red ochre, and almost every dancer wore one or two rows of white shells on the arm, the rattling of which while they were dancing supplied the place of music. . . .

At Pate and Malicola, in the New Hebrides, every family, or every few families, have a cluster of drums. These are made from trees hollowed out like a canoe and fixed into the ground, rising about six feet high. . . . from ten to twenty of them are fixed in a cluster at a few feet apart from one another. They emit when struck a hollow funereal sound, and are employed to furnish music at their dances and on other occasions. . . . The natives of Aneiteum sing beautifully, greatly surpassing anything I have heard among the New Zealanders.

In Aneiteum the natives believe in and worship superior beings called *Natmasses*. Their mode of worship is thus: they select long-shaped stones, from three to eighteen inches long, and pile them up under a banyan tree. They suppose that the spirit of the divinity resides in each of these stones. There is generally a small chip broken off one corner of the stone, at which the spirit goes in and out. Offerings of food of various kinds are presented before these piles of Natmasses. . . . They have an order of priesthood, but it is usually held by the chiefs, who thereby increase their influence. A future state of rewards and punishments is believed in; but heaven partakes much of the character of earth. . . . as the priests . . . look on the missionaries with a very jealous eye, they have been very reluctant to communicate any information bearing upon the religious beliefs of the natives. Their deities are all reputed as malignant beings, and hence fear, and not love, is the leading motive in their worship. *Naijerun* is one of the chief divinities: in moral attitudes he is very like Satan. . . .

In 1848 a Presbyterian Mission was established on Aneiteum, under the auspices of the London Missionary Society. There are at present two families connected with this mission. There are five stations on the island; four are occupied by native teachers from Samoa or Raratonga, and visited by missionaries who reside at the fifth. The population of the island is 3000. . . .

– *The New Zealand Government Gazette*, 6th May, 1851

ALASTAIR REID
'Hauntings'

The most distinguished Gallovidian of his day, Alastair Reid, who born in Whithorn in 1926, has spent much of his life on the staff of the New Yorker *and 'in exile' in Spain and in Central and Southern America. His* Whereabouts. Notes on Being a Foreigner, *published by Canongate in Edinburgh in 1987, should be on every Galloway bookshelf. This collection of essays, including* Digging Up Scotland, Hauntings, Notes from a Spanish Village, *and* Other People's Houses, *is a liberating exploration of his very personal peregrinations from 'his personal Eden' in Whithorn through and between different worlds and different languages.*

✝

I was born in a village called Whithorn, in the soft southwest of Scotland. It was my beginning; and, reaching back to it, I realize that for me it has remained in a time warp of its own – my personal Eden, in that although it was lost, the aura that comes back with remembering it stems from a time when house, family, garden, village and friends were all I knew of the world, when everything had the glow of wholeness, when I had no idea of the passing of time except as anticipation. . . .

Whithorn lies close to the tip of one of the southern fingers of the part of Scotland known as Galloway: isolated, seldom visisted, closer across the Irish Sea to Northern Ireland than it seems to the rest of Scotland; closer, too, to Ireland in the softness and cadence of its speech. It is rich, low-lying, carefully cultivated dairy country, with a few small fishing ports, and has a douce, mild climate, thanks to the proximity of the Gulf Stream, which has made certain Galloway gardens famous for their exotic transplantings. Whithorn was also a beginning for my parents. . . . It was my father's first charge, a village of some seven hundred, embracing the surrounding farms. My parents firmly took root there, my father healed over from the war, which nevertheless always troubled his memory, my mother had a house to turn into a household, and in later years they always spoke of these beginnings as a lucky time in their lives, for Galloway contains the kindliest of people in that flinty country – all in all, a good place to begin in.

In shape, Whithorn looks much like a child's drawing of a village: built on a slope, it has a single main street – the houses on each side of it joined in a single facade, no two of them, however, exactly alike – which widens like a mandolin as it descends to a semblance of a square, where the shops cluster, where the bus pulls in. The street narrows again and runs to the bottom end of the village, where, in our day, the creamery and the railway station stood adjacent to each other. Every morning, the miniature beginnings of a train would start out from Whithorn: a wagonful of full milk churns from the creamery destined for Glasgow; a single passenger coach, occasionally carrying those who had business in the outside world. Whithorn was a place easy to learn by heart. All round it lay the farms and, beyond them, infinitely, the sea.

As minister, my father had the gift of the manse to live in (the houses of Scottish ministers are always called manses), and the manse in Whithorn was an outpost, set apart from the village. From the main street, under an old arch bearing Whithorn's coat of arms, a lane led, first, to the small white church that was my father's charge, surrounded by a well-kept graveyard, where we sometimes practiced our reading from the gravestones. The lane continued past the church, crested a small rise, and ran down, over the trickle of a stream, to the white gates of the manse. A gravel drive led up to the manse, past a long, walled garden on the right; a semicircle of huge elm and beech trees faced the house from across the drive. Behind the house were stables and outhouses, and all around lay green fields. If you trudged across them, careful in summer to skirt the golden edges of standing oats and barley, you reached the sea – an irresistible pilgrimage. . . .

Whithorn was not at all well-to-do but thrived, rather, on the comfortable working equilibrium of that countryside. Some of its inhabitants went to sea, fishing, but most farmed; the creamery kept the dairy herds profitable; and the place had a kind of self-sufficient cheer that it needed, for it was truly at the end of a long, far line – it and its small seaport village, the Isle of Whithorn, a few miles beyond it, on the coast. There were not many comings and goings, and, so isolated, the people became their own sustenance, and had the warm grace of the countryside. Seven hundred people, if they do not actually know one another, know at least who everyone is. . . .

We had a network of friends on the surrounding farms, some of which were close enough for us, when we reached a certain age, to point ourselves like crows toward them, navigating the fields and stone dikes in between. I loved the days on the farm – the rituals of milking, still by hand; the work that changed according to season and weather – and I used to stay over at one farm, Broughton Mains, for haying in June, and for the golden weeks of harvest in late August: days we passed in the field, helping or playing; days punctuated by the women bringing hampers of food they had spent the morning preparing; the fields orderly at the end of the day, the bound oats in their rows of standing clumps; days that felt like rites. After we had left Whithorn, I would go back to Broughton Mains for the peak of the harvest, immemorially, for there that drama of abundance crowned the whole year.

We spent as much as we could of the daylight of our lives then outdoors, the house a headquarters among the fields and climbable trees, or a shelter on days of rain or raw weather. Sometimes we would be recruited in a body to help in the garden – a string of small bearers, baskets of weeds on our heads. My world at that time embraced five villages, a dozen farms, a river, and three beaches, some houses we visisted often, a countable number of friends we knew by name. We sailed sometimes on a fishing boat out of the Isle of Whithorn, and we often watched five or six local boats come in with their catches, sometimes with herring for the taking. My father preached there on odd Sunday evenings, in a small white church that protruded into the harbor, waves sometimes leaving their spray on its latticed windows during the service. Galloway mostly has soft winters and early springs, and we learned and looked for signs of growing, we followed the progress of the garden and the sown fields surrounding us, we eavesdropped on the farms, trying to pick up nuggets of country wisdom, and we practiced looking wisely at the sky. . . .

– A. Reid, Whereabouts, pp. 74–80

8

SCHOOLS AND SCHOOLMASTERS: PATRONS AND PUPILS

✝

The 1616, 1646 and 1696 Acts established a framework for what was something like 'a national system of education' in Scotland. Parochial schools with salaried schoolmasters existed in virtually every parish in 'Lowland' Scotland, including Dumfries and Galloway, through most of the eighteenth century and the nineteenth century. In each parish heritors were responsible for providing a school building and paying the teacher's salaries; in burghs this fell to the councils.

What this meant in practice changed over the years with local arrangements becoming more and more divers and inchoate throughout the later eighteenth century and the nineteenth century. A great deal depended on local resources and circumstances and the calibre and attitudes, hopes and expectations of landowners, proprietors, tenant farmers and clergy, and the willingness or inability of people to work together and accept their responsibilities. Any generalisations about the uniqueness of excellence of educational provision in Scotland between 1696 and 1872 needs to be tested against the realities of the situation at different times and in different counties and parishes. The Church of Scotland parish ministers had a very important role in appointing schoolmasters and taking part in regular visitations by Presbytery committees. Presbyteries had the power to depose schoolmasters, for example if they joined the Free Church post-1843 or if charged with lapses in the standard of behaviour expected of them. Mr James McKie was dismissed from Buittle parish school in 1861 for drunkenness at the 1860 Candlemas Bleeze and on the occasion of receiving his half-yearly salary.

Education was neither compulsory (until 1872) nor free (until after 1889). This presented enormous problems for children from lower-income households, as the money set aside from parish poor funds was generally sufficient to allow access for only a very few boys. Girls were far less likely to be given the opportunity to take up places at parochial schools in general. Another related problem was that attendance at parochial schools was often irregular or intermittent, either because parents could not pay the fees or because they required their children at home for seasonal farm work. Many private schools, entreprenurial ventures of a dubious quality, for example James McMeekin's school at Whithorn, attracted pupils just because their fees were at a much lower level. Private schools in the towns, Dumfries, Moffat, Kirkcudbright, Stranraer, included establishments for the daughters of prosperous tenant farmers, merchants, shipbuilders and shipowners. . . .

Schoolmasters received a salary from the parish, but this was supplemented by the fees they collected in relation to the subjects they taught (Latin and Greek were at a higher rate), and benefits amassed at the traditional collection of gifts from pupils at the Candlemas Bleeze. They often had other sources of income from work as session clerks and precentors. James Wallace at Kirkcolm, for example, was the parochial schoolmaster for forty-five years up to 1855, and was also the session clerk for thirty years, and then latterly also inspector and collector for the Poor Board. It must have been difficult when appointing a candidate to a school to assess their qualifications: few students graduated, as the evidence of having certificates denoting that they had attended classes at university was sufficient in itself.

In many of the larger parishes any one school, wherever located, was too far away from many homes. Some parishes had two parochial schools, for example Dalry with Stroanfreggan, with the second school funded at a lower rate, for example, Rerrick and Balmaghie. In Dumfries, Kirkcudbright, Wigtown and Stranraer the town schools were or became 'Academies' with boarding sections; and a number of other parochial schools became Boarding Academies or 'Grammar Schools' (Glenluce, Borgue, Leswalt, Whithorn, Bankend). Sometimes, however, a local group established their own private school, for example in Old Luce parish, where Crowes School was opened c. 1854 by farmers who subscribed 'a few pounds annually for the teacher, they being satisfied with his service.'

Parishes with substantial endowments from gifts and legacies from Glasgow and London merchants and West Indian planters (Closeburn, Caerlaverlock, Tynron, Dalry, Balmaclellan, Crossmichael, Borgue) were rich in comparison to their neighbours.

The 1872 Act established 984 school districts, each with school boards, and a national system of inspection. Attendance officers were appointed to encourage 'compulsory' attendance of children from five to thirteen years of age. Defaulting was still common, and quarterly fees were still collected until after 1889.

Although an interest in innovation in educational methodology was a significant part of the Scottish Enlightenment (see Chapter 3 for the courses on elocution and eloquence in Dumfries, part of the Enlightenment enthusiasm to eradicate Scotticisms approved of and pursued by David Hume, Adam Smith and Sir John Sinclair), there were few really useful and practical textbooks. The Treatise of Education *by George Chapman (1723–1806), the schoolmaster of the Dumfries Burgh or Grammar School from 1747 to 1774, was a wise and practical guide to good educational practice. It went into a fifth edition in 1792.*

Chapman was born at Alvah in Banffshire and studied at King's College in Aberdeen, graduating MA in 1741. He was the schoolmaster in Alvah parish from 1739 to 1743. He was allowed a substitute in 1739 and 1740 while at university. After four years as an assistant in the Grammar School of Dalkeith, he was appointed as conjunct master of the Grammar School of Dumfries with Robert Trotter, continuing as schoolmaster from 1750 to 1774. He also ran a successful boarding house section. He retired to a farm at Inchdrewer in Banffshire from 1781 to 1787! However, having married Katharine Dutchfield and with two daughters Katharine and Mary, born in 1789 and 1791, he moved south to Edinburgh in 1793 and established a new Academy at Liberton Kirk. The curriculum included Latin, Greek, Geography, Book-keeping and French, on the plan of teaching in his Treatise *(extra-curricular charges 24 guineas a year for Board and Lodging, 30 shillings a year for Washing if required, Perquisites 1 guinea to the Assistant Master William Cruickshank and 5 shillings to the Servants at the New Year).*

He remained famously popular in Dumfries and 'Dr Chapman's Scholars' had annual reunions in Hunters Tavern in the Writers Close in Edinburgh.

✝

A TREATISE ON EDUCATION

In the first period of life, when the child is most susceptible of impressions, he is surrounded with persons of low education and of weak minds. In the lowest rank of mankind, this circumstance cannot be avoided; but it is also very frequently the misfortune of children born in the middling stations, where it might be avoided. The consequence is, that he borrows their ideas, he imbibes their prejudices, he adopts their manners. . . . (p.17)

The progress of children at a public school will always depend upon the constitution of the school, and the number of the scholars, as well as the abilities of the schoolmaster. The more the school is crowded and the care of the master divided, the more will the notice which he can take of individuals be diminished. But if he have not a proper number of ushers to assist him, the inconveniences of a crowded school will be much greater.... This must naturally happen when there are several forms, or classes, of boys, all in the school at one time, learning different lessons, and consequently requiring his inspection and assistance. For as he can only attend to one of the classes at once, the other classes, and especially the younger boys, will be tempted to prattle and to trifle away their time: their noise too will be very disturbing to the elder and more studious scholars ... the teacher ... will find himself under the disagreeable necessity of using compulsive methods to silence this noise and to check this turn for dissipation and disorder. Hence his spirits will be wasted by degrees and his temper soured.... Nor is it doing justice to the elder boys, to employ them often, much less every day, in teaching the principles of language or even the lower authors. ...

The number of boys in each class, perhaps, should not be above ten or twelve; if it be much greater, it will prevent their improvement, and especially if they are young.... If they are generally under nine or ten years of age, or if the schoolmaster is obliged to teach a variety of things at once, as English, Latin, writing, arithmetic, it cannot be supposed that one person can give proper attention to more than twenty when so young, and so variously employed. But if his pupils are more advanced in years, and if they are to be taught the Latin authors, with as much geography, history and rhetoric as ought to be comprehended in the study of the classics, he may, in that case, be able to teach from twenty-five to thirty-five, if they can be ranged into two or three forms, without prejudice to their studies.... (pp. 48–53)

Of the Lower Ranks.... There is none so mean in his birth, or so indigent in his circumstances, who is not, in this respect at least, intitled to the care of the public.... To reconcile the lowest class of mankind to the fatigues of constant labour and the otherwise mortifying thoughts of a servile employment, pains should be taken to convince them, when young, that subordination is necessary in society; that they ought to submit to their masters or superiors in every thing that is lawful; that nature has formed us for action; that happiness does not consist in indolence, or in the possession of riches, nor in the gratification of sense, nor in pomp and splendid equipage, but in the habits of industry and contentment, in temperance and frugality, in the consciousness of doing our duty in the station in which we are placed.... But if there should arise among them a boy of an extraordinary capacity, he should be brought forward in his studies and carried through classical and academic learning; for such a boy is to be considered as a child of the public; and every well-disposed person who has it in his power will think himself obliged to contribute to his assistance. . . . for it is reasonable to suppose that geniuses of the first rate may sometimes be found among the lower, as well as the higher classes, of mankind. . . . (pp. 62–65)

Those who are destined for agriculture should be instructed in the simplest principles of mechanics, the nature of the different soils in the parish or county where they reside, the culture adapted to them, and the methods of the best farmers in this island. This will not appear so chimerical or useless, if we consider the laudable progress which some of our gentlemen have already made in improving their estates . . . it would both inspire them with an early taste for this useful art and direct them in the exercise of it. . . . (p.72)

Beside the public schoolmaster, already established, or to be established in every parish there should be one or more teachers of the English language in boroughs and populous villages, in proportion to the extent and populousness of the place. In like manner there should be, in every considerable town, teachers of Book-keeping, Geometry, Drawing, Algebra, Navigation, and Mechanics. These should explain the nature of trade to such as are intended for that way of life and give them, amongst other things, a just idea of the produce and manufacturers of this island and the branches of commerce which it carries on with foreigners and with its own colonies. The French tongue, if required, may be taught at separate hours. As for writing and arithmetic, they should be taught, as well as the English language, in the parish schools. . . . (p.78)

On Education . . . Of Women. . . . the very meanest among them should be taught to read the English language, to sing the church tunes, and to write. To this may be added the common rules of arithmetic, if they discover an inclination to learn them. Above all, the greatest care should be taken to instruct them in the principles of religion and morality, and to superintend and direct their conduct. For this purpose they should be sent to the parish-schools, either in company with the boys, or rather by themselves, and at different hours. . . . In forming their minds, particular care should be taken to point out those qualities which are most ornamental to their sex, such as cleanliness, neatness of dress, modesty, sweetness of temper, industry, sobriety, frugality. . . . They should also be carefully instructed, when young, in all the branches of domestic oeconomy, especially in the dressing of victuals, in sewing, spinning, and knitting. To be mistress of these and the like accomplishments will be a considerable advantage to a young woman: it will help to recommend her to a husband; it will compensate to her the want of a fortune. . . . (p.84–85)

Of Children . . . Of their Bodies. . . . Their exercises should be manly; they should be repeated at proper intervals, and suited to their constitutions, that they may be strengthened, and not exhausted, by them: They should be such as require address and give the body an agility and graceful motion. Such are those of the hand-ball, bowls, walking, riding; and within doors, the shuttle-cock, dumb-bell, chamber-horse, etc., Dancing, and perhaps fencing too, if the circumstances of the parents admit of them, may be very proper: they contribute, like other exercises, to health; but they contribute, above all others, to a genteel air and a graceful carriage of the body. If the children are to follow handicraft employments, their exercises . . . should have some relation to those employments. They should likewise be encouraged to do several things in the mechanical way and particularly to make, as well as contrive, the play-things which they use. . . . (pp. 116–17)

– G. Chapman, *A Treatise on Education. In two parts. With the Authors Method of Instruction*, 5th edition, 1792

Education. The Miss Hendersons (Kirkgate, Dumfries) beg leave to inform their friends and the public that they propose continuing to board and instruct YOUNG LADIES in the different branches of *Female Education*; and they flatter themselves, that they will be able to do great justice to any young Ladies, who may be placed under their care, having engaged an experienced Assistant in every respect qualified to teach all the variety of Needle Work, Filligrane, Gum Flowers, etc . . . the strictest and unremitted attention will be paid to the improvement of the young Ladies under their tuition. . . .

– *DWJ*, 3rd March, 1789

Thomas Huddleston, Cook and Confectioner in Dumfries, begs leave to acquaint his friends and the public that, as he has taken home his daughter and her children, he intends commencing his former business in all its branches, viz. he teaches young Ladies cookery and pastry: he also proposes to dress funeral entertainments, and to board young Ladies and Gentlemen as formerly, on the most reasonable terms. . . .

– *DWJ*, 2nd June, 1778

Needle-work, Gum-flowers, etc. Margaret and Ann Wylie beg leave to inform their friends and the public, that they will open a School, the first week of March next, to teach the following branches of education, viz. White and Coloured Seam of all kinds, Drawing and Painting, Embroidery and Lace, Shell-work and Gum-Flowers, Tambour and Dresden work, Millinery, Washing and Dressing, etc. They will likewise take in Washing and Dressing, Child-bed linens, and every kind of White and Coloured Seam, to work. . . . Their School room will be in the first Closs below the Long Closs, until the term of Whitsunday; when they will remove to a light and well-aired house in the New Entry; nearly opposite to the New Assembly Hall. Dumfries, Feb. 8, 1779.

– *DWJ*, 16th February, 1779

Dumfries Monday 12 April. Mr Dinwiddie will commence the following classes: A French class at seven in the morning. A Class of Arithmetic for Ladies, at eight in the morning. A Course of Arithmetic for Ladies, at eight in the morning. A Course of Geography. Also, on Monday the 5th April, at four in the afternoon, A Course of Experimental Philosophy at Kirkcudbright.

– *DWJ*, 30th March, 1779

The parish-school of Ruthwell, presently taught by Mr Farish, was publicly examined in presence of the minister, heritors, elders, and a number of other gentlemen, when the scholars went thro' their several exercises of reading English, and repeating pieces of Prose and Verse with great justness and propriety. The Latin-scholars acquitted themselves properly, and shewed that they were well grounded in Grammar, as far as they had advanced they produced specimens of their Writing, Arithmetic and Book-keeping, to the intire satisfaction of all present; and the Gentlemen most willingly give this public intelligence of their hearty approbation of Mr Farish's diligence, success and merit, as a teacher. Mr Farish continues to teach English after the newest and most approved method, Latin, Arithmetic, Book-keeping and the Elements of Mathematics, in all their different branches, as Land Surveying, Gauging, Navigation, Geography, etc. etc. and, as he has very good accommodation, proposes to take in boys for boarding and education, at the most reasonable rates. . . .

– *DWJ*, 17th August, 1779

Wanted, At Martinmas next, or very soon thereafter, for the Parish of Glencairn, A Schoolmaster, well qualified to teach besides English and

Writing, Latin, Arithmetic, and Book-keeping. He will also be expected to act as Precentor, and Session-clerk, if desired, and it will be an agreeable circumstance, if he teach Church-music. The annual amount, at an average, of Schoolmaster's salary, quarter-wages, perquisites, Precentor's and Session-clerk's dues, for several years, have been £25 sterling, besides a Dwelling-house at Minniehive. A diligent and acceptable teacher may expect a very numerous School. Candidates are to undergo examination, and to produce satisfying certificates of their good principles and moral character. More particulars may be known, by applying to the Rev. Mr. Grierson at Glencairn manse.

– DWJ, 30th October, 1798

Wanted in the parish of Crossmichael, Two Schoolmasters, to teach English, Latin, Writing, Arithmetic, Book-keeping, and Church Music. One of these teachers is to keep a Free School, to which is annexed a salary of ten pounds sterling, a good house and garden, and gratuities at Candlemas. The other will receive a salary of 200 merks Scots, a good house and garden, quarterly fees, and Candlemas gratuities. Also wanted, one to teach English and writing, for two guineas per annum, and fees and gratuities as above. All the teachers, if able and diligent, may expect to be well attended. . . . the 31st day of March next . . . the elections are to take place at the Church.

– DWJ, 18th February, 1794

A Schoolmaster Wanted for the Barony of Dalswinton, capable of teaching Latin, Writing, Arithmetic, Book-keeping, and English grammatically. Besides teaching the usual school hours, he will have to attend Dalswinton house for an hour or two each day, to keep Mr Miller's books. The Salary will be £15 per annum, with a House and Garden in the Village of Dalswinton; and the School wages will amount to a considerable sum, if the Schoolmaster is careful. . . .

– DWJ, 13th February, 1798

Of Leswalt. . . . There is a school-house near the church, where the youth are taught for about five months in the year; but towards the summer season they are generally called off, to assist their parents in country matters. There is also a school at one of the villages; but the perquisites are small, and no salary has been paid for near 50 years; hence learning must be at a low ebb.

– Rev. John Rose, 'Parish of Leswalt', *OSAS*, vol. III, 1790–91, p. 322

Of Stonykirk. . . . There are two schools in the parish, both in wretched order as to houses; and the salary only 100 merks. There may be above 130 scholars at them, for four months in the year, but after the 1st of March, the number declines down to 20 or thereabouts.

– Rev. Henry Blain, 'Parish of Stonykirk', *OSAS*, vol. II, 1790–91, p. 54

Of Stranraer. . . . The magistrates built a very convenient school-house a few years ago. The schoolmaster's salary is £11. The number of scholars 60 or 70. With quarter wages, and the different perquisites commonly attached to the office, it may be worth between £40 and £50 a year. There are some private schools also; some of them pretty numerous in scholars.

– Rev. John Coulter, 'Parish of Stranraer', *OSAS*, vol. I, 1790–91, p. 365

Of Caerlaverlock. . . . Dr John Hutton . . . was born in this parish. . . . He was . . . physician to King William and Queen Mary and physician general to their armies and hospitals: In which station he acquired an ample fortune, and died in 1712. . . . In 1708 Dr Hutton . . . mortified £1000 sterling; the interest of £900 of which was destined for support of the native poor of the parish, payment of schoolmasters, maintaining bursars at the schools, and repairing the church and manse. . . . The whole sum . . . now yields an annual rent of £183. . . .the whole annual income of the parish is now £193, which is thus expended:

To the grammar school at Bankend	£30	0	0
To the English school at Blackshaw	15	0	0
‖ ‖ at Highmains	7	0	0
‖ ‖ at Keltoun	7	0	0
To the maintainance of six poor boys as bursars at the school of Bankend, each of whom receive annually £3-4-6 for four years	19	7	0
After they leave school, they receive each 7s. 6d. for 4 years more, to assist in the payment of apprentice-fees, if bound to any trade	2	5	0

. . . what remains of the income, is devoted to the buying of books for the schools, and poor scholars; building and repairing schoolhouses, church and manse; and relieving accidental distress. . . .

– Rev. William McMorine, 'Parish of Caerlaverock', *OSAS*, vol. VI, 1791, pp. 27–31

The Last Will and Testament of Samuel Douglas of Jamaica,
2nd August, 1798

... I Samuel Douglas late of Tavannah in the Province of Georgia in North America, but now of the Island of Jamaica ... this my last Will and Testament ... as to my Estate and plantation known by the name of Windsor Castle ... in the parish of Saint Mary in the Island of Jamaica containing by estimating nine hundred acres ... with all and singular the Negro and other slaves, except my negro man slave named Thomas Men I intend to Manumise and set free, and also the Cattle, Horses, Mules, Sheep and all the remaining Household furniture and Stock thereon that is not particularly bequeathed ... I hereby give full power and authority to my Executors ... to sell and dispose thereof ... to raise the sum of £10,000 Capital for the establishing of a free school to be named Samuel Douglas formerly of the Island of Jamaica free school the interest thereof to be applied to and for the education of ten or more or as many as the interest of the said fund will support indigent children of honest and respectable parents born in the parishes of Kirkmabreck and Penningham in the county of Galloway N.B., the former being the place of my own and the latter of my parents nativaty. the said sum of £10,000 to be raised as soon after my decease as can be conveniently done ... and the three acres of land purchased in the county of Galloway in Scotland and the school house and garden wall built previous to the commencement of the institution. ...

and I do hereby nominate and appoint William Douglas, Esq. of Castle Douglas, and Samuel Douglas, of the City of London, Merchant ... Anthony Stocks, formerly chief justice of the province of Georgia ... now of the inner temple of the city of London aforesaid, Barrister of Law, and Samuel McClymont and Hugh McClymont of the town of Girvan, Merchants, and the Surveyor ... together with the Minister and the three oldest Elders in each of the aforesaid parishes for the time being to be perpetual Trustees and Managers of the before mentioned Institution or charity. ...

the children to be admitted to the benefit of this charity to be continued for a period of four years and then discharged and all vacancies to be immediately filled up and none of such children shall be received into such charity under four years nor above ten years of age, and the girls are to be instructed in Needle work a considerable part of each day for the last year ... and the boys are for the last year ... to be instructed in navigation Surveying Geography and other useful sciences, and both boys and girls are to be taught church music ... and the ... Schoolmaster to be allowed a salary of £80 per annum for bed, board and teaching the scholars to speak and read the English in its greatest purity and also to teach the scholars writing and arithmetic, and my will further is that each scholar shall have the yearly sum of £20 allowed out of my estate for bed, board and clothing and washing ... and that the ... Schoolmaster and every one of the scholars who shall be able to walk ... attend divine service the first day of every new year where a pew is to be purchased and made ready for them in the parish church ... the girls to be dressed in white with each a red ribbon sash around the waist and her hair in ringlets down the shoulders, to be powdered and to be adorned with artificial or natural flowers, and the boys to be dressed in great coats with white waistcoats and trousers tyed with a ribbon above the ankle to have a white stock and bands hanging down the bosom to have a little green silk bonnet on their heads set round with flowers, and ... the Minister of the Parish or any young Probationer shall be engaged to compose and preach a sermon suitable to the occasion and for which he is to be paid £2 2s., and all and each of the inferior Kirk officers to be paid 5s. for their trouble in attending. ...

    – From a typescript copy of the original will. See also EMU, 1971

Letters from Thomas Rainy, Dominica, to the Rev. Samuel Smith, Borgue

Dominica, 26th April, 1801 ... After a lapse of more than fifty years, I find I retain but a very imperfect knowledge of the inhabitants, or even of the different parts of my native parish Borgue. ... I have lately heard, with some concern, that the latin and greek languages are no longer taught in the school of Borgue: from my opinion of the good sense of the inhabitants I can scarcely believe this report. The study of these dead languages in the very early part of youth tends to open and expand the mind, to habituate it to think and reflect and to prepare it for more useful studies. ... What sum, beside the present emoluments, might be required to engage a schoolmaster well qualified to teach the latin and greek languages, the elements of Geometry, etc. ... Speculative politicians have long been struggling for a reform in the state: had half as much been done towards reforming the schools for educating youth, the effects would have been of lasting benefit to the nation. ... Your most hum. Servt., Tho. Rainy.

Dominica, 1st Sept., 1801 ... I had but too much reason to conclude that the school in Borgue had long been conducted in such a manner as would contribute but little toward the improvement of the scholars. For a young man Mr Alexander McCourty who arrived here about eighteen months ago told me he had for some months acted in the capacity of schoolmaster there and in some other parishes although a stranger to the dead languages and but little acquainted with the English tongue. I am sorry to find that the present emoluments are not sufficient to engage a gentleman sufficiently well qualified to instruct so considerable a number of scholars as usually attend the school. . . . I suppose one schoolmaster might be engaged to teach Reading Writing Arithmetic and Book-keeping. The other to teach the latin and greek languages, and the elements of mathematical science and the application of that science to the most usefull purposes of life – the scholars to pay in some proportion to the value of the several branches they are taught. the children of the poor to have their education and school-books without fee or reward. I mean that the branches of education I have mentioned should be taught with care and accuracy and not in the loose and slovenly manner that was but too generally practised in my time. . . .

Dominica, 6th July, 1802 . . . The stagnation in the sale of west India productions at the markets of Europe; and the scarcity of ships to convey our produce to England have left a great part of our last crop still on hand and as yet I have not sold nor shipped any part of my last crop. I usually sold my coffee before the month of March. . . . But in order that this inconvenience may no longer deprive the parishioners of the benefit of my offer I have by this opportunity written to my friend James Woodbridge Esquire of Richmondgreen Surry to remit you on my account three thousand pounds sterling. . . . of this 3000£ the yearly interest of a sum not less than two thousand and not more than two thousand four hundred pounds, I mean to be applied toward improving the school education of youth and the annual interest of the remainder to be applied toward relieving the poor of the parish of Borgue. . . . much, very much will depend on a judicious choice of the teachers who should be gentlemen of good moral characters of mild and engaging dispositions to enable them to accommodate their instructions, in some degree, to the different tempers and humors of their scholars. . . .

I am far from supposing that many of the parishioners will be disposed to keep their sons at school long enough to acquire a competent knowledge of latin and greek . . . but whether or not they will embrace the opportunity this will afford them must be left to their own determination. . . . Considering my advanced age and the distance between the mother country and this Island it would be highly improper for me to have any control over the money. . . . But permit me to recommend that the money be placed at interest by the advice and consent of the Minister and principal Heritors usually residing in the parish who may also make choice of the teachers. . . .

And from a letter to David Blair of Borgue – Dominica 18th March, 1805. . . . I have also to thank you most sincerely for the very friendly part you have taken in forwarding and compleating the school, trusting that through your benevolent attention and that of the other gentlemen concerned it may prove a nursery of erudition, piety and virtue. . . .

– *Letters from the Rainy Trust Minute Book, Kirkcudbright County Council Records*

KIRKINNER, WHITHORN AND THE GALLOWAY ESTATE

The descriptions taken from the personal reminiscences of former pupils of the parochial and private schools in Kirkinner and Whithorn parishes suggest something of the scale of the rural poverty and deprivation in late eighteenth- and early nineteenth-century Wigtownshire. The work undertaken by the Earl and Countess of Galloway to improve the condition of the people was remarkable as it was necessary.

Randolph Stewart, the 9th Earl (1800–1873), inherited the Galloway Estates in the Stewartry of Kirkcudbright and Wigtownshire in 1834. The Earl, who had been the Member of Parliament for Cockermouth from 1826 to 1831, and his wife, Harriet Blanche, a daughter of the Duke of Beaufort, were perhaps inspired by the ideas of Lord John Manners and the Young England movement and Disraeli's novels. Together they orchestrated and financed a formidable programme of educational and social welfare initiatives across Minnigaff, Penninghame, Wigtown, Kirkinner, Sorbie and Whithorn parishes over the next forty years. They built many new three-bedroomed houses for their tenants and advanced annual premiums for the best kept cottages and gardens; organised the Galloway House Clothing Club and provided dinners for the 170 members in the Servants' Hall; paid the school fees for children who would otherwise have been unable to go to Minnigaff parish school or Mr Wilson's school at Garlieston; organised receptions at Galloway House for 210 local schoolchildren, with prizes for everyone; ran several schools with qualified teachers at their sole expense; for example, Lord Galloway's infant school for over a hundred pupils and Lady Galloway's school of industry for girls in Newton Stewart, a girls' school at Whithorn, a school at Pier Cottage, Garlieston, and a charity school at Cumloden Cottage. Two hundred and fifty children were invited from their schools to tea at

Cumloden. They coordinated and financed the Annual Shepherds' Games with dinner for up to 200 at the House o' Hill. And even 'day trippers' arriving at Garlieston on steamboats from Whitehaven were welcomed to the pleasure gardens and grounds at Galloway house and, amazingly, were allowed to go up to the top of the house to admire the scenery. Generous contributions, food, coal, blankets, money in amounts of £10, £15, £20 a time, were handed over to augment funds for the care of the poor in Wigtown and Whithorn, for the Wigtown Clothing Club, for a whole range of good causes.

The situation in the Rhins may have been even more serious than in the Machars. The 1847 Parliamentary Report on Pupils in Burgh Schools estimated that there were upwards of 400 juveniles in Stranraer alone who did not attend any school and were, indeed, 'in all probability under a baneful course of tuition in vagancy, idleness, filth, and incipient crime.' An Industrial School for boys and a Penny-a-Week School opened in Stranraer in 1850. By February 1851 the latter (fees no more than 1d a week) had 244 pupils.

✝

Barglass School, Kirkinner, in the 1790s

I believe that a picture of the miserable hovel called the Parish School, where I obtained the small portion of tuition which fell to my share at Barglass, will represent in a general way the most of the country school-houses in the west of Scotland at that time, 1790. The walls were of the roughest kind of rubble work – it would never do to call it mason work – say thirty feet in length by fifteen wide and perhaps eight high; one small window in each gable, eighteen inches square; one small door on the roadside, no window; two windows in back wall, east side, two feet six by one foot eight inches; roofed with oak poles, stript of the bark, which glittered like polished ebony from the smoke of many years, and thatched with straw; a *lum*, tight in the centre of the roof, of large dimensions, also of straw; the surface dug off the floor, raked tolerably smooth, and you have the school-room.

A round spot in the centre of the room, right under the lum, was paved with small stones for the fire-place in winter, beside which stood a small round table and an arm-chair, upon which sat the good, kind-hearted old teacher, Mr John McMillan, in all his glory. He was not a man of high talent nor much scholarship, but what he had was of sterling quality, and he meant well. There were three writing desks with benches to suit, of foreign timber, at one end of the room; the seats for the other classes were of a very homely character. They were old oak trees which had been dug out of the mosses of the neighbourhood, nearly as when they were found as far as polishing was concerned, and propped up to suit the length of the lower limbs of his majesty's young subjects, the props being rough blocks of stone or earthen sods. There was no use for hooks to hang cloaks upon, as there were no cloaks to hang.

The teacher's house consisted of a *but* and *ben*, and altogether superior to the school-room, though still a very uncomfortable cabin. Early in the present century the good old teacher and the old wigwam died together. A small, comfortable school-room was built close by the site of the old one, which has since been superseded by buildings beside the church more in accordance with the spirit of the times, comfortable palaces when contrasted with that which I have attempted to describe. . . .

Talented men and comfortable houses . . . were in the minority in Wigtonshire in the fag end of the eighteenth century. . . . The class books of the Barglass schoolboy were in rotation . . . The Shorter Catechism, Solomon's Proverbs in pamphlet form, Reading Made Easy, Old and New Testament, Barrie's or Mason's Collection, for advanced readers, and Dilworth's System of Arithmetic; but a pair of globes, a map, or black board would have frightened the Barglassians out of the old house. . . .

It is obvious that there was no use for a satchel in those days. The Collection and the Catechisms were thrust inside of the waistcoat, as he knew that one or more questions must be answered when he entered the school in the morning, and a Psalm every Monday. . . . But though the Barglassian had no satchel, there was one indispensable appendage. He must carry to school every winter morning, a turf peat. If he omitted to do so he would be jostled from the great fire which was kept blazing in the middle of the floor the whole day. A strict watch was kept by the early comers on all as they entered in the morning, and if any one came in without the peat a chorus of many voices would be heard shouting – 'Maister, he hisna a peat'. . . .

– *Samuel Robinson*, Reminscences of Wigtonshire, 1872, pp. 20–24. *For further information on Robinson, who was born in 1786 and died in 1875, see the introduction to the* Remiscences *edited by Innes Macleod: Old Galloway Papers, vol. 4, 1984*

Whithorn Burgh and Parish 1834
Parochial Schools 2 Instructors 2 Children at Parochial Schools From Lady Day to Michaelmas 1833 Males 74 Females 36 Total 110
Other Schools 7 Instructors 7 Children at Schools Not Parochial From Lady Day to Michaelmas 1833 Males 116 Females 87 Total 203

The instruction at the Parochial Schools consists of English reading and grammar, writing, arithmetic, geography, book-keeping, mathematics, Latin, Greek and French, etc.; these appear to be all the branches that are essentially necessary. The salaries of the masters amount to £58 10s., and the school fees to £48 annually. At the Schools not Parochial, the isntruction consists of English reading and grammar, writing, arithmetic, book-keeping, geography, navigation and mathematics. The correctness of the answers cannot be vouched for, as some of the teachers keep no accurate school roll, and are unwilling to make known the number of scholars and amount of school wages. . . .

– Education Enquiry Scotland 1834, 1837, pp. 738–39

Whithorn Past and Present (1880)

The ancient landmarks, links connecting the past with the present, are fast disappearing in Whithorn. Some ten or twelve years ago the thatched tenements in the burgh numbered between twenty and thirty. Now all these eyesore erections have vanished, save one, or perhaps two, and more modern buildings set up in their stead. Two magnificent houses . . . with shops attached are in course of erection on the ground formerly occupied by Cain's Smithy, a miserable tumble-down hut situated nearly opposite the present Coffee-House establishment.

The old manse also, pity to say, has just been levelled to the ground; and a very difficult business it was, say the workmen, for, like all ancient buildings which are more substantial than ornamental, it required the strongest physical force to sever its lead-like mortar-bound stone walls. The house stood on part of the glebe, and belonged to the late Rev. Mr. Jardine, whose widow has sold it, we understand, to Mr Vance, joiner, for the small sum of £10 . . . As it is, its demolition has yielded the purchaser a perfect quarry of stones to the erection of the houses above referred to. Some of the stones, from figures and devices stamped or chiselled out of them, bear unquestionable testimony to having originally come from the ruins of the celebrated monastery. . . .

The old manse was interesting in many respects. It was the residence of the parish minister up to 1813, when the new parish manse was built. Immediately on being vacated by the minister it was tenanted by the Parochial Schoolmaster at that time, Mr Carter, who continued to occupy it till his death in 1833, when it formed the abode of the minister's man and sundry other individuals. But for several subsequent years it was used as a Girls School, and latterly as a Soup Kitchen for the poor of the parish. . . .

– GA, 3rd June, 1880

Galloway Dominies

Isaac McConnel, who died at Dunoon on the 17th of June, 1872, at the age of 75, had been the schoolmaster in the Isle of Whithorn parochial side school for about 50 years. James McMeekin, who died aged upwards of 90 years on the 23rd of August, 1867, had a varied career including years spent as a schoolmaster and itinerant bookseller.

. . . Isaac McConnel . . . is now gathered to his fathers at a ripe old age. A few years ago, James McMeekin, still further advanced, in years passed away. He was also one to whom I was sent to imbibe knowledge, and with whom most of my schoolboy days in Galloway were passed. James was a man of many acquirements. He was sign-painter to the ancient burgh of Whithorn, land-surveyor for the surrounding district, teacher of navigation to those who wished, with power to command to go down 'to the sea in ships'; and also letter-writer to those who knew nothing of the three R's. James, for many years before his death, had retired from teaching and started an equestrian machine, in which he carried a stock of stationery to supply the outlying districts; and being rather 'a character', and somewhat of 'a wit', James was tolerably well patronised.

The school of honest James, in my days, would certainly have been the better of a visit from a sanitary insector. It consisted of 'a butt' and 'a ben', as we say in Glasgow, but without any internal divisions, so that James was at times 'monarch of all he surveyed'. But the peat reek was at times a bar to the extent of his vision. James's school stood alone on the Green in Whithorn: it was airy and pleasant in summer, but in winter matters changed materially for the worse. Each scholar, to support the fire department, had to bring a peat per day, which was gradually taken from the peat stack at the door on going out to school and was thus often very wet. When the fire at each end of the school was endeavoured to be set in operation from these refractory materials, the production of smoke was much in excess of flame. The door being just about the middle of the building, any fresh air which struggled to get in was met by the smoke, which frequently found its way out by the same opening; and the air in the chimneys not being made sufficiently hot, resolutely kept its place against all comers. The density was thus greatest at the two extremes where the fires were being coaxed to burn; and when James ventured into these regions, though he bulked large at all times, he was altogether lost in the peat reek. He would then appear somewhat in the manner of a dissolving view getting into focus, and take his seat at his desk, which was in the middle of the school and directly opposite the door. James would then take a survey of the whole domain, and to any noisy or trifling scholar the *big* or the *wee tawse* was sent as a messenger, with a certainty of aim in which long practice had made him tolerably perfect; and the truant, by law established, had to carry the tawse to the desk and receive a number of *scuds* of the hand, in weight and number proportionate to James's idea of the transgression.

But Candlemas day was *the day* to see James in 'full feather' – his soft and kindly nature seemed to be full and running over on that day; desks and forms were mostly set aside or arranged for the day's enjoyment. The floor was swept clean by the girls, and being 'mother earth' and innocent of wood, it was well watered and made ready for the dance, to the lively fiddle of old John Kennedy. James, having at no time any leanings to what is now called 'Good Templarism', would produce some few bottles of 'the ardent', most likely the famous Bladnoch, several jugs, hot water and sugar; and being surrounded with all these utensils, he would produce a compound, not very potent, but hot and sweet, with a jug of which and glass in hand, the larger boys would set off through the school to supply the 'good cheer' to their fellows; but for those of more tender years, sweeties and such-like dainties were in store. Meantime, on went the dance, the joy *was* unconfined, and in a friendly way some of the old scholars would look in, to mix among and enjoy the fun. McConnel's scholars, passing home from their less pretentious enjoyments, I have seen looking in at the windows; and if James saw any who had been at one time in his school, he would send out for them to join in the merriment.

I give no opinion as to whether this was right, but I give it as a matter of history. The whole affair was always orderly, and finished with the larger boys giving 'a convoy', or possibly going the whole length home with the boy who was called 'the king' on account of the amount of 'his offering', the same being observed by the girls to 'the queen' . . . James and Isaac were both men completely in earnest, and wished to teach as much as possible in the least time.

– Notes by 'A Gallovidian in Glasgow', *GG*, 6th July, 1872

'Improving the condition of the labouring classes'
The Galloway Estates. The Earl and Countess of Galloway take a very lively interest in improving the condition of the labouring classes upon the Galloway estates, by affording them facilities for the education of their families, and improving their dwellings. Betwixt Whithorn and Glen Trool in Minnigaff there are seven schools of various kinds (chiefly schools of industry for girls and infant schools), in active operation under well qualified teachers, at the sole expense of his Lordship and Lady Galloway; besides which, they are never backward in co-operating with

others in furthering the great cause of religious and moral education. The infant school roll at Newton-Stewart generally numbers above a hundred. In respect to dwellings his Lordship has erected many dwellings on his estate, each containing, besides a small kitchen or living room, three small bedrooms, which is the amount of accommodation considered needful for a married couple with a family of boys and girls. These when erected in a substantial style, with foreign timber and slated roofs, cost from £80 to £90 each. *Dumfries Herald.*

– *GA*, 6th November, 1851

Parish of Sorbie (December 1838)

Education. Total number of Schools in the parish, 5; parochial schools, 1; unendowed schools, 4. Among these there are two female schools, one of which is supported by Lady Galloway, and conducted upon the Lancastrian system. . . . One of the schools of Garlieston has been long famous for navigation, and the practical branches of mathematics. The parochial teacher . . . salary is £25 13s. 3¾ d.; and the amount of school fees may be rated at £64 per annum. The yearly expense of education at the parochial school is . . . Reading of English, 12s.; reading and writing, 14s.; arithmetic, 16s.; Latin or Greek, 20s.; book-keeping by single entry, 20s.; book-keeping by double entry, £2 2s.; mensuration 7s. 6d.; trigonometry, 7s. 6d.; navigation, 21s. . . . .

– Rev. E.W. Davidson and Rev. A. Forrester, *NSAS*, 'Wigtonshire', 1845, p. 34

Parish of Penninghame (December 1838)

Education. There are nine schools in this parish; one parochial, three endowed, and the rest unendowed. . . . There is an infant school about to be opened on an endowment by the Earl of Galloway. . . . Of the endowed schools, one has a salary of ten pounds a year from the Earl of Galloway, with a school-room and dwelling-house *rent free.* . . .

– Rev. Samuel Richardson, *NSAS*, 'Wigtonshire', 1845, pp. 190–91

Parish of Minnigaff (February 1842)

Education. Besides the parochial school, there are two other in the parish; one at Bargrennan . . . built by subscription; and another at Stranord, in the mines district, built chiefly at the expense of Lady Heron Maxwell and Mrs Stewart of Cairnsmuir. . . . The teacher at Bargrennan has, in addition to the school fees, the sum of £5 allowed by the Earl of Galloway. The fees do not exceed £10. He generally resides two or three weeks alternately with those farmers who have children at school, otherwise it would be impossible to exist on the scanty remuneration he receives for his labours. The teacher at Stranord has no salary; his emoluments do not exceed £20 a year, a sum inferior to the earnings of a labourer in constant employment. In addition to those schools, the Countess of Galloway has a charity school near Cumloden Cottage, where 25 girls are instructed in reading, writing, arithmetic, and needle work, by a female teacher. Besides those children whom the parochial teacher is bound to teach gratuitously, the Earl of Galloway pays for the instruction of 20 children in the common branches of education at the parish school; and Lady Heron Maxwell and Mrs Stewart pay £2 yearly to the teacher at Stranord for the instruction of young children. . . .

Many parts of the parish are so distant from any school, being from six to ten miles distant over moors and bogs, as to prove a serious obstacle to attendance. The population is thinly scattered, and the families are mostly those of shepherds. They, however, display a laudable solicitude for the instruction of their children, and several of the families unite to procure a person, generally a young lad, to teach them, as it is impossible to assemble the children together daily for this purpose. The teacher usually goes the round of each family, remaining a week or fortnight in each, and the children bring their victuals with them, and remain for the same period, and thus an itinerating school is formed alternately in each other's houses. . . .

Charitable Institutions. There is no friendly society or saving bank in the parish. A clothing club was instituted a few years ago by Lady Galloway. The contributors deposit 1d. or 2d. weekly, as they choose; at the end of the year, her Ladyship adds to the sum deposited one-half of the amount, and, for this sum, the depositor receives an order on a draper in Newton-Stewart for what articles of clothing he may wish. . . .

– Rev. M.S. Johnstone, *NSAS*, 'Kirkcudbrightshire', 1845, pp. 141–43

Lady Galloway's Girls' School, Newton Stewart. . . . entirely maintained by the Countess of Galloway . . . teacher Miss Masson. . . . *Lord Galloway's Infant School.* Teacher, Miss Starke; pupil teachers, Misses Adams, Thomson, and Walsh. . . . Lord Galloway receives no Government aid for the school. . . . This school and the neighbouring girls' school were founded a good many years ago by the munificent liberality of Lord and Lady Galloway, for the benefit of the children of Newton-Stewart, and have ever since been maintained by them. . . . The school buildings are not only admirable, but form a most picturesque feature of Newton-Stewart; while the playground attached to them is such as all schools ought to have, but such as few do. The Infant

School . . . numbers about 130 scholars. . . . The day begins with prayer . . . Scripture lesson, object lesson, picture lesson follow in rapid succession, varied every four or five minutes by manual and pedal and capital exercises – by noddings and beckings and bowings, by turnings to the door and window, by prostrations to the floor, by twistings of wrist joints and knuckle joints, by angles made by fingers and arches made by arms. Then come songs, whose subjects range from mathematical definitions to the virtues of milk and the manufacture of butter. Then more lessons, embracing pictorial sketches from the Old Testament, dissertations upon the structure of the elephant, and lay sermons from the text that 'a stitch in time saves nine', illustrated by the curious fact that small holes in stockings undarned are apt to become big ones. . . . Then senior classes read well and spell well, write a little to dictation, and show a perfect acquaintance with the multiplication table and the simple rules of arithmetic. . . .

– *GG*, 1st April and 8th April, 1871

Festivities at Galloway House. On Friday, the 2d January current, Lord and Lady Galloway entertained the children attending the various schools in the district, which are so liberally endowed and supported by these two distinguished individuals, to a sumptuous tea, and amongst them were a number of boys taught at Mr Wilson's school in Garliestown, at the expense of the noble lord. The children, numbering 210, assembled in the large and magnificent hall . . . graced with five beautiful Christmas trees, profusely covered with useful and valuable prizes. . . . The children . . . proceeded in regular marching order along the extensive passage to the colonade, singing an appropriate piece on the march. The colonade being the banqueting hall for the youngsters, was enclosed and fitted up with a variety of evergreens . . . here was the ripe orange hanging in great profusion on the trees and the chrysanthemum in various hues and colours, with many other exotics. . . . the Countess of Galloway gave a prize to *every scholar* present, assisted by the Lady Caroline Stewart and the Lady Helen. . . . his lordship had provided a violin player, whose exertions were most effective in keeping the little ones in the most happy dancing mood. . . . The mothers of the children were also entertained to tea. And a number of his Lordship's respectable tenants in this neighbourhood were invited . . . There were upwards of 300 present, young and old. . . . *Corres. of Courier.*

– *GA*, 8th January, 1854

Cottage Premiums. For several years past the Earl of Galloway has given premiums for the cleanest and best-kept cottages on his Lordship's estates in the parishes of Minnigaff, Sorbie, Penninghame, Wigtown, Kirkinner and Whithorn. . . . The annual value of each cottage, with the ground attached, not to exceed £5 sterling, old cottages not only allowed but invited to enter into the competition. The roof of the cottage, whether of thatch or slate, to be in good repair, interior clean and orderly; windows free of broken glass, clean, and affording the means of ventilation; dunghills and all other nuisances to be removed from the front and gables and offices kept clean – preference given to competitors who, in addition to these requisites, are cleanly and tidy in their persons and families, and display the greatest taste in ornamenting the exterior of their houses, and the ground in front and at the gables. In judging of the gardens, the sufficiency and neatness of the fences, cleanness of the ground, neatness of the walks, quality of the crops, and general productiveness of the garden will be kept in view. . . . In the parish of Minnigaff: 1st prize, David Cochran, Cardorcan, 20s.; 2d do, John Henderson, Borgan Larg, 15s.; 3d do, James McGarva, do, do, 10s.; 4th do, Alexander Stewart, Boreland, 5s. . . .

– *GA*, 23rd November, 1854

The Annual Shepherds' Games at House o' Hill. In these days when financial reform associations, agricultral associations, and innumerable associations of divers kinds are holden in every quarter, we have to record another sort of gathering, which, we are sorry to say, is too seldom got up in . . . Galloway. The one to which we allude is held annually at the House o' Hill, where all sorts of gymnastic games are practised, and which gives the Minnigaff herds an opportunity of communicating to one another. . . . This affair is got up under the patronage of the Earl of Galloway, who distributes among the competitors a plentiful supply of the good things of this life, in the shape of substantial refreshments. . . .

– *GA*, 18th May, 1849

Monday 5th April, 1847 . . . upwards of 700 people at the House o' Hill Games. . . . Long Race on the public road . . . half a mile out and the same distance in . . . seven competitors . . . stripped to shirt and trousers . . . barefooted . . . 1st, Archibald McGuffie, Tannylaggie, 10s.; 2d, John McCrae, Carseriggan, 5s.; 3d, James Grierson, 2s. 6d. . . . Putting or throwing the stone . . . this season carried off by a stranger. . . . Short race on public road, barefooted. . . . Hop-step-and-jump. . . .

Long Leap, with running race. . . . High Leap, with running race. . . . High Leap, with running race. 1st prize, Wm Kirkland, Pinvalley; 2d, Samuel

Hewetson, Baltersan; 3d, Edward Maxwell, Esq., Kirrouchtree. . . .

Then followed an excellent dinner, to which betwixt one and two hundred sat down. . . .

Then followed the wrestling – 12 competitors, and, after all, an old man, said to be sixty years of age, came off victorious. . . . what must he have been in the ranks of our Cavalry two score years ago?

Steeple Chase – in my opinion by far the best race of the day – the ground selected being very uneven – part peat-bog, with high breast to climb – then level moor, soft, then hard – then meadow, with ditches and burns to cross – then high hill – dyke to cross into rough rocky ground descending down to level meadow – fences to cross again, and so on to the winning post – all this accomplished barefooted – 8 or 10 started, about the half only came in. . . .

Shepherds Race (exclusively for shepherds on the Galloway estate) – 1st, James McGarva, Lay; 2d, William Hutcheson, Auchenlick; 3d, Henry Adams, Holm.

– GA, 8th April, 1847

SCHOOL LOG BOOKS

Cairnryan, Whinnie Liggate (Kirkcudbright), and Birleyhill (Durisdeer)

Some log books were kept in parochial schools before the 1870s. The 1872 Education Act (Scotland) required head teachers in public schools to keep a Log Book (as well as detailed Registers), in which they noted attendances and the reasons why children failed to come to school. This was important because after 1873 the annual government grant paid out for each school was determined by (a) the average attendance in the year up to 30th April (at 4s. per pupil) and (b) on the success of pupils in examinations taken each year by inspectors. A fixed rate was paid for each pupil passing, for example, 3s. for reading or writing or arithmetic, 2s. for history or geography or grammar, and 1s. for singing. In 1883, for example, the Whinnie Liggate School Grant was

47 Average Attendance	*£15 5 6*	*Passes Reading 31*	*Writing 33*	*Arithmetic 32*
8 Infants	*3 4 0*	*= 96 less 4 = 92*	*£13 16 0*	
Grant under Art. 19D	*10 0 0*	*Grammar and History, etc. 40 = £8 0 0*		
	Total = £50 5 6			

Attendances fluctuated alarmingly. Some parents may have been unable or reluctant to pay school fees; others depended on the extra household income brought in by older children. Compulsory officers brought in to to try to persuade parents to send their children to school do not seem to have had much success in the 1870s. And temporary settlement was another problem as children often left at the end of May, when their parents flitted to work on farms in different parishes.

Extracts from the reports of the inspectors and from instructions from the School Boards were sometimes entered in the log books, for example on 28th March, 1883, the Teachers of Townend, Townhead and Whinnie Liggate Schools were 'specially requested by the Board to discountenance and put down the practice hitherto existing of children asking subscriptions from the Public for presentations to be made to the Teachers at Christmas.'

Trained for two years at the Church of Scotland T.C. in Glasgow or the Edinburgh Normal, the head teachers at these small rural schools seem very young, at 20, 21, and 24 years, for the positions they were taking up. Several moved on after a year to three years. On the other hand James Connell was head teacher at Birleyhill from 3rd October, 1876 until he died on 8th May, 1916. Their qualifications varied from the 3:3 of George Oliver at Cairnryan to a 1st Division, 2nd Year from Archibald McKinney at Glasgow in December 1875. McKinney, who succeeded William Armstrong at Whinnie Liggate in January 1876, was almost at 20 a veteran, having spent five years as a pupil teacher at Kirkcolm School in Wigtownshire.

The log books are a good local history source – for the condition of the school buildings, the length of the Summer and New Year Holidays, the accents and aptitudes of the pupils, singing or groaning at Birleyhill, and for absences for working in the woods or turnip hoeing or gathering shellfish or for the Duke's birthday or for attending Hiring Fairs or Cattle Shows or farm sales or for getting the messages in Stranraer. . . .

✝

Extracts from the Whinnie Liggate School Log Book 1866–70

1866 15 January	Mr Archibald Millar left, to take charge of Townend School, Kirkcudbright.
	Mr James McNicol appointed. . . . Trained in Est. Ch. Training College, Glasgow, 21 years of age – 2 years in training – served an apprenticeship as P.T.
30 January	Abolished 'Mother's Catechism' for the junior class – gave oral lesson on the Creation instead.
29 March	Day of humiliation for the Cattle Plague.
25 May	Holiday for the Queen's Birthday.

18 June	Bible lessons badly prepared, attendance small – children engaged at farm work.
20, 21, 22 June	Holidays for Bazaar.
24 September	John McDougall from Kilmun Parochial School began his duties as successor to James McNicol, who has accepted Nitshill school, Glasgow. J.McD. has been trained two years in Glasgow Est. Ch. Training College. His Parchment Certificate is 2:3.
1867 14 January	Punished and admonished two boys for quarrelling. Margaret Brown began to teach sewing, Jane Rae being held as resigned on account of absence.
5 April	Received Summary of Inspector's Report, which is as follows. All the scholars who had made the necessary attendances were presented for examination, the higher standards being well filled. On the whole the percentage of failures is considerably greater than at my last visit, a result due principally to bad spelling in the fourth and fifth standard. The fact that the oral spelling is good seems to show that the scholars are not sufficiently exercised in writing to dictation on paper. As regards Arithmetic the scholars show themselves expert and accurate with very few exceptions, and there is the usual amount of Geography and Grammar. My Lords will expect a much better report of the spelling next year.
1868 7 February	Lady Isabella and Miss Hope from the Isle visited the School. Attendance thin, on account of the inclemency of the weather.
13 February	Mrs Muir and Company visited the School.
17 February	Attendance very thin, on account of this day being the Cotmen's hiring fair at Castle-Douglas.
18 March	The Revd Messrs Underwood, Cowan, Milligan, Edgar, Thomson, and Wark, as a Committee of Presbytery, examined the School.
23 June	Attendance thinner on account of the children getting employment at turnip hoeing.
Closed school	7 August to 21 September.
7 October	Admonished and threatened those who injured the wood work of the School in any way.
23 October	One of the children got his leg broken by falling from a tree.

1869 16 October	Mr William Armstrong was, on the 29th of September appointed . . . in Whinnie Liggate. He is 24 years of age, and his class of Certificate is 2:2. He has been trained two years at the Glasgow Est. Ch. Training College. Since leaving that Institution in December 1867, he has been engaged as Assistant in Riccarton Parish School, Ayrshire.
2 November	A number absent at out-door employment – Preparing turnips for feeding sheep during winter.
1870 20 January	Mr Stark, Land Steward to the Earl of Selkirk, visited the School.
2 February	The Earl of Selkirk visited the School for the purpose of examining the damp wall.
21 March	Inspector's Report. Mr Armstrong is proceeding steadily well with the reorganization of the School. The progress already made is very creditable and there is good promise of more. . . . A cupboard for books and slates is required.

Extracts from the Log Book of Cairnryan G.A. School, Parish of Inch 1864–69

1864 16 January	Saturday. It is our custom to meet only on alternate Saturdays.
18 January	Mr William Jack, Esq., H.M. Inspector of Schools, visited and examined the School.
21 March	Garden work commencing. . . . Vacation 13 August to 26 September
26 September	Commenced with an attendance of 27, 13 boys and 14 girls.
27 November	Weather calm and settled, a number of school boys engaged fishing Whitings.
11 December	Seldom a visitor – this does not improve the manners of the children.
25 December	A dancing class in the village – greatly interfering with home preparations.

(School continues 25, 26, 27, 28, 29, 30 December. 30 December as Play Saturday)

1 January	Sunday
2 January	A Holiday
3 January	A Holiday

9 January	The Dancing Class is hurting the progress of our work.
30 January	The Dancing Class is now finished and gives me great relief.
8 February	Unless strictly put down the children would trifle with the hours of meeting.
7 March	School Staff George Oliver 3:3 Agnes Watson S.M.
22 March	Attendance still small as many of the children are busy at field work, as well as collecting shell fish.
1 April	Children largely engaged in gathering whelks and other shellfish.
9 April	Play Saturday
16 April	School Saturday
28 April	Time for collecting shellfish now drawing to a close.
23 June	Attendance affected by a practice which prevails of sending children on messages.
3 July	The attendance is greatly lessened during the weeding season which occurs during the latter part of June and the greater part of July.
6 November	My connection with the school is now drawing to a close.
7 November	My resignation has a tendency to keep the attendance small.
28 November	Doing my duty under the most disheartening circumstances.
30 December	Saturday. Ended my connection with the school this day.
1866	Temporary teacher John Wilson Janaury 9 – 19.
25 January	John Henderson aged 21 entered on the duties of teacher in Cairnryan School. . . . Trained for a period of 2 years in Edinburgh Normal School. My first school.
30 January	Rev. A. Murdoch Parish Minister visited the School.
2 February	Pupils commenced drawing on slates from copy on black-board. Manifested considerable zeal.
9 February	Grouped the various classes for a collective lesson. Rev. A. Murdoch gave a look in.
15 February	Children boisterous and difficult to manage owing to the crowded state of the school-room. 44 present.
21 February	Mr Jamieson F.C. Minister looked in for a short time in the afternoon.

5 March	School Staff. John Henderson. Agnes Watson S.M.
29 March	No school. Day of humiliation and prayer for the cattle plague.
9 April	School Report (Wm Jack). The examination to-day was conducted under some difficulties as the Register kept by the late Master could not be found. . . . The School building continues unimproved: they are certainly miserably cold in winter and must be too close in Summer. The number learning sewing is very small. . . . My Lords cannot continue to make Grants to the School while it is carried on in the present unsatisfactory building.
10 April	The attendance of the boys is most discouraging. Whenever a day's labour can be procured the bigger boys are kept from school.
4 May	It is customary with the parents to purchase their groceries in Stan[r] on Friday. This lessens our attendance on that day.
27 July	The smallness of the school-room renders our work very unpleasant in this weather.
Closed 3 August – 10 September	
11 September	Attendance 10 boys and 13 girls. . . .
5 November	Winter scholars dropping in.
6 November	Some of the children are away from school with the mumps.
13 November	Generally devote two half hours in the week to singing. One on Tuesday and the other on Friday.
6 December	Seldom a visitor looks in.
31 December	This being New Year week only 25 were present.
1867 1 January	A holiday.
2 January	The same.
4 March	Examination by a Committee of Stranraer Presbytery.
27 March	Three of my most regular attenders left school to-day as their father, who is a Coast-guard, has been removed to another station.
3 April	School Report. . . . Mr Henderson is an excellent teacher. . . . from the arrangement of the desks and forms, the amount of floor space available for the formation of Classes is much too small, and the damp appearance of the end walls of the School makes me think that the Room must be cold in Winter.

7 October	We have 50 present to-day.
21 October	Some additional scholars.
27 November	Had to send a boy home as the measles are in the family.
29 November	An endless drilling of backward children.
31 December	Dismissed for the holidays.
1868 6 January	School reopens.
24 January	A great storm has been raging all day. It was miserably cold.
5 February	The largest attendance I have had – 64.
11 March	School Report . . . reminds the Board that the Master's Salary must hereafter amount to at least £43 to satisfy Article 64.
29 April	It is somewhat difficult to get the Shorter Catechism repeated with accuracy.
14 May	Lost three scholars this week owing to their father's removal to the Isle of Man.
29 June	It is a sore punishment to teach for a day in this School in the summer months.
1869 25 February	School Staff John Henderson 2:2.
26 March	The new School premises erected under peculiar difficulties by the Proprietor seem thoroughly to meet the requirements of the locality. Dimensions of School-Room Length 41' 3" Breadth 15' 8" Height 15' 1". Occupied for the first time on 31st May, 1869.

Extracts from the Log Book of Birleyhill School, Durisdeer 1873–77

1873 10 October	Mr Alexander MacPhee commenced as Teacher. Number present 25. Pupils very bad speakers. They pronounce all a's as in fall, o's as in gross.
17 October	The children close their lips when speaking, raise the voice at every comma, instead of sustaining it. Started singing. Their first effort resembled a groan.
24 October	Number present to-day 52.
31 October	Number present on Monday 67.
1874 2 – 9 January	New Year Holidays.
16 January	Two new pupils, Margaret Paterson and Margaret Kelly.
23 January	Average attendance 73.2.
22 May	A number of pupils left school this week, their parents leaving the district. Received from Clerk of

	School Board intimation of examination of pupil teachers at Dumfries by Her Majesty's Inspector. John Blackley stands as a candidate.
3 July	School Inspection. Present 45 Boys 28 Girls.
	Alexander MacPhee. Certified Teacher Second Class Eliza MacPhee Sewing Mistress John Blackley Pupil Teacher.
10 July	Attendance irregular owing to hay cutting.
23 October	School closed on Friday to allow masons and joiners to get on with flooring the school.
27 November	Sarah E. Whiteley pupil in First Class left for England.
11 December	Very keen frost this week. Roads almost impassable, thes now lying in wreaths from three to four feet deep.
1875 29 January	Suffering much annoyance from tradesmen. . . . boys not learning anything good from tradesmen.
26 February	Tradesmen finished with inside of school interruption from September 1874 to 1 March 1875.
1 July	John Blackley left and Grace Blackley took his place as Pupil Teacher.
1876 11, 18 and 25 February	School closed on account of measles and fever.
17 March	Snow at Birleyhill nearly level with hedges. Road from Birleyhill to Belstane fairly blocked up with snow. Average 32.
31 March	What sort of an appearance am I to make before Her Majesty's Inspector. . . . For last seven weeks the school has nearly been as good as closed. Grace Blackley confined to house with cold.
29 September	Alexander MacPhee left Birleyhill Pub. School on Friday 29 Septr for Durisdeer Pub. School.
3 October	Opened the school with an attendance of 50 pupils . . . James Connell.
7 October	Inspector's Report. . . . G. Blackley has passed fairly under Article 19(e).
20 October	Pupil Teacher very diligent and attentive in her work and preparation of Lessons.
1877 26 January	This being the Local Hunt was observed as a Holiday.
23 February	Gave the children Music Books to-day. . . . Their ability to read by sight is only very fair yet. Commenced with 'Ye banks and braes.'

30 March	Examined to-day Grace Blackley's class – found them in a very satisfactory state.
18 May	A great decrease in the attendance this week . . . chiefly amongst the higher classes. Those above 13 years have left and gone to work in the woods.
27 May	The attendance this week still worse. . . . The officer is made acquainted with it and has sent letters to a few asking them to send their children to school. The School Fees were collected on Monday morning at 10 o'clock.
4 July	School inspected. Present 33 boys, 29 girls. James Connell, C.T. 3cl. Grace Blackley, P.T. 2 yr. Mary Simpson, S.M.
8 August	Summary of Inspector's report. . . . G. Blackley has done fairly. . . . now P.T. 3rd year.
28 September	School Board Officer called to-day for the purpose of looking after absentees.
30 November	Monday being the Duke's birthday a few . . . were absent from home with their parents.
27 December	Closed the school at 1 o'clock on Monday, the afternoon and Tuesday being observed as holidays on account of having a Christmas Tree in the School. On Wednesday morning none came forward but three boys. It had been a severe snow storm during the night – did not open the school. On Thursday only about half came forward and the most of them being wet and cold dismissed them at 12 o'clock. To-morrow and next week will be observed as New Year Holiday.

Whinnie Liggate is on the B727 north-east of Kirkcudbright; Cairnryan is north of Stranraer; and Birleyhill is on the Drumlanrig side of Durisdeer parish west of the River Nith (map ref. NS 843014).

The log books, K5 82/1, W5 21/1, and D5 16/1, are part of the collection of County Council records in the Ewart Library, Dumfries.

9

TEN NOVELS AND FIVE PLAYS

†

It was difficult to decide which to choose and which to discard. Mary Curran's The Country Ones *(1975) and Sir Denis Forman's* Son of Adam *(1990), beautifully recorded and partly 'schoolroom' centred narratives about growing up, one in a country cottage near Newton Stewart and the other in a country house near Moffat, are a record of very different life styles. The comic dialect Dumfries-shire tales by Joseph Laing Waugh (1868–1928) and John McNeillie's* Wigtown Ploughman *were also reluctantly set aside, as were* Three Loves *and* A Spell for Old Bones. Three Loves *(1932) by A.J. Cronin (1896–1981), the author of* The Citadel *(1937) and* The Keys of the Kingdom *(1942), is partly based on his own experiences as a schoolboy boarded out to St Joseph's College in a Dumfries thinly diguised as 'the Pearl of the Eastern Lowlands'.*

A Spell for Old Bones (1949) by Eric Linklater (1899–1974) is a very strange political fairy tale about the war between two giants, Furbister from Wigtown Bay and Od McGammon of 'Greater Carrick'! McGammon is the more sophisticated great dictator figure, preferring to be known as 'the Caretaker of Carrick'. It has some rather good jokes about 'square-faced Romans' in southern England, about 'Institutes for Friends from Over the Border' and 'the Institute for the Reinstatement of Necessary Ideas', and a puzzling ending in which 'Love ruled the land and women were its ministers'.

Hannay's Ned Allen *and Gracie's* The Grey Glen *are not lost 'great novels' discovered and should be regarded as stories of essentially very local interest. Henderson's* Lockerbie *is a thoroughly researched 'documentary novel' and a valuable record of social and economic conditions at the very beginning of the nineteenth century. The* Expedition of Humphry Clinker, Guy Mannering *and* Redgauntlet *are essential reading. The* Great Detectives *contains two classic examples of popular books of this particular type set unmistakably in the milieu of the 1930s.* The Lilac Sunbonnet *and* Sir Quixote of the Moors *should be in every local collection.*

Scott's Doom of Devorgoil *is a Gothic melodrama so awful that not even a Scottish National Theatre would want to include it in their repertoire.* The Gipsey of Derncleugh *is a snappy short play by a popular writer. The* Mumming-plays *collected by Gregor are examples of the 'resurrection' folk drama found at one time all over southern and central Scotland and perhaps going as far back as pre-Reformation Halloween and Hogmanay celebrations. McLellan's* Torwatletie *is a good and neglected comedy by a very professional craftsman.*

✝

TOBIAS SMOLLETT
The Expedition of Humphrey Clinker (1771)

Smollett was born at Dalquhurn in Dunbartonshire in 1721. He attended the University of Glasgow and after an apprenticeship in Glasgow went to London and then as a ship's surgeon to the West Indies. He maintained a modest living in London as a surgeon in Downing Street and in Chelsea. He died in 1771.

Humphrey Clinker, his last book, was mostly written while he was in Italy for his health. It takes the form of a series of eloquent, immensely readable and gently satirical letters written by the elderly squire Matthew Bramble from Monmouthshire, his sister Tabitha and her maid Winifred Jenkins, and his nephew and niece, Jerry and Lydia Melford. Humphrey Clinker, the postillion on their 1766 tour of Britain, is, it transpires, Mr Bramble's son, and the journey ends in three agreeable marriages.

The same stories of the inns and roads and people they encounter in their journey appear under the pen of the various correspondents. Crossing at Berwick, Smollett takes his little group to Edinburgh, Glasgow, Dumbarton and Inveraray, before returning to England by Lanark in Clydesdale and Dumfries in Nithsdale.

✝

To Sir Watkin Phillips, Bart. of Jesus College, Oxon.
Dear Knight, Once more I tread upon English ground, which I like not the worse for the six weeks' ramble I have made among the woods and mountains of Caledonia; no offence to the *land of cakes, where bannocks grow upon straw.*... we went some miles out of our road to see Drumlanrig, a seat belonging to the Duke of Queensbury, which appears like a magnificent palace erected by magic, in the midst of a wilderness. It is indeed a princely mansion, with suitable parks and plantations,

rendered still more striking by the nakedness of the surrounding country, which is one of the wildest tracts of Scotland. This wilderness, however, is different from that of the Highlands; for here the mountains, instead of heath, are covered with a fine green sward, affording pasture to innumerable flocks of sheep. But the fleeces of this country, called Nithsdale, are not comparable to the wool of Galloway, which is said to equal that of Salisbury Plain. Having passed the night at the castle of Drumlanrig, by invitation from the duke himself, who is one of the best men that ever breathed, we prosecuted our journey to Dumfries, a very elegant trading town near the borders of England, where we found plenty of good provision and excellent wine, at very reasonable prices, and the accommodation as good in all respects as in any parts of South Britain. If I was confined to Scotland for life, I would choose Dumfries as the place of my residence. Here we made inquiries about Captain Lismahago, of whom hearing no tidings, we proceeded by the Solway Frith to Carlisle. You must know that the Solway sands, upon which travellers pass at low water, are exceedingly dangerous, because, as the tide makes, they become quick in different places, and the flood rushes in so impetuously that passengers are often overtaken by the sea, and perish.

In crossing these treacherous Syrtes with a guide, we perceived a drowned horse, which Humphrey Clinker, after due inspection, declared to be the very identical beast which Mr Lismahago rode when he parted with us at Felton Bridge, in Northumberland.

This information, which seemed to intimate that our friend the lieutenant had shared the fate of his horse, affected us all, and above all our aunt Tabitha, who shed salt tears, and obliged Clinker to pull a few hairs out of the dead horse's tail, to be worn in a ring as a remembrance of his master; but her grief and ours was not of long duration; for one of the first persons we saw in Carlisle was the lieutenant *in propria persona*, bargaining with a horsedealer for another steed, in the yard of the inn where we alighted. . . . He told us he had inquired for us at Dumfries, and been informed, by a travelling merchant from Glasgow, that we had resolved by return by the way of Coldstream. He said that in passing the sands without a guide, his horse had knocked up; and he himself must have perished, if he had not been providentially relieved by a return post-chaise. . . .

Yours always,
J. Melford.

Carlisle, September 12.

To Dr. Lewis.

Dear Doctor, The peasantry of Scotland are certainly on a poor footing all over the kingdom . . . The country people of North Britain live chiefly on oatmeal, and milk, cheese, butter, and some garden-stuff, with now and then a pickled herring, by way of delicacy; but flesh-meat they seldom or never taste; nor any kind of strong liquor, except twopenny, at times of uncommon festivity. Their breakfast is a kind of hasty pudding, of oatmeal or pease-meal, eaten with milk. They have commonly pottage to dinner, composed of cale or cole, leeks, barley, or big, and butter; and this is reinforced with bread, and cheese made of skimmed milk. At night they sup on sowens or flummery of oatmeal. In a scarcity of oats, they use the meal of barley and pease, which is both nourishing and palatable. Some of them have potatoes; and you find parsnips in every peasant's garden. They are clothed with a coarse kind of russet of their own making, which is both decent and warm. They dwell in poor huts, built of loose stones and turf, without any mortar, having a fireplace or hearth in the middle, generally made of an old millstone, and a hole at top to let out the smoke.

These people, however, are content, and wonderfully sagacious. All of them read the Bible, and are even qualified to dispute upon the articles of their faith; which, in those parts I have seen, is entirely Presbyterian. I am told that the inhabitants of Aberdeenshire are still more acute. . . .

On the little river Nid is situate the castle of Drumlanrig, one of the noblest seats in Great Britain, belonging to the Duke of Queensbury; one of those few noblemen whose goodness of heart does honour to human nature. I shall not pretend to enter into a description of this palace, which is really an instance of the sublime in magnificence, as well as in situation, and puts one in mind of the beautiful city of Palmyra, rising like a vision in the midst of the wilderness. His grace keeps open house, and lives with great splendour. He did us the honour to receive us with great courtesy, and detain us all night, together with above twenty other guests, with all their servants and horses, to a considerable number. The duchess was equally gracious, and took our ladies under her immediate protection. . . .

From Drumlanrig we pursued the course of the Nid to Dumfries, which stands several miles above the place where the river falls into the sea; and is, after Glasgow, the handsomest town I have seen in Scotland. The inhabitants, indeed, seem to have proposed that city as their model; not only in beautifying their town and regulating their police but also in prosecuting their schemes of commerce and manufacture, by which they are grown rich and opulent. . . .

Yours,

Manchester, Sept. 15.   Matt. Bramble.

SIR WALTER SCOTT AND DUMFRIES AND GALLOWAY

Sir Walter Scott (1771–1832) knew Drumfries-shire fairly well. He had 'raided' Liddesdale on seven annual tours in the 1790s; he stayed with the Duke and Duchess at Drumlanrig on several occasions after 1812 and at Hoddom Castle with his friend, Charles Kirkpatrick Sharpe, and had visited Moffat and Caerlaverock Castle. His brother Thomas married Elizabeth McCulloch of Ardwall and Scott himself visited Gatehouse-of-Fleet in 1793 on 'professional business' in connection with the McNaught of Girthon case. His knowledge of Galloway, as far as personal observation is concerned, was however, slight. Scott, in Edinburgh, received from Joseph Train (see Chapter 3) and Sharpe a vast archive of tales, traditions, ballads, songs and poems.

Scott's novels Guy Mannering *(1815) and* Redgauntlet *(1824) and his play* The Doom of Devorgoil *(1830) are located in Dumfries and Galloway, and in* Old Mortality *(1816),* The Bride of Lammermuir *(1819), and* The Heart of Midlothian *(1818) he variously used stories and characters derived from Dumfries and Galloway originals. Jeanie and Effie Deans in* The Heart of Midlothian, *for example, were based on Helen and Tibbie Walker from Dalwhairn in Irongray parish. Helen set out on foot for London c. 1736 to obtain a royal pardon for her sister, who was in prison in Dumfries, having been found guilty on a charge of child murder. The story was sent to Scott by Helen Lawson of Girthhead, the wife of Thomas Goldie of Craigmuie. The story of Lucy Ashton,* The Bride of Lammermuir, *was based on different version of the 1699 marriage of David Dunbar, younger, of Baldoon and Janet Dalrymple, the daughter of Lord Stair. C.K. Sharpe's notes to Scott included Andrew Symson's poems 'On the unexpected death of the virtuous Lady Mrs Janet Dunbar, Lady Baldoon, younger' and his 'Funeral Elegie' for David Dunbar, who died in March 1682 (see Chapter 11, and Chapter 4 for R. Wodrow's notes).*

Scott's novels are usually read in the Magnum Opus editions of 1829 to 1833. These contain the extremely useful and lengthy introduction and prefaces and an 'improved' or expanded text: sometimes even the title has been altered. Old Mortality, *for example, was originally in 1815 'Tales of My Landlord, collected and reported by Jedidiah Cleishbotham, Parish-Clerk and Schoolmaster of Gandercleugh . . . The Tale of Old Mortality'. Many of the additions were provided by Joseph Train, whose correspondence with Scott began in 1814. The later editions included, for example, and virtually verbatim from Train, the story of Cooper Climent (Scott refers to Girthon rather than Borgue), the Memorandum of Robert*

Paterson's Funeral Charges in February 1801, and his expenses for the 4th of February, 1796, found in his pocket-book after his death. . . . 'To drye Lodgings for seven weeks . . . To Four Auchlet of Ait Meal . . . To 6 Lippies of Potatoes . . . To Lent Money at the time of Mr Reid's Sacrament . . . To 3 Chappins of Yell with Sandy the Keelman. . . .' Sandy the Keelman or 'Old Killybags' dealt in the keel or chalk purchased by farmers.

The original 1816 text, edited by Douglas Mack, is now available in the Edinburgh Edition of the Waverley Novels (1993).

Although Robert Paterson (1715–1801) or 'Old Mortality', who travelled throughout southern Scotland cutting and recutting memorial inscriptions to the Covenanters, came from Balmaclellan, The Tale of Old Mortality is about the Ayrshire and Lanarkshire Covenanters and real battles and fictional sieges in 1679. Their unlovely names, the Rev. Peter Poundtext, the Rev. Gabriel Kettledrummle, and 'the insane preacher', Habbakuk Meiklewrath, go all too well with their terrible fanaticism. The sermons preached before battle as are extraordinary as they are frightening.

Paterson, unsurprisingly, was not unique, nor were the inscriptions on the Covenanting monuments the result of a spontaneous outpouring of sentiment. Many were rather the product of a calculating propaganda devised fifty or more years after the events they commemorated. Note the report in the Edinburgh Evening Courant *of 1–4 November, 1728:*

> *Separatists in and about Dumfries, who retain the Title of Cameronians, have dispatched 3 of their Number to Magus Muir of Fife, to find out the Burial-place of Thomas Brown, Andrew —————, James Weed, John Clyde, and John Weddell, who were there execute during the Caroline Persecution, for being in Arms at Bothwel Bridge, etc., and have marked the grounds in order to erect a Monument with an Inscription like that of the Martyrs Tomb in Grayfriers Church Yard, to perpetuate the Zeal and Suffering of their men.*

Guy Mannering *was always the most popular of Scott's novels in Galloway – probably for the wrong reasons. Local enthusiasts argued long and furiously about the precise identification and location of Kippletringan, Portanferry, Ellangowan, Derncleugh and Dirk Hatteraick's Cave. However it is most unlikely that Scott paid any attention at all to the details of the geography of the Galloway landscape, let alone which castle or town or village might or might not be which. The debate was taken very seriously in Galloway and* Guy Mannering *locations were first rank (world class!) tourist attractions for decades. The inn at Ravenshall, for example, was kept busy with summer visitors in the*

1860s and kept a ladder available exclusively for the accommodation of parties to explore their Dirk Hatteraick's Cave.

As in so many of Scott's novels, the heroes and heroines are hardly inspiring and the plot almost slips into a muddle of unlikely coincidences. Everything changes in the scenes in which the gypsy with star quality, Meg Merrilies, and the comic support turn Dominie Sampson, appear. The fascination with the gypsy who disregards the laws and rules of society, an exotic creature who, as J.M. Barrie put it, 'belongs to the footlights', remains undimmed.

Redgauntlet *suffers from the use of the epistolary format. Ploughing through the letters from Fairford and Latimer is an unattractive proposition for modern readers. The descriptions of the spear fishing on the Solway and of the attack on the salmon fishing station at the mouth of the Nith by a mob with guns, fish-spears, iron-crows, spades and blundgeons, are memorable. Again it comes alive when we meet the blind fiddler Willie Steenson, Wandering Willie, 'the best fiddler that ever killed thairm with horse-hair', and little Benjie, 'cramming a huge luncheon of pie-crust into his mouth with one hand, while in the other he held a foaming tankard, his eyes dancing with all the glee of a forbidden revel; and his features, which have at all times a mischievous archness of expression, confessing the full awareness of stolen waters, and bread eaten in secret.'*

Scott's plays, Halidon Hall *(1822),* Macduff's Cross *(1823),* Auchindrane, or the Ayrshire Tragedy *(1830), and* The Doom of Devorgoil *(1830) are almost forgotten. The* Doom, *original title* The Fortunes of Devorgoil, *was begun in 1816, but completed only in 1830. Scott was an enthusiastic follower and patron of the theatre in Edinburgh and London and had many friends amongst actors and theatre managers, particularly Daniel Terry and the comedian Frederick Yates of the London Adelphi Theatre. He had hoped that Terry would put the* Doom *on the stage as a thoroughgoing Gothic memodrama with songs, 'The sun upon the lake is low', 'O, Robin Hood was a bowman good', and 'Bonny Dundee'. In fact stage performances based on* Rob Roy, Jeanie Deans *and* Guy Mannering *had been popular and successful. Terry had produced a version of* Guy Mannering *in 1816. Scott, however, had neither the time nor the patience to turn into a viable play the tale about Plunton Castle, forwarded by Train but originating with Mr Broadfoot, the schoolmaster at the clachan of Penninghame, or the stories of Closeburn and Hoddom Castles from Sharpe. The* Doom *was actually performed at the Pitlochry Festival in 1950. It was acclaimed as 'a dusty museum piece' and that was being kind.* However, *as always with Scott, it does have a wonderful role, Sage Master Melchisedek Gulcrammer, crying out for a Duncan Macrae or an Alastair Sim, with some splendid lines and jokes, not least at the expense of the Principal of Glasgow University and his philosophers. Did this have some special significance c. 1816–1830?*

✝

Guy Mannering, or The Astrologer

The desultory and long-winded narraive of the laird was interupted by the voice of someone ascending the stairs from the kitchen story, and singing at full pitch of voice. The high notes were too shrill for a man, the low seemed too deep for a woman. The words . . . seemed to run thus:

> Canny moment, lucky fit:
> Is the lady lighter yet?
> Be it lad, or be it lass,
> Sign wi' cross, and sain wi' mass.

'It's Meg Merrilies, the gypsy, as sure as I am a sinner,' said Mr Bertram. The Dominie groaned deeply, uncrossed his legs, drew in the huge splay foot which his former posture had extended, placed it perpendicularly, and stretched the other limb over it instead, puffing out between whiles huge volumes of tobacco-smoke. 'What needs ye groan, Dominie? I am sure Meg's sangs do nae ill.'

'Nor good either,' answered Dominie Sampson, in a voice whose untunable harshness corresponded with the awkwardness of his figure. They were the first words which Mannering had heard him speak; and as he had been watching with some curiosity when this eating, drinking, moving, and smoking automaton would perform the part of speaking, he was a good deal diverted with the harsh-timbre tones which issued from him. But at this moment the door opened, and Meg Merrilies entered.

Her appearance made Mannering start. She was full six feet high, wore a man's greatcoat over the rest of her dress, had in her hand a goodly sloethron cudgel, and in all points of equipment, except her petticoats, seemed rather more masculine than feminine. Her dark elf-locks shot out, like the snakes of the Gorgon, between an old-fashioned bonnet called a 'bongrace', heightening the singular effect of her strong and weather-beaten features, which they partly shadowed, while her eye had a wild roll that indicated something like real or affected insanity.

'Aweel, Ellangowan,' she said, 'wad it no hae been a bonnie thing an the leddy had bene brought-to-bed, and me at the fair o' Drumshourloch, no kenning nor dreaming a word about it? Wha was to hae keepit awa the

worriecows, I trow? Ay, and the elves and gyre-carlings frae the bonny
bairn, grace be wi' it? Ay, or said Saint Colme's charm, for its sake, the
dear?' And without waiting an answer she began to sing –

> Trefoil, vervain, John's-wort, dill,
> Hinders witches of their will;
> Weel is them that weel may
> Fast upon St. Andrew's day.
>
> Saint Bride and her brat,
> Saint Colme and his cat,
> Saint Michael and his spear,
> Keep the house frae reif and wear.

This charm she sung to a wild tune, in a high and shrill voice, and, cutting
three capers with such strength and agility as almost to touch the roof of
the room. . . .

'Weel, Meg, and how mony gypsies were sent to the tolbooth?'

'Troth, but three, Laird, for there were nae mair in the fair, by myself, as
I said before; and g e'en gae them leg-bail, for there's nae ease in dealing
wi' quarrelsome fowk. And there's Dunbog has warned the Red Rotten and
John Young aff his grunds, black be his cast! He's nae gentleman, nor
drap's bluid o' genetleman, wad grudge two gangrel puir bodies the
shelter o' a waste house, and the thistles by the road-side for a bit cuddy,
and the bits o' rotten birk to boil their drap parritch wi'. Weel, there's ane
abune a'; but we'll see if the red cock craw not in his bonnie barnyard ae
morning before day-dawing.'

'Hush, Meg, hush, hush! that's not safe talk.'

'What does she mean?' said Mannering to Sampson, in an undertone.

'Fire-raising,' answered the laconic Dominie.

'Who or what is she, in the name of wonder?'

'Harlot, thief, witch, and gypsy,' answered Sampson again. . . .

Chapter VII ('The Inhabitants of Dernclough') A tribe of these itinerants,
to whom Meg Merrilies appertained, had long been as stationary as their
habits permitted in a glen upon the estate of Ellangowan. They had there
erected a few huts, which they denominated their 'city of refuge', and
where, when not absent on excursions, they harboured unmolested, as the
crows that roosted in the old ash-trees around them. . . . The women spun
mittens for the lady, and knitted boot-hose for the laird, which were
annually presented at Christmas with great form. The aged sibyls blessed
the bridal bed of the laird when he married, and the cradle of their heir

when born. Then men repaired her ladyship's cracked china, and assisted the laird in his sporting parties, wormed his dogs, and cut the ears of his terrier puppies. The children gathered nuts in the woods, and cranberries in the moss, and mushrooms on the pastures, for tribute to the Place. . . .

The breach of peace between the house of Ellangowan and the gypsies of Derncleugh: The latter could not for some time imagine that the war was real, until they found that their children were horsewhipped by the grieve when found trespassing; that their asses were poinded by the ground-officer when left in the plantations, or even when turned to graze by the road-side, against the provision of the Turnpike Acts. . . .

When matters came to this point, the gypsies, without scruple, entered upon measures of retaliation. Ellangowan's hen-roosts were plundered, his linen stolen from the lines or bleaching-ground, his fishings poached, his dogs kidnapped, his growing trees cut or barked. Much petty mischief was done, and some evidently for the mischief's sake. On the other hand, warrants went forth, without mercy, to pursue, search for, take, and apprehend; and notwithstanding their dexterity, one or two of the depradators were unable to avoid conviction. . . .

Chapter VIII: At length the term-day, the fatal Martinmas arrived, and violent measures of ejection were resorted to. A strong posse of peace-officers, sufficient to render all resistance vain, charged the inhabitants to depart by noon; and as they did not obey, the officers, in terms of their warrant, proceeded to unroof the cottages and pull down the wretched doors and windows. . . .

Meg Merrilies . . . was standing upon one of those high, precipitous banks which . . . overhung the road; so that she was placed considerably higher than Ellangowan, even though he was on horseback; and her tall figure, relieved against the clear blue sky, seemed almost of supernatural stature. . . . On this occasion she had a large piece of red cotton cloth rolled about her head in the form of a turban, from beneath which her dark eyes flashed with uncommon lustre. Her long and tangled black hair fell in elf-locks from the folds of this singular head-gear. Her attitude was that of a sibyl in frenzy, and she stretched out, in her right hand, a sapling bough which seemed just pulled. . . .

'Ride your ways,' said the gypsy, 'ride your ways, Laird of Ellangowan, ride your ways, Godfrey Bertram! This day have ye quenched seven smoking hearths – see if the fire in your ain parlour burn the blyther for that. Ye have riven the thack off seven cottar-houses – look if you ain roof-tree stand the faster. Ye may stable your stirks in the shealings at Derncleugh – see that the hare does not couch on the hearthstane at Ellangowan. Ride your ways, Godfrey Bertram – what do ye glower after our folk for? There's thirty hearts there that wad hae wanted bread ere ye had wanted sunkets, and spent their life-blood ere ye had scratched your finger. Yes, there's thirty yonder, from the auld wife of an hundred to the babe that was born last week, that ye have turned out o' their bits o' bields, to sleep with the tod and the blackcock in the muirs. . . .'

Redgauntlet

Letter III: Of Dumfries, the capital town of this country, I have but little to say. . . . They are a sturdy set of true-blue Presbyterians these burghers of Dumfries; men after my own heart, zealous for the Protestant succession.

Letter IV: I crossed over the open downs which divided me from the margin of the Solway. When I reached the banks of the great estuary, which are here very bare and exposed, the waters had receded from the large and level space of sand, through which a stream, now feeble and fordable, found its way to the ocean. The whole was illuminated by the beams of the low and setting sun . . . over a huge battlemented and turretted wall of crimson and black clouds . . . setting rays glimmered bright upon the wet surface of the sands, and the numberless pools of water by which it was covered, where the inequalities of the ground had occasioned them being left by the tide.

The scene was animated by the exertions of a number of horsemen, who were actually employed in hunting salmon . . . they chased the fish at full gallop, and struck them with their barbed spears, as you see hunters speared boars in the old tapestry. The salmon, to be sure, take the thing more quietly than the boars; but they are so swift in their element, that to pursue and strike them is the task of a good horseman, with a quick eye, a determined hand, and full command of his horse and weapon. . . .

I caught the enthusiasm of the sport, and ventured forward a considerable space on the sands. The feats of one horseman, in particular, called forth so repeatedly the clamorous applause of his companions, that the very banks rang again with the shouts. He was a tall man, well mounted on a strong black horse, which he caused to turn and wind like a bird in the air, carried a longer spear than the others, and wore a sort of fur cap or bonnet, with a short feather in it. . . .

Letter IV: I shall never forget an impudent urchin, a cowherd, about twelve years old, without either brogue or bonnet, barelegged, and with a very indifferent pair of breeches – how the villain grinned in scorn at my landing-net, my plummet, and the gorgeous jury of flies which I had assembled to destroy all the fish in the river. I was induced at last to lend the rod to the sneering scoundrel, to see what he would make of it; and he not only half filled my basket in an hour, but literally taught me to kill two trouts with my own hand. This, and Sam having found the hay and oats, not forgetting the ale, very good at this small inn, first made me take the fancy of resting here for a day or two; and I have got my grinning blackguard of a Piscator leave to attend on me, by paying sixpence a-day for a herdboy in his stead. . . .

Letter VII: . . . Joshua . . . then proceeded to expatiate on every sort of rustic enormity of which he accused Benjie. He had been suspected of snaring partridges – was detected by Joshua himself in liming singing birds – stood fully charged with having worried several cats, by aid of a lurcher which attended him, and which was as lean, and ragged, and mischievous, as his master. Finally, Benjie stood accused of having stolen a duck, to hunt it with the said lurcher, which was as dexterous on water as on land. I chimed in with my friend, in order to avoid giving him further irritation, and declared, I should be disposed, from my own experience, to give up Benjie as one of Satan's imps. . . .

The Doom of Devorgoil, A Melo-Drama
Dramatis Personae
> Oswald of Devorgoil, a decayed Scottish Baron.
> (Bauldie) Durward, a Palmer (formerly Prior of Lanercost)
> Leonard, a Ranger (son of Devorgoil)
> Lancelot Blackthorn, a Companion of Leonard, in love with Katleen
> (Melchisedek) Gulcrammer, a conceited Student (Sage Master Gullcrammer, the new-dubb'd preacher)
> Owlspiegle and Cockledemoy, Mashers, represented by Blackthorn and Flora
> Spirit of Lord Erick of Devorgoil
> Peasants, Shepherds, and Vassals of Inferior Rank
> Eleanor, Wife of Oswald, descendant of obscure Parentage
> Flora, Daughter of Oswald
> Katleen, Niece of Eleanor.

Preface: . . . written, for the purpose of obliging the late Mr Terry, the Manager of the Adelphi Theatre, for whom the Author had a particular regard. The manner in which the mimic of goblins of Devorgoil are intermixed with the supernatural machinery, was found to be objectionable, and the production had other faults, which rendered it unfit for representation.

. . . The general story of the Doom of Devorgoil was founded on an old

Scottish tradition, the scene of which lies in Galloway. The crime . . . is similar to that of a Lord Herries of Hoddam Castle, who is the principal personage in Mr Charles Kirkpatrick Sharpe's interesting ballad, in the *Ministry of the Scottish Border*, vol. III, p. 352. . . .

The story of the Ghostly Barber is told in many countries; but the best narrative founded on a passage, is the tale called Stummé Liebé. . . . I think it has been introduced upon the English stage in some pantomime, which was an objection to bringing it upon the stage a second time. (pp. i–iii)

Act I Scene I
The Scene represents a wild and hilly, but not a mountainous country, in a frontier District of Scotland. The flat Scene exhibits the Castle of Devorgoil, decayed and partly ruinous, situated upon a Lake, and connected with the Land by a Drawbridge, which is lowered. Time – Sunset. . . .

Katleen.
    Dungeons for men, and palaces for owls;
    Yet no wise owl would change a farmer's barn
    For yonder hungry hall – our latest mouse,
    Our last of mice, I tell you, has been found
    Starved in the pantry; and the reverend spider,
    Sole living tenant of the Baron's halls,
    Who, train'd to abstinence, lived a whole summer
    Upon a single fly, he's famish'd too;
    The cat is in the kitchen-chimney seated
    Upon our last of faggots, destined soon
    To dress our last of suppers, and, poor soul,
    Is starved with cold, and mewling mad with hunger! . . .

Melchisedek Gullcrammer . . . enters from the side-scene. His costume is a Geneva cloak and band, with a high-crowned hat; the rest of his dress in the fashion of James the First's time. . . .

Gullcrammer.
    Right comely is thy garb, Melchisedek;
    As well beseemeth one, whom good Saint Mungo,
    The patron of our land and university
    Hath graced with license both to teach and preach –
    Who dare opine thou hither plod'st on foot?
    Trim sits the cloak, unruffled is thy band,

And not a speck upon thine outward man,
Bewrays the labours of thy weary sole.   (Touches his shoe, and
                                          smiles complacently)
Quaint was that jest and pleasant!. . .

Gullcrammer.
        . . . The crofts of Mucklewhame –
        Destined for mine as soon as heaven and earth
        Have shared my uncle's soul and bones between them –
        The crofts of Mucklewhame, old man, which nourish
        Three scroes of sheep, three cows, with each her follower,
        A female palfrey eke – I will be candid,
        She is of that meek tribe whom, in derision,
        Our wealthy southern neighbours nickname donkeys –

Durward.   She hath her follower too, when thou art there.

Gullcrammer.   I say to thee, these crofts of Mucklewhame,
        In the mere tithing of their stock and produce,
        Outvie whatever patch of land remains
        To this old rugged castle and its owner. . . .
        Master of Arts, by grace of good Saint Andrew,
        Preacher, in brief expectance of a kirk,
        Endow'd with ten score Scottish pounds per annum,
        Being eight pounds seventeen eight in sterling coin –
        Well, then, I say, may this Melchisedek,
        Thus highly graced by fortune – and nature
        E'en gifted as thou seest – aspire to woo
        The daughter of the beggar'd Devorgoil. . . .

Act II – Scene I
    Oswald.
        Confound the pedant! Can you read the scroll.
        Or can you not, sir? if you can, pronounce
        Its meaning speedily.

        Gullcrammer. Can I read it, quotha!
        When at our learned University,
        I gain'd first premium for Hebrew learning, –
        Which was a pound of high-dried Scottish snuff,
        And half a peck of onions, with a bushel
        Of curious oatmeal, – our learn'd Principal
        Did say, 'Melchisedek, thou canst do any thing.'. . .

Gullcrammer (looks at the scroll, and mutters as if reading)
    Hashgaboth hotch-potch –
    A simple matter this to make a rout of –
    Ten rashersen bacon, mish-mash venison,
    Sausagian soused-face – 'Tis a simple catalogue
    Of our small supper – made by the grave sage
    Whose presience knew this night that we should feast
    On venison, hash'd sow's face, and sausages. . . .

Act III Scene I
  Gullcrammer.
    . . . I love the bell that soon shall tell the parish
    Of Gabblegoose, Melchisedek's incumbent –
    And shall the future minister of Gabblegoose,
    Whom his parishioners will soon require
    To exorcise their ghosts, detect their witches,
    Lie shivering in his bed for a pert goblin,
    Whom, be he switch'd or cocktail'd horn'd or poll'd,
    A few tight Hebrew words will soon send packing?
    Tush! I will rouse the parson up within me,
    And bid defiance – (A distant noise) In the name of Heaven,
    What sounds are these! – O Lord! this comes to rashness!
                 (Draws his head down under the bed-clothes)
(Duet outwith, between Owlspiegle and Cockledemoy) . . .

Gullcrammer (who has again raised himself, and listened with great terror to the Duet)
        I have heard of the devil's dam before,
        But never of his child. Now, Heaven deliver me!
        The Papists have the better of us there, –
        They have their Latin prayers, cut and dried,
        And pat for such occasion – I can think
        On nought but the vernacular. . . .
  Owlspiegle and Cockledemoy. Both.
    . . . For all of the humbug, the bite, and the buz,
    Of the make-believe world, becoems forfeit to us,
    Halloo, halloo,
    The blackcock crew,
    Thrice shriek'd hath the owl, thrice corak'd hath the raven,
    Here, ho! Master Gullcrammer, rise and be shaven! . . .
(Owlspiegle shaves Gullcrammer, while Cockledemoy sings)
    Father never started hair,

Shaved too close, or left too bare –
Father's razor slips as glib
As from courtly tongue a fib.
Whiskers, moustache, he can trim in
Fashion meet to please the women;
Sharp's his blade, perfumed his lather, –
Happy those are trimm'd by father!. . .
(Owlspiegle cuts his hair, and shaves his head, ridiculously) . . .

Cockledemoy.
Sir, you have been trimm'd of late,
Smooth's your chin, and bald your pate;
Lest cold rheums shoud work you harm,
Here's a cap to keep you warm. . . .

Gullcrammer.
. . . (As he puts on the cap, a pair of ass's ears disengage (themselves)
Upon my faith, it is a dainty head-dress. . .

DOUGLAS W. JERROLD
The *Gipsey of Derncleugh*
(with the stage business, situation and directions, as
. . . performed at Sadlers Wells Theatre . . . 26th August, 1821)

Douglas Jerrold (1803–57) came from a family of strolling players. His father was the manager of a theatre in Sheerness; his mother's family came from Scotland. He had a long career as an actor and playwright, as a regular contributor to Punch, *from its first issues in 1841, and to many radical periodicals, and as an editor and publisher with a conscience. Pallbearers as his funeral included Dickens and Thackeray.*

His successes in the Coburg, the Haymarket, Covent Garden and Drury Lane theatres included Sally in our Alley, Black-Eyed Susan, Time Works Wonders, *and* Mrs Caudle's Curtain Lectures, *and a popular song* 'Jimmy Green's Tour', *in the 1826 musical,* Tom and Jerry in France.

The Gipsey of Derncleugh, *a stage version of Scott's* Guy Mannering, *with Mrs Egerton as Meg Merrilies and Mr Elliott as Dominie Sampson, was presented as a play in three acts. It was, however, a very short play designed to be performed on an evening with another play or with 'interludes' and songs or a pantomime. It included gipsy choruses and glees, and lively professionally written repartee in Act II between Meg and Dominie Sampson.*

✝

Derncleugh. Enter Sampson, reading, U.E.R.H.

Samp. The road appears somewhat uneven – where am I? – my book hath – Derncleugh! – Prodigious! – Lack-a-day! what could have brought me hitherto? – I will abscond.

Meg Merrilies appears, R.H.

Meg. Stay! – Do you know me, Abel Sampson?

Samp. Meg Merrilies! Prodigious! I will perambulate.

Meg. Stand! Whither are ye going?

Samp. Out of bad company; that is – home.

Meg. 'Tis long since we met, Abel Sampson.

Samp. Yes: but plagues will come sooner or later.

Meg. Me and mine have been long from here.

Samp. As doubtless the neighbouring hen-roosts can certify.

Meg. But the time is come. He that drove us from this once bonny place sleeps unmindful of the work: but there is one that calls us to our native spot; he shall feel the gipsey's power. We owe the dead a debt; we'll pay it to the living claimant.

Samp. Woman! thy words are explicable syllables. I am not comprehensive. . . .

Meg. Know you this spot?

Samp. I do. It is where you once dwelt, most accursed; that is, most accurate.

Meg. Aye, Abel Sampson; there blazed my hearth for many a day; and there, beneath the willow, which then hung its green garland o'er the brook, I've sat and sung to Harry Bertram songs of the old time –

Samp. Witch rhymes and incantations. I wish I could abscond.

Meg. The tree is withered now, never to be green again; and old Meg Merrilies will never sing blythe songs more. But I charge you . . . not to forget Meg Merrilies, but to build up the old old walls in the glen for her sake, and let those that live here be too good to fear the beings of another world; for if e'er the dead come back among the living, I'll be seen in this glen many a night after these crazed bones are mouldered in the grave. . . .

Jerrold also included a 'spectacular' Act II, Scene IV, with ample opportunity for the special effects which were such an important part of theatrical productions at this time.

Scene IV. Portanferry. Hatteraick attacking the Custom-house with party – Custom-house blazing – the Bridewell broken open – Bertram is seen in the hands of the Smugglers – Gabriel is one with Gipsies, who, under the appearance of assisting the Smugglers, are watching the safety of Bertram – Dandie, Jack Jacobs, and others rush on – a picture is formed, leaving Bertram in a doubtful situation. End of Act II.

Meg Merrilies is, of course, a great part for a 'star' actress:
Act III. Scene I. . . .

Meg. I am no good woman: the country kens I am bad enough, and may be sorry enough that I am no better; but I can do what good woman cannot, and does not do. I can do what would freeze the blood o' them.

Samp. Verily, 'tis Satan's betrothed. . . .

DAVID HANNAY OF CARLINGWARK
Ned Allen (1849)

David Hannay (1794–1864) of Lochbank and Carlingwark at Castle Douglas and, from 1823 to 1848, of Auchenfranco, was the son of James Hannay of Blairinnie in Crossmichael parish. James Hannay was a Glasgow merchant who at different times owned Barmoffity and Boghall in Kirkpatrick-Durham and Auchenfranco in Lochrutton. David's brothers, Robert (1789–1868) and John (1798–1868), were repsectively an advocate and a Writer to the Signet. David died in Islington, London, in his 71st year.

His novel, Ned Allen, *is not a lost masterpiece. It was published in London and Edinburgh in 1847 and then in London in 1849. The second half tails away badly into a dull story of country house entanglements and finance. But Ned Allen himself is interesting. He left Glendarroch village and the Glasgow Broomielaw in 1739, aged twelve years, for Bristol and Jamaica, and comes back in 1778 to Aulton (perhaps New Galloway, or a heavily disguised Castle Douglas) with a fortune made in Guiana. Ned Allen is worth looking at for the description of the scramble for votes in a fictitious parliamentary contest in 1780 for the county seat (Kirkcudbrightshire?) taken by 40 votes to 38, and for the Five (Dumfries?) Burghs (which included Kirkcudbright); for the challenge*

between teams of 35 curlers (assembled by the Rev. James Grierson of
Aulton and the Rev. Nathaniel Gordon of Rainton (Girthon?), based on
the actual challenge in 1777 between the ministers of Urr and Kirkpatrick-
Durham; for the description of the county town of Raeburn
(Kirkcudbright); for the glorious, and unusual for the period, clerical
scandal 'safely' located in the Highland presbytery of Kirkdrochat; and for
his Hilltap fair (Keltonhill), which ended with a splendid collieshangie
between two hundred Irishmen and the local worthies. Mr Allen dies aged
91, leaving all his relatives most splendidly prosperous.

✝

Tuesday morning comes forth calm, clear, and bright, and chill as the
most enthusiastic curler could desire; the ice firm as adamant and smooth
as polished silver, the slightest touch will propel the massive
stone. . . . These weapons of peaceful war, though all formed of the same
material, and having a general resemblance, yet differ in weight, size,
shape, and other respects. The most common and approved shape is that
of mother earth, from whose kind bosom they are torn, the orange shape,
or oblate spheroid; but as there are no bounds to human fancy, so the
varieties of construction and form are endless. Some choose the flat,
others the round model; some the heavy, others the light weight; they
who are dexterous at running a port, that is, taking a straight line to the
tee, through dangers and difficulties innumerable, to displace an enemy or
establish a friend, prefer the pineapple, or stilton cheese shape. Strength
and tenacity in the stone, and polish below where it comes in contact with
the ice, are, of course, objects of prime consideration. . . . The player, as he
delivers his stone, watches it with eager anxiety; and should it diverge
from the course intended, twists and contorts his body, in the foolish
hope of lessening its eccentricity, letting imagination triumph over
reason.

Soon the peculiar vocabulary of the game is in full utterance. The
unlearned hear, with wonder, of tees, hogs, hog-scores, in-rings, out-
rings, drawing up, roaring up, and numberless other terms and
phrases. . . .

The game had continued with great spirit, and pretty equal success, for
about three hours, when suddenly an alarm arose that the ice had given
way, and that a man was drowning . . . 'It's Jack Tamson faun into a
wallee!' cried two voices at once. . . .

– Ned Allen, vol. I, pp. 60–63

Raeburn . . . Its population did not exceed three thousand and . . . its suburbs and streets had a deserted look, a listless and idle air; here and there, a respectably dressed functionary, or decent tradesman, might be seen, loitering on the pavement, or a clergyman, in sombre garb, waiting the arrival of his brethren for the meeting of presbytery; but no stir or bustle, rattling of carriage or cart was heard, indicative of trade or business. Tippling and indolence were the besetting sins of Raeburn, natural yokefellows, reciprocating kindly, and dragging their victims, by sure and slow steps, to the insatiate abyss. The town had its occasional gaities; and, though the arts and sciences were little cultivated, it boasted of a good subscription library, and was not behind its sister boroughs in a due appreciation of those gradations, and distinctions of ranks, so necessary in a well balanced commonwealth, and so generative of the benvolent affections, the society of Raeburn being divided into no fewer than five well defined circles.

– *Ned Allen*, vol. I, pp. 99–100

Hilltap Fair . . . Here congregated, from the neighbouring towns, all the pedlars, hucksters, dealers in liquor, gingerbread, confectionery, and toys, and not a few of the drapers, ironmongers, and other tradesmen, who supplied goods in general demand by a country population; and here also congregated a very numerous class of tradesmen of a less respectable cast, keepers of menagéries with their huge caravans, exhibitors of giants and savages in a less ambitious way, theatrical heroes and heroines, dazzling the sight by the splendour of their spangles and feathers, dancing bears and monkeys, nine pins, pick the garter, and pea and thimble men; and not a few of the light-fingered and quick-handed craft, who delight in crowds. . . .

Hilltap . . . was likewise a mart for horses, cattle, and wool, and was attended by the dealers in those commodities from most of the counties of Scotland and the north of England, as well as by the gentlemen, clergymen, and farmers of the district. Here the lads, and the lasses too, had an opportunity of exchanging their hard won wages for such articles of use of fancy as they desired, meeting with distant relatives, reviving old friendships and loves, or forming new ones. . . . in the families of the farmers and cottars, particularly with the children, the day was one of unmingled joy and happiness . . . the evening was sure to bring with it large supplies of gingerbread, mint cake, toffy, sweeties, and other varieties, with whistles, tops, cups and balls, suxpenny drums, penny trumpets, etc. . . .

In a well enclosed field, close to the village, crowds were collected, placing caravans, erecting tents, booths and stalls. . . . At the inns of the village, which were very numerous, every third house being one, the preparations for mastication and inbibition were, of course, on a gigantic scale. . . . The friends had a look at the horse fair, where Vesey pointed out some good galloways, but could see nothing of blood or high breeding. . . .'

– Ned Allen, vol. II, pp. 74–81

S.R. CROCKETT
The Lilac Sunbonnet (1894)

Crockett may be best remembered for his adventure stories, The Raiders, The Men of the Moss Hags. . . . The Lilac Sunbonnet, *with people it is possible to care about and with real pathos, tension and humour, is more exciting than most of his historical novels. It is the story of Ralph Peden, a candidate for the ministry of a church whose clergy and elders are so vicious and bigoted that there are only two congregations left in Scotland, one in Edinburgh and one at Dullarg in Galloway. He is a young man 'sufficient of a hero. And not too much. . . . He had been told that women were an indispensable part of the economy of Providence.' He discovers that true orthodoxy is less important than love and common human decency. Helping him on his way are his 'Winsome' Winifred Charteris, 'whose butter was the best (and commanded the highest price) of any that went into Dumfries market on Wednesdays,' and whose fair hair, 'crisping and tendrilling over her brow . . . went scattering and waving over her shoulders wonderingly, like nothing on earth': Jess Kissock from the Herd's House at Craig Ronald, who contrives to persuade the Catholic laird to run off with her to Gretna; Andra Kissock, a lad who 'always lied from the highest motives' . . . . and had 'elevated the saying of the thing that was not, to the height of a principle'; and the peace of the Galloway Hills.*

✝

There are High-lands and Alp-lands there of sky-piercing beauty. But to Galloway, and specially to the central glens and flanking desolations thereof, one special beauty belongs. She is like a plain girl with beautiful eyes. There is no such country like her in the world for colour – so delicately fresh is the rain-washed green of her pasture slopes, so keen the viridian of her turnip-fields when the dew is on the broad, fleshy, crushed leaves, so tender and deep the blue in the hollow places. (Chapter 36)

And there is that 'muckle sumph', Saunders Mowdiewort, the minister's man, who 'howks the graves ower by at the parish kirk-yard', feckless, procrastinating, a 'cuif', a widower in search (perhaps) of a wife. . . .

The grave-digger went on: 'It's a strange thing love – it levels a'. Noo there's me, that has had a wife an' burriet her; I'm juist as keen aboot gettin' anither as if I had never gotten the besom i' the sma' o' my back. Ye wad never get a besom in the sma' o' yer back?' he said, inquiringly.

'No,' said Ralph, smiling in spite of himself.

'Na, of course no; ye havna been marrit. But bide a wee; she's a fell active lass, that o' yours, an' I should say' – here Saunders spoke with the air of a connoisseur – 'I wad say that she might be verra handy wi' the besom. . . .

When ye are young an' gaun coortin', ye dinna think o' thae things. But bide a wee till ye gaun on the same errand the second time, and aiblins the third time – I've seen the like, sir – an' a' thae things comes intil yer reckoning, so to speak. . . .

It's no in youth to think o' thae things – no till it's ower late. Noo, sir, I'll tell ye, when I was coortin' my first, afore I gat her, I could hae etten her, I likit her that weel; an' the first week efter Maister Teends mairrit us, I juist danced, I was that fond o' her. But in anither month, faith, I thocht that she wad hae etten me, an' afore the yar was oot I wussed she had. Aye, aye, sir, it's waur nor a lottery, mairriage – it's a great mystery.'

'But how is it, then, that you are so anxious to get married again?' asked Ralph . . .

'Well, ye see, Maister Ralph . . . I'm by inclination a social man, an' the nature o' my avocation, so to speak, is a wee unsocial. Fowks are that curious. Noo, when I gang into the square o' a forenicht, the lads 'll cry oot, 'Dinna be lookin' at my gate, Saunders, an' wunnerin' whether I'll need a seven-fit hole, or whether a six-fit yin will pass.' Or, maybe the bairns 'll cry oot, 'Hae ye a white skull i' yer pooch?' The like o' that tells on a man in time, sir. . . .

Ye see, mairriage mak's a man kind o' independent like. Say, for instance, he has been a' day at jobs up i' the yaur an' it's no been what ye micht ca' pleasant crunchin' through green wudan' waur whiles. Noo, we'll say that juist as a precaution, ye ken, ye hae to run ower to the Black Bull for a gles or two at noo's-an'-nan's. . . .

Weel, ye gang hame to the wife aboot the gloamin', an' ye open the door, an' ye says, says you, pleesant like, bein' warm aboot the wame, 'Guid-e'en to ye, guidwife, my dawtie, an' hoos a' thing been gaun on wi' ye the day?' D'ye think she needs to luik roon' to ken a' aboot the Black Bull? Na, na, she kens withoot even turnin' her head. She kenned by yer verra fit as ye cam' up the yaird. She's maybe stirrin' something i' the pat. She turns roon' wi' the pat-stick i' her haund. 'I'll dawtie ye, my man!' she says, an' *whang* afore ye ken whaur ye are, the pat-stick is acquaint wi' the side o' yer heed. . . . It's an odd thing hoo jooky a made-up lee is whan ye want it in time o' need!' (Chapter 27)

JOHN BUCHAN
Sir Quixote of the Moors. Being Some Account of An Episode in the Life of the Sieur de Rohaine (1895)

This early Buchan novel, set in seventeenth-century Scotland, begins in Ayrshire by the Water of Doon, where Jean, a French adventurer and 'an experienced man of the world, versed in warfare and love, taverns and brawls', encounters first the Dragoons, more 'like Cossacks than Christians', butchering the hill folk, and then the unlovely fanaticism of the Covenanters. Escaping into the Dumfries-shire hills, he ends up at the Manse of Lindean, somewhere beyond Nithsdale and nearer to the peat hags and hills behind Eskdalemuir and the top of the Ettrick Water, where 'many of the godly' find shelter. The geography is none too convincing.

The folk in the manse, although all kindness and charity, lack 'any grace or sprightliness in their lives'. Nevertheless he finds himself falling in love with Anne, the daughter of the manse. 'She had wonderful eyes – the most wonderful I had ever seen. They were grey in the morning and brown at noon day, now sparkling but for the most part fixedly grave and serene.' (pp. 118–119) It all, of course, ends badly, since honour and promises made matter more than love. But Anne is such a wholly believable creation that it is difficult not to speculate. Is this Buchan, at 24, in love? Badly? Unhappily?

✝

. . . I changed the subject of our converse, and asked if she ever sang.

'Ay, I have learned to sing two or three songs, old ballads of the countryside. . . . I will sing you one if you wish it.' And when I bade her do so, she laid down her work, which she had taken up again, and broke into a curious plaintive melody. I cannot describe it. 'Twould be as easy to describe the singing of the wind in the tree-tops. It minded me, I cannot tell how, of a mountain burn, falling into pools and rippling over little shoals of gravel. Now 'twas full and strong, and now 'twas so eerie and wild that it was more like a curlew's note than any human thing. (pp. 126–27)

... I have seen many dancers, great ladies and country dames, village lasses and burgher wives, gipsies and wantons, but, to my honour, I never saw one dance like Anne. Her body moved as if by one impulse with her feet. Now she would bend like a willow, and now whirl like the leaves of the wood in an autumn gale. She was dressed, as was her wont, in sober brown, but sackcloth could not have concealed the grace of her form. The firelight danced and leaped in her hair, for her face was turned from me; and 'twas fine to see the snow of her neck islanded among the waves of brown tresses. With a sudden, swift dart she turned her face to the window, and had I not been well screened by the shadows, I fear I should have been observed. But such a sight as her face I never hope to see again. The solemnity was gone, and 'twas all radiant with youth and life. Her eyes shone like twin stars, the even brown of her cheeks was flushed with firelight, and her throat and bosom heaved with the excitement of the dance. Then she stopped exhausted, smiled on Eff, who sat like a cinder-witch all the while, and smoothed the hair from her brow.

'Have I done it well?' she asked.

'As weel as he did it himsel,' the child answered. 'Eh, but you twae would make a bonny pair.' (pp. 142–43)

... I had come almost to feel an affection for her. She was so white and red and golden, all light and gravity, with the shape of a princess, the mien of a goddess, and, for all I knew, the heart of a dancing-girl. She carried with her the air of comfort and gaiety, and the very thought of her made me shrink from the dark moors and ill-boding errand as from the leprosy. (pp. 150–151)

... I have told you ere now how my feelings toward Anne had changed from interest to something not unlike a passionate love. It had been a thing of secret growth, and I scarcely knew it, till I found myself in the midst of it. I tried to smother it hourly, when my better nature was in the ascendant, and hourly I was overthrown in the contest. I fought against terrible odds. 'Twas not hard to see from her longing eyes and timorous conduct that to her I was the greater half of the world. I had but to call to her and she would come. And yet – God knows how I stifled that cry. (p. 157)

T. G. GRACIE
The Grey Glen (1928)

Thomas Grierson Gracie (1861–1934) lived, worked and brought up his family in Wanlockhead. In his Songs and Rhymes of a Lead Miner *(1921), in for example, his poem 'Emergency Pump, Level No. 4' and his song 'Level No. 6', he takes us down to encounter some of the fears and dangers –*

Sometimes ye think ye've got it, frae a hunerwicht o' bricks' – he lived with every day. Gracie, however, had another life. He was an accomplished musician – his hobby was the study of music and musical instruments – and worked his violin at concerts and balls, at kirns and merry-makings. In hard times it was his fiddle which 'kept the pot boiling and the bairns fed'.

Level No. 6, to the tune 'Bound to be a Row', is a great rousing song:
> *Come a' ye jolly miners an' listen tae ma sang,*
> *An' then in pity drap a tear as doon the vale ye gang,*
> *For a puir unlucky chappie wha's been in mony a fix,*
> *An' is noo a powny driver doon in Level No. 6. [Verse 1]*

Chorus
> *In Level No. 6 – in Level No. 6*
> *Yer sorrows are nae far tae seek,*
> *In Level No. 6. . . .*

> *The miners doon in No. 6 are awfu' han's tae sweer;*
> *Gang and hear them for yersel' gin ye think that I'm a leear;*
> *There's the Billys and the Sandys, the Taffys and the Micks,*
> *Cosmopolitan is jist the word for Level No. 6. . . .' [Verse 5]*

The Grey Glen *is a short romantic novel set in the Wanlockhead of 1860. The simple story of Davy and Jeanie is an opportunity to share some of the life experiences of the mining community: the village sports, where surprisingly the two-mile steeple chase takes precedence; the Leadhills Winter Fair; disasters and funerals; and Hogmanay with the village band and the work party parades on the second day.*

Leadhills Winter Fair. This fair was held on the last Friday of October annually, and was a red-letter day in the two villages. . . . carts were seen approaching in the early morning from Lanarkshire and Dumfriesshire loaded with fruit and all wares likely to command a ready sale at the fair. The miners of the two villages were also in evidence driving in the sheep and cows they had for sale. These were, for the most part, cattle they were not prepared to fodder through the winter months, and if the sharp-witted dealers from Biggar, Lanark, or Dumfries could discover that a poor miner had not sufficient hay to feed the animal he was offering for sale through the winter they took full advantage of the position and the poor man had generally to accept a very low price. . . .

The fair was held on the Vennel Head, a large square, and the different vendors of goods vied with each other in securing the most favourable position for their stalls. The morning and part of the afternoon was taken up in the buying and selling of cattle, and the real fun of the fair did not begin till the evening. The flare of naphtha lamps lighting up the different stalls showed them up to greater advantage; it also showed the faces of a crowd of humanity composed of farmers, shepherds, miners and their wives, farm-servants, and the rosy-cheeked maidens of the two villages hanging on to their stalwart swains, one and all dressed in holiday attire and bent on an evening's fun.

There was a variety of ways in which the youths could get rid of their hard-earned cash, such as 'The Wheel of Fortune', rifle ranges, 'Aunt Sally's'; 'Prick the Garter', fairin' the lassies at the fruit stalls, indulging in liquor at the bar, or in dancing penny reels in the hall of the old Inn. . . . The older and married people used their savings in the purchase of clogs for their bairns, who had probably run barefooted since the month of April, and in articles of household use. . . . The fun was kept up till eleven o' clock. . . . Some time before this Davy and Jeanie had taken their homeward way. . . . (pp. 41–42)

New Year's Rejoicings. . . . It was a red-letter day for the bairns – a treat in food and drink that would not be repeated till the year had run its course. . . . The village band marched from point to point in the village . . . and its stirring music brought old and young out of doors. . . .The second day's rejoicing was in the form of party parades. The men worked in parties of four, six, eight or more, and these parties would visit and revisit each others' houses and sometimes two or three parties would join forces. . . . In a company of twenty, Davy and Jeanie were enjoying themselves. This party was led by a fiddler, who was followed by Jamie, the clown, a great length of a man, six feet four in his socks. To add to his stature he wore a tall lum hat and in his hand he held a sheepskin bucket on which he was beating time to the music. . . . On reaching their first house of call, the fiddler played and Jamie drummed until they had all found seats or standing room inside. . . . (pp. 44–47)

THOMAS HENDERSON
Lockerbie: A Narrative of Village Life in Bygone Days (1937)

Thomas Henderson (1877–1964) was brought up in Lockerbie and started in practice as a solicitor in 1904. His short twenty-page pamphlet, Recollections of Lockerbie *(n.d.), contains some of his earliest recolletions: the railway smash in May and the great gale in December 1883; being taken by train from Lockerbie to Beattock for Moffat and hence by coach to St Mary's Loch, the driver and guard both in scarlet coats and top hats; using a penny-farthing bicycle, as did two his father's apprentices in the bank who travelled from Lochmaben every morning on their high bicycles; sliding on the duck pond at Muirhead; and shivering in the railway carriages until the porters arrived with the copper pans, filled with hot water that constituted the only heating.*

His Lockerbie *(1937) is set in the period of the Napoleonic Wars just before 1815. It allows us to discover the town along with Mrs Macdonald and her daughter Rose and son Ronald, who have come from Edinburgh to live there. It contains some vivid and detailed descriptions of Lockerbie life, including communion in the church, curling matches, and the Lockerbie Fair. Thomas Henderson's other publications included* The Four Royal Towns of Lochmaben *(1953).*

✝

. . . the kindly landlady hastened to relieve their minds by assuring them that she had no doubt but she would be able to get a wee pitcher o' butter for them some gate.

As for fleshers, there's twa in the village, she explained. The yin is Jessie Bell, wha haes her shop fornenst the Black Bull, an' the tither is Wullie Rae, wha haes his shop in the Square. For the maist part they sell kippered saumon an' saut beef in the winter, but they are baith killin' oftener noo. Fermers are beginning to grow turnips in their feels, an' no juist in their gerdens, an' tae spreed lime on their lan' an' fodder's getting mair plentifu' for winter keep. When a sturdy or braxy sheep was killed, or a beast that wasna' da'en ower weel, the bellman* went through the toon tae let the fowk ken that fresh beef was to be got. She could, she said, aye gie them a bit saumon† as she kippered a guid wheen barrels o't every backend and that keepit her gaun a' winter.

*The bellman had also a drum. One of his duties was to parade the street, drumming the lieges to bed at 10 p.m. and out of bed at 6 a.m. In an old and somewhat lengthy poem by Dr Gibson, who had lived sometime at Halldykes and afterwards in Lockerbie, and who ultimately settled in England, there appear the following verses:

Reminiscences of Lockerbie

Aul' Lockerbie! Aul' Lockerbie! the dear wee toon to me!
Where never fleyed, a boy I played, and roved a younker free,
Wi' heart sae licht that life was bricht, as never mair it shall,
For never mair I'll ramble where I drank o' Bessie's wal'.

Yes! dear to me is Lockerbie, its houses wee an' big,
Its *Up the gate*, its *Doon the gate*, its *Cross* an' *Through the brig*,
Its closes mirk, its stumpy kirk, its fu' and thrang kirkyard.
Where cauld an' deep some dreamless sleep I wish dour death had spared.

A hame to me was Lockerbie when half its roofs were theek,
An' jeests, an' jaums, an' gapin' lums, a' black japann't wi' reek;
When monie were the middens nerr the whunstane causey't street;
But cosie aye its hearthstanes lay afore the stranger's feet.

Then Lockerbie had sichts to see at race times an' at fairs.
Wi' Jocks and Jeans, strang chiels an' queens, in scores an' scores o' pairs;
An' gledging oot the roads abott or the fair had weel begun,
We'd watch the braw, braw lassies a' pu' on their hose and shune. . . .

Willie Corrie, Sandy Moray, then a licht amang the Whigs,
An' hairy-faced Bill Vairy wi' his wife, gaun selling' pigs;
Funny speakin' Peggy Meekin, wi' the meetin' nose an' chin,
An' Robbie Rule, aul' noisy tule, whase drum made sic a din.

† Salmon were plentiful in the rivers, and great numbers were caught by means of lights and leisters, and sold for 2d per lb. Servants when hiring stipulated that they would not get salmon more than twice a week. (pp. 16–17)

. . . In course of time the Lammas Fair arrived. . . . There were at this time in Lockerbie two principal Fairs and ten markets. One of the Fairs was held at Lammas and the other at Michaelmas, when moderate tolls were levied by the proprietor of the estate. At the ten markets all were free. There were also in winter weekly markets, principally for pork, which was brought from all quarters of the surrounding country to be disposed of. It is recorded that £1000 worth and more of pork would be bought by bacon curers in one day at these weekly markets. For lamb and wool markets Lockerbie had been celebrated for generations. . . .

Several days before the Fair day the carriers' carts brought in additional stores, and travelling merchants and packmen arrived in increasing numbers. On the day before the Fair quite a number of men of a distinctly better class were seen in the street. . . . Some of these were the substantial flockmasters from Upper Nithsdale, Upper Annandale, Moffat Water, Eskdale, Ettrick, Yarrow, Ewes, Teviotdale, Liddlesdale and Tweedside, who had come on horseback to sell their annual crop of lambs. These lambs had for days, and even for weeks, been driven to the Fair by the shepherds over the numerous drove roads which intersect almost every parish. The others were the buyers, many of whom had travelled from far south of the Borders to purchase lambs for their own pastures, and for the smaller farmers who bought from them.

These substantial visitors gave the narrow street and the market square a lively, busy and prosperous appearance, and the shopkeepers were busy selling snuff, tobacco and pipes, flints and tinder boxes, gunpowder, pellets, caps and wads for muzzle-loading guns, whipcord, bundles of quills, small knives for shaping the quills into pens called pen knives, and such personal articles that men like to purchase for themselves. In front of the tradesmen's premises were exhibited bags of nails made by the village nailers, peat barrows, milking hannas, tubs and pails all were coopered, flails for threshing corn, pump trees bored and ready for the well, wooden harrows and ploughs, carts with improved spoke wheels which attracted considerable attention, candle moulds and innumerable other articles. Practically everything was made by hand, and there was work and wages for all.

. . . There were also carts from Carlisle, Annan, Dumfries, Moffat, Lochmaben and many other places with barrels of ale, refreshment stalls, and the merchandise of the drapers, bootmakers, basket makers, provision and other merchants. . . . The roads and drove roads were full of shepherds with streaming plaids and flocks of sheep. . . . the street was full of stalls from the King's Arms down almost as far as the Secession Meeting House. The centre of the square was taken up for the most part with refreshment, drapery, haberdashery and other stalls. Pies and tarts, gingerbreads and brandy snaps, sweets of all descriptions, and the latest finery from the city were on sale, besides crockery, candle wicks, walking sticks, shepherds' crooks, whips, boots, shoes, clogs, horn spoons, snuff mulls, caps, bonnets, and an endless variety of other wares which thousands of country folks saw but once a year. . . .

Each trade appeared to have apportioned to it defined stances along the street and in the Market Square, and housewives were already busy examining homespun cloth and linen. These, she was informed by the chairmen, were woven by hand-loom weavers who regularly came to the fair from Dumfries, Castle Douglas, Thornhill, Annan, Moffat, Lochmaben, Ecclefechan, and many other small villages.... (pp. 190–196)

... The street was thronged from morning till late at night with merry lads and lasses clad in holiday attire, and with more matured and sedate folks, old soldiers with wooden legs and musicians in faded cloth playing the fiddle, the melodeon, and the flute.

On the Village Green were stalls laden with crockery, snaps and gingerbread, snuff, lace, ribbons, buttons, pipes, tobacco, tinder boxes, candle moulds and cottons, and many other articles; there were also quacks, mountebanks, fat women and dwarfs, competitions at wrestling, climbing the greasy pole, sack races, and hunting pigs with soapy tails; also mimic operas, men swallowing fire, and pedlars giving their goods away for nothing in order to attract the crowd and telling truths well mixed with lies, and many other shows and amusements. The glib-tongued salesmen harangued and earnestly counselled the onlookers and passers-by not to miss the rare opportuniy now within their reach, and never likely to occur again of purchasing some special article at a price far below its value. One would almost have thought that all the strolling musicians in Scotland were present. Fiddlers, blind and otherwise, and performers on tin whistles abounded. Leather lunged ballad singers, clad in sailor costume, in most cases minus the usual number of arms and legs, whose stentorian voices were heard above the surrounding din, chanted, cap in hand. Then there were the inevitable philanthropic individuals selling among other things, shillings for sixpence, and nimble-fingered adepts at the three-card trick and wheel of fortune plying their vocations of relieving the verdant innocent of his hard-earned slender means. Occasionally some stalwart rustic, who had imbibed not wisely but too well, was to be seen in the centre of an admiring circle with his staff in one hand and his plaid in another, performing a hornpipe with a vigour and agility that a dancing dervish might have envied, as his blushing sweetheart vainly endeavoured to persuade him to behave himself, while his faithful collie sat staring in dumb amazement at the unwonted spectacle. The air was full of the joyous shouts and the merry laughter of the excited groups of young folks, who with fingers pressed upon their waists, skipped high to the music of the Tulloch Reel, mid hoochs and hoos and loud hullos.... (pp. 201–202)

It is interesting to compare this description with the article on 'A Day in Lockerby, During the Lamb Fair' in the Dumfries Monthly Magazine *of*

September 1825. This may have been written by Dr J. Erskine Gibson (see Chapter 13), who has an article, 'A Country Kirn', in the August 1825 number. He died 19th January, 1833, aged 30.

Lockerbie is a neat, cleanly little town, with perhaps eight hundred inhabitants.... Besides the lamb and wool market held upon the hill, there is an annual fair on the same day in the town.... Even the sage inhabitants of Dumfries itself flock to it in hundreds.... Over the whole surface of the hill were scattered tents at various distances; along its summit westward ran a long line, resembling at a distance a street of irregularly-built white-washed houses; and eastward, southward, and northward of these stood various little groups.... Some of the tents were covered with blankets, and some with canvas ... while some sported the more primitive covering of sheep-skins; but all were white, and in excellent keeping with the colour of the lambs that stood in thousands among them.

On entering the town.... Here were crowds of people, of all descriptions.... Here marched a party of soldiers, with fifes, drums and drum-sticks tied upon their backs, who had come from Dumfries to beat up for recruits, and who were cursing the long roads, and the more fortunate passengers who dashed past them in gigs and on horseback; there swaggered onward a number of sleight-of-hand men, many of them Irishmen, in very ragged habilments; alongside of a string of carts laden with their luggage, walked a multitude of hucksters, male and female, engaged in edifying conversation at the highest pitch of their voices; in another place there stalked on with heavy pace various young and old labouring people, who intended to hire, and who, to render their object known, had stuck in their hats or their breasts a green twig pulled from some tree by the wayside....

From every door issued swarms of bare-footed and bare-headed children; some of whom would stand stock-still, and gaze with open mouths and eyes on every object that passed; others would call out to the young lads and lasses, 'country cubbies!' and then get behind them and pluck their skirts; while others would brandish a 'potstick' or a ram's horn spoon, and slap the old farmers' horses upon the buttocks as they jogged slowly past them....

At the east end of the town was placed a small 'show' of Punch and his wife, and other such rarities, in front of which stood a fellow fantastically dressed and with his face painted in a most hideous manner ... soliciting the 'ladies and gentlemen' to 'walk in' and behold the most wonderful things in the world for 'only twopence'.

... I set out Dumfriesward, full of sweet musings upon the lovely and loving lasses of Lockerbie.... Since then I have employed all my philosophy to ascertain why in this place, above all others, so much social frankness and humorous originality of character prevail.... Then, thought I, these pecularities must be indigenous to the climate, and of an infectious nature; and upon this ground have I now planted my foot, until some greater philosopher shall overthrow me; a task which he never can accomplish, without satisfactorily explaining, upon some other principle than climatic influence, why people forget every every ailment, excepting the head-ache, in Lockerby Lamb Fair.

DMM, September 1825, pp. 213–19

THE GREAT DETECTIVES
Inspector French and Lord Peter Wimsey

Freeman Wills Crofts (1879–1957), who was educated at the Methodist and Campbell College in Belfast, worked until 1929 as a railway engineer for the Belfast and Northern Counties Railway. For his detective, Inspector French (see The Hog's Back Mystery *and* Inspector French and the Starvel Tragedy*), the mystery was usually not so much 'Who done it?' as 'How did they manage to do it?'. The answers were usually found as the result of meticulous investigation of railway timetables, stations, platforms and ticket offices, and even cars, bicycles and boats.*

In Sir John Magill's Last Journey *(1930) on the overnight boat train from Platform 12 in Euston Station to Stranraer, it emerges that Magill had been murdered between Dumfries and Castle Douglas. French works his way patiently between Euston, Carlisle, Dumfries, Castle Douglas, Newton Stewart, Glenluce and Stranraer stations, plus Larne and Belfast. At Castle Douglas station neither the signalman nor the porter, not even the booking clerk, had seen the motor car, but the porter knew a man who had ...*

✝

French ... set off in quest of the youth.

'Aye,' said the young worthy, when at last they had tracked him down to his lair. 'I saw a car all right, but I didna see ony one wi' it. Ye see, I came off the London train an' I walked home. I live half a mile along the Dumfries road. Well, when I came to yon wee wicket gate on the far side o' the railway – ye ken the place, sairgent? – the car was there. It was parked up against the side o' the road, headin' for the toun.'

 . . . Castle Douglas station is of the ordinary roadside type of a double line passing between two platforms. The town lies on the 'down' or south side of the railway, the side for Stranraer, and on the down side also are the station buildings. At the west end of the station, beyond the platforms, and close to the junction for Kirkcudbright, there is a bridge over the railway. This carries the main road from Castle Douglas to Dumfries. A row of houses fronts this road on the station side, being separated therefrom by a field and narrow belt of trees. Some hundred yards or more beyond the bridge the road takes a slight bend and at this bend was the wicket gate. French stopped at the gate and looked about him. . . . (pp. 180–181)

Dorothy L. Sayers (1893–1957) had two aunts and an uncle who lived in Kirkcudbright. She enjoyed several autumn holidays at 14A High Street and also stayed with the Dignams at the Anwoth Hotel in Gatehouse-of-Fleet. She liked, perhaps even loved, Kirkcudbright and Galloway. Unfortunately The Five Red Herrings *(1931) is not her most successful book. Please compare the brilliant and atmospheric* The Nine Tailors *(1934), which is set in her own home country, the Fens, where 'flood-water and tide-water' meet the wind. The six suspects in the* Five Red Herrings *are all artists in Kirkcudbright and Gatehouse. One of them, Strachan, had been reading* Sir John Magill's Last Journey *'by a Mr Crofts'. Lord Peter Wimsey and Bunter are in Kirkcudbright enjoying 'the simple life' in a studio up a cobbled close with a blue gate. Sayers places them in an Inspector French type plot replete with essential railway timetables, lost bicycles, significant tickets punched in triplicate, and a panoply of stationmasters, booking clerks and porters. It is very old indeed and doesn't really work. A pity, because her description of Kirkcudbright and of the road to Newton Stewart is excellent.*

✝

The artistic centre of Galloway is Kirkcudbright, where the painters form a scattered constellation, whose nucleus is in the High Street, and whose outer stars twinkle in remote hillside cottages, radiating brightness as far as Gatehouse-of-Fleet. There are large and stately studios, panelled and high, in strong stone houses filled with gleaming brass and polished oak. There are workaday studios – summer perching-places rather than settled homes – where a good north light and a litter of brushes and canvas form the whole of the artistic stock-in-trade. There are little homely studios, gay with blue and red and yellow curtains and odd scraps of pottery, tucked away down narrow closes and adorned with gardens, where old-fashioned flowers riot in the rich and friendly soil. There are studios that are simply and solely barns, made beautiful by ample proportions and high-pitched rafters, and habitable by the addition of a tortoise stove and gas-ring. . . . (pp. 7–8)

The road from Kirkcudbright to Newton Stewart is of a varied loveliness hard to surpass, and with a sky full of bright sun and rolling cloud-banks, hedges filled with flowers, a well-made road, a lively engine and the prospect of a good corpse at the end of it, Lord Peter's cup of happiness was full. He was a man who loved simple pleasures. He passed through Gatehouse, waving a cheerful hand to the proprietor of the Anwoth Hotel, climbed up beneath the grim blackness of Cardoness Castle, drank in for the thousandth time the strange Japanese beauty of Mossyard Farm, set like a red jewel under its tufted trees on the blue sea's rim, and the Italian loveliness of Kirkdale. . . . The wild garlic was over now, but the scent of it seemed to still hang about the place in memory. . . . Then the salmon-nets and the wide semi-circular sweep of the bay, rosy every summer with sea-pinks, purple-brown with the mud of the estuary, majestic with the huge hump of Cairnsmuir rising darkly over Creetown. Then the open road again, dipping and turning. . . . (pp. 16–17)

TWO GALLOWAY MUMMING-PLAYS
COLLECTED BY WALTER GREGOR

Balmaghie. *The following mumming-play is performed by the school children at Hallowe'en. There are seven actors, three of whom carry sticks or swords. (1) Bauldie, wearing a 'fause face' [a mask], commonly black, dressed in a big coat, and carrying a stick as a sword; ordinary cap on head. (2) The Captain, dressed in the same way. (3) The General, dressed in the same way. (4) The Doctor, wearing a mask, black with red spots on chin, cheeks, and brow, with a big 'tile' hat on head, a stick in one hand, and a bottle of water in the other. (5) Peggy, face painted white, wearing an old dress down to her heels, an old mutch, with an old umbrella in hand. (6) Policeman, face painted black, with no red spots, wearing a big black coat, a big brown paper bag on his head, with a stick in his hand. (7) Weean, face painted white, wearing a small frock, and ordinary hat with ribbons.*

All except the Doctor enter the kitchen. They are asked 'What do you want?' They answer by singing 'Gentle Annie' or any other school song. Then speaks –

Bauldie.	Here comes I, Bell Hector;
	Bold Slasher is my name.
	My sword is buckled by my side,
	And I am sure to win this game.

General.	This game, sir! This game, sir!
	It's far beyont your power.
	I'll cut you up in inches
	In less than half an hour.

Bauldie.	You, sir!
General.	I, sir!
Bauldie.	Take out your sword and try, sir!

(They fight; the General is killed)
(One runs and calls the Doctor)

All.	The Doctor.

The Doctor enters.

Doctor.	Here comes I, old Doctor Brown,
	The best old Doctor in the town.
All.	And what diseases can you cure?
Doctor.	I can cure all diseases, to be sure.
All.	What are they?
Doctor.	Hockey-pockey, jelly-oakey,
	Down amongst the gravel.

(The Doctor gives the General a draught from the bottle, and he starts to his feet)

Laurieston.	*The following version is played here.*

Hector, Slasher, the Doctor, Beezlebub. Three of the actors enter the house and say:

> Hallowe'en, Hallowe'en comes but once a year,
> And when it comes we hope to give all good cheer.
> Stir up your fires, and give us light,
> For in the house there will be a fight.

Hector.	Here comes I, bold Hector;
	Bold Hector is my name.
	With my sword and pistol by my side
	I'm sure to win the game.

Slasher.	The game, sir! The game sir!
	It's not within your power;
	For I will cut you up in inches

	In less than half an hour.
Hector.	You, sir!
Slasher.	I, sir! (*They draw swords and fight*)
Hector.	Do, sir; die, sir! (*Slasher falls*)
Hector.	Oh, dear! what's this I've done!
	I've killed my brother's only son.
	A Doctor! Ten pounds for a doctor!
	What! No doctor to be found?

Doctor enters.

Doctor.	Here comes I, old Doctor Brown,
	The best old Doctor in the town.
Hector.	What diseases can you cure?
Doctor.	All diseases, to be sure.
	I have a bottle by my side,
	All mixed with polks (?) and eggs;
	Put it in a mouse's blether,
	Steer it with a cat's fether;
	A drop of it will cure the dead. (*Some of the medicine administered to Slasher*)

Hector.	Get up, old Bob, and sing a song.
Slasher.	Once I was dead and now I'm alive.
	God bless the old Doctor that made me survive.

Beelzebub comes forward

Beelzebub.	Here comes I, old Beezelbub,
	And over my shoulder I carry my clogs,
	And in my hand a frying-pan;
	So don't you think I'm a jolly old man?
	And if you think I am cutting it fat,
	Just pop a penny in the old man's hat.

– Gregor, *Further Report on Folklore in Scotland*, British Association for
the Advancement of Science, 1897, pp. 459–461

ROBERT McLELLAN
Torwatletie, or the Apothecary. A Scottish Comedy in Three Acts (1946)

*Robert McLellan (1907–1985) wrote several excellent light comedies in
the 1930s and 1940s. These included* Toom Byres, *on the sixteenth-
century Borders feud betwen the Kerrs and the Scotts;* Jamie the Saxt, *set
in the Edinburgh of 1591–94;* The Flouers o Edinburgh, *in the*

eighteenth-century Canongait; and a one-act play, The Changeling, *set in an Armstrong cot-house in the Debatable Land near the meeting place of the Wauchope and the Esk.*

Torwatletie *was first performed by the Unity Players in the Queens Theatre in Glasgow in November 1946 with a stellar cast, including Roddie McMillan as the Laird o Torwatletie and the great Duncan Macrae as the Reverend Joshua MacDowell. The play was published by William MacLellan in Glasgow in 1950. It is set near the village of Kirkronald (?Auchencairn or Dundrennan) in the Presbytery of Kirkcudbright in 1716, when there may still have been some ill-tempered rivalry in the Stewartry between Episcopalians and Presbyterians. As the Laird's sister, Mirren, has it in her 'grace' –*

> *For what we are aboot to receive may the Lord be thankit. May he prosper the cause o the true Kirk, and gar the licht o His Mercie shine on aa its members. May He bring ilka singin, sweirin, tea-drinkin, horse-racin Episcopalian sinner to a true understaundin o the error o his ways, and veesit ilka Jacobite rebel wi the eternal torment o the lowin brunstane pit. (p. 12)*

The Laird's house is conveniently near Port Yerrack, where the smugglers bring in their cargoes of 'speerits'. As the Laird says – 'I'm tellin ye the trith when I say that I haena set een on a smuggler this seeven or eicht year. When I want ocht I juist hing a sheet frae the tap winnock o the doocot, and the stuff's lyin at the doocot door airly the neist mornin.' He pays for it by taking his siller to Doctor Dan, the barber in Kirk Raw, when he goes to get his wig dressed. The Kirk Session are aye after Doctor Dan for witchcraft – 'he wad like to think himsell a doctor, and spends the feck o his nichts ower a big black pat, steering awa at aa sorts o queer concoctions he gars folks drink when they're seik.' (p. 22)

The Laird takes his religion lightly –

> *I dout we'll juist hae to put up wi the presbyteries efter aa, for we micht as weill be governt by them as by bishops appeynit by an imposter like German Geordie. . . . ye ken I was nae Episcopalian afore the Revolution. When ye were the curate o Kirkronald I neir set fute inside yer kirk door. And though I gied ye yer bite and sup whiles efter ye were rabblet oot o't I did it oot o peety for ye and no for ony principle. And to tell ye the truth, Willie, whan I did allou ye to convert me it was juist oot o anger at Jean MacMorran. She reportit me ance to the Kirk Session for sweirin, and they fined me twal pund Scots. (p. 18)*

Unfortunately the Moderator of the Presbytery of Kircudbright sends him a new 'chaplain' [Presbyterian] and the Laird, to his great

indignation, finds that he is expected to pay him a salary of five pounds
sterling and his board and washing ['guid gowd flung doun the stank!']

✝

Laird.	I canna understaun what wey ye were sent here, Maister MacDowell. We hae a chaplain already.
MacDowell:	His name, Laird?
Laird:	To tell the trith I hae forgotten it. We aye juist caa him Wanert Willie. He was the meenister o Kirkronald afore the Revolution.
MacDowell:	I see. An Episcopalian. Tell me, Laird: daes he bide here aa the time?
Laird:	Na na, but he looke in aye i' the passing, and bides for a day or twa.
MacDowell:	That'll explain the haill maitter. Ye see, Laird, the ceevil authorities hae taen it into their heids that the employment o gangrel Episcopalian preachers affords ower muckle scope the noo for intrigue on behalf o the exiled Stewarts, and they hae determined to discourage the practice, as prejudicial to the safety o the realm.
Laird.	I see.
MacDowell:	Ay. They hae askit the moderators o the district presbyteries to send oot proper chaplains to aa the families concerned.
Laird:	Sae that's the way o't. Ye hae been sent to the hoose to spy on me. Weill, Maister MacDowell, ye'll be wastin yer time. I neir fash wi politics.
MacDowell:	I'm glad to hear it, Laird, but I'm nae poleetical spy, if that's what ye think. I hae been sent here as yer chaplain, and ye'll fin me conscientious in that capacity. Tell me, noo: daes this Wanert Willie, as ye caa him, see that ye haud regular faimily worship?
Laird.	Weill, whan he's here he whiles puts up a bit prayer at nicht amang the servants, and he aye says a bit grace for us when we sit doun to oor meal.
MacDowell:	I see. Daes he encourage ye to conduct ony worship for yer faimily or the servants when he isna here?
Laird:	I canna say he daes.
MacDowell:	I see. Daes he examine ye aa regularly in the carritches?
Laird:	I believe he had the servants weill acquant wi the carrtiches

	when he cam here at first. Nae dout they could mak no a bad show yet.
MacDowell:	I see. And what sort o show could ye mak yersell, Laird?
Laird:	Me! I haena rin through them sin I was a laddie.
MacDowell:	It's juist as I thocht, Laird. I dout I'll hae to mak some gey drastic cheynges in the conduct o yer affairs. We'll stert wi a service for the haill hoose ilka nicht efter supper, and I'll tak yer dochter and yersell for scriptural instruction i' the efternunes aye for mebbe twa hours.
Laird:	Dae ye mean through the week?
MacDowell:	Ay. On the Saubbath we'll hae prayers efter breakfast, afore ye set aff for the forenune service at Kirkronald. Syne we'll hae prayers efter denner, afore ye set aff for the service i' the efternune. Efter the fower hours I'll examine ye aa in the carritches, and efter supper we'll read ower a chapter or twa and sing a wheen psalms, and hae a guid lang warstle wi the Lord in prayer afore we gang to bed.
Laird:	I see. Ye're gaun to keep us aa gey thrang.
Ailie	(Giving her father a meaning look):
	Daddie, is it not time ye were takin yer medicine?'

(pp. 53–55)

Perhaps it is hardly surprising to find that Act III 'degenerates' into a splendid farce with secret passages, candles, a press door, a downstage bed, a Jacobite in hiding, and a new wife (Mirren) for the manse at Balmagown. The Laird gets rid of his 'chaplain' and his troublesome sister!

10
FOUR SHORT STORIES

†

The first Scottish short stories were the old word-of-mouth tales of battles and deeds of valour, of ghosts and of local scandalous doings. These in turn became the source material for the compilers of chapbooks, for example The Life of Daniel Dancer, *the remarkable miser and* The Coalman's Courtship to the Creel-Wife's Daughter, *the literature of the people and sold in vast quantities by itinerant packmen throughout Scotland in the eighteenth century. Some were printed in Kirkcudbright and Newton Stewart. Sir Walter Scott's* Wandering Willie's Tale *in* Redgauntlet *(1824) and* The Two Drovers *in* Chronicles of the Canongate *(1827) are part of the evolution of the short story into a recognised specialised form.*

The layin' o' Susie's Ghaist *is very much still part of the older world of the telling of tales. The author, S.M.C., a poet living in London who writes lyrics for street songs, uses some of the repertoire he learned from Barbara Russel. He has an intimate knowledge of Lochmaben folk, including their Surgeon-apothecary and Man-midwife, and of Dumfries street life around the Butter Market, the Bank Vennel, Saint Peak's warehouse, and the inn where honest Andrew encounters Gibbie and his sodger catchers for Lord Peahool's battalions. Too diffuse to be regarded as a classic short story, it is nevertheless a very interesting attempt to bring together several themes and sub-plots in a two-part contribution to* The Scots Magazine *of 1807. Sonsie Susie with her skill in making bargains emerges triumphant!*

John Nicholson (1777–1866), who was born in Tongland parish, had one life as a weaver and as a soldier in the Scots Greys before settling down in Kirkcudbright c.1820 as a printer, bookseller, publisher and antiquarian. His newspaper, the Kirkcudbright Stewartry Times Galloway Register and Advertiser, *ran for at least 381 issues from 1859 to 1866. His publications consisted of chapbooks and more substantial volumes, including Mackenzie's* History of Galloway *(1841),* The Coloured Atlas of Galloway *(1843), and his own collection of* Historical and Traditional Tales . . . connected with the South of Scotland *(1843).* Janet Smith *(a better title would have been 'An Ample and Bountiful Provision') is a good short story with a strong sense of time and place and local identity and an appropriate economy of scale.*

Samuel Crockett (1859–1914) from Little Duchrae in Balmaghie parish – the 'Rutherford' to make up the S.R. was added in 1883 – was the Free Church minister at Penicuik from 1886 until 1895, when he became a full-time author. His short stories, written for various magazines and journals, including The Christian Leader *and* The People's Friend, *were published in six volumes,* The Stickit Minister *(1893)*, Bog-Myrtle and Peat *(1895)*, The Stickit Minister's Wooing . . . *(1900)*, Love Idylls *(1901)*, The Bloom o' the Heather *(1908) and* Young Nick and Old Nick *(c. 1910). Crockett was at his best when he was writing about ministers, foolish, ridiculous, stickit, pompous, drunken, and about sanctimonious elders and congregations. He could be very funny indeed, for example his description of Dr Roger Drumly 'who got a D.D. for marrying a professor's daughter (and deserved a V.C.)' in* The Colleging of Simeon Gleg *(1895), and his story of the minister's daughter, Elizabeth Catherine Haldane, who takes over and turns upside down the life and work of the highly unsatisfactory minister of Cairn Edward, the Rev. Ebenezer Shaw, in* The Biography of an 'Inefficient' *(1895). The bitter* Heather Lintie *(1893) – 'God is more merciful than man' – and* The Tutor of Curleywee *(1893), about the Minister of Education in Her Majesty's Government at the Back House of Curleywee – 'We keep a tutor' – have been included in modern collections of Scottish short stories.* By Right of Salvage, *from* Young Nick and Old Nick *is a gentle and amusing little tale about the field-night of the Whinnyliggate Choral Union!*

The title of Elliot Dickson's My Bagdad *(1896) is very misleading. It is not a travel book. His 'My Bagdad', to be taken in the sense of the quotation from Addison, 'Having ascended the high hills of Bagdad', is the splendid Cairnharrow hill in Anwoth parish above and between the prehistoric complexes at Cairnholy and Cauldside. The photograph opposite the title-page is a Poulton view of Gatehouse-of-Fleet showing the two dams and the toll house at the east end of the town! Dickson presents as his teller of tales one Michael McTear, shepherd of Knocknain and perceptive literary critic. Crockett, he says, 'had dune some guid work, but naething to what he'll dae if he tak's time – but only if he tak's time.' The greater part of the book is taken up with McTear's story of 'The Copelands of Meikle Dornal' (Chapters V to XI). The story of 'Joseph Andrew Kirkpatrick' is Chapter II. It is not clear whether the polisman was a real person in office some time after 1840, or if it is just a good story. R.C. Johnstone, the police officer at Cairnryan, who died on 30th April, 1854, was an old pensioner who had served overseas for many years in the Connaught Rangers.*

The *short story, which appears in many collections, is R.B.*

Cunninghame Graham's Beattock for Moffat *(1902), the train journey of Andra, 'the anticipated corpse', from London back to Beattock – 'He'll hae a braw hurl onyway on the new Moffat hearse.' The hearse is 'sort of Episcopalian lookin', wi' gless a' roond, so's ye can see the kist.'*

Beattock for Moffat *and three other classical stories, L.G. Gibbon's* Smeddum *(1933), G.M. Brown's* Celia *(1967), and Alun Richards'* The Former Miss Merthyr Tydfil *(1993) span the period from the 1900s to the 1990s.*

The sketches of Galloway life by Ian Niall and I.A.N. Henderson in Country Life *and* The Scottish Field *in the 1970s, although not strictly speaking short stories, should be mentioned here as enjoyable contributions to local history. Try Niall's* A Taste Lost Forever (Country Life, *9th August, 1979) on real farm cheese managed with paddle and rake as compared to the 'axle grease and caoutchoue' factory product: and Henderson's* Mrs Pennell *[the minister's wife par excellence] and the occasion of English 'Keep Fit' visitors giving a demonstration to the Borgue Rural, and* Jimmy Raphael *and the Borgue Carpet Curling Club* (The Scottish Field, *September and December, 1974).*

'THE LAYING O' SUSIE'S GHAIST'
A Tale

On Friday last, when overhauling a Jew's wallet, in quest of certain vestments, which the fellow solemnly declared were little the worse, a stranger, whose *latter end* plainly demonstrated the nature of his errand, crossed the Alley, and in the broadest Scotch I think I ever heard, thus accosted the Israelite, 'Ha'e ye gat onie breeks i' your bag?' Struck with the oddity of his address, and the well-known dialect of my native country, I looked stedfastly at the man; and, on carefully examining his features, I thought I discerned something like unto the lights and shades of a three-year auld dream, that savour'd much of ancient acquaintance; but when or where the supposed intimacy existed, I could not, for the life of me, recollect. 'Neibor,' said the stranger, for by this time I had ceased to rummage Nathan's wallet, and fastened mine eyes on Sawney, as if he had been Daniel's ram with seven heads and ten horns, 'Neibor,' said he, 'ye think ye'll ken me again.'

'Indeed, Sir,' said I, 'both your dress and your address are so very kenspeckle, that it would be no hard matter to single you out fifty years hence. Nevertheless . . . the seemingly indecent liberty I have just now been taking with your phiz must not be attributed to insolent curiosity, but to a well-grounded supposition that you and I are no strangers to each other.' 'That may be,' replied my good-humoured countryman, 'but foul fa' me gin I can say as meikle wi' a clear conscience. Whare come ye frae?'

Nathan was got out of all patience with our colloquy – his eyes were fixed on our wants, and his soul was ransacking our pockets. . . . The son of Jacob crammed his wallet with cast-off raiment, slung it to his back, and made the best of his way to rag fair, cursing us both for a pair of lowsey pennyless rogues. . . . the hides of some people's children are so confoundly drench'd and soaked in the dirty tan-pits of commerce, that nothing less than a two-edged sword will penetrate the almost invulnerable mail; and this observation will hold good from the vender of periwinkles and lily-white mussuls, up to the dealer in buckram and Brussel's lace. . . .

Saunders and I being now left to our meditations, a mutual explanation took place. He gave me a hasty sketch of his life, which, poor fellow, savoured not of frankinsence and myrrh; but when he mentioned the place of his nativity, the very spot where all my unadulterated joys and juvenile pastimes were fostered, I could contain myself no longer, every feature in his face became quite familiar, and I instantly recognised one of my most ancient and valuable cronnies. 'Gude life, David Waugh,' said I, 'is this you?'

'Conscience,' quoth David, 'its nae less a man; but in gude's name wha are ye?'

I looked wistfully in his face, and kindly enquired for the unlucky accomplice who used to assist him in bigging up the auld wives' winnocks and lums wi' breckans an' strae, to gaur them trou that mirk Mananday was come back again. He knew me in a moment and a scene of mutual congratulations took place altogether indescribable. But the open street was not a fit place to unbosom ourselves. We retired to his very garret where I am about to give a faithful account of the sequel, and in a trice were as happy as baps and yill could possible make us. 'Twa blyther hearts the lee-lang night, ye wadna faund in Christendie.'

In the course of our conversation, I was given to understand that time had made strange havock amongst my youthful companions. The *laddies* and the *lassies* were giving away their sons and daughters in marriage. The young men were laying aside their bonnets at weddings and kirsenings, to consecrate the haggies and the sheepshead, and the grown up *maids* were become grandmothers. As for the *auld fowk*, few remained above the turf indeed. He moreover told me that Bauldy Tuneham's curlie-headed Davie, after serving a regular apprenticeship to Patie Doddlewhanger the sow-libber o' Lochmaeban, had commenced Surgeon-apothecary and Man-midwife, and actually excelled in the art of jalap making, tooth-drawing and blood-letting, insomuch that the very hair of every college-taught practitioner in the neighbourhood was standing on end. That Sawney Mucklewraith, alias slavering Sawney Sumph, as we used to call him, had lately been warned by the spirit to lay aside his lap-stone, and become a gospel expounder; that he had got hold of the Apostle's opinion, 'he that marrieth doeth well, he that marrieth not, doeth better,' laid it upon his canonical anvil, and hammered it into a long-winded palaver in praise of celibacy, and that all the mouldy maids and frost-bitten batchelors in Galloway had joined his standard, fully resolved to banish the image of God from the face of the earth. In short, I was made acquainted with every prominent transaction worthy of notice since my departure from Scotland.

And how is *Barbara Russel?* said I, worthy woman, dead or alive, I am in duty bound to pray for her welfare. 'Barbara Russel!' quoth David, giving his head a melancholy shake, 'is amang the mools many years ago.' The blood instantly rushed into my face – ungrateful wretch, said I to myself, here hast thou been squandering away the vigour of thy manhood like an ungodly reprobate, in 'stringing blethers up in rhyme for fools to sing,' without so much as once mentioning the name of thy kind benefactress who, in early life, stored thy mind with so many rural tales and pleasing anecdotes: tales that in due time will doubtless enrich the stall, the basket, and the pannier of Andrew Bishop, Mrs Armstrong and Daniel Mackenzie. The worthy auld proverb, 'Better late mend than ne'er do weel', presented itself to my recollection, and I immediately resolved to hand the name of Barbara Russel from oblivion by presenting to the public some of her bonnie tales and queer stories.

Davie ... highly applauded my scheme and gladly volunteered his services in assisting me, having derived equal benefit with myself from Barbara's legendary loquacity. We immediately set our brains to work, and after critically examining the whole catalogue, were humbly of opinion that *The laying o' Susie's ghaist* was by far the best in Barbara's collection; but alas, on taking down the unfortunate tale from the skelf of recollection, nothing but scraps and tatters and broken fragments presented themselves; not a single verse remained harmless and skaithless. The truth is simply this – time had so gnawed and worried the story that little more than the bare bones could be collected. Devil take it, said I, what a misfortune; but no matter, the tale cannot, must not be lost: though like unto an auld plaid three part eaten by the mice and the moths, we'll e'en darn up the holes with good substantial prose, and so let it pass.

Gentle reader, tax me not with wishing to impose a child of my own begetting upon a generous, discerning public, for the legitimate offspring of honest Barbara . . . deceit is like unto a Bond Street lounger arrayed in the garments of Rag-fair, who hies him away to the Coffee-house, calls for his wine, and sits down upon a *heckle*. . . . But honest truth, conscious that the character he assumes is his own and that the raiment he wears is the produce of his father's sheep-bughts and his thrifty mother's spinning wheel, composedly takes his seat among the elders of the land, or marches alang the plain stanes, turning out the burnt side of his skin like a Dinscore laird on Rood-fair day.

Having thus lopped off every twig and bough at the which even perishing suspicion could possibly grasp, I shall do myself the honour of laying before your worship one of Barbara's Russel's favourite tales. It is written in a sort of humdrum blank kind of verse, or rather barbarously versify'd prose, and . . . miserably rent and tatter'd; but as I humbly propose to stitch the remants together with prose yarn, it is to be hoped that the general tone of the story will lose noting of its primitive twang. Our bard, after solemnly invoking his beloved mistress, Jenny McWhilter, as was customary in the ages of Chivalry (for here I must remark thast *the laying o' Susie's ghaist* is certainly a tale of great antiquity) proceeds as follows, viz.

> Good people all,
> Baith lairds an' souters, lend an apen lug.
> Down wi' your seams, ye souple-gabbit taylors,
> Lang-wundit cheftains o' the clashin' clan,
> An' blank na wi' your goose, Ye clashin' wives,
> Around the ingle draw in oure your creepies,
> An' steik your luntin' cutties i' your gabs,
> An' beek your shins, while I, wi' cannie skill,
> Sing o' a ghaist, the verra wale o' ghaists,
> That e'er in house or hauddin faund a howff.
> – Lang syne whan lair, that bogle-scanrin' loon
> Was but a bairn, an' hadna' coost his hippen,
> Nor wi' his patent specks bestrade the snout,
> O' haly priest, or waddlin' domonie;
> Whan yelling deils in ilka dowie heugh,
> At gloarein claw'd their een, an sallying forth,
> Flappit their sooty wings an' flew awa',
> To fley our graunies – waifa' times indeed . . .

The poet then regales us with a long palaver in praise of rural superstition . . . I shall e'en make it a pass over. His bardship then begins the story:

> In thae auld times, ye clep'd the days o' yore,
> Nae matter whan or where, dwalt Andrew Waddle,
> Snug in a cozie biggin, snodly theiket
> Wi' strae an' divets. Elspa Howe, his mither,
> Cloutit the sarks, an' darn'd the hose and stockins.
> An' bred'd the maut, an' beuk the scons an' bannocks
> A thriftier lucky ne'er essay'd to mak',
> A bawbee o' her boddle. Bught an' byre,
> Like breckans, thrave beneith the sonsie e'en
> O' Susie Duff, whase braed substantial back
> Right weel did bruik a lade o' bottle'd strae,
> Or umphquill gimmer smoor'd amang the snaw,
> Or stately midden creel – but waes my heart,
> Twa score o' gimmers had gane glibly bye,
> Sin' Tibby Twaddle 'Hey my kitten' sang
> To her wee Susie – What was warst o' a',
> The chiel's grown scant o' mense, an', fy for shame,
> Had nowther ca'd her hinny, do dawty,
> But late and a'er threipit she wad die
> The warst o' deaths – I darna gie't a name.

Andrew Waddle is next laid upon the table and carefully dissected by our author. He calls him

> A buirdly hash, a gawsy gousmalogie,
> A yird-tormenting mailen plowderin' slovan,
> Wha ne'er cou'd straik a scythe nor swing a souple,
> Nor hirsel up his breeks without twa hechs
> An' half a dizzen grains. At kirn or brydle,
> Whan ither lads anent their dawties habbit,
> To 'Jenny dang the weaver', 'Athol brose',
> Or 'Braes o' Cupar', Andrew, like a sumph,
> Or waefu' hawkie in an unco loan,
> Ay sought a secret howf, a lanely neuk,
> Wherein to straik his chin an' count the kipples.

Yet, notwithstanding the sluggishness of his disposition, it would appear from the sequel of this wonderful tale, that Andrew, to use our Bard's own words, 'was made o' flesh an' blude.' It seems that on Rood fair morning Susie Duff kail-bladed her basket, and loaded it with eggs and butter; and that Andrew untether'd the colt, kaimed his tail, and furbished him up for the market. They repaired to Dumfries for the purpose of vending their respective wares; but it grieves me to declare that the sequel of this eventful expedition to the provincial metroplis is no more. Indulgent reader, kindly permit me to make it a pass-over and set down the principal dramatis personae of the ensuing farces at the end o' the auld brigg, without any further ceremony; for there I humbly propose putting Andrew gracefully a striddle upon his colt, to the end that he may appear with credit to himself on the sands, and then conduct Susie in safety to the mid steeple. . . .

Well dost thou know, that from siller Sawney's, till such time as thou comest to the New-kirk, little or nothing is done in the way of business, I mean in the way of sweet-hearting, but no sooner dost thou face to the right, and gettest thine eye on the barber's sign directly facing scrub Haliday's shop, than 'hey go-mad' is the order of the day. . . . I will not give thee a catalogue of Susie's sensations, when she beheld

> Bonnie Leesie Waugh
> An' Femie Grey, Bess Cleugh, an' Kirsty Grieve,
> Alang wi' Davie Fyfe an' Jamie Twaddle,
> Blythly gaffain' in Will Harran's shop,
> An' trying on the gluves; the brydal gluves,
> An' spiering' for his fashionable prents
> His silks, his musline, lace, an' ither braws,
> From London just arriv'd –

And . . . I will not tell thee how envy gnawed her maiden heart when she described

> Gomral Jenny Spence frae Annandale
> Gaun linkin' check for chou wi' Johnny Jardine;

But I will accompany Susie to the butter market and there leave her to the patronage of a generous public. Let us now go in search of honest Andrew.

> Poor harmless hash – Scarce had he canter'd by
> The Smiddie door, whare yill an' Fairntosh,
> An' het Lochend frae gill an' chappen hisses
> Down deacon Johnston's house, Gibbie Glaive
> The sodger catcher, on him gat his e'e,
> An' spier'd the price of Bawsy: 'Just eight notes,'
> Our trooper rowit, for his thrifty mither
> Declared the sonsy brute was wordy o't.

Gibbie knew his man at first sight and affixed, by anticipation, the cockade to his bonnet. He caused Andrew to dismount and, on taking an actual survey of Bawsy, swore by gad that he was a fine animal and would well become any gemman whatever; but countryman, continued Gilbert, you ask a great deal too much. Andrew being of a different opinion, remounted his steed and was about to depart, *sans ceremonie*, when the crafty crimp laid hold of his bridle. 'My good friend,' rejoined Gibbie, 'why in such haste? I am much in love with the horse indeed, but as I never could find in my heart to strike a dry bargain, we never can come to terms without the assistance of a spiritual friend. Suppose we should retire to this here tavern and see what can be done over an exhilirating bowl?' As Andrew could start no legal objection to this proposition, he stabled his colt, and repaired with our quondam serjeant to an apartment in the back settlement of the house.

Scarcely had they taken their chairs, when the bowl was brought in, escorted by three or four country-looking lads, for so poor Andrew took them to be, whom Gibbie very kindly invited to a glass, as it was fair-time. 'They ca'd the bicker aft about,' but ne'er a word of Andrew's colt and the eight notes; except when Gibbie contrasted his merits and external appearance with Lieut. General Striddle's charger, which of course terminated in fabour of Bawsy. Indeed the discourse took quite a different turn, for Gilbert began to give some account of his prowess in Holland and Flanders, places where he very justly remarked many brave Scotsmen became *lairds*. The strangers in their turn spoke of America and the East Indies, or golden world, with equal warmth, and marvelled how so many spirited young men could loiter at their mither's hip in poverty and rags, when ease and affluence was so easily obtained abroad. I myself, continued one of them, have reason to bless the day I went to serve his Majesty. On facing the wide world with a gun on my shoulder, I was poor, penniless, and contemptible; now, I am possessed of wealth and independence. I cut my way to fame and fortune through the ranks of the foe.

Gibbie resumed the discourse by observing that a genteel young man of Andrew's appearance, sabre in hand, and mounted on a spirited steed, such as he was about to dispose of, could not fail of being caressed by the noble and gallant chiefs, whom his Majesty had lately commissioned to chastise the insolent Gauls and the haughty Dons, and enquired if our hero had ever turned his thoughts to a military life, because, continued Gilbert, my Lord Peahool called last night at my apartments, wishing to know if I could recommend him fifteen young men of character to fill up the vacancies occasioned by promotion in his lordship's battalions, the which, on my approval, will be ranked as follows, seven Captains, five

Lieutenants, three Cornets, and a kettle-drummer.

Andrew now began fairly to smell a rat. Though a simpleton, nature had furnished him with a quantum of that clumsy commodity commonly called mother wit, or rather pure instinct, which plainly told him that his companions 'were just nae better than they shou'd be,' and therefore to prevent the possibility of a *coup de main* as much as possible he carefully laid his left leg over his right, clenched his fists, and barricaded his breeches pockets with his elbows, lest an evil disposed shilling should intrude itself upon the premises in his Majesty's name. Yet, notwithstanding all this precaution, I have every reason in the world to believe that the poor simple soul would have been entrapped after all had his guardian angel not snatched him from their vulture fangs.

The day was not wearing awa, and tho' the colt and the eight notes were no longer talked of, yet, as one bowl very naturally begetteth another, and as water sanctified with the spirit has a great tendency to lull the judgment asleep, Andrew's vigilance was so far relaxed that he began to survey our black-legged quorum with a less suspicious eye, and even entertained some straggling thoughts that they were true men, able and willing to befriend him. In order, therefore, to recompence Gibbie for the miraculous account he gave of his wonderful exploits and hair-breadth 'scapes in the low countries, Andrew lifted up his voice and began to treat him with blind Harry's heroic narrative, 'how Wallace fished in Irvine water', and had actually got to the end of the second line when, as I before hinted, his great deliverer rescued him.

Susie, it seems, had disposed of her cargo sooner than could reasonably have been expected, and wishing to make the grand tour of the fair, went in search of Andrew. Here it may be necessary to acquaint the intelligent reader that in the infancy of this unco tale . . . though no sort of private cuddling or squeezing of hands was ever witnessed between the parties, yet it so happened that whenever Andrew deemed it necessary to visit Crummy, and Hawkie, and Gairy, Susie also deemed it necessary to muck the byre; and contrairwaise, when the latter milked the cows, the former was sure to be saunterin' about the bught. In fine, common report declared that Susie Duff was Andrew Waddle's 'only joy an' dearie o',' because, quoth the rude tongue of every rustick, 'like ay draws to like.'

But to proceed – at the head of the Bank vennel, Susie forgather'd wi' lang Will Shittleton, an' at him spier'd gin he had seen ought of Andrew? William answered in the negative and she continued her route. Further down the street, a little before thou comest to Saint Poaks's warehouse, Sandy Yerkin, the town souter, was in like manner accosted by our fair maiden, and returned the same answer. Whereupon Susie Duff resolved to reconnoitre the sands in person, and actually penetrated thro' the cattle market, in defiance of both nowt and cuissars, enquiring at every body she met for the object of her wishes, but all to no purpose.

At length Providence directed her interrogations to the lug o' a callan wha held naigs for black Rab Gallowtree, the Kelton-hill horsecowper. 'What sort of chiel is he?' quoth the laddie. 'He's a weel looking lad,' quo Susie, 'wi' black curlie hair, an' a saut an' pepper coat on, riding a bawsent colt.' 'A weel looking lad,' replies the youth, 'riding a bawsent colt wi' a sait an' pepper coat on: hasna he a rough tautit head, a lang thrawn din snout, an' a muckle moo?'

'Trowth,' quo Susie, 'the lad's nose is nowther sae ill faur'd, nor his mou sae muckle to mak' a ferlie at: he had a braid scone bonnet on his head, a grey plaid thrawa about him, an' a pair o' blue boot hose on.'

'Oad,' quo the callan, 'it's the verra man after a': I saw him an' Gibbie Glaive gaun into the monkrey a wee blink afore twall.'

'An' where awa's the monkrey, my bonnie man?'

'Just there,' quo the laddie, pointing with his finger.

Now in olden times this monkrey was a *Nunnery*. Christian reader, it was a tippling house, situated on the sands of Dumfries, inhabited by an athletic Abbess of the first order of Cyprians, to the which, as might naturally be expected, all the riff raff of the metropolis resorted. But Susie knew nothing of this circumstance; so into the monkrey she went, just as Andrew had rehearsed the second line of his heroic story, 'Wallace a fishing for diversion goes'. His well-known nicker led her to the scene of conviviality just in the nick of time to prevent a spurtle blade from dandling at his belt and a dog-skin wallet from decorating his shoulders. . . .

Suffice it then to say that the prying eye of woman soon descried what sort of company Andrew had got into, that her resolution tempered with prudence extricated him from peril, that her eloquence enraged the mob, and surrounded the unfortunate monkrey with hostile rungs, which compelled Gibbie and his blackguards to 'mak' their heels defend their heads'; and lastly, that her superior skill in the art of bargain-making sold the colt for eight notes and a crown.

London, 1807

S.M.C.

– *The Scots Magazine*, 1807, pp. 263–266 and 493–497

JANET SMITH
{'An ample and bountiful provision'}

Old Janet Smith lived in a cottage overshadowed by an ash tree, and flanked by a hawthorn, called Lasscairn, so named, in all probability, from a cairn of stones, almost in the centre of which this simple habitation was placed, in which, even within the period of my remembrance, three maiden veterans kept rock and reel, bleezing hearth and reeking lum. They were uniformly mentioned in the neighbourhood as the 'lasses o' Lasscairn'; though their united ages might have amounted to something considerably above threescore thrice told. Janet, however, of whom I am now speaking, had been married in her teens, and her husband having lost his life in a lime quarry, she had been left with an only child, a daughter, whom, by the help of God's blessing, an her wee wheel, she had reared and educated as far as the Proofs and the Willison's. This daughter having attained to a suitable age, had been induced one fine summer evening, whilst her mother was engaged in her evening devotion under the shade of the ash tree, to take a pleasure walk with Rob Paton, a neighbouring ploughman, but then recently enlisted, and to share his name and his fortunes for twenty-four months to come. At the end of this period she found her mother nearly in the same position in which she had left her, praying earnestly to her God to protect, to direct and return her 'bairn.' There were, however, two bairns for the good old woman to bless, instead of one, and the young 'Jessie Paton' was said to be the very picture of her mother. Be that as it may, old Janet, now a grannie, loved the bairn, forgave the mother, and, by the help of an additional wheel, which, in contra-distinction to her own, was denominated 'muckle' she, and her *broken hearted deserted daughter*, contrived, for years to earn such a subsistence, as their very moderate wants required. At last a severe fever cut off the mother, and left a somewhat sickly child at about nine years of age, under the sole protection of an aged and enfeebled grandmother. It was in this stage of old Janet's earthly travail that I became acquainted with her and her *daughter*, – for ever after her mother's death, the child knew her grandmother by no other name, and under no other relation.

Janet had a particular way, still the practice in Dumfries-shire, of dressing or preparing her meal of potatoes. They were scraped, well dried, salted, beetled, buttered, milked, and ultimately rumbled into the most beautiful and palatable consistency. In short, they became that first, and, beyond the limits of the south country, least known of all delicacies, 'champit potatoes'. As I returned often hungry and weary from school, Janet's pot presented itself to me, hanging in the reek, and at a considerable elevation above the fire, as the most tempting of all objects.

In fact, Janet, knowing that my hour of return from school was full two hours later than hers of repast, took this method of reserving me a full heaped spoonful of the residue of her and her Jessie's meal. Never whilst I live, and live by food, shall I forget the exquisite feelings of eager delight with which that single overloaded spoonful of beat or *champit* potatoes was devoured. There are pleasures of sentiment and imagination of which I have occasionally partaken, and others connected with what is called the heart and affections; all these are beautiful and engrossing in their way and in their season, but to a hungry school-boy, who has devoured his dinner 'piece' ere 10 o'clock A. M., and is returning to his home at a quarter before five, the presentiment, the sight, and, above all, the taste and reflection connected with the swallowing of a spoonful – and such a spoonful! – of Janet Smith's potatoes, is, to say nothing slightly or extravagant, not less seasonable than exquisite. As my tongue walked slowly and cautiously round and round the lower and upper boundaries of the delicious load, as if loath rapidly to diminish that *bulk*, which the craving stomach would have wished to have been increased, had it been ten-fold, my whole soul was wrapt in Elysium; it tumbled about, and rioted in an excess of delight, a kind of feather bed of downy softness. Drinking is good enough in its season, particularly when one is thirsty; but the pleasures attendant on the satisfying of *the appetite* for me! – This is assuredly the great – the master gratification.

But Janet did not only deal in potatoes, she had likewise a cheese, and on pressing occasions, a bottle of beer besides; the one stood in a kind of corner press or cupboard, whilst the other occupied a still less dignified position beneath old Janet's bed. To say the truth of Janet's cheese, it was not much beholden to the maker. It might have been advantageously cut into bullets or marbles, such was its hardness and solidity – but then, *in those days*, my teeth were good – and, with a keen stomach, and a willing mind, much may be effected even on a 'three times skinned sky blue!' The beer – for which I have often adventured into the 'terra incognita' already mentioned, even at the price of a prostrate person and a dusty jacket – was excellent – brisk, frothy, and nippy – my breath still goes when I think of it. And then Janet wove such long strings of tape, blue and red, white and yellow, all striped and variegated like a gardener's garter! I shall never be such a beau again, as when my stockings on Sabbath were ornamented with a new pair of Janet's well-known, much-prized, and admired garters.

It was, however, after all, on Sabbath that Janet appeared to move on her native element. It was on Sabbath that her face brightened, and her step became accelerated – that her spectacles were carefully wiped with the corner of a clean neck-napkin, and her Bible was called into early, and almost uninterrupted use. It was on Sabbath that her devotions were poured forth – both in family and private capacity – with an earnestness and a fervency which I have never seen surpassed, in manse or mansion – in desk or pulpit. There is, after all, nothing in nature so beautiful and elevating, as sincere and heart felt, heart-warming devotion. There is a poor frail creature, verging on threescore and ten years, with an attendant lassie, white-faced, and every way *shilpy* in appearance. Around them are nothing more elevating or exciting than a few old sticks of furniture, sooty rafters, and a smoky atmosphere. Surely imbecility has here clothed herself in the forbidding garb of dependence or squalid poverty! the worm that crawls into light through the dried mole hill, all powdered over with the dust from which it is escaping, is a fit emblem of such an object, and a condition. But over all this, let us pour the warm and glowing radiance of genuine devotion! The roots of that consecrated 'ash' can bear witness to those half articulated breathings, which connect the weakness of man with the power of God – the squalidness of poverty with the radiant richness of Divine grace. Do those two hearts which, under one covering, *now* breathe forth their evening sacrifice in hope and reliance – do they feel – do they acknowledge any reliance with the world's opinions, the world's artificial and cruel distinctions? If there be one object more pleasing to God and to the holy ministers of his will, than another, it is this – age uniting with youth, and youth with age, in the giving forth into audible, if not articulate expression – the fulness of the devout heart.

Lord W——, whose splendid residence stands about fifteen miles distant from Lasscairn, happened to be engaged in a hunting expedition in the neighbourhood of this humble and solitary abode, and having separated from his attendants and companions, he bethought him of resting a little under a roof, however humble, from which he saw smoke issuing. But when he put his tumb to the latch, it would not move; and after an effort or two, he applied first his eye, and lastly his ear, to the key-hole, to ascertain the presence of inhabitants, the solemn voice of fervent prayer met his ear, uttered by a person evidently not in a kneeling, but in an erect posture; he could in short distinctly gather the nature and tendency of Janet's address to her maker. She was manifestly engaged in asking a blessing on her daily meal; and was proceeding to enumerate, in a voice of thanksgiving, the many mercies with which, under God's good providence, she and hers had been visited. – After an extensive enumeration, she came at last to speak of that *ample provision* on which she was now imploring a blessing. In this part of her address, she dwelt with peculiar cheerfulness, as well as earnestness of tone, on that goodness which had provided so bountifully for her, whilst many, better deserving than she, were worse circumstanced; the whole tenor of her prayer tending to impress the listener with the belief that Janet's board, though spread in a humble hut, must be at least amply supplied with the necessaries of life. But what was Lord W.'s surprise, on entrance, to find that a round oaten bannock, toasting before a brick at a peat fire, with a basin of whey – the gift of a kind neighbour – composed that *ample and bountiful provision* for which this humble, but contented and pious woman expressed so much gratitude. – Lord W—— was struck with the contrast between his own condition and feelings, and those of this humble pair; and, in settling upon Janet and her inmate £6 a-year for life, he has enabled her to accommodate herself with a new plaid and black silk hood, in which she appears, with her granddaughter, every Sabbath, occupying her well-known and acknowledged position on the lowest step of the pulpit stair, and paying the same respect to the minister in passing, as if she were entirely dependent on her own industry and the good will of her neighbours as formerly.

– *Historical and Traditional Tales* . . . published by John Nicholson, Kirkcudbright, 1843, pp. 113–19

S.R. CROCKETT
By Right of Salvage
['The field-night of the Whinnyliggate Choral Union']

The time, by chance, was Christmas Eve. But it was in the Scotland of thirty years ago, so the fact made no difference. The Scriptures had not declared it unto them. The minister was silent on the subject, or spoke only to fulminate against prelatic Englishers, and others who 'regarded times and seasons.'

But it was the field-night of the 'Choral Union,' and the little Whinnyliggate schoolhouse had never been fuller. There was a light snow on the ground – a sprinkling only, for the frost of December had been long and black.

Many a man there had a back stiff with the slow lift and drive as he sent the channel-stone up the rink. But the 'Singing School' Concert – ah, that brought out all in the upper end of the parish who were neither deaf nor bedridden.

If you had gone to the four little steps that led up to the steep schoolhouse brae, you would hardly have seen the light from the windows for the heads clustering without and within. The younger men, who had had to take care of the horses and see them safely stabled at the smithy or at Gatehead farm, arrived late, and mostly found themselves without seats. But in revenge they stood about the windows, and even threw conversation lozenges in the direction of the half circle about the precentor, where the singers were fluttering the lace sleeves of their best gowns and shaking their ringlets, one on each side falling low on the shoulder, rebelliously, and tossed back with the prettiest shake of the head.

They were only awed by the waving baton of Robert Affleck of the Garioch, noble-hearted man and excellent musician, who only looked ridiculous when he began to sing. That is – to those who did not know him.

Those who did thought nothing of the strange screwing of the mouth, the twitching nostrils, or the rise and fall of the shaggy black eyebrows, as he twanged the turning-fork and prepared to attack the fortress of 'Ring the Bell, Watchman!' or even the 'Watch by the Rhine.' For it was the time of the Franco-German War, and, in English versions, warlike songs ravaged the remotest country parishes, otherwise haunts of ancient peace.

Here and there a greybeard elder shook his head and confided to his brother in office: 'If they were to sing the Hunderdth Psalm it wad fit them better than a' that clinkum clankum! Hear to thae craiturs. "Ring, ring, ring!" Ye wad think it was a smiddy. I tell ye what, Dumglass, I'm no on wi' thae vain sacrifices.'

'There's the harps,' suggested Drumglass in the speaker's ear. 'If you and me are on the road Up Yonder, we had better be gettin' accustomed to the like o' that!'

But the Hallelujiah Chorus, murdered wilfully, in the first degree and without extenuating circumstances, silenced both office-bearers. They remained, critic and apologist, with dropped jaws till the final 'Amen' seemed to escape through a broken roof.

The little stove in the centre on its red sandstone foundation was growing ruddy when at last the benediction was said, then the door was opened, and those nearest it fell out as turnips fall from an over-full cart when both pins are out and the back-board comes away with a clatter.

Mr Goodlison the minister was going from group to group, buzzing compliments. His wife was shaking her long side curls at him from the doorway as a signal to be done and come away home to his supper. She held ready in her hands the minister's white knitted comforter. Abraham was so sensitive to colds, so forgetful and careless, and withal so cunning that (will it be believed?) he would sometimes sneak into the soiled linen cupboard and get out a worn shirt and collar, which she had put away, alleging as an excuse (when taxed with his crime), that 'a stiff one choked the word of God in a man's throat.'

But the young people were all outside early arranging their affairs. Those who could walk home had generally their companions trysted long beforehand. The moon was at its full of course. Indeed Christmas Eve had been chosen for the festival entirely on this account.

Those living at greater distances drove. One or two well-to-do married farmers had their gigs. But such hurried homegoings by no means satisfied the young people. The longest farm carts had been covered with a thick felting of sacks along the shelving sides. The cart bottom was deep in straw, while all the rugs and coverlets in the house had been requisitioned for the homecoming.

There was much laughter. Invitations, audacious and mock tender, rang through the air. Young men who were to sit in the corner to drive, offered more quietly special accommodation by their sides, and promised to be 'douce.' There was but one of all the singers who stood aloof, showed no preference, accepted no invitation of all those laughingly or wistfully extended to her.

Alison Cairns, called from her rebellious locks 'curly', pouted disdainfully apart. Roy M'Farlane asked her, 'majorin' the worth of his turnout like an auctioneer. He retired snubbed. Andro Crossmyloof ventured in, was refused and fell back amid the muttered jeers of his comrades.

But the other girls, who envied Curly her good looks and her position as premier soloist, said loud enough for each other to hear, 'Oh, Will Arnott has gone home with Lizzie Baker.'

It was not true, but Alison Cairns turned her face away towards the sheeted hills that stood up white on the farther side of the loch.

She did not believe it of Will. Of course not. She knew why these girls said it, and she smiled pleasantly at the nearest, Bell Burns, ruddy even in the moonshine.

'I will wait,' she said, 'there's never a lad in this end of the parish worth the snap of a finger!'

'Come with us, Ailie,' cried Jeannie Begbie, more tenderhearted than the others, reaching a hand to help her up.

'Let her bide if she's sae upsettin', the proud madam!' murmured the more jealous. 'Drive on, Roy!'

Now there was enough of truth in all this to hurt, and Alison Cairns felt very angry indeed to be thus publicly shamed. Will Arnott had promised to be there waiting for her, and – No, no, it was impossible. She knew Will. There must be some accident. She was sure there must be some accident. All the same a sudden resolve came to her. The little strongly shod foot stopped tapping the hard beaten snow on which the wheels of many gigs and carts had executed fantastic curves and circles in turning.

In another moment the minister and his wife came out. Mrs Goodlison was busy rectifying the set of the white comforter about her husband's neck, for well she knew that, in Scotland at least, a minister's throat is his fortune.

'Bless me,' said the minister, 'is that not one of the maids I see going alone round the turn at the smithy?'

Well he knew that it was not good Whinnyliggate custom to permit anything of the kind. The young men ought to be ashamed of themselves. Now in his time –

'Should not I – ?' he stammeered. 'Should not *we*, Marion – that is, I do not like any of the young women returning home alone at this time of night.'

But Marion pulled him round sharply. The comforter was not yet entirely to her mind and she gave it an extra twitch because he was talking nonsense.

'We will do no such thing, Abraham,' she said. 'You will go doucely home with this old woman here present, and then you will take your milk-gruel while it is hot. Then to bed you will go like a decent man! As for the lassie it will only be Jess Kelly from the Greystone, she has only the corner to turn at any rate. And yonder is Will Arnott with an empty gig following her up!'

'Good night, Will,' the minister called out.

'Good night, sir,' said a voice from the gig, with an unusual strain in it.

'Why, what's the matter, Will?' cried the minister, stopping in spite of the forward tug of a wifely hand on his arm, 'what's that on your face? Blood?'

'Only a bit of a spill, sir,' said Will Arnott. 'Someone let fall a lantern in front of Bess as we drove out of the innyard, and before I could get her mastered she tumbled me out at the Well corner.'

'Come your ways into the Manse, Will,' said Mr Goodlison, 'it's well that these things should be seen to at once.'

'No thank you, sir,' said Will, 'it's nothing and – there's the mare – she's not to be trusted even yet – and –'

'What, Will?'

'Did you happen to see –' (Will had a delicacy in mentioning names) –

'a young lady waiting?'

'Who was to go home with you, William?' said the minister's wife, who loved to get to the point in such matters.

'Ah, well – that is to say, I hoped, I expected Miss Alison Cairns,' the youth stammered, occupying himself with the mare's restlessness to hide his own growing confusion.

'Alison,' said Mrs Goodlison reassuringly, 'oh, of a certainty she will have found a seat in one of the long waggons. I saw Roy M'Farlane speaking to her before she left the schoolroom.'

'Oh, thank you – no doubt,' said Will Arnott, as little reassured as possible. 'Goodnight, madam; good-night, Mr Goodlison!'

For Will had been at College and was accounted by far the most mannerly young man in the parish. He was a favourite also with the minister's wife, who thought him much too good for any of the village or even for the farmer's daughters.

But the minister, in spite of fifty years and a strict *régime* of comforters, had a warm spot in his heart for honest swains.

'I saw somebody that looked like Ailie Cairns,' he called out as Will drove off, 'going round the smithy turn a minute or two ago!'

'Nonsense – it was only the Kelly lass from the Greystane!' interrupted his wife. But Will had whipped up the mare, and by this time was rounding the turn himself.

'Oh, these young people,' said the minister's wife, 'they think of nothing else but lovemaking! I wish they were more awake to their higher duties.'

'Remember the Long Loaning, Marion!' said Mr Godlison, giving his wife's arm a quick squeeze under his.

'For shame, Abraham – think of your age and position!'

'I am thinking!' said Mr Goodlison, and they walked all the way home, silent both of them.

Meanwhile Will Arnott was on the trail as hard as the mare could go, and indeed she laid herself well done to her work, as if she knew her master's heart. The corner came. They flashed round the quick turns about Greystane and up the long alley of beech and birch, their naked twigs winnowing in the moonlight. No Ailie was to be seen. The avenue to the bridge and beyond it as far as Willowbank, white on its hill, glimmered pearly pale, delicately patterned by the branch shadows, all the way to the knoll from which you look down on the loch.

Instinctively Will laid the whiplash along the mare's glistening side. Bess bounded forward, and, eager on his chase, Will let her go.

It seemed as if he reached the top of the Urioch brae in a dozen strides.

As they topped the rise something moved behind a broom bush on the steep face from which in summer the children dig pignuts. Bess, quick to resent anything after the sting of the whiplash in the avenue of birches, laid back her vicious ears, set her head between her knees, and went down the steep hill at full gallop.

Now at the foot was the smallest sort of burn, twinkling and murmuring half-hidden in summer, but now, of course, frozen stiff. Then came three awkward turns, where aleady more than one man had found his end. A little beyond Bess swerved to the left, where was only a steepish rough bank, down which the wheels skidded. She struck the ice of the Bogle Thorn Pool, which broke beneath her weight. Then a black column of water rose churning in the frosty air. It was crested with white – the broken snow-covered ice of the pool. It sank, and all was still. To the watcher behind the whin bushes on the brae only a little black patch broke the white uniformity of the lake, a blot irregularly shaped but, as it seemed, no bigger than a man's hand.

How Alison Cairns got out of her hiding-place, how fast she crossed the crisp meadow-grass, hard as iron underneath, how she found herself standing on the verge of splintered ice, she never knew.

She saw a whiplash floating, that which had done all the mischief. The butt was still held down under the water. Something told her there was a chance. She dared not hesitate. Still less dared she pull. For she knew that the whip might be her only guide to hand that held it.

Taking firm hold of the branch of a scraggy thorn which overhung the pool, Alison let herself down into the water. She did not feel the chill. She only felt herself sinking. The branch snapped and she swerved in the direction of the outer edge of the ice. She felt her feet entangled. Then suddenly they rested firm. Down the whip handle a hand had come as if by magic into hers. She pushed violently shorewards, striking what was beneath her feet to give her an impetus, and the face of Will Arnott had come up close to hers, starkly white and wet under the moon.

She laid her hand on the branch – a stronger branch, then on the roots of the whins. There was a long struggle, but Will was out on the snow – silent, cold, and it seemed dead, on the steep, rough bank.

Then quite suddenly Alison's courage deserted her. She threw her arms about his face, crushed it against her, crying out, 'Oh, Will, Will, forgive me, do forgive me.'

At that moment she felt this horror was all her fault, and she wept over him, chafing his hands and wooing the life that would not come back into her sweetheart's body.

'I have killed him. I – I – who loved him!'

So busy was Ailie that she had not heard the jingle of horse-accoutrement on the road above. Two men slid down the embankment, leaving another in the waggon.

'What's this, what's this, Ailie?' said her father, standing tall and grave beside her.

'It's Will,' she sobbed, giving way completely now that all was over. 'I frighted the horse and drowned him!'

Her father was bending over Will Arnott. He was a quick, brusque man, and generally ordered everybody about, but he was gentle that night.

'Let us get him first to the mill,' he said, 'and then you, Rob, drive Alison home as fast as may be –'

'I shall stay with Will,' she cried. 'I must – I killed him. But I only meant to frighten him. He had made me wait at the school gate. Oh, father, I, am not wet – or cold! Indeed I am not!'

Her father sucked a little, low, comprehensive whistle between his lips.

'Whew-ew!' he murmured. 'So, Master Will!'

And in ten minutes all were safe in the millhouse – Will in bed and the miller's wife bustling about to find dry clothes for Ailie out of her daughter's store.

The next morning David Cairns strode into the room, flicking his high riding-boots free of snow. Alison sat with Will's hand in hers, and strangely enough, did not seem in the least abashed.

'Now, young people,' said her father, 'be good enough to tell me the meaning of all this.'

With a faint smile and happy eyes Will referred him to his daughter.

'If it had not been for Ailie,' he said, 'I would have been lying beside Bess in the pool at the bogle Thorn!'

'*And* then?' said Mr Cairns, turning to his daughter.

'Will is mine,' affirmed that young woman brazenly. '*I* saved him and *I* mean to keep him! Besides, he needs someone to keep him from careering madly about the country.'

'And if it had not been for me,' said Mr Cairns, 'pray where would the pair of you have been?'

'*Dear* father!' said Ailie, laying her hand upon his arm with the treacherous affection common to daughters on such occasions.

– S.R. Crockett, *Young Nick and Old Nick*, London *c.* 1910, pp. 100–12

ELLIOT DICKSON
The Polisman of Cairnryan, or, Blessed are the Peacemakers

Joseph Andrew Kirkpatrick, that was polisman of Cairnryan, was what may be called a kenspeckle man. He was above the average height, but balanced this by never holding up his head, which was 'fine an' lairge'. He wore his mutton-chop whiskers with a quiet dignity befitting one of Her Majesty's servants. He was a full-bodied man, whose breeks were aye baggie-kneed. He was a married man, too, and had a family of two daughters and a son.

Up till the time of which I am going to write, Joseph Andrew did not know what it was to have 'a case'. Indeed it probably never entered his mind that he would ever be forced to the cruel necessity of laying hands violently on any man. Perhaps it was because he never had had to do so that he was once on the point of promotion. Of course unpaid country Justices of the Peace are not anxious to have cases brought before them. However, Joseph Andrew Kirkpatrick's merits were inquired into, and it was decided 'that he remain where he is for the time being; his faithful service being entered in the books.'

Now it was not any, or all, of these facts or qualities...that made...the Cairn polisman the noteworthy man that he was. In addition to what has been said of him ... he was a logician, a man well-skilled in comparative geography – it may hap of all Galloway (omnes Gallowa) – long years before a single text-book on the subject had been prepared for 'the standards'; a man whose methods of approximating populations, whether in the Stewartry or in the Rhins, was incontrovertible. . . .

If a stranger happened to arrive at the Cairn, as Cairnryan was mostly called, Joe Kirkpatrick, who was almost always on his beat, or his stand, supporting the bieldiest corner of the inn, was the one from whom information was most invariably sought. Oh yes, strangers did come to Cairnryan sometimes: five had visited it the year before the big snaw, and odd people now and again had seen it between that time and 1840. . . . No doubt he had often to be asked several times before the idea got fairly home, but when once it did get there, the polisman was a sight. He would stand with feet a good way apart as if to strengthen the whole triangular body at the highest point of the vertex, the cranium. He would put the forefinger of the right hand into the open palm of the left, and there he would stand, with head turned to the right, a little off the perpendicular, and remember it was a 'fine an' lairge heid', looking for all the world like what a wise hen does when she tries to squint up sidewise at the hand that throws her the corn.

Then the metaphysical calculations in comparative geography would begin: 'Ye would like to ken hoo far it is frae the Cairn to New Luce?' Then, after a pause, 'Frae the Cairn to New Luce! Umphum! Aye, na! Weel, let me see, na!' Then there would be many dab-dabbings in his left palm with the forefinger of his right hand. 'Let me see, na! Let me see!' By and by his face would lighten up as the inspiration came upon him, and he would exclaim, 'Aye, man, that's it! Aye, that's it!' And then more directly to the questioner, 'It's juist aboot the same as frae Stranraer to Balgreggan.' Stranraer was the starting-point for all measurements in the western part.

If Joseph's answer did not give satisfaction to the questioner, the polisman would smile in a sort of commiserating way 'to think that ony edicate man didna ken where Balgreggan was.' But Joseph would try again, and after some more dab-dabbings would be sure he had done it, when he exclaimed, 'Maybe a wee bittie mair than frae Stranraer to Kirkcolm.' Any one who could not grasp that was, in Joseph Andrew's opinion, hardly fit to be allowed to go about alone.

Still, if the visitor had time to wait on, Joseph Andrew Kirkpatrick, polisman and logician, would try again; he had often found out that he had been lucky the third time, at least people often left him after that. He always took the first two measurements from Stranraer, and the third one from what, in his opinion, was the eastern capital, Newton Stewart. 'Weel,' he would say, after an extra time's dabbing, 'surely this'll dae ye! Oh, aye; surely this'll dae!' But there was not so much hope in the tone as there was at first: 'It's juist the very same as frae the Newton to Birlennan Hill, a bittock o' this side o' Kirkcowan!' Joseph had little hope of the traveller who failed to take in such an explicit answer as that.

Then, again, his method of approximating populations in Galloway was . . . too clear to be called in question. When the query was put to him, say, as to the population of Whithorn, Joe would put himself into the very same attitude as he had done when he was asked about the distance to a particular place. He was much averse to change of attitude or anything else. Some ill-natured people said that he carried this unchanging principle into such small details as his linen. . . .

Well, after the question had got home, the dab-dabbing would be repeated for a little while, the forefinger of the right hand in the palm of the left, and then Joseph thus: 'There's Jackson's, an' Thomson's, an' McAndrew's, an' Routledge's an' McCracken's o' the Bull.' He would go over the names again, counting them off on his fingers a second time. Then the same pleased light as before would break over his countenance as he drew his conclusions: 'Five! Aye, juist that. Ye would like to ken the size o' the Whitterun: weel, it's aboot five times as lairge as the Cairn.' . . . The five parties whose names were mentioned by Joseph Andrew Kirkpatrick were the holders of public-house licences. There was one place of refreshment in Cairnryan, and as Joseph had, strangely enough, a wonderful knowledge of the names and numbers of such houses in many of the towns within the Rhins and Stewartry, he was never at a loss as to the populations, comparatively.

The only case that Joseph ever had was one of much notoriety in the place Cairnryan. . . . the Cairn lies on the east side of Loch Ryan, 'strecht fornest Kirkcolm,' as Joe Kirkpatrick in his matchless lucidity would have said. A passing boat had run short of vegetables. The seamen were Hollanders, more likely from Paysly, came ashore to steal, about eight o' clock on a beautiful September morning. The foraging party landed not two hundred yards from the constable's dwelling. Near at hand was a splendid field of cabbages and turnips to which the men of the sea helped themselves freely. The owners protested, but to no purpose. At length, under these painful circumstances, they took a step which to this day is spoken of at the Cairn as a bold action, they sent for the polisman.

The messenger who was sent to call the representative of law and order arrived at Kirkpatrick's house all too soon; he reached the police office, a but and ben, at thirteen minutes *to* nine. Now by this I mean thirteen minutes *from* nine. 'To say thirteen minutes *to* nine is just to confuse country folk. An' am sure for your nine-twenties, an' your twelve-fifties, an' your three-seventeens, I never did un'erstan' them, an' I needna try.' . . . Well, as I have said, the messenger arrived at thirteen minutes to nine. It was proved afterwards, and that conclusively, that by the inn clock it was eleven minutes to the hour, and the clock was found to have been two minutes fast. . . .

Now it was well known in the Cairn that Joseph Andrew Kirkpatrick did not 'cry' for his trousers till 'ten minutes from nine' morning by morning. But this early summons roused him and excited him. Hurriedly the great man got dressed, and without taking his porridge, without shaving even, although it was the Saturday morning and he had never before gone out on a Saturday morning without having shaved – Hurriedly, I say, he set out from his house looking stern and inexorable.

But soon he bethought himself of the proprieties: he slackened his pace after the first twenty yards. Were not the eyes of the Cairn upon him? Was not that Jims Hughes, and that Saunders Hanna, not to speak of several stages of McMeekins, McDowalls, and Neillies, eyeing him as if they would ogre from him what he had determined to do? So he began to walk more coolly and deliberately. Deep down in his heart, too, was there not the earnest hope that the men of the sea would all be away before he reached the place? When he bethought himself he called himself many ugly names for having hurried as he had done.

With look averted from the vegetable patch, and gazing away seaward towards Kirkcolm Scar, Joseph, the 'polis', pursues with leaden feet the way. He draws nearer. There is silence among the onlookers. Such a sight had never been seen in the Cairn. Will the great man's wrath begin to blaze at once? Will he take the law into his own hands? In the memory of living man such a thing had never happened.

Joseph Andrew Kirkpatrick at length reached the prisoners: they had not escaped as he had hoped.

'Whit the deevil dae ye mean by comin' to steal in braid daylicht?' he thundered. 'Ha'ye nae sense ava? Could ye no ha'e come when fowk were a' sleepin'. It's the hangtest stupit thing I ever heard o' onybody daein'.'

Thus he raged and stormed, 'stupit deevils' being the most polite name he gave them. It was truly exasperating! To think that he, a real man of peace, who had never troubled any Justice with a prisoner, should have been brought out of his bed at such an unusual hour and hurried into this 'thiefin' business', all on account of the stupidity of a pack of long-boot men – it was really too bad! 'An' thiefin' at sic a time o' the day. Dasht, a Galloway wean wad ha'e kent better.'

Even then Joseph would have been more than glad if he could have let 'the case' off. But the owners of the patch would not hear of it; they had had so many of their vegetables stolen by passing boatmen. For this stubbornness and inhumanity Joseph upbraided them sternly. 'What could ye no ha'e been up earlier in the mornin' for' (Oh, Joseph!) 'an' stoppit thae silly sowls afore they began' (Oh, Patrick!) 'You lyin' routin' in your beds, an' puir stupit deevils stealin' your neeps an' kail in Gude's daylicht.'

Then, after thinking over the affair for a little – really he did not know what to do – he turned on the owners of the patch and gave them a great say-away for having been up so early. 'If you had been in your beds like dacent Christian fowk till ten meenutes frae nine, thir stupit craters wad ha'e gotten aff in peace.'

But nothing would do; Joseph could not get out of it. The case was taken before the Justice, and soon after that Kirkpatrick retired. He lived to a good old age, but he never cared to speak about the long-boots who stole the neeps till he was at his third (glass). But after that . . .!

Just in finishing the sketch Michael McTear said something about

Glasserton Kirkyard and a tombstone with the letters so much worn already that perhaps it would not be wise to spend time searching for it. Originally the inscription may have read:

> Joseph Andrew Kirkpatrick,
> For many years Policeman at Cairnryan.
> 'Blessed are the peacemakers.'
>   – E. Dickson, *My Bagdad*, London 1896, pp. 25–36

11

POEMS, PROLOGUES AND SONGS

✝

*There are the professionals, the craftsmen who wrote for a living –
Hannay, Ferguson, Burns, MacDiarmid – and there are the others. It was
tempting to include the great John Gay (1685–1732) of* The Beggar's
Opera *and* Polly *(Macheath in the West Indies) with the former. The
Duke and Duchess of Queensberry were his most generous and patient
patrons, entertaining him at their London house in Burlington Gardens,
at Amesbury near Salisbury, at Middleton Stoney near Bicester in
Oxfordshire, and at Drumlanrig in Dumfries-shire in the late 1720s. It is
possible, and perhaps probable, that he wrote some of his most important
late work at Drumlanrig.* The Beggar's Opera *was first performed on 28th
January, 1728.* Polly *was banned by Walpole on 12th December, 1728 to
the enormous disgust of Kitty, Lady Catherine Hyde, the Duchess of
Queensberry. When* Polly *had finally its first performance on stage in
London in London on 19th June, 1777, Kitty, aged 76, was there.*

*The others include packmen, doctors, ministers, blacksmiths, farmers,
fishermen, excise officers, labourers, booksellers and the happily
anonymous. Some received considerable acclaim in their own lifetime,
although the self-conscious rusticity and 'untutored fancy' can today be
difficult to take. As always in Scotland it was all too tempting to attempt to
follow and imitate Burns, when much that went into print would have
been better left in the secrecy of the writing-desk. Quite crude versifying
can, however, often make excellent source material (places and people) for
local historians.* Moffat Wells, *for example, provides a useful picture of the
people who went there and the facilities the town offered.*

✝

PATRICK HANNAY
A Happy Husband or, Directions for a Maide to choose her Mate. As also, A Wives Behaviour towards her Husband after Marriage (1619)

Patrick Hannay was from the Kirkdale line of Hannays, as Marshall's commendatory verse in the 1622 edition of his friend master's *poems makes clear. He was a court poet to James VI and I in London, composing elegies, songs, sonnets, epitaphs, and longer works including* Philomela, The Nightingale, *where we find this elegant description:*

> The Maple with a skarry skinne
>   Did ʒpread broad pallid leaues:
> The quaking Aʒpine light and thinne
>   To th'ayre light paʒʒage giues:
>   Reʒembling ʒtill
>   The trembling ill
> Of tongues of womankinde,
>   Which neuer reʒt,
>   But ʒtill are preʒt
> To waue with euery winde.

The Happy Husband *is full of practical, sensible advice. It is still a delight to read and, no doubt, a textbook for marriage guidance counsellors.*

> To chooʒe aright, know from what ʒtock he's grown;
> The *birth* ʒuits beʒt, is neereʒt to thine owne:
> Diʒlike makes higher *Birth* deeme lower baʒe,
> Lower will neuer by thy *Birth* take place:
> In *Man* the fault is more to be excus'd,
> Who of low *birth* (for *beauty*) hath one chus'd;
> His lightneʒʒe therein euer loue is deem'd,
> Yet as *his place*, his *Wife* ʒhall be eʒteem'd.
> But when a *Woman* of a noble race
> Doth match with *Man* of farre inferiour place,
> Shee cannot him innoble, he is ʒtill
> In place as ʒhee firʒt found him, good, or ill. . . .
>
> To alter that's not able, yet we know
> Oft *Men* of worth haue come of *Parents* low:
> For Parents place is not the Childrens merit,
> Yet it addes grace, if they their worth inherit;

If not, it addes to ʒhame: for from *high race*
Vertue's expected due to ʒuch a place. . . .

  No *Gamefter* let him be: for ʒuch a *Man*
Shall ʒtill be loʒer, doe the beʒt he can;
His *mind* and *money* it frets, and deʒtroyes
And waʒts the precious *time* he here enioyes. . . .

Vpon this Earth there is no greater *Hell*,
Then with ʒuʒpecting *Iealouʒie* to dwell.
See that his *humors* (as neere as may be)
Doe with each *humor* of thy *minde* agree;
Or elʒe *contention*, and *diʒʒention* ʒtill,
Will bar your ʒweet content; while the ones *will*
The others doth reʒiʒt, Loue cannot be
'Twixt *fire* and *water*, they will ne're agree:
True friendʒhip muʒt expreʒʒe 'twixt *man* and *wife*,
The *comfort*, ʒ*tay*, *defence*, and *port* of life. . . .

✝

ANDREW SYMSON
Teacher, Publisher and Poet

Outed as an Episcopalian clergyman, Andrew Symson (c. 1638–1712)
moved to Edinburgh to begin a new career as a publisher and bookseller
in the Canongate. In his Tripatriarchon *(1705), written at Kirkinner in*
the 1670s and 1680s, he has to struggle with a Middle Eastern folk culture
with complicated family ties (Abraham and his father's daughter), in-
group and out-group marriage, sacred and profane prostitution, sibling
rivalry, incest (Lot and his daughters), concubinage, adultery and
polygamy. The confusion is amazing, for example in Abraham's
explanation for calling Sarah his sister:

And yet, when as I did her Sister call,
I told the truth, although I told not all:
She was (though not the daughter of my mother)
My Fathers daughter; thus I was her brother.
Yea and (good women are not over rife)
I lik'd her well; and she became my wife.

Deliberately creating teaching situations on good agricultural practices, he points out that the servants of Isaac:

> ... Some of them did keep
> His beasts in order, some again knew how
> To order things belonging to the plow,
> Sow, harrow, weed, reap, and bring the corn,
> Tread out and thrash the same (may we not scorn
> Th' old native Irish? who were wont to sever
> The corn and straw, by burning both together:
> A lazy fashion): some again had skill
> To grind the corn, and make it pass the mill,
> And some to bake it...

And in his Funeral Elegie *to David Dunbar, younger of Baldoon, who died in 1682, he again manages to include praise of his excellent attention to agriculture:*

> He knew full well how to behave at court,
> And yet but seldome did thereto resort;
> But lov'd the country life, choos'd to inure
> Himself to past'rage and agriculture;
> Proving, improving, ditching, trenching, draining,
> Viewing, reviewing, and by those means gaining;
> Planting, transplanting, levelling, erecting
> Walls, chambers, houses, terraces; projecting
> Now this, now that device, this draught, that measure,
> That might advance his profit with his pleasure.
> Quick in his bargains, honest in commerce,
> Just in his dealings. ....

✝

WILLIAM DOUGLAS OF FINGLAND
Annie Laurie (c. 1700)

William Douglas wooed and lost Annie Laurie (1682–1764), the daughter of Sir Robert Laurie of Maxwelton. She married Alexander Ferguson of Craigdarroch in 1709.

> MAXWELTON banks are bonnie,
> Whare early fa's the dew;

Whare me and Annie Laurie
    Made up the promise true;
Made up the promise true;
    And never forget will I,
And for bonnie Annie Laurie
    I'd lay down my head and die.

She's backit like a peacock,
    She's breastit like a swan,
She's jimp about the middle,
    Her waist ye weill may span;
Her waist you weill may span,
    And she has a rolling eye,
And for bonnie Annie Laurie
    I'd lay down my head and die.

Lady John Scott, Annie Laurie (c. 1834–35)

Lady John Scott (1810–1900), the daughter of John Spottiswoode of Spottiswoode, married Lord John Douglas Montagu Scott in 1836. Her version of the song has a new third stanza and a completely different and rather dull second verse. The tune, which she had made before to fit the words of an old ballad, Kempye Kaye, was adapted c. 1834–35 for her new song.

MAXWELLTON braes are bonnie,
    Where early fa's the dew,
And it's there that Annie Laurie
    Gie'd me her promise true;
Gie'd me her promise true,
    That ne'er forgot sall be;
But for bonnie Annie Laurie
    I'd lay doun my head and dee.

Her brow is like the snaw-drift,
    Her neck is like the swan,
Her face it is the fairest
    That e'er the sun shone on;
That e'er the shun shone on,
    And dark blue is her e'e;
And for bonnie Annie Laurie
    I'd lay doun my head and dee.

Like dew on the gowan lying
   Is the fa' o' her fairy feet;
And like winds in summer sighing
   Her voice is low and sweet;
Her voice is low and sweet,
   And she's a' the world to me,
And for bonnie Annie Laurie
   I'd lay doun my head and dee.

✝

ROBERT FERGUSSON
'Dumfries' (1773)

Robert Fergusson (1750–74), the poet for Edinburgh, Leith and Fife, was respected, indeed revered, by Robert Burns. His vivid poetry, with its joyous fairs and bacchanalian celebrations, its finely observed fisherfolk and farmers and city gossips and dandies, and irreverent satire of the unco good and Sabbath-centred 'respectability' ('Leith Races', 'Caller Oysters', 'The Farmer's Ingle', 'Braid Cloth', 'Auld Reekie') was an inspiration for Burns. Although hardly vintage Ferguson, 'Dumfries', written during a three day visit from Edinburgh in September 1773, is a neat town poem. His Dumfries is a fresh, healthy and prosperous town. Verses 3 and 4 are omitted here:

The gods sure in some canny hour,
To bonny Nith hae ta'en a tour,
Whare bonny blinks the caller flow'r,
   Beside the stream,
And sportive there hae shawn their pow'r,
   In fairy dream.

Had *Kirkhill* here but kent the gate,
The beauties on Dumfries that wait,
He'd never turn'd his canker'd pate
   Of satire keen,
Whan ilka thing's sae trig and neat
   To cheer the ein. . . .

Had Horace liv'd, that pleasant sinner,
That loo'd gude wine to synd his dinner,

His muse tho' dous, the de'il be in her,
       She'd lous'd her tongue,
The drink cou'd round Parnassus rin her
       In blythest song.

Nae mair he'd sung to auld Maecenas
The blinking ein o' bonny Venus,
His leave o' them he'd taen at anis
       For Claret here,
Which Jove and a' his gods still rain us
       Frae year to year.

O Jove, man, gie's some orrow pence,
Mair siller, an' a wie mair sense,
I'd big to you a rural spence,
       An' bide a' simmer,
An' cald frae saul and body fence
       Wi' frequent brimmer.

✝

DAVID DAVIDSON
Thoughts on the Seasons (1789)

David Davidson (1760–1828) had a varied career in England as a tutor to the Duke of Somerset and as a schoolteacher in the 1780s in Salisbury and Lymington. On returning to his native Stewartry he ran an 'Academy or Boarding School for Young Gentlemen' (or 'The Grove Academy' or 'Davidson's Academy' or 'Davie Davie's School') in Castle Douglas. He was also a printer and publisher and, with his son Anthony S. Davidson (1798–1867), he began the Castle Douglas Miscellany *in 1823.*

His long Thoughts on the Seasons, *published in London in 1789, followed James Thomson's* Seasons *(1726–30), but 'adapted for Scotland'. The best sections are located on 'The Village Green' on a Summer Evening:*

They whisked about the good brown ale,
       An' bumpered round the claret;
The whiskey ran frae reaming pails–
       Some lasses got their skair o't–

The cook-maid she was wond'rous spruce,
    An' bobbit in the entry–
She wadna taste it butt the house,
    But pried it in the pantry.

– and at 'Kelton-hill Fair', where he uses the 'East Galloway dialect'.

Summer. Kelton-hill Fair
Frae touns an' distant villages thick crowds
Press, thronging, to the Fair, to pass the day
In harmless merriment.–The reaming caups
Are nimbly handed roun'; an' social mirth
Sits, fidging, on ilk' turf throughout the Hill. . . .

An' sic a sight sure ne'er was seen
    O' lads an' ruddy lasses;
Some thither went to show their shoon,
    An' some to tak their glasses.
Upo' the Hill, nags, men, an' boys
    A' through ither fast did bicker;
Some here sat selling Tunbridge toys,
    An' there some sat wi' licker
                In kaigs, that day.

An' there was ginger-facèd Moll,
    Wi' sweeties frae Kirkcu'brie;
An' calf-reed carrier Samuel Noll,
    Nae better than he should be.
An' there was nimble-fingered Ben,
    Wha frae the whins cam' jumpin;
An' beggars frae the auld Brig-en',
    Amang the croud cam' limpin
                To thieve, that day.

An' there was pluke-faced Willie Kell,
    Wi' brandy in a barrel;
An' Jemmy Neal an' Geordy Fell,
    Wha baith cam there to quarrel.
An' there sat leering Lily Scott
    Upo' a green truff laughin',
Wha sold for tippence plack the pot

The best yill i' the clachan,
                    Sae brisk, that day.

Great was the noise o' chapman lads,
    An' muckle was the bussle;
Wi' girls wi' gingerbread in dauds,
    An' boys wi' bawbee whussles.
Some tippling chiels gaed to the tent,
    To hansel Leezy Waldron;
An' drank until their wymes were stent,
    Like only drum or cauldron,
                    Wi' punch, that day.

The lasses, now, in twa's an' three's,
    Cam' sweating up the entry;
Nell, Jean, an' Sue, frae Ba'maghie,
    An' sic misca'èd gentry.
Their sweethearts met them at the gate,
    Just at the hour expected;
But squintin Susy took the pet,
    Because she was neglected,
                    An' scorned, that day. . . .

                    – *Thoughts on the Seasons*, 1789, pp. 51–55

†

ROBERT BURNS
John Anderson my Jo (1790)

Robert Burns (1759–96) became the tenant of Ellisland farm in June 1788. He packed into the last eight years of his life an almost impossible workload: for three years a farmer, although he had to assist him a first-rate ploughman in William Clark from Annan, who died in 1843 at the age of 76; from September 1789 an Excise officer, riding, in 1790, 200 miles a week on his duties; as still a working poet and a collector of bawdry; as a collector and editor of songs for James Johnson's Scots Musical Museum *and George Thomson's* Select Collection of Original Scottish Airs for the Voice; *as a great songsmith (words and music); and as a man with extended family commitments and a vast range of outside interests from the Dumfries Theatre and heraldry to the Monklands Library.*

His John Anderson my Jo, *although originating in a fairly crude early-eighteenth-century song, turned out to be the most perfect and sensitive of all his songs:*

> John Anderson my jo, John,
>   When we were first acquent;
> Your locks were like the raven,
>   Your bony brow was brent;
> But now your brow is beld, John,
>   Your locks are like the snaw;
> But blessings on your frosty pow,
>   John Anderson my Jo.
>
> John Anderson my jo, John,
>   We clamb the hill the gither;
> And mony a canty day, John,
>   We've had wi' ane antither:
> Now we maun totter down, John,
>   And hand in hand we'll go;
> And sleep the gither at the foot,
>   John Anderson my Jo.

The Deil's awa' wi' th' Exciseman (1792)

Burns moved into Dumfries in November 1791. This song has a wild, careless, carefree and infectious rapture. Burns himself, however, was an efficient, hard-working, conscientious and very ambitious career officer, as his letters to his superiors and his aristocratic patrons seeking support for his advancement and promotion make very clear:

> The deil cam fiddlin thro' the town,
>   And danc'd awa wi' th' Exciseman;
> And ilka wife cries, auld Mahoun,
>   I wish you luck o' the prize, man.

Chorus

> The deil's awa the deil's awa
>   The deil's awa wi' th' Exciseman,
> He's danc'd awa he's danc'd awa
>   He's danc'd awa wi' th' Exciseman.
>
> We'll mak our maut and we'll brew our drink,
>   We'll laugh, sing, and rejoice, man;

And mony braw thanks to the meikle black deil,
  That danc'd awa wi' th' Exciseman.
    The deil's awa & c.

There's threesome reels, there's foursome reels,
  There's hornpipes and stratspeys, man,
But the ae best dance e'er cam to the Land
  Was, the deil's awa wi' th' Exciseman.
    The deil's awa & c.

Burns and the Dumfries Theatre

Burns was an enthusiastic supporter of the theatre in the Old Assembly Rooms in Irish Street and of the elegant New Theatre which opened in Dumfries on 29th September, 1792 under the management of Mr Williamson of the Theatre Royal, Haymarket, London, and Mr Sutherland. Dumfries, with a population of only c. 6,000, was really too small to maintain in the long-term a first-rate professional resident company. The bravado and the scale of the productions in 1792 and 1793 is remarkable. On 21st November, 1792, for example, the company presented a comedy, The Dramatist, *with four songs added including 'The Blue ey'd Lassie', words by Burns and music by Robert Riddell of Glenriddell, a Scots interlude, 'Hooly and Fairley', and a Pantomime, 'The Death of Captain Cook', with elaborate scenery and costumes. Alexander Nasmyth, perhaps at the direction of his patron Patrick Miller of Dalswinton, provided at least one stage setting.*

  Burns wrote addresses and prologues for the benefit nights of Mr Sutherland on 31st December, 1789 and 21st November, 1792, for Mrs Sutherland in February or early March 1790, and for the 'simple, wild, enchanting' Miss Louisa Fontenelle (1773–1799) on 26th November, 1792 (on 'The Rights of Women') and on 4th December, 1793. It is highly likely that the invitation in his 1790 Prologue:

    Is there nae Poet, burning keen for Fame,
    Will bauldly try to gie us Plays at hame?

was one that the always ambitious and enterprising Burns might well have taken up after completing his song collection commitments. Tam o' Shanter *as a play with special effects?*

Robert Burns: Scots Prologue for Mrs Sutherland's Benefit Night at the Dumfries Theatre, 1790

What needs this din about the town o' Lon'on?
How this new Play, and that new Sang is comin?
Why is outlandish stuff sae meikle courted?
Does Nonsense mend, like Brandy, when imported–
Is there nae Poet, burning keen for Fame,
Will bauldly try to gie us Plays at hame?
For Comedy abroad he need na toil,
A Knave an' Fool are plants of ev'ry soil:
Nor need he hunt as far as Rome or Greece,
To gather matter for a serious piece;
There's themes enow in Caledonian story,
Wad shew the Tragic Muse in a' her glory.

Is there no daring Bard will rise and tell
How glorious Wallace stood, how hapless fell?
Where are the Muses fled, that should produce
A *drama* worthy of the name of Bruce?
How on *this* spot he first unsheath'd the sword
'Gainst mighty England and her guilty Lord,
And after many a bloody, deathless doing,
Wrench'd his dear country from the jaws of Ruin!
O! for a Shakespeare or an Otway scene,
To paint the lovely hapless Scottish Queen!
Vain ev'n the omnipotence of Female charms,
'Gainst headlong, ruthless, mad Rebellion's arms.
She fell–but fell with spirit truly Roman,
To glut that direst foe,–*a vengeful woman*;
A *woman*–tho' the phrase may seem uncivil,
As able–and as wicked as the devil!
[One Douglas lives in Home's immortal page,
But Douglases were heroes every age:
And tho' your fathers, prodigal of life,
A Douglas followed to the martial strife,
Perhaps, if bowls row right, and Right succeeds,
Ye yet may follow where a Douglas leads!]

As ye have generous done, if a' the land
Would take the Muses' servants by the hand,
Not only hear–but patronise–defend them,
And where ye justly can commend–commend them;

And aiblins when they winna stand the test,
Wink hard, and say, 'The folks hae done their best.'
Would a' the land do this, then I'll be caition,
Ye'll soon hae Poets o' the Scottish nation,
Will gar Fame blaw until her trumpet crack,
And warsle Time, and lay him on his back.

    For us and for our Stage, should ony spier,
'Whase aught thae Chiels maks a' this bustle here?'

My best leg foremost, I'll set up my brow,
We have the honor to belong to you!
We're your ain bairns, e'en guide us as ye like,
But, like guid mothers, shore before ye strike;
And grateful still, I trust, ye'll ever find us:
For gen'rous patronage, and meikle kindness,
We've got frae a' professions, sorts, an' ranks:
God help us!–we're but poor–ye'se get but thanks!

New Theatre, Dumfries. . . .
For the Benefit of Miss Fontenelle on Wednesday, December 4, 1793 will
be presented
A Comic Opera (never acted here) called '*THE HAUNTED TOWER.*'
Written by Mr Cobb; Music by Storace.
Baron of Oakland, Mr Scriven, Lord William, Mr Clarke,
And Lord Edward, Mr Williamson, Lady Elenor, Miss Harley,
And Adela, Miss Fontenelle.
End of act 2d, a new Scots Air called '*THE BANKS OF NITH*'.
The words by Mr Burns; the music by Robert Riddell of Glenriddell,
Esq. –
To be sung by Miss Fontenelle.
End of the Play, '*A NEW OCCASIONAL ADDRESS*',
Written by Mr Burns, to be spoken by Miss Fontenelle.
To which will be added (by particular desire) A Musical Farce,
    called '*THE VIRGIN UNMASK'D*'.
    Lucy, Miss Fontenelle.
After which will be performed, A Grand Spectacle,
    called '*The Siege of Valenciennes*'.
Founded on a series of interesting events, in the late operations of the
combined armies on the Continent. Accompanied by *Machinery* and
Action. Giving a comprehensive idea of whatever is most striking in the
progress and termination of a Siege; particularly, the working in the

Trenches; the Preparation and Explosion of a Mine; and the manner of effecting and entering a Breach.

To finish with a General View of the STORMING PARTY; Their getting possession of the Horn Work; and the Consequent Capitulation and Surrender of THE TOWN. The whole built upon well known facts, and respectfully offered to the Public, as some Illustration of the present Military Movements on the Great Theatre of War. Tickets and Places for the Boxes to be had at the usual places; and of Miss Fontenelle, at Mr Kemp's, Cabinet-maker. – Boxes, 3s. – Pit, 2s. – Gallery, 1s. –

Doors to be opened at Six, and to begin precisely at Seven o'clock.

— *DWJ*, 3rd December, 1793

✝

DAVID McCULLOCH OF ARDWALL
'Todlen hame'

Robert Burns may have collected Todlen hame *by David McCulloch of Ardwall, who died in 1793, on his journey through Galloway in June 1794 when he travelled from Gatehouse to Kirroughtree with John Syme and David McCulloch, jun.. David McCulloch's children included James Murray McCulloch (see Chapter 7), Elizabeth, who married Thomas Scott, the brother of Sir Walter Scott, and David McCulloch jun. (1769–1825), who was a good-hearted friend of Burns. Burns sent a copy of 'Todlen hame' to Robert Cleghorn in Edinburgh in August 1795, and specifically mentions that it was by the* late *David McCulloch:*

When wise Solomon was a young man o' might,
He was canty, & liked a lass ilka night;
But when he grew auld that he was na in trim,
He cried out, 'In faith, Sirs! I doubt it's a sin!'
 Todlen hame, todlen hame,
 Sae round as neep we gang todlen hame.–

But we're no come to that time o' life yet, ye ken;
The bottle's half-out – but we'll fill it again:
As for Solomon's doubts, wha the deevil cares for't!
He's a damn'd churlish fallow that likes to spill sport.–
 Todlen &c.

A bicker that's gizzen'd, it's nae worth a doit;
Keep it wat, it will haud in – it winna let out:
A chiel that's ay sober, is damn'd ill to ken;
Keep him wat wi' gude drink – & ye'll find him out then.–
   Todlen &c.

May our house be weel theekit, our pantry ay fu',
Wi' rowth in our cellar for weetin our mou';
Wi' a tight, caller hizzie, as keen as oursels,
Ay ready to souple *the whistle & bells!!*
   Todlen hame & c.

✝

JOHN LAUDERDALE OF KIRKINNER
Poems chiefly in the Scottish Dialect (1796)

John Lauderdale, who was born about 1740, left County Antrim in Ireland and settled in Kirkinner parish in Wigtownshire in the late 1780s or early 1790s. He may well have been one of the radical 'infatuated Presbyterians' or Croppies who had to get out of Ulster to escape the attention of the government. He continued to espouse in Kirkinner radical views on Irish, British and local politics. He had been in the Army and had some expertise as a quarryman, which gave him some employment in Kirkinner; he ran a little village shop bearing the sign of a willow rod with a herring and potato at opposite ends; he also tried running a private school without much success. It may have been his wife, Mary Conchie, who really kept the family together, dealing in eggs and poultry and selling leeches gathered in the swamps.

The 100-page Poems *published in 1806 was clearly an attempt to imitate the success of Robert Burns, but without the same education and talent. His best work is probably when he is poking none-too-gentle fun at local figures, for example the* Curdandy *poems about the Seceder Robert Alexander, a baker in Wigtown and church officer in Mr Ogilvie's church.*

The Galloway Farmer's Song

How canty is the farmers life,
If fou o' care, he's free frae strife,
Wi' plenty o' guid peat
To mak his fire, to brew, to bake,

To warm his fingers, gif they ache;
To roast or boil his meat.

His harvest in, his grain well sold,
His beer well brew'd, his gain well told,
Will gar him raise his voice;
His horses strong, his pleugh at wark,
His flails a' going wi' a jerk,
To mak his heart rejoice.

How can men say that times are bad?
They surely must be reckoned mad,
When barley's fifty-five!*
Our rents are low, an' cattle dear,
Four pounds a head, a year auld steer,
How can he miss but thrive.

This blessed war, begun by Pitt,
We farmers hope, he'll near submit
But feight it out fu' friskey;
And if frae hame he'll sow dissensions
Amang the Chonana, and Conventions,
We'll drink his health in whiskey.

*Twelve bushels

✝

JOSEPH TRAIN
The Cabal o' Witches: A Cantata

Joseph Train (see Chapter 3) included some powerful images in his Poetical Reveries (1806) of the old alternative world of kelpies and goblins and bogles and brownies ('Spunkie'; or, 'The Wan'er'd Wight') and witches and devils ('The Witch o' Inverness'). 'The Cabal o' Witches' take their revenge on a pious hypocrite who had accused his neighbours of being witches or warlocks, hanging his effigy in a fire and singing a Grand Chorus while 'Still pricking it with skivers here and there'.

First Witch   Her skin as rough as any rasp

Was like the belly o' an asp;
Her whiskers taper'd like a cat's;
Her een was like a water rat's;
Her feet were webbed like a duck's. . . .

Second Witch　　Her cap was made o' adder's skin,
Wi' spider muslin lin'd within.
An' dead men's eyes, an' sinews strung,
As ornaments about it hung. . . .

Third Witch　　This hag was what in each degree,
The devil's mother's said to be.
Ten teats from her black body hung,
To which as many imps were clung;
An' straight between her glowring een,
Each hellish fury there was seen. . . .

Grand Chorus　　Round about the ingle turn him,
Throw in greasy bones an' burn him;
Rip his belly, tear his eyes out,
Give them to the first, who cries out.
Let his empty skull be drest
For a Willie-wag-tail's nest. . . .
Take the bowels from his body,
On the fire here mak them ready;
Strew his ashes in the air,
Ne'er to be remember'd mair. . . .
Fiends infernal bear his soul
To your dreary dark abode. . .
– *The Poetical Reveries of Joseph Train*, 1806, pp. 105–12 and
pp. 123–24

✝

WILLIAM NICHOLSON
The Braes of Galloway (1814)

William Nicholson (1783–1849) was born at Tannymas in Borgue parish. His father, who was from Mouswald in Dumfries-shire, has been described as a carrier and 'crofter'. His older brother, John Nicholson, became a publisher and author in Kirkcudbright. Their mother, Barbara Houston, had a rich store of tales and traditions which she passed on to them. The family moved to Kempleton in Twynholm and to Barncrosh in Tongland, before settling in the village of the Red Lion [Ringford], where he went to school.

Like many young Scots he took to the road as a packman selling shawls and ginghams. He was also a teller of tales, collecting old traditions and ballads for his Tales, in Verse, and Miscellaneous Poems *(1814). His most important work was the* Brownie of Blednoch, *which was included in the* Dumfries Monthly Magazine *(1825), a Galloway version of the 'Bodach' of Carrick, the 'Doonie' of Nithsdale, the 'Glashan' of Man, or the 'Grugach' of Ireland.*

'The Braes of Galloway' is his version of an old chapman or tinker plea sung about or to a lassie to persuade her to come to live in Galloway:

> O Lassie, wilt thou gang wi' me,
> And leave thy frien's i' th' south country –
> Thy former frien's and sweethearts a',
> And gang wi' me to Gallowa?
>
> O Gallowa braes they wave wi' broom,
> And heather-bells in bonnie bloom.
> There's lordly seats, and livin's braw,
> Amang the braes o' Gallowa.
>
> At e'en, whan darkness shrouds the sight,
> And lanely, langsome is the night,
> Wi' tentie care my pipes I'll thraw,
> Play 'A' the way to Gallowa'.
>
> Should fickle fortune on us frown,
> Nae lack o' gear our love should drown.
> Content should shield our haddin' sma,
> Amang the braes o' Gallowa.

> [Verses 1, 5 and 6 of 6, and Chorus]

Compare the North-East version recorded by the late great Jeannie Robertson –

> For I say bonnie lass it's will ye come wi' me
> Tae share your lot in a strange country

> For tae share your lot when doon fa's a'
> An' I'll gang oot owre the hills tae Gallowa'.

. . . But to have heard her sing it is something one can never ever forget.

✝

MOFFAT WELLS, HO!!!

. . . All pains and diseases poor mortals endure,
Here with speed find a happy infallible cure,
Thy box, O Pandora! no further can go;
Then, invalids! haste ye to – Moffat Wells, ho!

Are you teased with rhuematics, or pestered with gout
Are you bilious, or nervous, or not very stout,
Have you been in the hands of Quack Doctors, or so;
To renovate health, haste to – Moffat Wells, ho!

If a doctoring further you think you have need,
Here are plenty 'aye ready' to blister or bleed,
Prescribe what your case suits, and make their charge, O;
Then haste, instant haste straight to – Moffat Wells, ho!

Are you wrong in your stomach, or wrong in your head,
No more of absorbents or jackets you'll need,
Here health, rosy health soon returning, will show
The paramount virtues of – Moffat Wells, ho!

But if high in health's boom, you are young, fresh and fair,
And have merely a wish to enjoy a change of air,
To flirt and to gossip and pass for a beau,
Then haste, instant haste ye to – Moffat Wells, ho!

Here are billiards and bowls, and grand rooms for a dance,
Fiddlers, frizeurs, and players, from England and France;
Here are parties select, and clubs, just so so,
As their purses and ranks suit, at – Moffat Wells, ho!

Whate'er your taste be, for the serious or joke,

Divines you'll meet here, with some witlings of note,
You'll find men of great talents, aye and many a round O
Like hoops moving round you, at – Moffat Wells, ho!

. . . Here the grave soon turn gay, the stupid turn witty,
The fool becomes wise, and the plainest wax pretty,
Here the bloom of each beauty unfaded shall blow
When washed by your waters, sweet – Moffat Wells, ho!

Here lovers no longer need mourn or complain,
Old maids here enjoy what they sighed for in vain,
And young ones the joys of sweet Hymen soon know
With the lovers they longed for at – Moffat Wells, ho!. . .

[*C. Bankside*, 14th May, 1817]
– *DGC*, 20th May, 1817

†

GEORDIE WISHART
To the Honourable the Provost and Bailies of the Royal Burgh of Kirkcudbright (*c.* 1821)

Geordie Wishart was the chief salmon fisher on the Dee. He rented the lower part of the river from the burgh of Kirkcudbright. He was also a storyteller and professional versifier. The poem was collected by a gentleman who left Kirkcudbright in 1821 and returned with it from Indiana in 1880, when he recited the piece from memory. James Waugh was the town officer and bellman or town crier. James Herries was employed by the town as a sort of 'criminal officer' to deal with tramps and troublemakers: unfortunately he spent too much time on his many journeys in inns and was drowned at Palnackie travelling 'under night'. Wishart is replying here to a demand for rent!

When times were good, I was content
Yearly to pay my fishing rent;
But now the times are altered sair,
The fish grown scarce, nae cash to spare,
Which makes a body quake for fear
That Waugh or Herries may appear,
Unwelcome folk as you do ken,

When they do visit honest men:
You may believe me when I say,
The rent is mair than I can pay.
                              [*George Wishart*, Fish House]
                              – *KA*, 1st October, 1880

✝

ROBERT SHENNAN
'Rough Meg and the Midges' (1831)

Robert Shennan (c. 1782–1866) was a tenant on the estate of the Rev. Dr David Lamont of Ironcrogo, the minister of Kirkpatrick-Durham parish, to whom he dedicated his Tales, Songs and Miscellaneous Poems . . . Descriptive of Rural Scenes and Manners, *Chiefly in the Scottish Dialect (Dumfries, 1831). Robert Shennan, jun., who died in Dunedin, New Zealand, in January 1859, was described as late of Lairdlaugh, Kirkpatrick-Durham. Robert Shennan died at Barmoffity on 27th December, 1866.*

His poems are interesting as a record of local occasions, the 'Fair' and 'Races' at Kirkpatrick-Durham, and 'Rowley-Powley wi' the Pins'. The village Debating Society seems to have played an important part in his life and several of his poems were written specifically for Society meetings, for example 'The Gudeman and Johnny' for the question 'Are charity balls proper or not?' 'Rough Meg and the Midges' deals with an ever-present Scottish problem!

The sun to the westward was slippin' away,
When Maggie was making a wee pickle hay,
And the impudent midges got under her claise
And she swore she was never sae fash'd in her days,
For they buzz'd and they flutter'd, they kittled and bit,
And she curs'd, and she raged, and she stamp'd wi' her fit,
But she breeked her coats and got rid o' them there,
Though still they were thrang 'bout her head and her hair,
And bit her dun haffits, she curs'd them again,
And wish'd that the Devil wad send for his ain,
But Satan was busy and just let them stay,
And she couldna get raking and coling her hay;
She started, she rubbed, and hundreds fell dead,

But still some were biting her hands and her head;
Till her patience run out, and her heart turned sair,
And she left the hay-bog in a fit of despair.
'I wonder,' she cried, 'what it is I have done,
That Providence always upon me doth frown;
My sister was neither sae clever nor bonny,
Yet she got a husband wi' plenty o' money,
And bonny wee bairns, a' weel happ'd and fu',
While I hae got nought but a cat and a cow;
And I canna for midges get wonnin' my hay. . . .'

✝

'O.Z.'
'Epitaph on the Deceased Thomas McCarlie' (1836)

*Tam McCarlie was a noted character and poet in Stranraer. He was almost
certainly a suter (or souter), i.e., a cobbler or shoemaker.*

Our bard is gane whom we'll mis sairly,
The great immortal Tam McCarlie;
Grim death, I trow, has nick'd him fairly,
It comes in turns;
A poet like him ye'll meet but rarely,
Except in Burns.
Puir Tam, he liked a wee drap drink,
Whene'er the bawbees he could clink,
But death cam for him in a blink
And tane awa'
Our poet, whom I really think
Could verse them a'.
Tam was a son o' Crispin's tribe,
Wi' coat o' mail an' horse did ride;
Two suters gaed on every side,
To guard our bard.
But noo his corpse away does glide
To yon kirk-yard.
In his last will he did desire,
His hammer to gang to J——e B——r,
To break his coals to mend his fire

In time o'need.
But Tam he has ascended higher,
I wish him speed.
                    – *The Galloway Register*, 7, 1st September, 1836

†

ROBERT KERR
'My First Fee' (1843)

Robert Kerr (1811–48) was born at Midtown of Spottes near Haugh of Urr. His father, a native of Dunscore, was a farm labourer. His mother, Janet Shennan, came from Kirkpatrick-Durham. He went to Hardgate parish school under Mr William Allan, and worked as a young lad on farms in the area. After three years c. 1826–29 at 'The Pack', that is as an itinerant trader or packman in Essex, he came back to Urr parish as a ploughman on Redcastle farm. He was able to save up enough money to take on the tenancy of Bogue farm near Garlieston in the autumn of 1848, but died of pneumonia at Redcastle on the 30th of September.

His poems are carefully planned. The longest, 'Maggie o' the Moss' (1844), is a lively story about auld Witch Maggie, who lived in a cottage near Redcastle. She had been hired by 'Clootie' and so was feared by poor and rich alike.

> What e'er she ask'd for, nane refus'd her:
> But every farmer strove to please
> The hag, wi' milk, and meal, and cheese. . . .
> For they,wha Meg's petitions spurn'd,
> Had cairts, and carriages o'erturn'd;
> Their horse gaed mad, and ran like stags,
> Till some got broken arms, and legs;
> The best kye in the byre gaed yell;
> Some died, some couldna raise themsel'. . . .
> And aft, at nicht, ane black as soot,
> Wha seem'd to wear a cloven foot,
> Wad visit Meg's. . . .

Maggie, with many a Caledonian grannie, attended an international conference of witches at the North Pole, a 'United Nations' of Esquimaux witches 'mounted upon bears in raws' and 'southern hags on kangaroos' and 'Indians on bamboos'.

A collection of his poems, edited by M.M. Harper, was published by Thomas Fraser of Dalbeattie in 1891. It included 'My First Fee' and 'The Widow's Ae Cow' (1844), both first published in the Dumfries Courier. *'My First Fee' may well be based on some of his own experiences as a herd boy.*

My mither was wae, for my faither was deid,
An' they'd threaten'd to tak' the auld hoose owre oor heid;
Her earnin's grew scanty, the meal was got dear,
An' the auldest o' five, I could whyles see the tear,
When she cam' hame at nicht, glisten bricht in her een,
Half hid, as if't didna juist want to be seen;
I spoke na a word, but my wee heart wad ache,
An' I wished I was big, for my puir mither's sake.

There were fermers aroun' wanted herds for their kye,
And my mither had said she had ane that wad try;
I mind hoo I trembl'd, half fear, an' half joy,
When a maister ca'd on us to look at the boy:
He bade me stan' up, an' he thocht I was wee,
But my frank, honest face, he said, pleased his e'e;
He wad tak' me, and try me ae half-year, an' see,
For a pair o'new shoon, an' a five shillin' fee.

We were gled to hear tell o't, the bargain was struck,
An' he gied me a saxpence o' earles for luck;
My trousers an' jacket were patch'd for the day,
An' my mither convoyed me a lang mile away,
Wi' charges an' warnin's 'gainst a' kin o' crime,
An' rules she laid doun, I thocht hard at the time:
If the kye should get wrang, I was never to lee,
Though they sent me awa' but my shoon or my fee.

Sae I fell to my wark, an' I pleas'd unco weel –
But a word or a wave, an' I plied han' or heel;
But my troubles cam' on, for the fences were bad,
An' the midsimmer flees made the cattle rin mad;
An' in cauld blashy weather, sair drenched wi' the rain,
Whyles wee thochts o' leavin' wad steal owre my brain;
But wi' courage, I dashed aye the tear frae my e'e,
When I thocht o' my shoon, an' my five shillin' fee.

An' Martinmas brocht me my lang-thocht-o' store,
An' proudly I coonted it twenty times o'er;
An' lang years hae fled, in a fortunate train,
But I never ance met wi' sic raptures again.
The sailor, juist safe through the wild breakers steer'd,
Proud Waterloo's victor, when Blucher appeared,
Ne'er felt what I felt, as I placed on the knee
O' a fond-hearted mither, my five shillin' fee.

†

JAMES KENNEDY, SANQUHAR'S VETERAN BARDIE
'Stanzas on the Novel Improvements of Mr Anderson, Farmer, Drumore'

As the Poet was wand'ring, his poems to sell,
Chance led him to call where a farmer does dwell,
A farmer of fame, he had ne'er seen before,
His name's Anderson, and his farm is Drumore.

A more sage cultivator, for tilling the ground,
In the South of auld Scotia is rare to be found;
His 'tatoes and turnips, and gay golden grain
Wave yellow in autumn, o'er well cultivated plain.

For rearing of cattle, there's none may exceed:
The Ayrshire's his fav'rite – he's fond of the breed –
The fat he oft ships to the land of the Rose,
Where John Bull is aye ready a bargain to close.

Fine mares – most prolific for draught or for rein,
For cart, plough, or harrow, or coursing the plain,
Their owner reward, with some fifty per cent.,
His coffers to swell, or in payment of rent.

The Anderson stock met preferment by far,
And gained the first prize at the shows of Stranraer;
His stallions, for symetry, took the first prize,
His mares and his foals were preferred likewise.
And last, tho' not least, new improvements in store. . . .

Close drains are in progress at each lane or turn,
That empty themselves in the mill-turning burn:
For a' kinds of meldry the miller's complete,
Makes finest of flour from our own native wheat.

The byre is tidy, and handsome withal,
Each cow is possessed of a fine roomy stall,
A grate drains the urine, conveyed by a sewer
To a tank made of metal, that holds it secure.

A pump throws it into a barrel or stand,
From thence carted off as manure to the land:
Of its virtues so rare, the half's not been told,
To the farmer more precious than Ophir's fine gold. . . .

The subject is worthy the son of the lyre,
But Sanquhar's hoar Bardie begs leave to retire. . . .
                              – *GA*, 31st August, 1849

✝

JAMES TROTTER
'The Wee Bruckit Lassie' (1864)

This poem was first published in the Kirkcudbrightshire Advertiser *of 1st July, 1864 with James Trotter (1842–99) taking on the rather thin disguise of 'Seumas-mac-an-doctor, Dalry, Glenkens'. After qualifying in Medicine in Glasgow, Dr James Trotter practised in Bedlington in Northumberland. His prolific output included the 71-verse* Clachan Fair *in Dalry with 'sweetie stalls like wooden walls', a gypsy lass (no lang since cadging some prison kail in Wigton jail) with 'laulin' lungs an' talkin' tongue' crying out 'her tairts an' pies' and 'brandy drops or gingersnaps', and 'Glasca rogues in Hielan' togs', races between Carsphairn and Dalry men, farmers sorting out their brass in 'Sutton's grand hotel', and a right collieshangie in 'Sibbal's Inn' –*
> *But mony a lass will sell the pass*
> *Nine months this very nicht, man.*
But not, we may safely conclude, 'this wee, wee bruckit lassie, that milks her mammie's cow'.

The sun has set, the gloamin's come, the day has glided by,
The lassies liltin' through the broom, are ca'in' hame their kye;
I'll dauner doun the clachan brae to meet the ane I lo'e –
My wee, wee bruckit lassie, that milks her mammie's coo.

Wha wadna lo'e this wee bit thing, sae winsome and sae free,
The smilin' dimple o' her chin, her merry twinklin' e'e;
Her hair sae artless hangin' doun, but shaded frae her broo –
My wee, wee bruckit lassie, that milks her mammie's coo.

Yestreen, when up the Mulloch Knowe, I set her on my knee;
Says I – 'Wee Jessie, will you leave your frien's and come wi' me?'
She lap doun on the grass, and cried – 'I wadna gang wi' you' –
My wee, wee bruckit lassie, that milks her mammie's coo.

And when I asked her for a kiss, she turned and looked sae shy,
Affected wonder in her face, sae modest and sae coy;
Then, wheelin' roun', she stamp'd her fit – 'Sic tricks I'll no aloo' –
My wee, wee bruckit lassie, that milks her mammie's coo.

She gangs on Sundays to the kirk, sae bonnie and sae braw,
And, haith, my wee thing bears the gree, the belle amang them a';
But then she winna court wi' me, she's far owre young to woo –
This wee, wee bruckit lassie, that milks her mammie's coo.

✝

JOSEPH HEUGHAN OF AUCHENCAIRN
'Whar I the trade o' smithery on did ca'

Joseph Heughan (1837–1902) was born in Auchencairn on the 1st of January, 1837; his mother and father died on the 20th of January and the 20th of February of the same year. He was brought up by his grandfather on his mother's side at West Knockwhillan croft near Collin Mill. He grew up to become the blacksmith in Auchencairn, 'a great soul in a massive body'. He was also a stonemason, adding Latin inscriptions to headstones; a bookbinder; a cabinetmaker; and a skilled metalworker making working tools at his forge and exquisite miniature ploughs, trivets, candleholders and scales. Note the plough now in the Stewartry Museum in Kirkcudbright which he made in 1872 at a scale of 'twa inches to the fit'.

As a poet [occasional pen name Mulciber Veritatis] he had an amazing range from scholarly paraphrases of Virgil into Scots to love poems [Supplicatio Amatoris], and dramatic poems [Sennacherib], to humorous verses in the Galloway dialect, for example 'The Wooer's Flicht'

Puir ell-wan' Johnnie canna sleep
Since Jeanie gaed awa',
The saut tears thro' his winkers dreep,
His een's like meltin' snaw.
He's blearie and weary,
The chiel's gane nearly doylt,
Wi' mournin' and yearnin',
His fair physog is spoilt. . . .

She'll soon be to oor clachan back,
Should nae minyar o'ertak' her,
His mind will then be aff the rack,
When handy he can smack her.
He'll daft be, and saft be,
Her mou' he'll slaver ower,
He'll slaik her and straik her,
And test his courtin' power. . . . [verses 1 and 5 of 8]

A modest and truly good man he called his great work on world affairs 'Here awa', there awa'. His reverent description of God is curiously impressive:

Though nae ee can him see, yet he is, yet he is,
Though nae ee can him see, yet he is,
Though nae ee can him see,
He was an' aye will be
King o' Immensity,
Micht is his.

†

ALEXANDER ANDERSON
'Railway Surfaceman, Kirkconnell'

Alexander Anderson (1845–1909) ws born in Kirkconnell, Dumfries-shire. He was the youngest in a family of six boys and one girl. They moved to

Crocketford when he was three years old and he attended the village school there. His first work was labouring in a quarry near Kirkconnell. At the age of 17, and for the next 18 years, he was a surfaceman and plater employed by the Glasgow and South-Western Railway (hence the pen name 'Surfaceman'). The creative urge to write poetry, and to learn several languages, was in him from an early age. From 1870 onwards he found a ready market for his poems in The People's Friend *and* The People's Journal, *and also in* Good Friends *and* Cassell's Magazine. *In 1880 a post was found for him as Assistant Librarian at the University of Edinburgh.*

His first book, A Song of Labour and Other Poems *(1873) sold out its 2,000 copies in a fortnight. Many of the poems are about mischievous children (always boys) – 'The Deil's in that bit bairn', 'The Paidlin Wean', 'Maggie's Wean', 'The Unco Bit Wean', as compared to the ever helpful 'Oor Sis'; and another popular theme was the pathos of 'A Dead Child', 'The Child's Grave', 'The Mother and the Angel', and 'Oor Johnnie'.*

His third book, Songs of the Rail *(1878), was also successful, although many of the poems on railway engines and fatal accidents on the line – 'Rid of his Engine', 'Old Wylie's Story', 'Jim's Whistle' – are ponderous in the extreme. The first verse of the 'Song of the Engine'*

> IN the shake and rush of the engine,
>   In the full, deep breath of his chest,
> In the swift, clear clank of the gleaming crank,
>   In his soul that is never at rest;
> In the spring and ring of the bending rail,
>   As he thunders and hurtles along,
> A strong world's melody fashions itself,
>   And this smoke-demon calls it his song.

and Stood at Clear, *with only twenty-six lines, are exceptions:*

> . . . . Naught around in the night was seen
> Save the glimmer of lamps, where the crash had been.
>
> Right across the six-feet way,
> One huge hulk, engine and tender lay,
>
> While the wailing hiss of the steam took the air,
> By fits, like the low, dull tone of despair. . .

'Jim, old mate,' I said in his ear,
'They will ask you a question – can you hear?'

Then I saw through the grime that was on his face,
A white hue coming with slow, sure pace;

And upon his brow by the light of the lamp,
Other dew than the night's lay heavy and damp.

'Speak to him – quick!' they bent and said,
'Did the distant signal stand at red?'

Broken and slow came the words with a moan,
'Stood – at – clear,' and poor Jim was gone. . . .

The Two Angels and Other Poems (1875) is an altogether more accomplished and varied collection. The subjects include landscapes and scenery, 'A Walk to Pamphy Linns' near Sanquhar; schools and schooldays, 'Ledgie Cooper', who kept a school on the Crawick, and 'The Old Schoolhouse'; characters, 'The Fiddler o' Boglebriggs', 'Daft Ailie'; and children's verses, 'Dingle Doozie', 'Cockie-Roosie-Ride', and 'The Bowgie Man' with his cry:
    Mithers fash'd wi' steerin' weans, Pit them in my pock?
The post popular and best-remembered were probably the extravagantly sentimental, ['my deid'] 'Jamie's Wee Chair', 'Jenny Wi' The Airn Teeth'

> Mithers hae an awfu' wark
> Wi' their bairns at nicht –
> Chappin' on the chair wi' tangs
> To gi'e the rogues a fricht.
> Aulder weans are fley'd wi' less,
> Weel aneuch, we ken –
> Bigger Bowgies, bigger Jennies,
> Frichten muckle men.

and *'Cuddle Doon'*:

> The bairnies cuddle doon at nicht,
>   Wi' muckle faucht an' din;
> O, try and sleep, ye waukrife rogues,
>   Your faither's comin' in.

They never heed a word I speak;
    I try to gie a froon,
But aye I hap them up, an' cry,
    'O, bairnies, cuddle doon.'

An' just afore we bed oorsel's,
    We look at oor wee lambs;
Tam has his airm roun' wee Rab's neck,
    An' Rab his airm roun' Tam's.
I lift wee Jamie up the bed,
    An' as I straik each croon,
I whisper, till my heart fills up,
    'O, bairnies, cuddle doon.'

The bairnies cuddle doon at nicht
    Wi' mirth that's dear to me;
But sune the big warl's cark an' care
    Will quaten doon their glee.
Yet, come what will to ilka ane,
    May He who sits aboon
Aye Whisper, though their pows be bauld,
    'O, bairnies, cuddle doon.'

[Verses 1, 5 and 6 of 6]

There is a story that when he was an old man Alexander Anderson was sitting one day on a hillside above Kirkconnell. 'Aye,' he said, 'it's a bonnie world. If the next half is ane like, it will dae.'

✝

ROBERT ADAMSON
'The Peat Machine'

A Robert Adamson, probably the father of the poet, died at Little Dyke, Dalton in November 1877. The son, born in Yorkshire, was brought up at Isle of Dalton and went to Dalton parish school. He lived with his family at Collin and worked as a labourer and plasterer in the building trade. He died at Rosebank Cottage, Collin on the 17th of September, 1913 in the 75th year of his age.

His collected poems, Musings in Leisure Hours *(Dumfries 1879) is an excellent local history source, for example the 'Lines Composed on the Co-operative Store newly commenced in the town of Lockerbie' or the unique 'Kirkmichael Manse and the Rats' [They're gaun about like droves of sheep/Bound for the Langholm Fair']. In 'The Peat Machine' he describes in 27 verses the local enthusiasm for Henry Clayton's apparatus on Lochar Moss near Racks Station in 1875: with a six-horse power engine it rolls off 60 tons of moss each day and presses and moulds it into peats. Just about everyone comes to see the prodigy:*

> There's lots of men about the Racks
>   That long have idle been;
> They'll get a job at digging moss
>   For this new peat machine. . . .
>
> Sic squads of folk are gathering up,
>   The like was never seen;
> Baith rich and poor are gaun like stour
>   To see this peat machine. . . .
>
> There's cotton weavers by the scores,
>   O'er frae the banks of Mein,
> Baith swamp and thin, thrang looking on
>   At this new peat machine.
>
> There's farmers there wi' dandy carts
>   Frae's far off as Kirkbean;
> They've heard the tidings, and have come
>   To see this peat machine.
>
> There's lots o'shepherds coming next
>   Frae's far off as Loch Skene,
> Wi' crooks and plaids and great big dogs,
>   To see this peat machine. . . .
>
> There's Taffy Helen frae Hightae,
>   Her bonnet's trimmed wi' green;
> She's on the road wi' Bauldy's Jock
>   To see this new machine. . . .
>
> There's Turkey Will o'er frae Smallholm,
>   And his big daughter Jean;

They're wheeling o'er the Carthat Brae
To see the big machine. . . .

✝

GORDON FRASER
'Wha wrote an' sang o' Wigtown'

*Gordon Fraser (1836–90) trained in Wigtown under Mr Walter
Malcolmson, whose business as druggist, printer and stationer/bookseller he
took over. He also, as a 'Certificated Teacher of Phonography', took classes
in Pitman's system of shorthand in Wigtown, Port William, Garlieston and
Stranraer, and was employed as a shorthand writer in Carlisle Law Court.
A very useful historian, his books on* Wigtown and Whithorn: Historical
and Descriptive Sketches *(1877) and* Lowland Lore, or the Wigtownshire
of Long Ago *(1880) include many extracts from local records.*

The Poems *he published in 1885 have an infectious enthusiasm that can
be overwhelming, for example the chorus to 'Peggy Broon':*

Oh! Peggy Broon, sweet Peggy Broon, ye're the joy o' a'
    my heart;
What pain I am sure for you I endure, when I'm called frae
    you to part!
Oh! Peggy Broon, sweet Peggy Broon, ye're lovelier than
    the rose;
For you I cud greet till the tears at my feet rin doon frae
    the tap o' my nose.

*His account of the wedding of 'Tilda McGraw' brings in the many locals
'wha honoured the nuptials'.*

There was Andy M'Minn frae the farm o' Drumjin,
    An' wee drouthy Tam frae the Back o' the Wa';
Jean Clune frae the brig, lookin' gaudy an' trig –
    A cousin, I think, o' my Tilda M'Graw.

Lang Sandy M'Lean, wha seemed a' skin an' bane;
    Frae Sorbie a couple o' hizzies sae braw;
An' Saunners M 'Tier frae the farm o' Balsier –
    A' folk that respected douce Tilda M'Graw

Tam Broon an' his Jenny cam' roun' frae Kivernnie,
    Frae Kirkland there cam' douce auld Andy M'Graw;
An' Tibbie M'Clurg a' the way cam' frae Borgue –
    For Tibbie was auntie tae Tilda M'Graw. . . .

The Misses Colquhoun frae the farm o'Baldoon;
    Kirkinner some dizzen sent trippin' awa';
The Blains frae Westmains, an' auld Cook frae the Crook,
    A' witnessed the weddin' o' Tilda M'Graw. . . .

Fraser was the unofficial town poet and chronicler of local events, composing verses for all occasions, including concerts by The Wigtown Town Band *and by the* Wigtown Young Men's Mutual Improvement Association *(for the latter a 'Poetical Rhapsody'). Many of the poems were very long, for example his overview of the history of* Wigtown Toon, *including –*

We've a braw wee bit Square here in Wigtown toon
On a spot that was yinst desolation a' roun',
        Whaur ducks, swine, an' geese
        Might roam as they please,
        An' luxuriate at ease
            Here in Wigtown toon.

and his description of 'The Guid Auld Toon o' Wigtown' –

Upon a gently sloping hill,
Where Simmer flo'ers their balm distil,
An' wi' sweet scent the breezes fill,
        There stan's the toon o' Wigtown. . . .

Here Business rows a leisure oar,
Grasps not at boundless earthly store;
If ends are met it asks no more,
        But leeves content at Wigtown.

Nae helter-skeltering here an' there;
Peace frae the clouds aboon her Square
Extends her olive wand sae fair,
        An' blesses cannie Wigtown. . . .

As a bookseller and publisher Fraser would surely have been pleased to see Wigtown in 2000 as a 'Book Town'. He died on the 23rd of February 1890:

> An' when the call to rise is given,
> An' sinners to their doom are driven,
> May I an' mony mair to heaven
>   Ascend frae oot o' Wigtown.

✝

ROBERT LOUIS STEVENSON
'To S.R. Crockett On receiving a Dedication'

Crockett was still the minister of the Free Church at Penicuik when his The Stickit Minister *was published in 1893. With his finely tuned flair for public relations and marketing he dedicated the book to Stevenson in exile in Vailima: 'To Robert Louis Stevenson of Scotland and Samoa I dedicate these stories of Grey Galloway land where About the Graves of the Martyrs The Whaups are crying – his heart remembers how.'*

Stevenson, with his long-held interest in the Covenanters, was almost overwhelmed with these 'words that brought tears' to his eyes every time he looked at them: 'I wish I could be buried there – among the hills, say, on a head of Allermuir – with a table tombstone like a Cameronian.'

Stevenson's poem was included in the eighth limited edition (1894) of The Stickit Minister *and in later editions.*

> Blows the wind today, and the sun and the rain are flying,
>   Blows the wind on the moors today and now,
> Where about the graves of the martyrs the whaups are crying,
>   My heart remembers how!
>
> Grey recumbent tombs of the dead in desert places,
>   Standing-stones on the vacant wine-red moor,
> Hills of sheep, and the howes of the silent vanished races,
>   And winds, austere and pure:
>
> Be it granted me to behold you again in dying,
>   Hills of home! and to hear again the call;

Hear about the graves of the martyrs the peewees crying,
And hear no more at all.

☦

G.G.B. SPROAT
'Bonnie Gallowa'

George Gordon Byron Sproat (1858–1927) was born at Nethertown of Almorness in Buittle parish. He followed his father, John Sproat, into a farming life, first as tenant in High Creoch on Cally estate and then in Boreland of Anwoth, where he was the friend and neighbour of Lord Ardwall. In buying Borness estate from Mr Fairhurst and Borgue estate from Mr Pringle he became a substantial laird as well as a working farmer. His own special interest was in breeding Galloway cattle, in particular belted Galloways. The collection of his poems, The Rose o' Dalma Linn and Other Lays o' Galloway, *published in Castle Douglas in 1888, contains some fine work, including 'Craignair', 'The Auld Scotch Songs', and the 'Epitaph to a Reisty Horse'. The song 'Bonnie Gallowa', set to music by George Faed Hornsby, was published by Adam Rae in Castle Douglas in September 1896. It has become something of a Galloway anthem.*

Epitaph on a Reisty Horse
Here lies 'The Midge,' both stiff and stark,
    This suits her to a tee;
She never took the road for wark,
    But often took the gee.
If she had lived till ninth o' June
    I meant to try her pace,
But, lo! I found her race was run
    Before she ran her race.

Bonnie Gallowa'
Wha but lo'es the bonnie hills,
Wha but lo'es the shinin' rills;
Aye for thee my bosom fills –
    Bonnie Gallowa'.

Land o'darkly-rollin' Dee,
Land o' silvery windin' Cree,

Kiss'd by Solway's foamy sea –
Bonnie Gallowa'.

Wreathes o' glory roun' thee weave,
Gory land o' fearless Thrieve,
Heroes' deeds your sons achieve –
Bonnie Gallowa'.

Ance ye had a king your ain,
Wha your laurels ne'er wad stain,
Focht your foes wi' micht an' main –
Bonnie Gallowa'.

Wha 'mang Scotia's chiefs can shine?
Heroes o' the Douglas line,
Maxwells, Gordons, a' are thine –
Bonnie Gallowa'.

Land o' birk and rowan tree,
Land o' fell and forest free,
Land that's aye sae dear to me –
Bonnie Gallowa'.

✝

A NATIONAL POET FOR SCOTLAND?

Christopher Murray Grieve or Hugh MacDiarmid (1892–1978) wanted to become a, or more probably the, national poet for Scotland. Unfortunately his political allegiances, from fascism in the 1920s to Stalinist communism to republican nationalism and his occasionally bizarre ideas (on 'the coming war between Britain and the United States' – 1939, and 'England is our enemy' – 1940), left him alienated and isolated from his own countrymen. His best work may be the poems in which he celebrated in a loving and kindly way the life of his father, James Grieve, 'Fatherless in Boyhood', country life, his own personal Eden in the Muckle Toon of Langholm, and his wanderings in the hills of Eskdale.

Country Life (1925)
Ootside! . . . Ootside!
There's dooks that try tae fly
An' bum-clocks bizzin' by,
A corn-skriech an' a cay
An' guissay i' the cray.

Inside! . . . Inside!
There's golochs on the wa',
A craidle on the ca',
A muckle bleeze o' cones
An' mither fochin' scones.

The Dog Pool (1931)
Oot o' the world and into the Langholm!
There's mony a troot in the auld Dog Pool
Livelier, praise be, than ocht you can write.
Lean owre as you used to ga'en to the school
And see the broon shadows and ivory beaks
  Bonnier than ony book bespeaks.

Or when there's a spate and the water's as black
As Maxton's hair and as noisy as Kirkwood
Wha'd no watch it withoot wantin' to think?
Tech, ony man that isna a stirk would.
It'll be time to think when the Esk rins dry.
  Watch it noo while it's still ga'en by.

Catch it noo – for even as I speak
The fish may be gaspin' on dry land there
And the hindmaist wave o' the Esk gang roon'
The curve at Land's End to be seen nae mair
And a silence still waur for a sang to brak'
  Follow the row the waters mak'.

12

HEROES AND HEROINES

✝

Heroes and Heroines (is there any equivalent in Scots? – Braw Lads and Braw Lasses?) are respected for their courage, whether in peace or war, and for their persistence, patience, enterprise and endurance in following the path of duty as they see it. It does not follow that because 'heroes' must have ideals that they are therefore 'good' people. We may, for example, think that Carlyle was deeply misguided and perverse in his political judgements and his view of the world, but still see him as an 'heroic' figure.

In Victorian Britain the élite of all heroes were the explorers and the missionaries who, like David Livingstone, between 1849 and 1873, combined both roles. Among this élite were Sir John Ross (1777–1856) from Inch manse, for his expeditions to the White Sea and the Arctic in 1812, and his 1818 and 1829–33 searches for a North-West Passage; his nephew, Sir James Clark Ross (1800–62), for Arctic exploration (1819–27 and 1829–33), and his major (1839–43) expedition to the Antartic; Captain Hugh Clapperton (1788–1827) from Annan, for the 1823 expedition across the Sahara from Tripoli to Lake Chad; John Duncan (1805–49) from Culdoach near Kirkcudbright, for his part in the 1842 Niger expedition, and the exploration of the Kong Mountains and Dahomey and the coast between the Lagos and Niger rivers (1845–46); and John Thomson (1858–95) from Gatelawbridge near Penpont and Thornhill, for his achievements on the East Central African expedition to Lake Nyasa and Lake Tanganika (1878–80), and for his discoveries en route to Lake Victoria via the Great Rift Valley (1882), and in north-west Nigeria (1885) and the Upper Congo (1890).

Sir Samuel Halliday Macartney (1833–1906) from Auchenleck in Rerrick parish, who took a degree in Medicine at the University of Edinburgh, had a splendidly adventurous life: in the Crimea and at Constantinople (1855–57), in India during the Mutiny, to China with the British invasion force in 1860, as a civil mandarin in the Chinese Imperial service and for twelve years director of the arsenal at Nanking. In 1876 he was appointed as Counsellor and English Secretary in the Chinese Legation in London. He retired to Ken Bank above Dalry.

For enterprise and initiative, albeit on a lesser scale, add E.A. Hornel (1864–1933) for his thirteen-month (1893–94) visit to Japan with George Henry (1858–1943), during which, and under difficult circumstances, they studied Japanese art at Nagasaki, Yokohama, Tokyo and at Kanazawa, China and Kamakura, three villages on Tokyo Bay.

After the explorers and the missionaries came the great engineers, whose ranks included Thomas Telford (1757–1834) from Glendinning in Westerkirk parish. 'The Colossus of Roads' was so completely modest and self-effacing that it is very difficult to find any letters or reminiscences that do justice to him at all. Only a magnificent coffee-table book of drawings and photographs of his works, from the Ellesmere Canal (1793–1805), the Menai Suspension Bridge (1819–26), St Katherine's Docks (1824–38), the Gotha Canal in Sweden, and the Caledonian Canal (1803–23), could do that.

The remarkable contingent of Scots in eighteenth-century Russia included Dr James Mounsey (1710–73) from Skipmyre farm in Tinwald parish. Beginning as a lekar in St Petersburg Naval Hospital in 1736, he retired to private practice in Moscow in 1756 as a Lieutenant-General in the Army, and then became first physician to the Empress Elizabeth and Chief of the Medical Services in Russia. He retired to Scotland in 1762 to Rammerscales estate, which he purchased in 1758. In 1766 Mounsey obtained a position in Russia for Dr John Rogerson (1741–1823) from Lochbrow near Lochmaben. Rogerson became physician to the Empress Catherine the Great in 1786 and remained in Russia until 1816. He purchased Dumcrieff near Moffat in 1805 and Wamphray estate in 1810.

Scholars as heroes might include John Dalrymple, Lord Stair (1619–95), philosopher, lawyer, judge, Lord President of the Council, and author of The Institutes of the Law of Scotland; *William Todd (1774–1863), the dominie of Kirkmaiden parish from 1799 to 1843 and then Free Church schoolmaster in Drummore, mathematician, antiquarian, maker of clocks and sundials and globes and beehives, a collector of tales and traditions, a man of high temperance principles; Alexander Murray (1775–1813), the shepherd's son form Dunkitterick in Minnigaff parish with a special genius as a linguist, minister of Urr parish, and Professor of Oriental Languages in the University of Edinburgh; James Clerk Maxwell of Glenlair (1831–79), country laird and Professor of Experimental Physics at Cambridge, and ranked along with Newton and Einstein for his research on the theory of the structive of atoms and molecules; and Sir Herbert Maxwell of Monreith (1845–1937) for a life of public service as MP for Wigtownshire (1877–1906), chairman of the Royal Commission of the Ancient and Historical Monuments of Scotland, President of the Society of*

Antiquaries of Scotland, and author of books on topography, place-names, local and national history, trees, gardens, fresh-water fishes, salmon and sea-trout, and gentle genteel reminiscences.

This chapter includes some of 'the great and the good' who were famous and a few of the hundreds of others out there.

THE HOWDIE
Ann Young of Dalry and some Man-Midwives and Quacks

Most midwives, or 'howdies', in rural areas remote from Edinburgh, Glasgow and Aberdeen, even at the end of the eighteenth century, still utilised skills derived from oral tradition and work experience. A programme of instruction, examination and registration of midwives had been developed in Edinburgh after 1726 and in Glasgow after 1740, and the first formal courses in midwifery for medical students in the University of Edinburgh were begun under Thomas Young (1756–80) and Alexander Hamilton (1780–1800). Midwives in Edinburgh in the 1760s received certificates recording that they had attended courses of lectures on the Theory and Practice of Midwifery and the Lying-in Ward of the Royal Infirmary.

Ann Young had a busy and useful life as a midwife in Dalry from c. May, 1769. She trained in Edinburgh and refers specifically in her notes to her 'old companions' there, 'Fanny Barnet, Ann Fraser, Ann Levingston, Ann Ramage, Bell Burt, Jean Lowriston, Jean Moody, Miss Wilson and Miss Rutherford'. She kept a detailed record of her cases in the Glenkens and Parton, Balmaghie, Crossmichael and Kelton parishes, and of the payments received from her clients, landowners, clergy, tenant farmers, millers and others (or rather their wives). Some of her accounts were for substantial sums, for example £5-3s. on March 9th, 5s. on June 10th, one guinea on August 7th, and two-and-a-half guineas on August 10th, 1793 from Mr Spalding Gordon of Holm. It is interesting to see that she also mentions baptisms in some cases.

The public in Dumfries and Galloway had a confusing choice from an assortment of surgeons and male-midwives, local howdies (some with a very dubious reputation), doctors and doctoresses, itinerant quacks swarming like locusts through the nation, and resident quacks. The two at the Clachan and Kirk of Penninghame almost constitute a local industry of quackery. Few, however, sound as dangerous as Mrs Bernard from Berlin! It is difficult not admire their marketing techniques which would hardly be inappropriate in 2001.

✝

Ann Young's Notebook

1788 January	2	James McKie, Kelton, was born at 6 in the morning – 5s.
	23	For attending Mrs Dickson, Laurieston – 5s.
February	8	For attending Mrs McNaught, Blairmuck – 5s.
	15	David Gordon McWhay was born at 8 at night – 5s.
	16	Jean Smith Livingstone was born at 5 at night – baptised the 19th – 4s.
	20	For attending Mrs Copland in Poundland – 2s.6d.
March	9	John McMin Wilson, Crossgates, was born at 12 o'clock forenoon – baptised the 16th – 5s.
April	21	Delivered Mrs Geddes in the Woodfoot of Balmaghie of a dead boy, between 5 and 6 in the morning. She died herself about 10 minutes after – 5s.
	22	Mary Colville, in Collin, was born at 6 at night – 2s.6d.
July	4	Robert Fowler was born at 10 o'clock forenoon, Parton Kirk – 5s.
September	16	Nancy Dronnan, Greenlaw, was born between 8 and 9 in the morning – baptised the 21st – 5s.
	20	Grizel McLellan, Mains, was born at 3 in the afternoon – baptised the 22nd – 6s.
	28	Margaret Carter, at Kelton, was born at 2 o'clock afternoon – baptised the 30th – 6s.
October	3	Anne Miller, at Parton Kirk, was born at 3 o'clock afternoon – 2s.
	9	Agnes McGowan, at the Risk, was born about 1 o'clock afternoon – baptised the 11th – 5s.
		Agnes McKane, at Cairny-yard, was born December 3rd, between 6 and 7 at night – 5s.
1789 January	11	For attending Mrs Glendonwyn, of Parton – £1 – ls.
	26	Robert Blacklock, at Crossmichael Kirk, was born about 11 o'clock forenoon – 4s.
February	2	Jean Wallace, at the Locks, was born at 5 in the morning – 5s.
	12	William Hall, at Crossmichael Kirk, was born at 8 at night – baptised the 15th – 4s.

	24	Ebenezer McKaw, at High Park, was born at 2 in the morning – 5s.
	29	William Knox, in the Mill, was born at 4 afternoon – baptised the 30th – 6s.
March	11	William Kinon, in the Knowetop, was born at 4 in the morning – baptised April 5th – 5s.
April	7	Thomas Edgar, in Campdougal, was born at 4 afternoon – 5s.
May	23	Robert Gill, at the Mill Cassey, was born – 2s.6d.
July	11	For attending Mrs Durham, at Lochenbreck – 5s.
	25	Peter Brown, at Tintum, a twin, was born between 2 and 3 in the morning – 5s.
August	1	For attending Mrs Carlie, at the Underwood – 2s.6d.
October	7	Forenoon, 11 o'clock, Hellen Gordon, in Crogo, was born – 10s.6d.
December	12	James Whitrock, at Balmaghie Kirk, was born between 1 and 4 in the morning – 3s.
	21	Between 3 and 4 in the morning, Elizabeth McGuffog, in Gerringtoun, was born – baptised the 29th – 7s.
1790 January	1	For attending Mrs Kim, in Clarkbrand – 4s.
	7	At 10 at night, Agnes Thomson, at Kelton Mill, was born – baptised the 9th – 5s.
February	15	For attending Mrs Copland, in Poundland – 5s.
March	12	Delivered Mrs McLellan, at Crossmichael Kirk, of a dead child – 5s.
April	20	David Wilson, in Crossgates, was born at 4 in the afternoon – baptised the 20th – 5s.
	25	At 1 in the morning, George Steedman McWhay was born – 5s.
	26	Betty Ferguson, at the Hole, was born at 3 in the morning – dead – 2s.6d.
May	10	James Haffie, in Crofts, was born at 6 in the morning – baptised same day – 5s.
	13	Agnes Muir, in the Threve Mains, was born at 1 of clock forenoon – baptised the 20th – 10s.
	28	Janet McConchie, in Drumglass, was born between 9 and 10 forenoon – 13s.
September	21	Mary Kelvie, at Crea, a twin, was born between

11 and 12 at night – baptised the 25th – 6s.

October	14	Between 1 and 2 in the morning, delivered Mrs McFarlane, in Crofts, of a dead boy – 5s.
December	19	At 5 in the morning, Francis Brown, at the Boat of Livingston, was born – 5s.
	25	At 3 in the morning, delivered Mrs Campbell of Springfield of a girl, in the seventh month, that lived about an hour – £1 – 6s.

Alex. Brown, Surgeon and Man Midwife . . . having now begun business in this place, opposite the Head of the Friars Vennel . . . though but a young practitioner . . . he lately attended three courses of lectures on Chemistry and Pharmacy, Eight on Anatomy and Surgery, etc., etc., besides Dissecting for a Class of Anatomy last Winter in Edinburgh.

– *DWJ*, 28th October, 1794

I. Linton, surgeon and man-midwife, intend to begin business next week at Kirkpatrick-Fleming.

– *DWJ*, 30th May, 1797

Neilson Rae, Surgeon, Apothecary and Man-Midwife, has commenced business at Gatehouse of Fleet . . . 7th August, 1797.

– *DWJ*, 15th August, 1794

The Wake of the Suicide

[A short story – Jenny Lightfoot finds herself pregnant]
'When I first kenn'd mysel' in this way, I applied to auld Barbara Hemlock the howdie, and she undertook to cause a miscarriage, wi' her yerbs an' her bitters, as she has dune to mony a ane forbye: but Barbara's skill has had nae effect – An' now there's nought for me but the Black Stool, and the Gansell o' the Haly Ban.'

– *The Castle Douglas Miscellany*, 48, 14th June, 1824, pp. 378–381

'Poetical Essays'. *The Quack*
Not long since, in a market-town,
A Quack acquired vast renown,
He talk'd so loud, and talk'd so long,
He half-bewitch'd the rural throng. . . .
From stage aloft, as from a rostrum,
He puff'd his wonder-working nostrum. . . .
He bled, drew teeth, nor fail'd his potions,

All-powerful, to give store of motions. . . .
Ye Quacks of each degree and station,
Who swarm like locusts thro' the nation,
Soul-Quacks, or Body-Quacks, in short,
Quacks all, from dunghill up to court. . . .
Without remorse, rob, cheat, and plunder,
Rewarded for each theft or blunder.

– *SM*, 41, 1779, p. 623

James Lindsay, at Kirk of Penninghame, near Wigtown, Galloway, Takes this method of acquainting the Public, That he received from his father, when on his death-bed, a recipe (which he used with success upwards of forty years) for curing the Bloody-flux, Head-ache, Pains in the Stomach, and Heart-burn, and now proposes to issue it for the benefit of mankind. Any person afflicted with either of the above disorders, will be faithfully served with the medicine, by applying to the above James Lindsay. His price for curing the Flux is five shillings, and for other disorders one shilling. No cure no pay.

– *DWM*, August 8th 1775

Charles Ferguson in Clachan of Penningham (who has for a number of years practised curing the Bloody Flux and Pain in the Stomach) begs leave to inform the Public, That, as his sight is decayed, he has given up business in favour of Jean McCulloch, his housekeeper. Those therefore, who apply to the said Jean McCulloch, may depend on being faithfully served with medicine and a receipt for the application of it. . . .

– *DWM*, October 3rd, 1775

. . . James Sharp, late miner and engineer at Leadhills, now living at Morton Mains, is possessed of an effectual Cure for that desperate disease the bite of a mad dog in man or beast, which he had applied with success for many years, as he can evidence by Certificiates, which he will produce if required, from great numbers of respectable people within the Synod of Dumfries and elesewhere, some of whom were Cured that were not infected till six or eight months after they were bit. His price for beasts is half a Crown a-head, and where there are a great number he is more moderate, as also when any of the human kind are bit or infected. As his residence is not certain at present, any person who wants his assistance will get notice of him by enquiring at Andrew Black Inn-keeper at the Spread Eagle, or Mr John Martin of Glengaber. . . .

– *DWJ*, 13th April, 1779

That Doctress Ann Morris intends setting out from Dumfries on Thursday next for the Stewartry and Shire of Galloway, where she intends to practise Physic in all its branches. . . . there are many in this town and neighbourhood who can attest the wonderous cures performed by her on persons who were given over by the Doctors and Surgeons, she . . . will soon confirm their most sanguine hopes, by performing many cures almost beyond belief. . . . she will be at Gatehouse on Friday and Saturday, at Ferrytoun of Cree on Monday, Tuesday and Wednesday, at Newtonstewart on the Saturday or Monday following, and at Wigton some . . . days thereafter.

– *DWM*, October 10th, 1775

Mrs Bernard, Dentist from Berlin, begs leave to acquaint Gentlemen and Ladies of the neighbourhood and Town of Dumfries that she has appointed Robert Jackson, Printer, to be sole vender, there, of her well known Liquid for cleaning and fastening the teeth, into which a cloth being dipped, and the teeth rubbed therewith, it renders them white as alabaster, how black soever they formerly were; it eradicates the scurvy, causes the gums to adhere closely, though ever so much decayed, and prevents the teeth from rotting: it will likewise cure the Tooth-ache in half a minute, and sweetens the breath by using it thrice a week, a Tea spoonful at a time. Its sovereign virtues and efficicacy have been repeatedly experienced by the nobility and gentry at the German Spa, Bath, Bristol, Scarborough, Buxton, and in every city and principal town in Great Britain and Ireland. . . . They are sold at . . . One Guinea the bottle; Half a Guinea the half bottle; and Five Shillings and Three pence the quarter bottle.

– *DWM*, September 17th, 1776

PATRICK MILLER OF DALSWINTON
Cheap and Wholesome Bread

The third son of the laird of Barskimming in Ayrshire and Glenlee in the Stewartry, Patrick Miller (1731–1815) had a rich and varied life as a storekeeper in Virginia and as a merchant in Greece and the Levant and in Leith; as an Edinburgh banker as a partner in Mansfield Ramsay and Co. and as Deputy Governor of the Bank of Scotland; and as the proprietor of the estates of Southfield near Edinburgh, Pitnacree in Perthshire, and Dalswinton in Dumfries-shire, of collieries and a harbour at Pittencrieff and Brucehaven in Fife, and of 22,000 acres on the Ohio river in

Kentucky. 'The Inventor of Boats' was famous for his experiments in naval architecture and artillery (carronades or 'pacifiers'). He built at his own expense the 'double ship' called The Experiment *(1787), the 'triple vessel'* The Edinburgh *(1787), and, with William Symington and James Taylor, the Dalswinton* Pleasureboat cum Steamboat *(1788). He was also the generous and protective patron of Alexander Nasmyth and Robert Burns.*

Always immensely public-spirited, he was experimenting at Dalswinton in 1800 in making cheap and wholesome bread with potatoes and wheat and barley flour. As ever, he had no false modesty in adverstising his wares.

†

To the Editor of the Dumfries Weekly Journal.
Sir, I send you the following Receipt for making cheap and wholesome Bread. It is the result of a good many experiments which I have carried on of late, with a view to assist the industrious labourers who have families in this neighbourhood. . . . The calculations are made from the present prices of potatoes and grain in Dumfries market.

Receipt. Boil six pounds of potatoes, then peel and mash them well, adding salt to your taste. In this state, when cold, they will weigh four pounds, which, at a half-penny per pound of the six pounds of raw potatoes, is 3d. One pound of wheat flour cleaned from the ends, and a small part of the bran, will cost 2½ d. One pound of barley meal will cost the same 2½ d. Cost of the materials 8d.

No water is used in mixing and kneading, as the potatoes take up the flour and meal. The dough, pressed out into the form of cakes or bannocks, is toasted on a griddle or the iron plate of a stove. The above mixture produces four pounds ten ounces, when baked and cold, of good wholesome bread; and when warm, is more palatable than oatmeal bread – and the cost is a trifle under 1¾d. the pound; whereas a pound of oatmeal costs 4d. the present price of a pound of oatmeal, which produces exactly, when baked into a cake and allowed to cool, one pound weight. Bread made from potatoes and flour without barm, or from flour of wheat and barley meal without potatoes, is not so good or palatable as the bread from the mixture in the Receipt.

If every industrious man in the kingdom, who has a family, were, soon after the close of harvest, to purchase 200 lbs. of potatoes, a bushel of wheat, and a bushel and a half of barley, not to be used till he saw it would carry him on, without going to market, to the time of the next harvest; I am of opinion it would form an excellent national magazine, having the effect to prevent disturbances on account of the high prices of grain, and to prevent monopolies in that article, if there be such a thing. It would also, when there was an evident general deficiency in the crop, afford the Government a sufficient time to provide against the evil. And surely, an honest industrious man with a family, who may not have money to purchase this annual store, will obtain credit for the small sum required for a purpose so laudable. . . . P. Miller, Dalswinton, 12th April, 1800.

– DWJ, 15th April, 1800

WARRIORS

Hugh Paisley, Kirkmahoe Parish – A Waterloo Veteran

We have this week to record the death of Hugh Paisley, a Waterloo veteran, who died at Dalswinton village on 17th ult., in the 88th year of his age. The deceased was born at Quarrelwood, in the parish of Kirmahoe, on the 14th February, 1777, and enlisted in the Hopeton Fencibles when stationed in Dumfries, at the early age of 17. He served on board his Majesty's ship *Isis*, 50 guns, at the victory of Copenhagen, on the 2d of April, 1801. He then went to South America, where he fought under Lieut.-General Whitelock, and was wounded in the head by a *coup de sabre*, and taken prisoner along with the whole brigade. Mr Paisley having recovered both health and freedom, did not remain long inactive, but forthwith proceeded to Portugal, and under Sir Arthur Wellesley took an active part in the Peninsular campaign.

He was present at the battle of Vimiera, 21st of August, 1809; and marching into Spain with Sir John Moore, he was taken captive during the famous retreat from Corunna. He remained a prisoner of war five years and four months in a French prison, and after his liberation he again followed his old commander, now Duke of Wellington, and fought on the three memorable days which closed with the final overthrow of Napoleon at Waterloo.

From the time of his entering the service till 1815, Paisley's life was one of incessant activity in his country's cause, except when suffering from wounds and imprisonment; and he was well entitled to and had worthily won the pension and discharge which he obtained after 24 years of service. . . .

He had a vivid recollection of Burns visiting the village of Quarrelwood in his official capacity. The boys followed the bard, recognising him to be a man of mark, and manifesting their curiosity and interest by catching the yellow tops of his long boots, also the tails of his coat, and repeating over some of the poet's lines concerning the 'poacher's court.' The deceased was an advanced Liberal in politics, of the study of which he was very fond, and entered into discussion with great ability. He was much noticed for his remarkable wit. . . . He was well stored with useful reading . . . and possessed a commanding flow of words, lighted up at times by expressive phrases, which came forth with unpremeditated play. . . . The deceased was of humble birth, but of a truly noble mind. . . . it will be many long years before the recollection of Hugh Paisley will be effaced from the memory of the good people of Kirkmahoe. . . . (*Dumfries Standard*).

– *KA*, 10th March, 1865

Auld Grog Willie: General Sir William Stewart

The extravagant review of General Stewart's life in The Oracle *captured one essential aspect of his character. He was brave to the point of being foolhardy, reckless, six times seriously wounded, in war too easily struck with 'battle frenzy', warm-hearted and popular with his men. He was known as 'Auld Grog Willie' because he gave his men extra allowances of rum, which Wellington rightly insisted he paid for himself. Like General Sir John Moore (1761–1809), he was very good at establishing and maintaining an* ésprit de corps *through devising imaginative exercises, including swimming, cricket, and football, for the men in his Rifle Corps and by organising a regimental benevolent fund and a regimental school.*

William Stewart (1774–1827), the second son of the 7th Earl of Galloway, went to war at an early age in March 1786 as an ensign in the 42nd Foot. Over the next twenty-eight years he fought in seventeen campaigns, in the West Indies, Martinique, Guadaloupe, San Domingo, with the Austrian and Russian armies in Italy in 1799, in command of the marines on board Nelson's flagship at Copenhagen in 1801, in Sicily and Egypt (1806–09), and in the Peninsular War in Spain, Portugal and France (1810–11 and 1812–13) at Albuera, Vittoria, the Pyrenees, Nivelle, Nive, Orthez, and Toulouse. He retired to Cumloden in 1814. He was also MP for Saltash (1795) and for Wigtownshire (1796–1802 and 1812–16).

During the Peninsular War Stewart was one of Wellington's problem generals. He was, yes, a splendid fighting man, but 'muddle-headed' and disobedient. 'With the utmost zeal and good intentions he cannot obey an order' (Wellington, 6th December, 1812). In spite of his blunders and insubordination Stewart had friends and influence at the War Office and Wellington failed in his attempts to have him kept in Britain.

Charles Oman's History of the Peninsular War *(7 vols., 1902–30)*

*includes a detailed account of the Battle of Albuera on the 16th of May,
1811. Stewart, as the divisional commander of Colborne's, Hoghton's and
Abercrombie's brigades, took it upon himself to launch an offensive on his
own initiative: Colborne's three leading battalions were caught on open
ground by French and Polish cavalry, the 2nd Hussars and the 1st Lancers
of the Vistula, and virtually annihilated with 58 out of 80 officers and
1,190 out of 1,568 men killed, wounded or captured (Oman, IV, 1911,
376–400). In his second tour there were other examples of blunders and
insubordination in the November 1812 retreat from Salamanca and at
Maya in July 1813 when Stewart, attracted at daybreak by news of
fighting elsewhere, abandoned his command. 'Sought in vain for many
hours . . . the long-lost William Stewart at last appeared on the scene and
assumed command' at 2 p.m. The other Stewart, of course, was seen at the
Battle of Saint Pierre on 13th December, 1813, when, in a desperate
situation, he himself led the 71st in a charge after their commander, Sir
Nathaniel Peacock, had galloped off to the rear showing 'the white feather
in unmistakenable style' (Oman, VII, 1930, 270–273). Peacock was
subsequently cashiered.*

*Stewart's independent and impetuous streak was probably always there
in his make-up. There is only a fine line between boldness and rash
incompetence. His comrade-in-arms, Nelson, had described him as 'the
rising hope of our Army', and Stewart had indeed played an important
part with Col. Coote Manningham, General Moore and Col. Kenneth
Mackenzie in introducing new infantry tactics. His plan in 1799 for
creating a corps of riflemen, specially trained marksmen and skirmishers,
for independent operations and reconnaissance activities, was based on his
experience with the Austrian army in Italy, where he saw for himself how
effective the Croatian and Tyrolese light infantry were in a campaign.
With the enthusiastic support of the Duke of York, he established an
Experimental Corps of Riflemen which became the 95th Regiment. The
95th, along with other light infantry units, including Moore's 52nd and
Mackenzie's 90th, eventually became the famous and successful Light
Division.*

*Stewart was a close personal friend of Horatio Nelson and his privately
published* Cumloden Papers *(1871) included an excellent description of
Nelson's bold and decisive battle plan at Copenhagen and some of the best
'Nelson touch' stories.*

✝

The Oracle, vol. 1, No. 3, February, 1832. Published in Wigtown
by Thomas Tait

The honourable Lieutenant General Sir William Stewart. . . .
In prefixing this illustrious name to our present Number, we beg our
Readers will pardon our presumption. . . . We disavow all ambitious and
vain-glorious intentions of attempting to add to that generous and gallant
gentleman's reputation; but we thought it *right* and *necessary* that the
pages . . . of the first periodical established in his native County, should
boast some notice of the First Hero of the Province, and the most beloved
and chivalrous General of the British Army.

A Soldier from his earliest youth, Sir William Stewart fought and bled
on many bright fields. . . . His proud and independent soul could not
stoop to adulation and flattery; he disdained to importune his superior
officers for well merited mention in the official dispatches; and despising
the babbling of the Newspapers, he indignantly spurned the purchased
applause of a mercinary Press, and the servile verses of Hireling Bards.
He left his own fame to take care of itself; and to the gallant hearts of his
devoted companions in arms, of whom, alas! few escaped the glorious
and sanguinary fields of Spain, to unfold the heroic character and
splendid actions of their bravest Leader.

Magnanimous and disinterested, he boldly and fearlessly asserted the
right of his Officers and men to well earned applause, while, conscious of
merit, he neglected his own fame, and although adored by the whole
Army, was equally neglected by the General in Chief. But the British
Army contained no braver Soldier, or more daring and enterprising
General, than Sir William Stewart. . . . instead of breaking the high spirit
of his troops by unnecessary harshness and rigidity of command, he was
always most anxious to promote the interests of his Officers, and most
kind and indulgent to his men; And in return he was universally admired
and beloved, and the meanest soldier hailed him as an assured Friend and
a steadfast Protector.

The Roland of the English Army, his impetuous and chivalrous
courage impelled him into the fiercest and sternest combats; and like Ney,
and Massena, his *Coup d'oeil* always rapid and profound, became more
vigorous and piercing in the midst of battle. When the French Infantry
were pouring on with their well known gallantry and vehemence; when
their Cavalry rode fiercely over every thing, and their guns played hotly
with grape, ranged over the whole field; then it was that General Stewart
was himself.

Firm and undaunted he rapidly glanced over the whole scene; at once
his commanding judgment seized the *ensamble*, and the true object of the

combinations of his skilful antagonists, and throwing himself among his men, and cheering loudly, he charged headlong upon the masses in his front, and bodly arrested the operation of the enemy when in full execution; then it was that his lofty and gallant bearing was most conspicuous; and his Soldiers electrified, and maddened with enthusiasm, furiously followed their beloved Chief over every obstacle, and charged and cheered, as if whole armies were at their back. In dangerous and critical moments, when defeat and ruin were imminent, and the unhappy thought of retreat and disaster arose in less determined minds, his sanguine spirit only gloried in the stern and desperate struggle, and resolved on death or victory, he firmly stood his ground, and often by some sudden burst or gallant dash redeemed the reeling fortune of the day, and gave another Laurel to the British Arms.

It was thus he greatly distinguished himself at Vittoria, the Pyrenees, Orthes, and Toulouse; and although at Albuera, that 'glorious field of grief', his untamed and boiling courage overlaid his judgment and nearly sacrificed a whole Brigade, he quickly remedied his fault, and again mounting the fatal hill with a second Brigade, and twice wounded, he bravely maintained that fierce and dangerous fight.

For his splendid services on these occasions he, on one day, the 24th June 1814, thrice received the thanks of the House of Commons, and acknowledged the honors conferred on him in three admirable speeches, which exhibit his noble and generous character in its true light. . . .

CRIMEAN WAR LETTERS TO STRANRAER AND NEWTON STEWART

The Crimean War (1854–56), in which a Great Britain mesmerised by Liberal jingoism and hatred of Tsar Nicholas, joined with the mountebank dictator's France, Cavour's Piedmont, and Turkey to attack Russia, was an unnecessary military adventure. Almost the only result of the Treaty of Paris at the end of the war was to perpetuate Turkish rule over the Christian peoples of Serbia, Bulgaria and Armenia. A Baltic expedition apart, the war consisted of the 'allied' assault on Sebastopol, from which the Russian fleet patrolled the Black Sea. The folly of the politicians was paralleled by the incompetence of the War Office and the British and French commanders, Lord Raglan and General St Arnaud. Their failure to provide adequate clothing, food, shelter, medicines and hospital facilities during the siege of Sebastopol was soon seen in Britain as a scandal. The British newspapers and their war correspondents were, in contrast, remarkably efficient in sending in and publishing reports from the Crimea.

The Charge of the Light Brigade during the battle of Balaclava on 25th October, 1854, was an extravagant example of mad courage. Of the 697 officers and men of the 8th and 11th Hussars, the 4th and 13th Light Dragoons and the 17th Lancers, only 198 returned. Lt. Col. Sir William Gordon (1830–1906) of Earlston in Borgue parish, who was in the 17th Lancers, was wounded five times, but survived the Charge to attend the last reunion in 1900. Private John Wilson, also of the 17th Lancers, the son of James Wilson, sometime landlord of the Commercial Inn in Gatehouse-of-Fleet, was killed by a shell burst.

Two of the first Victoria Crosses, made of cannon taken at Sebastopol, were presented to Lt. William James Montgomery Cunningham of the Rifle Brigade (later Lt. Col. Sir William Cunningham of Kirkbryde, Maybole and Lagwinnan, Portpatrick) and Corporal (later Sergeant) John Ross of the Royal Sappers and Miners. Ross, from Stranraer, won his V.C. for his gallantry at the Redan on 8th September, 1855.

The letters sent home from Sebastopol and Balaclava show the tenacity and bravery of the British soldiers in the face of extreme difficulties and danger, and the extent to which they had had to depend on the 'good people' at home who sent out trench boots, warm clothing, and gifts of tobacco, cheese, and whisky, etc. Some regiments, including the 91st, were stranded in Greece waiting for transport to the Crimea: Private John McKeand wrote home from Piraievs on 15th July, 1855 to his cousin, a manufacturer in Newton Stewart, describing not the war, but the architecture of Greece!

✝

Sergeant James Black, 14th Regiment: 'In Camp before Sebastopol, March 12th, 1855'
[Black had recently promoted from Corporal to Sergeant. At night he was in an advanced post not above 100 yards from the Russians, without any shelter and 'the shot and shell flying round us'. His letter begins 'Dear Parents'.]

Sometimes there will be about ten or twelve killed of a night... our country has done very well for us by giving us warm clothing ... and the ladies of Aberdeen gave our regiment a present of warm clothing – so we were able to keep out a little of the frost ... I was a long time off duty with frost-bitten feet after the months of December and January, but they are getting better. . . . Some men . . . lost both their feet and some their hands, others their fingers and ears, and we used to have from six to seven deaths a day. . . It is five months since I have had my clothing off. . . and we sleep with our belts and sixty rounds of cartridges in our pockets. . . . We expect to attack Sebastopol very soon now. . . .

I am sitting on my comrade's knapsack, with my own on my knee, while I am writing this letter. . . the noise of the guns would split your head. . . I have often cursed my hard fate, and before the tears would be half down my cheeks, they would be frozen. . . . All things are very dear down at Balaclava. The bread is 1s. a pound, cheese 2s. a pound, butter 3s. a pound, and so everything rates the same, except tobacco, tea, and sugar, which are cheap. . . .

I have seen Robert McQueen of the Sappers. I had also seen John Boyle of New Luce, that used to be on service with me: he is in the Sappers.

Robert McQueen of the Royal Sappers and Miners: 'Camp before Sebastopol, Monday morning, 9th April'
[*McQueen's father lived in Hanover Street in Stranraer*]

I have just arrived from the trenches; I scarcely got to camp before they opened fire, so I am very glad I was not down when they opened fire, for the party that was in the rear of us could scarcely get to camp. I am sitting now writing this amid roars of cannon, louder than any thunder you ever heard. There were eight of us had a very narrow escape of being shot: we were working at No. 7 battery, opening the embrasures; at the same time there was an alarm that the Russians were advancing on our works. We, the Sappers, had the word to always retire in rear of the infantry in case of an attack. . . . we were retiring to the rear of the infantry, when all at once a volley of musketry came about our ears from the party that was to protect us. . . . At about the same time the outline picquet of the 17th Regiment were retiring into the trenches, they were fired on by their own men, wounding three of the poor fellows. . . . the Regiment that fired on us . . . there was no heed taken of it, as it is an old trick of theirs. . . .

We have plenty of ammunition and plenty of artillery, but the enemy have no men to work their guns, which is a good job for us. But perhaps it is only policy in them for to entice us to storm the place, but . . . the generals in command know that, for the Russians have got every inch of it mined, so you may guess what a sacrifice of life there would be on all sides. . . . Thank God I am not afraid of the Russian round shot or shell either, but there is no use in thinking that way. There is despatches just come up that our artillery are making splendid practice – they are knocking the enemy's batteries to pieces. . . .

It is very wet weather now . . . continual rain. . . . But thanks to the good people at home for sending us plenty of warm clothing and other necessaries, we, the Royal Sappers, have got a pair of long boots that come up above the knee, known better by 'trench boots', also a first-rate oilskin and a hairy cap, so we defy old Nicholas himself to come through to wet us. The fine luxuries the noble and generous people at home sent us, such as sugar, tea, butter, and sundry articles, instead of us getting them at wholesale prices, we have to pay above 50 per cent above retail price; so you can see how we have been cheated.

George Dingwall: 'Balaklava, April 27th, 1855'
[*The letter is to his brother and sister in Stranraer*]

We are very comfortable now, since we have got the wooden huts, 24 men in each one, also better rations; and change now, not biscuit and pork one day and pork and biscuit the other; we got preserved vegetables, potatoes, fresh meat, twice a week, bread the same. It is a farce to see us going to the front to do duty in the trenches; we all get mounted on mules, horses, and ponies, with our accoutrements, our haver-sacks, calabashes, and firelocks slung across our shoulders – it is a strange sight; we are called the Highland cavalry.

We had a near escape for our lives the week of the siege, we were accoutred 26 hours, working all day under a tremendous fire, above 400 guns of the Allies playing on the Russian forts. There are some ugly sights here. We marched from the front at night to Lord Raglan's quarters: he saw us all satisfied with coffee. Sir Colin Campbell came with us to the railway, he saw us all settled in the waggons, and but a few minutes more and our position was very different. There is a great incline in the railway; the one-half of us went down all right; the remainder went off the line. The navvies did not put on the brakes in time, and they had no power on the waggons – down we went like a shot – we all knew what would be the upshot when we came to the turn of the rails, but before we got that length the navvies heard us coming at such speed that they knew we would go through the waggons in front, so they threw planks across the rails; and when the waggons came to that part of the rails, waggons and men were flying in the air, officers and men alike. It was a miracle so few were killed: we had only 2 killed, 1 had his leg cut off, 16 were bruised, and 2 navvies killed; I escaped myself, landing on my back on a mound of earth.

Since then I have been twice in the advanced trenches, the last time 300 of us as a storming party. . . . We are close friends to the Russians at present – within 40 yards of their pits. Sebastopol was very strongly fortified. Some batteries mounted one hundred guns. When I was up at the bombardment on the 12th, the Round Tower was in ruins, only one gun working: I was standing in the advanced trench and saw a 3-inch shell thrown right into the centre of it, making both men and stones fly into the air. The next day they sent out a flag of truce to take away their dead; I believe they could build batteries with their bodies. . . . The General wants to save as many lives as possible by silencing their forts. Dear Brother – they may say at home that it will never be taken, but that is all stuff, it will be taken, and that before long; the officers can scarcely refrain the men for making for the breach every night.

. . . you must be tired of this long letter, perhaps it will be the last one, but I hope not. Dear Sister, I never saw the newspapers you mentioned, I would like to get one . . . the Scotch servant lasses sent out paper, pens, and ink, tobacco and pipes, and tin cases to us, also cheese forbye; the merchants in Glasgow sent us out Scotch whisky that gives us three glasses a day, so you see we are a great deal better off now. This is badly wrote, but I am standing sentry.

William Summers, 93d Highlanders: 'Kamara, September 14, 1855'
[*This letter is to his father and mother in Newton Stewart*]

I had very little time since I came back from Kertch, and ever since was in the trenches with my regiment, and a very dangerous job it was. There was shot and shell of every kind coming amongst us. . . . I have stood in the trenches and seen my comrades falling around us 3 or 4 at a time. . . . It would make one tremble to see the poor fellows in their wounds, some with their heads blown off, legs and arms broken, and some of them halved through the middle. . . Between the English and French, Turks and Sardinians, we have an army of about 200,000 and there is more coming. . . . If you see Mr Neilson's father . . . tell him that he is well. . . .

Alexander Farish, 6 Company, Scotch Fusilier Guards: 'Sebastopol, 14th September, 1855'
[*A letter to his parents in Newton Stewart*]

. . . the Russian stronghold in the Crimea is taken from them, after about 6 hours hard fighting. . . . I was as fatigued the other day, carrying the dead Russians out of the hospitals . . . in the town of Sebastopol.

GA, 5th April, 3rd and 24th May, and 4th October, 1855

CHRISTIAN SOLDIERS

The Rev. William McKergo of New Luce – 'to the Greenland whaling'

William McKergo (1772–1854) was neither a distinguished theologian nor the minister of a fashionable church, and he was nearly forty before he was presented to New Luce. But as a country boy who financed his university studies by manual labour and by going to the Greenland whaling as a ship's surgeon, he deserves the greatest respect for his courage and perseverance (see also Innes Macleod (ed.), To the Greenland Whaling, 1979, for Alexander Trotter's journal of his 1856 whaling expedition).

✝

The late Rev. W. McKergo . . . minister of new Luce . . . was a native of the parish of Inch. . . . His early life was a hard struggle with penury. By his earnings as a herd boy and as a farm servant, he was enabled to attend the parish school, and to push his way to the University. . . . The old professors of Glasgow College . . . Young, Jardine, Milne, Findlay, Jeffrey, and Principal Taylor, in the latest years still remembered and spoke of the awkward country lad, the hard working student. . . . Winters spent in studying the languages and philosophy at college were succeeded by summers of manual labour in the country. Having attended the classes of anatomy, surgery, and medicine, he obtained a situation as surgeon in a Liverpool whale ship, and made several voyages to the Arctic region. The salary he thus obtained enabled him to prosecute his studies for the holy ministry. In 1805 he was licensed by the Presbytery of Stranraer to preach the gospel, and was employed for some time as assistant in the parishes of Whithorn in Galloway and Symington in Ayrshire. The parish of New Luce having become vacant. . . . Mr McKergo was presented. He was ordained minister of the parish on the 6th March, 1811.

. . . He was imbued with a deep love of nature and delighted to trace the marks of the wisdom and goodness of the Creator. The scenes amid which he spent his early days were indelibly impressed on his mind. The wonders of the Arctic regions he was wont to describe with peculiar enthusiasm.

He was fond of Greek and Hebrew literature, and was often found with his Homer and his Hebrew Bible. . . . For many years he entertained the idea that the translation of the Psalms was susceptible of improvement and he went so far as to overture the General Assembly to undertake a new version.

About thirty or forty years ago Mr McKergo was the popular preacher of the district. In the days of tent preaching the green was crowded when he ascended the tent. His powerful voice admirably fitted him ... and he greatly delighted in it.... During the last three years his powerful herculean frame had been perceptibly giving way. ...

— *GA*, 14th September, 1854

Jessie McClymont: A Missionary's Wife (an extraordinary 'ordinary' woman)

Jessie McClymont (1821–1885) married the Rev. John Inglis (see Chapter 7) at Corriefeckloch on 11th April, 1844. He had been ordained in 1843 as a missionary by the Reformed Presbyterian Church of Scotland to work in New Zealand. They left for Wellington in July 1844. In 1852 they were settled in the island of Aneityum in the New Hebrides. His own account, A Missionary's Wife: being a sketch of the life and character of Mrs Inglis, of the New Hebrides Mission, *was published privately in Edinburgh in 1885.*

✝

[Jessie McClymont] ... was born at Corriefeckloch, in the parish of Minigaff ... on the 15th of April, 1821. Her father, John McClymont, was a well-known and much esteemed farmer, and for a long time a leading elder in the Reformed Presbyterian congregation in Newton-Stewart. Her mother, Jane Murray ... was the daughter of a highly respectable elder in one of the Secession congregations in Stranraer. Jessie ... was the eldest of a family of eleven, of whom eight were daughters and three were sons. ... After utilising what the locality could supply, she had to be sent to Newton-Stewart, Stranraer, Ayr, and Manchester, to supply what was lacking at home. When her education ... was completed in one of the best ladies' schools in Manchester, she returned home, at the age of fourteen ... and for the next nine years ... she was her mother's right hand in the upbringing of the younger children.... she was carefully examined (by Dr Symington of Stranraer) and on his report was admitted by the Session to the full fellowship of the Church in 1838. ...

Three months after our marriage we sailed from London to New Zealand and joined the Reformed Presbyterian Mission to the Maoris. After eight years we removed to the New Hebrides, in which mission she laboured for twenty-five years. On our return home she spent four years, three in London and one in Kirkcowan, assisting me to carry through the press the Aneityumese Old Testament and some other native books, including the Aneityumese grammar and dictionary. She was thus publicly employed in missionary work for thirty-seven years. During the last four years of her life she has lived retired in Kirkcowan. . . .

From the very first she set herself, as a duty, to acquire a knowledge of the native language, both in New Zealand and in the New Hebrides. She had a considerable knowledge of the Maori language . . . her knowledge of it was limited compared with her knowledge of the Aneityumese. . . . there was not a word in common use the meaning of which she did not know; and before long she spoke it with great readiness and fluency. . . . When we went to Aneityum, as she knew nothing of the language, she went to the morning-school, and commenced a class of eight or ten little girls in the alphabet. . . . By and by, as the work grew upon her, she had to give up her attendance at the morning-school, and confine herself to a Bible-class on the Sabbaths and on the Wednesdays. She instituted a forenoon sewing-class for the women on certain days of the week, which was largely attended. She also established a boarding-school, or a school of industry, for girls and young women. She began with two, but they went on increasing till she had at times as many as sixteen. . . . My wife undertook to clothe the girls and teach them, but their parents or friends were to supply them with food. . . . They most of them became teachers' wives, and in after years exercised a salutary influence on the community. . . . in its order her Sabbath Bible-class . . . was 'as round as Giotto's circle' and her week-day sewing-class, often numbering forty to fifty, was equally well arranged. . . . She trained the girls living on the premises so thoroughly that they were able to act as monitors under her; and when these large classes were collected, she divided them, and set one of her own well-trained girls over every class of four or five to teach them. . . .

At meetings of the Mission Synod we often sat twenty for dinner and all other meals for a week or ten days at least. . . . The captain of the *Dayspring* said that she could have conducted the commissariat department of a man-of-war. . . . she was up every morning at four o' clock. . . . she had at her back from twenty to thirty of her best-trained natives, mostly teachers and teachers' wives, whom she had trained herself, and brought there for the occasion. . . . To provide food during that time for missionaries and their families, to the number of thirty or more, and an equal number of native servants, required some forethought. Accordingly for two or three weeks previously she advertised for fowls and bought every one that was brought to her till her coops were full. She spoke to every fisherman on the shore to keep her supplied with fish during the meeting; she had spoken to eight or ten of the chiefs to supply her daily with so many baskets of taro, each man on his day; and she had pigs and goats ready to be killed as they might be required. On such occasions, in addition to these, she provided in abundance yams, bread-fruit, bananas, cocoa-nuts, pine-apples, sugar-cane, oranges, etc., according to the season.

. . . She prepared a dozen bedrooms, the majority of them extemporised, as a matter of course, but all of them supplied with everything necessary. . . .

In the islands, in the first years of the mission, a twelvemonths' stores had always to be ordered at once, and they had to be ordered always six months, sometimes twelve months, before they were received; on one occasion two years' supplies had to be ordered at once. . . .

She was the first to introduce the making of arrowroot on Aneityum. . . . The natives of Aneityum have contributed upwards of £2000 for Bibles, books, and missions, the proceeds of arrowroot. Other islands, viz., Tanna, Aniwa, Eromanga, Efate, and Nguna, have all followed the example of Aneityum; the work is going on, and extending year by year. . . .

Her great familiarity with the language was of very important service to me in translating, revising and editing the Scriptures. . . . There are nearly a million words in the Aneityumese Bible, and perhaps more than 120,000 stops. Now to read twice through the entire Bible, name these million words each time, and be certain that each word is correctly spelled, and also name twice over each one of those 120,000 stops, and see that each is inserted in its proper place . . . is the drudgery of literature. . . . In this department of mission-work she laboured conscientiously and successfully for twenty-nine long years, from the time she went to Aneityum till four years before her death, when the entire Bible, the first part of the Pilgrim's Progress (abridged), the Hymnal, the First Catechism, the Shorter Catechism, and the Grammar and Dictionary were all printed. . . .

. . . although, like Jacob, she did not attain the days of the years of the life of her fathers – her mother died at 76, her maternal grandmother at 86, and her paternal grandmother at 91 – yet . . . every day of her life, from her fourteenth year to her sixty-fifth, she had done a full woman's work.

. . . She was a thorough manager, unsurpassed as a housekeeper; she was neatness itself in her person, her dress, and her household arrangements. She knew what her income was, and not only always kept within it, but left a large margin for contingencies. . . .

. . . as she judged herself . . . there was nothing remarkable, nothing brilliant, nothing romantic, nothing out of the way. She was not specially clever, not specially talented, not learned, not accomplished . . . One of the great lessons of her life lay in this, that she was in no way extraordinary herself, and did no extraordinary work during her life; she was nothing but what any ordinary woman may be. . . . She laid all her plans in good time beforehand, and always carried them out with quietness and decision. . . .

JOHN RUSKIN, DR JOHN BROWN, AND JOAN RUSKIN AGNEW

John Ruskin (1819–1900) was the one essential arbiter of good taste and excellence in art and architecture in nineteenth-century Britain. His Modern Painters *(1843–60) completely changed the contemporary assessment of Turner's work and promoted the Pre-Raphaelite 'Brotherhood' who shared his devotion to medieval Italian art, and* The Stones of Venice *(1851–53) brought about a new interest in and general enthusiasm for Gothic architecture.*

Ruskin himself had family links with Galloway and Perthshire. His father was born in Edinburgh and went to the Royal High School. Dr John Brown (1810–82), a medical practitioner in Edinburgh and a friend of Hugh Miller and Thackeray, was also the sympathetic and 'truest friend' of Ruskin over the years. Ruskin's personal life was a mixture of tragic farce (his marriage to Euphemia) and farcical tragedy (his obsession with Rosa de la Touche betwen 1854 and 1875). He came to depend on Joanie, Joan Ruskin Agnew, who had looked after his widowed mother and helped him to cope with the near madness of the last decades of his life. 'What I have myself since owed to her – life certainly, and more than life, for many a year.'

Joanie, who married the artist Arthur Severn, was the daughter of George Agnew (of the Lochnaw line) and Catherine Tweddale; Joanie's grandfather, James Tweddale, was a brother of Ruskin's grandmother, also a Catherine Tweddale. George Agnew's house in Wigtown, on the site of the later County Buildings, is illustrated in Fraser's Penny Guide *to* Wigtown and Neighbourhood *(1879).*

Ruskin's Praeterita *. . . Scenes and Thoughts perhaps worthy of memory in my past life and his* Fors Clavigera *are immensely long and virtually shapeless books; but he was always capable of the most wonderful lyrical passages, for example, on his leaving the Lakes by train in 1871 –*

There was not much to look at through the driving, and gradually closer driven rain – except the drifting asbout of the seagulls, and their quiet dropping into the pools, their wings kept open for a second till their breasts felt the water well; then closing their petals of white light like suddenly shut water flowers.

The blind man who gave singing lessons was the prodigious Andrew Denniston of Whithorn, who died on 17th October, 1897, in his 76th year. He took senior and junior music classes, lectured, organised choral societies and concerts between Dalbeattie and Stranraer between the 1840s and the 1880s. He was also a major figure in the Temperance movement in Galloway. His repertoire ranged from sacred music to glees and his own party pieces, inluding the The Whithorn Soiree.

The minerals referred to in the Praeterita (as 'crystals') included a collection which he presented to the Museum in Kirkcudbright.

Ruskin's enthusiasm for Christy Minstrels, especially the Moore and Burgess Company, is recorded in his Fors Clavigera, particularly an account of his visiting the Minstrels in St James's Hall in London with Burne-Jones.

✝

John Ruskin: Fors Clavigera
Whithorn, October 3rd, 1883.

As the sum of Sir Walter's work at Melrose, so here the sum of St. Ninian's at Candida Casa, may be set down in few and sorrowful words. I notice that the children of the race who now for fifteen hundred years have been taught in this place the word of Christ, are divided broadly into two classes: one very bright and trim, strongly and sensibly shod and dressed, satchel on shoulder, and going to and from school by railroad; walking away, after being deposited at the small stations, in a brisk and independent manner. But up and down the earthy broadway between the desolate-looking houses which form the main street of Whithorn, as also in the space of open ground which borders the great weir and rapid of the Nith at Dumfries, I saw wistfully errant groups of altogether neglected children, barefoot enough, tattered in frock, begrimed in face, their pretty long hair wildly tangled or ruggedly matted, and the total bodies and spirits of them springing there by the wayside like its thistles, – with such care as Heaven gives to the herbs of the field, – and Heaven's Adversary to the seed on the Rock.

There are many of them Irish, the Pastor of Whithorn tells me, – the parents too poor to keep a priest, one coming over from Wigton sometimes for what ministration may be imperative. This the ending of St. Ninian's prayer and fast in his dark sandstone cave filled with the hollow roar of Solway, – now that fifteen hundred years of Gospel times have come and gone.

This is the end: but of what is it to be the beginning? Of what new Kingdom of Heaven are *these* children the nascent citizens? To what Christ are these to be allowed to come for benediction, unforbidden?

– *Fors Clavigera*, vol IV, Letter 92

John Ruskin: Praeterita

I have never yet spoken of the members of my grandfather's family, who either remained in Galloway, or were associated with my early days in London. Quite one of the dearest of them at this time, was Mrs Agnew, born Catherine Tweddale, and named Catherine after her aunt, my father's mother. She had now for some years been living in widowhood; her little daughter, Joan, only five years old when her father died, having grown up in their pretty old house at Wigtown, in the simplicity of entirely natural and contented life: and, though again and again under the stress of domestic sorrow, untellable in the depth of the cup which the death-angels filled for the child, yet in such daily happiness as her own bright and loving nature secured in her relations with all those around her; and in the habits of childish play, or education, then common in the rural towns of South Scotland: of which, let me say at once that there was greater refinement in them, and more honourable pride, than probably, at that time, in any other district of Europe; a certain pathetic melody and power of tradition consecrating nearly every scene with some past light, either of heroism or religion. . . .

. . . they all ended in my driving to No. 1, Cambridge Street, on the 19th April, 1864: where her uncle (my cousin, John Tweddale) brought her up to the drawing-room to me, saying, 'This is Joan.' I had seen her three years before, but . . . only I had a notion that she would be *nice*, and saw at once that she *was* entirely nice, both in my mother's way, and mine; being now seventeen years and some – well, for example of accuracy and conscience – forty-five days, old. . . .

Thus far Joanie; nor virtually have she and I ever parted since. I do not care to count how long it is since her marriage to Arthur Severn; only I think her a great deal prettier now than I did then: but other people thought her extremely pretty then, and I am certain that everyone *felt* the guileless and melodious sweetness of the face. Her first conquest was almost on our threshold; for half an hour or so after we had reached Denmark Hill, Carlyle rode up the front garden, joyfully and reverently received as always; and stayed the whole afternoon; even (Joan says) sitting with us during our early dinner at five.... And, on another occasion, after he had been to meet the Queen at Dean Stanley's, in describing to us some of the conversation, he made us laugh by telling how, in describing to Her Majesty the beauty of Galloway, that 'he believed there was no finer or more beautiful drive in her kingdom than the one round the shore of the Stewartry, by Gatehouse of Fleet', he got so absorbed in his subject that, in drawing his chair closer to the Queen, he at last became aware he had fixed it on her dress, and that she could not move till he withdrew it!

... Joan herself had real facility and genius in all rightly directions. She had an extremely sweet voice, whether in reading or singing; inventive wit, which was softly satirical, but never malicious; and quite a peculiar, and perfect, sense of clownish humour, which never for an instant diminished her refinement, but enabled her to sing either humorous Scotch, or the brightest Christy Minstrel carols, with a grace and animation which, within their gentle limits, could not be surpassed. She had a good natural faculty for drawing also, not inventive, but realistic; so that she answered my *first* lessons with serviceable care and patience.... very soon, also, she was able to help me in arranging my crystals, and the day divided itself between my mother's room, the garden, and the drawing-room, with busy pleasures for every hour.... and although ... I had learned Scott's own Edinburgh accent with a precision which made the turn of every sentence precious to me ... yet every now and then Joanie could tell me something of old, classic, Galloway Scotch, which was no less valuable to me than a sudden light thrown on a chorus in AEschylus would be to a Greek scholar....

For myself, the impressions of the Solway sands are a part of the greatest teaching that ever I received during the joy of youth: for Turner, they became the most pathetic that formed his character in the prime of life, and the five *Liber Studiorem* subjects, *Solway Moss*, *Peat Bog*, *Scotland*, *The Falls of Clyde*, *Ben Arthur*, and *Dumblane Abbey*, remain more complete expressions of his intellect, and more noble monuments of his art, than all the mightiest after work....

Joanie tells me she has often heard the fame of the *real* Wandering Willie spoken of: he was well known in travel from the Border right into Galloway, stopping to play in villages and at all sorts of out-of-the-way houses, and, strangely, succeeded by a *blind woman* fiddler, who used to come led by a fiddler; and the chief singing lessons in Joanie's younger days were given through by Galloway by a *blind man*, who played the fiddle to perfection....

... my little Joanie sang me yesterday, 13th May, 1889, 'Farewell, Manchester' and 'Golden Slumbers,' two pieces of consummate melody.... And still I have not room enough to say what I should like of Joanie's rarest, if not chiefest merit, her beautiful dancing. *Real* dancing, not jumping, or whirling, or trotting, or jigging, but dancing, – like Green Mantle's in *Redgauntlet*, winning applause from men and gods, whether the fishermen and ocean Gods of Solway, or the marchmen and mountain Gods of Cheviot....

– Praeterita, vol. III, 1888, passim

Letters: Dr John Brown

[Letter CCVI. Dr John Brown to his son, April 1870.]

Galloway Arms, Newton Stewart, Sunday.

My dear John, We came here last night from Kirkcudbright. On Friday morning we started from Dalbeattie in a waggonette, and went along a very picturesque road to Dundrennan Abbey, a fine ruin. We saw the burying-place of Lord Barcaple's father and people.... Yesterday morning we left in a waggonette and drove up the Dee (it is very beautifully wooded all about K.) to Barcaple, such a pleasant, half-highland place, such a plain gentlemanly place, so like himself, everything first-rate, no superfluities or show, beautiful grounds and offices.... We thrn drove across a high ridge with a great view of the big hills all heathery and rocky, and came to Gatehouse-of-Fleet, a pretty little town, called so from being at the Gate of Cally.... The present man has no children, and it goes to some distant man. We then started off along the Coast for Ravenshall, a little roadside inn close to Dirk Hatteraick's cave, and an old castle, the original of Ellangowan. The rocks and coast are very fine. We thought of sleeping and spending to-day there, but that was impossible. We got poached eggs and cheese and scones and *Robert Younger's* excellent ale.... We then drove on to Creetown, intending to get a dog-cart and go on to this place, but the cart was there, the horse not, so we had to wait 2 hours till the train. I supertended a game at 'Bools' (marbles) in the street, and saw justice done, with some difficulty. We had a mile and a half to walk to the station, and we saw a pretty little dark-eyed girl of 12. I spoke to her, and found she was going to meet her father and little brother, who were coming home from Berwickshire, where they had been stone-dyking since Ocotober.... We got here past 8; it (the Galloway Arms) is very old, but very clean and well-appointed, with a wonderfully grand little sitting-room....

– Letters of Dr John Brown, 1909, pp. 200–201

[Letter CCXLVIII. Dr John Brown to John Ruskin]
23 Rutland Street, Edinburgh, 20th May 1874 (Sunday)

My dear Friend – It is good in you to write. We will know by and by what you have been doing and thinking and feeling in the Sistine Chapel. . . . I was in Galloway with my John for 5 days last week; the air as clear and cold as ice, the trees awfully brilliant and differentiated (a horrid word). The wood Hyacinths covering acres of brushwood like *snow* dust of sapphires, quite wonderful; at one place, Ravenshall, between Gatehouse and Creetown, we stopped the carriage, and stared. The very horses, I think, wondered. Then we went from Newton Stewart to Loch Trool, a real little Highland loch, savage and sweet, granite and heather, and oak and birch, and Merrick quite near it, 3000 feet high. . . . Yours ever affectionately, J. Brown.

– Letters, p. 230

J. M. BARRIE
Dumfries and Gretna Green Revisited

James M. Barrie (1860–1937), of A Window in Thrums *(1889),* The Little Minister *(1891),* Quality Street *(1901),* The Admirable Crichton *(1902),* Peter Pan *(1904),* Dear Brutus *(1971), and* Mary Rose *(1920), was a pupil at Dumfries Academy from Autumn 1873 to 1878, when he went up to the University of Edinburgh. He was aye a precocious wee laddie – 'At twelve or thereabout' I put the literary calling to bed for a time, having gone to a school where cricket and football were more esteemed' (*Dumfries Academy Magazine, *1st May 1911). He wrote his first bits, *The Rekollections of a Skoolmaster, *in May 1875, and his first play, *Le petit drame sensational, en six tableaux – Bandelero the Bandit, *the following year. A 'staggerer' or melodrama 'in six scenes and fifteen minutes', in which Barrie himself played all his favourite characters in fiction (from Ballantyne, Hope and Marryat) rolled up into one 'Smike' and with two awful stage robber villians, Gump and Benshaw, it was performed at the end of December 1876 in the English Room at the Academy and again at the Crichton Institution in January 1877. There followed a first-class sensation in Dumfries, when a local minister took the opportunity at a School Board meeting to attack the three plays, *Off the Line, Paul Pry, *and* Bandelero, put on by the Academy Dramatic Club as 'grossly immoral'. A good start for a career as a playwright by any standards!*

In his tribute to his old Mathematics teacher, Mr John Neilson, on his retirement, Barrie described how when the shades of night began to fall, certain young mathematicians shed their triangles, crept up walls and down trees, and became pirates in a sort of Odyssey that was long afterwards to become the play of Peter Pan. *For our escapades in a certain Dumfries garden, which is enchanted land to me, was certainly the genesis of that nefarious work. We lived in the tree tops, on cocoa-nuts attached thereto, and that were in bad condition; we were bucaneers, and I kept the log-book of our depradations, an eerie journal without a triangle in it to mar the beauty of its page.*

– Dumfries Academy Magazine, 16, December 1924

Unfortunately Barrie only occasionally wrote about his Dumfries days. In A School Revisited *he described his adventures in pedestrianism.*

✝

One day we walked to Carlisle, and so I got into the papers for the first time, under the heading, 'Plucky Pedestrianism.' I remember how, after that, our mathematical master, whom hundreds of men, once boys at that school, now revere, and none more than I, used to stump a young gentleman dull at figures with this tremendous problem: 'If two boys walk from this town to Carlisle, a distance of thirty-three miles, in eight hours and a quarter, how long would one boy take to walk the same distance, going at a rate of four miles an hour?' That boy covered his slate with solutions, but to no avail.

The merry boy and I walked twenty-four miles one morning, and I had to play in a football match that afternoon, after which I was missed from the school for a month. . . .

– The Success, 24th August, 1895

Barrie's 'Gretna Green Revisited' appeared in the English Illustrated Magazine *of January 1886. A long article, including a review of the history of the Scottish Marriage Emporium, it is useful for the description of late nineteenth-century Springfield and Gretna Green and the Langholm clientele:*

The one bumpy street of Springfield, despite its sparse crop of grass, presents to this day a depressed appearance, a relic of the time when it doubled up under a weight of thundering chariots. At the well-remembered, notorious Queen's Head I stood in the gathering gloom watching the road run yellow, until the last draggled hen had spluttered through the pools to roost, and the mean row of white-washed shrunken houses across the way had sunk into the sloppy ground, as they have been doing slowly for half a century, or were carried away in a rush of rain. Soaking weeds hung in lifeless bunches over the hedges of spears that line the roads from Gretna; on sodden Canobie Lea ... dirty piles of congealed snow were still reluctant to be gone; and gnarled tree trunks, equally with palings that would have come out of the ground with a sloppy gluck, showed a dank and cheerless green. Yesterday the rooks dinned the air, and the parish of Gretna witnessed such a marrying and giving in marriage as might have flung it back fifty years. Elsewhere such a solemn cawing round the pulpit on the tree tops would denote a court of justice, but in the vicinity of Springfield, it may be presumed, the thoughts of the very rooks run on matrimony.

A little while ago Willum Lang, a postman's empty letter-bag on his back, and a glittering drop trembling from his nose, picked his way through the puddles , his lips pursed into a portentous frown, and his grey head bowed professionally in contemplation of a pair of knock-knee'd but serviceable shanks. A noteworthy man Willum, son of Simon, son of David, grandson by marriage of Joseph Paisley, all famous 'blacksmiths' of Gretna Green. For nigh a century Springfield has marked time by the Langs. ... Willum's predecessors in office reserved themselves for carriage runaways, and would shake the lids from their coffins if they knew that Willum had to marry the once despised 'pedestrians.'. ... But those were the great clattering days, when there were four famous marrying shops: the two rival inns of Springfield, that washed their hands of each other across the street, Mr Linton's aristocratic quarters at Gretna Hall, and the toll-bar on the right side of the Sark. ...

Willum Lang's puckered face means business. He has sent for by a millworker from Langholm, who, having an hour to spare, thinks he may as well drop in at the priest's and get spliced; or an innocent visitor wandering through the village in search of the mythical smithy; or by a lawyer who shakes his finger threateningly at Willum. ... The room in which the Gretna Green marriages have been celebrated for many years is a large rude kitchen, but dimly lighted by a small 'bole' window of lumpy glass that faces an ill-fitting back door. The draught generated between the two cuts the spot where the couples stand, and must prove a godsend to flushed and flurried bridegrooms. A bed, wooden and solid, ornamented with divers coloured clothes dependent from its woodwork like linen hung on a line to dry, fills a lordly space. The monster fireplace retreats bashfully before it into the opposite wall, and a grimy cracked ceiling looks on a bumpy stone floor, from which a cleanly man could eat his porridge. ...

It is not for Willum Lang to censure the Langholm millworkers, without whose patronage he would be as a priest superannuated, but if they could be got to remember whom they are married to, it would greatly relieve his mind. When standing before him they are given to wabbling unsteadily on their feet, and to taking his inquiry whether the maiden on their right is goodly in their sight for an offer of another 'mutchkin': and next morning they sometimes mistake somebody else's maiden for their own. When one of the youth of the neighbourhood takes to him a helpmate at Springfield his friend often wiles away the time by courting another, and when they return to Langholm things are sometimes a little mixed up. The priest, knowing what is expected of him, is generally able when appealed to, to 'assign to each bridegroom his own', but one shudders to think what complications may arise when Willum's eyes and memory go. . . . sometimes . . . a second marriage by a minister is not thought amiss. . . . (pp. 316–317)

CARLYLE
The Lost Hero

The life of Thomas Carlyle (1795–1881) was recorded in great detail in his own Reminiscences *and his wife's* Letters, *from his childhood in the house his father and uncle, both stone masons, built in Ecclefechan c. 1791, to studying at the University of Edinburgh and teaching at schools in Annan and Kirkcaldy, his marriage to Jane Welsh Carlyle (1801–66) in 1826, and the years (1828–34) at Craigenputtock in the Dumfries-shire hills, west of Dunscore and Glenesslin, and then in London, and in particular in Cheyne Row in Chelsea. His enormous reputation rested essentially on his great books on* The French Revolution *(1837),* Oliver Cromwell's Letters and Speeches *(1845), and* The History of Frederick II of Prussia *(1858–65), and his controversial critical essays in* Sartor Resartus *(1838) and* On Heroes and Hero-worship and the Heroic in History *(1841).*

Carlyle certainly saw himself as a heroic figure living in a diseased society and virtuously, vehemently, violently, viciously condemning all the things he loathed: democracy and the British system of parliamentary government; Disraeli and his Second Reform Bill which extended the right to vote; the emancipation of Black slaves in the West Indies as an abdication of responsibility and a convenient self-deception; the smugness of the absurdly optimistic liberal/radical middle nineteenth-century consensus and all their 'philanthropic, emancipatory, constitutional, and other anarchic revolutionary jargon', hence his clever parodies of the

'*Universal Abolition of Pain Association*' *and the* '*Sluggard and Scoundrel Protection Society*'.

Just as his own life was governed by ideals of hard work, thrift and decent economy, so in the world at large he saw work as the first essential, a sacred duty: so people, Blacks, Whites, must be compelled to work, by force if necessary. 'It is the everlasting privilege of the foolish to be governed by the wise... this is the first "right of man"' (Latter-Day Pamphlets, *1850*).

Any close examination of Carlyle's obnoxious views on the Irish, the Slavs, the Jews, the Gauchos of Paraguay, and the freed and formerly slave population of Jamaica, Dominica, and Old South in the United States of America, may well lead us to conclude that the world would have been a better place and Carlyle a less lonely and bitter man in his old age if he had spent more time playing draughts and rather less time writing about the politics, economics, and social anthropology of countries he had never been to and did not understand.

An excellent discussion of Carlyle's Occasional Discourse on the Nigger Question *(1849) and* Shooting Niagara: and After *(1867) can be found in* British Historians and the West Indies *(1966) by Eric Williams, the eminent historian and onetime Prime Minister of Trinidad and Tobago.*

✝

From Carlyle's Occasional Discourse

... if the Black gentleman is born to be a servant, and, in fact, is useful in God's creation only as a servant, then let him hire not by the month, but by a very much longer term. That he be *hired for life*, really here is the essence of the position he now holds! How to abolish the abuses of slavery, and save the precious thing in it. ...

Do I, then hate the Negro? No ... I decidely like poor Quashee; and find him a pretty kind of man. With a pennyworth of oil, you can make a handsome glossy thing of Quashee, when the soul is not killed in him. A swift, supple fellow; a merry-hearted, grinning, dancing, singing, affectionate kind of creature, with a great deal of melody and amenability in his composition. This certainly is a notable fact: the black African, alone of wild-men can live among men civilized.

– Fraser's Magazine, November, 1849

In Shooting Niagara *a furious Carlyle wrote:*
By far the notablest case of *Swarmery*, in these times, is that of the late American War, with settlement of the Nigger Question for

result. . . . One always rather likes the Nigger; evidently a poor blockhead with good dispositions, with affections, attachments, – with a turn for Nigger Melodies, and the like; he is the only Savage of all the coloured races that doesn't die out on sight of the White Man; but can actually live beside him, and work and increase and be merry. The Almighty Maker has appointed him to be a Servant. . . .

Poor Dominica itself is described to me in a way to kindle a heroic young heart . . . Population of 100 white men (by no means of select type); unknown cipher of rattlesnakes, profligate Niggers and Mulattoes: governed by a Piebald Parliament of Eleven (head Demosthenes there is a Nigger Tinman), and so exquisite a care of Being and of Wellbeing that the old Fortifications have become jungle . . . an Island capable of being taken by the crew of a man-of-war's boat. And indeed it was nearly lost, the other year, by an accidental collision of two Niggers on the street, and a concourse of other idle Niggers to see. . . .

– *Macmillan's Magazine*, August 1867

Poor naïve Carlyle, imagining that by 1826 he had satisfactorily solved the world's problems meditating on 'long solitary rides' or 'glowerin out over' the merse and the Solway and could thereafter look 'down on the welterings' of his poor 'fellow creatures'.

Thomas Carlyle on his father, James Carlyle, and his uncles John, Frank and Tom

. . . the boys were accustomed to all manner of hardship, and must trust for upbringing to nature, to the scanty precepts of their poor mother, and to what seeds or influences of culture were hanging as it were in the atmosphere of their environment. Poor boys! they had to scramble, scraffle, for their very clothes and food. They knit, they thatched for hire, above all they hunted. My father had tried all these things almost in boyhood. Every dell and burngate and cleugh of that district he had traversed, seeking hares and the like. He used to tell of these pilgrimages. Once I remember his gun-flint was tied on with a hatband. He was a real hunter, like a wild Indian, from necessity. The hares' flesh was food. Hareskins (at sixpence each) would accumulate into the purchase money of a coat. All these things he used to speak of without either boasting or complaining, not as reproaches to us, but as historical merely. . . . His hunting years were not useless to him. Misery was early training the rugged boy into a stoic, that one day he might be the assurance of a Scottish man.

– J.A. Froude (ed.), *Reminiscences of Thomas Carlyle*, vol. I, 1881, pp. 36–37

Postcript by Thomas Carlyle to a letter by Jane Welsh Carlyle,
10th September, 1838

... My mother, many years before, on the eve of an Ecclefechan Fair, happened in the gloaming to pass one Martha Calvert's door, a queer old cripple creature who used to lodge vagrants, beggars, ballad-singers, snap-women, etc., such as were wont, copiously enough (chiefly from the 'Brig-end' of Dumfries), to visit us on these occasions. Two beggar-women were pleasantly chatting, or taking sweet counsel, outside in the quiet summer dusk, when a third started out, eagerly friendly, 'Come awa; haste; t' ye first rush o' ye tea!' (general tea inside, just beginning, first rush of it far superior to third or fourth!)

'God's Providence'. Peg Ir'rin (Irving), a memorable old bread-and-ale woman, extensively prepared to vend these articles at Middlebie Sacrament, could not by entreaty or logic (her husband had fought at Bunker's Hill) extort from the parish official (ruling elder) liberty to use the vacant school-house for that purpose, whereupon Peg, with a toss of her foolish high head (a loud, absurd, empty woman, though an empty especially of any mischief), 'Ah, well; thou canna cut me out of God's Providence.'

    – J. A. Froude (ed.), *Letters and memorials of Jane Welsh Carlyle.*
    Prepared for publication by Thomas Carlyle, vol. I, 1883, p. 110.

Postscript by Carlyle to a letter by Jane Welsh Carlyle to John Sterling,
Esq., Falmouth, January–February 1842

Shortly after this letter came ill news from Templand ... February 26, 1842, her mother had departed; that 'first stroke' mercifully the final one.... I followed to Liverpool two days after.... The same night I went by mailcoach (no railway farther for me) to Carlisle, thence through Annan, etc., and was at Templand next morning for a late breakfast. Journey in all parts of it still strangely memorable to me. Weather hard, hoar-frosty, windy; wrapt in an old dressing-gown with mackintosh buttoned round it, I effectually kept out the cold, and had a strange night of it, on the solitary coach-roof, under the waste-blowing skies, through the mountains, to Carlisle. It must have been Saturday, I now find, Carlisle market-day. Other side of that city we met groups of market-people; at length groups of Scotch farmers or dealers solidly jogging thither, in some of whom I recognised old schoolfellows! A certain 'Jock Beattie,' perhaps twelve years my senior, a big good humoured fellow finishing his arithmetics, etc., who used to be rather good to me, him I distinctly noticed after five-and-twenty years, grown to a grizzled, blue-visaged sturdy giant, sunk in comforters and woollen wrappages, plod-

plodding there, at a stout pace, and still good-humouredly, to Carlisle market (as a big bacon-dealer, etc., it afterwards appeared), and had various thoughts about him, far as he was from thoughts of me! Jock's father, a prosperous enough country-carpenter, near by the kirk and school of Hoddam, was thrice-great as a ruling-elder (indeed, a very long-headed, strictly orthodox man), well known to my father, though I think silently not so well approved of in all points. 'Wull Beattie' was my father's name for him. Jock's eldest brother, 'Sandy Beattie', a Probationer (Licentiate of the Burgher Church), stepping into our school one day, my age then between seven and eight, had reported to my father that I must go to Latin, that I was wasting my time otherwise, which brought me a Ruddiman's *Rudiments*, something of an event in the distance of the past.

At Annan, in the rimy-hazy morning, I sat gazing on the old well-known houses, on the simmering populations now all new to me – very strange, these old unaltered stone-and-mortar edifices, with their inmates changed and gone!... Six miles farther, I passed my sister Mary Austin's farmstead in Cummertrees... At Dumfries, my Sister Jean, who had got some inkling, was in waiting where the coach stopped; she half by force hurried me over to her house, which was near, gave me a hot cup of tea, etc., and had me back again in plenty of time. Soon after 10 a.m. I was silently set down by the wayside, beckoned a hedger working not far off to carry my portmanteau the bit of a furlong necessary, and, with thoughts enough articulate and inarticulate, entered the old Templand now become so new and ghastly. ...

The day of the household sale, which was horrible to me, I fled away to Crawford Churchyard (20 miles off, through the pass of Dalveen, etc.), leaving my brothers in charge of everything; spent the day there by my mother-in-law's grave and in driving hither and back; the day was of bright weather, the road silent and solitary. ... It was not till the beginning of May that I got actually back to Chelsea, where my poor sorrow-stricken darling with Jeannie, her Liverpool cousin, had been all this while. ...

– ibid., pp. 140–45

Letter from Jane Welsh Carlyle to Thomas Carlyle, 27 **August,** 1843; *and postcript by T.C.*
... I have realised an ideal, having actually acquired a small sofa, which needs to be covered, of course. ... Never fear! this little woman knows what she is about; the sofa costs you simply nothing at all! Neither have I sillily paid four or five pounds away for it out of my own private purse. It

is a sofa which I have known about for the last year and half. The man who had it asked £4. 10s. for it; was willing to sell it without mattress or cushions for £2. 10s. I had a spare mattress which I could make to fit it, and also pillows lying by of no use. But still, £2. 10s. was more than I cared to lay out of my own money on the article, so I did a stroke of trade with him. The old green curtains of downstairs were become filthy; and, what was better, superfluous. No use could be made of them, unless first dyed at the rate of 7d. per yard; it was good to get rid of them, that they might not fill the house with moths, as those sort of woollen things lying by always do; so I sold them to the broker for thirty shillings; I do honestly think more than their value; but I higgled a full hour with him, and the sofa had lain on his hands. So you perceive there remained only one pound to pay; and that I paid with Kitty Kirkpatrick's sovereign, which I had laid aside not to be appropriated to my own absolutely individual use. So there is a sofa created in manner by the mere wish to have it. . . .

T.C. . . . At Linton in the forenoon, I noticed lying on the green, many of them with Bibles, some 150 decent Highlanders; last remnant of the old 'Highland reapers' here; and round them, in every quarter, such a herd of miserable, weak, restless 'wild Irish,' their conquerors and successors here, as filled me with a kind or rage and sorrow at once; all in ragged grey frieze, 3,000 or 4,000 of them, aimless, restless, hungry, senseless, more like apes than men; swarming about, leaping into bean-fields, turnip-fields, and out again, asking you 'the toime, sir.' I almost wondered the Sabbatarian country did not rise on them, fling the whole lot into the Frith. . . .

– ibid., pp. 253–55

Reminiscences, completed between Autumn 1866 and 2nd January, 1867
Next 26th of May (1826) we went all of us to Scotsbrig (a much better farm, which was now bidden for and got), and where, as it turned out, I continued only a few months, wedded, and to Edinburgh in October following. . . .

   With all its manifold petty troubles, this year at Hoddam Hill has a rustic beauty and dignity to me, and lies now like a not ignoble russet-coated idyll in my memory; one of the quietest, on the whole, and perhaps the most triumphantly important of my life. I lived very silent, diligent, had long solitary rides . . . my meditatings, musings, and reflections were continual; my thoughts were wandering (or travelling) through eternity, through time, and through space, so far as poor I had scanned or known. . . . This year I found that I had conquered all my scepticisms, agonising doubtings, fearful wrestlings with the foul and vile and soul-murdering Mud-gods of my epoch; had escaped as from a worse than Tartarus, with all its Phlegethons and Stygian quagmires, and was emerging free in spirit into the eternal blue of ether, where, blessed be heaven! I have for the spiritual part ever since lived, looking down upon the welterings of my poor fellow-creatures, in such multitudes and millions still stuck in that fatal element, and have no concern whatever in their Puseyisms, ritualisms, metaphysical controversies and cob-webberies, and no feeling of my own except honest silent pity for the serious or religious part of them, and occasional indignation, for the poor world's sake, at the frivolous secular and impious part, with their universal suffrages, their Nigger emancipations, sluggard and scroundrel Protection societies, and 'unexampled prosperities' for the time being! What my pious joy and gratitude then was, let the pious soul figure. . . .

– J. A. Froude (ed.), *Reminiscences of Thomas Carlyle*, vol. I, 1881, pp. 286–87.

Deaths. On the 26th ult. at Dalbeattie, aged 88 years, Mr James Ker, clog-maker, a person of . . . superior intellectual endowments. Thomas Carlyle was instructed by the deceased in the game of draughts.

– *KA*, 7th July, 1865

13

SPORT AND USEFUL RECREATION

†

Seventeenth- and eighteenth-century legislators and eighteenth- and nineteenth-century clerical commentators drew a line between useful, respectable and government-approved sport, archery, for example, at the Bairns' Bow Butts on the Dumfries Whitesands, and wapenschaws, for example, with 'harquebuss and culverin' for the Dumfries Siller Gun; and vulgar, 'irrational' sports which tended to 'demoralize the people', as the Rev. James Donaldson of Canonbie put it in 1836. The latter included kayles or cloish or 'ninepins', and football, bull-baiting and cock-fights, which attracted mobs bent on violence and mischief. The evidence for the eighteenth century in Dumfries and Galloway is thin, and unfortunately the ministers compiling the Statistical Account entries in the 1790s and 1830s/1840s only occasionally deigned to mention sport, and usually only curling and quoits, the most popular leisure activities in every parish.

Newspaper advertisements show the huge popularity of horse racing c. 1780–1820, both at recognised racecourses, Tinwald Downs outside Dumfries, Kirkpatrick-Durham and Creetown, and at country fairs, for example at Haugh of Urr, Castle Douglas, Rhonehouse and Gatehouse-of-Fleet. Crowds of spectators came to the races, for example, to the Sands of Luce for the match in January 1803 for 20 guineas a side between Mr McKinnell's Miss Kennedy, got by the Duke of Hamilton's Washington, and Mr Ross's grey mare, got by the Earl of Eglinton's Fingal. This race was run as 'a three-mile heat right out', and Mr Ross's mare, with a boy of five stones as jockey, bolted or left the course, so there was 'but little entertainment to the crowd' [DWJ, 18th January, 1803].

There were some early curling clubs (Sanquhar 1774, Wanlockhead 1777), but a whole series of new clubs (Anwoth and New Abbey 1820, Penninghame 1829, Kelton 1831, etc.) were established in the 1820s and 1830s. The appearance of clubs with the use of lochs or ponds for curling, of open land for quoiting, and of 'grounds' for cricket, dates in Dumfries and Galloway mostly to the second and third quarters of the nineteenth century. All sorts of curling challenge matches, 'battles' between parishes, and tournaments (for example, between Anwoth, Borgue, Girthon, Kirkmabreck, Tongland and Twynholm) were organised. Regional and national events were on a much larger scale. The North of Scotland versus the South match in February 1853 and the January 1854 competition between Carrick, Kyle and Cunningham for the Earl of Eglinton's trophy were each contested by some 1,500 curlers. The enthusiasm for curling is perhaps best illustrated by the development by Newton Stewart curlers in 1853–54 of the remote White Loch of Drigmorn (NX 469758) for early and late season ice. The loch was at about 1850 feet, between Auchinleck and Loch Dee, and 3½ miles from a road.

High stakes, heavy gambling and cash prizes were an important part of nineteenth-century sport at the highest level, for example, the Grand Quoiting Match at Carlisle in September 1850 between Rennie of Alva, the Scottish champion, and Heywood, the Oldham 'don', for 100 guineas a side; and the Golf Grand Match at North Berwick in August 1849 for £200 between Allen Robertson and Tom Morris of St Andrews and J. and W. Dunn of Musselburgh. Bets were placed at cricket matches on and between innings, hence the allegations even in eighteenth-century England of games being 'fixed' and 'bought and sold'.

In the Borders and Dumfries and Galloway town and village cricket clubs flourished from the 1850s, for example, Dumfries, Langholm, Closeburn, Stranraer (1856), Newton Stewart (1859) and Wigtown (1859), and 'county' matches between Dumfries-shire and 'United Galloway', for example, at the Kirroughtree Club Ground, became regular summer features. The players in the September 1854 game were in cricket costume with respectively blue and red caps. Cricket bats, balls and stumps had been more or less standardised by 1835, but it was very difficult to produce decent pitches and safe outfields, so most games were played over two innings for each side, with sometimes a return match later in the afternoon or evening.

Patronage was important in persuading new players to take up cricket. The Earl of Galloway's sons, Lord Garlies and the Hon. Randolph Stewart, were keen and competent players and organised their own Cumloden side. Guests at Cumloden, notably the Hon. Granville Somerset, an excellent batsman, took part. Lord Garlies and Granville Somerset also played for the United Galloway team. Matches were also arranged between teams got up by Mr Ogden of the Excise and Capt. Walters of the Cairnsmore Mines, with Lord Garlies and his brother in the Mines side. Some small villages, for example Blackcraig, had their own cricket team by the 1870s. Groundsmen and professionals, Sgt. Bunch at Dumfries and Craven at Kirkcudbright, were employed by the 1880s and 1890s, and feelings ran high between supporters of local town teams.

'Sport and Useful Recreation' included a vast range of activities – fox

hunting, stag hunts, otter hunting, coursing clubs, regattas on Lochryan and the Castle Loch, Lochmaben, ploughing matches, wrestling, bicycle races, tug of war contests, athletic games (for the Shepherds' Games at House o' Hill see Chapter 8), football, golf, bowling, dancing, walking or pedestrianism, debating societies, Mutual Improvement Associations, Mechanics Institutes, Temperance Societies, and the club activities of the Volunteers.

BULL-BAITING AND COCK-FIGHTING

Reginald of Durham's Life of St Cuthbert includes an account of Ailred of Rievaulx's visit to Kirkcudbright on 20th March, 1165, the day of the feast of St Cuthbert. There was a tradition of tying a sacrificial bull to a stake to be baited by the young men of the town. One young lout who had been rebuked by Ailred and had turned on him, telling him to mind his own business, was then gored by the bull, another miracle of divine retribution! [Reginald of Durham, De admirandis Beati Cuthberti virtutibus, Surtees Society, I, 1835, pp. 178–179] *There are occasional references to bullbaiting in eighteenth-century Scotland, for example, at Cockenzie Fair on 27th October, 1720, when 'excellent Bull-baiting, with a variety of other Diversions' was advertised in the* Edinburgh Evening Courant *of 18th–20th October, 1720.*

Robert Trotter, the schoolmaster of the Burgh School in Dumfries from 1724 to 1747 and jointly headmaster with George Chapman until 1750, was an eminent scholar. His Grammaticae Latinae Compendium . . . in usum Scholae Drumfrisiensis *(Edinburgh 1732) is a good example of an eighteenth-century school textbook. The school rules laid down by the Town Council at the time of his appointment included special provision for cock-fights on Fastern's E'en [the English April Shrove Tuesday].*

✝

That at Fastern's Even, upon the day appointed for the cocks fighting in the schoolhouse, the under teacher cause keep the door, and exact no more than twelve pennies Scots for each scholar for the benefit of bringing in a cock to fight in the schoolhouse; and that none be suffered to enter that day to the schoolhouse but the scholars, except gentlemen and persons of note, from whom nothing is to be demanded; and what money is to be given in by the scholars the under teacher is to receive and apply to his own use for his pains and trouble; and that no scholars except who pleases shall furnish cocks, but all the scholars, whether they have cocks or not, are to get into the school. Those that have none paying 2s Scots as forfeit. . . .

– William McDowall, *History of the Burgh of Dumfries* (1867), 1906, p. 550

Cock-Fighting. Dumfries. On Wednesday the 25th instant, a Main of Cocks will be fought in the New Room, at the George Inn here, between some Gentlemen of the Town and Country, for Two Guineas the Battle and One Hundred Guineas the Main. To begin fighting at eleven o'clock. Admission 2s. 6d. each.

– *DWJ*, 24th February, 1795

Cock-Fighting in Cannobie. We had been induced to think that this disreputable and brutalising amusement had disappeared, at least, from this part of the country, and that any person who had the smallest respect for his character and credit, would indignantly repudiate the idea of allowing his name to be associated with the patrons and promoters of such disgraceful exhibitions. We are sorry to find, however, that in this opinion we have been in error. Only a few days ago, a prize cock-fight came off in the parish of Cannobie, under the patronage of two squires, whose names figure in honourable proximity with those of Cock Bobbie and an underling menial of the Duke of Buccleuch's. Your readers will not be surprised to learn that when such a moral and manly exhibition was to take place in this favoured parish, the cock-fighters were accommodated with a piece of rich holm land for the purpose, within half a mile of the barren moss where the Free Church congregation were interdicted by a 'Christian Nobleman' from meeting for public worship.

– *DGS*, 14th May, 1845

Miscellaneous Observations. . . . Till within these last four years cock-fights were very common, with all their vile accompaniments, and more particularly at the village of Rigg.

– Rev. James Roddick, *Parish of Graitney* (revised March 1834), *NSAS*, 1845, p. 272

My Father, Dr Robert Trotter . . . the famous Muir Doctor in his day . . . was fond of the games and sports then common in the Glenkens, such as draughts, backgammon, putting the stone, throwing the hanmmer, channel-stanes alias curling, etc.; and only a few days before his death . . . he went with me to two Cock-fights, one of them on

Dalarran Holm and the other on the Washing-Green, New-Galloway. . . . He died 14th March, 1815, aged 76. . . .

Cockfighters. He attended the Fairs, Races and Cock-fights at that time, and for years afterwards. The death of my father, and the emigration of Willie Sinclair to Canada, may be said to have put an end for ever to the annual Candlemas Cock-fights in the Glenkens. The leading men at these sports were Willie Sinclair, Robert Manson, William Corson, Cubbox, and old James Wyllie, the bedal of Kells.

– Dr Robert Trotter of Auchencairn and Dalry (1798–1875),
My Autobiography to 1862

KYLES OR KEEL PINS OR CLOSH

In the summer of 1834, as the servants of Mr Bell in Banjoin, in the parish of Balmaclellan, were casting peats on Ironmacannie moor, when cutting near the bottom of the moss, they laid open with their spades what appears to be the instruments of an ancient game, consisting of an oaken ball, 18 inches in circumference, and seven wooden pins, each thirteen inches in length, of a conical shape with a circular top. These ancient 'Keel Pins,' as they are termed by Strutt in his *Sports and Pastimes of the People*, were all standing erect on the hard till, equidistant from each other, with the exception of two which pointed towards the ball that lay about a yard in front, from which it may be inferred that they were overthrown in the course of the game. The ball has been formed of solid oak, and from its decayed state, it must have remained undisturbed for centuries, till discovered at a depth of not less than twelve feet from the original surface.

In the excavations making at Pompeii, utensils are often found seemingly in the very position in which they were last used. This may be accounted for by the awful calamity that suddenly befel that devoted city, but what induced or impelled the ancient gamesters in the wilds of Galloway, to leave the instruments of their amusement in what may be considered the midst of the game, is more difficult to solve. . . . These remnants of antiquity are now in my possession.

– [Communication from Mr Train] – 'Relics', in William Mackenzie,
The History of Galloway, 1841, vol. 2, pp. 66–67 of Appendix.
The 'keel pins' or kyles found on Ironmacannie moor are now in the Museum of Scotland.

Kayles. Kayles, written also cayles and keiles, derived from the French term quilles, was played with pins, and no doubt gave origin to the modern game of nine-pins; though primitively the kayle-pins do not appear to have been confined to any certain number ... the two engravings ... from a Book of Prayers ... the pastime of kyles is playing with six pins. ... another drawing on a Ms. in the Royal Library ... the pastime is played with eight pins; and the form of these pins is also different, but that might depend entirely upon the fancy of the makers. One of them, in both cases, is taller than the rest.

The arrangement of the kayle-pins differs greatly from that of the nine-pins, the latter being placed upon a square frame in three rows, and the former in one row only. The two delineations here copied represent that species of the game called club-kayles, jeux de quilles à baston, so denominated from the club or cudgel that was thrown at them.

Closh. The game of cloish, or closh, mentioned frequently in the ancient statutes, seems to have been the same as kayles, or at least exceedingly like it: cloish was played with pins, which were thrown at with a bowl instead of a truncheon, and probably differed only in name from the nine-pins of the present time.

– Joseph Strutt, *The Sports and Pastimes of the People of England*, 1834, pp. 270–272

The medieval Ironmacannie 'keel pins' were perhaps used for a game of cloish by an itinerant band, for example an English army reconnaissance patrol in the reigns of Edward I or Edward III: if they were abandoned this obviously could have been because the patrol had to take to their heels in a hurry in the face of a sudden attack.

Rowley-powley or skittles was popular at eighteenth- and nineteenth-century fairs. Robert Shennan (1831), for example, described Kirkpatrick-Durham fair where

> *Rowley-powley wi' his pins*
> *Was kittle for a body's shins.*

The oddly named Dumfries Rowley-Powley Curling Club (president, Alex. Robson, surgeon and vice-president, Wm. Brown, writer) may have been in some way part of this tradition, or it may simply have been a club for 'roly-polys', that is for happily plump gentlemen who enjoyed their puddings. ...

†

A DAY AT THE RACES

In January 1769, Mess. Maxwell of Dalswinton and Blair of Dunrod laid a wager of £200 Sterling, Which of them should ride soonest from Dumfries to Kirkcudbright? which is about 27 miles. Mr Blair being taken ill on the road, seven miles short of Kirkcudbright, yielded the race at that place, gave bill for the sum lost, and died before the bill became due.

Mr Maxwell sued Mr Blair's heir for payment; who pleaded in defence the Scots statute 1621; whereby it is declared, that all money won at cards and dice, or in wagers at horse-races, above 100 merks Scots, belongs to the poor of the parish. . . . the court in July found, That the statute was not in desuetude; and appointed the kirk-sessions of Dumfries and Kirkcudbright, and the kirk-session of Kelton, in which parish Mr Blair gave up the race, to appear for their interests. . . .

– *SM*, 36, 1774, pp. 718–19

A Fair to be holden at Haugh of Urr . . . the Lady Fair . . . on the estate of Captain Laurie of Redcastle, at the Haugh of Urr, on the first Tuesday after of fourteenth . . . August 1788. Considerable entertainment is expected from the following Races, viz. A Horse Race for a new Saddle and Bridle; As Also, An Ass Race – A Race of Men – Another of Women – all for suitable prizes. The whole under the direction of respectable characters.

– *DWJ*, 5th August, 1788

The Patrick'smas Fair, in Kirkpatrick-Durham . . . will be held on Thursday the second day of April, at which there will be various prizes for Foot Races in the afternoon . . . And on Friday . . . the following prizes will be offered for Horse Races, viz. Three Guineas for the first Race – One Guinea for the second Race – and One Guinea for the third Race. . . . The Horses that run for the second prize must belong to persons resident in the parish of Kirkpatrick, and must have been in their custody at least four weeks before the Race. . . .

– *DWJ*, 17th March, 1789

Dalton Races. On Thursday the 5th day of September, 1797, there will be run for at Dalton, an excellent good Saddle, the best of three three-mile heats, by Horses and Mares who never won a prize of £50, also, a set of good Cart Harness, by common Draught Horses, together with Bridles, etc. . . .

– *DWJ*, 29th August, 1797

Creetown Races. There is to be run for, over the beautiful course of Creetown, on Thursday the 6th of May 1802, the Subscription Purse of Five Guineas, by horses that never won a ten guinea prize . . . also, on same day, the Ladies Subscription of Two Guineas, for a Trotting Match by saddle or country horses. . . .

– DWJ, 20th April, 1802

CURLING AND SKATING

Last week a Grand Curling Match was to have been played between the parish of Ruthwell and the parish of Irongray for a considerable sum, but, on a supposed inferiority in the latter, they paid two Guineas to Ruthwell, which was the fine agreed upon in case of failure.

We hear from Mousewald, that on Thursday last a Grand Curling Match was played on a Board below that village, between the parish of Mousewald and the parish of Ruthwell, for dinner and drink, in which the former came off conquerors with ease: And on Friday another was played between the parish in Mousewald and that of Dalton, also for dinner and drink, of which the former had greatly the superiority.

– DWJ, 13th January, 1778

The Curling Society at Sanquhar have agreed that a Match shall be played on Tuesday first, being the 8th instant, or on the first lawful day suitable for that purpose, betwixt 40 men of the name of John, and the same number of the name of William, all within the burgh, for 40 pints of spirits, 40 pints of porter, 40 two-penny loaves, and 40 lbs. of cheese; and that these Curlers shall meet at the Cross, by nine o'clock in the morning of the day they are to play, and shall march to the ice in five divisions, each by the side of his antagonist, armed with his ice-stone, besom, etc. – and that this *Curling Regiment* shall be attended by a Band of Music, to and from the place of action: – and, it is further agreed upon, that the above 80 Curlers are to play other 80 of different names, all within the burgh, for double the number of pints of spirits, etc.

(Signed) Alexander Turnbull, Praeses.

– DWJ, 8th January, 1793

On Friday the 29th ult. a Curling Match took place in the parish of Crossmichael, the married men against the unmarried, at which the latter came off victorious, by a superiority of upwards of thirty shots. The match was for the benefit of the poor of the said parish; and we are happy to state, that upwards of Ten Guineas have been collected, which has afforded a very seasonable relief to many persons in indigent circumstances.

DWJ, 23rd February, 1813

Newton Stewart, 14th Jan. – A bonspeil was played to-day betwixt the parishes of Penninghame and Minnigaff, forty of each side. The agreement between the parties was that every player should pay 1s., so that the whole amounted to £4 sterling, which will be given to the poor of these parishes, £1 to Minnigaff, and £3 to Penninghame, they being victorious.

– *DWJ*, 17th January, 1826

The Annan curlers have long been in the practice of playing an annual match between the east and west ends of the town, which is divided into two nearly equal portions by a ditch known by the name of the Fosse. This match, which is commonly called the *Fosse Match*, came off on Tuesday last, and terminated for this season in favour of the Eastendians. The day was rather soft, which, in some degree, lessened the pleasure of the sport; but the game passed over with perfect harmony, and the winners and losers, after partaking together of 'beef and greens' in the Blue Bell inn, spent the evening together with the utmost cordiality.

The annual competition by the four rinks composing the Carlaverock curling club, for the silver medal, took place on Tuesday the 15th instant, when, after a keen contest conducted with the greatest good humour, victory declared in favour of the rink directed by Mr Thomas Clark, Locherbank.

– *DT*, 17th January, 1833

Amusements. In the winter season, curling and skating are very common amusements. During hard frost, some of our lochs present a very gay and animating appearance. The skater performs his evolutions – the stone thunders along the ice amid the cheers of the spectators – the graceful forms of the fair move up and down on the slippery promenade, giving additional interest to the scene. Curling levels all distinctions – the laird and the labourer, the master and the servant, the clergyman and the clown, are all on an equality at this game. . . .

Rev. James Fergusson, 'Parish of Inch (1839)', *NSAS*, 1845, p. 89

We shall not . . . attempt any minute description of the numerous scenes of strife between tried and stalwart men, which we have witnessed in our neighbourhood within the last ten days: as, for example . . . on the Whinny Leggit Loch, on Monday last, between the sturdy burghers of Kirkcudbright and the chivalrous predial section of the parish, wherein the latter body mightily prevailed and, without other aid or protection than their own skill and indomitable resolution, carried off triumphantly the palm of victory; or, another affair . . . of deep regard to those immediately concerned, which came off at the same time and place – a contest exceedingly well sustained and won hard by the winner for a boll of meal for distribution among the poor of the burgh. Let us rather . . . record the great and decisive event of the day . . . of the pitched battle of Kirkcudbright against the world renowned Borgue, on the Earlston pond (in Borgue). On this memorable occasion the belligerents were led forth and drawn up in order of battle in two divisions, under the able generalship on the Borgue side of Mr W. Sproat of Borness and Mr Alexander Brown of Carlton; and on the Kirkcudbright side of Mr James Williamson of Bombie and Mr James Duff of Upper Sypland. . . . The war cry of swoop! swoop! resounded. Whack! and whack! against each other went their missiles, thrown by no feeble arms. For a time the issue of the strife seemed doubtful. Fickle fortune with her usual syren smile suspended her laurel, now over one brow, and then over that of another of the generals. But as time progressed apace, the Invincibles of Borgue snatched the trophy from the undecided goddess' hand, Borgue gaining by three shots over Mr Williamson and Carlton by seven over Mr Duff. . . . Long may we live to see such battles and such bloodless strifes. . . .

– *GA*, 25th January, 1850

John Boyd, Esq. of Milton, against Dr David Lamont. At Kirkpatrick Kirk, the second Monday of January, 1777 years, in presence of me, James Muirhead, minister of Urr, notary public . . . Compeared John Boyd of Milton, Esq., who in the personal presence of Dr David Lamont, minister in Kirkpatrick-Durham, did solemnly and legally protest that on Thursday last the said Dr David Lamont did most pompously and ostentatiously and vaingloriously challenge, provoke, and defy him . . . to find twenty-four curlers belonging to the parish of Urr and bring them, with their stones, tramps, brooms, and other implements of ice playing, to a certain horsepond or goosedub, magnificently called Lochpatrick, lying within a certain moor denominated by Mr John Coltert of Areeming, Lochpatrick Barony. That the said Dr David Lamont did most incredibly and hyperbolically affirm that he would find twenty-four curlers within the parish of Kirkpatrick-Durham able and willing to play a bonspiel for a decent dinner, and necessary drink, against the said curlers of Urr, upon the said gutter of Lochpatrick, though it is well known that the said parish of Kirkpatrick-Durham scarcely contains twenty-four inhabitants, excepting moor collies and the sheep they persecute.

That the said John Boyd, Esq., not willing to contradict a dignified clergyman otherwise than by a fair opposition of facts, did muster and assemble twenty-four curlers out of eighty-five which may be readily found in the said parish of Urr. That he did this day conduct the said curlers of Urr to the aforesaid goosedub of Lochpatrick . . . where he found the said Dr David Lamont in company with four persons, whom he denominated the curlers of Kirkpatrick-Durham, one of them being possessed of a channelstone which he had stolen from Mr John Thompson, merchant at Haugh-of-Urr, and which he, the pilferer, had greatly diminished with a mill-pick, for certain reasons not very creditable, which he gave as his apology, when the stone was taken back by its real owner. That the said Dr David Lamont did there confess . . . that the remaining twenty of Kirkpatrick curlers, who were undeniably absent, had either forgot to attend, or had been supernaturally intimidated, or had left their habitations in quest of dead sheep, an avocation indispensible to the existence of his parishioners and their families in the present season of the year. That the said Dr David Lamont also declared his whole parish could hardly afford dinner and drink for such a multitude as now invaded it, seeing that their whole wethers had been sold at Martinmas, their tups had extenuated by procreation, their ewes gone with young, and their hens devoured by the fumerts. And that therefore the said Dr Lamont was both unwilling and unable to contend in a match of curling with the said John Boyd, Esq. . . .

I was persuaded that the said Dr David Lamont had criminally transgressed against the convenience and interests of the said John Boyd, Esq., as well as the credit of Kirkpatrick-Durham. . . .

Same time and place compeared the said Dr David Lamont, who required . . . that I should receive and insert his answers . . . First, That previous to Thursday last he had been promised by several of his parishioners respectable quantities of tarry wool and ewe milk cheese to pray for foul water and an early spring for the good of the sheep; and on Sabbath last he did, in consequence, exert himself mightily, and never doubted but that the weather would have broke yesterday, and the spring season commenced this morning early, whereby he imagined himself in safety to challenge and defy the said John Boyd, Esq., as narrated in the protest. Secondly, That though his parish was not yet so numerous as to exhibit twenty-four effective curlers, his parishioners were generally prolific, as he could prove from the records of his session, and might in a short time beget and bring up a number sufficient for supplying the deficiency he had now accession to deplore. Thirdly, As to the stated number of his parishioners, he was often obliged to the Godly parish of Troqueer for a temporary supply; that his parish at any rate supported those needy wanderers, he was resolved to assume them as his own property, and that next season he would erect a city for their accommodation. Fourthly, That so soon as he could lead twenty-four curlers from the parish of Kirkpatrick-Durham he would infalliably meet the said John Boyd, Esq., upon the Loch of Meikle Milton, where they would contend against an equal number of gentlemen curlers belonging to the parish of Urr; that the said twenty-four curlers belonging to each parish should, at the direction of their respective leaders, be divided into three companies, one of which should plan for an abundant dinner, another for plenty of drink and the third for ten stones of meal to the poor of the parish that should prove victorious. . . .

– *KA*, 20th June, 1862

Female Curling! To such a height has the manly game of curling arrived of late in Keir, that on Tuesday last two rinks of blooming maids, the one from the estate of Capenoch, the other from that of Waterside, met on the *Ged* Loch, to contest the palm of victory. . . . Hundreds of spectators met at an early hour, some purely from amusement, others to gaze with delight on the fair forms of their sweethearts. . . . Nothing could have been more unfavourable than the state of the weather, the thaw having been fairly commenced and the bright luminary above shining with unabated splendour throughout the whole day. . . . And though standing ancle deep in water, it was wonderful to see how patiently they endured the cold, and to witness the vigour of a female arm. The *curling* broom they managed with as much dexterity as the *household* one, and the channel-stone as the distaff. . . . the veterans of Capenoch . . . beat those of Waterside only by a single shot. The evening was spent with as much hilarity as the day, the rattling sound of the stone having given place to the spirit-stirring sound of the fiddle. . . .

– *DWJ*, 16th February, 1830

QUOITS

The game of quoits . . . quoits are not only made of different magnitudes to suit the poise of the players, but sometimes the marks are placed at extravagant distances, so as to require great strength to throw the quoit home; this, however, is contrary to the general rule, and depends upon the caprice of the parties engaged in the contest.

To play at this game, an iron pin, called a hob, is driven into the ground, within a few inches of the top; and at the distance of eighteen, twenty, or more yards, for the distance is optional, a second pin of iron is also made fast in a similar manner; two or more persons, as four, six, eight, or more at pleasure, who divided into equal parties are to contend for the victory, stand at one of the iron marks and throw an equal number of quoits to the other, and the nearest of them to the hob are reckoned towards the game.... Formerly in the country, the rustics not having the round perforated quoits to play with, used horse-shoes, and in many places the quoit itself, to this day, is called the shoe.

– J. Strutt, *The Sports and Pastimes of the People of England*, 1834, pp. 76–77

Quoiting [pronounced kiting]

Quoit Playing. – On Friday se'ennight, a grand match of quoits was played on the spacious green before Dalswinton House (the proprietor having kindly given his consent), betwixt the parish of Closeburn and the united quoit club of Locherbriggs and Tinwald. After the ground had been taken up, four different rinks were formed, and twelve players selected from each side; when after a keen contest of several hours duration, fortune smiled upon the exertions of the merry men of Locherbriggs and Tinwald. The victors, it appeared, had been successful at three rinks, and unsuccessful in one, though even here there was such an equality of play that the winning shot had to be determined by admeasurement. At the termination of the game, a ponderous *grey hen* of excellent aquavitae was placed in the centre of the green, round which the honest rustics assembled, and by dint of quaichs, dram glasses, etc. contrived to help themselves to copious and well timed libations. C.G.S. Menteath, Esq., W. McAlpin Lennie, Esq. and Mr Menteath, jun. honoured the party with their presence – an honour of which the quoitmen felt justly proud, and for which they testified their gratitude by pledging their visitors' healths in rapturous bumpers. . . .

DWJ, 18th October, 1822

Quoiting Match at Leswalt. A match (the result of a challenge by the victors) took place here on the evening of Saturday, on the farm of Dinduff, between Mr Alex. McWilliam, miller, Soleburn Mill, and Mr

Wm. McLean, gamekeeper, Leswalt: against Mr Erskine, blacksmith, Barnultock, and Mr Sinclair, blacksmith, Stranraer. After having played an hour and a half, victory was declared in favour of Messrs. McWilliam and McLean by a majority of six shots.

– GG, 16th July, 1870

Grand Quoiting Tournament, Castle Douglas ... held alternate years in Castle Douglas and Kirkcudbright ... at farm of Whitepark ... refreshment tent Mr Wm Rankine, Globe Hotel ... 100 entries ...

All Comers –	1st £7	R. Kirkland, Mauchline
	2nd £3.10s	Wm. McElveen, Mauchline
	3rd £2	T. Smith, Dumfries.

– GG, 13th August, 1870

CRICKET

Cricket Match at Annan. We have always been persuaded, and experience bears us out, that athletic exercises, enjoyed as an amusing pastime, as foot-ball, cricket, quoits, etc., is more conducive to the health – yes, to the elasticity and nervous strength of the body, and consequently to the clear and unclouded atmosphere of the imperishable part of man – 'the pure ethereal soul' – than games of a more sedentary and less interesting nature. Under these circumstances, it affords us no small pleasure to record a match at cricket, which *partly* came off at Annan on Friday last, the 9th inst. between the married men and the single, and caused great interest to the lovers of this manly game. The following is the result of the first inning:

Married	Runs	Single	Runs
Mr Little, ct. by Maxwell	8	Williamson, ct. by Benson	4
Mr Turnbull, run out	29	Willis, bd. by Turnbull	21
Mr Benson, bd. out by Ray	0	Hind, not out	37
Mr Little, Jun., bd. by Hind	4	Ray, bd. by Little	2
Mr Hudson, run out	5	L. Benson, do. do	0
Mr Skelton, bd. by Johnson	6	Maxwell, stumpt out	1
Mr Smith, bd. by Ray	0	Johnson, ct. by Little	1
Mr Hope, bd. by do.	0	I. Nelson, ct. Benson	3
Mr Blalock, not out	3	Cleminson, bd. by Little	8
Mr Downie, bd. by Ray	0	Dalgliesh, ct. by Skelton	1
Byes	12	Byes	1
	67		79

The game will be terminated on Monday, when good play is expected. . . . The butting of Messrs Hind and Turnbull was excellent, as also the fielding of Mr Skelton. After the contest . . . the party adjourned to our friend Hudson's, of the Steam-Packet Tavern, and spent an hour or two in social and harmonious revelry.

– DT, 13th June, 1838

The unmarried came off victorious by about 10 notches. . . .

– DT, 20th June, 1838

Cricketting. Some time ago the good old English game of crickets was introduced into this quarter, and clubs have been formed. On Wednesday . . . two of these, viz. the Kirrouchtree and Penninghame House Clubs met 'in fell array' on the Kirrouchtree cricket ground. The day was fine, and the ground in excellent condition. On the toss-up for innings, which was won by Kirrouchtree, Messrs Maxwell and Millar assumed the 'bats', but were speedily bowled out by Messrs Stopford and Tighe, and the other eleven as speedily followed, so that, when all their 'stumps' were down, they only scored 29. Penninghame then went in and scored 85. Nothing daunted, although with small prospect of success, Kirrouchtree again came to the post, and by the beautiful play of Mr Millar, they scored 105; whereas Penninghame, in the second innings, only scored 34, making a total for Penninghame of 119 shots, whilst Kirrouchtree had 134, being a majority of 15 runs in favour of Kirrouchtree. Ample refreshments of good old English cheer – bread and cheese and ale – were plentifully supplied on the ground, not only to the players, but likewise to the spectators. . . .

– GA, 18th August, 1853

Cricket Match. On Saturday last the first match this season took place on the cricket ground at Kirroughtree between the Cumloden and Kirroughtree cricket clubs, eleven players aside. . . . A large assemblage of ladies and gentlemen were present and witnessed the game. . . . Lord Garlies and Mr Edward Maxwell here tossed for the innings – Kirroughtree went in first. Amongst the players in the Kirroughtree side were the following gentlemen – D.B. Hope Johnstone, E. Stopford Blair, yr., of Penninghame, Mr Tighe, Mr Edward Maxwell . . . . in the Cumloden side, Lord Garlies, the Hon. Randolph Stewart, Hon. Granville Somerset. . . . There were also three gentlemen of the Inland Revenue service playing in the Cumloden side.

Kirroughtree 60 and 23 Cumloden . . . after very superior

play . . . 111 . . . . and the Hon. Granville Somerset, before being run out, scored no fewer than 63 runs.

– *GA*, 31st August 1854

Newton Stewart Cricket Return Match. . . .
      Cumloden Club 37 and 95
      Kirroughtree Club 24 and 51 for 6 when night coming in. . . .
In the second innings the play was beautiful. . . . Superior batting of Mr Thompson of Bladnoch. . . .

– *GA*, 7th September, 1854

Newton Stewart . . . Kirroughtree Cricket Club . . . Friday 22 August . . . between cricket teams of Mr Ogden of the Excise at Bladnoch versus Capt Watters of the Cairnsmore Mines, whose side won by an innings and 96 runs. . . . Lord Garlies and his brother, the Hon. Randolph Stewart, took part. . . .

– *DGS*, 27th August, 1856

Blackcraig v. Stranraer Rovers. This match came off at Palnure on Saturday last on the usual ground and resulted in an easy victory for Blackcraig by an innings and 26 runs. . . . The highest scorer on the Blackcraig side was Mr Thomas Hannah, who, by careful cricket, ran up the respectable score of 28. . . . So far the Blackcraig club has been victorious in every match this season, although it has been six times in action.
Stranraer 17 and 41 Blackcraig 84 (including 25 extras). . . .

– *GA*, 4th July, 1878

Cricket Kirkcudbright v Gatehouse of Fleet at Gatehouse. . . .
Kirkcudbright 24 Gatehouse of Fleet 19 for 6. . . .
unfortunately a discussion arose as to a decision given by one of the umpires, and the game came to a sudden termination. . . .

– *KA*, 20th September, 1880

Kirkcudbright. Benefit Cricket Match. . . . The last match of the season will be played in Kirkcudbright on Saturday . . . between Dumfries and the local team, and the proceeds from the gate will be for the benefit of Geo. Craven, the Kirkcudbright professional.

– *KA*, 26th August, 1892

Kirkcudbright v. Dalbeattie. Played at Dalbeattie on Saturday afternoon before a large crowd in the final tie for the Galloway Cup. The visitors had an exceptionally strong team, and included Craven, their old professional. Dalbeattie lodged a protest against his playing, on the ground that he was not a member of the club, and was brought for that match. . . . Boyd and Brown opened the Kirkcudbright innings . . . the professional . . . punished the bowling severely and . . . got 34 by good cricket . . . The innings closed for 136. None of the Dalbeattie batsmen played the bowling with any confidence . . . The innings closed for 29 (Four batsmen were bowled by Craven and another was out lbw to Craven).

– KA, 18th August, 1893

FOX HUNTING, OTTER HUNTING AND COURSING

A number of Noblemen and Gentlemen met at Dumfries Oct. 1 and had a week's sport. One pack killed a fox each hunting-day, and another had good sport at hare-hunting. The fox-chaces were very long and over fine grounds. There were two balls, at which a numerous company of Ladies and Gentlemen made a brilliant appearance.

– SM, September, 1750

Fox Hunt. The Glasserton and Balgreggan Hounds on Thursday last had a capital run . . . Reynard was started on the farm of Clenry, in the neighbourhood of Castle Kennedy Loch . . . a northward . . . run for 17 miles . . . the fox lost in Glenapp near to Capt. Kennedy's of Finnart. . . .

– GA, 8th April, 1852

Fox Hunting in Balmaghie. For some time past Mr Reynard has been paying us frequent visits, and making himself rather familiar with some of the poultry roosts in the neighbourhood, until it was thought proper to advise Mr Macallum of his depradations. . . . on Saturday morning he started for Dornall Hill, being a favourite retreat of theirs, with a good retinue of armed men, and a number of boys from the village as followers, all anxious to find some at home. Fortunately he was, for scarce had the hounds been uncoupled, and the sound of 'hark forward' echoed through the hills, till three fine foxes were on foot trying to make off for safer lodgings. One broke earlier than the others, but was soon brought to a halt by a broadside from Mr Ivy Campbell of Craig. Other two took straight to Livingstone Wood, with 'Melody' not far in the rear. There the pursuit turned on one, while the other was allowed to escape; and after a few of his cunning movements inside the cover, which allowed the hunter time to arrive with more hounds, he found himself completely surrounded in Finniness Wood, and being hard pressed by the hounds he ventured too near the range of Mr David Clark, whose certain aim made him share the same fate as his mate. . . . Both brushes were presented to Master C. Congreve of Mollance, for his kind assistance.

– KA, 20th January, 1865

Staghunting. The Cally hounds met at Barharrow Farm on Friday of last week, and an excellent day's sport followed. The coverts adjacent failed to hold a stag, and consequently Colonel Murray Baillie gave the order for Gaitgil, where an outlier had recently been seen. Drawing up towards the mansion house, it was not long before the field heard the music of the pack. Crossing the avenue the stag made for the open, and from the way hounds picked up the line it was at once seen that with any luck at all followers were in for a gallop.

Running a short right-handed ring in the direction of Barharrow, the stag retraced its steps to where it had been found, but the hounds were close behind and soon forced their quarry to quit. Breaking away in the direction of Glenterry with the pack close behind, the pace was a cracker, and those of the field who wished to ride well up had no time to pick and choose places over the formidable fences. The chase continued over the large pastures of Barharrow, and it appeared at one time as if the woodland of Knockbrex was this good stag's objective, but this proved to be wrong, as the deer was viewed a field ahead of the hounds making towards Enrick. Clearing the high stone wall which surrounds Cally policies it shook off all further pursuit, as the Master gave orders for the pack to be whipped off after a most sporting hunt of some 75 minutes without a check.

– GG, 3rd January, 1914

Otter Hunt. An otter hunt . . . took place . . . Monday in our neighbourhood. The hounds employed were those of Mr Lomax . . . there were seven couples in the field. The dogs threw off at Portrack about 8 o'clock, and after beating the banks of the river for some time, they found at Friars' Carse. The otter was a singularly large and active male, and held the dogs and their masters in busy and eager pursuit for not less than three hours. He first took up the water till he reached the lint mills above Blackwood house, when, finding himself hard pressed in his natural element, he determined to try the land, and accordingly slipped into the wood, where, however, he was soon followed and backed. He again reached the water, which he threaded downward as far as Auldgirth-bridge. There he was again driven to land, but as his strength was now exhausted, and in an attempt to retrace his steps, he was intercepted and killed on one of the walks in front of Blackwood house. No hunt of the kind that has taken place for a very long time has afforded so great and so continued and spirit-stirring enjoyment. . . .

– *DWJ*, 6th August, 1834

On Monday the Carlisle Otter Hounds commenced operations in the Annan water. . . . At half-past six o'clock, Sandy, looking remarkably smart in his new uniform of scarlet jacket and white flannels, the master, Mr Robinson Carr, and a number of subscribers to the pack, left Carlisle for Annan, the meet being at the bridge there. . . . Since the meet on Friday last the celebrated hound 'Old Thunder, the father of the pack', has died. On Monday last, at Kirtle, the first meet of the season, the old hound unfortunately fell from a bridge, a distance of about twenty feet. . . . On Tuesday morning, about half-past seven, the pack cast off from Annan Bridge. . . . they had gone about half a mile up, where the first mouth was given and the otter was taken in the mill-race where Old Thunder had his first hunt. This is a portion of the river where the hounds generally find, and the otter took shelter behind some stones. . . . He was hunted for some time in the river . . . he went back to the mill-race . . . he took the bank into the wood, but the hounds coming upon the land drag, he was obliged to seek shelter again in the river. This time, however, his strongold was impregnable, and 'move on' was the word. After proceeding a little further up the river to near Mount Annan, where an island divides the stream, a second otter was started beneath the rocks in very deep water. . . . First on one side and then on the other the hounds 'dragged' their prey, up and down the flat they followed him with their exciting music, the otter frequently showing himself to the spectators on the bank. In this way the sport carried on until about two o'clock, when, deep water favouring the otter, the varmint was lost and the hounds were called off for the day. . . . The hounds were taken up to Ecclefechan for the night, and on Wednesday morning will cast off at Hoddam Bridge. (*Carlisle Journal*)

– *KA*, 12th May, 1865

Early on Saturday morning week the Carlisle pack tasted the first blood of the season. . . . the river was hunted to Kirtle Bridge. Here a drag was taken and followed to Mossknowe. . . . The only person up at the death with the huntsman was the Kirkpatrick tailor, who had moved his feet

almost as fast as his needle.... Sandy returned to Carlisle with his
prize.... The otter was a fine dog, about 22 pounds in weight and four
feet in length. (*Carlisle Journal*)

– KA, 23rd June, 1865

Wigtownshire Coursing Club ... Programme of their Meeting on the 4th
October, 1870 and the following days.... *The Wigtownshire St Leger*,
An Open Stake for Greyhounds, being Puppies of 1869 ... Entry, £3.
10s.... *The Galloway Stakes*, A Club Stake for Greyhounds of all
ages ... Entry, £1. 10s., with £10 added by the Club, £5 by the President
and £5 by the Vice-president ... *The Baldoon Cup* for Greyhounds of all
ages ... Entry, £5.10s.

– GG, 18th June, 1870

Wigtownshire Coursing Club ... Tuesday 4th October morning Port
William road end ... Wednesday 5th October at Balfern gate (over the
Grounds by kind permission of the Earl of Galloway) ... President Lord
Stair, Vice-president Lord Garlies ... meeting supervised by the Earl of
Galloway and Mr Vans Agnew ... *Wigtownshire St Leger* ... 1st/2nd
Prizes £60/£20; 3rd/4th Prizes £8 each....

– GG, 8th October, 1870

WRESTLING

The Langholm Lamb Fair ... Races and Wrestling. Saturday, 27th July, 1844.
... Forty-eight Wrestlers entered the ring:

Third Round	Stood	Fell
	John Irving, Laversdale	John Thompson, Pattieshill
	Hugh James, Boggside	Joseph Little, Cumwhitton
	Mark Norman, Low Hyket	G. Turnbull, Breakinhillrig
	John Atkinson, Kingwater	John Phillips, Crackrope
	Joseph Elliott, Croglin	George Phillips, Glebelands
	John Jackson, Bolton Fell	William Oliver, Mains
Fourth Round	Stood	Fell
	Hugh James	Joseph Elliot
	John Jackson	John Irving
	Mark Norman	John Atkinson
Fifth Round	Hugh James	John Jackon

Hugh James beat Mark Norman (the odd man) and thus became champion of the wrestling ring and caried off the head prize. . . .
– GA, 1st August, 1844

Langholm Sports . . . took place on the Wednesday. They consisted of wrestling, hurdle-racing, hack races, pony races, etc.. A goodly number of wrestlers entered for the prize of six pounds and there was a fair muster of the 'dons' including Hugh James, William and Alexander Scott of Newcastleton, Jared Armstrong, Tom Batey, John Irving of Laversdale, and a number of others from Newcastleton and Bewcastle. The principal prize was won by Wm Jackson of Newcastleton, a young 'un and a light 'un, who received two pounds. . . . (*Carlisle Journal*)
– GA, 7th August, 1845

Kirkcudbright Exhibition and Gymnastic Drill
The annual exhibition of Captain McConchie's class took place in the Town Hall on Friday last before a large and enthusiastic audience. Formerly the class was composed of boys who attended the Academy. This year the ranks have been opened to girls attending that institution and Miss Bell's school. . . . The display comprised such well known and popular items as squad drill, physical drill with arms, sword, dumb-bell, bar-bell and Indian club exercises, scarf-drill and maze. . . .
– KA, 15th July, 1892

CYCLING

Adapted to childhood, youth and age – it takes the working man to his work, the business man to his business, the doctor to visit his patients, the policeman to run criminals to earth, the postman on his daily round, and even our friends the tramps are beginning to recognise the advantages of Cycling.

It is also beginning to play an important part in Military tactics. Nearly every brigade, not only of regulars but also of volunteers, has its cyclist corps, which is told off to do special duty where rapid transit from place to place is a consideration. Which of us did not feel proud of our Galloway lads when two years ago they brought home from the far south the Blue Ribbon of volunteer cycling. . . .
– 'Lecture on Cycling' by G.M. Stark, Gatehouse-of-Fleet, 1896

100 Mile Bicycle Race in the Stewartry

Within recent years cycling has become very popular in the Stewartry, and has now gained a permanent footing as one of our most health-giving and recreative pastimes.... Mr Morrison, watchmaker, Dalbeattie, offering a silver cup with the option of a gold badge as 1st prize and two silver badges as second and third prizes ... were competed for yesterday (Thursday) in a 100 mile handicap race for all classes of bicycles. The course chosen for the race was from Castle Douglas to Newton Stewart via Gatehouse, and back – 66 miles, then from Castle Douglas to Maxwelltown via Crocketford, and back to Castle Douglas – 34 miles.... only 6 competitors put in appearance at the start.

At 9.30 a.m. the cushion tyre machines, which were allowed half-an-hour's start, were promptly dispatched from the Cross, the riders being J. Watt, J. Gray, and R. Thomson, all of Dalbeattie.... a large crowd gathered to witness the start at 10 a.m. of the pneumatic tyre machines, which were placed scratch, and ridden by J. McMurray, Castle Douglas; D. Barbour, Maxwelltown; and J. McCann, Dalbeattie. Immediately after the start of the race an unfortunate accident happened through Barbour running over a cat, causing the rider to fall from his machine. McCann, who was following closely behind, was also thrown, and his machine badly damaged, causing him to retire from the race. Barbour, however, was fortunate in getting the loan of another machine, and proceeded after some delay. McMurray, who was paced by Alexander of Edinburgh, the 50 mile Waverley Road champion, did not get off without a mishap, for his tyre burst shortly before reaching Gatehouse on the return journey, and he was compelled to ride Alexander's machine. About 2.40 p.m. Gray arrived at Castle Douglas; McMurray at 2.45; and Barbour at 3.5. By this time great excitement prevailed as to the finish when McMurray arrived at Castle Douglas from Maxwelltown at 5.30, his time for the 100 miles being 7½ hours, an average of 13⅓ miles an hour....

               – *KA*, 24th June, 1892

A 10-mile championship race ended in a fiasco at Creetown. The rider of the only solid-tyred machine was given about a mile of a handicap and when the starting pistol was fired he was the only one who heard it as the main field was so far away. Officials were unable to stop him to make a fresh start and the lone rider returned to claim the cup. The committee deeply regretted the disappointment caused to the rest of the competitors....

               – *KA*, 3rd September, 1892

FOOTBALL

Wigtown, Jan. 13, 1826. . . . Old New Year's day passed off as usual, with much bustle and parade; two foot-ball matches were well contested, and the parties marched in two and two with drums beating and colours flying to the Town-house, where copious libations of the mountain dew made them all 'unco happy', and, as there was no scarcity on the field, it was little to be wondered at that so many of their spouses were to be seen arming them home tack and tack; and when the full influence of het pints and shooting matches are taken into account, it was no wonder many of them made 'an unco lee way', and that some actually upset.

– *DWJ*, 17th January, 1826

The Football Craze. . . . Kirkcudbright 16 June, 1892 . . . Football in this district is carried to a most immoderate length, and is monopolising the time and energy of our youths to an extent which is very unfair. Our young men will engage in no other sport, they will discuss no other topic. In the evening they congregate at the field, later they may be heard at our street corners, on Sundays they repair in bands to the fields and woods, and their one and only theme is football. Now, football is essentially a winter game, and it is manifestly unfair that it should be carried over through the summer to the hurt of other forms of recreation. Our local volunteer companies cannot get their men to attend parades – they are at football; our rowing club . . . languishes for lack of members . . . and so with our cricket, cycling and other clubs. From October to May is the proper time for it; during the other months it is quite unreasonable, and the leather might very well give place to the rifle, the oar, or the bat. . . . Dropkick.

– *KA*, 17th June, 1892

Young Corner Loafers in Kirkcudbright

Every city, town and county in our country is infested more or less with common loafers and Kirkcudbright is preeminently infected with this plague which for some reason or other the police are unwilling or unable to put down. At the corners where men congregate after their day's work is done no one is annoyed or molested when passing. This is not the case however at the corner of St Mary Street and Gladstone Place. This is the favourite gathering place after dark of a few choice specimens of rudeness, blasphemy, obscenity and general mischief that could not be matched in any other town. Their ages range from ten to sixteen years and evidently they are the sons of respectable well-to-do parents who perhaps are under the delusion that they are receiving good moral training at the Band of Hope or at the Bible Class, for Sabbath night in particular is a night of high carnival with them, for then doors are kicked, stones are thrown, windows are broken or besmearched with filth, and they run from their depradations round the square back to their favourite corner where peaceful passers-by are assailed with oaths, groans and language too vile to mention.

They are cunning cowards of the lowest grade, for on week-nights they will leave their corner a few minutes before the ten o'clock train arrives and move over by the station door and platform. Why? Because they know the police will be up at their remote corner when the train arrives. Bible Classes or Bands of Hope leave no impression on youths constituted of such brutish natures and demoralised minds. When they go out to our large cities to find situations they are the material that will ultimately swell the number of the great unwashed, tobacco-chewing, beer-guzzling city corner loafers.... Parents are to blame for allowing their offspring such liberties and being out of sight for hours at night. Home chastisement is sadly neglected and this results in the authority of the parent being ignored, education a complete sham, Bible Classes a worse ditto! and the lads having formed no taste for anything refined join with gladness the street-corner academy to graduate finally as depicted above.... Hyades.

– *KA*, 22nd April, 1892

AT THE DANCING

The following curious incident, which happened a few days ago, may be depended on as a fact: John McCaa, a farmer near New Galloway, walking out with his son, who was playing on a fiddle, stopped for some time on the hill of Troch of Hows, when John looking accidentally over his shoulder, observed two hares standing upright, and rubbing their pates as if they were listening to the music. He then desired his son to play a reel, on which they immediately began to dance, and continued for a considerable time, until John's laughter drove them away.

– *DWJ*, 17th September, 1793

Peter a Dick's Peatstack. A favourite dancing *step* with the peasantry, performed by giving three *flegs* with the feet, and two stamps with the heel alternately; such is the simple dance, the movement of the feet correspond to these words when said at the same time; indeed, the noise the feet makes seems to speak them – *Peter a Dick*, *Peter a Dick*, *Peter a Dick's Peatstack*. It is commonly the first *step* dancing masters teach their pupils; the A, B, C, etc. of dancing science, when the scholars become tolerate at *beetling it*; they are next taught to *fleup* through the *side-step*; then *Jack on the Green*, *Shawintrewse*, and other *hornpipes*, with the *Highland Fling*, mayhap; these dances are all got pretty well by the feet in the *first month*, with sketches of *foursome*, eightsome reels, and some country dances; but if the scholars attend the *fortnight* again of another *month*, they proceed at great length into the labyrinths of the art.

A *light heel'd sooter* is generally the dancing dominie; he fixes on a barn in some *clauchan* to show forth in; he can both fiddle and dance, at the same time; can cut double quick time, and *trible Bob Major*; he fixes on, and publishes abroad when his *trial night* is to come on, so the young folks in the neighbourhood doff their *clogs*, and put on their *kirk-shoon*, these being their *dancing pumps*; off they go to the *trial*, which, if it be a good turn-out, he tries no more, but begins teaching directly. . . . in the second (month) the *Flowers of Edinburgh*, mayhap; *Sweden* and *Belile's Marches*, with other hornpipes, and country dances many, such as the *Yillwife and her Barries*, *Mary Grey*, *The wun that shook the barley*, etc., with the famous *Bumpkin Brawley*; yes, and they will even dare, some times to imitate our Continental neighbours over the water, in their *waltzing*, *alimanging*, and *Cotillion trade*; ay, and be up with the Spaniards too, in their *quadrilles*, *borellos*, and *falderalloes* of nonsense; so out-taught, they become fit to attend *house-heatings*, *volunteer* and *masonic balls*, what not. Partners are taken to the *practeezings* and *balls*; these girls, whom boys chose thus to *partner* them, are commonly beloved by them for ever afterwards; indeed, *love* is first felt by thousands at dancing-schools; to those sweet dears, *ribbons*, *lockets*, and *strings o' beads* are brought, to adorn their fair bodies. . . . Dancing is a famous amusement, but, like every art, I have known some better at it who were never taught than those who were; who could give a *hooh* and a *crack* with their heels, in a wonderful funny original manner.

– Mactaggart, op. cit., 1824, pp. 379–80

Our Modern Belles (1827)

Amongst the higher circles of our females, it must be confessed that phthisis, tabes, diseases of the spine, nervous habits, dyspepsia, etc., are becoming very frequent. Nothing can be more absurd or prejudicial to health than the present mode of rearing and educating our young ladies. As soon as they are out of leading strings, they are braced up in stays and are not permitted to eat till satisfied, lest they should grow coarse and strong like country wenches. They are not suffered to go out except in delightfully fine weather, and then only for an hour or so in the day. Should there be a breeze of wind or a refreshing shower, they are not allowed to venture abroad, or, if they do go out, they are wrapt up in cloaks and hoods and drawn along at horses' heels. . . . When they enter their teens, the stays are curiously fitted up with bars of tempered steel and whale-bone. . . . To procure a delicate complexion and a slender waist, they are sparing in their diet and lace their stays and pin their clothes, until respiration is even painfully performed. Flannels and warm clothing are little used in the winter months, as they tend to increase the bulk of the wearer and acquire her the appellation of stout – an epithet most disgusting to all our modern belles. On the day of an assembly, the dandyzettes must eat almost nothing – a little bit of something solid, two mouthfuls of beefsteak or biscuit and water – nothing more, even a cup of tea would be out of the question! Then the maid must pull the stays to the utmost pitch of tightness, at the risk of losing her place. The neck, shoulders and arms must be bare, and the feet cased in silk stockings and wafer-soled sandals. The danger of catching cold is not worth considering, when compared with the havock meditated by such a show of charms.

The assembly, too, would be shockingly vulgar were it to begin before the industrious citizens are snoring soundly in their beds: and, when the sun begins to emerge from his chambers in the east, these light-hearted, light-footed ladies of the town are heard scampering homewards in carriages, to the horrid annoyance of Bacchanalians, thieves and drowsy watchmen. Now-a-days, when we say that a lady is in full dress for a ball or an assembly, we mean little more than that she is scarcely dressed at all. . . .

Spending years of a valuable life in reading novels, plays and poetry, in playing on musical instruments, drawing, singing, dancing, dressing, and card-playing, with smattering French and building pastry castles, is injurious to both body and mind. Yet these, with a little fanciful unprofitable needle-work, and a formal stiffness in the ordinary movements of the body, comprehend nearly the whole system of education taught at some of our boarding-schools. Nature never intended their constitutions to be worn out by any such absurd practices. If we wish our young ladies to possess health, fresh complexions, stout nerves and exhilarating spirits, we must recommend the abolishing of that useless, cumbersome, unnatural and mischievous piece of dress, ycleped stays, corsets or boddice, till they have attained at least their twentieth year. . . . They ought to rise early and go early to bed, to walk much or ride on horseback, to spend their hours of employment in learning what may be useful through life and endeavour to blend profitable instruction with amusement. During spring and summer a walk, ride or other moderate exercise before breakfast is singularly salutary to most constitutions and gives an agreeable zest and relish for food. . . .

Reading at proper intervals well chosen books, newspapers, ladies' magazines and the like, and learning to write a good legible hand, are of the first and highest importance to every young lady, as she requires to be able to hold conversation easily upon general subjects and correspond with her acquaintances upon the ordinary topics of life. But that pining love-sick habit of making the tour of the circulating library is hurtful in the extreme. Wading through so many volumes of fictitious nonsense tends not only to enervate the frame, but also to give girls a wrong idea of the world. . . . Let them think upon the industry, the early hours and housekeeping maxims of their grand-mothers and great-grand-mothers, let them reflect upon the blessing of health and the value of time . . . and let them not forget that one short hour spent in religious meditations will afford them more real happiness and peace of mind than a whole lifetime spent in pursuit of vanity. . . .

We have a class of females in Dumfries-shire, and I believe every other place has its share of them, who, from their sitting at work from an early hour in the morning till a late hour at night, are subject to phthisis, dyspepsia, etc.. I mean milliners, mantua-makers, straw-hat-makers, dress-makers, tambourers, sempstresses, and the whole family of sewing girls. Their number here is very great and they are frequently crowded into small apartments, or backshops, and sometimes work the whole night. When consulted by any of these female artificers, I have almost universally recommended a walk, morning and evening, in suitable weather or a retirement for a while to the country. . . .

– Dr J. Erskine Gibson, surgeon, Dumfries, and one of the surgeons of the Dumfries Dispensary, *A Medical Sketch of Dumfriesshire*, Dumfries, 1827, pp. 14–18

A Popular Song
Where Are All The Young Men Gone, or the town is rifle mad
Oh! where are all the young men gone,
It really is a shame,
Our state is hard to think upon,
I wonder who's to blame, I wonder who's to blame, I wonder
who's to blame.

There was a time when Tom and Fred,
An hour or two might kill,
In pleasant chat, but now instead,
They have to go to drill. . . .

Good gracious 'tis too bad,
And I for one begin to think,
The Town is Rifle mad,
And I for begin to think The Town is Rifle mad.

I only wish I could find out,
Who cook'd this mighty stew,
For what the fuss is all about
I cannot tell, can you? I cannot tell, can you? I cannot tell, can you?

I only know, I sorely miss
My usual promenade,
For now Tom's only answer is,
I'm order'd on parade. . . .

Good gracious 'tis too bad,
And I for one begin to think
The Town is Rifle mad,
And I for one begin to think The Town is Rifle mad.

– Written by John Brougham about 1860. Music by I.M. Jolly – and
with a superb Tom 'Graduated Tint' Packer cover.
                          – *Collected c. 1970 in Kirkcudbright*